"That Men may know from the Rising to the
Setting of the Sun that there is no one besides Me.
I am the Lord and there is no other.
The One forming Light and creating Darkness,
causing Well-being and creating Calamity;
I am the Lord who does all these."

[Isaiah 45.6, 7]

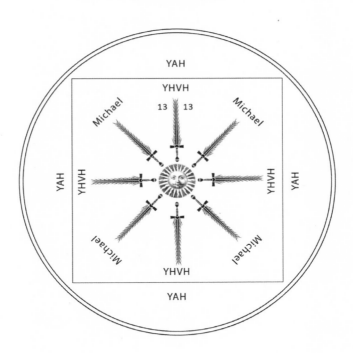

"I am the Lord your God, who Brought you Out
of the Land of Egypt, out of the House of Slavery.
You shall have no other gods before Me."

[Exodus Chapter 20.2, 3]

Holy Menorah being taken away by the Romans after the destruction of the Second Temple 70 AD

The Secret of the Breast Plate

Author- Vashisht Vaid

"All Spiritual Things and Spiritual Matters should be Examined Only by the "Inner Mind" also known as the "Spiritual Eyes", Otherwise looking at them with Worldly Eyes, One is Liable to make Grave Mistakes..."

– Vashisht Vaid

The Secret of the Breast Plate

Copyright © 2015

Author:
Vashisht Vaid
www.Outfinitevision.com

Publisher:
The Divine Vision
Fifth Printing

Graphics:
Kevin Vancio | kevinvancio.com

ISBN: 978-1-329-04623-8

Printed in U.S.A

Preface

This Particular Book named "The Secret of Breast Plate " by the Grace of the MOST HIGH came in Existence, as One Very Important Key Pertaining to the "Secret of the Breast Plate" was somehow left out from my earlier books, which are related to the Wisdom of the Famous Prophet King Solomon, the "Chosen Son of GOD", and the Wisest King of the Israelite's as mentioned in "1 Chronicles 17.13" of the Holy Bible.

To properly explain the Importance of this Holy Key, which holds the "Secrets of the Breast Plate" which had been worn by the High Priest of Israelite's since AARON's Time, as per the Command of the MOST HIGH, it was required for me to go in details of Other Various Spiritual Aspects, which are clearly mentioned in the various chapters of the Holy Bible, which include both the Old and the New Testaments, as the Chapters of the New Testament in reality Mirrors the Holy Wisdom of the OLD TESTAMENT, which is contained in its various chapters.

Most People of the Modern World now only consider the Holy Bible as a "RELIGIOUS BOOK, but in Reality, it is a True store House of Most Valuable Codified "GODLY WISDOM", which was revealed through HIS Chosen Prophets in times of "SPIRITUAL NEEDS", and is now readily Available to "All MANKIND", who in their Short Lived Incarnated Human Lives may have Consciously linked with their True HIGHER SELVES, commonly known as their "SOUL CONSCIOUSNESS", and thus have attained the GODLY GIFT of "SPIRITUAL EYES" to Reverently Pry through its HIDDEN SECRETS, and in this reference Prophet EZEKIEL, the Chosen "Son of Man", a title bestowed upon Him by the Graceful Conscious WORD of the LORD- GOD HIMSELF as repeatedly mentioned in his dedicated chapter, thus said in the HOLY BIBLE, which Clearly States:

"Then the WORD of the LORD came to Me saying, "Son of Man, You live in the Midst of the Rebellious House, Who have EYES to See, but DO NOT SEE, Ears to Hear, but DO NOT HEAR; for they are a Rebellious House. [Ezekiel 12. 1, 2.]

Later on JESUS CHRIST, the "Chosen Son of GOD", incarnated many hundred years later after Prophet EZEKIEL also clearly said, as recorded in the Gospel of Matthew in the Holy Bible, which states:

"Therefore I speak to them in Parables; because while SEEING they DO NOT SEE, and while HEARING they DO NOT HEAR, Nor do they UNDERSTAND.

But blessed are Your EYES, because they SEE; and Your EARS, because they HEAR.

For Truly I say to You, that Many PROPHETS and RIGHTEOUS MEN desired to SEE what You SEE, and did not SEE it; and to HEAR what You HEAR, and did not HEAR it. [Matthew 13. 13, 16, 17.]

Jesus Christ has been quoted again the Gospel of Mark in the Holy Bible, which states:

'For Nothing is Hidden, except to be revealed; nor has anything been SECRET, but that it should come to LIGHT. If any MAN has Ears to HEAR, let Him HEAR.'' [Mark 4. 22, 23.]

The same message was recorded by John, to which the Angel of the Church in Laodicea wrote:

"He who has an Ear, let Him Hear what the SPIRIT says to the Churches." [Revelation 3. 22].

This Esoteric book of Holy Wisdom will thus serve the Evolutionary Purpose of all the downtrodden faithful and Loyal servants of the "MOST HIGH", the One and Only CREATOR LORD – GOD of the Various Hierarchical orders of the Angelic HOSTS, who ALL in Reality are his Created Servants, the So called "ELOHIM", who merely act as his servant Co - Creator's, originally created by His "Desire Mind Vital Energy Impulses", to Consciously and Unconsciously manifest in differentiated grades of evolutionary consciousness, just like in building of a house, first architectural plans are required, and then based upon these plans a firm ground and a strong foundation is required upon which the House is built by various grades of construction workers, , so they can first create the differentiated dimensional plane frequencies and then to manifest in them various animated Kingdoms of differentiated conscious, embodied by the Hierarchical levels of Various Visible and Invisible "Entities and Beings", as well as just to assist HIM in HIS Evolutionary Plan and Purpose, they thus were supposed to act "FAITHFULLY" in their Various Assigned Duties to carry out HIS desired Wishes.

The LORD GOD, the "MOST HIGH", with their help and assistance later on Created the Human Beings and all other living visible and Invisible Creatures of this Planet Earth, so they can cyclically and Systematically attain their Vital Spirit Conscious Expansion in the 3 dense dimensional Vital Frequency worlds of ASSIAH, YETZIRAH, and BRIAH, which have been earthier thus manifested with HIS Divine Grace upon this Planet Earth, and then after acquiring all the necessary Material World Experience related to the Conscious Expansion of their Solar Consciousness termed as the SPIRIT, they all were required as per the Evolutionary Plan and Purpose, then to Consciously become a radiant Individualized Conscious part of their "Collective Solar Conscious Existence", through a Divine Merger.

And this Book of Holy wisdom will thus serve all the faithful subjects of the MOST HIGH, as a great tool in their "SPIRITUAL QUEST", to Consciously understand and Comprehend, according to their Indwelling Mind "SPIRITUAL CAPACITIES", the Plan and Purpose of the Unknowable MOST HIGH, for whom his Chosen Son, the Great King Solomon erected the First Grand House of Worship in Jerusalem, as well as for all those who "Consciously Do Their Best" to uphold the Universal law of "Will to do Good", during their short lived incarnated Human Lives upon the Physical plane of this Planet Earth.

Vashisht Vaid

Jesus Christ shown in the heavens as the Fixed Cross, with the Four Constellation symbols shown on Four corners, as shown in Ezekiel's Vision, which are from top left to right, Scorpio, Aquarius; bottom left to right, Leo and Taurus.

SECRETARIAT OF STATE
—
FIRST SECTION - GENERAL AFFAIRS

From the Vatican, 29 October 2012

The Secretariat of State is directed by His Holiness Pope Benedict XVI to acknowledge the eight volumes authored by Mr. Vashisht Vaid and sent to him by Outfinite Visions Inc.

The Secretariat of State also expresses His Holiness's acknowledgement of the respectful sentiments which prompted this presentation.

Peter B. Wells
Monsignor Peter B. Wells
Assessor

Acknowledgment by Pope Benedict XVI 2012

A Brief Note About The Author

Mr. Vashisht Vaid was born in a Hindu Mohyal Brahmin family in Delhi India, and since childhood being a student of science, he has been interested in the esoteric knowledge about this great Brahmanda [universe]. During his life he has personally come across various thousands of years old higher dimensional great ancient Siddha's and Maharishi's, who can take a physical form at their desired "Will". Mr. Vashisht Vaid also visited the esoteric Kailash Mountain of Tibet China in 2002. and currently lives in New Jersey U.S.A. He has also participated in the Millenial Prayer as an invited guest to the Thanks-Giving Square Foundation in Dallas, Texas.

The Masonic Library & Museum
OF THE DISTRICT OF COLUMBIA

Robert F. Drechsler, *Past Grand Master*

5428 MacArthur Blvd., N.W.
Washington, DC 20016-2524
Tel: (202) 686-1811
Fax: (202) 686-2759

Ramachandra N. Swamy
50 Cragwood Road Suite No. 104
South Plainfield, NJ 07080

May 28, 2013

Dear Mr. Swamy,

This letter is to let you know that we have received the following publications by Vashisht Vaid:

Who are Devas [Angels] and what Happens after Physical Death? Vols. 1, 2 &3
The Secrets of Cosmic Energy Portals "Nakshatras" Vols. 1 & 2
Brahmandic Gyanum Universal Knowledge
Thy Evolutionary Plan
The Codified Mysteries
The Esoteric Collections
The Secrets of Astrology
The Radiant Words of Love & Wisdom

Thank you for the donation of the above listed books to the Grand Lodge Library of Free and Accepted Masons in the District of Columbia.

Regards,

Robert F. Drechsler PGM

Acknowledgment by past Grand Master Robert F. Drechsler 2013

Rosicrucian Park
1342 Naglee Avenue • San Jose, CA 95191
408•947•3600 FAX 408•947•3677
www.rosicrucian.org

July 3, 2013

Ramachandra N. Swamy
50 Cragwood Road, Suite 104
So. Plainfield, NJ 07080

Dear Ramachandra,

Thank you very much for your recent gift of Books on Esoteric Knowledge by the Most Reverend Vashisht K. Vaid, published by The Outfinite Visions Inc., a New Jersey Not for Profit Corporation, to our beloved Order.

Our time-honored teachings aid sincere students by giving them techniques by which they can learn to direct their own lives, experience inner peace, and become active participants in the spiritual advancement of humanity. With the help of devoted members like you, the light of the Rosicrucian Order will shine ever more brightly as a bountiful source of wisdom, peace, and Universal Love.

Thank you for helping our Order fulfill its highest goals.

With best wishes for Peace Profound,
Sincerely and fraternally,

Julie Scott

Julie Scott
President

Acknowledgment by President Julie Scott 2013

THE CHURCH OF JESUS CHRIST OF LATTER-DAY SAINTS
OFFICE OF THE FIRST PRESIDENCY
47 EAST SOUTH TEMPLE STREET, SALT LAKE CITY, UTAH 84150-1200

June 4, 2015

Kevin Vancio
Outfinite Visions
P.O. Box 0416
Springfield, NJ 07081

Dear Mr. Vancio:

I have been asked by President Cecil O. Samuelson to acknowledge your letter and the book entitled *The Secret of the Breast Plate* by Vashisht Vaid.

Sincerely yours,

Brook P. Hales
Secretary to the First Presidency

Acknowledgment by President Cecil O. Samuelson 2015

June 2, 2015
Month of the Sacred Heart of Jesus
Year of Consecrated Life

Mr. Kevin Vancio
Assistant
Outfinite Visions
P.O. Box 07081-0416
Springfield, NJ 07081

Dear Mr. Vancio:

Thank you most sincerely for the copy of the book, *The Secret of the Breast Plate,* by Vashisht Vaid. Your thoughtfulness is deeply appreciated.

With prayerful best wishes, I am,

Faithfully in Christ,

Timothy Michael Cardinal Dolan
Archbishop of New York

Acknowledgment by Archbishop of New York
Timothy Michael Cardinal Dolan 2015

UNIVERSITY OF CALIFORNIA

BERKELEY • DAVIS • IRVINE • LOS ANGELES • MERCED • RIVERSIDE • SAN DIEGO • SAN FRANCISCO      SANTA BARBARA • SANTA CRUZ

1111 Franklin Street
Oakland, California 94607-5200
Phone: (510) 987-9074
Fax:(510) 987-9086
http://www.ucop.edu

June 8, 2015

Outfinite Visions
Post Office Box 07081-0416
Springfield, New Jersey 07081

Dear Mr. Vancio:

As you requested, I am pleased to acknowledge receipt of the autographed copy of *The Secret of the Breast Plate* that you recently sent to University of California President Janet Napolitano. The President appreciates your thinking of her and has asked me to thank you for sharing this book with her.

With best wishes,

Sincerely,

Cecile M. Cuttitta
Director
Presidential Communications

Acknowledgment by President Janet Napolitano 2015

14

PRINCETON
UNIVERSITY

President's Room
Nassau Hall
Princeton, New Jersey 08544-0015

June 18, 2015

Mr. Kevin Vancio
Outfinite Visions
P.O. Box 07081-0416
Springfield, New Jersey 07081

Dear Mr. Vancio:

    I am writing to acknowledge receipt of *The Secret of the Breast Plate* by Vashisht Vaid. Thank you for sending a copy of the book to Princeton University.

Sincerely,

Erin Graham
Executive Assistant

Acknowledgment by Executive Assistant of Princeton University, Erin Graham 2015

Dear Renée,

Thank you so much for taking the time to send us a signed edition of _The Secret of The Breast Plate_, by Vashisht Vaid. We appreciate your thoughtfulness.

We are praying God fills you with His strength, peace, love and healing touch. We are believing that He will bless you with abundant favor and open doors of opportunity, as He fulfills His plans for you.

~Joel & Victoria Osteen~

Acknowledgment by Joel & Victoria Osteen 2015
Senior Pastor of Protestant Church

Rhodes College

—1848—

OFFICE OF THE PRESIDENT

July 24, 2015

Renée Fishel
Assistant, Outfinite Visions
P.O. Box 07081-0416
Springfield, NJ 07081

Dear Renée,

Our office is in receipt of the signed copy of the book, "The Secret of the Breast Plate," by Vashisht Vaid. Many thanks.

Sincerely,

Meredith Hicks

Meredith Hicks
Office Assistant to the President
Rhodes College

Acknowledgment by Assistant to the President 2015
Meredith Hicks, Rhodes College

(More letters of Acknowledgment in back of book)

Breastplate of Kohen Gadol, the "High Priest" of Israel.

2 Onyx stones, each stone has engraved 6 names of tribes of Israel

The Breastplate of Judgement (Choshen) with 12 precious stones [Sardius, Topez, Caruncle, Emerald, Sapphire, Diamond, Ligure, Agate, Amethyst, Beryl, Onyx, & Jasper]

Hidden in the Breastplate of Judgement contains the Urim and the Thummim

Ephod embroidered with blue, purple, scarlet and gold

Incense of Fragrence full of enjoyment for His glory

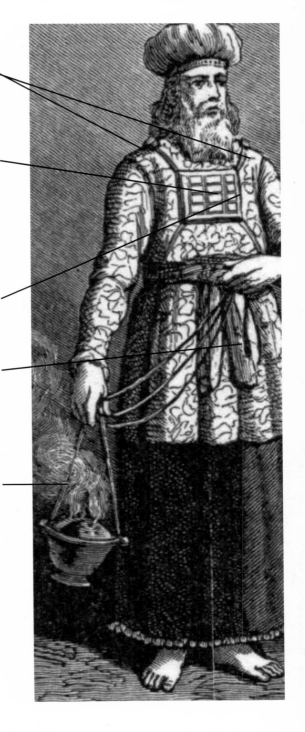

Description of the High Priest Garments

Dedication

This book is dedicated to the "Outfinite Supreme Council", who are the true conceivers of the grand experiment commonly known as the "Infinite Universe".

PRIEST   HIGH PRIEST.   LEVITE.

Ancient dress code of the Levites [The Priesthood]

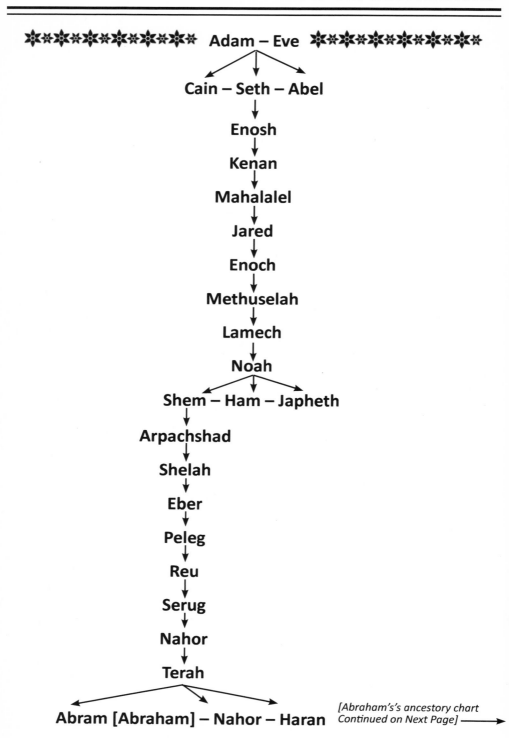

Adam – Eve

Cain – Seth – Abel

Enosh

Kenan

Mahalalel

Jared

Enoch

Methuselah

Lamech

Noah

Shem – Ham – Japheth

Arpachshad

Shelah

Eber

Peleg

Reu

Serug

Nahor

Terah

Abram [Abraham] – Nahor – Haran

[Abraham's's ancestory chart Continued on Next Page] ⟶

Abram [Abraham] – Nahor – Haran

Maid Wife **Hagar** · Concubine Wife **Keturah** · Wife **Sarah**

Ishmael ←----------------------------→ Isaac

🌸 12 Princes named:

Zimran – Jokshan – Medan – **Midian** – Ishbak – Shuah

1) Nebaioth, 2) Kedar, 4) Mibsam, 5) Mishma

3) **Adnan [Adbeel]**, 6) Dumah, 7) Massa, 8) Hadad

9) Tema, 10) Jetur, 11) Naphish,

🌸 [Progenitor of Adnani Tribe in North]

12) **Qahtan [Kedemah]** 🌸 [Progenitor of Qahtani Tribe in South]

Esau – – Jacob [Israel]
Children of 12 Tribes

Maadd Ibn Adnan

Nadhar Ibn Maadd

Mudar Ibn Nadhar

Ilyas Ibn Mudar

Mudrikah Ibn Ilyas

Khuzaymah Ibn Mudrikah

Kinanah Ibn Khuzaymah

Al-Nadar Ibn Kinanah

Malik Ibn Al-Nadar

Fihr Ibn Malik

🌸 [Progenitor of Banu Quraysh Tribe]

Jethro (Reuel) [Priest of Midian's]

Wife **Leah**

✡ ✡ ✡ ✡ ✡ ✡
Reuben – Simeon – Levi – Judah – Issachar – Zebulun

(Daughter) **Zipporah** *married to:* → ✡ **Moses – Aaron**

[Mose's] **Nun** [Servant]

Joshua

Gershon – – **Eliezer**

Wife **Rachel**
✡ ✡
Joseph – Benjamin

✡ ✡
Manasseh – Ephraim

Bilhah [Rachel's maid]
✡ ✡
Dan – Naphtali

Zilpah [Leah's maid]
✡ ✡
Gad – Asher

☪ *[Prophet Muhammad's ancestory chart Continued on Next Page]*

By command of God to Moses the Levite Priest's from Levi clan, were established and thus taken out of the original 12 TRIBES to perform their priestly duties who later on in the land of Canaan were given 48 cities to live.

🛡 *[King Solomon's ancestory chart Continued on Next Page]*

Ishmael lineage through Fihr Ibn Malik continued...

Ghalib Ibn Fihr

↓

Luay Ibn Ghalib

↓

Kab Ibn Luay

↓

Murrah Ibn Kab

↓

Kilab Ibn Murrah   [Kuraja- 373 AD]

↓

Qusai Ibn Kilab – – **Zuhrah** Ibn Kilab

[Kusaja- 400 to 480 AD]   [Progenitor of Banu Zurah Tribe]

↓

Abd Manaf Ibn Qusai

↓

Hashim Ibn Abd Manaf   [Progenitor of Banu Hashim Tribe]

↓

Abd Al Muttalib Ibn Hashim [Shayhah or Shajba]

↓

Abd Allah Ibn Abd Al Muttalib [Abdullah]

↓

Abu Al Qaism Muhammad Ibn Abd Allah
[*PROPHET MUHAMMAD - 570 AD to 630 AD]

↓

Fatimah (Daughter) Ibn Abu Al Qaism Muhammad
[605 AD]

↓

Hasan Ibn Ali – **Hussein** Ibn Ali   [Grandson's
[625 AD]   [626 AD]   of prophet
                                Muhammad]

↓

Descendant Muslim's having title names of: **Sayyad's, Sharif's, Ashraf's**

Isaac lineage through Jacob [Israel] lineage continued...

[Children of Leah]
Reuben – Simeon – Levi – Judah – Issachar – Zebulun

Perez
Hezron
Ram
Amminadab
Nahshon
Salmon
Boaz
Obed
Jesse
David [Daud]
***GREAT KING "SOLOMON"** [Suleyman]
Rehoboam
Abijah
Asa* ← *King's during* **Prophet Elija**
Jehoshaphat‡
Joram [Jehoram] *King's during* **Prophet Elisha** "Man of God"
Ahaziah [Jehoahaz]
Joash
Amaziah*
Uzziah [Azariah]* *King's of Judah during* **Prophet Isaiah**
Jotham
Ahaz
Hezekiah*
Manasseh
Amon *King of Judah during* **Prophet Zephaniah**
Josiah ←
Jehoiakim [Eliakim]
Jeconiah [Jehoiachin]- [Enslaved to Babylon]
Pedaiah [Shealtiel]
Zerubbabel
Abiud [Jushab-Hesed]
Eliakim
Azor
Zadok   **Hananiah**
Achim   **Shecaniah**
Eliud   **Shemaiah**
Eleazar   **Neariah**
Matthan   **Elioenai**
Jacob
Joseph   → **Hodaviah,**
(Mary's   → **Eliashib,**
Husband)   → **Pelaiah,**
                → **Akkub,**
                → **Johanan,**
                → **Delaiah,**
                → **Anani**

Jesus Christ
[God's begotten son]

ORIGINAL 12 TRIBES

1) Reuben, 2) Simeon, 3) Levi , 4) Judah, 5) Dan, 6) Naphtali,

7) Gad, 8) Asher, 9) Issachar, 10) Zebulun,

11) Joseph, 12) Benjamin

✳✳✳✳✳✳✳✳✳✳ ✳✳✳✳✳✳✳✳✳✳ ✳✳✳✳✳✳✳✳✳✳

NEW 12 TRIBES

1) Reuben, 2) Simeon, 3) Judah, 4) Dan, 5) Naphtali, 6) Gad,

7) Asher, 8) Issachar, 9) Zebulun, 10) *Ephraim,

11) *Manasseh, 12) Benjamin

GREAT KING "SOLOMON" [Suleyman]
Son of King David, born in the
lineage of the Tribe of Judah

*Joseph's two son's Ephraim and Manasseh replaced Joseph as per the wishes of Jacob [Israel] to form two new tribes, and later on the command of God, members of the Levi clan were taken out as per the instructions of the "Lord" to become Priests during "Moses and Aaron's" time. Since then Levites were considered as members of the priesthood by all the new 12 tribes.

25

"And it came about the same night, that the word of God came to **NATHAN**, saying, "Go and tell **DAVID** My servant, 'Thus says the Lord, "You shall not build a house for Me to dwell in." And it shall come about when your days are fulfilled that you must go to be with your fathers, that **I WILL SET UP ONE OF YOUR DESCENDANTS AFTER YOU, WHO SHALL BE OF YOUR SONS**; and I will establish his kingdom. He shall build for Me a house, and I will establish his throne forever. **I WILL BE HIS FATHER, AND HE SHALL BE MY SON;** and I will not take My lovingkindness away from him, as I took it away from him who was before you. **BUT I WILL SETTLE HIM IN MY HOUSE AND IN MY KINGDOM FOREVER AND HIS THRONE SHALL BE ESTABLISHED FOREVER.**" [1 Chronicles 17 Verses 3, 4, 11, 12, 13, 14.]

The Secret of the Breast Plate

Part 1

The Secret of the "Breast Plate'" which was to be worn by the "High Priest" [Kohen Gadol], who was chosen from the decedents of Aaron" and thus belonged to the "Tribe of Levi" before he could Enter the "Holy of Holies"[Kadosh Hakadashim], the revered sacred place of the "Most High" in the Temple of King Solomon situated in the "City of King David" in Jerusalem during "Yom Kippur" [Jom ki pur -day of Atonement. The 'word "Kippur" meaning "Atone" in Hebrew Language].

According to the "Holy Bible" as mentioned in the Chapter 28 of Exodus, Verses 2, 4, and 15 to 30, the Lord – God of Israel [Most High] instructed Moses to make a "Breast Piece of Judgment" to be worn by the High Priest "Aaron" Chosen by the "Lord – God" himself, so by wearing it, he can make the required atonement for the "Sons of the 12 Tribes".

In the great Temple of King Solomon dedicated to the "' Most High '" in Jerusalem, there were two very important chambers known as the "Palhedrin Chamber'", and the "Avitnas Chamber", which were meant for the "Spiritual Conscious Expansion " of the "'Kohen Gadol" [High Priest], in which he was supported by the revered Prophets and Seers of his time along with the myriad of invisible Spiritual angelic entities and beings of the "Lord – God", as to properly purify his "Indwelling Mind Consciousness" before entering the "Holy of Holies" on the day of atonement, by first reviewing the "Lords Instructions" as given to "Moses" and written down in the five books of Torah and then discussing it with the appropriate chosen "Prophet of the Lord – God" of his times in the "Palhedrin Chamber", while in "Avitnas Chamber" he offered "Incense" by repeatedly singing praises as the "Glory to the invisible Most High".

The Kohen Gadol [High Priest] thus for 7 days prior to the "Yom Kippur" prepared himself to be endowed with "Spiritual Blessings", so he can enter the "Holy of Holies" protected by the "Spiritual Blessings", the only time of the year during which anyone went inside its holy precinct's, and in such preparations he followed all the prescribed purification and preparation practices which included five immersions in a Mikvah [Ritual Bath] , and four changes of clothing, which were sprinkled with "Holy Spring Water", which contained the burnt ashes of "Red Heifer".

During the Time of the wise and great King Solomon, whom as per the "Holy Bible", the "Lord God of Israel" himself called as his loving "Son" [1 Chronicles 17.13], the High Priest [Kohen Gadol] was "Zadok" and the chosen Prophet of the "Most High" was the "Prophet Nathan".

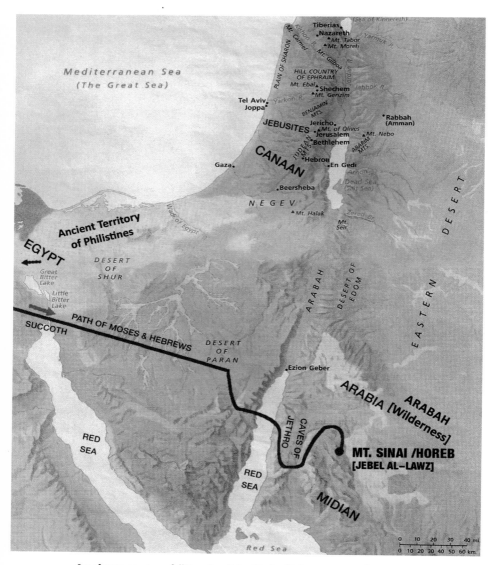

Ancient route of "Exodus" to Holy "Mount Horeb–Sinai"

The Secret of the Breast Plate

Part 2

According to the "Holy Bible " the great Prophet 'Moses" was chosen by the "Most High" as his mouth piece, as mentioned in this verse of "Holy Bible", which states " Now then go, and I even I, will be with your mouth, and teach you what you are to say""" [Exodus 4. 12].
The "Holy Bible" states that later " In the third month after the sons of Israel had gone out the land of Egypt, on that very day they came into the wilderness of Sinai", and camped in the wilderness in front of the mountain [Exodus 19.1,2]

The wilderness of Sinai was named after the "Sin", the ancient name of our "Moon", as the whole ground area was lit on full moon nights, and the holy mountain which is situated in this wilderness of Sinai was known as the mountain of "Rab or Reb" meaning "God", or simply "Mount Horeb", also termed as "Mount Sinai" being associated with the wilderness of Sinai.

As per the "Holy Bible', to this "Mountain of God" or Mount – "HoReb" much later during the reign of King AHAB of Israel, the great Prophet "ELIJAH", the Tishbite returned when the "Sons of Israel" became "Utterly Corrupt". In this reference the "Holy Bible" states that, " The angel of the Lord came again a second time and touched Elijah and said; Arise, Eat, because the journey is too great for you. So he arose and ate and drank, and went in the strength of that food 40 days and 40 nights to "Horeb", the mountain of God. Then he came there to a cave, and lodged there; and behold, the word of the Lord came to him, "What are you doing here Elijah?'. And he said "I have been very Zealous for the Lord, the God of hosts; for the "Sons of Israel" have forsaken Thy Covenant, torn down Thine altars, and killed Thy Prophets with the Sword. And I alone am left, and they seek my life to take it away". [1Kings 19 verses 7 to 10].

Prophet Elijah returned to Mount Horeb about 575 years later after Moses, as per the holy bible which states that, "480 years after the Sons of Israel came out of Egypt, during the 4th year of King SOLOMON'S reign the "House of God" was started to be built in Jerusalem, and the great King Solomon reigned for a total of 40 years, then his son King REHOBOAM reigned for 17 years, then King ABIJAM reigned for 3 years, then King ASA reigned for 41 years in JERUSALEM, and in the 38th year reign of King ASA, AHAB, the son of OMRI became King over ISRAEL, who did EVIL in Sight of the Lord, "MORE THAN ALL'" who were before him" [1 Kings Chapters 6 to 17].

Mount "Horeb" also known as the Mount "Sinai", is the sacred place where "Moses" received his 10 commandments from Lord – God of Israel, the revered most benevolent One and Only "Most High", upon 2 Tablets made of Stone from the Holy Mountain HOREB, who as per the Holy Bible also made earlier covenant's with their "Fore Fathers" . The Holy Bible states that after the great Flood "'GOD spoke to NOAH and to his Sons with him. Saying, NOW BEHOLD, I MYSELF DO ESTABLISH MY COVENANT WITH YOU, AND WITH YOUR DESCENDANTS AFTER YOU" [Genesis 9.8,9]

Later the "MOST HIGH" Lord - God made Covenant with Abram also changing his Chaldean name ABRAM given in the city of UR by his father TERAH to "ABRAHAM", regarding which the Holy Bible states, "Now when ABRAM was Ninety Nine Years old, the Lord appeared to ABRAM and said to him, I AM GOD ALMIGHTY, WALK BEFORE ME AND BE BLAMELESS. AND I WILL ESTABLISH MY COVENANT BETWEEN ME AND YOU, AND I WILL MULTIPLY YOU EXCEEDINGLY". And Abram fell on his face, and GOD talked with him saying, "AS FOR ME, BEHOLD, MY COVENANT IS WITH YOU, AND YOU SHALL BE THE FATHER OF A MULTITUDE OF NATIONS. NO LONGER SHALL YOUR NAME BE CALLED ABRAM, BUT YOUR NAME SHALL BE ABRAHAM; FOR I WILL MAKE YOU THE FATHER OF A MULTITUDE OF NATIONS". [Genesis 17.1,2,3,4,5]

Later on the Almighty "MOST HIGH" kept his covenant with ABRAHAM'S Son ISAAC, when he appeared to him in the night during the "Quarrel of Wells", regarding this episode which occurred during ISAAC'S Life, the Holy Bible states "And the Lord appeared to him the same night and said, I AM THE GOD OF YOUR FATHER ABRAHAM; DO NOT FEAR, FOR I AM WITH YOU. I WILL BLESS YOU, AND MULTIPLY YOUR DESCENDANTS, FOR THE SAKE OF MY SERVANT ABRAHAM". [Genesis 26.24]

Part 3

The Lord God of Israel also renewed his covenant with JACOB, the Son of ISAAC, and the grandson of ABRAHAM, by blessing him, regarding which the Holy Bible states, "GOD appeared to JACOB again when he came from Paddan –aram, and HE blessed him. And God said to him, Your name is JACOB; You shall no longer be called JACOB, But "ISRAEL" shall be your name." Thus HE called him ISRAEL. GOD also said to him, I am God Almighty; Be fruitful and multiply; A nation and a company of nations shall come from you, And Kings shall come forth from you. And the land which I gave to ABRAHAM, and ISAAC, I will give it to you, And I will give the land to your descendants after you [Genesis 35.9.10.11.12]

Much later MOSES was reminded by GOD about the Covenant at Mount "HOREB", the "Mountain of God", which he earlier made with ISRAEL and his Forefathers, and was thus MOSES was told by HIM, regarding which the Holy Bible states "HE said also, I AM THE GOD OF YOUR FATHER, THE GOD OF ABRAHAM, THE GOD OF ISAAC, AND THE GOD OF JACOB." Then MOSES hid his face, for he was afraid to look at GOD.

Then MOSES said to GOD, Behold, I am going to the sons of ISRAEL, and I shall say to them, "The GOD of your fathers have sent me to you." Now they may say to me, "'What is his name?'", what shall I say to them? And GOD said to MOSES, "I AM WHO I AM "; and HE said, "Thus you shall say to the Sons of Israel, "I AM" has sent me to you". [Exodus 3. 6, 13, 14]

The "MOST HIGH" Lord – God further added, "'THEN YOU SHALL SAY TO PHARAOH, THUS SAYS THE LORD, "ISRAEL" IS MY SON, MY FIRST BORN". [Exodus 4.22]

The Holy Bible further states that the "'MOST HIGH " Lord God told MOSES, "AND AGAINST ALL THE GODS OF EGYPT, I WILL EXECUTE JUDGMENTS - I AM THE LORD". [Exodus 12.12]
And all the People of this Planet Earth by now, very well know, this Undeniable 'HISTORICAL FACT" that since the day the MOST HIGH", Who is the One and Only "'True Creator – Observer'", and the ALMIGHTY Unknowable "LORD GOD" of the Universe, ""EXECUTED HIS JUDGMENT AGAINST ALL THE GODS OF EGYPT'", the Many Millennial

Old "'Ancient Egyptian Religion'" of various so called "'GODS AND GODDESSES'" Crumbled to Pieces, and in the due course of only just 1 Millennium after MOSES and the children of ISRAEL left EGYPT, it was Totally Annihilated from the "Ancient Land of the Mighty Pharaoh's", with its Complete "'ELIMINATION and EXTINCTION, FOREVER", Never to be "'Established Again'" in the Ancient Land of Egypt..

MOSES said to the LORD, " Please , LORD, I Have Never Been Eloquent, Neither Recently Nor In Time Past, Nor Since Thou Hast Spoken To Thy Servant; For I Am Slow Of Speech And Slow of Tongue." And the LORD Said to Him, "WHO HAS MADE MAN'S MOUTH? OR WHO MAKES HIM DUMB OR DEAF, OR SEEING OR BLIND? IS IT NOT I, THE LORD?" "NOW THEN GO, AND I, EVEN I, WILL BE WITH YOUR MOUTH, AND TEACH YOU WHAT YOU ARE TO SAY".
But He said, "Please, LORD, now send the message by whomever THOU Wilt." [Exodus 4. 10, 11, 12, 13]

Then the Lord Said to MOSES. "SEE I MAKE YOU AS A """"GOD""""" TO PHARAOH, AND YOUR BROTHER AARON SHALL BE YOUR PROPHET" [Exodus 7.1]

Many People of this Planet Earth, and their counterpart INVISIBLE ENTITIES AND BEINGS, who still believe in the Pantheons of their "GODS AND GODDESSES" Systems, and who are part and parcel of their Various FAITHS AND BELIEFS " and thus daily Worship them consistently through various rituals, fail to UNDERSTAND this "MOST IMPORTANT UNDERLYING FACT" that their "" ALMIGHTY GODS AND GODDESSES" were also Created by "SOMEONE MUCH MORE HIGHER THAN THEMSELVES", and thus WHO through his "DIVINE WILL" AND "'DESIRE MIND" FULL OF "LOVE", WHICH IS BASED UPON "ONE AND ONLY" UNIVERSAL LAW OF "WILL TO DO GOOD" thus brought THEM in their Various Levels of "HIERARCHICAL EXISTENCE", to reverently perform their required duties, thus existing Unconsciously, Sub Consciously, Semi Consciously, Consciously, Super Consciously, and Ultra Consciously in their own differentiated spherical dimensional levels which were known to the ancient WISE SEERS AND PROPHETS in Hebrew Language as the "'SEPHIROTS OR SEFIRA'S"

In the 3 main dense worlds of this Planet Earth, which are known as the 3 dense Spherical dimensional planes of Human Existence, and which have been termed since ancient times by the "WISE SEERS

AND PROPHETS", who faithfully performed their "REQUIRED DUTIES" as the Servant Workers of the "MOST HIGH", as the "DIMENSIONAL SEPHIROT'S" of "ASSIAH, YETZIRAH, and BRIAH", of which the 2 Higher Dimensional Planes are usually invisible to Most Incarnated Humans Beings, who are incarnated upon the dimensional plane commonly known as the SEPHIROT OF ASSIAH of this Planet Earth, all the CONSCIOUS AND UNCONSCIOUS CREATIONS OF THE "UNKNOWABLE CREATOR", WHO ARE JUST EXISTING AS THE VARIOUS HIERARCHICAL ORDERS OF "ENTITIES AND BEINGS" IN THEIR OWN DIFFERENTIATED LEVELS OF CONSCIOUS EXISTENCE, AS PER THE "PLAN AND PURPOSE OF THE UNKNOWABLE CREATOR – OBSERVER LORD – GOD OF THE UNIVERSE, WHO WAS KNOWN TO THE GREAT AND WISE "'KING SOLOMON", THE MOST FAMOUS KING OF ALL TRIBES OF ISRAELITE'S, AS THE UNKNOWABLE "MOST HIGH" LORD – GOD OF THE INFINITE UNIVERSE, FOR WHOM HE BUILT THE GREAT "'TEMPLE HOUSE'" IN JERUSALEM, THE CITY OF HIS FATHER DAVID, they are required to properly perform their "REQUIRED DUTIES'", and to act just only as the "'CO – CREATORS" as per the "EVOLUTIONARY PLAN AND PURPOSE OF CONSCIOUS EXPANSION" established by the Unknowable "MOST HIGH" in all the subjectively and objectively manifested "SEPHIROTS of CONSCIOUS EXISTENCE", and thus "CYCLICALLY" Expanding also their Own Indwelling Consciousness, by willfully existing as the "TRULY FAITHFUL SERVANTS AND WORKERS" of their ONE AND ONLY UNKNOWABLE "CREATOR – OBSERVER" of the ENTIRE INFINITE UNIVERSE, who since Very Ancient Times has been known to the ENLIGHTENED SEERS AND PROPHETS" as the "MOST BENEVOLENT, MOST BENEFICENT, THE MOST MERCIFUL, THE ONE AND ONLY, TRUE "LORD – GOD" OR THE "MOST HIGH'" OF THE SUBJECTIVELY AND OBJECTIVELY MANIFESTED "'UNFATHOMABLY HUGE INFINITE UNIVERSE'" IN THE "CELESTIAL SPACE".

Ancient Menorah etched on a rock at Mount Horeb–Sinai – Saudi Arabia

Mount Sinai on the left and Mount Horheb on the right in Saudia Arabia

The Secret of the Breast Plate

Part 4

More than 3000 years have passed, since the Children of Israel were led out of Egypt by the Grace of the "Most High" through the humble services of his faithful Servant Moses, who per the wishes of the Unknowable MOST HIGH", as stated in the "Holy Bible" was made as a "GOD" to the Ruling Mighty Pharaoh of ancient Egypt, and his brother Aaron assisting him a "PROPHET" [Exodus 7. 1]

But most of the "Biblical Scholar's" of the modern physical dimensional world, without having the Clear Consciousness of "Spiritual Zest" like their ancient "'Sages and Prophets" had, who considered themselves nothing more than the "Humble Servants of their Lord – God "Most High", who since very ancient times made Covenant with their forefathers, have yet failed to understand the underlying "Plan and Purpose", which he devised for the "Children of Israel", which was absolutely required for them to wander in the wilderness for 40 years to reach the promise land, which is physical reality is only about 200 miles from where they originally left in Egypt.

To have some basic understanding of the 'Plan and Purpose", of the "MOST HIGH", which he devised for the "Children of Israel", let us contemplate upon it through a very "Spiritual Mind", rather than using our everyday worldly "Personality Mind", and then wholeheartedly examine some basic facts which are related to this entire "Episode of Exodus" as written in the "Holy Bible".

According to "Holy Bible", the time that the Sons of Israel lived in Egypt was Four Hundred and Thirty Years. And it came about at the end of 430 years, to the very day, that all the hosts of the LORD went out from the land of Egypt [Exodus 12.40, 41]. So it had been long time since Israel [Jacob] brought his entire family to dwell in the land of Egypt, and during this long time period they became Mightier [Wealthy] than the local Egyptians, as stated in this particular verse "Now a new king arose over Egypt, who did not know Joseph. And he said to his people, "Behold, the people of the Sons of Israel are more and mightier than we. Come, let us deal wisely with them, lest they multiply and in the event of war, they also join themselves to those who hate us, and fight against us, and depart from the land." So they appointed taskmasters over them to "Afflict Them with Hard Labor". And they built for Pharaoh Storage cities, named PITHOM and RAMESES. But the more they afflicted them, the more they multiplied and the more they spread out, so that they were in dread of the Sons of Israel. [Exodus 1. 8, 9, 10, 11,12]. [Please Note, that the same thing Happened upon this planet in Germany Occupied Areas of the Physical Plane, during World War II Time Period]

During the passing of over 4 centuries, most children of Israel now living for many generations in Egypt, started following the "Traditions and Culture" including food habits of the Ancient Egyptians, who worshiped myriad of "Gods and Goddesses", whose "Very Names" defined their various divine attributes, and that is why as per the "Holy Bible" MOSES asked the LORD – GOD "Behold, I am going to the Sons of Israel, and I shall say to them, "The GOD of your Fathers has sent me to you". Now they may say to me, "WHAT IS HIS NAME?' What shall I say to them?"[Exodus 3. 13].

Now when the "MOST HIGH" Lord – God delivered the Sons of Israel safely from Egypt, they were in huge numbers regarding which the Holy Bible states, "Now the Sons of Israel journeyed from RAMESES to SUCCOTH, about Six Hundred Thousand Men on foot, aside from children. And a mixed multitude also went up with them [Egyptian Relatives, Friends, and their Slave Workers], along with flocks and herds, a very large number of Livestock. [Exodus 12. 37, 38].

The Holy Bible further states " Thus the LORD saved ISRAEL that day from the hand of Egyptians, and ISRAEL saw Egyptians dead on the Seashore. And when ISRAEL saw "THE GREAT POWER", which the LORD has used against the Egyptians, the People "FEARED THE LORD"', and they "BELIEVED IN THE LORD ", and in "HIS SERVANT MOSES". [Exodus 14.30, 31].

If anyone through inner mind contemplation pays "Spiritual Attention" to this "Important Verse" then they will notice, that even after so many earlier miracles which were performed by MOSES, the Faithful Servant of the unknowable "MOST HIGH", most "Sons of Israel", and the mixed multitude of People, who were used to the "Egyptian Magic', which was usually performed by the "Magician Priesthood" of the Egyptian Gods, still did not properly FEARED OR 'BELIEVED IN THE LORD ', and in "HIS SERVANT MOSES" till then.

Part 5

Most incarnated Human Beings, and their counterpart invisible "Entities and Beings", who exist in the dense dimensional spherical plane of ASSIAH of this Planet Earth, which is also commonly termed as the "Physical Plane" and known by the Mystics as the "Sephirot or Sefira" of the Human Life existence, which is meant for the utilization of their animated dense human form, usually "'FAIL TO UNDERSTAND" this very basic fact, that the "Spiritual Wisdom" can only be comprehended with a "Spiritual Mind" and not a everyday "'Personality Mind", which the incarnated human beings normally utilize to learn the material aspects of their physical life existence, daily dealing with the "Illusory Glamour" of this dense material plane. And now with the advent of Physical "Sciences and Technology", they have further created an "Virtual Illusory Reality", which generally keeps their "Personality Minds'" more occupied in "ILLUSION and DELUSION" during their short lived Human Lives", and only the Enlightened Human Beings, who have expanded their indwelling mind consciousness through rigorous practices can also make use of "VIRTUAL REALITY", for HIGHER SPIRITUAL PURPOSES to advance the UNIVERSAL LAW OF WILL TO DO GOOD, commonly known as the "'Divine Love", during their short lived Human Form existence.

The Spiritually advanced persons having "One Pointed Goal" to "Consciously" get in touch with their "Solar Consciousness" or their "SPIRIT", also known as their "True Higher Self" are in reality "'SPIRITUAL'", but they "'May or May not" be Religious, as the basic reason for the formation of Religions since ancient times upon this physical plane of planet earth, as per the Plan and Purpose of the "Most High", the unknowable "CREATOR – OBSERVER" Lord- God of the Universe, was to provide an evolutionary path which was made for the lower stages of evolutionary conscious expansion, like the children during their Childhood Schooling are generally required to follow certain dress codes or sit in a assigned spot of their class rooms, so that their "Personality Minds" can become stable and absorb the teachings with much more attention.

The "Spiritual Wisdom", as compiled and written by the ancient SEERS AND SAGES, who with their "Spiritual Mind's" could Consciously Hear and Talk, and thus communicate with the angelic co – creator servants of the "Most High"', especially the Chosen PROPHETS, who could directly communicate with the unfathomable consciousness of the unknowable "MOST HIGH", the One and Only "LORD – GOD" of the Universe, who can also JUDGE ALL OTHER --- "GODS and GODDESSES", who themselves are also part of HIS subjectively and objectively manifested CREATION , and his such "MOST HIGH" status is clearly mentioned in this verse of "Holy Bible", which states "Against all the Gods of Egypt, I WILL EXECUTE JUDGMENTS – I AM THE LORD" [Exodus 12.12].

Most Human Beings of this Planet Earth are "'TOTALLY UNAWARE" of this "IMPORTANT FACT'" that before MANKIND was created upon this Planet by the "MOST HIGH" Lord – God, of the Universe, HE had already created his various "SERVANT HELPERS", who are existing as the Myriad Hosts of various Hierarchical Angelic Groups. Of whom some were allowed by him to act as co – creator Gods and Goddesses as his faithful servants.

The "Most High" Lord God also "CREATED" through his desire mind vital energy, Various Types of Invisible "'Elemental", which were required to set up his various Visible Kingdoms, [Mineral, Plants, Animal and Human Kingdoms] by supplying them with their proper forms, who Primarily existed in their differentiated levels in CONSCIOUSLY, SEMI CONSCIOUSLY, and UNCONSCIOUSLY states, about which the Holy Bible give us some IMPORTANT HINTS in the following Verses of GENESIS, which explains the CREATION of the "MOST HIGH".

"Then God said, "LET US" make Man in Our image, according to "OUR" likeness; and let them rule over the fish of the sea and over the birds of the sky and over the cattle and over all the Earth, and over every creeping thing that creeps the Earth."[Genesis Chapter 1, Verse 26].

Anyone who pays close attention to this "IMPORTANT VERSE" will clearly notice, that this verse of the very first chapter of the Holy Bible" is clearly stating that the "MOST HIGH" had already Created his "SERVANT HELPERS", who were assisting HIM as "Co – Creators" in the formation of a Human Beings, and these SO CALLED GODS are the very same ones WHO "'WILLFULLY" LATER ON CONSPIRED AGAINST THE "MOST HIGH" and through their DEFORMED and MUTATED MINDS WENT AGAINST HIS EVOLUTIONARY PLAN AND PURPOSE, WHICH IS BASED UPON THE UNIVERSAL LAW OF WILL TO DO GOOD." And that is why later on he had to PUNISH" these "CORRUPTED MIND" "GUILTY ONES" to uphold the UNIVERSAL LAW OF "WILL TO DO GOOD",, Who were worshiped for many thousands years in the Land of Egypt, when he spoke to his Humble Servant MOSES thus clearly explaining in this verse of "Holy Bible", which states "AGAINST ALL THE GODS OF EGYPT, I WILL EXECUTE JUDGMENTS – I AM THE LORD" [Exodus 12.12].

The Holy Bible further clarifies the presence of the Angelic Servant Helpers of the "MOST HIGH" in this next Verse of GENESIS, which state, "Then the LORD – GOD said, "Behold, the MAN has become like "ONE OF US", knowing good and evil; and now, lest he stretch out his hand, and take also from the tree of life, and eat, and live forever". [Genesis 3.22]

Much later his son JESUS CHRIST, who himself incarnated upon this earth just as a Human Being was fully aware of this fact that the Unknowable Lord – God, The "MOST HIGH", not only can "JUDGE and DESTROY" the Corrupt Human Beings but also can JUDGE ALL THE GODS OF THIS EARTH , AND THUS EXECUTE HIS JUDGMENTS AGAINST THEM .

The Holy Bible Quotes JESUS CHRIST in this IMPORTANT VERSE, which states, "AND DO NOT FEAR THOSE WHO KILL THE BODY, BUT ARE UNABLE TO KILL THE "SOUL"; BUT RATHER FEAR "'HIM'", WHO IS ABLE TO DESTROY BOTH "SOUL AND BODY" IN HELL". [Matthew 10.28]

The High Priest

39

Man and Woman created by LORD GOD in "His" own image

The Secret of the Breast Plate

Part 6

In the physical plane, known in Hebrew Language as "SEPHIROT OF ASSIAH", which is the domain of incarnated human beings, and their counterpart invisible Angelic Beings to dwell in, during very ancient times, when the created ANGELIC SERVANT HELPERS of the Most Beneficent, the Most Benevolent, the "MOST HIGH', were TRULY FAITHFUL to him, He cheerfully allotted them "INDIVIDUALIZED SPECIFIC POWERS" to perform their specific duties related to the evolution of invisible and visible kingdoms of planet earth, and thus to act as Co – Creators in the three dimensional spheres of "ASSIAH", "YETZIRAH", and "BRIAH", which over the passing of time they willfully "MISUSED", and thus became totally CORRUPT, and due to this very reason the Evolving Human Beings, who were gradually evolving for their conscious expansion under the "'care and guidance" of these Angelic Beings, who were also acting as the Sons of God, themselves became Fully CORRUPT, and thus started the illegal worship of these so called Gods and Goddesses, upon this Planet Earth.

The "Holy Bible" regarding this "Wholesale Corruption" clearly explains in the following verses of GENESIS, which state:

"Now it came about when men began to multiply on the face of land, and daughters were born to them, that the Sons of GOD saw that the daughters of men were beautiful; and they took wives for themselves, whomever they chose.

Then the Lord saw that the wickedness of man was great on earth, and every intent of the thoughts of his heart was only evil continually. And the LORD was sorry that "HE" had made man on the Earth, and "HE" was grieved in "HIS" heart. And the LORD said, "I WILL BLOT OUT MAN WHOM I HAVE CREATED, FROM THE FACE OF LAND, from man to animals to creeping things and to birds of the sky; for I AM sorry that I have made them".. But "NOAH" found favor in the eyes of the LORD..

Now the Earth was CORRUPT in the Sight of GOD, and the Earth was filled with violence. And GOD looked on the Earth, and behold. It was CORRUPT; for all FLESH had CORRUPTED their way upon the Earth.

Then GOD said to NOAH, "The End of All Flesh has come before "ME"; for the Earth is filled with violence because of them; and BEHOLD I AM ABOUT TO DESTROY THEM WITH THE EARTH.

Thus NOAH did; according to ALL that GOD had COMMANDED him, so he did. [Genesis 6, 1, 2, 5, 6, 7, 8, 11, 12, 13, 22]

Thus "HE" blotted out every living thing that was upon the face of the Land, from Man to Animals to Creeping things, and to Birds of the sky, and they were blotted out from the Earth; and only NOAH was left, together with those that were with him in the ark [Genesis 7. 23]

Then GOD spoke to NOAH and his sons with him, saying "NOW BEHOLD I MYSELF DO ESTABLISH MY COVENANT WITH YOU, AND WITH YOUR DESCENDANTS AFTER YOU. [Genesis 9. 8, 9]

During the "'Very Ancient Vedic Time's" after the event of great flood, in the fertile lands of Bhartavarsha [India] only the Unknowable "Most High God" was worshiped, through "Fire Oblations" whom the Vedic Seers and Sages in Sanskrit Language called as the "Maha Ishvara"meaning "The Great Lord – God". He was reverently worshiped by All Human Beings as well as by All the Invisible Angelic Beings. The "Most High" Lord - God being "'Unknowable" thus could not be ever known by Anyone, and whose Conscious attributes were only perceived by all named in Sanskrit as the "Agni" meaning "Fire", thus "Holy Fire" was the only Visible Element composed of live ethereal essences, which defined his "Divine Presence" upon this Planet Earth.

Although the "MOST HIGH" blotted out everyone upon the physical plane of ASSIAH through the Great Flood, which is recorded in various religious literature's of this planet Earth, "HE" being the "Most Merciful" did not destroy the two higher planes of this Planet Earth namely "YETZIRAH", and "BRIAH", but surely rebuked his Created Angelic Children the so called "Gods and Goddesses' 'of the Human Races with Severe Judgment's, who willfully indulging in Corrupt Behavior over the passing of Time [Descending Wheel of Time] went astray from their required prescribed duties.

But then over the passing of time these Corrupt Angelic children of the Most High also willfully plotted against their Most Benevolent creator Father "The MOST HIGH", and thus willfully Conspiring against him then heinously back stabbed his ineffable LOVE and TRUST.

Much Later when the situation went out of hand, The Lord - God "MOST HIGH" did not wanted to cause any destruction again, as mentioned in this verse of Genesis in "Holy Bible", which states, "The LORD said to HIMSELF "I" will Never Again "CURSE" the ground on account of Man, for the Intent of Man's Heart is "EVIL" from his Youth; and I will never again destroy every living thing, as "I" have done. [Genesis 8. 21],

But these MOST CORRUPT GODS and GODDESSES in the ENTIRE UNIVERSE who are living in various visible and invisible dimensions of this Planet Earth took illegal advantage of His Benevolence, and thus started again "Full Scale Open Corruption" in All the Countries and Nations of this world, penetrating all forms of Governments and established religions, which they supported by unquenchable greed and power to control others through the falsified "Concept of Money".

But the Lord - God "MOST HIGH" instead of destroying Human Beings and all other living creatures of this Planet Earth, "HE" again made a covenant with a direct descendant of NOAH, whom he blissfully renamed from ABRAM to ABRAHAM,

NOAH'S descendants till then were again wrongfully indulged in the unlawful practices of worshiping these So Called "GODS and GODDESSES, who were the very reason of the earlier worldwide corruption upon this planet earth.

Regarding this matter of again worshiping the So Called "Gods and Goddesses after the Great Flood, who themselves are nothing but the CREATION of the Unknowable "MOST HIGH", and thus NOAH's descendants performed this wrong act rather than worshiping their ONE AND ONLY UNKNOWABLE TRUE CREATOR, who is generally referred to, by all "Entities and Beings of the three dimensional plane worlds of "ASSIAH, YETRIAH and BRIAH" as "THE "MOST HIGH"", and the worship of Gods and Goddesses by NOAH'S Descendants has been clearly mentioned in the "Chapter of Joshua" in the Holy Bible, which thus states in the following verses:

"And JOSHUA said to ALL the people, thus says the "LORD", the "GOD OF ISRAEl,", " From Ancient Times Your Fathers Lived beyond The River Namely "TERAH", The Father of ABRAHAM, and the Father of NAHOR,

""""""AND THEY SERVED OTHER GODS"""""". Then "I" Took your father ABRAHAM Beyond the River, and led him through "'ALL THE LAND OF CANNAN", and multiplied his descendants and gave him ISSAC.

And to ISSAC. "I" gave JACOB and ESAU, and to ESAU, "I" gave Mount SEIR, to possess it, but JACOB and his SONS went down to EGYPT.

Then "I" sent MOSES and AARON, and "I" Plagued EGYPT by what "I" did in its midst; and afterward "I" brought you out. [Joshua 24. 2, 3, 4, 5]

Then GOD spoke to NOAH and his sons with him, saying "NOW BEHOLD I MYSELF DO ESTABLISH MY COVENANT WITH YOU, AND WITH YOUR DESCENDANTS AFTER YOU. [Genesis 9. 8, 9]

44

Part 7

In the Story of Creation as per the "Holy Bible", the Unknowable LORD GOD clearly Commands NOAH that "Only You Shall Not Eat Flesh with its Life, that is its "BLOOD" [Genesis 9. 4]. And the very reason is that the Blood contains tiny indestructible particles of "LIFE FORCE" now known by the modern day scientists as "SOMATIDS", which can be seen through high magnification electronic Microscope.

The Human Being incarnated upon this physical plane of "ASSIAH", shares "Physio-Chemical Life Processes" with all "animals"[Mammal , Birds etc.], who belong to animal kingdom of this planet earth, and on the physical plane [ASSIAH] it is totally indistinguishable from them except humans has been given by the ineffable grace of the "Most High" a gift of "Individualized Mind". Therefore all humans are having an "Animal Personality" or in Hebrew the "Nefesh HaBehamit", which is empowered by extremely minute "Somatids" in the blood, which perform the "physio-chemical life processes" for vital animation.

Regarding this "Life Force" of individualized "Personality Conscious" which is present in the blood, the "Holy Bible" in the "Chapter of Leviticus" states " For the Life of the flesh is in the blood, and I have given it to you on the Altar to make atonement for your souls; for it is the blood by reason of the life that makes atonement. Therefore I said to the Sons of Israel, No person among you may eat blood, nor may any "Alien" who sojourns among you eat blood [Leviticus 17.11, 12]

In the ancient Hindu Literature, the Sanskrit word "SOMA" defined the "Nectar of Gods", which was the "Secret of Immortality", as the Soma Particles just like these "Somatids", were Indestructible to all types of Heat as well as to Radiation. Only a handful of learned people may know, that just like the ancient Chaldean Hebrew – Aramaic name for "Moon" has been "SIN", similarly the Ancient Sanskrit name for Moon has been "SOMA" in the Ancient India.

Not too many Human Beings are aware of this "Most Important Fact", that many millions of years ago when the "Conscious Expansion Experiment" based upon the Universal Law of "Will to do Good" utterly Failed, and was thus condemned due to "Unquenchable Corruption and Greed", "All Life" by the ineffable Grace and due to the timely intervention of the unknowable "MOST HIGH" was systematically transferred from Moon [SIN - SOMA] to this Planet Earth, through the proper use of this "Vital Life Energy Containing SOMATID particles, which are now found in all types of growing visible and invisible Earthly Kingdoms having vitality in differentiated levels of consciousness, of which the 4 visible kingdoms of growth are [1] Mineral Kingdom as the "Growing Crystals" have in them the required life force, [2] Plant Kingdom, [3] Animal Kingdom, and the [4] Human Kingdom, and the 3 Invisible Kingdoms which exist below the level of Visible Mineral kingdom, as well as in all invisible kingdoms [Realm of Angelic beings and Departed Forefathers], which exist above the visible level of Human Kingdom, of which "ALL" of the incarnated Human Beings, have some type of "Conscious and Unconscious" Glimpses during their Physical body Sleep time, when their indwelling consciousness temporarily detach from their physical bodies and thus leave on the ethereal magnetic currents from their physical bodies, but still connected with it through an shining invisible "Vital Cord of Vital Energy - Force", with a silvery hue, which continually provides the "Life Force" known in Hebrew language as the "Nishmat Chaim" coming from the higher mental plane world of "BRIAH" as the "Neshama" [Vital Force of Mind Consciousness], to the incarnated Human Body thus living incarnated in the "SEPHIROT OF ASSIAH", for its required animation during the course of their "Physical Plane Life", whom the Great Wise Preacher King SOLOMON referred to as the "SILVER CORD" in the "Chapter of ECCLESIASTES of the "Holy Bible", which gets cut from the physical body at the time of "Physical Death".

In reference to this "Silver Cord", these most important verses of the "Holy Bible" states "Remember HIM before the SILVER CORD is Broken, and the Golden Bowl [Auric Body] is crushed, the pitcher by the well is shattered and the wheel at the cistern is crushed; then the dust will return to the earth as it was, and the "SPIRIT" will return to GOD who gave it. [[Ecclesiastes 12. 6, 7].

"Near death Experiences", which many people of this world have, during their short lived incarnated human lives, this invisible "SILVER CORD" of vital force is only "Partially or Temporarily" Cut, and during this time period their indwelling personality consciousness [NEFESH] immediately becomes "Very Small" and in its such tiny existence, it is able to consciously see all around this physical plane world with a 360 degree angle view, as all particles of their "RUACH" body simultaneously corresponds to the extended "'Sensation of View'". The very basic reason for such 360 degree view is that, the vital conscious particles of their "Ruach Bodies', which literally compose it, are magnetically charged and are of "Liquid" in nature as compared to the dense physical body particles of an incarnated Human Being, and being thus in their "ethereal magnetic liquid state", they are thus constantly in motion, not like their counterpart dense physical body particles, which compose the two human eyes for the "Sensation of Sight", which are fixed in their cone socket frame work, which thus only allows them the "front view abilities". In this dense physical plane of ASSIAH, all incarnated human beings, using their "Ruach Body" during such astral travels during their sleep time enter various levels of the Dream World, and thus feels like having thousands of eyes with a 360 degree angle view, just like the ancient Prophets ISAIAH and Ezekiel mentioned in their divine visions.

And in such near death experiences, those people thus in their tiny vital forms enters in this "Silver Cord" preparing to go back to the "Higher Dimensional Plane of Yetzirah [Astral Plane]", from where they originally incarnated in the dense physical plane of Assiah, to have an incarnated physical body to acquire material world experience, so they as per plan and purpose of the "Most High" can enhance and expand their indwelling personality consciousness during their short lived human lives, which is connected with this invisible "Silver Cord" to their higher dimensional plane of BRIAH'S "Spiritual Consciousness" [NESHAMA], and this "Silver Cord" being Hollow at that particular moment appears to them as a "Tunnel of Light", but if this temporary cut of this silver cord gets healed, due to various reasons which may include "Their physical plane time is not yet finished, or Unfinished Business of the Soul" or an extra boost of vital help provided through "Prayer Energy of the Spiritual Well Wishers" their Vital Cord Connection gets joined back again, and thus fixed for the indwelling personality consciousness to come back to dwell again in their physical bodies to fulfill their "Unfinished Spiritual duties".

This "Silver Cord of Vital force" is very elastic in nature, which can easily be stretched for thousands of miles instantly at the "'speed of light'" during the physical body sleep time commonly known by human beings as the "Dream Time", as per the "Desire Mind" requirements of the "Indwelling Human Consciousness" [Nefesh], to penetrate the

"Invisible Ethereal Higher Dimensional Zones", which then become visible during such "Astral Travel" to our ethereal bodies having "Ruach"[Electromagnetic Vital Consciousness, which is generally defined since ancient times by the "Seers and Sages" as the flowing "Wind", which we all humans during our incarnated lives consciously or unconsciously use in such "Astral Travels".

When we use our ethereal bodies "unconsciously" in such travels, then we do not remember the dreams upon waking up back in our physical bodies, except we have a undeniable feeling as a strange sensation that we dreamed, while we remember the dreams, sometimes to a great extent when we use our ethereal bodies in "Semi or Sub Conscious" mind states. When we use our ethereal bodies "Consciously" during our sleep time, as well as during the contemplating upon the "Spirit" or the "Higher Mind Solar Consciousness" known as the art of "Spiritual Meditation", thus entering the higher dimensional invisible ethereal levels, of which the ancient Prophets were very well aware, then we can interact with the higher dimensional "Entities and Beings", including some of our departed family members and friends, who had departed from this physical plane due to their physical death, and who may be present in the various sub levels of the higher dimensional zones, and thus in those cases we fully remember our dreams and all such interactions which took place in the "Higher Dimensional Levels" upon waking up back in our physical bodies.

An important fact to be noted that the outer most Periphery of the invisible dimensional zone of "SEPHIROT of YETRIRAH", which becomes visible to the indwelling human consciousness during sleep time, extends all the way to the physical boundaries of our visible "MOON".

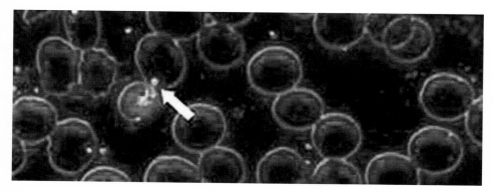

Somatid's

Part 8

The Astral Body known in Hebrew as "Ruach", which is connected with the physical body through the "Silver Cord of Vital force", regarding which the "CHOSEN - SON of GOD", the Most Wise KING SOLOMON mentioned in the Holy Bible. Regarding King Solomon being the chosen "SON of GOD", is clearly stated in the "Holy Bible" in its chapter "1 Chronicles 17. 13, 14". The Most Wise King of the "Holy Bible", thus properly mentioned about this Silver Cord in the "'Book of Ecclesiastes chapter 12 verse 6'", whose many other Important Works related to HIS deep understanding of True "SPIRITUALITY", which during his Life Time was directly provided to HIM by the ineffable grace of his INVISIBLE CREATOR FATHER OF THE UNIVERSE – The "MOST HIGH", the LORD – GOD of ISRAEL, were then properly compiled and written down in great details by the PROPHET NATHAN, the Humble Servant of God, as mentioned in the "Holy Bible" and were later on deceitfully lost, regarding which the "Holy Bible" clearly states, "Now the rest of the ACTS of SOLOMON, from FIRST to the LAST, Are they Not written in the records of NATHAN the PROPHET? [2 Chronicles 9. 29].

These most important records were "Willfully" OMITTED due to a full-scale conspiracy against HIM, by those Jealous members of "PRIESTHOOD" and their supporters, who first under the "Demonic Spell" of the So Called invisible GODS and GODDESSES, earlier sided with his brother to be the "king of Israel" against the wishes of the "MOST HIGH", who earlier chose him as "HIS SON", as per the Holy Bible, and after KING SOLOMON'S passing away, they later willfully joined the Evil King JEROBOAM, who became the King of the 10 Tribes of ISRAELITE'S out of the Total 12 Israelite Tribes, with the "invisible help", which was provided to him by the so called "GODS and GODDESSES", who earlier also provided JEROBOAM, refuge in the Land of Egypt, to live under the protection of their henchman Pharaoh, from where their LORD – GOD "MOST HIGH" during the time of MOSES delivered them from the "Bondage's of Slavery".

Most people fail to understand this basic FACT, that JEROBOAM is the Evil One, the "First King of Israelite's" since the time of Exodus, when MOSES, about 516 years earlier, liberated them under the command of the "MOST HIGH", the Most Revered and One and Only "'TRUE

CREATOR GOD" of the Entire Universe, the Lord – God of ISRAEL and ABRAHAM, from the Slavery of the Egyptian Pharaohs, whose very minds were Corrupted with the invisible help of these so called """"EGYPTIAN GODS and GODDESSES"""". In this regard the holy bible states "Now it came about in the FOUR HUNDRED and EIGHTIETH year after the SONS of ISRAEL came out of the Land of Egypt, in the FORTH year of SOLOMON'S reign over ISRAEL, in the month of "ZIV", which is the Second Month, that HE began to build the HOUSE of the LORD" [1Kings 6. 1]. And per the Holy Bible we also know that "Thus the time that SOLOMON reigned in JERUSALEM over all ISRAEL was FORTY years. And SOLOMON slept with his fathers and was buried in the city of his father DAVID, and his son REHOBOAM reigned in his place [1 Kings 11. 42, 43]. Thus the children of ISRAEL got openly DIVIDED for the first time after 516 years of their liberation from the slavery of Egyptian Pharaoh's [480 – 4 + 40 = 516 years].

JEROBOAM whose HEART got controlled by the GODS and GODDESSES of EGYPT, under their "MIND CONTROL" techniques, then deceitfully persuaded all the Children of the Tribes of ISRAEL except the TRIBE of JUDAH, to willfully SIN against the "MOST HIGH" by putting them upon the wrong path of "IDOL WORSHIP", who made him their king as per the "Holy Bible", 1 Kings 12. 20, which state "'And it came about when ALL ISRAEL that JEROBOAM had returned, that they sent and called him to the assembly and made him KING over ALL ISRAEL, NONE but the TRIBE of JUDAH followed the House of DAVID. [1 Kings 12. 20].

In regard to the Controlling of the HEART of the King JEROBOAM, by these so called CORRUPT GODS and GODDESSES, the "Holy Bible" states. "And JEROBOAM said in his HEART, Now the Kingdom will return to the House of DAVID. If these people go up to offer sacrifices in the HOUSE of the LORD at JERUSALEM, then the HEART of this PEOPLE will return to the LORD, even to REHOBOAM, King of JUDAH; and they will kill ME and return to REHOBOAM, KING of JUDAH". So the King "'CONSULTED'" [Most Probably the "'CORRUPT members of the PRIESTHOOD'" whose minds got controlled by the "Demonic Powers" having a underlying desire to Follow the IDOL WORSHIP], and made """"TWO GOLDEN CALVES"""""""", and he said to them, "IT IS TOO MUCH FOR YOU TO GO UP TO JERUSALEM; """"""""""""BEHOLD YOUR GODS, O ISRAEL, THAT BROUGHT YOU UP FROM THE LAND OF EGYPT""""""""." [1 Kings 12. 26, 27, 28].

Now Looking at all these "'Biblical Facts'", the "Main and Most Important Question" arises that "How come the "LEVITE PRIESTHOOD", the ""chosen Sons"" of "MOSES and AARON", as well "'ALL THE OTHER SONS OF ISRAEL'" kept "'QUIET'" to such "DISGRACE AND ABOMINATION", to their DELIVERER, the "LORD – GOD of ISRAEL, the "MOST HIGH", the "ONE" and "ONLY", who with his "Godly Love", made """"""COVENANTS""""""""""" with their FOREFATHERS, since from the "Very Beginning" of the TIME, and again during the ancient times of "NOAH, ABRAHAM, ISAAC, JACOB, and MOSES", and thus did not "revolted against their such Abomination King JEROBOAM with a Zeal"?,

Had they really Become so """"CORRUPT"""", that they really "FORGOT" that it was NOT the "'GOLDEN CALF GOD'" of EGYPT, which brought them out of the "LAND OF EGYPT, and Gave MOSES the 10 COMMANDMENTS upon Mount HOREB, to be Duly placed in the "ARK OF COVENANT", but the Most Benevolent and Merciful "LORD GOD", Whom the Great King SOLOMON and his father King DAVID called as the """"MOST HIGH"""""?

The Astral Body or the "Ruach", when compared to the Dense Physical body in its acquired shape, is very much similar to the Physical Body, which is known in Hebrew as "Nefesh", which during the incarnated human life of an human being act as an "Animated Form Container" which we normally call the "Human Body" of "flesh and blood", for the indwelling "Personality Consciousness" to exist inside it. During its life duration time, and due to this very fact that "Ruach" is composed of "Tiny Astral Particles" which are made up of "'Invisible Magnetic Ethereal liquid", the 99 percent particles of this Astral Matter of "Ruach", which are present in the "Auric Shell" of a Human Being, which invisibly exist in the shape of a "Vital Energy Egg" around the physical body, thus totally enclosing it, which being the particles of "Ethereal Mist" are invisible to the naked human eye during our awake state, thus densely cling to their counterpart physical body through magnetic attraction, and even fully penetrate it.

And during the incarnated lives of human beings being, these "Ruach" Particles stay close to the shape of their Physical Form bodies due to their magnetic attraction with the dense animated matter, and thus constantly go on intermingling with it for a long period of time, and due to their inherent magnetic nature, they then develop a memory of their counterpart physical human form, and during the Astral travel time

51

in which the sleeping human beings "consciously or unconsciously" enter the various Dream world's differentiated dimensional Zones, which technically are the further differentiated conscious levels of the dense 4 ethereal sub planes levels and 7 Astral sub planes levels, which exist just like their counterpart Physical plane world, which also has various differentiated time zones levels in which various countries and nations exist having in them from highly technologically advanced areas, to totally backward rural areas of human existence in which they live similar to ancient way of life, and during such dimensional travels during the sleeping of physical body, the Ruach particles keep their such "Misty Ruach Forms" intact, which riding upon the ethereal magnetic currents of the higher dimensional planes, gets temporarily detached from the physical form embodying the human mind consciousness still attached to physical body with this "SILVER CORD", we consciously or unconsciously utilize RUACH during our dream world travels.

Upon physical death, when the animating life energy providing "Silver Cord's" connection gets broken from the physical body, these "Ruach Misty Forms" hold their shape for certain period of TIME, according to their corresponding physical form with which they were used to, but afterwards they can also change their shape to a new form according to the underlying desire of their "conscious mind", which is the CONSCIOUSNESS of the departed "Personality', if that particular person chooses to do so in their new level of higher dimensional plane existence [YETZIRAH], which is normally invisible to most incarnated human beings, during their physical plane existence of this Planet Earth.

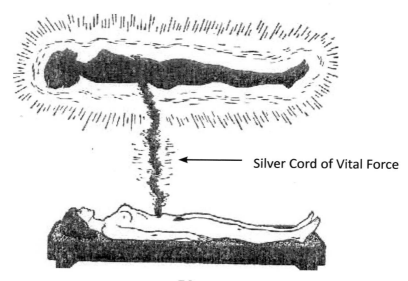

Silver Cord of Vital Force

Part 9

Regarding the existence of these so called "Gods and Goddesses", who themselves are nothing more but just a "MERE CREATION" brought into existence by the Ineffable Grace of the "MOST HIGH", through the "EVENTUATION PROCESS" according to the thoughts or the "DESIRE MIND" vital Consciousness Reflections of the Unknowable "MOST HIGH", and are thus just embodying a "'Little More Expanded Consciousness'" than their counterpart evolving "Human Beings", whom now they illegally Control and thus treat just as any other member of the evolving Lower Animal Kingdom, even though the "Holy Bible" clearly states that these created Hierarchical "Beings and Entities" later known to the "Human Beings" as the so called invisible "Gods and Goddesses" of various religions were "'PRESENT'" at that particular time, as the Faithful "SERVANT'" HELPERS of the "LORD-GOD", to assist HIM in their specific duties, when the LORD – GOD, the "MOST HIGH", the "UNKNOWABLE LORD – GOD" of the Entire Universe, created for the first time the "Human Being" upon this Planet Earth, who Earlier ALSO created the "HEAVENS and the Earth", regarding which the "Holy Bible" clearly mentions in its very first verse of the very first chapter, which states "IN THE BEGINNING GOD CREATED THE HEAVENS AND THE EARTH" [GENESIS 1,1],

Regarding the Creation of the "Human Being", the "Holy Bible" also clearly states in its first chapter that, "Then GOD said, Let ""US""""" make "'MAN" in """"OUR"""""" IMAGE, according to """"OUR"""" likeness; and let """"THEM""""" rule over the Fish of the Sea and over the Birds of the Sky and over the Cattle and over all the Earth, and over every creeping thing that creeps on the Earth." [Genesis 1. 26].

The plurality words in this particular verse existing as the words of "US" and "OUR" clearly defines the presence of these INVISIBLE SERVANTS of the "Most High", performing their intended specific roles in the creation of MAN upon this Planet Earth, and the word "THEM" in this Verse denotes, that as per the Plan and Purpose of the unknowable "MOST HIGH", to start with the MAN was intended to later DUPLICATE himself upon this Planet Earth.

But over the Passing of "'Evolutionary Cyclic Time'" upon this Planet

Earth, his "Created Servant worker's", the so called "GODS and GODDESSES" themselves became "Totally Corrupt", of which the smallest time cycle is composed of just a "Day and Night", regarding which the Holy Bible states in the story of CREATION in its very first chapter of Genesis, in which it is written "And there was EVENING and there was MORNING, a THIRD day. Then GOD said, "Let there be lights in the expanse of the Heavens to separate the Day from Night, and let them be for SIGNS, and for the SEASONS, and for DAYS and YEARS; and let them be for lights in the expanse of the Heavens to give light on Earth"; and "IT WAS SO" [Genesis 1. 13, 14, 15.]

"NOTE; The Holy Words of unknowable "MOST HIGH" known as """SO BE IT"""" or commonly termed as "AMEN" by the Ancient "Seers and Sages" is the Godly PROCLAMATION in the "EVENTUATION PROCESS of the CREATION, during which "HE" filled with "DIVINE LOVE" thus performed this Act of "CREATION" through "'HIS DESIRE MIND", which is based upon the Universal Law of "WILL TO DO his 'GOOD".

The Holy Bible Further states "And GOD made the Two Great Lights, the Greater Light to govern the Day, and the Lesser Light to govern the Night; "HE" made the stars also. And GOD placed them in the expanse of the HEAVEN'S to give light on Earth, and to govern the Day and Night, and to separate the Light from Darkness; and GOD saw it was good. And there was Evening and there was Morning, a FOURTH Day". [Genesis 1. 16, 17, 18, 19.]

These so called' 'TIME CYCLES" were thus established at the Very start of "CREATION", which as per the "Evolutionary Plan and Purpose" of the "MOST HIGH" are required for the "Conscious Expansion" of all visible and invisible "CREATED ENTITE'S AND BEING'S", who all are just the subjective and objective "CREATION'S" manifested or eventuated out of the DESIRE MIND of the "MOST HIGH", thus subjectively and or objectively, existing in their various differentiated states of "Conscious Existence", in the differentiated "Sub Levels and Zones" of the "3 Dense Dimensional Worlds", which are known in Hebrew Language as the "SEPHROTS of ASSIAH, YETZIRAH, and BRIAH", so all "Entities and Beings" during their "Life duration Cyclic Existences", being thus mounted upon the "Wheel of Time" can "Periodically" qualify themselves, to finally enter the Higher Most Dimensional World, known in Hebrew Language as the "SEPHIROT of ATZILUTH", which is meant for all the Human Beings to dwell in by finally attaining the "RADIANT

CONSCIOUS WISDOM OF LIGHT" and thus finally exist consciously free from the bondage's of the 3 dense dimensional worlds of "ASSIAH, YETZIRAH, and BRIAH, as the "LIGHT BEINGS' 'in the "HOUSE and KINGDOM of the LORD – GOD the MOST HIGH, as mentioned in the verse of HOLY BIBLE regarding the earlier SON OF GOD "'KING SOLOMON", which states "I WILL SETTLE HIM IN MY HOUSE AND IN MY KINGDOM "FOREVER", AND HIS THRONE SHALL BE ESTABLISHED "FOREVER" [1 Chronicles 17.14]

JESUS CHRIST later Chosen SON of GOD also talks of Many Mansions or Dwelling Places, which are present in his "FATHER'S HOUSE" [SEPHIROT of ATZILUTH] regarding which the "Holy Bible" clearly states " IN MY FATHER'S HOUSE ARE MANY DWELLING PLACES; IF IT WERE NOT SO, I WOULD HAVE TOLD YOU; FOR I GO TO PREPARE A PLACE FOR YOU [John 14. 2]

But these invisible SERVANTS of the MOST HIGH, the so called GODS and GODESSES themselves became so Corrupt that they illegally installed CORRUPT HUMAN BEINGS in High Positions of Human Societies, which were segregated by them, through the concept of "Cast, Creed and Religious Belief systems", and also through the "Deceitful and illegal Inducing" of "Animalistic Nature thought forms" in their evolving minds, through the Wrongful Use of their "Mind Controlling Power Vibrations", which are the underlying "'Traits of Corruption'", and which upon this Planet Earth's Material World are primarily related to the basic two main factors, known as the Vices of "UNQUENCHABLE GREED" to own and Hoard Material Things, and "UNDYING LUST" to illegally control "All OTHER KINGDOMS" of Nature through mutated and deformed consciousness, which also include to illegally control other evolving members of the "HUMAN RACES" through "FALSE PRDE", in the name of so called Material world "NAME and FAME", who innocently evolving upon the lower levels of the "EVOLUTIONARY CHAIN LADDER" totally depend upon them, for their Everyday Survival in this Dense Physical Plane of the Planet Earth.

These are the same so called invisible "Entities and Beings", who are invisibly present upon this Planet Earth since a Very Long Time, and commonly worshiped as the "Gods and Goddesses" by various societies of Human Beings of this planet earth, who "WILLFULLY" Backstabbed their one and only "CREATOR LORD – GOD", the "ALMIGHTY through heinous Conspiracy, who at the very beginning of "Creation" filled with

"Divine Love" thus "TRUSTING" them as his "CREATED CHILDREN", gave them "Certain Powers" to independently perform their proper duties, by existing in their Hierarchical Groups as his reliable "SERVANTS", to act merely as "Co- Creators Servants" to firmly uphold the Universal Law of "WILL TO DO GOOD", but instead they themselves became CORRUPT, and thus conspired against him, forgetting this BASIC FACT, that their CREATOR FATHER, the MOST HIGH is always " UNKNOWABLE ", and thus TOTALLY IMPOSSIBLE for them to Understand his "PLAN and PURPOSE", which is based upon the ONE and ONLY Universal Law of "WILL TO DO GOOD".

But over the passing of time upon this planet earth, they forgot all about their CREATOR LORD, the MOST HIGH, and thus they collectively with their deceitful hearts became Deformed and Mutated in their originally "Pure Consciousness" and thus permanently lost their statues of "Beings of Light", and under their Corrupt Control since then this Planet in the Entire Solar Universe has become a undesirable Place of Pain and suffering's, and such Corrupt Status of this Planet Earth is still continuing to this Very Day, even So many Prophets, Seers and Sages including the Redeemer Son of God has physically appeared Time and Again to guide and save evolving "Human Races" and their Counterpart so called invisible GODS and GODDESSES from their "Permanent Elimination, Annihilation and thus Total Extinction".

"IN MY FATHER'S HOUSE ARE MANY DWELLING PLACES; IF IT WERE NOT SO, I WOULD HAVE TOLD YOU; FOR I GO TO PREPARE A PLACE FOR YOU [John 14. 2]

Part 10

The so called "Gods and Goddesses" of this planet Earth, who are prevalent in its all worldly religions, existing in various disguises, like all the "Invisible "Angelic Beings", who are innocently worshiped as the "Gods and Goddesses", by many Human Beings instead of the ONE and ONLY True Creator, "LORD – GOD, the unknowable MOST HIGH, as these all ANGELIC BEINGS are themselves, just the mere Desire Mind "CREATIONS" of the "Unknowable "MOST HIGH", and are in fact the "True Source" of "All CORRUPTION" and "Illegal Activities, which are now "Openly Prevalent" upon this Planet Earth, and they are the "'VERY SAME ONES'", under whose Command their Henchmen, the So called "High Positioned Leaders" of various Human Societies, "Willfully" Commit mostly unpublicized White and Dark Collar "CRIMES".

The Advanced Vedic Seers and Sages of Ancient India, were fully aware of this undeniable fact, and they thus only "Worshipped Him" and No One Else", referring him in their Original Vedic Sanskrit Literature as the unknowable "Tata" or "Tat Purusha". They were also aware of this celestial fact that his "Holy Presence" was always observed by Human Beings, in the form of the "Holy Fire", whom they named as "AGNI". And this unknowable "Great GOD", or the ONE AND ONLY LORD of all other LORDS, they later on named as the "MAHA ISHVARA", meaning in English the "GREAT LORD GOD OF ALL", to whom they offered their Sacrifices of Holy Oil in the Holy fire.

But after the willful backstabbing of their MOST BENEVOLENT LORD GOD, by his these "Invisible Creations" of the Most High, in a High Level Deceitful Conspiracy against HIM also thus naming as the "STUPID OR BHOLA", THEY WILLFULLY TOTALLY BETRAYED HIS "DIVINE LOVE AND TRUST", and then they through their henchmen's, the so called Left Hand Rishi – Muni's of the Dark agendas who prolonged their own miserable lives with the blood Energy of the innocent Creatures, made new books in the name of Hindu Religion and thus illegally added to the ancient Vedic Religion the worship of these "SO CALLED - GOD AND GODDESSES".

To Curb and Correct this "ILLEGAL ACT, and their "WRONGFUL DEMONIC ACTIVITIES" being carried on in "HIS NAME" upon this planet earth, the Divine Consciousness of the MOST HIGH" himself took a Human Birth in ancient times of India, but these CORRUPT Ones who since long time are in full control the "4 invisible Ethereal planes" or the 4 invisible sub planes of the dense physical plane [ASSIAH – BHU LOKA] of this planet earth , which has authority given to them, [his unfaithful Servant workers], earlier by the MOST HIGH himself to determine the place and race of the Human Birth upon the Physical Plane [ASSIAH], of Planet Earth, which are ethereally situated in the dimensional confinements of Physical Plane [ASSIAH- BHU LOKA], deceitfully gave him a unpleasant "Birth" in the Pathetic Conditions of a "JAIL" of "MATHURA"", in which his Parents already were ILLEGALLY IMPRISONED before HIS birth, by their Henchman, who was NONE other than the DIVINE CHILDS Own Maternal Uncle, the Notorious King named "KAMSA OF MATHURA".

This Divine Incarnation of the MOST HIGH is now worldwide known as KRISHNA", who later openly informed the whole WORLD through his follower – friend "ARJUNA", against the illegal worship of these so called GODS and GODDESES, his earlier "CREATION'S" to manifest before HE Created MANKIND upon this planet earth, who with the "PASSING of TIME", themselves became the True Source of all Material "CORRUPTION", which since then, for a very long time is prevailing upon this Planet Earth, and this DIVINE INFORMATION is now known as the Sacred Text of "BHAGWAT GITA", an important part of the 'HINDU EPIC MAHABHARTHA" , in which he explained, but still not in very "Harsh Words", as he was full of Divine Love of the Unknowable MOST HIGH, and was "STILL HOPING" for them to "CHANGE FROM THEIR EVIL WAYS", regarding which the "Bhagwat Gita States":
""All MEN of """"""SMALL INTELLIGENCE"""""", who worship the so called "GODS and GODDESSES", their acquired FRUITS from such WORSHIP are "LIMITED and TEMPORARY", and THOSE who WORSHIP these "GODS and "GODS and GODDESSES" go to them and thus "JOIN THEM" [[AFTER THEIR PHYSICAL DEATH], but MY DEVOTEES, no matter how they may WORSHIP ME, they in the "END" then "JOIN ME"". [Bhagwat Gita Chapter 7, Verse 23].

These so called "Gods and Goddesses" not only infiltrated upon this planet earth just the East, or Mesopotamia, Babylon and Egypt, but their Worship was done earlier in the great Continent of Atlantis of the West, situated in the confinements of "Atlantic Ocean", which ultimately became "TOATLLY CORRUPTED" and thus Got Ultimately "Totally

Destroyed" along with their Ancient Religion, just as the all other Ancient "GODS and GODDESSES" religions were ultimately destroyed in ancient Egypt, Mesopotamia, Babylon, as well as in Ancient Greece and Rome.

Although later on, the Surviving Descendant of Atlantis still carried on the Ritual Worship of these Gods and Goddesses in South and North Americas, but ultimately they were also wiped out.

And the "LORD- GOD", the "MOST BENEVOLENT" – "THE MOST HIGH", then made new Covenants with the Faithful Children of later Human Race, of which the Most Notable are "NOAH, and ABRAHAM", whose Descendants Currently live in the 3 religions of this World, known as the JUDAIC HEBREWS or JEWS, CHRISTIANS, and MUSLIMS.

Abraham looking towards the heavens

59

"Then NOAH built an Altar to the LORD, and took of every clean animal and of every clean bird and offered "Burnt Offerings" on the altar. [Genesis 8. 20].

Since Very ancient Times upon this planet earth, in all the past and present world religions of this world, the "Burning Fire" apart from other Elements of Nature, has been always considered as one of the "Main Divine Attributes" of the Unknowable "Most High", who is One and Only Creator LORD- GOD, the "MOST HIGH" of the Universe, and the Main reason for such consideration is because "Fire and its Heat known as the "Energy of LIGHT" are the life giving attributes of the "Solar Sun", which are most important vital necessities for the survival of all Plants and living Creatures as well as the Human Beings of this Planet Earth.

"Fire" apart from Water is considered as the "Purifying Element" upon this Physical plane [ASSIAH], since ancient times by the Human Beings of Various Ancient Cultures, , and many of those ancient culture's physical existence, is nowhere to be found now, as many of their dwelling areas established upon the physical plane's existence, got submerged under the rising waters of the Oceans, due to the SINS of the Most Corrupt invisible caretaker "Entities and Beings" of this planet and their henchmen human worshipers, who willfully indulged in them and thus betrayed their "MOST LOVING, One and Only, CREATOR FATHER", by totally routing his "LOVE and TRUST", and also deceitfully conspired against him.

In this heinous and immoral act of total betrayal, they thus "ILLEGALLY" took over his "GRAND POSITION" and "Universe's Most High Spot" by becoming the "FALSE MOST HIGH" themselves for "Certain Time Duration's", during their agreed upon "cyclic group rotation", which consisted of the 7 Most Corrupt Entities, who devised their conspirator plan, and jointly put in action against their beloved "CREATOR FATHER", whose consciousness is also present upon this physical plane of this planet connected with various "FORMS and SHAPES".

These so called Gods and Goddesses, who by willfully hijacking the evolutionary process, which is based upon universal law of "WILL TO DO GOOD", through total "deceit and betrayal" willfully changed the evolutionary plan and purpose of the MOST HIGH to this low level upon this Planet Earth, that now most people of this world, having their indwelling "Personality Consciousness" embodied in their human forms in the name of "civilization and advancement" have lost their interest in "TRUE SPIRITUALITY, and thus zealously believing in their various religious Dogmas are killing one another in the name of the "MOST HIGH', rather than following the universal law of "WILL TO DO GOOD", which is supposed to be upheld by "All" as per the plan and purpose of the MOST HIGH" rather spend their short lived physical life duration's following corrupt and unspiritual ways of "HOOK and CROOK", thus gone spiritually blind after lusting for "Illusory Material Gains".

Regarding the "Light Conscious Attributes" of the "Most High", which since the ancient times has been represented by "FIRE", the "Holy Bible" explains in its very first chapter of Creation [Genesis] stating, " Then GOD said, "LET THERE BE LIGHT", and there was LIGHT. And GOD saw that LIGHT was GOOD; and GOD separated the LIGHT from Darkness. And GOD called the Light day, and the DARKNESS HE called night. And there was evening and there was morning, one day. [Genesis 1. 3, 4, 5.]

Afterwards, for the first time, the Holy Bible talk of "FIRE", which was used for Holy Ritual known as the "BURNT OFFERINGS", which were offered by "NOAH to the "LORD- GOD" after he and his family were saved from the FLOOD, by the LORD – GOD, as NOAH already made covenant with HIM, regarding which the "Holy Bible" states, "Then NOAH built an Altar to the LORD, and took of every clean animal and of every clean bird and offered "Burnt Offerings" on the altar. [Genesis 8. 20].

Then again the "FIRE" is mentioned in Holy Bible during ABRAHAM'S Time, with whom THE "MOST HIGH" LORD – GOD, also made a Covenant, regarding which the "Holy Bible" states "And ABRAHAM took the wood of the Burnt Offerings, and laid it on ISSAC his son, and he took in his hand the "FIRE" and the knife. So the two of them walked on together. And ISSAC spoke to ABRAHAM his father and said "MY FATHER!" And He said, "Here I Am my Son." And he said, Behold, the "FIRE" and the wood, but where is the Lamb for the Burnt Offering?" [Genesis 22. 6.7]

'And ABRAHAM took the wood of the Burnt Offerings, and laid it on ISSAC his son, and he took in his hand the "FIRE" and the knife. So the two of them walked on together. And ISSAC spoke to ABRAHAM his father and said "MY FATHER!" And He said, "Here I Am my Son." And he said, Behold, the "FIRE" and the wood, but where is the Lamb for the Burnt Offering?" [Genesis 22. 6.7]

Tree

Cave

Elijah's cave at Holy Mount Horeb – Saudi Arabia

The Secret of the Breast Plate

Part 12

According to "Holy Bible", after death of SARAH, ABRAHAM took another wife named "KETURAH", regarding which the 'Holy Bible' states, "Now ABRAHAM took another wife, whose name was KETURAH. And she bore to him ZIMRAN, and JOKSHAN, and MEDAN, and "MIDIAN", and ISHBAK, and SHUAH. And the Sons of "MIDIAN" were EPHAH, and EPHER, and HANOCH, and ABIDA, and ELDAAH. All these were the Sons and Grandsons of Abraham through KETURAH.

Now ABRAHAM gave all that he had to ISAAC; but to the sons of his Concubines, ABRAHAM gave gifts while HE was still living, and sent them away from his son ISAAC "EASTWARD - TO THE LAND OF EAST". [Genesis 25. 1, 2, 4, 5, 6].

Later on, the descendants of "MIDIAN" the Son of ABRAHAM through KETURAH, established themselves in the areas near East including Babylonia, and the surrounding areas now known as the North West IRAN, and the South east TURKEY, and with the passing of time subsequently became Mighty and Powerful to establish themselves as the "GREAT MIDIAN EMPIRE" in the ancient world, which also covered the areas east and south of CANNAN", which included the land of modern day SAUDI ARABIA, in whose territories the Holy Mountain of GOD named MOUNT "HOREB - SINAI" is also situated, later also known as the "JEBEL HOREB" and "JEBEL MUSA" meaning the "Mountain of MOSES".

Many people are unaware of this "Important fact", that the Holy Mount HOREB and the Mount SINAI are the two adjacent or joined peaks of the "Same Large "Mountain" having the same base, thus existing right next to each other, the physical Mount HOREB peak is on the right side, which has the Ancient Cave to which Prophet ELIJAH went and Lodged there, as mentioned in the Chapter of "1 Kings 19. 8, 9" of the Holy Bible, and the physical Mount SINAI is situated on the Left Side of Mt. HOREB'S Peak having its "darkened and burnt out" crystallized peak due to the ancient "FIERY FLAMES", which in the ancient times represented the divine conscious attributes of the "MOST HIGH", and was known in the ancient times as the "FIERY MOUNTAIN of GOD", of which now all the HOLY FLAMES are totally "All Gone Out", and have thus become TOTALLY EXTINGUISHED since for a long time due to full scale "'Worldwide Corruption'", and due to "Total Betrayal" of the Divine "LOVE and KINDNESS" of The "LORD- GOD, the MOST HIGH", by "ALL HIS CREATIONS", which also include his "Invisible Created Servants" the so called Angelic Beings, acting out their specific roles to the Human beings as the so called "GODS AND GODDESSES", who themselves became an unwanted "Part and Parcel" of this Worldwide Corruption, as well as the Created "Visible Human Beings", who knowingly or unknowingly followed their Most Corrupt and Deceitful agendas, against the Evolutionary plan and purpose of the "MOST HIGH", who were originally lovingly created by HIM in HIS Own Image as mentioned in the Chapter of Genesis in the Holy Bible [Genesis 1. 26].

As per the Holy Bible, when Prophet ELIJAH was lodging in the cave of Mount HOREB during ancient times, the word of LORD came to HIM, regarding which the Bible states:

" So ELIJAH arose and ate and drank, and went in the strength of that food forty days and forty nights to HOREB, the mountain of GOD. Then he came there to a cave, and lodged there; and behold, the word of the LORD came to him, "WHAT ARE YOU DOING HERE, ELIJAH?"

And he said, "I have been very zealous for the LORD, the GOD of HOSTS [Angels]; for the Sons of Israel have forsaken Thy COVENANT, torn down Thine Altars and killed Thy Prophets with the Sword, And I alone am left; and they seek my life, to take it away."

So HE said, "GO FORTH, and Stand on the Mountain "BEFORE THE LORD". [Toward Mt. SINAI – which is Next door to Mount HOREB]. And behold, the LORD was passing by! And a Great and Strong Wind was rending the MOUNTAIN'S [Both HOREB and SINAI], and breaking in pieces the rocks before the LORD; but the LORD was not in the Wind. And after the Wind an Earthquake, but the LORD was not in the Earthquake. And after the Earthquake a "FIRE", but the LORD was not in the "FIRE"; and after the "FIRE" a sound of "GENTLE BLOWING". And it came about when ELIJAH heard it, then he wrapped his face in his mantle, and went out, and stood in the ENTRANCE OF THE CAVE. And behold, a voice came to him and said, "WHAT ARE YOU DOING HERE, ELIJAH?" [1 Kings 19. 8, 9,]

Since their father ABRAHAM'S time they carried on their offerings to the "MOST HIGH" as their great ancestor's NOAH and ABRAHAM did in their own times through the use of "Sacred Fire". The priesthood of MIDIAN were also known as the "MAGI'S". The Medians being the descendants of ABRAHAM always associated their HOLY OFFERINGS with "FIRE" which consciously related them with the divine presence of "MOST HIGH", and during the time of much Later MIDIAN Kings, "ZOROASTER" of ancient Persia [Modern day IRAN] embodied this "Sacred Fire" divine aspect of the unknowable "Most High", which is related to everyone's vital consciousness expansion, in his new found religion, now known as the "Zoroastrianism" or the "Parsi Faith", which is the same Holy "FIRE" which is related to the MOST HIGH as his divine conscious attribute aspect of the desire mind.

The MIDIAN"S, much later established "ECBATANA" as their capital city situated at the foot of Mount Alvand, regarding which the "Holy Bible" mentions it in reference to the decree, which was made by King "CYRUS" concerning the "House of GOD in JERUSALEM", which states as follows:

" Then King DARIUS issued a decree, and search was made in the archives, where the treasures were stored in BABYLON. And in ECBATANA in the fortress, which is in the "Province of Media", a Scroll was found and there was written in it as follows: "Memorandum – In the first year of King CYRUS, CYRUS the King issued a decree: concerning the House of GOD at JERUSALEM, the place where sacrifices are offered, be rebuilt and let its foundations be retained, its height being 60 cubits and its width 60 cubits; with three layers of "Huge Stones", and one layer of timbers. And let the cost be paid from the Royal Treasury, and let the Gold and Silver utensils of the temple of GOD, which NEBUCHADNEZZAR took from the Temple and brought to BABYLON, be returned and brought to their places in the Temple in JERUSALEM; and you shall put them in the House of GOD". [Ezra 6. 1, 2, 3, 4, 5.]

Elijah's Grotto at Mount Carmel

Mount Carmel, Israel

Most Human Beings of this Planet Earth dwelling in different continents, and belonging to various Faiths, Casts and Creeds, fail to understand the Underlying "FACT" that the Unknowable "MOST HIGH" LORD – GOD of the subjectively and objectively manifested UNIVERSE and embodying in his Desire Mind, its Differentiated Dimensional Configurations known as "The Matrix", since very ancient times has been defined by the Sages and Seers as the "Great Lord God" [Maha Ishvara in Sanskrit Language], Who being utterly "Peaceful and Joyful" is an Embodiment of the Great Qualities of "LOVE and COMPASSION" in the Infinite Universe, and is thus Totally "Immersed and Filled" with the "DIVINE LIGHT of "VITAL ETHEREAL CONSCIOUSNESS".

So Most People of this World fail to understand this basic FACT that Any Kind of "PAIN and Sufferings" which are related to the conscious aspect of "Emotions and Feelings" is ABSOLUTELY not a part of "HIS" Indwelling Consciousness, but they are WRONGFULLY in existence upon this planet earth for a long time due to the "Backstabbing and Betrayal" of HIS "Love and Trust", by HIS Created Invisible Servant Helpers, the so called GODS and GODDESSES, who were Earlier CREATED by Him upon this Planet Earth as well as in the Entire Solar System, through the application of HIS inherent "Will Power" of the "Desire Mind", which is known as the manifesting "Process of Eventuation", and who were considered by HIM as his "Created Children", and were thus given certain "Powers" to independently use them, by acting as the "Co – Creators" in the 3 Main dense dimensional of this Planet Earth known in the Hebrew Language as the "SEPHIROTS of ASSIAH, YETZIRAH, and BRIAH", to perform their Certain Required Duties as per "HIS Evolutionary Plan and Purpose" established through "His Desire Mind", which is "ABSOLUTELY" based upon the Universal Law of "WILL TO DO GOOD", and over the passing of time, it was "Willfully Defiled by "Very Those", whom "HE" fully trusted to perform their required duties, and thus they "The So Called Gods and Goddesses", became the underlying cause of all types of "CORRUPTION" which then in its various "Mutations and Deformations" caused the "PAIN and SUFFERINGS to come in effect upon this Planet Earth, in the evolutionary cyclic lives of all evolving visible and invisible "Entities and Beings", who unknowing the "BASIC FACTS" regarding Planet Earth's Evolution, now Consider the "Corruption" in their evolving Lives as a "'Normal way of the Evolutionary Process", which is wrongfully now taking place upon this Planet Earth.

Since Very ancient times The CREATOR – OBSERVER, The "MOST HIGH" has been defined upon this Planet Earth as the "Very One", who is MOST BENEFICENT, THE MOST BENEVOLENT, THE MOST MERCIFUL – LORD GOD of "ALL", whom the ancient Seers, Prophets, Sages, and Saints called as the unknowable "GREAT LORD OF THE FLAMES", as the Divine Fire, which appeared through his "Desire Mind", never needed the help of any objects for it to burn, and thus left no residue behind it, which thus represented "HIS" Vital Conscious Attributes of "LIFE", greatly needed and required by all planetary entities and beings for their "Conscious Expansion", which embody the attributes of "MIND".

And since the ancient times all "FIRE" which burnt by itself upon this planet earth, without the visible aid of any physical objects was thus considered HOLY, as it depicted the invisible attributes of HIS physical presence upon this physical plane [ASSIAH] of this planet Earth.

The Huge Mountain Peak of "Mount SINAI ", which is adjacent to the peak of "Mount HOREB", is not a Volcanic Mountain as many may now consider, but was such a Holy Place in the ancient times, where the "Fiery Flames" Burnt by Themselves, sometimes also associated with thunder and lightning.

The second chapter of Holy Bible known as "EXODUS" is very much associated with the "LORD – GOD OF THE FLAMES", the "MOST HIGH", whom MOSES, later on defined in the 4th Chapter of Deuteronomy, which in the Holy Bible clearly states, " For the "LORD YOUR GOD" is a """"CONSUMING FIRE"""""", A Jealous GOD" [Deuteronomy 4. 24].

During the Time of MOSES, some of the Descendants of MIDIAN, who was a son of ABRAHAM through KETURAH as mentioned in "Genesis 25. 1, 2", were dwelling in rock hewed caves at the base of the Holy Mountain HOREB, and were thus known as the "Cave People, the Cave Dwellers" or the "JETHRO", which was just their 'Title Name', and their MIDIAN PRIEST was named "REUEL" as mentioned in Holy Bible, which states:

"When Pharaoh heard of this matter, he tried to kill MOSES. But MOSES fled from the presence of the Pharaoh and settled in the land of MIDIAN; and he sat down by a well. Now the Priest of the MIDIAN had seven daughters; and they came to draw water, and filled the troughs to water their father's flock. Then the Shepherds came and drove them away, but MOSES stood up and helped them, and watered their flock. When they came to "REUEL" their father, He said, "Why have you come back so soon today?" [Exodus 2. 15, 16, 17, 18].

Caves of Jethro in Saudi Arabia

Prophet Elijah

View from inside the Elijah Cave at Mount Horeb– Saudi Arabia

Most Incarnated Human Beings as well as their counterpart Invisible Angelic Beings, who dwell in any of the three dense dimensional planes [ASSIAH, YETZIRAH, and BRIAH], of this Planet Earth, are totally unaware of the Highest ethereal plane of this solar Universe, to which this Planet Earth itself also belongs, which was formed at the very start of its subjective manifestation in the "Dense Cosmic Ethereal Zone" of the Huge Milky Way Galaxy's vital energy parametric confinements, which the very ancient sages and seers termed as the "The First" or "The Ancient Plane" also termed as "The Plane of Truth", because it consist of "Pure Vital Consciousness", which is Free from any type of "CORRUPTION".

This 1st dimensional plane out of the Seven main dimensional planes of conscious existence of our Solar Universe, came into existence by the cyclically outward Energy Bursts of "Vital Consciousness Energy" from its centrally located "Cosmic Energy Point", about which the Highly advanced Seers, Prophets and Sages, with the Grace of the unknowable "Most High", who is also known as the "Lord of the Flames", became aware of, and thus named it "EIN SOPH" in Hebrew Language.

The ancient Vedic Seers of India, who worshiped "only" the unknowable "Most High" or the unknowable "Lord of Flames" and his conscious attributes of FIRE, WATER etc., instead of worshiping his "Created Servants", which later became known as the so called "Gods and Goddesses" termed this centrally located "Cosmic Energy Point" in their Sanskrit Language as the "PARA - BINDU".

His devotees, with the ineffable grace of the unknowable "MOST HIGH" who is embodiment of "LOVE", thus became aware of this highest or the 1st dimensional plane, which is composed of liquid ethereal matter of "PURE VITAL CONSCIOUSNESS", coming out of the "Cosmic Energy Point"known as the "EIN SOPH", having a Bluish Color Luminous Fire, which does not Burn, and thus all the ethereal particles of this liquid matter luminously glow.

So the "Fiery Flames", which appeared out of mountains in the dense physical plane by themselves became thus holy, as they represented the Conscious Attributes of the unknowable "MOST HIGH". In Northern India, there is such a place, which still exist named "JWALA JI", near the city of KANGRA, in the Himachal Pradesh, which in the ancient times of "Dvapara Yuga" as mentioned in the Hindu Epic Mahabharata its "TIRATH PARVA" [Pilgrimage Section], were known as "SAPTA CHARU", meaning the "SEVEN CONSUMING FIRES", but after the conspiracy against the Creator – Observer of the Infinite Universe, the unknowable "Maha Ishvara" or the MOST HIGH, are now attributed to the Goddesses, rather than the "MOST HIGH" himself, as it was originally attributed to him in the ancient "Vedic Times".

There is another such place on the Mountain top adjacent to Muktinath Shrine in the country of Nepal, inside a goddess temple where the "Bluish Flames" cover the flowing waters of Cold Water Stream, which flow inside the Temple Precinct, but are now covered with removable slates, thus hidden from the eyesight view of its common visitors.

And the most famous of all in the ancient world was the Mount SINAI adjacent to the peak of Holy Mount HOREB, the Holy Mountain of LORD – GOD, now situated in Saudi Arabia, from which the consuming flames were hurled out day and night from its Holy Peak, and were visible for a great distance of many hundred miles in the nightly skies, of which we have the only written records, which define it in great details in the Holy Bible.

It is first mentioned in the Holy Bible along its wilderness in its 2nd chapter known as "The Exodus" which defines it as the "Flaming Mountain of God" regarding which the Holy Bible states:

"Now MOSES was pasturing the flock of JETHRO, his father in law, the Priest of MIDIAN, and he led the flock to the WEST Side of the Wilderness, and came to HOREB, the mountain of GOD. And the angel of the LORD [The Created Servant of the Most High], appeared to HIM in a 'blazing fire' from the midst of a 'Bush' and he looked, and behold, the bush was burning with fire, yet the bush was not consumed. So MOSES said, "I Must turn aside now, and see this marvelous sight, why the bush is not burned up."

When the LORD [The MOST HIGH], saw that he turned aside to look, GOD called to him from the midst of the bush, and said, "MOSES,

MOSES!'' And he said ''HERE I AM.''

Then HE said, ''Do not come near here; remove your sandals from your feet, for the place on which you are standing is the ''HOLY GROUND''. HE said also, ''I AM THE GOD OF YOUR FATHER, THE GOD OF ABRAHAM, THE GOD OF ISAAC, AND THE GOD OF JACOB.'' Then MOSES hid his face, for He was Afraid to look at GOD. [Exodus 3. 1, 2, 3, 4, 5, 6.]

Eternal flame burning, behind a waterfall in Chestnut Ridge, Shale Creek Preserve, in western New York state USA.

The Prophet Elijah at Mount Horeb

The LORD – GOD, THE MOST HIGH, through his CHOSEN PROPHETS Time and Again tried to convey the proper facts to confused MANKIND of this Planet Earth, who are having distorted minds , that all other so called invisible GODS and GODDESSES, were just his mere CREATION, who all were just created according to his Evolutionary Plan and Purpose through the outpouring vital impulses of His Desire Mind in the Eventuation Process, as HIS servant Helpers, to exist in an hierarchical order with certain limited set of powers to perform their required duties, but HIS Own Creation, the human beings of many nations and belief systems, in the modern world still create their own so called visible Gods – Goddesses in the shape of various IDOLS, so they can worship VERY THOSE, whom they have themselves created to exist Objectively!

The Prophet ISAIAH clearly states regarding it in Holy Bible thus explaining LORD'S words, which say:

"That Men may know from the rising to the setting of the SUN, that there is NO one besides ME. I am the LORD, and there is NO other. The ONE forming LIGHT and creating DARKNESS, Causing "Well Being" and Creating "Calamity"; I AM THE LORD WHO DOES ALL THESE. [Isaiah 45. 6, 7.]

Prophet "ELIJAH", the Tishbite, the chosen prophet of GOD after the Passing away of the Prophet King Solomon, considered as SON by the MOST HIGH as mentioned in "1 Chronicles 17. 13", was very aware of the FIERY Attribute of the LORD – GOD, "THE MOST HIGH", who CREATED through the WILL POWER of his DESIRE MIND, known as the "PROCESS OF EVENTUATION", ALL the So called "Other GODS and GODDESSES" of this Planet Earth, THE MYRIAD OF ANGELIC HOSTS, ALSO KNOWN AS "THE ELOHIM", to Co - Exist in his subjectively and objectively manifested creation, thus existing in the "vitally vibrating" various dimensional planes and their sub planes of this Solar Universe having their own tonal colors and sound frequencies, as well as upon the dimensional planes of this Planet Earth, so they can humbly assist him as his 'Loyal Servants", and HE then Trusting them like his created children thus allowed them certain types of powers and their related underlining knowledge, to actively perform their required duties in the 3 Main dimensional plane worlds, which are the Dimensional Sephirot's of "ASSIAH, YETZIRAH, and BRIAH, known in Sanskrit Language as the TRILOKAS, which were earlier manifested as per HIS Evolutionary Plan and Purpose, which is based upon Universal Law of "WILL TO DO GOOD", but unfortunately these are the very "SAME ONES", who willfully Betrayed His Love and Trust, by backstabbing HIM in a wide spread conspiracy.

As per the Holy Bible, the Prophet ELIJAH, proved this Universal FACT of the SUPREMACY of The MOST HIGH above "ALL" other, the so called God's, who is the "One and Only", CREATOR - LORD GOD of all other GODS and GODDESSES, when he Called upon the grace of the "LORD GOD" and thus showed the GLORY OF MOST HIGH to all those Children of Israel, who wrongly started again worshiping the Most Corrupt EGYPTIAN GODS like the "BAAL", who were the prime reason in the Bondage of their Ancestor's during MOSES time in Egypt, regarding which the Holy Bible clearly states:

"And ELIJAH came near to All the People and said, "How long will you hesitate between two opinions? If the LORD is GOD, follow HIM; But if BAAL, follow HIM." But the People did not answer him a word.

Then ELIJAH said to the People, "I alone am left a prophet of the LORD, but BAAL'S Prophets are 450 Men. Now let them give us Two Oxen; and let them choose one Ox for themselves and cut it up, and place it on the Wood, but put no FIRE under it; and I will prepare the other Ox, and lay it on the Wood, and I will not put FIRE under it. Then you Call on the Name of your GOD, and I will Call on the Name of the LORD, and the GOD who answers by "FIRE", HE IS GOD." And all the people answered and said, "That is a Good Idea".

So ELIJAH said to the Prophets of BAAL, "Choose One Ox for yourself and prepare it First, for you are Many, and Call on the Name of your GOD, but put no FIRE under it". Then they took the Ox, which was given them, and they prepared it and called on the Name of BAAL from Morning until Noon saying, "O BAAL, Answer US." But there was No Voice, and No One answered. And they leaped about the Altar which They made.

And it came about Noon, that ELIJAH Mocked them and Said, Call out with a Loud Voice, for he is GOD; Either He is Occupied or Gone Aside, or is on a Journey, or perhaps He is Asleep and needs to be Awakened."

So they Cried with a Loud Voice and "Cut Themselves" according to their "Custom" with "Swords and Lances" until the Blood Gushed out on them. And it came about when Mid-day was Passed, that they Raved until the Time of the Offering of the Evening Sacrifice; but there was No Voice, No One Answered, and No One Paid Attention.

Then ELIJAH said to ALL the People, "Come Near to Me." So All the People came near to Him. And He repaired the "ALTAR of the LORD" which had been "Torn Down". And ELIJAH took Twelve Stones according to the Number of the Tribes of the Sons of JACOB, to whom the word of the LORD had come, saying, "ISRAEL shall be your Name."

So with the stones He built an Altar in the Name of the LORD, and He made a trench around the Altar, large enough to hold Two Measures of Seed. Then He arranged the Wood and Cut the Ox in pieces and laid it on the Wood, and He said, "Fill Four Pitchers with Water and pour it on the Burnt Offerings, and on the Wood." And He Said, "Do it a Second Time", and They did a Second Time, and He Said, "Do it a Third Time", and They did it a Third Time. And the Water flowed around the Altar, and He also filled the Trench with Water. Then it came about at the Time of the Offering of the Evening Sacrifice, that ELIJAH the Prophet came near and Said, "O LORD, THE GOD OF ABRAHAM, ISAAC, and ISRAEL, Today Let it be Known that "'THOU ART GOD in ISRAEL'", and that "'I Am THY SERVANT'", and that I Have Done All These Things at "THY WORD".

"Answer Me, O LORD. Answer ME, that this People May Know that THOU, O LORD ART GOD, and that THOU HAST TURNED THEIR HEART BACK AGAIN." Then the FIRE OF THE LORD Fell, and CONSUMED the Burnt Offering, and the Wood, and the Stones, and the Dust, and Licked up the Water that was in the Trench. And when All the People Saw it, they Fell on their Faces; and they Said, ""THE LORD, HE IS GOD; THE LORD HE IS GOD,""

Then ELIJAH said to them, "Seize the Prophets of BAAL; Do Not let One of them Escape." So they Seized Them; and ELIJAH brought Them down to the Brook of KISHON, and Slew Them there. [1 Kings. Verses 21 to 40]

Eziekel's Visions of GOD

In the Ancient times, the Seers, Prophets, and Sages were CHOSEN by the Ineffable Grace, and as per the "Desire Mind Wishes" of the "UNKNOWABLE MOST HIGH", who is the One and Only "TRUE LORD – GOD", the CREATOR FATHER of the Entire UNIVERSE, so they can Humbly Perform their respective duties during their Incarnated Human Lives, according to his "Divine Evolutionary Plan and Purpose", which is based upon One and Only Universal Law of "Will to do Good".

These CHOSEN ones, who were from the different races of MANKIND, but all being descendants from the Lineage of the Created ADAM the first Human, were then given "Extrasensory Powers" by the grace of the MOST HIGH, so they can have Divine Hearing and "Divine Vision", for the purpose of Divine Communication, so they can properly understand HIS Instructions to be carried out upon the Physical Plane of this Planet Earth. These Extra Sensory Powers are now known as the divine gift of " Clair-audience", and "Clairvoyance" by Human Beings, like the Chosen Ancient Ones from the time of NOAH were given by the Grace of the MOST HIGH, through which they freely communicated with the MOST HIGH and thus clearly understood his Instructions, whose title since very ancient times is known to all the Angelic Beings as "THE LORD OF FLAMES".

But since an ILLEGAL and Huge Conspiracy was stirred up by the "Mutated Mind Leaders" of the hierarchical groups of the CREATED SERVANT HELPERS, the invisible Creations of the MOST HIGH, some time ago upon this Planet Earth, who illegally utilizing their Vested POWERS thus "WILLFULLY" Back-stabbed HIS Ineffable LOVE and TRUST, and thus became THEMSELVES, the ILLEGAL RULERS of this "Planet Earth, which happened due to their "CORRUPTED MIND CONSCIOUSNESS", and then promoting themselves into 7 Main Angelic Groups, commonly known as the so called GODS and GODDESSES of various Faiths and Religions of this world, thus established their OWN Hierarchical Orders to govern various Visible and Invisible Kingdoms of this Planet Earth, and then started taking TURNS to Cyclically become the "FALSE MOST HIGH" for Certain Time Duration's, and under their deceitful controls this Beautiful Planet Earth since then, has become a CORRUPT PLANET filled with

PAIN and SUFFERINGS for the MOST "Entities and Beings", except their Certain Chosen Followers, who "Willfully" following the illegal path of Materialism in the dense Physical world, full of unquenchable GREED and LUST in the name of so called WHITE COLLAR CIVILIZATION, which are Purely Animalistic Instincts and Desires, rather than the HEAVENLY Path of SPIRITUALISM, or the Proper Evolutionary Path of "Liberation from all the Mental Bondage's of the 3 dense Material Worlds", which was originally made and established according to the Evolutionary Plan and Purpose for the Human Beings, who in the ancient past were bestowed for the first time upon this planet Earth, with the divine attribute of "INDIVIDUALIZED MIND" by their Most Loving CREATOR FATHER, the Unknowable MOST HIGH, and thus following their "Deceitful Agendas", they still continue to Extend and Prolong their CORRUPT WAYS against the Universal Law of "Will to do Good".

Now under the CORRUPT INFLUENCE of these SO CALLED GODS and GODDESSES of this Planet Earth, who illegally became the Deceitful Modern Rulers of this Beautiful Planet Earth, every Street Corner "Astrologer, Palm or Tarot Card Reader" claim to have the Extrasensory Divine Powers of "Clair - audience", and "Clairvoyance", which were "ORIGINALLY", meant "ONLY" for the Chosen Few, who according to the Holy Books are known as the Venerable "Prophets, Seers and Sages" of the "MOST HIGH", who as per "HIS" Desire Mind impulses were incarnated filled with HOLY SPIRIT, reincarnating "Time and Again" in this Physical Plane World of "ASSIAH" to bring the HUMANITY upon the right path of SPIRITUALITY rather than the path which they were knowingly or unknowingly following pertaining to the "SOUL DESTRUCTION" which is the wrongful path of CORRUPT MATERIALISM.

These Chosen Prophets in the Ancient Days were willfully shown by the Grace of MOST HIGH through the extra sensory power of perception now known as the 'CLAIRVOYANCE" the FIERY" attribute of the MOST HIGH, which exist in the form of RADIANT BLUISH PARTICLES composing the HEAVENLY SEA of Radiant and Peaceful "NON BURNING FIRE" in the Highest Plane of the Solar Universe, which is known as "THE PURE PLANE OF UTMOST TRUTH" encompassing also the Cosmic Energy Point "EIN SOPH". also known in Sanskrit Language as the "ADI or the SATYAM LOKA", and the JOYFUL VITAL ETHEREAL HEAT of this "DIVINE FIRE" Gradually Aids in the CONSCIOUSNESS EXPANSION of ALL Entities and Beings, which Consciously or Unconsciously Exist and thus Dwell, in the Numerous differentiated sub plane Tonal Frequencies [color and sound vibrations of Divine Light], in the 3 MAIN differentiated DENSE SPHERICAL DIMENSIONS of this Planet Earth, which are known as the "SEPHIROT'S of ASSIAH, YETZIRAH, and BRIAH".

During the Dreadful Time of EXILE for the "Sons of Israel", such a Divine Vision was granted to the Prophet "EZEKIEL" by the grace of the MOST HIGH, when the praying cries of the "Children of Israel" were heard by their LORD GOD, the MOST HIGH, who were exiled due to all their inequities by following the so called GODS and GODDESSES, and thus "WILLFULLY" breaking their COVENANT with their LORD – GOD, which was earlier made in the ancient times by their Forefathers.

Regarding this Extrasensory Vision of Prophet EZEKIEL, the "Holy Bible" States:

"The Word of the LORD came expressly to EZEKIEL the Priest, son of BUZI, in the Land of CHALDEANS by the river CHEBAR; and there the hand of the LORD came upon him. And as I Looked, behold, a Storm Wind was coming from the North, a Great Cloud with "FIRE" Flashing forth continually and a "BRIGHT LIGHT" around it, and in its Midst something like Glowing Metal in the Midst of the "FIRE".

In the Midst of the Living Beings there was something that looked like BURNING COALS of "FIRE", like Torches darting back and forth among the Living Beings. The "FIRE was BRIGHT", and LIGHTNING was FLASHING from the "FIRE".

Now above the Expanse that was over their Heads there was something resembling a Throne, like LAPIS LAZULI in appearance; [Lapis Lazuli is BLUISH in Color], and on that which resembled a Throne, High up was a figure with the appearance of a MAN. Then I noticed from the appearance of "HIS" loins and upward something like glowing Metal that looked like "FIRE" All Around Within It, and from the appearance of "HIS" loins and downward I saw something like "FIRE"; and there was "RADIANCE" around "HIM".

As the appearance of the Rainbow in the clouds on a Rainy Day, so was the appearance of the Surrounding "RADIANCE". Such was the appearance of the Likeness of the "Glory of the LORD". And when I saw it, I fell on My Face and heard a Voice Speaking. [Ezekiel 1. 3, 4, 13, 26, 27, 28.]

"Then "HE" said to me, "SON of MAN", I AM sending you to the Sons of ISRAEL, to a "REBELLIOUS PEOPLE", who have rebelled against "ME"; they and their "FATHERS" have Transgressed Against "ME" to this Very Day.

And "I" am sending you to Them, Who are "STUBBORN and OBSTINATE" Children; and You shall say to them, "'Thus Says the LORD GOD.'" As for them, whether they "Listen or Not" – for they are a "REBELLIOUS HOUSE" - They will Know that a PROPHET has been Among Them. [Ezekiel 2. 3, 4, 5.]

"The Word of the LORD came expressly to EZEKIEL the Priest, son of BUZI, in the Land of CHALDEANS by the river CHEBAR; and there the hand of the LORD came upon him. [Ezekiel 1. 3]

Since the Wide Spread Conspiracy against the MOST HIGH took place upon this Planet earth, most Human Beings incarnated under the Wrong Conscious Spells of these Conspiring Servants of the MOST HIGH, the so called Gods and Goddesses, which are certain Hierarchical Groups of Invisible Angelic beings who WILLFULLY BETRAYED "HIS" Unconditional LOVE and TRUST and thus Themselves became the Illegal "CORRUPT RULERS" of this Planet Earth, thus in their short lived Human Lives mostly take "No Interest" in Willfully Understanding the "True Spiritual Aspects" of this Subjectively and Objectively manifested Universe, which are related to their own "Higher Selves" radiant Solar Consciousness, which is commonly known as their "SOUL CONSCIOUSNESS", although Some Scientists of this world have clearly understood the "Material Aspects" of this Universe to a great degree, that "ALL MATTER IS NOTHING ELSE BUT DENSIFIED VITAL ENERGY, HAVING PARAMETRIC BONDAGE'S".

As far as the Human Beings of this Planet Earth are Concerned, their indwelling "PERSONALITY CONSCIOUSNESS" embodied in their formulated incarnated Human Bodies, in which they having the conscious attribute of "Individualized Mind" thus dwell upon the Dense Physical Plane to exist gaining the Material world Experiences during their "Short Lived Duration's" is in FACT just a Tiny Extended Part of their "Vital Ethereal Conscious Energy", which has been Known to the ancient Seers, Prophets and Sages as their "SOUL CONSCIOUSNESS".

This is an Undeniable Fact that "IT is NOT SO", that the MOST HIGH, the Unknowable Creator LORD – GOD of this subjectively and objectively manifested Infinite Universe is Unaware of the CORRUPT and BETRAYAL DEEDS and PATHETIC BEHAVIOR of his "CREATED SERVANT'S", but being a TRUE UPHOLDER of the Universal Law of "Will to do Good", and full of "DIVINE LOVE" due to HIS MOST BENEVOLENT Nature, for many MILLENNIUM, HE has shown his Unfathomable "Patience and Mercy" regarding this "Grave Matter" to both these MOST CORRUPT ENTITIES and BEINGS, now having a Totally DEFORMED, DERANGED, and MUTATED Consciousness, who with their DECEITFUL MINDS have WILLFULLY HIJACKED HIS Divine Evolutionary Plan and Purpose, and their MULTITUDE HOARDS of FOLLOWERS including the Human Beings of this Planet Earth, Most of Whom have ABSOLUTELY NO KNOWLEDGE of this HEINOUS CONSPIRACY formulated by their So called Venerable "GODS and GODDESSES".

Time and again, the MOST HIGH through HIS Desire Mind Conscious Reflection's, had Willfully Sent Conscious energy impulses through his CHOSEN PROPHETS upon this Planet Earth to Properly Warn all the Evolving Entities and Beings of this Planet regarding the "Utmost Grave Dangers" they Collectively Face, but Most Humans belonging to various Faiths, casts and Creeds, having "Animalistic Level Consciousness" thus Devoid of the "SPIRITUAL ENLIGHTENMENT", which thus keep them "Mentally Bound" in the Desires, which are related to "Material World Glamour", have always thus Willfully ignored HIS Such Warnings.

The Holy Prophet JEREMIAH tried to explain the CONSECRATION PROCESS of the MOST HIGH, during his time to his fellow Human Beings that the Unknowable LORD – GOD through HIS "Desire Mind" impulses Willfully "CHOOSES", "HIS" Ordained PROPHETS, long before they are born upon this Planet Earth, regarding which the Holy Bible States:

"Now a Word of the LORD came to Me Saying; "Before "I" formed you in the Womb, "I" Knew You, And before You were born "I" Consecrated You; "I" have appointed You a Prophet to the Nations."

Then the LORD stretched out HIS Hand and Touched My Mouth, and the LORD Said to Me, "Behold, "I" have put MY words in Your Mouth. See "I" have appointed You this Day over the NATION'S and over the KINGDOMS, To PLUCK UP and to BREAK DOWN, To DESTROY and to OVERTHROW, To BUILD and to PLANT".

And "I" will pronounce MY JUDGMENT'S on them Concerning All their WICKEDNESS, Whereby They have FORSAKEN ME and have offered Sacrifices to OTHER GODS, and WORSHIPED the WORKS of their OWN HANDS.

"And they will Fight against You, But they will NOT OVERCOME YOU, for I AM WITH YOU to DELIVER YOU," declares the LORD. [Jeremiah 1. 4, 9, 16, 19.]

Regarding the JUDGMENT of the MOST HIGH also against these Corrupt

Invisible Controllers of this Planet Earth, "PROPHET ISAIAH" has Clearly Warned in the "Holy Bible", which states:

"And All the HOSTS of the HEAVEN will WEAR AWAY, And the Sky will be Rolled Up like a Scroll; All their HOSTS will also WITHER AWAY as a LEAF WITHERS from the VINE, Or as One WITHERS from the FIG TREE. [Isaiah 34. 4].

Most Incarnated People and their Counterpart Invisible Angelic Beings of this Planet Earth have thus far "NOT" Understood and thus Completely Failed to Properly Comprehend this Very Basic FACT, that the Unknowable LORD – GOD, "THE MOST HIGH" being HIMSELF, an "True Upholder" of the Universal Law of "Will to do Good" has shown so far HIS "UTMOST PATIENCE" regarding the ILLEGAL and CORRUPT BEHAVIOR and WRONGFUL DOINGS and ILLEGAL ACTIVITIES of HIS "'Visible and Invisible CREATIONS", which include "All the Various Orders" of the So Called Created Hierarchical Entities and Beings, who Consciously or Unconsciously dwell in the Many differentiated Dimensional Planes and the Sub Planes of this Solar Universe, thus Existing and Evolving in the "Differentiated Tonal Frequencies" of its Objectively Manifested Planet Earth.

The Prophet ZEPHANIAH, a Chosen PROPHET of the MOST HIGH clearly warned "ALL" regarding their CORRUPT DEEDS, regarding which the Holy Bible states:

"Therefore Wait for ME, declares the LORD, For the Day when "I" rise up to the Prey. Indeed MY Decision is to Gather Nations, To Assemble Kingdoms, To Pour Out on Them MY INDIGNATION, ALL MY BURNING ANGER; FOR ALL THE EARTH WILL BE DEVOURED, By the "'FIRE" of "MY ZEAL".

In that Day you will Feel "NO SHAME" BECAUSE OF YOUR "DEEDS", BY which You have "'REBELLED AGAINST ME'''; For then I will REMOVE YOU FROM YOUR MIDST, YOUR PROUD EXULTING ONES, And You will NEVER be HAUGHTY on MY HOLY MOUNTAIN. But "I " will LEAVE among You a HUMBLE AND LOWLY PEOPLE, and they will take REFUGE in the NAME of the LORD. [Zephaniah 3. 8. 11]

Jewish High Priest with Holy Torah

Most People of this Planet Earth, as well as their invisible counterpart "Entities and Beings" including HOST'S of ANGELS who may be to a great degree Religious, and thus belong to a Particular Hierarchical Order of Certain "Faith and Belief System" of this Planet, but Yet are not Spiritually Inclined, meaning "NOT IN COMMUNICATION WITH THE UNKNOWABLE 'MOST HIGH'S" ETHEREAL VITAL CONSCIOUS IMPULSES, WHICH ORIGINATING FROM A CENTRALLY LOCATED COSMIC ENERGY POINT [EIN SOPH], THEN CONTINUOUSLY CIRCULATE IN THE FORM OF DIFFERENTIATED TONAL FREQUENCIES OF "COLOR AND SOUNDS", PERVADING ALL THE VISIBLE AND INVISIBLE DIMENSIONAL FREQUENCIES OF THE ENTIRE SOLAR UNIVERSE AS WELL AS THIS PLANET EARTH", thus MISERABLY FAIL to Understand and thus Properly Comprehend that all "HOLY BOOKS" literally contain the "Highest Form of Codified Wisdom", which can be "ONLY REVEALED" to THOSE CHOSEN FEW, Who are nor just Die Heart Religious Beings, but More So Consciously Exist upon this Planet as The Purely "SPIRITUAL BEINGS".

The HOLY BIBLE, whose very first FIVE CHAPTERS are termed as the "FIVE BOOKS OF MOSES" or just simply known as the TORAH, are the Highest Source of "CELESTIAL WISDOM" as it Contains the CODIFIED KNOWLEDGE and WISDOM not known Even to Many of the so Called Religious Leaders, which relates to the Evolutionary Plan and Purpose formulated by the Desire Mind of the UNKNOWABLE MOST HIGH, based upon the Universal Law of Will to do Good.

Let us closely look with an "Intuitive Spiritual Mind", at the Very First Verse of the First Chapter of the Holy Bible, So We can receive its Codified Wisdom by the ineffable grace of the MOST HIGH, which states:

"In the Beginning GOD Created the HEAVEN'S and the EARTH" [Genesis 1, 1]

Now if we have our Spiritual Minds Very Much Open to receive the Blessings of the Unknowable MOST HIGH, then we will notice that the word HEAVEN'S define the Plurality aspect of the "Invisible Celestial

Creations" of the MOST HIGH or the Various Vital Dimensional Planes of Differentiated Consciousness, known in Hebrew as the "Sephirot's" or the "Sefira", while the word "Earth" itself just defines the Singular aspect of the "Physical Plane Planet Earth".

Basically the word "Heaven" itself can be misleading to many of the evolving Human Beings, whose Evolving "Animistic Personality Consciousness" during their short lived incarnated life may be Totally Stuck in the Bondage's of the Material Glamour of this dense Physical plane life, and thus most of them may Consider a Short Lived Glamour's life of the Physical Plane World as their So Called Heavenly Existence.

The Word "Earth" of this verse, in the HOLY BIBLE in this particular case simply defines the Physical dimensional plane of Incarnated Human existence, and thus All Those Who have not yet come in Contact with their Higher Dimensional "SOUL CONSCIOUSNESS", which being totally SPIRITUAL in Nature thus exist in its SOUL Consciousness Form in the Heavenly world of BRIAH, and thus may NOT Comprehend the Underlying Essence of Wisdom, which this Very Important Verse of the Holy Bible Contains.

The Word "Spiritual" technically defines the "UNTAINTED PURE STATE OF VITAL ETHEREAL CONSCIOUSNESS", which Existing at the Dawn of Creation as the "Pure Vital Ethereal Essence", composed of the Desire Mind reflections of the Unknowable "MOST HIGH" thus permeate the Entire Vital Space of the "Cosmos", and thus is termed since ancient times by the Seers and Sages as the "SPIRIT", which then through the Desire Mind Vibration Impulses of the Unknowable Creator LORD - GOD, the MOST HIGH, thus Manifest in the differentiated frequencies of the "Heaven World's", which have been termed by the ancient Seers and Sages as the differentiated "Planes and Sub Planes" of conscious Existence, to "Subjectively and Objectively" exist as a Subjectively or objectively manifested "Vital Creation", having a particular differentiated state of consciousness, which ranges from the Initial state of "Unconsciousness" to the Highest state of "Ultra or Absolute Consciousness", which in fact is a mere refection of the differentiated "Desire Mind" Consciousness of the MOST HIGH, the UNKNOWABLE CREATOR, THE LORD GOD OF THE UNIVERSE.

Just like the Physical Plane of this Planet, which we Incarnated Human Beings commonly Call as the "Earth", by having a limited Scope of

Sensory Vision, which is based upon the vital vibrations, which all exist between the Red and Indigo color Tonal Frequencies, thus allowing us Only to Perceive those Particular Existence's which exist in its Tonal frequency boundaries, and which as per our Earthly Knowledge is teaming with innumerable species of life scattered worldwide in its four Main Classified Kingdoms namely ''Mineral', ''Plant'', ''Animal'' and ''Human'' Kingdoms, in which each specie is gradually evolving at its own Evolutionary pace thus gradually attaining the ''Conscious Attributes of Heavenly Spirit'' during their limited time incarnated life duration's, to finally become one with the ''Spiritual Mind'', which is a mere reflection of the Desire Mind Attributes of the Unknowable MOST HIGH.

Much later about the ''Kingdom of Heaven'', JESUS CHRIST, the Chosen Son of GOD, defined it in parables, regarding which the Holy Bible states:

'The Kingdom of Heaven is like a Treasure Hidden in the Field, which a Man found and Hid; and from JOY over it, He goes and Sells all that He Has, and Buys that Field.

Again, the Kingdom of Heaven is like a Merchant Seeking Fine Pearls, and upon finding ONE PEARL OF GREAT VALUE, He went and Sold All that He Had, and Bought It.

Again the Kingdom of Heaven is like a Dragnet cast into the Sea, and Gathering Fish of Every Kind; and when it was Filled, they drew it up on the Beach; and they sat down, and gathered the Good Fish into Containers, but the Bad they Threw Away''. [Matthew 13. 44, 45, 46, 47, 48.]

JESUS CHRIST further Clarified about the Beautiful Dwelling places of Existence in the Heavenly worlds as recorded in the Gospel of JOHN of Holy Bible, which States:

''Let Not Your Heart be Troubled; Believe in GOD, Believe also in ME. In MY FATHER'S House are many Dwelling Places; If it were NOT SO, I would have Told You; for I go to Prepare a Place for you''. [John 14. 2]

In the Codified Story of Creation which is mentioned in the First Chapter named Genesis of the Holy Bible, it further states:

"And GOD called the Light Day, and the Darkness HE called Night. And there was EVENING, and there was MORNING, One Day." [Genesis 1. 5]

This is a Great Verse of Spiritual Wisdom, as it clearly Highlights and thus Defines the Great Importance of the "EVENING and MORNING" Hours, which are created as the "IMPORTANT TIME ZONES" on the Very first Day of Creation by the Unknowable LORD GOD of the Universe, which since very ancient times have been known as such, to the Seers, Prophets, and Sages as the Time Periods of "TWILIGHT HOURS", which are Most Suitable for "Prayers and Supplications", as it is during these "Few Hours Period", where the interpenetrating Higher Dimensional Plane Portals then Get Opened up, and a "Spiritually Inclined Person" incarnated in the human form upon this Physical Plane of Planet Earth, can Directly and Much More easily "Get in Touch", with the Graceful Divine Conscious Energies of the "MOST HIGH", which constantly Circulate around, and thus Permeate each and every Zone of our Planet earth.

The Holy Menorah

Most Human beings are unaware of this BASIC FACT that all Crystals of the Mineral Kingdom, which is the lowest Manifested Kingdom visible to Mankind upon this Planet Earth, also has resonating "Vital Consciousness", because ALL the CRYSTALS GROW, and anything which Grows has "Animating Vital Consciousness", which is an attribute of the Evolving "MIND Consciousness", provided by the grace of MOST HIGH.

The Stone crystals of Highest Clarity since ancient times are thus considered more "Pure" in their embodied vital consciousness, than all other manifested Kingdoms of the Planet earth, and thus since ancient times they have been primarily used in various Spiritual and Religious practices by descendants of ADAM, as they are the Least tainted Manifested Kingdom of this Planet Earth which is not mixed up yet with the Worldly Desires of Illusory Glamour, which in the earlier stages of their objective manifestation, these Vices are not yet properly manifested in them, and through their proper prescribed methods, their user can willfully enhance his intended spiritual or worldly objectives, and these 12 Stone crystals were thus used as per the Instruction of the LORD GOD, "THE MOST HIGH" to be Mounted in this "Spiritual Breast Plate of Judgment".

All the Crystals of the Mineral Kingdom depending upon their Clarity thus Correspond and Resonate to the Vital Ray Energies of the Solar Sun, as well as the Vital Energies of Other Celestial existences "Especially" to the Subtle Vital Radiation Frequencies of the 12 Zodiacal Constellations", which are the "Fixed Markers" in the celestial space, as observed in the Nightly skies by the Human Beings of this planet earth since the Very Ancient Times.

Thus each Manifested Mineral Crystal ranging from the Clear White Crystals to those which have Different Color Hues, resonate to Different Tonal Conscious Vibration Frequencies of the Universe, and that is the Very basic reason why LORD – GOD instructed MOSES to make a "BREAST PLATE OF JUDGEMENT" having 12 Named CRYSTAL STONES mounted in four rows and three columns, each Horizontal Row having 3 different type of Stone Crystals, each One of which should resonate according to the "Vital Mind Collective Consciousness", of One of the 12 "Tribes", which were Named after the 12 Sons of ISRAEL [JACOB], whose names were also engraved upon them according to HIS instructions, thus making Each of these Crystal Stones like an Engraved Holy SEAL.

And apart from these Instructions "THE MOST HIGH" also instructed MOSES to put in the BREAST PIECE OF JUDGMENT the "URIM and the THUMMIM" to be worn over the AARON'S Heart, Who became the First High Priest [KOHEN GADULA] for the Sons of Israel as mentioned in the 28th Chapter of Exodus in Holy Bible [Exodus 28. Verses 1 to 30].

And these 12 named Crystals by the "MOST HIGH" were according to the 12 Tribes of the Israelite's, which were Originally based upon the 12 Children of JACOB, who as per Holy Bible was named by the MOST HIGH as "ISRAEL' [Genesis 35. 10], and according to Holy Bible each of the 12 Children of JACOB had their "Own Evolutionary Mind Consciousness", which under the Spiritual Guidance of the LORD – GOD, His servant JACOB clearly defined in a Codified Way, prophesying their CONSCIOUS ATTRIBUTES in the 49th Chapter of Genesis of Holy Bible, which state:

"Then JACOB summoned his Sons and Said, "Assemble yourselves that I may tell you what shall befall you in the days to come. Gather together and hear, O Sons of JACOB; and listen to ISRAEL your father.

REUBEN, you are My First born; My Might and Beginning of My Strength, Preeminent in Dignity and Preeminent in Power. Uncontrolled as WATER, you shall not have Preeminence, because you went up to your father's bed; then you defiled it- he went up to my couch.

SIMEON and LEVI are brothers; their Swords are Implements of VIOLENCE. Let My Soul not Enter into their Council; Let not My Glory be united with their Assembly; because in their ANGER they slew Men, and in their Self – Will they lamed Oxen. Cursed be their anger, for it is Fierce; and their WRATH, for it is CRUEL. I will disperse them in JACOB and scatter them in ISRAEL.

JUDAH, your Brothers shall Praise You; your hand shall be on the Neck of your Enemies; Your Father's Sons shall Bow down to you. The Scepter shall not depart from JUDAH, nor the Ruler's Staff from between His Feet, until SHILOH Comes, and to Him shall be the Obedience of the Peoples.

ZEBULUN shall dwell at the Seashore; and He shall be a Haven for Ships, and His flank shall be toward Sidon.

ISSACHAR is a strong Donkey, lying down between the sheepfolds. When He saw that a resting place was good, and the Land was Pleasant, He Bowed His Shoulder to bear Burdens, and became a Slave at Forced Labor.

DAN shall JUDGE His People, as one of the TRIBES of ISRAEL. DAN shall be a Serpent in the Way, a Horned Snake in the Path that Bites the Horse's Heels, so that His rider falls backward.

As for GAD, Raiders shall raid Him, but He shall Raid at their Heels.

And for ASHER, His food shall be Rich, and He shall yield Royal Dainties.

NAPHTALI is a Doe let Loose, He gives beautiful words.

JOSEPH is a fruitful bough, a fruitful bough by a spring; Its branches run over a Wall. The archers bitterly attacked Him, and Shot at Him and Harassed Him; but His Bow remained Firm, and His Arms were Agile, From the hands of Mighty One of JACOB [From there is the Shepherd, the Stone of ISRAEL], From the GOD of your Father Who Helps You, And by the ALMIGHTY who Blesses You, With the Blessings of Heaven Above, Blessings of the Deep that lies Beneath, Blessings of the Breasts and of the Womb. The Blessings of Your Father have Surpassed the Blessings of My Ancestors, Up to the Utmost Bound of the Everlasting Hills; May they be on the Head of Joseph, And on the Crown of the Head of the ONE distinguished among His Bothers.

BENJAMIN is a Ravenous Wolf; In the Morning He Devours the Prey, and in the Evening He Divides the Spoil.

All these are the Twelve Tribes of ISRAEL, and this is what their Father said to them, when He Blessed Them. He "Blessed" them, Every One with the Blessing Appropriate to Him. [Genesis 49. 1, 2, 3, 4, 5, 6, 7, 8, 10, 13, 14, 15, 16, 17, 19, 20, 21, 22, 23, 24, 25, 26, 27, 28.]

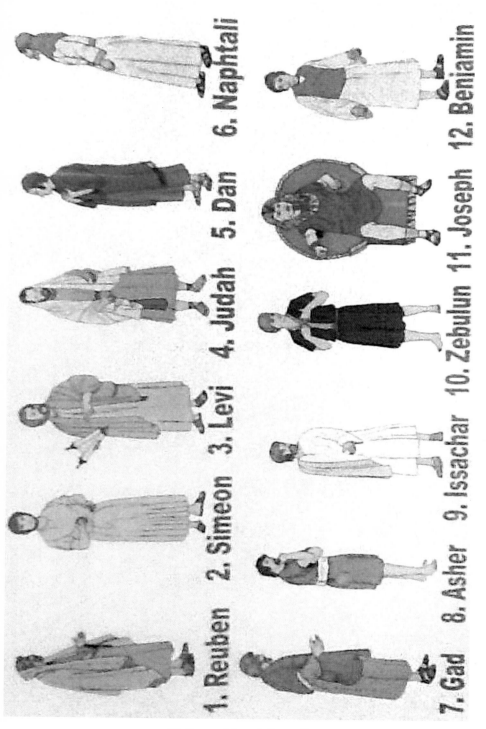

12 Sons of Jacob [Israel]

The Secret of the Breast Plate

Part 20

Although the Chosen Prophets of GOD after their incarnation upon this Planet, in the their Physical Appearance look very Similar to all Other Normal Human Beings of this Planet Earth, the Main difference between them is in the appearance of their Invisible "Casual Body", which is also the Seat of their "Soul Consciousness", which is Normally Invisible to the Most Human Beings of this Planet earth, as it is Composed of "'Rare Ethereal Matter" Electric in Nature, having Only "Good Feelings of Kindness and their thus created Thought forms", which Totally and Unconditionally Comply with the One and Only Universal Law of "Will to do Good".

All Incarnated Human Beings of this Planet, belonging to Various Faiths, Casts and Creeds, and also differentiated through their Various Colors and Races, thus inhabiting various regions of this Planet Earth, are in FACT Originally Created by the "Ethereal Vital Thought Forms" , which are Generated by the "Desire Mind Impulse's" of the ONE CREATOR LORD GOD, THE UNKNOWABLE "MOST HIGH", Who as per the Holy Bible Joyfully Created Them in HIS Own Image, according to HIS Likeness, through the assistance of "His Created Workers, the Servant Helpers", the So called Later Gods and Goddesses of this Planet Earth, Who were in reality his "Prior Creations", and are Clearly denoted by the Plural Word "US" in the Creation Chapter of the Holy Bible, which states:

Then GOD said, "Let US make Man in Our Image, according to OUR Likeness; and Let Them Rule over the Fish of the Sea, and over the Birds of the Sky, and over the Cattle, and over all the Earth, and over every Creeping thing, that Creeps on the Earth." [Genesis 1. 26].

But Since these "Prior Creations" of the Most LOVING LORD- GOD, the So Called Invisible "GODS and GODDESSES", Themselves Willfully Went Astray from his Evolutionary Plan and Purpose, and thus becoming themselves CORRUPT, then TOTALLY BETRAYED his LOVE and TRUST though the Gross MISUSE and Illegal Conduct of their "VESTED POWERS", the Whole Evolutionary Process since then, which is related to the Further Expansion of "SPIRIT CONSCIOUSNESS", has now unfortunately come to a TOTAL HALT and thus remains STANDSTILL, while the MATTER RELATED "PERSONALITY CONSCIOUSNESS in the name of Civilization has progressed in Leaps and Bounds to Technically advanced "New Heights".

This "Material Mind", which in reality is the "Personality Consciousness" of the Incarnated Human Beings, under the Guidance of these "DEFORMED and MUTATED MIND INVISIBLE ANGELIC BEINGS", their So Called "Angelic Hosts" or the "Gods and Goddesses", has thus created those Illusory Virtual reality tools which keep their Incarnated Fellow Human Beings "evolving consciousness" completely engrossed in the ILLUSORY WORLD REALITY, which is now prevalent everywhere upon the dense Physical Plane of this Planet Earth, which since ancient times is known to the Seers and Sages as the Dimensional Plane of ASSIAH.

Many of these "Artificial Intelligence Machines" now controlled by a handful of Corrupted Henchmen of these invisible, 'DEFORMED and MUTATED MIND INVISIBLE ANGELIC BEINGS", who themselves have totally lost their Touch with their Own "Spiritual Higher Selves", who are the Powerful and Elite Segment, sitting on top of the Human Society", engrossed in Material Profitability, which is related to Unquenchable GREED and the Fleeting Joy of Name and FAME, which are also the creations of Human Beings, have deprived the Large Masses to earn their daily livings thus forcing them also to alienate themselves from their "True Higher Selves" and get engrossed in the wrong path of "Involutionary Process", than moving forward toward their "Spiritual Evolution" as required per the Evolutionary Plan and Purpose of the Most Benevolent MOST HIGH.

This Gross Material aspect of This So Called Scientific Advancement has wrongfully labeled as the "Human Evolution", while it is in Fact in totally Contradiction to it, as in reality it is the "Human Involution" meaning indwelling Human Personality Consciousness Willful "INVOLVEMENT in MATTER" or in the ILLUSORY aspect of the "MATERIAL SCIENCES".

According to the Plan and Purpose of the LORD – GOD, the MOST HIGH, the "True Human Evolution", relates the indwelling "Personality Mind" consciousness of the incarnated Human Beings to the "True Established Evolutionary Process", which is meant for the CONSCIOUS EXPANSION of their "Higher Self" also termed as the "SOUL CONSCIOUSNESS", which itself is a PART and Parcel of the Differentiated Vital Ethereal "SOLAR

CONSCIOUSNESS'' existing in our Solar Universe, commonly known since ancient times in the Holy Books as the "SPIRIT". The indwelling "Personality Consciousness" Incarnated in a Human Form having the attributes of "Individualized Mind" is in fact just a "Tiny fraction" or a "Very Small portion" of his Radiant "SOLAR CONSCIOUSNESS", which since ancient times have been termed by the Learned Seers and Sages as the "SPIRIT".

Most People now with the advent of science and technology are so engrossed in the Mundane Glamour of their daily lives, that they have No time or Efforts spared to pay their Concentrated Mind Attention to the Evolutionary Plan and Purpose of their CREATOR LORD, the Invisible and Unknowable MOST HIGH, and thus many have wrongfully started in believing in "ONE HUMAN LIFE" agenda which is now propagated in the name of Civilization and a New Culture, by the Visible and Invisible henchmen of the DEMONIC MIND ENTITIES, which has thus absolutely stopped the Further Formation of their "CASUAL BODIES", which only expand in size according to those Conceived Live "THOUGHT FORMATIONS" which are related to their "Feeling and Emotions", which are based upon the universal law of "Will to do Good".

The Unknowable Creator LORD GOD, also known as the MOST HIGH, as well as the LORD OF THE FLAMES, Since Very ancient Times have shown his EXTREME PATIENCE toward HIS Visible and Invisible Creations upon this Planet Earth, and Time and Again Forgiven them for their Inequities and Corrupt Behavior by just only rebuking them with small Consequences, but now for their Long Survival which is in "Total Jeopardy", a full scale "RETURN and SURRENDER" is Required as per the Celestial Command, which follows the Inherent Instructions of the Universal Law of "Will to do Good".

During the ancient times, When Most of the Advanced Civilizations of Ancient world including those Evolving in the Fertile Lands of Sumeria and Egypt, wrongfully started worshiping his mere CREATIONS, the so Called "Gods and Goddesses", who were nothing more than HIS Servant Helpers, existing as the so called "The Hosts" or "The Elohim's", Who started to Expand their Corrupt Mind Agendas related to "MATERIALISM", then LORD GOD in those times Chose "MOSES" to deliver HIS people out of Material Bondage's, who got caught in the Deceitful activities of their Human Leaders, who at that time were the Mighty "Pharaohs of Egypt".

The Very Second book of Holy Bible starts with the "Life of MOSES", and thus Explains his Choosing by the MOST HIGH upon the "Mountain of God", and in regards to these so called Gods and Goddesses, in its Third Book named "LEVITICUS" the Holy Bible states:

Then the LORD spoke to MOSES, Saying, "Speak to ALL the Congregation of The Sons of ISRAEL and Say to Them, You shall be Holy, for "I" the LORD your GOD am Holy.

Every One of You shall reverence His Mother and His Father, and you shall keep MY Sabbaths; I AM THE LORD YOUR GOD.

Do not turn to IDOLS or make for Yourselves Molten Gods; I AM THE LORD YOUR GOD.

Now when you Offer Sacrifice of Peace Offerings to the LORD, you shall Offer it so that you may be accepted. It shall be eaten the Same Day you Offer it, and the Next Day; But what remains until the Third Day shall be Burned with "FIRE". So if it is eaten at All on the Third Day, it is an Offence; it will not be accepted. And Everyone Who Eats it will Bear His Iniquity, for He has Profaned the Holy Thing of the LORD; and that Person shall be cut off from His People." [Leviticus 19. 1, 2, 3, 4, 5, 6, 7, 8.]

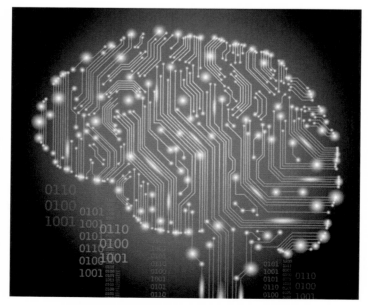

Mechanized computer brain

The Unknowable "Lord of the Flames", Who since Very Ancient Times has been referred to by Various Holy Seers, Prophets, and Sages of this Planet Earth as THE MOST BENEVOLENT CREATOR, "THE MOST HIGH", is in FACT, the Extended Consciousness Embodiment of the DESIRE MIND VITALITY of the ONE and ONLY CREATOR – OBSERVER, the UNKNOWABLE LORD GOD of the manifested "ENTIRE INFINITE UNIVERSE", which Contains Innumerable Number of HUGE GALAXIES, and their "Various Solar Star Systems" in its undefinable HUGE PARAMETRIC ETHEREAL SPACE, constantly resonating with the VITAL CONSCIOUS CURRENTS, which Originate from a "CENTRAL POINT", Which "Cyclically" permeate its various Visible and Invisible DIMENSIONAL LEVELS to keep it Animating through the Vital Churning Force of 'SPIRAL, CYCLIC, and CIRCULAR MOTIONS".

This Animating force having VITAL CONSCIOUSNESS is the basis of all "FREQUENCY VIBRATIONS', which manifest as the differentiated 'Subjective and Objective Realities", which are Comprehended by various Hierarchical Orders of Entities and Beings though TONAL COLORS AND SOUNDS, according to their own level of CONSCIOUSNESS EXPANSION, which accordingly as per the Evolutionary Plan and Purpose of the MOST HIGH, provide them the Necessary Sensory Attributes and related manifested Tools, so they can properly comprehend them.

The Holy Bible in its various Chapters hold the "Very Secrets", which are related to the "MOST HIGH -GOD CONSCIOUSNESS" and HIS SUBJECTIVE AND OBJECTIVE CREATION.

For Example, this Important Verse in the Holy Bible from the First chapter of the GOSPEL OF JOHN clearly states:

In the Beginning was the WORD, and the WORD was GOD. HE was in the Beginning with the GOD. ALL THINGS CAME INTO BEING BY HIM; AND APART FROM HIM NOTHING CAME INTO BEING THAT HAS COME INTO BEING.

IN HIM WAS LIFE; AND THE "LIFE" WAS THE "LIGHT" OF MEN. AND

THE LIGHT SHINES IN THE "DARKNESS", AND THE "DARKNESS DID NOT COMPREHEND IT." [John 1. 1, 2, 3, 4, 5.]

In these above Verses of the Holy Bible, the Conscious Attributes of the Unknowable MOST HIGH, or the LORD – GOD, who is the MOST BENEVOLENT and the LIFE GIVER has been defined as the Vital Consciousness of "LIGHT", which always SHINES IN THE "DARKNESS", And the "DARKNESS" meaning the DENSE MATERIAL CONSCIOUSNESS, stuck in the MATERIAL PLANE BONDAGE'S can thus never COMPREHEND IT.

And in the Verse 6 of Psalm 33 in the Holy Bible, which also pertains to the Conscious Attributes of the Unknowable MOST HIGH, or the LORD – GOD, it also clearly states:

"By the WORD of the LORD, the HEAVENS were made. And by the BREATH of HIS MOUTH all their HOST. [Psalm 33. 6]

This Particular Verse of Holy Bible like the Previous Important Verse thus clearly denotes the importance of "SOUND FREQUENCY VIBRATIONS", which existing as "THE HOLY WORD" or the FREQUENCY VIBRATIONS created as the "Vital Thought Forms", Originating from the DESIRE MIND of the MOST HIGH, which thus manifested the Various Differentiated Planes and their Sub- Planes, commonly known as the Subjective and Objective Heavens, having their own densities according to the Resonance of its "Key Note Vibrations, and their related Tonal and Sub Tonal Frequencies".

And the CYCLIC VITAL ETHEREAL ENERGY denoted in this Important Verse as the "BREATH OF THE MOUTH OF MOST HIGH", which technically in an Incarnated Human Being represents the "Inhalation and Exhalation Process", But in this Particular Verse it is codified for the "UNIVERSAL PROCESS OF EVOLVING CONSCIOUSNESS EXPANSION", or Just Simply the Process of "EVOLUTION AND INVOLUTION", which brought into manifestation, the various HIERARCHICAL ORDERS of Various ENTITIES and BEINGS to "UNCONSCIOUSLY OR CONSCIOUSLY" exist in these Differentiated Dimensional Planes, who are termed in the Holy Bible simply as the HOSTS, thus continue Moving according to the Evolutionary PLAN and PURPOSE of the MOST HIGH in a Forward Motion, by Continuously moving through the Vital Ethereal Space for their GRADUAL CONSCIOUSNESS EXPANSION, and for this very purpose they are Mounted upon the "Small and Large "Time Cycles", Composing the GREAT WHEELS of EVOLUTION, which are known as the "WHEELS OF TIME".

THE LORD GOD, THE MOST HIGH gave the Codified Understanding of these "WHEELS OF TIME" to the Prophet EZEKIEL, who saw them in His Holy Vision, and described them as such in great details, which is recorded in the Holy Bible, which states:

"And as I Looked, Behold, a Storm Wind was Coming from the North, a Great Cloud with FIRE Flashing forth Continually and a Bright Light around it, and in its Midst Something like Glowing Metal in the Midst of the FIRE" [Ezekiel 1. 4]

The "North East" Angular Direction since ancient times has been known to all the Advanced Ancient Seers and Sages, as the starting direction of All Creation upon this Planet EARTH, as well as the Holy Direction of the MOST HIGH, whose glory is represented by the North Easterly Direction of the Vital Solar Rays of the Rising Sun.

The Holy Bible regarding EZEKIEL'S Vision further states:

"And within it there were figures resembling Four Living Beings. And this was their appearance: they had HUMAN FORM".

And each went Straight Forward; wherever the SPIRIT was about to Go, without turning as they Went. In the Midst of the Living Beings there was something that looked like Burning Coals of FIRE, like Torches darting back and forth among the LIVING BEINGS. The FIRE was BRIGHT, and the LIGHTNING was flashing from the FIRE. And the LIVING BEINGS ran To and FRO like the Bolts of LIGHTNING.

Now as I looked at the LIVING BEINGS, Behold there was One WHEEL on the Earth beside the LIVING BEINGS, for EACH of the FOUR of Them. [Ezekiel 1. 5, 12, 13, 14, 15]

There are 4 different Major TIME CYCLES, known as the "WHEELS OF TIME", each ONE of Them related to ONE of the Four Major Dimensional Planes, which are known in Hebrew Language since ancient times by the SEERS and SAGES as the DIMENSIONAL SEPHIROT'S OF "ASSIAH, YETZIRAH, BRIAH, and ATZILUTH". The SEPHIROT of ASSIAH represents the PHYSICAL PLANE of this Planet Earth, the domain of Incarnated Human Beings, regarding which the Prophet EZEKIEL mentioned in the Above Verse as, "Behold there was One WHEEL on the Earth beside the LIVING BEINGS".

The Holy Bible further states regarding EZEKIEL'S VISION:

"The appearance of the WHEELS and their Workmanship was like Sparkling Beryl, and All FOUR of Them had the SAME FORM, their appearance and workmanship being as ONE WHEEL WERE WITHIN ANOTHER. [Ezekiel 1, 16]

As the Boundaries of all of these FOUR DIMENSIONAL PLANES INTERPENETRATE Each other, thus these FOUR WHEELS OF TIME are also CO – EXISTENT, and their Corresponding Interdependence and their CYCLIC Interrelationship, due to their INTERPENETRATION was thus Shown to Prophet EZEKIEL in this VISION OF GOD, through the Divine attributes of HIS Ineffable Grace, So that He Can share this Information to all those who were "GONE ASTRAY" from the Evolutionary Plan and Purpose of THE MOST HIGH, regarding which Prophet EZEKIEL further states in the Holy Bible:

"Now it came about at the end of SEVEN days that the WORD of the LORD came to ME saying, "Son of Man, I have appointed you a Watchman to the House of ISRAEL; whenever you hear a WORD from My MOUTH, WARN Them from ME. When I Say to the Wicked, YOU SHALL SURELY DIE; and you do not WARN Him or Speak Out to WARN the WICKED from His WICKED WAY that He may LIVE, that the WICKED MAN shall DIE in His INIQUITY, But His BLOOD I will require at Your Hand.

Yet if you have WARNED the WICKED, and He does not turn from His WICKEDNESS or from His WICKED WAY, He shall DIE IN HIS INIQUITY; But You have DELIVERED YOURSELF [Ezekiel 3. 16, 17, 18, 19]

Regarding the "SPIRIT OF THE LIVING BEINGS" or their "EVOLUTIONARY VITAL CONSCIOUSNESS", which is related to these FOUR WHEELS OF TIME, as depicted in the VISIONS OF GOD shown to Prophet EZEKIEL, the Holy Bible further states:

"Wherever they moved, they moved in any of the FOUR directions,

WITHOUT TURNING as They Moved. As for their Rims they were Lofty and Awesome, and the RIMS of All FOUR of Them were FULL OF EYES round them" [Ezekiel 1. 17, 18]

Here the Prophet EZEKIEL was shown by the Grace of MOST HIGH, the COLLECTIVE CONSCIOUSNESS of THE LIVING BEINGS having their INDIVIDUALIZED CONSCIOUS ATTRIBUTE depicted in this VISION as their "EYES", As Eye is Considered as the "CENTER of the SOUL CONSCIOUSNESS", but they all are still a PART AND PARCEL OF THE COLLECTIVE CONSCIOUSNESS of these Dimensional Planes, whereas the RIMS of these FOUR WHEELS in this Godly Vision depicted their indwelling SUB – PLANES thus composing in their totality the FOUR DIMENSIONAL PLANES, which are related to the FOUR GREAT WHEELS OF TIME, and are thus required for their Vital Existence to CYCLICALLY EXPAND in these FOUR DIMENSIONAL PLANES of ASSIAH, YETZIRAH, BRIAH and ATZILUTH.

Regarding these FOUR WHEELS, The Holy Bible further states:

"And whenever the Living Beings Moved, the WHEELS Moved with Them. And whenever the Living Beings rose from the Earth, the WHEEL rose also. Wherever the SPIRIT was about to Go, they would Go in that Direction. And the WHEELS Rose close beside them; for the SPIRIT OF THE LIVING BEINGS was in the WHEELS.

Whenever those went, these went; and whenever those "STOOD STILL", these "STOOD STILL". And whenever those Rose from the Earth, the WHEELS Rose close beside them; for the SPIRIT OF THE LIVING BEINGS was in the WHEELS". [Exodus 1. 19, 20, 21]

In these above verses the Holy Bible Clearly states that the EVOLUTIONARY WHEEL OF TIME pertaining to CONSCIOUSNESS EXPANSION can also COME TO A STANDSTILL, thus UNDULY TOTALLY HALTING THE GRAND EVOLUTIONARY PROCESS, as in these above Verses Prophet EZEKIEL also clearly said that the "SPIRIT OF THE LIVING BEINGS was in the WHEELS".

Four Creatures of Ezekiel's Vision, as depicted by the Earlier Christians

The Secret of the Breast Plate

Part 22

In the Vision of GOD, which EZEKIEL, the Chosen Profit by the Grace of MOST HIGH was allowed to View, He saw Figures having human forms in the Flashing Fire, regarding which the Holy Bible states:

"And as I Looked, Behold, a Storm Wind was coming from the North, a Great Cloud with FIRE flashing Continually and a BRIGHT LIGHT around it, and in its Midst Something like Glowing Metal in the Midst of the FIRE.

And within it there were figures resembling Four Living Beings. And this was their appearance: They had Human Form. Each of them had Four Faces and Four Wings.

And their Legs were straight and their feet were like a calf's Hoof, and they gleamed like Burnished Bronze. Under their Wings on their Four Sides were Human Hands. As for the faces and wings of the FOUR of them, their wings touched one another; their faces did not turn when they moved, each went straight forward.

As for the Form of their Faces, Each had the face of a MAN, All FOUR had the Face of a LION on the right and the Face of a BULL on the Left, and all FOUR had the Face of an EAGLE.

Such were their Faces. Their Wings were spread out above; each had two touching another Being, and Two Covering their Bodies. And each went Straight Forward; wherever the SPIRIT was about to Go, without turning as they went. [Ezekiel 1.4, 4, 6, 7, 8, 9, 10, 11, 12.]

Most people of this Planet Earth, till now are unaware of the SECRET and Most Important INFORMATION which was provided to the MANKIND, and His Many Generations to come upon this Planet, by the Ineffable Grace of the MOST HIGH, through this CODIFIED VISION never revealed before in the HISTORY of this PLANET EARTH, which through HIS LOVE and KINDNESS was thus given to Prophet EZEKIEL, and is thus Truly Related to the EVOLUTIONARY PLAN and PURPOSE of Conscious Expansion established at the very start by the MOST HIGH, the LORD - GOD.

The Four Figures Esoterically represent the Four Quadrants formed in the "Expanding Spherical Universe", later Represented by the Holy symbol of a CROSS in Various Ancient Cultures, as these Four Quadrants came into manifestation by the Desire Mind "Thought Forms" of the Unknowable Most High", whose Desire Mind consciousness also differentiated itself in Three Conscious Parts at the Very Beginning of the Creation, later to be known by the Human Beings of the Various Races as the "Holy Trinity". In Our Solar Universe, the Mathematical Number "Four" represents the Collective Consciousness of Jupiter, Whose Hebrew name is "TZEDEK" meaning the "RIGHTEOUS ONE".

In the 12 Constellation's of the Celestial Skies, Whose Cosmic Energy Radiations have a Major Impact upon the Evolving consciousness of "All" Visible and Invisible Evolving Kingdoms of this Planet Earth, who Consciously or Unconsciously "Co – Exist" in its Various Differentiated Dimensional Frequencies, Especially Effecting the Evolutionary Human Beings and their Counterpart Invisible Angelic Beings, as at the Very start of "Grand Experiment of Consciousness Expansion", which is termed as the "Evolutionary Process" of Conscious expansion, established for this Planet Earth, these "Close Knitted Cluster of Solar Star Systems" thus belonging to our "Milky Way Galaxy", were established by "LORD OF THE FLAMES" as the 'Fixed Energy Reservoirs" in the Celestial Skies, whose Cosmic Radiations since very beginning Daily impact this Planet Earth's evolving "Collective Consciousness".

According to the Gradual Conscious expansion Program established for the "Incarnated Human Beings" upon this Planet Earth, who Since Very Ancient Times Gradually Evolved upon this Planet through the "Timely Introduction" of "Various Human Races" and then their further Differentiated "Sub Races", according to the Desire Mind impulses of the Observing Unknowable "MOST HIGH", these Various "Star Groups" now known as the "Zodiacal Constellations", which at the very start of this Grand Experiment were originally established in Celestial skies only as a Group of "8" Zodiacal Constellations, thus related to the Mathematical Number of 8, which is considered as the "Conscious Totality" of the "Heavenly FATHER and HIS Mind Born SON", and this number 8 thus representing the "conscious totality" is the Mathematical Number of "Infinity", and is thus Symbolically Represented in the Mathematics by 'Two Adjoined Circles", which in reality is "A POINT AND a CIRCLE", representing in a CODIFIED way, the Cosmic "FATHER and the SON" Conscious Energy Relationship. The

Mathematical Number "8" is also the Mathematical number of Planet Mercury representing its Collective Consciousness, which objectively Exists close to the Objectively Manifested Body of the Solar Sun, and in later Times was thus known as the Wise "HERMES", upon whose basis, the word "HERMIT" Came to be Known for all those Human Beings, who were having Mystical Abilities associated with their Saintly Nature's.

By the "MUCH - Much Later Time" of Prophet 'EZEKIEL', the number of ZODIACAL CONSTELLATIONS in the Celestial skies had already risen to a total number of 12 Constellations, of which the TAURUS Constellation was represented by the shape of a "BULL" just like the Image of the "BAAL", which was worshiped by the Ancient Egyptians as their "Sacred Apis Bull", the Embodiment of their "Father God" whom they reverently called as the Embodiment of "Ptah Consciousness". Similarly the AQUARIUS Constellation was represented by the Shape of a "MAN". The LEO Constellation was represented by the Shape of a "LION", and the ancient symbolic shape of SCORPIO Constellation was that of an "EAGLE", whom the Ancient Egyptians Revered as the "PHOENIX BIRD, as well as an Important Symbol of their Venerated "GOD HORUS".

In the Vision of GOD, which Prophet EZEKIEL saw, as mentioned in the Holy Bible, in which it States:

"As for the Form of their Faces, Each had the face of a MAN, All FOUR had the Face of a LION on the right and the Face of a BULL on the Left, and all FOUR had the Face of an EAGLE".

The Prophet Ezekiel was shown in the Vision of GOD, the Codified Symbol of the "Fixed Cross", which through ages have existed in the Celestial Skies, Composed of the Symbols of the 4 Zodiacal Constellations, which consist of [1], "TAURUS", [2], "LEO", [3] "SCORPIO", [4] "AQUARIUS", which by much later times of Jesus Christ, the Chosen Son of GOD, this "FIXED CROSS OF THE HEAVENS", was symbolically represented later on by an Elongated armed "LATIN CROSS OF CHRISTIANITY", a CODIFIED SYMBOL OF THE UNKNOWABLE SOLAR LOGOS, the LORD – GOD of the ENTIRE SOLAR UNIVERSE, whose Conscious Expanding energies are meant for the Spiritual Advancement and Conscious Growth of All Evolving Human Beings of this Planet Earth, so that during their Short Lived Incarnated Human Lives, their Indwelling Personality Consciousness, which is mostly related to the

Desire Mind of this Material World can Consciously Come in contact with their Invisible Higher Selves, spiritually known as their "SOLAR CONSCIOUSNESS", and thus Consciously join it by becoming ONE with their SOUL CONSCIOUSNESS, before their Physical Death Occurs in this dense Physical Plane.

And this Holy Verse mentioning what the Prophet EZEKIEL saw, states:

"And their Legs were straight and their feet were like a calf's Hoof, and they gleamed like Burnished Bronze",

Which represent the Gleaming State of their Higher Conscious Mind shining like the "BURNISHED BRONZE" and represented by the Four Symbolic Faces of the MESSIAH ZODIACAL CROSS also known as the FIXED CROSS of the Celestial Heavens , which the "Children of ISRAEL" acquired after they Again Collectively made a "Holy Covenant" with the MOST HIGH during the time of HIS Chosen Servant MOSES and HIS High Priest AARON, and thus willfully left the practices of "Calf Worship" behind, symbolically represented in this Great Vision by their "Calf Hoofs", in which they were earlier Wrongfully indulged in during their Slavery Time Period in the Land of Egyptian Pharaoh's.

The FIRE and the SHINING BRIGHT LIGHT, which the Prophet EZEKIEL in His Vision Saw, regarding which the Holy Bible states:

"FIRE flashing continually and a BRIGHT LIGHT around it, and in its Midst Something like Glowing Metal in the Midst of the FIRE".

This Codified Verse technically represents the Circular Wheel Like motion of the CELESTIAL SPIRITUAL ENERGIES of this "FIXED" or the MESSIAH CROSS of the Celestial Skies, in which the EXPANDING CONSCIOUSNESS is represented by the FLAMING FIRE, which produce the SHINING BRIGHT LIGHT of the SPIRITUAL MIND, as the Human MIND, Since very Ancient Times has been symbolically represented by the Various Human Races by a symbol of "LIGHT", and now in our Modern time with a LIGHT BULB, and the "Something like Glowing Metal in the Midst of the FIRE" represents the PROTECTIVE ARMOUR for the "Children of ISRAEL created and thus provided by the DESIRE MIND THOUGHT FORMS of the Unknowable MOST HIGH.

The Secret of the Breast Plate

Part 23

In the Holy Bible, both the Prophet Elijah, the Tishbite from Gilead, and as per the Command of the LORD – GOD, the MOST HIGH, his Chosen Disciple Elisha from Abel – Meholah, both have been repeatedly termed Individually in the Holy Bible as the "Man of GOD", which are stated in these Particular Verses of the Holy Bible.

Prophet Elijah has been termed repeatedly as a "Man of God" in the following verses of the Holy Bible [1 Kings 17.18], [2 Kings 1.9. 11, 13.]

And with the performing of the Miracle of restoring a Dead Child back to Life, the Holy Bible confirms Him as the "Man of God" as stated in these following Verses:

"And Elijah took the child, and brought Him down from the Upper Room into the House and gave Him to His Mother; and Elijah said. "SEE YOUR SON IS ALIVE". Then the women said to Elijah, "Now I know that you are a MAN OF GOD, and the WORD of the LORD in your Mouth is TRUTH". [1 Kings. 23, 24].

The Holy Bible describes the appearance of Prophet Elijah in this Particular verses, which state:

"And he said to them, "What kind of Man was He who came up to meet you and spoke these words to you?" And they answered Him, "He was a Hairy Man with a Leather Girdle bound about His Loins." And He said, "It is Elijah the Tishbite".

And Prophet Elisha in the following verses of the Holy Bible has been also termed as the "Man of God" [2 Kings Chapter 4.7,16,21,22,25,27,40,42; Chapter 5.8,14,15; Chapter 6.9,10,15; Chapter 7.18,19; Chapter 8.7,8,11; Chapter 13.19].

Prophet Elijah has been always repeatedly quoted as saying in the Holy Bible, "As the LORD, the GOD of ISRAEL Lives, before whom I stand" [1 Kings 17.1], "As the LORD your GOD LIVES" [1 Kings 18.10], or "As the LORD of the HOSTS LIVES, before whom I stand" [1 Kings 18.15], which had deep Spiritual meaning, as It clearly explains that Prophet ELIJAH was fully aware of the Utmost Status of the MOST HIGH in the subjectively and objectively manifested Infinite Universe, that not only HE is the LORD – GOD of the Human beings but also the LORD GOD of all the Invisible HOSTS, the so called "ELOHIM".

During the times of Prophet Elijah another Prophet of LORD named MICAIAH, son of IMLAH Quoted the same WORD as Prophet ELIJAH earlier did, regarding which the Holy Bible states:

"But MICAIAH Said, "As the LORD Lives, what the LORD says to Me, that I will Speak." [1 Kings 22.14].

Later on Prophet ELISHA repeatedly said the same Word as earlier said by Prophet Elijah thus telling Him, "As the LORD Lives, and as You Yourself Live, I will not leave You." [2 Kings 2. 2, 4, 6.]

According to holy Bible, the "Man of God" ELISHA, just like JESUS CHRIST, also brought back a "dead lad" to life, as clearly narrated in 2 Kings chapter 4 verses 32 to 37. It states "When ELISHA came into the house, behold the lad was dead and laid on his bed. So he entered and shut the door behind them both, and prayed to the Lord. And he went up and lay on the child, and put his mouth on his mouth, and his eyes on his eyes and his hands on his hands, and he stretched himself on him; and the flesh of the child became warm. Then he returned and walked in the house once back and forth, and went up and stretched himself on him, and the lad sneezed seven times and the lad opened his eyes. And he called Gehazi and said, "Call this Shunammite," So he called her, and when she came in to him, he said "Take up your son." Then she went in and fell at his feet and bowed herself to the ground, and she took up her son and went out. [2 Kings Chapter 4 verses 32 to 37].

The "Man of God" ELISHA also performed the miracle of food to feed the hungry, which was similarly performed later on by "Son of God", JESUS CHRIST during his time. In 2 Kings Chapter 4 verses 42, 43, 44, it's clearly written about this miracle in details, which state "Now a man came from Baalshalishah, and brought the "MAN OF GOD" bread of the first fruits, twenty loaves of barley and fresh ears of grain in his sack. And he said, "Give them to the people that they may eat." And his attendant said "What shall I set this before a hundred men?" But he said, "Give them to the people that they may eat, for thus says the Lord, They shall eat and have some left over". So he set it before them, and they ate and had some left over, according to the word of the Lord" [2 Kings Chapter 4 verses 42, 43, 44].

Similarly such a miracle of feeding the hungry was performed by Jesus Christ as narrated in chapter 14 of the Gospel of Matthew, which states, "And when it was evening, the disciples came to Him, saying, "The place is desolate, and the time is already past; so send the multitudes away, that they may go into the villages and buy food for themselves." But Jesus said to them, "They do not need to go away; you give them something to eat!" And they said to Him, "We have here only five loaves and two fish." And He said, "Bring them here to Me." And ordering the multitudes to recline on the grass, He took the five loaves and the two fish, and looking up toward heaven, He blessed the food, and breaking the loaves He game them to the disciples, and the disciples gave to the multitudes. And they all ate, and were satisfied. And they picked up what was left over of the broken pieces, twelve full baskets. And there were about five thousand men who ate, aside from women and children [Matthew 14 verses 15 to 21].

Much later JESUS CHRIST clearly stated in the Holy Bible, about JOHN THE BAPTIST, stating "For all the prophets and the Law prophesied until John, and if you care to ACCEPT it, HE himself is ELIJAH, who was to come. He who has ears to hear, let him hear." [Matthew 11.13, 14, 15]. Jesus again clarified about ELIJAH's reincarnation in the following verses "And his disciples asked Him, saying, Why then do the scribes say that ELIJAH must come first? And He answered and said ELIJAH is coming and will restore all things, but I SAY TO YOU that ELIJAH ALREADY CAME, and they did not recognize him, but did to him whatever they wished. So also the "SON OF MAN" is going to suffer at their hands. Then the disciples understood that He had spoken to them about JOHN THE BAPTIST" [Matthew 17.10, 11, 12, 13].

JESUS CHRIST was in close touch with ELIJAH, just like ELISHA was earlier in touch with ELIJAH and their meetings have been clearly stated in the Holy Bible, which was even witnessed by PETER, JAMES, and JOHN, his brother, as mentioned in these following verses "And six days later Jesus took with Him Peter, and James and John his brother, and brought them up to a high mountain by themselves. And He was transfigured before them; and His face shone like the SUN, and His garments became as white as light. And behold, MOSES AND ELIJAH APPEARED TO THEM, TALKING WITH HIM. And peter answered and said to Jesus, Lord, it is good for us to be here; if You wish, I will make three tabernacles here, one for YOU and one for MOSES and one for ELIJAH. While he was still speaking, behold, a bright cloud overshadowed them and behold a voice out of the cloud saying, 'This is My beloved Son, with whom I am well pleased, hear Him!' And when the disciples heard this they fell on their faces and were much afraid. And Jesus came to them and touched them and said, 'Arise and do not be afraid'; And lifting up their eyes, they saw no one, except Jesus Himself alone [Matthew 17.1, 2, 3, 4, 5, 6, 7, 8]. This same narrative of JESUS MEETING ELIJAH has been repeated in the GOSPEL OF MARK Chapter 9 verses 2,3,4,5,6,7,8 and in the GOSPEL OF LUKE Chapter 9 verses 28 to 37.

Just like PROPHET ELIJAH was a forerunner before PROPHET ELISHA, "THE MAN OF GOD", similar information is clearly mentioned in the GOSPEL OF LUKE about the spirit of ELIJAH incarnating as "JOHN THE BAPTIST" before the incarnation of the spirit of "SON OF GOD" to be incarnated as Lord JESUS CHRIST, as written in this following verse of Holy Bible, "The angel said to him, "Do not be afraid Zacharias, for your petition has been heard and your wife Elizabeth will bear you a son, and you will give him the name JOHN. And it is he who will go as a forerunner before Him in the SPIRIT AND POWER OF ELIJAH, to turn the hearts of the Fathers back to the children, and the disobedient to the attitude of the righteous, so as to make ready a people prepared for the Lord' [Luke 1.13,17].

The "MAN OF GOD" PROPHET ELISHA'S Spirit was upon JESUS CHRIST when crucified upon the cross about the 9th hour, Jesus cried out with a loud voice, "ELI, ELI, LAMA SABACHTHANI", meaning "My Lord, My Lord, why have you forsaken Me"? And some of those who were standing there, when they heard it, began saying, "This man is calling for ELIJAH". But the rest of them said. "Let us see whether ELIJAH will come to save him". And Jesus cried out again with a loud voice, and yielded up His spirit [Matthews 27.46, 47, 49, 50].

Prophet Elisha watching Prophet Elijah be carried off by chariots of fire.

A depiction of Golden Calf Idol Worship by sons of Israel

The image of a Calf depicted at Mount Horeb in Saudi Arabia

The WORD of GOD came expressly to Prophet Ezekiel, who was actually a Priest, son of Buzi living among the Exiles in the Land of the Chaldeans by the river Chebar, who was permitted to have a Divine Vision by the grace of the MOST HIGH, on the fifth of the month in the fifth year of King Jehoiachin's exile by the river Chebar in the land of the Chaldeans as mentioned in "Ezekiel 1. 1, 2, 3." In the Holy Bible.

By the Time of Prophet Ezekiel the Children of Israel had more or less forgotten the HOLY COVENANT, which Since the days of NOAH was reverently made for the FIRST TIME with the MOST HIGH, and then was also repeatedly made by their Patriarchs, which was reverently Kept and observed by HIS "Chosen Sons" and the "Holy Prophets". And thus by the time of Prophet Ezekiel, they willfully negating their Holy Covenant due to their Corrupt Minds filled with Unquenchable Greed and Lustful behavior to illegally Control others, like all those Humans, who worshiped the Invisible Animistic and Material Mind Creatures Entities, as their So called "GODS and GODDESSES", thus themselves started the Wrong practices of worshiping the "ANIMAL" Figures like that of the "BULL or a Calf", whose Molten and Carved Figures representing the "ANIMAL MIND CONSCIOUSNESS" have Much lesser Consciousness Expansion that that of an "Incarnated Human Being", and thus having more or less a "HERD Type GROUP CONSCIOUSNESS", the animals still do not possess the Fully Bloomed Conscious attribute of an "Individualized Mind", which all of the incarnated Human Beings of this Planet Earth Surely Possess during their short lived time duration's.

To Worship a lower Mind Creature as a "God or Goddess" is surely a Big Mistake, which is still being Carried on ignorantly in various Human Cultures, upon the physical plane of this Planet Earth, as such practices only attract those "'Doomed Invisible Consciousness Existences'", who earlier themselves willfully or ignorantly by performing such wrong practices during their incarnated human life duration's, are now thus stuck in the Invisible dimensional frequencies of this planet earth without having a dense physical form, and thus stay "mentally imprisoned" for Very long unimaginable duration's with animistic habits, after the demise of their physical bodies known to all Human Beings as the physical death.

It is hard to imagine, that the Human Beings of this Planet Earth, even in these modern times of rational thinking, all having the Conscious Attribute of Individualized MIND, whom the LORD – GOD Created in own Image, will foolishly pertain to such Degraded Worship Practices, and start worshiping the "CREATION" animated in its various aspects, rather than its Unknowable "CREATOR", the LORD – GOD, THE MOST HIGH.

During the turbulent times of Children of Israel, who were living in Exile in the land of Chaldeans, the LORD GOD, THE MOST HIGH, chose the Priest Ezekiel, to act as HIS Prophet, addressing him as the "Son of Man", regarding which the Holy Bible states:

Then HE said to me, "Son of Man stand on your Feet that "I" May speak with you!" And as HE spoke to me, the SPIRIT entered me and set me on My Feet; and I heard HIM speaking to me. Then HE said to me, "Son of Man, "I" am sending You to the Sons of Israel, to a REBELLIOUS People, Who have REBELLED AGAINST ME; They and Their FATHERS have TRANSGRESSED against ME to this very Day.

And "I" am sending you to Them, WHO are STUBBORN and OBSTINATE Children; and You Shall say to them, "THUS SAYS THE LORD GOD".

"As for Them, Whether They LISTEN OR NOT – FOR THEY ARE A REBELLIOUS HOUSE – They will know that a Prophet has been among them. And SON of Man, neither FEAR them nor FEAR their Words, though THISTLES and THORNS are with you and you sit on SCORPIONS; Neither FEAR their Words nor be DISMAYED at their Presence, for they are a REBELLIOUS HOUSE.

But you shall Speak MY WORDS to them, whether THEY LISTEN OR NOT, for they are REBELLIOUS. Now Son of Man, Listen to what "I" am speaking to you; Do not be Rebellious like that REBELLIOUS HOUSE. Open Your Mouth and EAT what "I" am giving you."

Then "I" Looked, Behold, a HAND was Extended to me; and Lo a SCROLL was in it. When HE spread it out before me, it was written on the FRONT and BACK; and Written on it were LAMENTATIONS, MOURNING, and WOE. [Ezekiel 2. Verses 1 to 10.]

Then HE said to me, "Son of Man", Eat what you Find; Eat this SCROLL, and Go, Speak to the House of Israel."

So I opened my MOUTH, and "HE" fed me this Scroll. And HE said to me. "Son of Man feed your Stomach, and fill your body with this SCROLL which "I" am giving you." Then I ate it, and it was SWEET as HONEY in my MOUTH. Then HE said to me, "Son of Man, Go to the House of Israel and speak my words to them. For you are NOT being sent to a People of UNINTELLIGIBLE SPEECH or DIFFICULT LANGUAGE, but to the HOUSE of ISRAEL, nor to many Peoples of Unintelligent Speech or Difficult Language, Whose Words you cannot Understand. But "I" have Sent you to Them WHO SHOULD LISTEN TO YOU; Yet the House of Israel WILL NOT BE WILLING TO LISTEN TO YOU, SINCE THEY ARE NOT WILLING TO LISTEN TO "ME". Surely the WHOLE HOUSE OF ISRAEL is STUBBORN and OBSTINATE".

'Behold, "I" have made your face as HARD as their FACES, and your FOREHEAD as HARD as their FOREHEADS, Like EMERY HARDER THAN FLINT, "I" have made your Forehead. Do not be AFRAID of THEM or be DISMAYED before THEM, though they are a REBELLIOUS HOUSE."

Moreover, HE said to me, "Son of Man, take into your HEART all "MY WORDS" which "I" shall Speak to You, and LISTEN CLOSELY. And Go to the Exiles, to the Sons of YOUR PEOPLE, and speak to THEM, and Tell them, whether they LISTEN OR NOT, "THUS SAYS THE LORD GOD".

Then the SPIRIT Lifted me Up, and I heard a Great Rumbling Sound behind me, "BLESSED BE THE GLORY OF THE LORD IN HIS PLACE." [Ezekiel 3. Verses 1 to 12.].

In the above mentioned verses of the Holy Bible Everyone who has been blessed with the gift of "Spiritual eyes" can clearly envision in His indwelling Spiritual Mind, that Even though the LORD GOD, THE MOST HIGH repeatedly Called the Sons of Israel as the "REBELLIOUS People, Who being STUBBORN and OBSTINATE Children; had willfully REBELLED AGAINST HIM; and thus They and Their FATHERS have Willfully TRANSGRESSED against HIM to that very Day, But being the MOST BENEVOLENT, MERCIFUL and THE TRUE UPHOLDER OF THE UNIVERSAL LAW OF "WILL TO DO GOOD", HE knowing Fully Well, that they WILL NOT BE WILLING TO LISTEN, still sent HIS Chosen Prophet, the Priest EZEKIEL among them, whom HE repeatedly addressed as the "Son of Man", to wake them UP from their UNLAWFUL TRANSGRESSIONS and CORRUPT BEHAVIOR, which is Mostly related to the ILLUSORY "'Material World GREED" upon this Planet Earth, as this wrongful Corrupt Behavior, which is related to the WORLDLY RICHES, PRIZED POSSESSIONS, MONEY CONTROL, and FLEETING GLAMOUR since the "TIMES OF MOSES" have repeatedly brought upon them their Untimely Doom, Death and Destruction.

A depiction of wrongful practices, which came in effect after the passing away of King Solomon. Shown here is the High Priest of the Ten Tribes, who seperated themselves from Judah, following the orders of their King Jeroboam, who re-established the wrongful practice of worshiping the Golden Calf.

Part 25

Since the Time of Prophet Moses, when the MOST HIGH, the "LORD GOD OF THE FLAMES" first appeared to Moses on Mount SINAI, the Fiery and Flaming Mountain of "LORD GOD, THE MOST HIGH", upon the Holy Place which Co- Exists next to the other Peak of His Holy Mountain named HOREB in Arabia, which also has the Holy Cave of Prophets, and then after the LORD Delivered the Children of Israel from the Bondage's of Egyptian Pharaoh, which took place after the passing of a long period of 430 years since the Time Of their First Settling in Pharaoh's Land which was due to the settlement of their Patriarch JACOB [ISRAEL] along with His Entire Family, regarding which the Holy Bible states:

"Now the time, that the Sons of Israel lived in Egypt, was Four Hundred and Thirty Years. And it came about at the end of Four Hundred Years, to the very day that all the HOSTS of the LORD went out from the Land of Egypt. [Exodus 12. 40, 41.]

But many Humans may not know this Important Fact, that many centuries before the deliverance of Israelite's from Egypt, The LORD – GOD, THE MOST HIGH already informed their Grand Patriarch ABRAM, who was later named by the Grace of the MOST HIGH as ABRAHAM, which took place during the Process of renewing a Holy COVENANT with Him, just like a Holy Covenant Was made by GOD in the Much Earlier Times with His Great Ancestor NOAH and his Children as mentioned in the Genesis Chapter, Which is the "Chapter of Creation" in the Holy Bible, regarding which it states:

"Then GOD spoke to NOAH and to His Sons with Him Saying, "Now Behold, "I" Myself do Establish MY COVENANT with you, and with Your Descendants after you." [Genesis 9. 8, 9.]

The Enlightening Grace of the MOST HIGH informed Patriarch ABRAHAM about his future Descendants, and their living in Slavery as Strangers in a Land not their Own, regarding which the Chapter of Genesis in the Holy Bible, clearly states:

And GOD said to ABRAM, "Know for CERTAIN that your descendants will be STRANGERS in a Land that is Not Theirs, where they will be ENSLAVED and OPPRESSED, FOUR HUNDRED YEARS." But "I" will Also "JUDGE the NATION" Whom They Will Serve; and After-ward they will come out with Many Possessions." [Genesis 15. 13, 14.]

And With MOSES and the Children of ISRAEL, the LORD GOD, THE MOST HIGH again renewed a COVENANT on THE FLAMING MOUNT SINAI, whom He delivered from the Agony of AFFLICTIONS caused due to Slavery in Egypt, regarding which the Holy Bible states:

And the LORD Said, "I" have surely seen the Affliction of My People Who are in Egypt, and have given heed to their CRY because of their Taskmasters, for "I" am AWARE of their SUFFERINGS. So "I" have COME DOWN to DELIVER them from the POWER of Egyptians, and to BRING THEM UP from that land to a GOOD and SPACIOUS Land, to a LAND FLOWING WITH MILK AND HONEY, to the Place of the Canaanite, and the Hittite, and the Amorite, and the Perizzite, and the Hivite, and the Jebusite. And now, behold, the CRY of the Sons of Israel has come to ME; furthermore, "I" have seen the OPPRESSION with which the EGYPTIANS are OPPRESSING THEM. Therefore, Come Now, and "I" will send YOU to Pharaoh, So that YOU may BRING MY PEOPLE, The SONS OF ISRAEL, out of Egypt."

But MOSES said to GOD, "who am "I", that "I" should go to Pharaoh, and that "I" should bring the Sons of Israel out of Egypt?" And HE said, "CERTAINLY "I" WILL BE WITH YOU, AND THIS SHALL BE THE SIGN TO YOU, THAT IT IS " I " WHO HAVE SENT YOU; WHEN YOU HAVE BROUGHT THE PEOPLE OUT OF EGYPT, YOU SHALL WORSHIP "'GOD'" AT THIS MOUNTAIN."

Then MOSES said to GOD, "Behold I am going to the Sons of Israel, and I shall say to them, "The GOD of Your Fathers has Sent Me to you.' Now they may say to me, 'What is His Name?' What shall I say to them?".

And GOD said to MOSES, "I AM WHO I AM"; and HE Said, "Thus you shall say to the Sons of Israel, "I AM" has sent me to you." And GOD furthermore said to MOSES, "Thus you shall say to the Sons of Israel. 'The LORD, the GOD of your FATHERS, the GOD of ABRAHAM, the GOD of ISAAC, and the GOD of JACOB, has sent me to you.' THIS IS MY NAME FOREVER, AND THIS IS MY MEMORIAL - NAME TO ALL GENERATIONS.

"GO and Gather the ELDERS of ISRAEL Together, and Say to Them,
The LORD, the GOD of YOUR FATHERS, the GOD of ABRAHAM, ISAAC,
and JACOB, has appeared to Me, Saying, "I AM INDEED CONCERNED
ABOUT YOU AND WHAT HAS BEEN DONE TO YOU IN EGYPT." So I said,
"I" WILL BRING YOU UP OUT OF THE AFFLICTION OF EGYPT, to the
Land of Canaanite, and the Hittite, and the Amorite, and the Perizzite,
and the Hivite, and the Jebusite, to a LAND FLOWING WITH MILK AND
HONEY."[Exodus 3. Verses 7 to 17]

Please Note that only if someone is looking at these Holy verses with
their INNER MIND OR their SPIRITUAL EYES FULLY OPEN. Then only
they will Truly Understand the Spiritual Importance of these Holy
Verses, containing the Higher Spiritual wisdom, as the LORD GOD
REPEATEDLY PROMISED THEM A "'LAND FLOWING WITH MILK AND
HONEY'", WHICH ARE CONSIDERED AS THE VEGETARIAN FOODS OR THE
JOYFUL FOODS WITHOUT EVER INVOLVING THE KILLING OF INNOCENT
ANIMALS, WHICH THROUGH THEIR REPEATED USE OF CONSUMPTION
QUICKLY ENHANCE SPIRITUAL NATURE OF A HUMAN BEING, AND THUS
SPIRITUALLY TRIGGERS HIS 'HIGHER SELF' SOUL MIND
CONSCIOUS EXPANSION".

After the Deliverance of the Sons of ISRAEL from their Affliction's,
which they suffered in Egypt, the LORD – GOD renewed HIS COVENANT
with MOSES and ISRAEL upon the HOLY GROUNDS of MOUNT SINAI,
the Flaming Mountain of GOD having HIS Divine Graceful Presence
regarding which the Holy Bible states:

Then GOD Said, "Behold, "I" AM GOING TO MAKE A COVENANT".
Before all your People "I" will Perform Miracles, which have not been
Produced in all the Earth, nor among any of the NATIONS; and all the
People among whom you live will see the WORKING OF THE LORD, for IT
IS FEARFUL THING THAT I AM GOING TO PERFORM WITH YOU.

Be Sure to Observe what I am Commanding you this Day; behold,
I AM GOING TO DRIVE OUT THE AMORITE BEFORE YOU, AND THE
CANAANITE, THE HITTITE, THE PERIZZITE, THE HIVITE, AND THE
JEBUSITE. "WATCH YOURSELF THAT YOU MAKE "' NO COVENANT '"
WITH THE INHABITANTS OF THE LAND INTO WHICH YOU ARE GOING,
LEST IT BECOME A SNARE IN YOUR MIDST. BUT RATHER, YOU ARE TO
TEAR DOWN THEIR ALTARS AND SMASH THEIR SACRED PILLARS AND
CUT DOWN THEIR ASHERIM – FOR YOU SHALL NOT WORSHIP ""ANY

OTHER GOD''', FOR THE LORD, WHOSE NAME IS JEALOUS, IS A JEALOUS
GOD – LEST YOU MAKE A '''COVENANT''' WITH THE INHABITANTS
OF THE LAND, AND THEY PLAY THE HARLOT WITH THEIR GODS, AND
SACRIFICE TO THEIR GODS, AND SOMEONE INVITE YOU TO EAT OF HIS
SACRIFICE; AND YOU TAKE SOME OF HIS DAUGHTERS FOR YOUR SONS,
AND HIS DAUGHTERS PLAY HARLOT WITH THEIR GODS, AND CAUSE
YOUR SONS ALSO TO PLAY HARLOT WITH THEIR GODS. YOU SHALL
MAKE FOR YOURSELF '''''NO MOLTEN GODS'''''. [Exodus 34. Verses
10 to 17.]

Then the LORD Said to MOSES, "WRITE DOWN THESE WORDS, FOR
IN ACCORDANCE WITH THESE WORDS "I" HAVE MADE A COVENANT
WITH YOU AND ISRAEL." So He was there with the LORD Forty
Days and Forty Nights; He did not Eat Bread or Drink Water. And He
wrote on the Tablets, "THE WORDS OF THE COVENANT", the "TEN
COMMANDMENTS". [Exodus 34. 27, 28.]

The Hebrews collecting Manna, for forty years on a vegetarian diet

Sons of Israel gathered in the wilderness before the flaming Mountain of Sinai– Horeb, in the land of Arabah

Joshua gathered all the tribes of Israel and called for the elders, heads, judges, and their officers, and they presented themselves before GOD

Part 26

Although THE "MOST HIGH", WHO IS THE "ONE and ONLY", CREATOR - OBSERVER - LORD GOD OF THE ENTIRE UNIVERSE, after the Great Flood Established HIS COVENANT with NOAH, and His Sons, and with their Descendants to come after them, as clearly stated in "Genesis 9. 8, 9." of Holy Bible, but unfortunately HIS Holy Covenant was NOT KEPT by NOAH'S Descendants, and they became ignorant about the LORD'S COVENANT and thus foolishly started worshiping his mere Invisible "CREATIONS", THE SO CALLED "OTHER GODS", whom they gave "Forms and Shapes" according to their MIND Desire's, regarding which MOSES Servant JOSHUA Clearly recalled, during His reviewing of ISRAEL'S HISTORY, regarding which the Holy Bible states:

Then JOSHUA gathered all the Tribes of ISRAEL to SHECHEM, and called for the Elders of ISRAEL and for their HEADS and their JUDGES and their OFFICERS; and they presented themselves before "'GOD'".

And JOSHUA said to all the People, "thus says the LORD, the GOD of ISRAEL, 'FROM ANCIENT TIMES YOUR FATHERS LIVED BEYOND THE RIVER, NAMELY, TERAH, THE FATHER OF ABRAHAM AND THE FATHER OF NAHOR, AND THEY SERVED ""OTHER GODS""'. THEN "I" TOOK YOUR FATHER ABRAHAM FROM BEYOND THE RIVER, AND LED HIM THROUGH ALL THE LAND OF CANAAN, AND MULTIPLIED HIS DESCENDANTS, AND GAVE HIM ISAAC. AND TO ISAAC I GAVE JACOB AND ESAU, AND TO ESAU "I" GAVE 'MOUNT SEIR' TO POSSESS IT, BUT JACOB AND HIS SONS WENT DOWN TO EGYPT. THEN "I" SENT MOSES AND AARON, AND "I" PLAGUED EGYPT BY WHAT "I" DID IN ITS MIDST; AND AFTERWARDS "I" BROUGHT YOU OUT. AND "I" BROUGHT YOUR FATHERS OUT OF EGYPT, AND YOU CAME TO THE SEA; AND EGYPT PURSUED YOUR FATHERS WITH CHARIOTS AND HORSEMEN TO THE RED SEA. BUT WHEN THEY CRIED OUT TO THE LORD, "HE" PUT DARKNESS BETWEEN YOU AND THE EGYPTIANS, AND BROUGHT THE SEA UPON THEM AND COVERED THEM; AND YOUR OWN EYES SAW "WHAT I DID IN EGYPT". AND YOU LIVED IN THE WILDERNESS FOR A LONG TIME." [Joshua 24. Verses 1 to 7.]

So the above passages of the Holy Bible clearly state that, NOAH'S Descendants forgot their Most Valuable and Holy Covenant, which was Established with them by the "THE MOST HIGH", and thus started worshiping so called Other Gods, who were just HIS "MERE CREATIONS".

The Hebrew word SEIR means "Hairy, Rough or sometimes a Goat", and the Mount SEIR of "ESAU" was mentioned by the Pharaoh Amenhotep III in his Temple Script at Soleb, dedicated to AMUN RE in ancient Nubia, which is now known as Sudan, whose descendant's He called as "Shasu" instead of "ESAU'S", as the location of SEIR is mentioned in the "Land of Shasu". Later Pharaoh Akhenaten rededicated this Temple to 'GOD ATEN', which was changed back again by his Son Pharaoh Tutankhamen.

JOSHUA, the faithful Servant of MOSES, also earlier accompanied MOSES to go up the Mountain of God –"MOUNT SINAI" regarding which the Holy Bible states:

Now the LORD said to MOSES, "Come Up to ME on the Mountain and remain there, and "I" will give you the Stone Tablets with the LAW and COMMANDMENTS, Which "I" have written for their Instructions." So MOSES arose with JOSHUA His Servant, and MOSES went up to the Mountain of God. [Exodus 24. 12, 13.]

After the Passing away of MOSES, LORD Chose JOSHUA to lead the Sons of Israel to the PROMISED LAND, regarding which the Holy Bible states:

Now it came about after the Death of MOSES, the servant of the LORD, that the LORD Spoke to JOSHUA the Son of Nun, MOSES Servant, Saying, "MOSES MY Servant is Dead; Now therefore Arise, Cross this JORDAN, You and All this People, to the Land 'WHICH I AM GIVING TO THEM, TO THE SONS OF ISRAEL', Every Place on Which the Sole of Your Foot Treads, I Have Given it to YOU, Just as "I" Spoke to MOSES. From this Wilderness and this LEBANON, Even as far as the Great River, the river EUPHRATES, All the Land of the Hittites, and as far as the Great Sea toward the Setting of the Sun, will be Your Territory. NO MAN will be able to Stand before you all the DAYS OF YOUR LIFE.

JUST AS I HAVE BEEN WITH MOSES, I WILL BE WITH YOU; I WILL NOT FAIL YOU OR FORSAKE YOU. Be Strong and Courageous, for you shall Give this People Possession of the Land WHICH "I" SWORE TO THEIR FATHERS TO GIVE THEM." [Joshua 1. 1, 2, 3, 4, 5, 6.]

Since the time of MOSES, the Proper Location and the True Whereabouts of MOUNT SINAI, The Flaming Mountain of GOD were clearly known to all the later descendant Children of Israelite's up to the time of the destruction of the 2nd Temple in Jerusalem, whose forefathers earlier accompanied MOSES during Exodus, wandering through it for FORTY YEARS, which was situated in the land of MIDIAN, whose surrounding areas around it was later Called by the Hebrews as the "ARABAH", later to be known as the Land of ARAB or ARABIA, , as the word "ARABAH" in their Hebrew language defines a Barren Wilderness, a Wasteland, or an Arid and Dry Plane. The Modern day Gulf of AKABAH in the Days of MOSES was known as the "EASTERN BRANCH OF THE RED SEA", beyond which lied the area belonging to the descendants of the Son of ABRAHAM named MIDIAN, which was thus known as the "Land of MIDIAN'S".

Regarding ARABAH the Prophet ISAIAH Clearly wrote, about which the Holy Bible States:

The wilderness and the Desert will be Glad, and the ARABAH will Rejoice and Blossom; like the Crocus. Then the Lame will leap like a Deer, and the Tongue of the Dumb will shout for Joy. For the Waters will break forth in the Wilderness and Streams in the ARABAH. [Isaiah 35. 1, 6.]

Moses in front of the grace of "Most HIgh", present in the burning bush

God's pillar of Fire giving light and protecting Moses and Children of Israel from the pursuing armies of Pharaoh

Since the grand Experiment of Consciousness began upon this Planet Earth, by the Desire Mind Vital Ethereal Impulses of the Unknowable LORD- GOD, who is known to his TRUE DEVOTEES as the "MOST HIGH", or the "FORMLESS FLAMING LORD GOD", Commonly Termed as the MOST BENEVOLENT - GREAT GOD or the "MAHA ISHVARA" in the Sanskrit Language of the ANCIENT EAST, WHO TO THE SO CALLED "'OTHER GODS AND GODDESSES'", AS WELL AS TO THE ANCIENT SEERS AND SAGES, HAS ALWAYS APPEARED LIKE A "HUGE COLUMN OF LIGHT" HAVING UNFATHOMABLE VITAL CONSCIOUSNESS, and who is also the Unknowable "GREAT LORD OF THE FLAMES", who Since Ancient Times Mostly prefers to dwell upon the Holy Mountains, but can also act out swiftly in the Plains, as per HIS desired Will, as HE is the "ONE and ONLY" LORD – GOD of ALL CREATION, and all so called "OTHER GODS AND GODDESSES" are his mere CREATED SERVANT HELPERS, with LIMITED vested powers to act just as "CO – CREATORS" as per HIS Desired Wishes.

In the ancient times, the Enemies of the Sons of Israel, foolishly thinking that their LORD GOD was Only the GOD of Mountains, engaged them to fight in the plains, but they were proved WRONG, as the GRACE of the MOST HIGH totally decimated them in the Plains, during their ILL WILLED Confrontation with the Sons of Israel, regarding which the Holy Bible States:

And the King of Israel went out and stuck the Horses and Chariots, and killed the Syrians with a great Slaughter. Then the Prophet came near to the King of Israel, and said to Him, "Go, Strengthen Yourself and Observe and See what You have to do; for at the turn of the Year, the King of Syria will Come Up against you."

Now the Servants of the King of Syria said to Him, "Their GODS are GODS of the Mountains, therefore they were Stronger than We; but rather Let Us Fight against them in the Plain, and surely we shall be Stronger than they. And do this thing; remove the Kings, each from His Place, and put Captains in their Place, and muster an army like the army you have lost, Horse or Horse, and Chariot for Chariot. Then we will Fight against them in the Plain, and Surely We shall be Stronger than they." And He Listened to their Voice and did so.

So it came about at the turn of the Year, that Ben – haddad mustered the Syrians and went up to Aphek to fight against Israel. And the Sons of Israel were mustered and were provisioned and went to meet them; and the Sons of Israel Camped before them like two little flocks of Goats, but the Syrians filled the Country.

Then a MAN OF GOD came near and Spoke to the King of Israel and Said, "Thus says the LORD, 'BECAUSE THE SYRIANS HAVE SAID, '"THE LORD IS A GOD OF MOUNTAINS, BUT HE IS NOT A GOD OF THE VALLEYS"; THEREFORE "I" WILL GIVE ALL THIS GREAT MULTITUDE INTO YOUR HAND, AND YOU SHALL KNOW THAT "I" AM THE LORD'".

So they camped one over against the other seven days. And it came about that on the seventh day, the battle was joined, and the Sons of Israel killed of the Syrians 100,000 foot Soldiers in One Day. But the rest fled to Aphek into the City, and the Wall fell on 27,000 men who were left. And Ben – hadad fled and came into the City into an inner Chamber. [1 Kings 20. Verses 21 to 30.]

During the Exodus Times of Moses, to protect Him and the Sons of Israel from the Pursuing Pharaoh and His armies, the LORD –GOD showed them all, HIS Unimaginable Divine Form, as a "PILLAR OF CLOUD with LIGHT" regarding which the Holy Bible states:

Then they set out from SUCCOTH and camped in ETHAM on the Edge of the Wilderness. And the LORD was going before them in a "PILLAR OF CLOUD" by Day to Lead them on the Way, and in a "PILLAR OF FIRE" by Night to give them LIGHT, that they might Travel by Day and by Night. HE did not take away the "PILLAR OF CLOUD" by Day, nor the "PILLAR OF FIRE" by Night, from before the People. [Exodus 13. 20, 21, 22.]

And as Pharaoh drew near, the Sons of Israel looked, and behold, the Egyptians were marching after them, and they became very frightened; so the Sons of Israel cried out to the LORD. Then they said to MOSES, "Is it because there were no graves in Egypt that you have taken us away to Die in the Wilderness? Why have You Dealt with Us in this Way, bringing Us out of Egypt? Is this not the Word that We spoke to You in Egypt, Saying, 'Leave Us Alone that We may Serve the Egyptians"? For it would have been better for Us to Serve the Egyptians than to Die in the Wilderness."

But MOSES Said to the People, "Do not Fear! Stand by and See the Salvation of the LORD, Which HE will accomplish for You Today; for the Egyptians whom you have seen today, You will Never See Them Again Forever, "The LORD will fight for You While You keep Silent." [Exodus 14. 10, 11, 12, 13, 14.]

And the Angel of GOD, Who had been going before the Camp of Israel, moved and went behind them; and the "PILLAR OF CLOUD" moved from before them and stood behind them. So it came between the Camp of Egypt and the Camp of Israel; and there was the Cloud along with the Darkness, yet it gave LIGHT at Night. Thus the One did not come near the Other All Night. [Exodus 14. 19, 20.]

And when Israel saw the Great Power which the LORD had used against the Egyptians, the People Feared the LORD, and they Believed in the LORD and in His Servant MOSES [Exodus 14. 31]

The Unknowable MOST HIGH to HIS Subjective and Objective Creations, who exist in various Manifested Dimensional Levels or the " VITAL ENERGY FREQUENCY VIBRATIONS of HIS DESIRE MIND Manifestation's, which are known to Highly Enlightened "Seers and Sages" as the Egg Shaped Spherical "HUGE THOUGHT FORMS", which also appear as Various Material Grade "SUBJECTIVE and OBJECTIVE Manifested Levels of Conscious Existence, as normally understood by "HIS CREATED, EVENTUATED, INVOLVED OR EVOLVED" Differentiated Conscious Level Existences, who CONSCIOUSLY or UNCONSCIOUSLY exist in their own Visible and Invisible DIFFERENTIATED Hierarchical Orders, and are commonly known as the various differentiated groups of "Entities and Beings" existing upon this Planet Earth, who by Misusing their Vested Powers acting out as the "co – Creators", thus WILLFULLY BETRAYED HIS INFINITE "LOVE and TRUST", which made this Beautiful Planet a "STORE HOUSE OF UNDUE CORRUPTION", which is especially prevalent in ALL the Leadership ranks of the differentiated Human Societies, which are Cyclically Evolving for their Consciousness Expansion upon this Planet Earth objectively existing in the "parametric ethereal space" known in Sanskrit Language as the "Akasha" of our "Solar Universe".

Establishment of Tabernacle in the wilderness

Children of Israel collecting their daily supply of Mana food in the wilderness

Part 28

Long before the arrival of MOSES, the MIDIANS, who lived in their caves around the Farthest End, from the base of the Holy Mountain of GOD, whose two adjacent peaks were known to them as Mount Horeb, and the Flaming Mount Sinai, for them it was a "Holy Place of Reverence" in the Land of ARABAH or in the immense Wilderness, and "REUEL", the father in law of MOSES, also known as the JETHRO, meaning a "Cave Dweller" was a Wise "Priest of Midian", who was also a Believer, and thus also revered the "MOST HIGH" – LORD GOD Humbly by following the footsteps of their great ancestor "ABRAHAM" whose children they were also, but through a different lineage than ISAAC, regarding which the Holy Bible states:

And MOSES told His Father in Law, all that the LORD had done to Pharaoh, and to the Egyptians for Israel's Sake, all the Hardship that had befallen them on the Journey, and how the LORD had delivered them. And Jethro REJOICED over all the GOODNESS which the LORD had done to Israel, in delivering them from the hand of Egyptians.

So Jethro Said, "BLESSED be the LORD, Who delivered you from the hand of the Egyptians, and from the hand of the Pharaoh, and WHO delivered the People from Under the Hand of the Egyptians. "Now I know that the LORD IS GREATER THAN ALL GODS; Indeed, It was PROVEN when they dealt proudly against the People."

Then Jethro, MOSES Father - in - Law, took a Burnt Offering and Sacrifices for GOD, and AARON came with All the "Elders of Israel" to Eat a Meal with MOSES Father – in – Law before GOD.

And it came about the Next Day that MOSES sat to Judge the People, and the People stood about MOSES from the Morning until the Evening. Now when Moses Father - in - Law Saw all that He was doing for the People, He said, "What is this Thing that you are doing for the People? Why do you Alone Sit as JUDGE, and all the People stand about you from Morning until Evening? And Moses said to his Father – in – Law, " Because the People come to Me to Inquire of GOD. When they have a Dispute, it comes to Me, and I Judge between a Man and His Neighbor, and Make known the Statutes of GOD and His LAWS."

And Moses Father – in – Law said to Him, "The Thing that You are Doing is "NOT GOOD". You will surely WEAR OUT, Both Yourself and these People Who are With You, for the Task is TOO HEAVY for You; You cannot do it Alone. Now Listen to Me; I shall Give You Counsel, and GOD BE WITH YOU. You be the People's Representative before GOD, and You Bring the Disputes to GOD, then teach them the Statutes and the Laws, and make known to them the Way in which they are to Walk, and the Work they are to Do. Furthermore, You shall Select out of all the People, Abel Men WHO FEAR GOD, MEN OF TRUTH, THOSE WHO HATE "'DISHONEST GAIN'"; and You Shall Place These over Them, as Leaders of Thousands, of Hundreds, of Fifties, and of Tens. And let them JUDGE the People at all Times; and let it be that every Major Dispute they will bring to You, but every Minor Dispute they themselves will JUDGE. So it will be easier for You, and they will bear the BURDEN with You.

If You Do this Thing, and GOD SO COMMANDS YOU, then You will be able to Endure, and all these People also will Go to their PLACE IN PEACE."

So Moses Listened to His Father – in – Law, and did All that He had Said. And Moses Chose Abel Men out of all Israel, and made them Heads over the People, Leaders of Thousands, of Hundreds, of Fifties, and of Tens. And they Judged the People at all Times; the Difficult Dispute they would bring to MOSES, But every Minor Dispute they themselves would Judge. [Exodus 18. Verses 8 to 26.]

The above verses of Holy Bible clearly explain that the LORD – GOD used his Humble Servant "REUEL" also known as "JETHRO", the MIDIAN PRIEST, who Himself did not belonged to the Direct Lineage of ISAAC, to Counsel His Son – in – Law MOSES. And upon His Such Wise counsel were then established for the first time in the History of Israelite's, the "FIRST JUDGES" for the Children of Israel, by the Servant of GOD MOSES, so they Properly Solve their Minor Disputes.

The Tent of Meeting in the wilderness

Elders discussing in the Tent of Meeting

Moses with Children of Israel in front of the Mountain of GOD

According to Holy Bible, after Delivering the Sons of Israel through the Services of His Chosen Servant MOSES from the Afflicting Hands of Egyptians, the LORD – God brought them out to his Holy Flaming Mountain, just like HE previously told Moses about it before HE sent Him to Egypt to Confront Pharaoh as mentioned in "Exodus 3. 12", so they can Properly Worship Him, just like their Elders used to Worship Him in the Ancient days, especially since from the Time of NOAH, all their Ancestor's reverently Worshiped HIM. But later on with the passing of time, they mostly forgot their Holy Covenant made Earlier with the "MOST HIGH", and thus went astray and started worshiping so called OTHER GODS and GODDESSES, in the Forms of Various Animals, who unfortunately possess Even Less Intellect and Wisdom than an Incarnated Human Being of this Planet Earth, like a So Called God in the Molten form of a "Calf" known as "BAAL", which was the favorite out of all those Egyptian God's for the Children of Israel, who Since the ancient times of JACOB [Israel], dwelt in the land of Egyptian Pharaoh's, as it was a child of "A Male Bull GOD" and a "Female Cow GODDESS", and thus a "CALF" became an Venerated object of Worship, as in their opinion it represented their "Combined Holy Consciousness", and per the Established Egyptian Religious Belief, the Form of a Male Apis Bull in the Land of Pharaohs represented the Consciousness of their Father God "PTAH", and the Female Cow represented the Consciousness of their Mother Goddess "HATHOR", and Some of the Children of Israel, who started following the Egyptian ways of Worship, thus went astray from the Worship of their Unknowable True LORD – GOD, who Himself created in the very beginning all the Mankind as Clearly mentioned in the Very First Chapter of Genesis in the Holy Bible, and HE Himself is also the Creator of all the Other So called GODS and GODDESSES [Elohim's], whom HE Created to Serve HIM, as per His established Evolutionary Plan of Conscious Expansion upon this Planet Earth, which was supposed to Continue through Reoccurring Cycles, which were known to the Ancient Seers, Prophets, and Sages as the "Wheels of Time" always Spinning, Spiraling and Churning, thus Going in a forward or in a "Counter- Clock" wise motion, moving through the "Vital Ethereal Space" of the Infinite Universe.

Regarding the Children of Israel Coming to the Holy Mountain of God after their deliverance from Egyptian Bondage's, the Holy Bible States:

In the third month after the Sons of Egypt had gone out of the land of Egypt, on that very day they came into wilderness of Sinai. When they set out from Rephidim, they came to the Wilderness of Sinai, and camped in the Wilderness; and there Israel Camped in Front of the Mountain.

And MOSES went up to GOD, and the LORD called to Him from the Mountain, Saying, 'Thus You shall say to the House of JACOB, and tell the Sons of Israel:

"You yourselves have Seen what "I" did to the Egyptians, and How "I" Bore You on EAGLES WINGS, and brought you to MYSELF. Now then, if YOU will KEEP MY COVENANT, then you shall be MY OWN POSSESSION AMONG ALL THE PEOPLES, FOR """ALL THE EARTH IS MINE"""; and YOU shall be to ME a KINGDOM OF PRIESTS and a HOLY NATION." These are the Words that YOU shall SPEAK to the Sons of Israel.'

So MOSES came and called the Elders of the People, and Set before them all these Words, which the LORD had commanded Him. And all the People answered Together and Said, "ALL THAT THE LORD HAS SPOKEN, '"WE WILL DO!'" And MOSES brought back the Words of the People to the LORD. [Exodus 19. Verses 1 to 8.]

These important Verses of the Holy Bible contain Codified wisdom of the LORD, as HE told MOSES on the Holy Mountain that "HE Bore THEM on EAGLES WINGS, and THUS brought THEM to HIMSELF". Much later When Most of Descendants of Israel and their Ruler Kings became Evil and Willfully Broke the Holy Covenant with their LORD – GOD, and thus became Totally Corrupt by Worshiping the so called "OTHER GODS" by making their Molten Animal Figures, and were thus Punished by the Wrath of GOD for their Such Evil Deeds, then During those Dreadful Times of their slavery, when they were exiled in Land of CHALDEAN'S, to again Remind the Children of Israel, HE Mercifully gave HIS Chosen Prophet EZEKIEL a Divine Vision, in which HE Showed Him these "DIVINE EAGLE WINGS", about which HE Long Before told MOSES upon the Flaming Holy Mountain, Which in a Codified Way represent the Cosmic Energy Radiations of the Scorpio Constellation needed for Human Consciousness Expansion, whose Ancient Symbol was an Eagle Bird or an "REINCARNATING PHOENIX BIRD" through REJUVENATION PROCESS, a CODIFIED MYTHICAL SYMBOL which technically represents the cyclic reincarnation of Human beings in the dense material world of this Planet Earth to attain material world experiences through emotions and feelings during their short lived time duration's, which are perceived by them as Tonal Color and Sound frequencies, regarding which the Holy Bible states:

And as I looked, behold, a Storm Wind was coming from the North, a Great Cloud with FIRE flashing forth continually, and a Bright Light around it, and in its midst Something like Glowing Metal in the Midst of the FIRE. And within it there were figures resembling Four Living Beings. And this was their appearance: they had Human Form. Each of them had Four Faces and Four Wings.

Under their Wings on their four sides were Human Hands. As for the faces and wings of the four of them, their Wings touched one another; their faces did not turn when they moved, each went straight forward.

And under the expanse, their Wings were stretched out Straight, one toward the other; each one also had two Wings covering their bodies on the one side and on the other.

I also heard the sound of their Wings like the Sound of Abundant Waters as they went, Like the VOICE OF THE ALMIGHTY, a Sound of Tumult, like the Sound of an Army Camp; whenever they Stood Still, they dropped their Wings. And there came a Voice from above the expanse that was over their Heads; whenever they stood still, they dropped their Wings.

As the appearance of the Rainbow in the Clouds on a Rainy Day, so was the appearance of the surrounding Radiance. Such was the appearance of the Likeness of the Glory of the LORD. And when I saw it, I fell on My Face and heard a Voice Speaking. [Ezekiel 1. 4, 5, 6, 8, 9, 23, 24, 25, 28.]

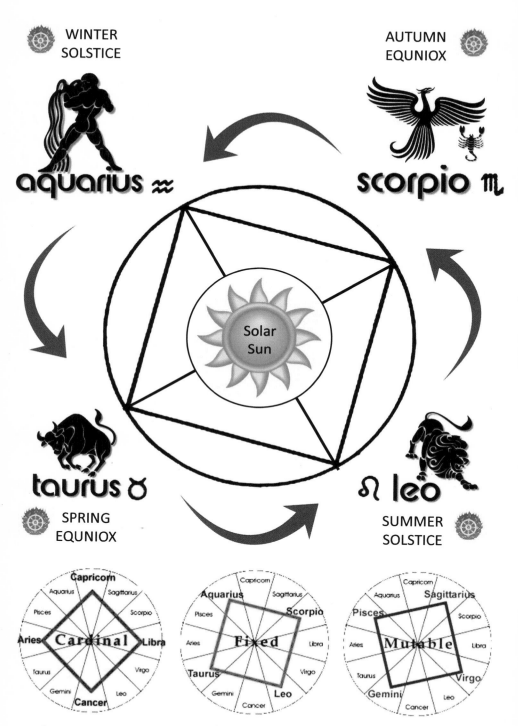

The Four Faces seen by Ezekiel in the visions of GOD, represent the Four constellation symbols of the FIXED CROSS of Heaven, and Four Flaming Wheels depicting the "Four Wheels of Time" related to 2 Solstices and 2 Equinoxes.

Part 30

Out of the many Available Religious Text Books, which have been given to the MANKIND over many MILLENNIAL, by the Holy Grace of the Unknowable CREATOR LORD, Who is reverently known to His Devoted Servants as the Unknowable "MOST HIGH", the Holy Bible in its current form containing Various Chapters of Enlightening Wisdom, which are Collectively known as the OLD TESTAMENT and the NEW TESTAMENT, is the FOREMOST in their Such Codified Group of Spiritual Literature, thus being a Unfathomable STOREHOUSE OF "CODIFIED WISDOM", which is related to the many "SPIRITUAL ESSENCES" of the SUBJECTIVELY and OBJECTIVELY manifested INFINITE UNIVERSE, which Exists in the Huge Parameters of the Vast VITAL ETHEREAL SPACE unimaginable for the Material Mind Human Beings to intellectually Fathom, as this Holy Bible was Compiled over Many Generation's, through HIS Graceful Divine Revelations, which were Properly Received by a Chosen Few as the "Spiritual Thought form Impulses", which penetrated deep in their evolving Aura Consciousness as the "DIVINE VISIONS, and were thus periodically given to the Receiving Minds of His Various Chosen Prophets and His humble Servants, which were also related to the Happenings of their Own Evolutionary Times.

In the Foreign Land of Chaldean's, during the Turbulent Times of Captivity for the Children of Israel, the Divine Visions of Prophet Ezekiel, Which Still being Highly CODIFIED, were Willfully Given to Him, by the Grace of the MOST HIGH in Great Details, which in fact was much earlier also Objectively Shown Continuously for Many Days to all the Thousands of Children of Israel, who moved along with HIS Humble Servant MOSES, after they were Delivered from the hands of the Mighty Pharaoh of Egypt, although their Grand Vision was Without all the Specific Details, which were later Envisioned by Prophet Ezekiel, when He was fully awake by the River CHEBAR, When the Heavens were Opened up to reveal Him the Codified Visions of GOD.

Let us again Closely Look and reexamine seeing with our "Inner Eyes" and not Just Mere Physical Eyes drenched in Material Glamour of the Material World, but filled with "HOLY SPIRIT" at these following verses of Holy Bible to receive the Ineffable Grace of MOST HIGH, with our "Spiritual Minds thus Fully Open", which state:

And the LORD was Going before them in a Pillar of "CLOUD" by Day to Lead them on the Way, and in a Pillar of "FIRE" by Night to Give them LIGHT, that they might travel by day and by night. HE did not take away the Pillar of CLOUD by Day, nor the Pillar of FIRE by Night, from before the People. [Exodus 13. 21, 22.]

Now reexamine the "Visions of GOD" given to Prophet Ezekiel regarding which the Holy Bible states:

And as I Looked, behold, a Storm Wind was coming from the North, a Great "CLOUD" with "FIRE" flashing forth continually and a Bright "LIGHT" around it, and in its midst Something like Glowing Metal in the Midst of the FIRE. [Ezekiel 1. 4.]

If our Spiritual Minds are open, then with the grace of MOST HIGH, we will surely perceive the Similarities of the Divine Vision seen by Prophet Ezekiel, which in Moses Time of Exodus was witnessed by the thousands of Children of Israel, except Prophet - Priest Ezekiel through his Spiritual Eyes and Humble Mind was able to further Penetrate and thus clearly See inside the midst of the "FIERY CLOUD", which represented the Divine Codified Graceful Wisdom of the MOST HIGH.

With our Spiritual Eyes still open Let us further examine Prophet Ezekiel's Visions of GOD, regarding which the Holy Bible States:

'And within it there were figures resembling four Live Beings. And this was their appearance: They Had Human Form. Each of them had four Faces and Four Wings.

As for the Form of their Faces, Each had the Face of a MAN, all Four had the face of a LION on the Right, and the Face of a BULL on the Left, and All Four had the Face of an EAGLE. Such were their Faces. Their Wings were SPREAD out ABOVE; EACH had Two Touching another Being, and Two covering their Bodies. And EACH went Straight Forward; Wherever the SPIRIT was about to Go, without turning they went. In the Midst of the Living Beings there was SOMETHING that Looked LIKE BURNING COALS OF FIRE, like TORCHES darting Back and Forth among the Living Beings. The FIRE was BRIGHT, and LIGHTNING was FLASHING from the FIRE. And the Living Beings ran to and fro like BOLTS OF LIGHTNING.

Now as I looked at the Living Beings, behold, there was ONE WHEEL on the Earth besides the Living Beings, for EACH OF THE FOUR OF THEM. The appearance of the WHEELS and their Workmanship was like Sparkling Beryl, and ALL FOUR OF THEM HAD THE SAME FORM, their Appearance and Workmanship being as if ONE WHEEL WERE WITHIN ANOTHER. Whenever they MOVED, they moved in ANY OF THEIR FOUR DIRECTIONS, without turning as they moved.

Wherever the SPIRIT was about to Go, they would go in that Direction. And the WHEELS rose Close beside them; for the SPIRIT OF THE LIVING BEINGS was in the WHEELS. Whenever those went, these went; and whenever those stood still, these stood still. And whenever those rose from the Earth, the WHEELS rose Close beside them; for the SPIRIT OF THE LIVING BEINGS was in the WHEELS'. [Ezekiel 1. 4, 5, 6, 10, 11, 12, 13, 14, 15, 16, 17, 20, 21.]

The four Faces which the Prophet Ezekiel saw of the Human Beings in his Divine Vision, represented the four important Constellations of the Zodiac, which create the MESSIAH CROSS in the Celestial Heavens, which has been represented since ancient times with such four Symbolic Shapes in the Zodiac. These Four Constellations through their Vital Cosmic Energy Radiations, play a major role in the Evolution and Sustenance of all living beings, who are evolving upon this planet earth.

The Zodiacal Constellation of the Aquarius is represented by the shape of a MAN, the Zodiacal Constellation of Taurus is represented by the shape of a BULL, the Zodiacal Constellation of Leo is represented by the shape of a LION, and the Zodiacal Constellation of Scorpio is represented by the shape of an EAGLE, which was its original Zodiacal form, and to CONFUSE THE EVOLVING HUMANITY, it got illegally changed to the current Form of a Scorpion by the Dark Conspiring Entities, who are none other than the SO CALLED INVISIBLE GODS and GODDESSES, and they easily accomplished it with the help of their High Positioned Corrupt Human Followers, who since a long time have been illegally ruling this Planet Earth, by establishing themselves upon the Top Posts of their Human Societies, to promote their Invisible CORRUPT MASTERS illegal and deceitful agendas, against the desired wishes of their One and Only True CREATOR LORD, THE MOST HIGH, who Originally Established the Evolutionary Plans for all evolving beings of this beautiful planet based upon universal law of "Will to do Good", which thus due to illegal and corrupt activities of these No Good deformed and mutated minds Entities and Beings has made this planet as an Undesirable PLACE OF UNDUE PAIN AND SUFFERINGS, for the Majority of Evolving Masses, in the Entire Manifested Universe.

Since the Very ancient times of establishing the Human races upon this Planet Earth, the four important time Periods of this planet Earth, have been known to the SEERS and SAGES as the "FOUR Cyclic WHEELS of TIME", which have always occurred at the same time periods without any major changes, during which the Solar Sun Appears to be passing through these 4 Zodiacal Constellations of the Celestial Heavens.

These four WHEELS of Time, are also interrelated just as the Prophet Ezekiel saw in His Divine Vision which as per the Holy Bible clearly states "As if ONE WHEEL WERE WITHIN ANOTHER. Whenever they MOVED, they moved in ANY OF THEIR FOUR DIRECTIONS, without turning as they moved", and these Continuously moving WHEELS of Time are known to the Learned Human beings as the [1] Autumn Equinox, [2] Winter Solstice, [3] Spring or Vernal Equinox, and [4] Summer Solstice. And the SPIRIT of the evolving Human Beings of this Planet Earth, who live their entire incarnated lives related to the TIME FACTOR, move with these four Wheels of Time, as these are the Major Periods of Human activity which is related to Sowing and Reaping of Harvests, as well as a The Important Time Period of Rest and Celebrations, which are important for their Incarnated Lives Sustenance and Survival.

In the ancient times, the Autumn Equinox occurred around 21st of September, during the time period of Solar Sun being in the Scorpio Constellation, and thus the celebration period for the Rejuvenation of the Mythical Egyptian Phoenix Bird, or the Hindu Garuda, which was later depicted by an Eagle Bird, which has been also venerated since Long by the ancient Indian tribes of the North and South Americas.

The New Year Celebrations for the Children of Israel known as "ROSH HASHANAH" also took place around this time, a time period of two days Celebration ending with the Holy day of atonement known as the YOM KIPPUR, which is observed 10 days later. The Vedic Hindu believers of "One Creator – Lord God", whom they referred to as their Unknowable Great Lord "Ishvara", also celebrated their 10 days period of Vijaya Dashmi, a Celebration of "Good Over Evil", during this Particular WHEEL of Time, later to be followed by their New Year known as Diwali.

The Time Period of Solar Sun's Rejuvenation or Rebirth in the Celestial skies also occurred during the Time WHEEL of "Winter Solstice", which occurred around 21st of December during the time period of Solar Sun being in the Aquarius Constellation, which is Zodiacally depicted by the shape of a MAN and thus the celebration period for the of SUN God's Birth or GOD'S SON Rejuvenation took place during this particular time, after it appeared to stand still "Dead" or "MOTIONLESS" in the Celestial skies for a three day period, and then again started its movement on 25th of December, Later to PASSOVER in a Easterly Motion to Cross the Northern Hemisphere Boundaries during the time WHEEL period of "Spring or Vernal Equinox", which always occurred around 21st of March during the time period of Solar Sun being in the Taurus Constellation, which is Zodiacally depicted by the shape of a BULL, during which also major religious festivities of the World religions related to the Coming Back of Spring Season took place, which included the Celebration of Passover, Easter as well as the Hindu, Sikh and Buddhist festivities of Spring Season.

The fourth WHEEL time period known as the "Summer Solstice" is related to the face of a LION, which was envisioned by Prophet Ezekiel, which occurs around 21st of June during the time period of Solar Sun, being in the Leo Constellation of the Celestial Skies, and thus the Right face of these Living beings was depicted by the grace of the MOST HIGH in the shape of a LION, as the Living Beings envisioned by Prophet Ezekiel ran to and fro like bolts of lightning, having their Solar Consciousness moving from the Left sided Bull face to the Right sided Lion face. The Sons of Israel since ancient times Celebrated their annual Holy "Festival of Weeks" around this time, which is also known in Hebrew Language as the Holy Festival of "SHAVU'OT".

Land of Chaldean's

149

The Egyptian "Gods & Goddesses" diminished to relics in museums

Part 31

Many of the so called Religious People of the Modern world of this Planet Earth, whose Desire Minds are mostly occupied with the "Material World Glamour" during their incarnated daily lives, and remember LORD - GOD, THE MOST HIGH, "Only" During the Time of their Various Afflictions, as well as Most of them only thank him during Few Times in a Year, mostly during their Religious Observance's and Holy Days, especially on "Thanksgiving Day" thus totally Fail to Understand the Underlying Fact that the "Bonding Love Relationship" between the "CREATOR and his CREATION" known in Spiritual terms as "THE HOLY COVENANT" due to Such Weak Bonding Relationships thus cannot Survive for a Long Period of TIME.

Since the time of Patriarch JACOB, whom the LORD – GOD named "ISRAEL", most of His Descendant Children who were Born and Raised in the Land of Pharaoh's, by the passing of time went astray from the proper understanding of their Unknowable LORD GOD, the MOST HIGH, because of the utter confusion which overpowered their human minds due to this main underlying fact, that The Mighty Egyptian Pharaoh's, who in fact were also Just Mere Mortal Human Beings like Anyone Else, as all Human life Problems of the Material World and Related Diseases also afflicted them, but they themselves, apart from their Many Varieties of So Called "Gods and Goddesses" were wrongly considered as "Living GODS" and thus wrongly venerated as such in their Mortal Human Forms, like Currently in Many Western Countries, even now Just Mere Mortal Human beings, who "For Sure" Die like any other Human Being of this Physical Plain World, are not any more afraid of the UNKNOWABLE TRUE LORD, to Openly Call themselves as a "LORD", because they are an esteemed member of the so called Political "HOUSE OF LORDS" created in their Human Societies, even though they are Just Mere Men just like Any Other.

When MOSES went back to Egypt and delivered Sons of Israel, the Message of the MOST HIGH, who is None other than the CREATOR LORD GOD of their Ancestor's and Forefathers, they were Reluctant to receive it and thus were mostly unresponsive due to their Own Personal Reasons, regarding which the Holy Bible states:

"So MOSES Spoke thus to the Sons of Israel, but they did Not Listen to MOSES on Account of their Despondency and Cruel Bondage." [Exodus 6. 9.]

But Later on, when MOSES left Egypt delivering Sons of Israel, from the Hands of the Mighty Pharaoh and their SO CALLED GODS, then at that time, a Great number of the Israelite's were following him, of which, many were still Confused and thus Unsure about their Future, regarding which the Holy Bible states:

Now the Sons of Israel journeyed from Ramses to Succoth, about Six Hundred Thousand Men on Foot, aside from Children. And a Mixed Multitude also went up with them, along with Flocks and Herds, a Very Large number of Livestock. [Exodus 12. 37, 38.]

Even though so many People Left Egypt following MOSES, many were still unsure and afraid of the Happenings which were taking place in their lives, and the MOST HIGH, who is the Creator of Entire Mankind, was fully aware of their unstable desire mind's ensuing "Thought Forms", regarding which the Holy Bible states:

Now it came about when Pharaoh had let the People Go, that GOD did not lead them by the way of the land of Philistines, EVEN THOUGH IT WAS NEAR; for GOD Said, "LEST THE PEOPLE CHANGE THEIR MIND WHEN THEY SEE WAR, AND THEY RETURN TO EGYPT."

Hence GOD led the People around by the way of the Wilderness to the Red Sea; and the Sons of Israel went up in a Martial Array from the Land of Egypt. [Exodus 13. 17, 18.]

Then the MOST HIGH, the LORD GOD OF FLAMES, to teach a Proper and Befitting lesson to the Mighty Pharaoh, and their so called OTHER GODS and GODDESSES hardened His Heart, as these so called OTHER GODS and GODDESSES are in fact just mere "HIS Created Servant Helpers", Originally Brought into Manifestation through the SPIRAL, CYCLIC, CIRCULAR Motions of Vital Energy Impulse Actions, which pertained to HIS Desire Mind's Vital Ethereal Energy Reflections, so that they thus Created, can Humbly Assist HIM in HIS Evolutionary plans upon this Planet Earth, which are Established based upon universal law of "Will to do Good" and are meant for everyone's Conscious expansion, and thus serve HIM by Looking after the Evolving Human Races as Independent

Co – Creators, by simultaneously existing parallel to the incarnated Human Beings, staying in their own Hierarchical Order Groups, and being invisible to the Human Beings, later on they were also started to be known as the so called Gods and Gods, but who liking their such "false status of deceitful reverence", which was WRONGFULLY given to them by the ignorant SUBJECTS of evolving Human Societies, then by Misusing their Allotted Powers themselves became TOTALLY CORRUPT, as well as Cruel and Ruthless, and thus WILLFULLY DEFILED, the Universal law of "Will to do Good".

And thus MOST HIGH to let MOSES know that HE is the ONLY TRUE LORD of the Entire Manifested Universe, HE gave Him Superior Powers which were above and beyond the Capacity of the Entire Pantheon of the GODS and GODDESSES of the Mighty and Powerful Egypt, whose so called GODS and GODDESSES since Last few Millennium's are now Long Forgotten on this Planet Earth, and whose Mighty and Powerful Man made Statues are now only Displayed in Museums, as "'Powerless Dead Objects'" all over the Human WORLD.

To Prove HIS Point, the "MOST HIGH", the LORD GOD of ABRAHAM, ISAAC, and JACOB, Earlier "Bestowed" upon MOSES with his Divine Grace those Vested Powers, which were FAR SUPERIOR than that of "ALL THE COMBINED POWERS OF GODS AND GODDESSES OF THE MIGHTY EGYPT", regarding which the Holy Bible states:

Then MOSES answered and Said, "What If They will not Believe, or Listen to What I Say? For they may Say, 'The LORD has not appeared to you'. And the LORD Said to Him, " What is in Your Hand?" And He Said, "A Staff". Then HE Said, "Throw it on the Ground." So He threw it on the Ground, and it became a Serpent; and MOSES fled from it. But the LORD said to MOSES, "Stretch Out Your Hand and Grasp it by its Tail" – So He Stretched out His Hand and Caught it, and it became a Staff in His Hand – that They may Believe that the LORD, the GOD of their FATHER'S, the GOD of ABRAHAM, the GOD of ISAAC, and the GOD of JACOB, has Appeared to You."

And the LORD furthermore Said to Him, "Now Put Your Hand into Your Bosom." So He Put His Hand into His Bosom, and When He took it out, Behold, His Hand was LEPROUS like SNOW. Then HE said, "Put Your Hand into Bosom again; and when He took it out of His Bosom, Behold, it was restored like the Rest of His Flesh.

And it shall come about that if they will not Believe You or Heed the Witness of the First Sign, They May Believe the Witness of the Last Sign. "But it shall be that If They will NOT BELIEVE EVEN THESE TWO SIGNS OR HEED WHAT YOU SAY, THEN YOU SHALL TAKE SOME WATER FROM THE NILE AND POUR IT ON DRY GROUND; AND THE WATER WHICH YOU TAKE FROM THE NILE WILL BECOME BLOOD ON THE DRY GROUND."

And the LORD Said to MOSES, "When You Go Back to Egypt, See that You Perform before Pharaoh all the WONDERS Which I have put in Your Power; But "I" will Harden His Heart, So that He will not let the People Go. "Then you shall Say to Pharaoh, 'Thus Says the LORD, "ISRAEL is MY SON, MY FIRST BORN". 'So I Said to you, "LET MY SON GO, THAT HE MAY SERVE ME"; But you have refused to let Him Go. Behold, "I" WILL KILL YOUR SON, YOUR FIRST BORN'. [Exodus 4. Verses 1 to 9, 21, 22, 23.]

Not only had the Lord vested in MOSES, HIS Divine Powers, which were Much Superior than the total Combined Powers of all the So Called "GODS and GODDESSES" of the Mighty Egypt, but HE also raised the Status of MOSES to become as a "GOD" Himself in front of the Mighty and Powerful Pharaoh, who Himself was considered as a Living God by His Subjective People, all over the Land of Egypt, regarding which the Holy Bible states:

Then the LORD said to MOSES, 'SEE "I" MAKE YOU AS "'GOD'" TO PHARAOH, AND YOUR BROTHER AARON SHALL BE YOUR PROPHET'. You shall Speak All that "I" Command You, and Your brother AARON shall Speak to Pharaoh, that He Let the Sons of Israel Go out of His Land. [Exodus 7. 1.]

Regarding the Planned action of the MOST HIGH against "'ALL THOSE'", the So called MIGHTY AND POWERFUL, Who during the Ancient Times of "EXODUS" Due to their Material Mind "FALSE PRIDE" were not ready to WILLFULLY Follow His COMMAND, and Who even now in these Modern Times of this Planet Earth are "NOT YET READY TO RETURN AND SURRENDER, AS PER HIS DESIRED WISHES", HE HARDENS THE HEARTS OF ALL THOSE VISIBLE AND INVISIBLE "ENTITIES AND BEINGS" WHO WILLFULLY CHOOSE TO GO AGAINST HIM, AND THUS "HE"PROPERLY PUNISHES THEM ACCORDINGLY. During the Times of MOSES, the LORD also HARDENED the Heart of RULING PHARAOH, and Executed HIS JUDGMENTS against """"ALL THE GODS OF EGYPT"""", as mentioned in the Holy Bible which states:

"And Against ALL THE GODS OF EGYPT, "I" WILL EXECUTE JUDGMENTS – I AM THE LORD." [Exodus 12. 12]

Regarding the LORD'S Justice Procedure known as the HARDENING OF THE HEART, which is meant for "All Those" WHO WILLFULLY IGNORE THE CREATOR LORD'S "'DESIRED WISHES AND COMMANDS'", the Holy Bible states:

'But "I" will HARDEN Pharaoh's Heart that "I" may Multiply MY SIGNS and MY WONDERS in the Land of Egypt. When Pharaoh will not Listen to You, then "I" will Lay MY Hand on Egypt, and Bring out MY HOSTS, MY PEOPLE, the SONS OF ISRAEL, from the Land of Egypt by """"GREAT JUDGMENT'S"""". And the Egyptians shall Know that "I" am the LORD, When "I" Stretch out MY Hand on Egypt, and Bring out the SONS OF ISRAEL from their Midst.' So MOSES and AARON did it; as the LORD commanded them, thus they did. [Exodus 7. 3, 4, 5, 6.]

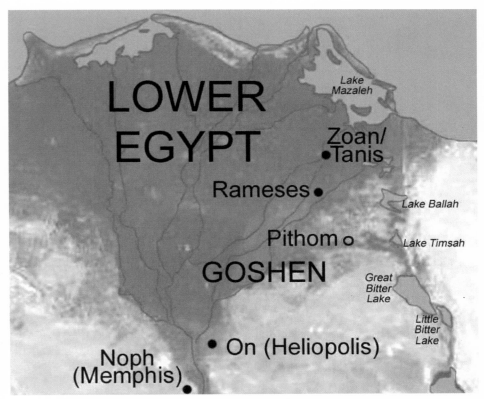

The cities of Ramses and Pithom, where Sons of Israel lived

Pharaoh Ramses II depicted in his chariot

Children of Israel under afflictions in ancient Egypt

Pharaoh Rameses II and God Ptah

Pharaoh Ramses II statue found at ancient city of Pithom

Moses in the wilderness with the Sons of Israel, who are gathering water from the rock which Mose's struck in Saudi Arabia

The Secret of the Breast Plate

Part 32

Since the time of Exodus, Many People of this Planet Earth, Who have not used their "SPIRITUAL EYES", and thus not used their Higher or "Inner Mind's" Filled with Enlightening "LOVE and DEVOTION" for their required Conscious Expansion, which Contains the Vital Ethereal Electro - Magnetic Conscious Energies of their Vibrating SPIRIT, while reading the Holy texts of Bible with mere mortal PHYSICAL EYES drenched in the Illusory Material Glamour of the three dense dimensional planes MATRIX known as the SEPHIROT'S of ASSIAH, YETZIRAH and BRIAH, Which are also known in the Eastern Wisdom in Sanskrit Language as the "TRILOKA'S", they thus have Utterly FAILED to Comprehend the Hidden Codified Spiritual Essence's, which glorifies the LORD GOD OF ISRAEL, and they have also thus failed to comprehend this important Point that "WHY DID THE LORD - GOD TAKE 40 YEARS TO "LEAD" THE SONS OF ISRAEL TO THEIR PROMISED LAND OF 'MILK AND HONEY', WHICH WAS PROMISED TO THEIR FOREFATHER'S ABRAHAM, ISAAC, AND JACOB, WHEN THEIR PROMISED LAND'S OUTERMOST BOUNDARIES WERE ACROSS THE JORDAN, ONLY 11 DAYS JOURNEY FROM MOUNT HOREB?"

The answer to this Important Question is written ALL OVER in the Various Chapters of the OLD TESTAMENT in the Holy Bible, and can be FULLY COMPREHENDED and thus GRASPED only, if any one pays a close Attention while looking at them, just not merely with Physical Eyes but with their "Spiritual Eyes" Fully Open to PROPERLY Understand the "Codified Words of Wisdom of GOD".

Let us start reviewing some of the HOLY VERSES with our Spiritual Eyes FULLY Open, so we can reverently get an understanding of the Divine Codified Wisdom, and thus become a partaker of the Ineffable Grace and Glory of the MOST HIGH, the Lord God of NOAH, ABRAHAM, ISAAC, JACOB and MOSES.

The Holy Bible Clearly States that MOSES addressed the children of Israel across the Jordan in the FORTIETH YEAR, according to ALL that the LORD had Commanded Him to Give to THEM, which is as follows:

'These are the Words which MOSES Spoke to all Israel across the Jordan

IN THE 'WILDERNESS', IN THE 'ARABAH', opposite Suph, between Paran and Tophel and Laban, and Hezeroth and Dizahab. It is ELEVEN DAY'S JOURNEY FROM HOREB by the Way of Mount SEIR to Kadesh – barnea.

And it came about in the Fortieth Year, on the First day of 11th Month, that MOSES Spoke to the Children of Israel, according to All that the LORD had Commanded him to give to them, after He had defeated 'SIHON', the King of Amorites, who Lived in Heshbon, and 'OG' the King of Bashan, who lived in Ashtaroth and Edrei.

Across the Jordan in the land of Moab, MOSES undertook to expound this law, saying, "The LORD our GOD spoke to US at HOREB, saying:

"YOU HAVE STAYED LONG ENOUGH AT THIS MOUNTAIN. Turn and Set Your Journey, and Go to the Hill Country of the Amorites, and to all their Neighbors in the ARABAH, in the Hill Country and in the Lowlands and in the Negev and by the Seacoast, the Land of Canaanites, and Lebanon, as far as the Great River, the River Euphrates. See, "I" have placed the Land before You; Go in and Possess the Land, which the LORD Swore to Give to Your Fathers, to ABRAHAM, to ISSAC, and to JACOB, to them and their descendants after them."

And I spoke to you at that time, saying, 'I am not able to bear the Burden of You alone. The LORD Your GOD has MULTIPLIED YOU and Behold, YOU ARE THIS DAY AS THE STARS OF HEAVEN FOR MULTITUDE. May the LORD, the GOD of Your Fathers. INCREASE YOU A THOUSAND-FOLD MORE THAN YOU ARE, AND BLESS YOU, JUST AS "HE" HAS PROMISED YOU! [Deuteronomy 1. Verses 1 to 11.]

These above Holy Verses give a Clear Indication that all those Sons of Israel, whom the LORD earlier delivered from the hands of Mighty Pharaoh in Egypt, so that they instead of worshiping and serving the so called Gods and Goddesses, who are just mere His Created SERVANT HELPERS, can instead Righteously Serve Him, Who is the "One and Only", THE TRUE CREATOR LORD GOD of the UNIVERSE, just as their Forefathers, NOAH, ABRAHAM, ISSAC, and JACOB did in the Ancient Times, but even after their Deliverance by the MOST HIGH, these Sons of Israel were still molded in their Old Ways of Egyptian Life, and even though from the Very Start, the LORD -GOD SHOWED THEM GREAT MIRACLES, Much More Powerful than the Combined Power of ALL THE EGYPTIAN GODS AND GODDESSES, they still Grumbled against MOSES and AARON comparing their Life in the Wilderness than that of the Very Life they had in Egypt, and many a Times openly Rebelled against them, by willfully not Heeding to the COMMANDS OF THEIR LORD GOD. So it took LORD – GOD "Forty Years" to create a New Generation of His "Strong Believers", who wholeheartedly depended upon HIM just like their Forefathers, NOAH, ABRAHAM, ISSAC, and JACOB did in the Ancient Times, regarding which the Divine Essence is contained in the above Verses, which were uttered by MOSES, the Mouthpiece of LORD, to all Israel across the Jordan IN THE 'WILDERNESS', IN THE 'ARABAH', in which they Clearly State that "The LORD Your GOD has MULTIPLIED YOU and Behold, YOU ARE THIS DAY AS THE STARS OF HEAVEN FOR MULTITUDE".

The LORD – GOD chose 40 Years Period as the "Appropriate Time Period" for the Consciousness Expansion of the "New Generation of Sons of Israel" who were raised in the Wilderness without any links to The Land of Egypt like their Fathers did, and who thus Wholeheartedly depended upon HIM, to come of Age in the Wilderness, as since the Time of the Patriarch ABRAHAM, the MOST HIGH, LORD – GOD earlier established 40 years for HIS Descendant's to come of AGE, so they can Mary and thus Multiply as mentioned in the above verses uttered by MOSES in the Wilderness, through Holy Matrimony, regarding the Holy Bible states:

'And ISAAC was "Forty Years" Old, When He took REBEKAH, the daughter of BETHUEL the Syrian of Paddan – aram, the Sister of Laban the Syrian, to be His Wife.' [Genesis 25. 20.]

Regarding the Miracles of the Most High, and the Continuous Various willful "Grumblings and Rebellions" of the Children of Israel, whom the LORD – God kindly delivered from the Afflictions of Egypt, all the Chapters of the Old Testament in Holy Bible are filled with Such Narratives, Which HIS Chosen Prophets 'Time and Again' used to Guide the Gone Away Astray Children of Israel, who after the Passing of their Wisest King Solomon, again came under the influence of dark Spells of the So called ancient Gods and Goddesses of Egypt through their devised wicked and deceitful plans, in which the Deranged Mind JEROBOAM got Chosen by the 10 Tribes of Israelite's, and thus got used by these Corrupt Gods and Goddesses as their MAIN and 'FRONT STOOGE' to willfully deviate the Children of Israel from the Holy COVENANT and thus from the Graceful Protection of their MOST

HIGH LORD – GOD of the Universe, and they thus willfully again started Worshiping "Those Very Culprits", who as per "Exodus 12. 40." in the Holy Bible, had HELD them earlier in the Egyptian Bondage's filled with Afflictions, for 430 years in the Land of Pharaoh's. These So called Corrupt Gods and Goddesses not only Corrupted the Minds of the Sons of Israel but after the passing of 521 years since the Children of Israel finally left the Land of Egypt during Moses time, a time period which is calculated as per the verses of the Chapters 1 Kings in Holy Bible, which clearly mentions that after 480 years of Exodus, the first Temple building was built, during the 4th year reign of King Solomon + 36 years of King Solomon's further reign out of his total 40 year reign period, and + then passing of 5 more years during his Son King Rehoboam's reign, thus totaling to 480 + 36 + 5 = 521 Years, these So called Gods and Goddesses also Sent their Stooge Pharaoh King "SHISHAK" of Egypt by impulsing Him to Attack Jerusalem, and thus destroyed the World Famous "Achieved Glories" of the "SON OF GOD" King SOLOMON as clearly stated of HIS SUCH DIVINE STATUS in "1 Chronicles 17. 13" of the Holy Bible, just like they also willfully Totally Destroyed the Glories of Pharaoh King AKHENATEN and His Beautiful City AMARNA, which was established by Him on the banks of River Nile in Egypt, when He Single-minded Courageously Rose against the Corruption and ILLEGAL and DECEITFUL AGENDAS of these so called GODS and GODDESSES of Egypt and their Established Priest Hood drenched in Evil Black Magic, who being CREATED SERVANTS of the Benevolent CREATOR LORD, then in a Wide Spread Conspiracy back stabbed their OWN CREATOR SOLAR LOGOS, THE UNKNOWABLE "MOST HIGH", Whom Pharaoh AKHENATEN thus not knowing His True name, like MOSES did, then called HIM as the LORD – GOD "ATEN" of the Universe.

Regarding the Attack of King SHISHAK of Egypt against Jerusalem, the Holy Bible States:

'Now it came about in the Fifth Year of King REHOBOAM that SHISHAK King of Egypt, came up against Jerusalem. And He Took Away the TREASURES OF THE HOUSE OF THE LORD, and the TREASURES OF THE KING'S HOUSE, and He Took EVERYTHING, Even Taking All the Shields of Gold, which SOLOMON had Made.' [1 Kings 14. 25, 26.]

Let us look further at some of the related Verses of the Holy Bible regarding the Miracles of the Most High, and the Continuous Various willful "Grumblings and Rebellions" of the Children of Israel, whom the

LORD – God delivered from the Afflictions of Egypt, with our "SPIRITUAL EYES" fully open, So that we can grab some of the Codified Divine Nectar of "Spiritual Holy Essence", which is embedded in them.

Pharaoh Shishak Battle Relief at Karnak, Egypt depicting the Hebrew captive slaves with their hands tied behind their backs and their necks tied together in a string of ropes during the invasion of Israel and Judah in 926 BC.

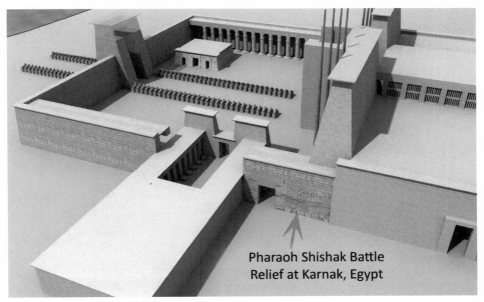

Pharaoh Shishak Battle
Relief at Karnak, Egypt

Moses & Aaron meeting in the wilderness of Mount Horeb, as per the command of LORD

FIVE BODY'S OF A HUMAN BEING

[1] NEFESH / Physical body

[2] RUACH / Desire Mind Form

[3] NESHAMAH / Mental Body

[4] CHAYAH / Causal Body

[5] YECHIDAH / Body of Collective Consciousness

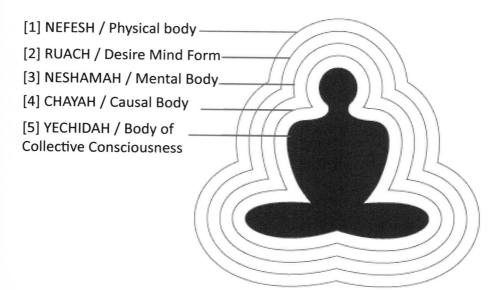

The Holy Bible clearly states that the MOSES and his brother AARON, who were known as per the Holy Bible as Levite's, as they were the descendant children of LEVY, the Son of JACOB, who was named by the grace of the "THE MOST HIGH" as ISRAEL, willfully followed LORD GOD'S commands without any Ensuing Doubts as they were readily cleared by the LORD, and thus became His Humble and Loyal Servants to carry out HIS Commands in delivering out, the Children of Israel from the bondage's of Egypt, Because LORD always clarified the ensuing doubts of their Minds by Properly answering their Questions, and thus providing them the Necessary Solutions as per their Requirements.

The Holy Bible also clearly states that MOSES was not "A POLITICIAN" like the many of so called WORLD LEADERS of Today, Who with Their Own Vested Interests are thus claiming to Lead the Evolving Humanity of this Planet Earth, as MOSES Himself declared to the LORD that He was not Eloquent, as well as Slow of Speech and Slow of Tongue, regarding which the Holy Bible states:

'Then Moses said to the LORD, "Please LORD, I have Never been ELOQUENT, Neither Recently, Nor in the Past, Nor Since Thou hast Spoken to Thy Servant; FOR I AM SLOW OF SPEECH and SLOW OF TONGUE."

And the LORD said to Him, "WHO HAS MADE MAN'S MOUTH? Or WHO MAKES HIM DUMB OR DEAF, or WHO SEEING OR BLIND? IS IT NOT "'I'" THE LORD?"

"Now then Go, and "I", Even "I", will be with YOUR MOUTH, and teach YOU What YOU ARE TO SAY."

But He Said, "Please LORD, Now Send the Message by Whomever THOU WILT." [Exodus 4. 10, 11, 12, 13.]

In these above Verses anyone, who have their Spiritual Eyes Fully Open can Clearly See and thus VISUALIZE, what kind of Personality MOSES had! And He humbly told about his Doubting Mind to the LORD – GOD. But at that particular Moment MOSES forgot to pay attention to this

Underlying FACT as clearly mentioned in Verse 27 of the Very First Chapter of the Holy Bible, which states:

"AND GOD CREATED MAN IN HIS OWN IMAGE, IN THE IMAGE OF GOD "'HE'" CREATED HIM; MALE AND FEMALE "'HE'" CREATED THEM. [Genesis 1. 27.]

So it is Important to remember for ALL THE INCARNATED HUMAN BEINGS OF THIS PLANET EARTH, THAT IT IS THE "MOST HIGH", "THE LORD OF THE FLAMES", Who to Start with CREATED THE HUMAN BEINGS UPON THIS PLANET EARTH, AND THUS GAVE THEM THE "INDIVIDUALIZED MIND CAPACITIES" WITH REQUIRED SENSORY ABILITIES, TO EXPAND THEIR EVOLVING "SOLAR SPIRIT" CONSCIOUSNESS, THROUGH AN EXTENDED VITAL ARM OF THE ETHEREAL SPIRIT CONSCIOUSNESS, Known to Prophets, Seers, and Sages, as THE "ETHEREAL CORD OF VITALITY", Whom THE WISE "KING SOLOMON" TERMED AS THE SILVER CORD in "ECCLESIASTES 12. 6" of the HOLY BIBLE, thus PROVIDING THE REQUIRED ANIMATION FORCE to their EVOLVING "EGO MIND " and their "INDIVIDUALIZED PERSONALITY CONSCIOUSNESS" Embodied in their 5 "Related Shaped Forms" composed of differentiated ethereal matters of the 3 dimensional plane worlds of "ASSIAH, YETZIRAH, and BRIAH", which are known in the HEBREW LANGUAGE AS:

[1] NEFESH, meaning the Composed Physical body of a Human Being, which is formed upon the frame work of the Vital Ethereal Body, composed of Live Elemental Essences of the 3 ethereal sub planes [2nd, 3rd, and Most Amounts of the 4th Vital Ether] of the Dense Physical Plane World [ASSIAH], whose vital frequencies are mostly invisible to ALL HUMAN BEING'S, especially to all those, whose Consciousness is Totally Polarized in the ILLUSORY MATERIAL WORLD GLAMOUR of this DENSE PHYSICAL PLANE WORLD of Planet Earth.

[2] RUACH, meaning the Desire Mind Form, which is related to the Dense Material Plane World Desires, or the "Lower Mind" body also known as the "DREAM BODY", WHICH WE CONSCIOUSLY OR UNCONSCIOUSLY USE IN THE DREAM WORLD ZONES, WHEN OUR DENSE MATERIAL PLANE "PHYSICAL BODY" IS ASLEEP, and the RUACH body is formed from the live elemental essences of Liquid Magnetic Matter, which thus being highly sensitive to magnetic charge of the "DESIRE MIND CONSCIOUSNESS - VITAL FORCE" Quickly Respond to the

Emotions and Feelings of the Human Mind.

[3] NESHAMAH, meaning the Mental Body, which is formed from the live elemental essences of Gaseous Electric Matter, which thus being highly sensitive to Electric charge of the "EXPANDING MIND CONSCIOUSNESS VITAL FORCE", whose very interest is only to uncover the HIDDEN TRUTHS related to HIGHER SELF, also known as the "SOLAR CONSCIOUSNESS", or the "SOUL MIND", which Vitally Exists upon the Mental Plane Dimension, also known as the SEPHIROT of BRIAH.

[4] CHAYAH, meaning the CAUSAL BODY, which through repeated incarnations of a Human Being upon the Dense Physical Plane [ASSIAH], Constantly Grows in Size, ONLY According to the AMOUNT OF GATHERING OF THE SPIRITUAL EXPERIENCES IN THE DENSE PLANE MATERIAL WORLD [ASSIAH], or during their Short Lived Incarnated Human Lives in the Dense Dimensional Plane of the Incarnated Human Beings upon this Planet Earth.

MOST INCARNATED HUMAN BEINGS OF THIS PLANET EARTH, WHO MAY HAVE ATTAINED PRESTIGIOUS DEGREES FROM TOP NOTCH UNIVERSITIES, ARE UNAWARE OF THIS "IMPORTANT FACT", THAT The HIGHER SELF or the SOUL CONSCIOUS MIND of All Human Beings is "ONLY INTERESTED" in the Spiritual Aspects of their Evolving Consciousness, and thus has ABSOLUTELY NO INTEREST in the Physical Mind Aspects of the EVOLVING PERSONALITY CONSCIOUSNESS. The CHAYAH is thus Considered as A BRIDGE TO HIGHER DIMENSIONAL PLANES OF THE INFINITE UNIVERSE and thus known as THE HOLY BODY OF TRANSCENDENCE, which after its FULL COMPLETION is TOTALLY FILLED WITH SPIRITUAL CONSCIOUSNESS EXPANSION, and WITH ITS EXPANDING MIND HEAT then GETS DESTROYED, and thus FREES THE EMBODIED "SOLAR CONSCIOUSNESS" from its PARAMETRIC ENCLOSURE, as this Solar Consciousness has been COMMONLY TERMED since ancient times, by THE SEERS, PROPHETS AND SAGES AS THE "SOUL", thus RELEASING IT PERMANENTLY FROM THE "FORM BONDAGE'S" OF THE 3 DENSE DIMENSIONAL PLANE WORLDS OF THIS PLANET EARTH, TO "CONSCIOUSLY EXIST" appearing as an "ETHEREAL RADIANT JEWEL" having an GLOWING EXISTENCE of "RADIANT BLUISH LIGHT".

[5] YECHIDAH, meaning the BODY OF COLLECTIVE CONSCIOUSNESS, thus EXISTING IN THE HIGHER DIMENSIONAL PLANE OF """"ATZILUTH"""",

A JOYFUL STATE OF CONSCIOUS EXISTENCE for the SPIRITUALLY EVOLVED CONSCIOUSNESS, HAVING ATTAINED A RADIANT SOLAR CONSCIOUS MIND, FILLED WITH BLUISH HUE OF "SOOTHING RADIANT FORCE", thus existing as a part and parcel of a much larger GROUP CONSCIOUSNESS.

These five bodies, which are composed of five types of differentiated Vital ETHEREAL Matter are also known as the "5 Koshas" in Sanskrit Language", which are Fully Utilized by the Evolving "SOUL" or the "HIGHER SELF" through repeated incarnations IN THE 3 DENSE MATERIAL WORLDS, KNOWN AS THE SEPHIROT'S OF "ASSIAH, YETZIRAH, AND BRIAH", WHOSE VIBRATING ETHEREAL DIMENSIONAL BOUNDARIES INTERPENETRATE EACH OTHER.

Just when the LORD gave commands to MOSES upon his Holy Flaming Mountain, HE then considering the DOUBTS OF HIS MIND, The Great LORD chose a HELPER for Him, His own brother AARON, regarding which the Holy Bible States:

'Then the Anger of the LORD Burned against MOSES, and HE Said, "IS THERE NOT YOUR BROTHER AARON THE LEVITE? "I" KNOW THAT HE SPEAKS FLUENTLY. AND MOREOVER, BEHOLD, HE IS COMING OUT TO MEET YOU; WHEN HE SEES YOU, HE WILL BE GLAD IN HIS HEART. AND YOU ARE TO SPEAK TO HIM AND PUT THE "WORDS IN HIS MOUTH"; AND "I", EVEN "I" WILL BE WITH YOUR MOUTH AND HIS MOUTH, AND "I" WILL TEACH YOU WHAT YOU ARE TO DO."

"Moreover He shall Speak for you to the People; and it shall come about that He shall be as a MOUTH for YOU, and YOU shall be as "GOD TO HIM". And YOU shall take in Your Hand this STAFF, with which YOU shall PERFORM THE SIGNS." [Exodus 4. 14, 15, 16, 17.]

Now the LORD Said to AARON, "Go Meet MOSES in the Wilderness." So He Went and Met Him at THE MOUNTAIN OF GOD, and He Kissed Him. And MOSES Told AARON, All the WORDS OF THE LORD, with which HE had Sent Him, and All the SIGNS, That HE had COMMANDED Him to do.

Then MOSES and AARON went and assembled All the Elders of the Sons of Israel; and AARON Spoke All the WORDS, WHICH LORD HAD SPOKEN TO MOSES. He then PERFORMED the SIGNS in the SIGHT OF THE PEOPLE. So the People BELIEVED; and when They Heard that the LORD was CONCERNED about the SONS OF ISRAEL, and that HE had seen their AFFLICTION, then they BOWED LOW and WORSHIPED. [Exodus 4. Verses 27 to 31.]

The Five Bodies of an Incarnated Human Being

THE 5 FORM CONTAINER'S ALSO KNOWN AS KOSHA'S
In 3 Dense Dimensional Sephirots "Spheres"

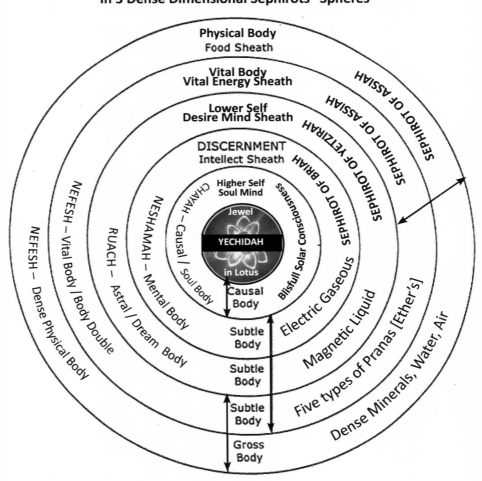

Pharaoh Seti I smiting his enemies on the Karnak wall of ancient Egypt

Ancient Egyptian priesthood worshiping Eagle-faced God Horus

Part 34

Most incarnated Human Beings of this Planet Earth, who living in an ongoing rat race of the Physical Plane Modern World with their desire minds in their Daily Lives, absolutely polarized in Emotions and Feelings, can be quickly swayed and thus easily tend to forget their Affliction's occurring upon daily basis in their incarnated Lives, through the Ethereal ELECTRO - MAGNETIC Mind Control Impulses, which also include Media and Debated Methods, which are thus daily bombarded upon them by their INVISIBLE MASTERS, commonly referred to as the so called Invisible "Gods and Goddesses", which encourage them and thus Deceitfully Lead them to LIVE their Short Lived INCARNATED HUMAN LIVES through CORRUPT AGENDAS which are TOTALLY CONTRARY TO WHAT IS WRITTEN IN THEIR "RELIGIOUS and SPIRITUAL BOOKS", and they are thus Invisibly Controlled like any other DOMESTICATED ANIMALS in the name of SO CALLED CIVILIZATION through the aid of their incarnated Henchmen, the Famous and Well Positioned World Leaders, Who thus Richly Established by acquiring Material Wealth are sitting on Top of their Human Societies, and thus knowingly or unknowingly aid in their such governance in the physical plane world, acting as their Most Effective Front Tools.

Although the Ancient Egyptian Pharaohs, who became Mighty and Powerful with the help of these invisible Corrupt GODS and GODDESSES, who themselves by going Astray thus BACK – STABBED their Own Creator LORD – GOD OF THE FLAMES, and thus Constructed Many Great Feats of Engineering upon the Physical Plane of this Planet Earth, they were Ruthless as any other Powerful Human Beings of their Times, and were Cruel in their Judgment's and Behavior as depicted upon the ancient Wall Murals, thus glorifying their Such Deeds and Feats.

During the Time of MOSES, "The LORD OF THE FLAMES", commonly known since ancient times by his devotees and worshipers as the "SUPREME BEING" or the "MOST HIGH" who is also known by HIS MANY TITLE NAMES, Which Include HIS Popular Title Names as the "MOST BENEVOLENT", "MOST MERCIFUL", and the "EMBODIMENT OF LIGHT", or Just Simply the "LORD – GOD", was fully aware of the inequities of these so called "Gods and Goddesses", Who in FACT are Just Mere His CREATED SERVANT HELPERS, who drenched in their own

EGOISTIC FALSE PRIDE through the Total Misuse of their Vested Powers, STUPIDLY THOUGHT and thus FOOLISHLY CONSIDERED that their One and Only "CREATOR - OBSERVER LORD" is "TOTALLY UNAWARE" of their "SUCH EVIL AND DECEITFUL AGENDAS", and their this Unlawful Reasoning for Such "ILL MINDED THINKING" was due to their Inadequate Understandings of HIS EVOLUTIONARY PLAN AND PURPOSE, Which is Based Upon One and Only Universal Law, which is "WILL TO DO GOOD".

And More so. because being themselves existing as the CREATED ENTITIES AND BEINGS, in this UNIVERSE Who are INVISIBLE to the Incarnated Human Beings, they FOOLISHLY THOUGHT, that the "MOST HIGH" being an "EMBODIMENT OF SOLAR LOGOS CONSCIOUSNESS" IN THIS SOLAR UNIVERSE thus EXISTS as an PARTICIPATOR as well as an OBSERVER OF THE GRAND EXPERIMENT OF CONSCIOUSNESS EXPANSION in HIS Created Universe, So "HE" is ONLY INTERESTED in the "SPIRITUAL ASPECTS" of HIS Subjectively and Objectively Manifested Creation, which "Thus Manifested" exists in the various Differentiated and Interpenetrating Egg Shaped Spherical Dimensional Planes in the VITAL ETHEREAL SPACE, which are governed by HIM through HIS RADIUS OF INFLUENCE, and HE will thus "CARE LESS'" FOR ALL WHAT GOES ON IN THE THREE DENSE MATERIAL WORLDS OF THIS PLANET EARTH, which since Ancient Times have been Known to the Seers, Prophets, and Sages in Hebrew Language as the Dimensional SEHIROTS [Spheres] of ASSIAH, YETZIRAH, and BRIAH, or in Sanskrit Language as the "BHU", "BHAVA", and "SVA" LOKA'S. But the "MOST HIGH" has "TIME AND AGAIN" Proved them "Absolutely Wrong", which has been Compiled and Written in great Details of the HOLY BIBLE, especially in its 2nd Chapter known to all Human Beings as the "EXODUS".

The LORD – GOD was Fully Aware of the Inequities of HIS Created Servant Helpers, who were "INVISIBLE" to the Human Beings, and the Materially Minded Majority of the Human Beings Without Paying much attention to the Underlying FACTS thus Revered them as their SO CALLED GODS AND GODDESSES Deceitfully Guided by their Luxurious Life Style Colorful PRIESTHOOD, but Strangely Worshiped them Mostly in the "SHAPE OF ANIMALS", who possess even "LESS CONSCIOUS ATTRIBUTES", than the Human Beings themselves, Or in the Venerated Shape of MOLTEN FIGURES OF MALE AND FEMALE HUMAN BEINGS, sometimes also combined with the shapes of Various Animal Features, who are Just MERE MORTALS like themselves.

Part 35

Although the Most HIGH, also known as the Unknowable Lord – God by most of His Staunch Visible Humans Followers, and Invisible HOST Devotees, who usually thus Address HIM, is the One and Only ABSOLUTE True Creator of the Universe, Which has been Subjectively and Objectively Manifested through His "Desire Mind" Vital Impulses, and in it HE is Carrying on the "GRAND EXPERIMENT" of Conscious Expansion, which is required for All the Visible and Invisible Entities and Beings to achieve HIGHER DIMENSIONAL LEVELS OF EXISTENCE, Who are thus Existing in its Various Differentiated Dimensional Frequency Levels, apart from HIS such status of Being the ABSOLUTE CREATOR, HE is also the CONSCIOUS OBSERVER of HIS Grand Experiment, an IMPORTANT FACT which is not known to many of HIS manifested HIERARCHICAL CREATIONS.

HIS continuous observance is thus absolutely required in this GRAND EXPERIMENT, which as per HIS Evolutionary Plan and Purpose is currently going on upon this Planet Earth, as apart from being the "Absolute Creator and Observer", HE is also the Upholder of the Universal Law of "Will to do Good", which is known to HIS Devotees and Followers as the "HOLY COVENANT", and thus Supposed to be PRACTICALLY KEPT in its HIGHEST ESTEEM.

When Ever "All Those", who are supposed to follow and thus keep HIS Holy Covenant, "Willfully Go Astray", then HE VISIBLY OR INVISIBLY CONSCIOUSLY PARTICIPATE AMONG THEM, to GUIDE them, SO THEY MIGHT BE ABLE TO SAVE THEMSELVES FROM THEIR LOOMING DOOM, SPIRITUAL DEATH, AND THUS "SOUL CONSCIOUSNESS" PERMANENT DESTRUCTION, ELIMINATION, ANNIHILATION AND EXTINCTION.

During the time of Exodus such was the case upon this Planet Earth, as then the MIGHTY EMPIRE OF THE PHARAOHS, who worshiped the so called GODS and GODDESSES, at that Particular Time of Human History was much more Advanced as compared to Most other Nations of the Known World, but they were not aware of this BASIC FACT, that these so called Invisible Gods and Goddesses themselves were just mere CREATIONS of their LORD OF THE FLAMES, who is also known as the Unknowable "THE MOST HIGH", and these Gods and Goddesses of Egypt started misusing their vested Powers, and thus willfully went astray from the Established Evolutionary Path, which all the Holy books of Various religions term as the "SPIRITUAL PATH", and they instead themselves indulged in the Wrong Material Path of Illusory Glamour, and thus their Human Followers enchanted with material world glamour also left the Evolutionary Spiritual Path, and willfully started proceeding upon the Wrong Path of Involution, which is Totally opposite to Spirituality thus developing more of their "LOWER MIND" Qualities, which are related to the Unquenchable desires of Dense Material Word Glamour.

When LORD GOD delivered Children of Egypt from the hand of Egyptians, People started believing in HIM as well in HIS Servant MOSES, but OLD HABITS DIE HARD, and even after Seeing So many Great Miracles, Time and Again People Grumbled, whenever problematic issues arose for them, and for this very reason LORD took 40 Years to patiently change their desire minds which were set in OLD WAYS through various perseverance's in the wilderness, before they finally proceeded toward their Promised Land, regarding which the Holy Bible states:

'And When Israel saw the Great Power, which the LORD had used against the Egyptians, the People Feared the LORD, and they believed in the LORD and in HIS Servant MOSES.' [Exodus 14. 31.]

Then MOSES and the Sons of Israel sang this Song to the LORD, and Said. "I will sing to the LORD, for HE is highly exalted; The Horse and its Rider HE has hurled into the Sea. Who is like THEE among the gods, O LORD? Who is like THEE, Majestic in Holiness, Awesome in Praises, Working Wonders? [Exodus 15. 1, 11.]

Then MOSES Led Israel from the Red Sea, and they went out into the Wilderness of SHUR; and they went three days in the wilderness and found no water. And when they came to Marah, they could not drink the waters of Marah, for they were bitter; therefore it was named Marah.

So the People GRUMBLED at MOSES, Saying, 'What shall we drink?' Then He CRIED OUT to the LORD, and the LORD Showed Him a Tree; and He threw it into the waters, and the water became Sweet. There HE made for them a STATUTE and REGULATION, and there HE tested them.

And HE Said, "IF YOU WILL GIVE EARNEST HEED TO THE VOICE OF THE LORD, YOUR GOD, AND DO WHAT IS RIGHT IN HIS SIGHT, AND GIVE EAR TO HIS COMMANDMENTS, AND KEEP ALL HIS STATUTES, I WILL PUT NONE OF THE DISEASES ON YOU, WHICH "I" HAVE PUT ON THE EGYPTIANS; FOR "I", THE "LORD", AM YOUR HEALER."[Exodus 15. Verses 22 to 26.]

Precession of the Apis Bull worshiped as an embodiment of God Ptah in ancient Egypt

White Manna looked like these Sabudana made from Cassava [Tapioca] Root in India

Cake Bread made from Sabudana [Tapioca]

During the time of Exodus, the Children of Israel rebelled many times in the wilderness against MOSES and their LORD, even though they had Time and Again, Seen and thus Fully Experienced, HIS immensely GREAT POWERS, as they Left Egypt, because their evolving minds were still CORRUPTED with all those DESIRES, which they assimilated in their "Personality Minds" during their Long Duration Stay in the Lands of Egypt.

During their 430 Years stay in Egypt, they were constantly impulsed illegally by the Corrupt Egyptian Priesthood, who acted as the Magicians for the ruling Pharaoh, as well as the Human Fronts for their Various Animal Shaped Egyptian Gods and Goddesses, with the magnetic energy thought forms created by the use of Chanting's as the Force of Sound Frequencies, which were Willfully Applied in their magical rituals, which then created Live Thought Forms composed of Lower mind Desires, Emotions and feelings, and to keep them in SLAVERY, thus bombarded them daily "without their knowledge" to enhance their Lower mind desires, mostly animalistic in nature, which then manifested in their brains as the "LIVE THOUGHT FORMS" of 'Lust and Greed', which all of a sudden then randomly formed and thus appeared in their Minds, which they innocently considered as their "Own Mind Thoughts", but these Lower Desire Mind "Thought Forms" were thus deceitfully introduced in their invisible egg shaped Auras, which then filtered to their Brains, by the illegal action of these so called Invisible Gods and Goddesses, who themselves originally rebelled against the Established Evolutionary Plan of their own CREATOR LORD- GOD, THE MOST HIGH, which is Clearly written in all Holy Books of this world as the Noble or "SPIRITUAL PATH, and they thus Illegally and Willfully took the entire Humanity of this Planet Earth upon the downward material path of Animalistic Lower Mind, which Since then has thus kept the entire Humanity engrossed in the Illusions of Material World Glamour for a Long Time.

Regarding the Corrupted State of their Minds, the Holy Bible states as follows:

'And the Whole Congregation of the Sons of Israel GRUMBLED against MOSES and AARON in the Wilderness. And the Sons of Israel said to them, "Would that We had Died by the LORD'S Hand in the Land of Egypt, when We Sat by the POTS OF MEAT, When We Ate BREAD to the FULL; For you have brought Us out into this Wilderness to Kill this Whole Assembly with Hunger." [Exodus 16. 2, 3.]

But LORD was fully aware of their Grumblings, as they missed the Flesh of Dead Animals, whom they craved, and which they were used to Eat in Egypt, but according to the evolutionary plan of conscious expansion in the dense physical world, to attain a Spiritual Mind and Inner Eyes, one should not consume dead animals as, their flesh tissues which in an animal during his incarnated life independently performed their required life supporting duties, thus supporting his animal form body, thus embodied their animal nature Lower Mind Consciousness impulses during their entire incarnated lives, and after being consumed by human beings, they then also enhanced their lower mind animalistic desires, and the ALMIGHTY LORD who instantly provided ABRAHAM in the ancient times a RAM for the performance of His burnt offerings as stated in "Genesis 22. 13.", for sure could have provided them their heartfelt desired MEAT, but for the Good of the Children of Israel, HE Willfully Chose Not to do so, and instead provided them White Mushrooms, sweet in Taste to Eat, whose perforated appearance underside of their canopy top looked like the shape of the sides of a Coriander Seed just like the Mushrooms of today look like, which was later named as MANNA by the Children of Israel, thus curtailing to a great degree their MEAT EATING FOOD HABITS, regarding which the Holy Bible States:

'Then the LORD said to MOSES, "Behold, "I" will Rain Bread from Heaven for You; and the People shall go out and gather a Day's Portion Every Day, that "I" may test them, whether or not they will walk in MY Instruction. And it will Come about on the Sixth Day, When they Prepare what they Bring in, IT WILL BE TWICE AS MUCH AS THEY GATHER DAILY".

And the LORD spoke to MOSES, Saying, "I HAVE HEARD THE GRUMBLINGS OF THE SONS OF ISRAEL; Speak to them, Saying, 'At Twilight You shall Eat Meat, and in the Morning you shall be Filled with Bread; and you shall know that "I" am the LORD Your GOD.' So it came about at Evening that the Quails came up and covered the Camp, and in the morning there was a Layer of Dew around the Camp. When the Layer of Dew Evaporated, Behold, on the Surface of the Wilderness there was a fine Flake – Like thing, fine as the hoarfrost on the Ground.

When the Sons of Israel saw it, they said to one another, 'What is it?' For they did not know what it was. And MOSES said to them, "It is the Bread which the LORD has given you to Eat. This is what the LORD has commanded, 'Gather of it every Man as much as He should Eat; you shall take an Omer a piece according to the number of Persons each of you has in His tent. And the Sons of Israel did so, and some gathered much and some little. When they measured it with an Omer, He who had gathered MUCH had No EXCESS, and He who had gathered LITTLE had no LACK; Every Man gathered as much as He should eat.

So the People rested on the Seventh Day. And the House of Israel named it Manna, and it was like Coriander Seed, White; and its taste was like WAFERS with Honey. Then Moses said, 'This is what the LORD has commanded, "Let an Omerful of it be kept throughout Your Generations, that they may see the Bread that "'I'" fed You in the Wilderness, When "'I'" brought You out of the Land of Egypt."

And the Sons of Israel Ate the Manna Forty Years, until they came to an Inhabited Land; they Ate the Manna until they came to the Border of the Land of Canaan. [Exodus 16. 4, 5, 11, 12, 13, 14, 15, 16, 17, 18, 30, 31, 32.]

In the next book of the 'Old Testament' which is the 3rd book of the Holy Bible named "NUMBERS", it is further stated that Even the LORD – GOD provided the Children of Israel all their Daily NEEDS with full supply of Food in the Wilderness, they Still went on Grumbling, Complaining, and thus Foolishly Wept due to their Animalistic greedy desires of the Lower Mind, which Kindled the Anger of the LORD, AND THE FIRE OF THE LORD BURNED AND CONSUMED SOME OF THEM.

White Corriander Seeds

179

Manna appeared like these Bdellium's

Part 37

Even though the LORD delivered the Sons of Israel from their Afflictions which they regularly faced in Egypt, they were still constantly complaining about their New-found Freedom, thus living in the wilderness, regarding which the Holy Bible States:

Now the People became like those who complain of adversity in the hearing of the LORD; and when the LORD heard it, His anger was kindled, and the FIRE of the LORD burned among them and consumed some of the Outskirts of the Camp. The People therefore Cried out to MOSES, and MOSES Prayed to the Lord, and the FIRE Died Out. So the name of that Place was called Taberah, because the FIRE of the LORD burned among them.

And the Rabble who were among them had GREEDY DESIRES; and also the Sons of Israel wept again and Said, "who will GIVE US MEAT TO EAT? We remember the Fish which we used to Eat Free in Egypt, the Cucumbers and the Melons and the Leeks and the Onions and the Garlic, but now our appetite is gone. There is nothing at all to look at except this MANNA."

Now the Manna was like Coriander Seed, and its appearance like that of BDELLIUM. The People would go about and gather it, grind it between Two Millstones, or beat it in the Mortar, and boil it in the Pot and make Cakes with it; and its taste was as the taste of cakes baked with Oil. And when the Dew fell on the Camp at Night, the Manna would fall with it.

Now MOSES heard the People weeping throughout their Families, each Man at the doorway of His Tent; and the Anger of the LORD was KINDLED GREATLY, and MOSES was DISPLEASED. So MOSES said to the LORD, "Why hast THOU been so HARD on THY Servant? And why I have not found favor in THY Sight, that THOU hast laid the Burden of All the People on ME? Was it I who Conceived all this People? Was it I who brought them forth, that THOU shouldest Say to Me, 'Carry them in your Bosom as a Nurse carries a Nursing Infant, to the Land which Thou didst Swear to their Father's'"?

"Where am I to get MEAT to give to all this People? For they Weep before me saying, 'Give us Meat that we may eat!' I alone am not able to carry all this People, because it is too burdensome for me. So if THOU art going to DEAL thus with me, Please Kill me at Once, if I have found favor in THY Sight, and do not let me See my Wretchedness."

The LORD therefore said to MOSES, "Gather for ME Seventy Men from the Elders of Israel, whom you know to be the Elders of the People, and their Officers, and bring them to the Tent of Meeting, and let them take their Stand with you. Then "I" will Come Down and Speak with you there, and "I" will take of the SPIRIT who is upon you, and put Him upon them; and they shall bear the burden of the People with you, so that you shall not BEAR IT ALL ALONE. And say to the People, Consecrate Yourselves for Tomorrow, and you shall EAT MEAT; For you have Wept in the Ears of the LORD, Saying, 'Oh that Someone would give us MEAT TO EAT! For we were WELL – OFF in Egypt.' Therefore the LORD will give you MEAT and you shall eat. You shall Eat, Not One Day, Nor Two Days, Nor Five Days, Nor Ten Days, Nor Twenty Days, But a Whole Month, until it comes out of YOUR NOSTRILS and becomes LOATHSOME to YOU; BECAUSE YOU HAVE "'REJECTED THE LORD'" Who is AMONG YOU and have WEPT before HIM, saying, 'WHY DID WE EVER LEAVE EGYPT'?"

But MOSES said, "The People among whom I am, are 600,000 on Foot; yet THOU hast Said, 'I WILL GIVE THEM MEAT IN ORDER THEY MAY EAT FOR A WHOLE MONTH.' Should Flocks and Herds be slaughtered for them, to be Sufficient for them? Or should all the FISH of the Sea be gathered together for them, to be Sufficient for them?"

And the LORD Said to MOSES, "IS THE LORD'S POWER LIMITED? NOW YOU SHALL SEE WHETHER MY WORD WILL COME TRUE FOR YOU, OR NOT."

So MOSES went out and told the People, the words of the LORD. Also, He Gathered Seventy Men of the Elders of the People, and STATIONED them around the Tent. Then the LORD came down in the CLOUD and Spoke to Him; and HE took off the SPIRIT who was upon Him, and Placed HIM upon the Seventy Elders. And it came about that, when the SPIRIT rested upon them, THEY PROPHESIED. But they did not do it again. But two Men had remained in the Camp; the name of one was ELDAD, and the name of other MEDAD. And the SPIRIT rested upon them [Now they were among those who had been registered, but had not gone out to the Tent]. And they PROPHESIED in the Camp. So a young man ran and told MOSES and said. 'ELDAD and MEDAD are Prophesying in the Camp,' Then JOSHUA the Son of NUN, the attendant of MOSES from His Youth, answered and said, 'MOSES My Lord, restrain them.' But MOSES Said to Him, 'Are you Jealous for My Sake? Would that ALL the LORD'S People were Prophets, that the LORD would PUT HIS SPIRIT UPON THEM!' Then MOSES returned to the Camp, both He and the Elders of Israel.

Now there went forth a Wind from the LORD, and it brought QUAIL from the SEA, and let them fall beside the Camp, about a day's journey on this Side, and a day's journey on the Other Side, all around the Camp, and about TWO CUBITS DEEP ON THE SURFACE OF THE GROUND. And the People spent all Day and all Night, and all the Next Day, and gathered the Quail [He who gathered Least, Gathered Ten Homers], and they Spread them Out for THEMSELVES all around the Camp.

While the MEAT was still between their Teeth, before it was chewed, the ANGER of the LORD was KINDLED against the People, and the LORD STRUCK the People with a VERY SEVERE PLAGUE. So the name of that place was called KIBROTH – HATTAAVAH, because there they buried the People, WHO HAD BEEN GREEDY. [Numbers 11. Verses 1 to 35.]

There is an ancient saying which states "You are What you Eat!", and the above verses clearly state that the desire mind of the Greedy People was still polarized Firmly in the old habits of Eating Animal MEAT, while the LORD – GOD, wanted to raise their indwelling consciousness, through the daily supply of HIS Heavenly Food, whom the House of Israel named as the "Manna", which he provided them for 40 Years in the Wilderness, so they can become a True SPIRITUAL FLOCK as per HIS Covenant, which HE made with their Elders since the ancient Times, and thus considered them as HIS Chosen People.

Much Later, the well versed Pharisee named SAUL, Who willfully became the Humble Servant of Resurrected JESUS CHRIST, the Chosen Son of the "MOST HIGH", later to be known as the World famous APOSTLE PAUL, was aware of the ILLS OF EATING "MEAT", as He Clearly stated in His Spiritual Thoughts written to "ROMAN'S" from His Confined cell in Rome, later to be known as the "Chapter of Romans" in the Holy Bible, which state:

"It is GOOD Not to Eat MEAT, Or to Drink WINE, Or to do anything by Which Your Brother Stumbles." [Romans 14. 21].

It was also Apostle Paul, who talked about in His letter to the Churches of Galatia, knowing full Well the Proper location of Mount Sinai, and it being in Arabia, and not in the land of Egypt, as about 300 Years later it was wrongly proclaimed by Helena, the Mother of King Constantine, regarding which the Holy Bible States:

"Now this Hagar is Mount Sinai in Arabia." [Galatians 4. 25.]

Also the above verses clearly explain as to how the "Prophets" of Israel" PROPHESIED, when the LORD would PUT HIS SPIRIT UPON THEM, just as what happened for the first time to the 70 Elders of Israel, whom MOSES, the Humble Servant of the LORD, as per HIS commands, Chose from the rest of his People.

"Now there went forth a Wind from the LORD, and it brought QUAIL from the SEA, and let them fall beside the Camp" [Numbers 11.31]

According to the Holy Bible, even though the GREAT LORD repeatedly showed His Immense Divine Mercy, and thus brought out the Sons of Israel from their everyday afflictions, which they suffered at the hands of their Taskmasters in Egypt, Many of the Children of Israel were still Rebellious and thus Obstinate in the Eyes of the LORD.

And the very reason for the Children of Israel having such Obstinate minds was due to their polarized desire minds, having animal type desires like, that of unquenchable Greed, which thus kept their evolving personalities consciously polarized in their "RUACH Bodies", which are composed of the Live Elemental Essences, which exist in the liquid magnetic Dimensional plane of YETZIRAH, and these invisible live essences are in fact very tiny elemental's, who respond to the magnetic impulses of the Desire Mind of Human Beings, which are commonly known as the sensations of feelings and emotions of Human Beings, which are related to the dense physical world's material objectivity. And being magnetic in nature, they collectively gather themselves and thus compose the "RUACH or the Astral bodies" of incarnating Human Beings, which are appropriately related to the desire or personality consciousness mind of an incarnated human being, and at the time of their birth in the Physical world of this planet earth, these elemental essences composing his RUACH body are related to the sensations of His Previous Birth's desire mind actions and reactions, and this RUACH body is also commonly known by the Human Beings as the "Dream State Body", which is consciously or unconsciously utilized by the Human Beings during their Mind Consciousness temporarily leaves the dense confinements of their physical body and thus is carried upon the liquid frequency vibrations of the magnetic plane ethereal matter, which is part of the YETZIRAH Dimensional Plane, and such consciousness state is known as the "Dream State" of a Human Being, when their Physical bodies are lying asleep.

This 'RUACH' body is also their future body of conscious existence, in which, after the severance of the "Silver Cord of Vitality" from their Incarnated Physical bodies they later on live to exist in the dimensional sphere of YETZIRAH, as the severance of the "Silver Cord then immediately causes the stoppage of the animating Vital Force, which was earlier provided to them through this invisible Vital Energy cord, and thus so called physical death occurs to their physical bodies.

These tiny elemental essences in fact do not possess the attributes of Intellect yet, but work instead with their magnetic instincts, and thus have Totally different evolutionary objectives than the incarnated evolving Human beings, as the evolving human beings according to the evolutionary plan of the "LORD OF THE FLAMES", have a higher goal to attain Higher Dimensional Heavenly world after their Physical Death, but these Tiny Elemental essences, who still do not possess a dense material physical form yet, thus have an opposite goal to somehow objectively gain a material form in the objectively manifested lowest Kingdom of nature in the Physical Plane of ASSIAH, which happens to be the objectively manifested Dense Mineral Kingdom, and through their instinct consciousness they thus firmly attach themselves, and thus correspond with those desire mind impulses of the Human Beings, which are related to the objects of the dense material world, and through such impulses they become more and more in tune with the magnetic energy vibrations of the dense physical plane of ASSIAH, which is also the daily life objective material world of the incarnated Human Beings.

Unfortunately most human beings are not aware of this underlying fact, that when the desire mind personality consciousness of an incarnated Human being is strongly polarized in the material world glamour, and thus having prominent animal desires of the lower mind involved in material objectivity of the physical plane world, he then becomes a prime candidate for these elemental essences to firmly take over the corresponding mental plane matter, which is present in his RUACH body, and which may thus keep him captive in bondage's of the next higher dimensional plane of YETZIRAH for a Very Long time after his physical death, thus slowing down his onward evolutionary progression, and "If and when", He might ever get Free from the bondage's of the RUACH body after its death, which happens due to having no more interest left in the material world desires, and then to proceed further to enter the Higher dimensional plane of BRIAH, to consciously live in His NESHAMAH Body, then Many a times in the Ensuing Struggle to free himself from his RUACH body, an Evolving Human Being, who earlier had His Desire Mind totally polarized in material world desires, may Permanently loose part of the ethereal mind matter, which originally belonged to his Personality's 'Desire Mind', which was related to his physical world's gained experiences, thus losing to these firmly clinging elemental essences, which gets entangled with their strong and overpowering magnetic instincts, and such a loss of "Mental Matter" to an evolving human being's consciousness is then unfortunately irreversible, which in the first place was meant to be fully recovered back, and thus totally filled with the Dense Material world experiences, by His Higher mind evolving "Solar or Soul Consciousness", which is stationed inside the Spherical Parameters of the higher mental plane's ethereal body, and thus constantly expanding in its Dimensional Size to finally reach the expanded "Point of Fullness", and such Fullness is Only acquired through the gained "SPIRITUAL EXPERIENCES" by the Human Beings in the 3 dense worlds, and this progressively expanding body of Spiritual experiences is known in the Hebrew language as the "CHAYAH" or in English as the "Causal Body".

After the full conscious expansion of the "CHAYAH" BODY through accumulation of various gained Spiritual Experiences, the spherical boundaries of "CHAYAH" body expands to its fullness, and then burst open to finally release the radiant "Solar Consciousness" commonly termed as the "SOUL", from the bonding limitations of the 3 dense dimensional planes of this Planet Earth, to consciously exist in its Bluish Hue Light Body, known in Hebrew as the "YECHIDAH" Body, thus Consciously existing as an Integral and extended part of the Collective Group Consciousness, which reflects the Desire MIND consciousness impulses of the unknowable "MOST HIGH", THE Supreme LORD GOD of the Entire Manifested Creation.

During the Long tenure of JACOB'S Descendants in the Land of Egypt, the Evolving Personalities of Many of the Children of Israel, being raised for 430 Years in the materially advanced culture of the Ancient Egypt, thus got affected due to the Glamorous Material Desires of their Lower Minds, which then became polarized in the Physical world's Material Glamour, and thus under the influence of the instinctual behavior of the elemental essences of their RUACH bodies, many of them Time and Again, thus foolishly forgot all the Powerful Miracles, which were consciously witnessed by them, and which their Great LORD repeatedly performed during their Deliverance from the Mighty Hands of Egypt, and under such deluded mind conditions they willfully rebelled and Constantly Grumbled against the Most Benevolent LORD GOD of their Forefathers.

When MOSES went up to the LORD - GOD upon the Holy Mountain, to receive HIS Commandments, they under the influence of the material world glamour quickly forgot their Holy Covenant, and to satisfy their Own Lower Mind Desire Urges, they made a Molten GOD in the Shape of a "CALF", an animal which possesses much less Mind Conscious attributes than any incarnated Human Being of this Planet Earth, regarding which the Holy Bible states:

Then the LORD spoke to MOSES, 'Go Down at once, for your People whom you brought up from the Land of Egypt, have CORRUPTED themselves. They have quickly turned aside from the Way, which "I" Commanded Them. They have made for themselves a Molten Calf, and have worshiped it, and Sacrificed to it, and said, "This is Your GOD, O ISRAEL, who brought you up from the Land of Egypt!"'

And the LORD Said to Moses, "I HAVE SEEN THIS PEOPLE, AND BEHOLD, THEY ARE AN '"OBSTINATE PEOPLE.'" [Exodus 32. 7, 8, 9.]

And AARON Said to them, "Tear Off The Gold Rings, Which are in the Ears of Your Wives, Your Sons, and Your Daughters, and Bring Them to Me." Then All the People Tore Off their Gold Rings, which were in their Ears, and Brought them to AARON. And He Took this from their Hand and fashioned it with a Graving Tool, and made it into a Molten CALF; and THEY SAID, "THIS IS YOUR GOD, O ISRAEL, WHO BROUGHT YOU UP FROM THE LAND OF EGYPT."
[Exodus 32. Verses 2,3,4.]

Part 39

Even though the Children of Israel, time and again in the Wilderness, willfully went against the commands of the LORD, their GOD, " known to them as "THE MOST HIGH", the most humble Servant of the LORD, 'MOSES', also himself being an upholder of the universal law of "Will to do Good", thus always pleaded on their behalf, so that He could make atonement for their grave SINS, regarding which the Holy Bible States:

'Then MOSES returned to the LORD, and Said, "Alas, this people has committed a great SIN, and they have made a GOD OF GOLD for themselves. But now, if THOU wilt, forgive their SIN – and if not, Please Blot Me Out from THY Book Which THOU hast written!"

And the LORD said to MOSES, "WHOEVER HAS SINNED AGAINST ME. "I" WILL BLOT HIM OUT OF MY BOOK. But Go Now, Lead the People, Where "I" Told You. Behold, My Angel shall Go before you; Nevertheless in the Day When "I" Punish, "I" will Punish them for their SIN."

Then the LORD Smote the People, because of what they did with the CALF, which AARON had made. [Exodus 32. Verses 31 to 35.]

Then the LORD spoke to MOSES, "Depart, Go up from here, YOU and the People whom you have brought up from the Land of Egypt, to The Land of which "I" Swore to ABRAHAM, ISAAC, and JACOB, Saying, 'TO YOUR DESCENDANTS "I" WILL GIVE IT.' And "I" will Send an Angel before You, and "I" will drive Out the Canaanite, the Amorite, the Hittite, the Perizzite, the Hivite, and the Jebusite.

Go up to a Land, Flowing with MILK and HONEY; for "I" WILL NOT GO UP IN YOUR MIDST, BECAUSE YOU ARE AN "OBSTINATE PEOPLE", LEST "I" DESTROY YOU ON THE WAY."

When the People heard this Sad Word, they went into Mourning, and None of Them put on His Ornaments. For the LORD has Said to MOSES, "Say to the Sons of Israel, 'YOU ARE AN OBSTINATE PEOPLE; SHOULD "I" GO UP IN YOUR MIDST FOR ONE MOMENT, "I" WOULD DESTROY YOU. Now therefore Put Off Your Ornaments from You, that "I" may know, WHAT "I" WILL DO WITH YOU.'

So the Sons of Israel stripped themselves of their Ornaments from Mount HOREB Onward. [Exodus 33. Verses 1 to 6.]

Now the Prime reason for LORD'S such Command about getting rid of their bodily Ornaments was to Consciously let the Desire Minds of the Children of Israel, get themselves FREED from Bondage's of the "Illusory World Glamour", as they still carried these 'Mental Bondage's' with them in the wilderness, even though their Physical Bodies were freed from the Bondage's and Afflictions of Egypt. It were these prized possessions, and the glamour of their Gold Ornaments, which made them SIN against the TRUE LORD – GOD, regarding which the Holy bible states:

'Now when the People saw that MOSES Delayed to Come Down from the Mountain, the People Assembled about AARON, and Said to Him, "Come, Make Us a GOD, Who will Go before Us; as for this MOSES, the Man Who brought Us up from the Land of Egypt, We do not Know What has Become of Him."

And AARON Said to them, "Tear Off The Gold Rings, Which are in the Ears of Your Wives, Your Sons, and Your Daughters, and Bring Them to Me." Then All the People Tore Off their Gold Rings, which were in their Ears, and Brought them to AARON. And He Took this from their Hand and fashioned it with a Graving Tool, and made it into a Molten CALF; and THEY SAID, "THIS IS YOUR GOD, O ISRAEL, WHO BROUGHT YOU UP FROM THE LAND OF EGYPT." [Exodus 32. Verses 1 to 4.]

Now After More than FIVE Centuries later, when with the Blessings of their LORD, the Children of Israel got Firmly established in the Promised Land, then after the Passing away of their Wisest King SOLOMON, who during HIS Life, made the Kingdom of Israel Glorious, and whom the LORD -GOD, Chose to be his SON as mentioned in Holy Bible, which states: "I WILL BE HIS FATHER, AND HE SHALL BE MY SON."[1 Chronicles 17.13.], the Children of Israel again Foolishly Acted, when they made JEROBOAM as the King of their Israel Tribes, except the TRIBE OF JUDAH, WHO FOLLOWED THEIR LORD - GOD, Regarding which the Holy Bible states:

'And it Came about when All Israel Heard that JEROBOAM had returned, that they Sent and called Him to the Assembly and made Him a King over ALL ISRAEL. """NONE""" BUT THE TRIBE OF JUDAH FOLLOWED THE

HOUSE OF DAVID.' [1 Kings 12. 20.]

And JEROBOAM Said in His Heart, "Now the Kingdom will Return to the House of David, If these People Go Up to Offer Sacrifices in the HOUSE OF THE LORD AT JERUSALEM, then the Heart of this People will 'RETURN TO THEIR LORD', Even to REHOBOAM King of JUDAH; and they will Kill Me and Return to REHOBOAM King of JUDAH." So the King CONSULTED, and made TWO GOLDEN CALVES, and He Said to them, "It is Too Much for You to Go Up to JERUSALEM; Behold YOUR GODS, O ISRAEL, THAT BROUGHT YOU UP FROM THE LAND OF EGYPT." And He Set One in BETHEL, And the Other He Put in DAN. NOW THIS THING BECAME A "SIN", FOR THE PEOPLE WENT TO WORSHIP BEFORE THE ONE, AS FAR AS DAN. [1 Kings 12. Verses 26 to 30.]

King Jeroboam consulted, and made 2 Golden Calves, and he said to them, "It is too much for you to go up to Jerusalem, behold your Gods, O Israel, that brought you up from the land of Egypt." And he set one in Bethel and the other he put in Dan [1 Kings 12.28,29].

Hebrew workers doing their chores in ancient Egypt

The Exodus of Hebrews from the land of Egypt

Part 40

Even though the LORD – GOD, the "MOST HIGH" made His chosen Servant MOSES as a 'GOD' for his brother AARON, as well as for the Pharaoh of Egypt, as mentioned in the Verses of the Holy Bible, many of the Children of Israel including some of His Close Associates, who All were led by MOSES, through the Grace of "MOST HIGH" out of the Land of Egypt, still questioned about His Such Close Relationship to the LORD.

And to receive the blissful Hidden Wisdom of these Narratives, by the Grace of the "MOST HIGH", let us closely examine some of the important Related Verses of the Holy Bible, with our Spiritual Eyes Fully Open, thus comprehending them as the imagined and Perceived Enlightened Live "THOUGHT FORMS", which will thus be envisioned by the Spiritual Eyes, and then will get vitally created in the Spiritual Matter of Our INNER OR HIGHER MIND, and thus firmly root themselves to further expand the Higher Dimensional Causal Body, which is known in Hebrew Language as the "CHAYAH".

Regarding the Humble MOSES, who being a Faithful and Humble Servant of the LORD, and regarding His Elevated status, which was Created and Bestowed upon Him by the Desired Will of the "MOST HIGH", to Exist as a "GOD" among Men, a Most Honorable Title among the Incarnated Human Beings, who are living upon the face of earth, about His Such Elevated Status, the Holy Bible Clearly States in the following Two Verses, in which the Great LORD is conversing with MOSES thus Mentioning Him and his Brother Aaron, which state:

"Moreover, He shall speak for YOU to the People; and it shall come about that He shall be as a MOUTH for You, and YOU shall be as "'GOD'" to Him. And you shall take in Your Hand this STAFF, with which you shall perform the Signs." [Exodus 4. 16, 17.]

Then the LORD Said to MOSES, 'SEE "I" MAKE YOU AS ""'"GOD"'"" TO PHARAOH, and Your brother AARON shall be Your Prophet'. [Exodus 7.1.]

And regarding People, Especially some of His Close Associates, still Doubting MOSES Personal Relationship with the LORD, and His such

Closeness to the "MOST HIGH", the Holy Bible in the following Verses Clearly States:

'Then MIRIAM and AARON Spoke AGAINST MOSES, because of the Cushite Woman, whom He had Married [for He had married a Cushite Woman]; and they Said, "Has the LORD Indeed Spoken Only through MOSES? Has He not SPOKEN through US as Well?" AND THE LORD HEARD IT.

[Now the Man MOSES was very HUMBLE, More than Any MAN, who was on the FACE of the EARTH]

And Suddenly, the LORD Said to MOSES and AARON and to MIRIAM, "YOU Three Come Out to the Tent of Meeting." So the three of them CAME OUT. Then the LORD Came Down in a PILLAR OF CLOUD, and STOOD at the Doorway of the Tent, and HE Called AARON and MIRIAM. When they both came forward, HE Said:

"HEAR NOW MY WORDS; IF THERE IS A PROPHET AMONG YOU, "I" THE LORD, SHALL MAKE MYSELF KNOWN TO HIM IN A VISION. "I" SHALL SPEAK WITH HIM IN A DREAM. NOT SO, WITH MY SERVANT "'MOSES'", HE IS FAITHFUL IN "'ALL'" MY HOUSEHOLD; WITH HIM "I" SPEAK MOUTH TO MOUTH, EVEN OPENLY, AND NOT IN DARK SAYINGS, AND HE BEHOLDS "'THE FORM OF THE LORD'". WHY THEN WERE YOU NOT "'AFRAID'" TO SPEAK AGAINST MY SERVANT MOSES?"

So the Anger of the LORD Burned Against Them, and HE Departed. But when the CLOUD had withdrawn from over the Tent, behold, MIRIAM was LEPROUS, as White as Snow. As AARON turned toward MIRIAM, behold she was Leprous. Then AARON Said to 'MOSES', "OH MY LORD, I Beg you, do not ACCOUNT THIS SIN to US, in which we have acted FOOLISHLY and in which WE HAVE SINNED, OH Do not let her be Like ONE DEAD, Whose Flesh is Half Eaten away, when He comes from His Mother's Womb!"

And MOSES Cried Out to the LORD, Saying, "Oh GOD, Heal Her, I Pray!' But LORD Said to MOSES, "If Her Father had but SPIT in Her Face, Would She Not Bear Her SHAME for SEVEN DAYS? Let Her be Shut Up for Seven Days Outside the Camp, and Afterward She may be Received Again."

So MIRIAM was Shut Up outside the Camp for Seven Days, and the

People did not Move On until MIRIAM was received again. [Numbers 12. Verses 1 to 15.]

In the above mentioned Verses, when We examine them through the depth of our Spiritual Eyes, we can clearly see, that finally the Inner Eyes of Aaron, the brother of MOSES also Got Opened during this Episode, regarding the Most Elevated Status of MOSES, which was Bestowed upon by the MOST HIGH Himself for His Faithfulness, and then at that Particular Moment, He addressed MOSES as His LORD, when according to these Verses He Said to MOSES "OH MY LORD, I Beg you, do not ACCOUNT THIS SIN to US, in which we have acted FOOLISHLY and in which WE HAVE SINNED."

But after this above mentioned episode, when LORD told MOSES to send some Spies to the LAND OF CANAAN, He then faithfully following the LORD'S Command, sent the Heads of the Sons of Israel along with JOSHUA, the Son of NUN, and CALEB, the Son of JEPHUNNEH, and with their findings, they returned back to the Camp at the end of forty days. But the men, who had gone out with Joshua and Caleb, although they certainly saw the fruitful land of Milk and Honey, as promised by the MOST HIGH, 'All of Them' except Joshua and Caleb, still gave out a Very Bad Report of their findings to the Sons of Israel, Saying, that the People Who Lived in the Land were STRONG and of Great Sizes, and thus they were Not able to Go AGAINST them, which caused the Overwhelmed People to REBEL AGAIN against the LORD, and His Faithful Servant MOSES, regarding which the Holy Bible States:

"And All the Sons of Israel GRUMBLED AGAINST MOSES and AARON; And the WHOLE CONGREGATION Said to Them, "Would that we have Died in the Land of Egypt! Or would that we had died in this Wilderness! And why is the LORD bringing us into this Land, to fall by the Sword? Our Wives and Our Little Ones will become Plunder; would it NOT be BETTER for us to RETURN to Egypt?"

So they said to One Another, 'Let us appoint a LEADER and return to Egypt.' Then MOSES and AARON fell on their faces in the Presence of All the Assembly of the Congregation. And Joshua, the son of Nun and Caleb the Son of Jephunneh, of those who spied out the land, tore their clothes; and they spoke to All the Congregation of the Sons of Israel, saying, 'The Land which we passed through to Spy out is an Exceedingly Good Land. If the LORD is Pleased with us, then HE will bring us into this land, and give it to us – A Land Which Flows with Milk and Honey. ONLY DO NOT REBEL AGAINST THE LORD; and do not fear the people of the land, for they shall be our prey. Their Protection has been removed from them, and the LORD IS WITH US; DO NOT FEAR THEM."

But the Congregation said to STONE THEM WITH STONES. Then the GLORY OF THE LORD APPEARED in the Tent of Meeting to ALL the Sons of Israel. And the LORD Said to MOSES, ""HOW LONG WILL THIS PEOPLE SPURN ME? AND HOW LONG WILL THEY NOT BELIEVE IN ME, DESPITE ALL THE SIGNS WHICH "I" HAVE PERFORMED IN THEIR MIDST? "I" WILL SMITE THEM WITH PESTILENCE AND DISPOSSESS THEM, AND "I" WILL MAKE YOU INTO A GREAT NATION, GREATER AND MIGHTIER THAN THEY." [Numbers 14. Verses 2 to 12.]

And the LORD Spoke to MOSES and AARON, Saying:

"HOW LONG SHALL "I" BEAR WITH THIS "EVIL" CONGREGATION, WHO ARE GRUMBLING AGAINST ME? "I" HAVE HEARD THE COMPLAINTS OF THE SONS OF ISRAEL, WHICH THEY ARE MAKING AGAINST ME. SAY TO THEM, "'AS 'I' LIVE, SAYS THE LORD, JUST AS YOU HAVE SPOKEN IN MY HEARING, SO "I" WILL SURELY DO TO YOU; YOUR CORPSES SHALL FALL IN THE WILDERNESS, EVEN ALL YOUR NUMBERED MEN, ACCORDING TO YOUR COMPLETE NUMBER FROM TWENTY YEARS OLD AND UPWARD, WHO HAVE GRUMBLED AGAINST ME. SURELY YOU SHALL NOT COME INTO THE LAND, IN WHICH "I" SWORE TO SETTLE YOU, EXCEPT CALEB, THE SON OF JEPHUNNEH, AND JOSHUA, THE SON OF NUN. YOUR CHILDREN, HOWEVER, WHOM YOU SAID WOULD BECOME A PREY – "I" WILL BRING THEM IN, AND THEY SHALL KNOW THE LAND WHICH YOU HAVE REJECTED. BUT AS FOR YOU, YOUR CORPSES SHALL FALL IN THIS WILDERNESS. AND YOUR SONS SHALL BE SHEPHERDS FOR FORTY YEARS IN THE WILDERNESS, AND THEY SHALL SUFFER FOR YOUR UNFAITHFULNESS, UNTIL YOUR CORPSES LIE IN THE WILDERNESS.

ACCORDING TO THE NUMBER OF DAYS, WHICH YOU SPIED OUT THE LAND, FORTY DAYS, FOR EVERY DAY YOU SHALL BEAR YOUR GUILT "'A YEAR'", EVEN FORTY YEARS; AND YOU SHALL KNOW """"MY OPPOSITION""""".

'I' THE LORD, HAVE SPOKEN, "'SURELY'" THIS 'I' WILL DO TO ALL THIS "'EVIL CONGREGATION'", WHO ARE GATHERED TOGETHER AGAINST ME. IN THIS WILDERNESS THEY SHALL BE DESTROYED, AND THERE THEY

SHALL DIE."

As for the Men, whom MOSES sent to Spy out the Land, and who returned and Made All the Congregation GRUMBLE Against Him, by bringing Out a Bad Report Concerning the Land, even those Men, who brought out the Very Bad Report of the Land, DIED BY 'PLAGUE' before the LORD. But JOSHUA, the Son of NUN, and CALEB, the Son of JEPHUNNEH remained ALIVE out of Those Men, Who went to Spy out the Land. [Numbers 14. Verses 26 to 38.]

Then the GLORY OF THE LORD APPEARED in the Tent of Meeting to ALL the Sons of Israel. And the LORD Said to MOSES, ""'HOW LONG WILL THIS PEOPLE SPURN ME? AND HOW LONG WILL THEY NOT BELIEVE IN ME, DESPITE ALL THE SIGNS WHICH "I" HAVE PERFORMED IN THEIR MIDST? "I" WILL SMITE THEM WITH PESTILENCE AND DISPOSSESS THEM, AND "I" WILL MAKE YOU INTO A GREAT NATION, GREATER AND MIGHTIER THAN THEY."
[Numbers 14. Verses 10,11,12]

While the MEAT was still between their Teeth, before it was chewed, the
ANGER of the LORD was KINDLED against the People, and the LORD STRUCK
the People with a VERY SEVERE PLAGUE. So the name of that place was called
KIBROTH – HATTAAVAH, because there they buried the People, WHO HAD
BEEN GREEDY. [Numbers 11. Verses 33,34]

The Secret of the Breast Plate

Part 41

Most of the Chosen People of God, Who Since ancient times have been known to the Sons of Israel as the "Enlightened Prophets" of the "MOST HIGH", were Consciously aware of this Hidden fact that the LORD God is really not interested in the Burnt offering's or Animal Sacrifices, as their 'BLOOD" IS IDENTIFIED WITH their Vital 'LIFE', as HE Instead Preferred"Milk as Honey" as the Proper Spiritual food for Divine Enlightenment, as HE mentioned about them Time and Again in the "Holy Bible" as the inherent Quality of Lands, which HE referred to the Sons of Israel as their Promised Land.

The Statute of Animal Sacrifice and Burnt offerings was established by the LORD for Two Main reasons, the First being that the Sons of Israel regularly craved for MEAT, to which they were used to as their daily diet, during their Long Stay in Egypt, and He saw them daily Grumbling and Crying about it in Wilderness as repeatedly mentioned in various chapters of Holy Bible starting First with the "Chapter of Exodus", which states:

'And the Whole Congregation of the Sons of Israel Grumbled against Moses and Aaron in the Wilderness. And the Sons of Israel said to them, "Would that we had died by the LORD'S hand in the land of Egypt, when we Sat by the POTS OF "'MEAT'", when we ate Bread to the Full; for you have brought us out into this Wilderness to kill this whole assembly with hunger.' [Exodus 16. 2, 3.]

And the Second reason, which is unknown to many Human Beings, is that the Invisible "Demons" were in fact the So called Various Animal Shaped Gods and Goddesses of Egypt, who being deceitful thus preferred to be displayed in the Shape of Lower Conscious Animals, and then with Grandeur Rites, they were thus Worshiped by the Human beings, thus making a Mockery of their "Evolutionary Higher Conscious" status, which is far superior to all Animals, which exist in the entire Animal Kingdom, as well as the Mockery of their Creator Lord of the Universe, commonly referred to as the MOST HIGH, Whom they Willfully Back- Stabbed, who as mentioned in the very first chapter of Genesis of the Holy Bible, in its Verse 27, delightfully created Humans at the Very start of Consciousness Expansion upon this Planet Earth, in HIS OWN IMAGE.

Out of the So called Egyptian Gods, the Main Important gods were Known as the God Ptah and Goddess Hathor, which were depicted in the Shape of a Male OX and a Female Cow, while the Important God Amon was depicted as a Ram or a Goat, and the God of Wisdom Thoth, and also the God Horus, both were depicted in the shape of birds, while later on Thoth was Replaced by the Shape of a Baboon, and to these so called Gods and Goddesses, the People of Egypt, regularly Sacrificed their domestic animals, and then later Eat their Sacrificed flesh, but many of them instead of eating well-done cooked meat, preferred to eat their grilled "Rare Meat" oozing out with their Blood.

And regarding the "Demonic Entities and Beings", who generally being INVISIBLE to the Incarnated Human Beings, Mainly Live and thus SURVIVE by working with the Magnetic Vibrations of the Earth, which are commonly referred to as their Abilities of INSTINCTS, just as all the Migratory Birds and the Whales also use these Magnetic Impulses of the Earth for their yearly Migrations.

These "Partial Conscious Live Entities" who are known to the Human Beings as the "Undead" or the "Demon's", who mostly became like this "Awful state of conscious Existence", by Willfully Choosing the Material World Plane "Glamour" during their incarnated physical lives upon this Planet Earth, and thus during their Physical Life duration's, they went Astray from the Established Evolutionary Spiritual Plan of the LORD, and then after their Silver cord of Animating vitality was Severed from their Physical bodies, they in their such Confused State of "DYING CONSCIOUS", some of their Desire Mind "ESSENCES", got Partially stuck to their "Putrefying Body Shells", due to their unfulfilled Material World desires. And they then thus got trapped and illegally captured by the Practicing "BLACK MAGICIANS", who are themselves eternally 'DOOMED', so they can willfully misuse them as their front stooges and helping hands in their own illegal and deceitful agendas, which are thus openly carried out through them as well as with the assisted help of their counterpart incarnated Human Beings, living incarnated upon the dense physical plane, who are the Noted Members of their established 'Secret Societies', who also being their 'FAITHFUL followers, thus then become their Visible FRONTS in all such Illegal actions upon this Planet Earth, in the name of "POLITICS", and all Such Maleficent Actions are commonly not noticed by the evolving general public, who are innocently immersed in this "Illusory Matrix" to carry on their daily lives just for their everyday survival, and For their Such Illegal Services, these

Invisible and Visible Black Magicians along with the Invisible Demons then "Well Place" their Doomed Followers upon the "Chosen Positions" of the Human Societies, as the GOVERNING LEADERS of the evolving Human Race, to carry on Unnoticed their "INVOLUTIONARY ACTIVITIES" instead of Proper Evolution in the MATRIX of the dense plane material world, and are thus themselves get Doomed FOREVER from any Further Spiritual Evolution.

The Wise "'Prophet King Solomon'", the Chosen Son of LORD, also Warned All Children of Israel in His Holy Writings, to Timely Wake Up from this Illusory "World Glamour", before their animating "Silver Cord" was Broken, regarding which the Holy Bible states:

"Remember HIM, before the SILVER CORD is Broken, and the Golden Bowl is Crushed, the Pitcher by the Well is Shattered, and the Wheel at the Cistern is Crushed; then the Dust will Return to the Earth as it was, and the SPIRIT will Return to GOD, Who Gave It."

"Vanity of Vanities," says the Preacher, "All is Vanity!"[Ecclesiastes 12. 6, 7, 8.]

These Invisible "Demons" thus PREFER the Bodies of Animals, as well as those of "Spiritually Less Evolved" Human Beings, who like themselves are living mostly through "Magnetic Instincts", thus similarly consciously polarized in Material World Glamour during their short lived Incarnated Lives, and are constantly using their Instincts, referred to as their WANT'S, which are related to the "Feelings and Sensations of Worldly Desire's", and they being unaware about the Evolutionary Plan of the "MOST HIGH", thus Unknowingly, allow these invisible "Demons" to act out their Illegal Agendas through their incarnated form bodies, which are thus willfully carried out against the Established Evolutionary Plan of the MOST HIGH, in the dense Worlds of this Planet Earth, and in this way their evolving consciousness thus easily correspond to the Deformed and Mutated consciousness of these "Demonic Entities and Beings".

This Hidden aspect of Animal Consciousness, is clearly stated in the Holy Bible, when much later JESUS CHRIST, the Chosen Son of God, Encountered the DEMONS, and knowing full well that they were DOOMED PARTIAL CONSCIOUS EXISTENCES, He then as per their wishes, Cast them out when they Clearly told Him to cast them out into the

Animal Herd, regarding which the Holy Bible States:
'And When HE had come to the other side into country of the
Gadarenes, two men who were Demon- Possessed met HIM as they
were coming out of the Tombs; they were so exceedingly Violent that
No One could Pass by that road. And behold, they cried out, saying,
"WHAT do we have to do with You, SON OF GOD? Have YOU come to
TORMENT us BEFORE THE TIME?"

Now there was at a Distance from there, a Herd of many Swine Feeding.
And the Demons began to Entreat HIM, Saying, "If YOU are going to
Cast Us Out, Send Us into the Herd of Swine." And HE Said to Them, Be
– Gone! And they came out, and went into the Swine, and Behold, the
whole Herd rushed down the Steep Banks into the Sea, and Perished in
the Waters. [Matthew 8. Verses 28 to 32.]

So during MOSES time, THE MOST HIGH LORD – GOD, to let the Ignorant
Children of Israel know, that ALL ANIMALS OF THIS PLANET EARTH,
WHO LIVE BY MERE INSTINCT ABILITIES, WHICH ARE GOVERNED BY
EARTH'S MAGNETIC FREQUENCY VIBRATIONS, HAVE LESS EVOLVED
CONSCIOUSNESS THAN All HUMAN BEINGS, WHO USE THEIR
INDIVIDUALIZED HIGHER MIND ABILITIES, THROUGH THE USE OF
COSMIC ENERGY "ELECTRIC" IMPULSES, AND FOR THIS VERY BASIC
REASON, THESE ANIMAL SHAPED DEPICTIONS, WHICH ARE TERMED
BY EGYPTIANS AS THE "GODS AND GODDESSES" TO EXIST IN THEIR
ELABORATE HUGE TEMPLES, AS THE HUMAN CREATED MOLTEN SHAPED
FORMS AND CARVED STATUES, THUS CANNOT BE THEIR "GODS
AND GODDESSES".

The Most high knowing full well, that it was very hard for the children of
Israel NOT TO CRAVE THE DESIRES OF EATING 'MEAT", thus established
the laws pertaining to the Slaughter of Animals, which they were earlier
performing as Sacrifices to the so called GODS in the Land of Egypt,
regarding which the Holy Bible states:

'Then the LORD Spoke to MOSES , Saying, "Speak to AARON and to His
Sons, and to All the Sons of Israel, and Say to Them, This is What the
LORD has Commanded, Saying, 'ANY MAN FROM THE HOUSE OF ISRAEL,
WHO SLAUGHTERS AN OX, OR A LAMB, OR A GOAT IN THE CAMP, OR
WHO SLAUGHTERS IT OUTSIDE THE CAMP, AND HAS NOT BROUGHT
IT TO THE DOORWAY OF THE TENT OF MEETING, TO PRESENT IT AS
AN OFFERING TO THE LORD, BEFORE THE TABERNACLE OF THE LORD,

"'BLOOD-GUILTINESS'" IS TO BE RECKONED TO THAT MAN. HE HAS SHED BLOOD, AND THAT MAN SHALL BE 'CUT OFF' FROM AMONG HIS PEOPLE.

THE REASON IS, SO THAT THE SONS OF ISRAEL MAY BRING THEIR SACRIFICES, WHICH THEY WERE SACRIFICING IN THE OPEN FIELD, THAT THEY MAY BRING THEM IN TO THE LORD, AT THE DOORWAY OF THE TENT OF MEETING TO THE PRIEST, AND SACRIFICE THEM AS "'SACRIFICES OF PEACE OFFERINGS'" TO THE LORD. [Leviticus 17. Verses 1 to 5.]

Regarding their earlier way of Sacrificing to the so called Animal Shaped Gods and Goddesses of Egypt, primarily the GOAT and the CALF – BULL shaped one's, the LORD clearly defined them as the "DEMON'S" in the following Verse, regarding which the Holy Bible States:

"AND THEY SHALL NO LONGER SACRIFICE THEIR SACRIFICES TO THE ""GOAT DEMONS"", WITH WHICH THEY PLAY "'THE HARLOT'". THIS SHALL BE A PERMANENT STATUTE TO THEM, THROUGHOUT THEIR GENERATIONS." [Leviticus 17. 7.]

Also All those incarnated human beings of this Planet, who are living in their physical form bodies, and might be well educated from Well – Known Civilized Universities of the Physical World, and May be Well Established upon the Top Posts in the Human Society, but in reality without their knowledge, they May be "Possessed" by these "Invisible Demons", and thus Crave to drink Animal Blood, and like to Eat their "Rare Meats" still drenched in Blood, regarding them the Holy Bible states:

'And any Man from the House of Israel, or from the Aliens, who Sojourn among them, WHO EATS ANY BLOOD, "'I'" will Set My Face Against that Person WHO EATS BLOOD, and will Cut Him Off from among His People.

FOR THE LIFE OF THE FLESH IS IN THE 'BLOOD', and "I" have given it to You on the Altar, to make Atonement for your SOULS; for IT IS THE BLOOD BY REASON OF THE LIFE, THAT MAKES ATONEMENT."

For as for the LIFE OF ALL FLESH, ITS 'BLOOD" IS IDENTIFIED WITH ITS 'LIFE'. Therefore "I" Said to the Sons of Israel, 'YOU ARE NOT TO EAT THE BLOOD OF ANY FLESH, FOR THE LIFE OF ALL FLESH IS ITS BLOOD; Whosoever Eats it, shall be Cut Off.' [Leviticus 17. 10, 11, 14.]

Spiraling ladder invisioned by JACOB. "JACOB came to a Certain Place and Spent the Night there, because the Sun had set; and He took one of the Stones of the Place and Put it under His Head, and Lay Down in that Place. And He had a Dream, and Behold, A LADDER WAS SET ON THE EARTH, WITH ITS TOP REACHING TO HEAVEN; AND BEHOLD, THE ANGELS OF GOD WERE ASCENDING AND DESCENDING ON IT. And Behold, the LORD Stood above it and Said, "'I AM THE LORD, THE GOD OF YOUR FATHER ABRAHAM, AND THE GOD OF ISAAC; THE LAND ON WHICH YOU LIE, I WILL GIVE IT TO YOU, AND YOUR DESCENDANTS." [Genesis 28. Verses 11,12,13]

The Unknowable Lord – God of the Universe, from whose Desire Mind's Vital Energy Reflections was first formed, a Centrally located Fiery Glowing "Point", known in Hebrew Language as the "Ein Soph", All Visible and Invisible Manifestations of the Universe were thus started with the VIBRATIONS OF HIS DESIRE MIND VITAL ENERGY, existing as the Vital Energy Frequency Vibrations, to subjectively and objectively start the Grand Experiment of Conscious Expansion, in its Unfathomable and Huge Radius of Influence, thus originating the three Basic Types of Universal Motions in the Vital Ethereal Space, commonly known as the Spiral, Cyclic, and Circular Motions, which caused the Differentiation's in the Unfathomable Cosmic Space, which is Composed of Vital Ethereal Matter having the full potential of Vital "Mind Consciousness" Growth, and the Dense matter thus Created, Composed of Dense or Slow Frequency Vibrations of Vital Cosmic Ether, thus manifested as becoming the Densest Matter in the Enclosed Outer Spherical side, and the Rare Matter having Higher Frequency Vibrations, thus brought in the rarer manifestations of frequency Vibrations, the differentiated Rarer or Spiritual Matter toward the Inside peripheries, just like the Churning Motion of the Milk Separates Butter from Milk, and thus brought in those Dense and Light Segregated manifestation's, which are the so called "Differentiated Dimensional Spheres', which are known in Hebrew Language as the "Sefira's, Sephora's or the Sephirot's".

And then in these Differentiated Dimensions, the various Visible and Invisible Hierarchical Orders were also Subjectively and Objectively Manifested, by the further action of HIS DESIRE MIND ENERGY, which is known to a Handful of HIS CHOSEN ONE'S as the "EVENTUATION PROCESS", to exist as various orders of Hierarchical Entitles and Beings, to Gradually Experience these differentiated Dimensional Spheres of Existence, and thus Consciously or Unconsciously exist in them, and Periodically and thus Gradually raising their indwelling consciousness toward Higher Degrees of their Segmented portions of "ETHEREAL SPIRIT", which is attained through the actions of Cyclic Motion supported by the Circular and Spiral motions, and thus following the Gradual Steps of the EVOLUTIONARY LADDER for their required Consciousness Expansion, as per LORD'S EVOLUTIONARY PLAN and Purpose based upon the Universal Law of "WILL TO DO GOOD", and this

"Evolutionary Ladder" was also Envisioned by the "PATRIARCH JACOB", according to His Own Comprehension of this "Incomprehensible Divine Fact", who was later named ISRAEL by the Grace of MOST HIGH, regarding which the Holy Bible states:

"Then JACOB departed from Beersheba, and went toward Haran. And He came to a Certain Place and Spent the Night there, because the Sun had set; and He took one of the Stones of the Place and Put it under His Head, and Lay Down in that Place.

And He had a Dream, and Behold, A LADDER WAS SET ON THE EARTH, WITH ITS TOP REACHING TO HEAVEN; AND BEHOLD, THE ANGELS OF GOD WERE ASCENDING AND DESCENDING ON IT.

And Behold, the LORD Stood above it and Said, "'I AM THE LORD, THE GOD OF YOUR FATHER ABRAHAM, AND THE GOD OF ISAAC; THE LAND ON WHICH YOU LIE, I WILL GIVE IT TO YOU, AND YOUR DESCENDANTS.

Your Descendants shall also be like the Dust of the Earth, and you shall Spread Out to the West, and to the East, and to the North, and to the South; and IN YOU, AND IN YOUR DESCENDANTS, SHALL ALL THE FAMILIES OF THE EARTH, BE BLESSED.

And Behold, I AM WITH YOU, and will Keep You, Wherever You GO, and will Bring You Back to This Land, for "I" WILL NOT LEAVE YOU, UNTIL "I" HAVE DONE, WHAT "I" HAVE PROMISED YOU.'"

Then JACOB Awoke from His Sleep, and Said, 'Surely the LORD is in This Place, AND I DID NOT KNOW IT.' And He was Afraid and Said, 'How Awesome is This Place! THIS IS NONE OTHER THAN THE "HOUSE OF GOD", AND THIS IS THE "GATE OF HEAVEN".

So JACOB rose Early in the Morning, and Took the STONE, that He had put under His Head, and Set it up as a PILLAR, and Poured Oil on its Top. And He called the Name of that Place 'BETHEL'; However, Previously the Name of the City had been 'LUZ'. [Genesis 28. Verses 10 to 19.]

But just after little more than Five Centuries later, the descendants of JACOB 'conveniently" forgot their 'Holy Covenant' with the LORD, which was Greatly Revered by All their Patriarch's, even More than THEIR Own LIVES, when their Chosen King JEROBOAM, Who was Chosen by the Rebellious Tribes of Israel to Rule them instead of their King REHOBOAM, the Son of Wise King Solomon, WRONGFULLY INSTITUTED the Worship of the molten form of a 'GOLDEN CALF' at the Holy Place of BETHEL, which their ancestor Patriarch very Well Understood after Envisioning it as the Holy Place which was "NONE OTHER THAN THE "HOUSE OF GOD", AND THE "GATE OF HEAVEN", regarding which the Holy Bible States:

'So the King Consulted and made Two Golden Calves, and He Said to Them, "It is Too Much for You to go Up to JERUSALEM; Behold YOUR GODS, 'O ISRAEL' THAT BROUGHT YOU UP FROM THE LAND OF EGYPT."

And He Set One in 'BETHEL', and the Other He Put in Dan. Now This Thing became a SIN, for the People went to Worship before the One, as far as DAN. And He made Houses on High Places, and made Priests from among all the People, who were not the 'SONS'S of LEVI'. And Jeroboam Instituted a Feast in the EIGHTH MONTH ON THE FIFTEENTH DAY OF THE MONTH, Like the Feast which is in JUDAH, and He went up to the ALTAR; thus He did in 'BETHEL', SACRIFICING TO THE CALVES, WHICH HE HAD MADE. And He went up to the ALTAR, which He had made in 'BETHEL' on the Fifteenth Day in the Eighth Month, EVEN IN THE MONTH, WHICH HE HAD 'DEVISED' IN HIS OWN HEART; AND HE INSTITUTED A FEAST FOR THE SONS OF ISRAEL, AND WENT UP TO THE ALTAR TO BURN INCENSE. [1 Kings Verses 28 to 33.]

But for Such a Heinous Crime, which was WILLFULLY COMMITTED BY JEROBOAM and His Subjects, THE SONS OF ISRAEL AGAINST 'THE 'MOST HIGH', THE 'GREAT LORD' , Who then WARNED THEM through HIS 'MAN OF GOD', a Holy Title with Which the Holy Bible first referred to PROPHET 'ELIJAH, THE TISHBITE' and thus MANY DO NOT KNOW that it was the Young Prophet "ELIJAH" known as the 'Man of God', Who Was Sent By God from JUDAH to Warn JEROBOAM at the Altar of BETHEL, and afterwards PROPHET ELIJAH appeared again about 60 years later, to Similarly Warn the King AHAB of ISRAEL, (King Jeroboam ruled 22 Years over Israel [1Kings 14.20], King NADAB Son of Jeroboam ruled 2 Years over Israel [1Kings 15.25], King BAASHA ruled 24 Years over Israel [1Kings 15.33], King OMRI ruled 12 Years over Israel, of which 6 Years at Tirzah, and 6 Years at SAMARIA, A New City He Built on a Hill named after its Owner named SHEMER, from whom He Bought the Hill for Two Talents of Silver[1 Kings 1 Kings 16. 23,24], who was followed by his Son AHAB to become the King over Israel, and thus the Time Passed from the King Jeroboam to King Ahab was a total of 60 Years [22+2+24+12 = 60 Years]), and after Jeroboam, the Later Kings of Israel also Continued to do the Evil Abominations to their LORD – GOD, THEIR "MOST HIGH", and Each of these Successive Kings of Israel Acted More and More Wickedly than their Predecessors, and thus Made the ENTIRE ISRAEL SIN.

Regarding the Warning given to King Jeroboam, by the MAN OF GOD, the Holy Bible States:

'Now Behold, there came a "MAN of GOD" from JUDAH to BETHEL BY THE 'WORD OF THE LORD', while Jeroboam was standing by the Altar to Burn Incense. And He Cried Against the ALTAR by the WORD of the LORD, and Said, ""O ALTAR, ALTAR, THUS SAYS THE LORD, """BEHOLD, A SON SHALL BE BORN TO THE HOUSE OF DAVID, JOSIAH BY NAME; AND ON YOU HE SHALL SACRIFICE, 'THE PRIESTS OF THE HIGH PLACES, WHO BURN INCENSE ON YOU', AND "'HUMAN BONES"' SHALL BE BURNED ON YOU.""'

Then He gave a Sign the Same Day, Saying, "This is the Sign which the LORD has Spoken, "'Behold, the Altar shall be Split Apart, and the Ashes which are on it, shall be Poured Out."'"

Now it came about, when the King Heard the Saying of the 'MAN of GOD', which He CRIED AGAINST the 'ALTAR in BETHEL', that JEROBOAM Stretched out His Hand from the Altar, Saying, "SEIZE HIM". But His Hand, which He stretched out against Him Dried Up, So that He could not draw it Back to Himself. The Altar was also Split Apart, and the Ashes were Poured Out from the Altar, according to the Sign, which the 'MAN of GOD' had given by the """WORD of the LORD"". And the King answered and Said to the 'MAN of GOD', "Please Entreat the LORD YOUR GOD, and Pray for Me, that My Hand may be restored to Me." So the "MAN of GOD" Entreated the LORD, and the King's Hand was restored to Him, and it became as it was before.

Then the King Said to the 'MAN of GOD', "Come Home with Me, and refresh yourself, and I will give you a Reward." But the 'MAN of GOD' Said to the King, " IF YOU WERE TO GIVE ME HALF YOUR HOUSE, I WOULD NOT GO WITH YOU, NOR WOULD I EAT BREAD OR DRINK WATER IN THIS PLACE. FOR SO IT WAS COMMANDED ME BY THE WORD OF 'LORD', SAYING, "'YOU SHALL NOT EAT NO BREAD, NOR DRINK

WATER, NOR RETURN BY THE WAY WHICH YOU CAME.'''

So He Went another Way, and did not return by the Way which He Came to BETHEL. [1 Kings 13. Verses 1 to 10.]

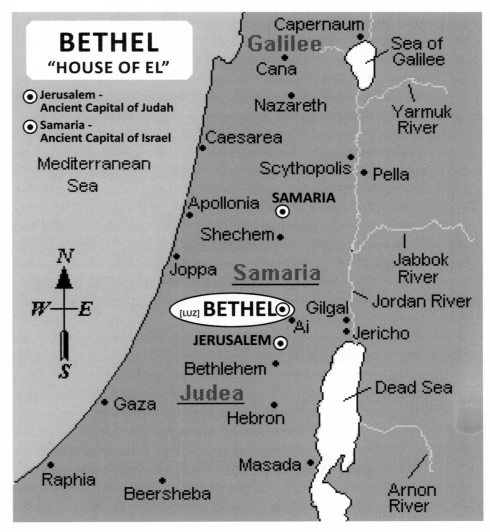

Then JACOB Awoke from His Sleep, and Said, 'Surely the LORD is in This Place, AND I DID NOT KNOW IT.' And He was Afraid and Said, 'How Awesome is This Place! THIS IS NONE OTHER THAN THE "HOUSE OF GOD", AND THIS IS THE "GATE OF HEAVEN". So JACOB rose Early in the Morning, and Took the STONE, that He had put under His Head, and Set it up as a PILLAR, and Poured Oil on its Top. And He called the Name of that Place 'BETHEL'; However, Previously the Name of the City had been 'LUZ'. [Genesis 28. Verses 16 to 19]

Tzitzit Tassel

During the time of Exodus, the Children of Israel, whose Ancestors known as the famous Patriarchs, who themselves were Chosen by the Grace of LORD, and with whom the LORD also made HIS Holy Covenant, their Descendants, who were delivered by His Grace from their Afflictions in Egypt, were Again and again breaking their Holy Covenant with their LORD - GOD, by Continuous Rebelling Against His Commands, and also Constantly Grumbling against the LORD'S Humble Servant MOSES, and His Brother AARON, then LORD understanding their "'Shortness of Memory'" regarding the Various Miracles, which they all Witnessed but easily and Conveniently Forgot, the LORD then Commanded Moses to tell all the Children of Israel, to make Tassels on the Corners of their Garments, so that it may HELP them to remember His Commandments, and also put upon these Tassels a CORD of BLUE Color, a Color which since ancient times, has been known by all the Enlightened Seers and Sages as the Spiritual Color representing the "HIGHER MIND'S VITAL CONSCIOUSNESS", as the Hidden Secret of the Blue Color is, that its Vital Vibration Frequencies represents the "'Devotional Feelings of Reverence'", which are Primarily related to the understanding of the Religious Texts, and thus these Faith related "Devotional Thought Forms" are reverently generated, being geared toward the unknowable "MOST HIGH", who is also the "'"'GOD OF THE SPIRITS OF ALL FLESH"'"'. Regarding this Holy Command of Tassels, the Holy Bible States:

'The LORD also Spoke to MOSES, Saying, "'Speak to the Sons of Israel, and Tell them, that they shall make for themselves Tassels on the Corners of their Garments THROUGHOUT THEIR GENERATIONS, and that they shall Put on the Tassel of Each Corner, A CORD OF BLUE.

AND IT SHALL BE A TASSEL FOR YOU TO LOOK AT, AND REMEMBER ALL THE COMMANDMENTS OF THE LORD, SO AS TO DO THEM AND 'NOT FOLLOW AFTER YOUR OWN HEART AND YOUR OWN EYES', AFTER WHICH YOU PLAYED THE HARLOT, IN ORDER THAT YOU MAY REMEMBER TO DO "ALL MY COMMANDMENTS", AND BE HOLY TO YOUR GOD. "'I AM THE LORD YOUR GOD'", WHO BROUGHT YOU OUT FROM THE LAND OF EGYPT TO BE 'YOUR GOD'; I AM THE LORD YOUR GOD.'" [Numbers 15. Verses 37 to 41.]

But the Holy Bible further mentions, that even with Such Clear Mandated Instructions from the LORD, the Children of Israel were still unable to mend their Rebellious Ways, and thus were unable to control their Negative Mind Impulses, which were related to their Lower Mind Desires, commonly known as the Animal Mind Instincts, regarding which the Holy Bible States:

'Now KORAH, the Son of IZHAR, the Son of KOHATH, the Son of LEVI, with DATHAN and ABIRAM, the Sons of ELIAB, and ON the Son of PELETH, Sons of REUBEN, Took Action, and they Rose Up before MOSES, together with Some of the Sons of Israel, Two Hundred and Fifty Leaders of the Congregation, Chosen in the Assembly, Men of Renown. And they Assembled Together Against MOSES and AARON, and Said to Them, "YOU HAVE GONE FAR ENOUGH, For ALL the Congregation are Holy, Every One of Them, and the LORD is in their Midst; SO WHY DO YOU EXALT YOURSELF ABOVE THE ASSEMBLY OF THE LORD?"

When MOSES heard this, He Fell on His Face; and He Spoke to KORAH and all His Company, Saying, "Tomorrow Morning, the LORD will Show Who is His, and Who is Holy, and will bring Him Near to HIMSELF; Even the One Whom HE will Choose, HE will bring near to HIMSELF. Do this; Take Censers for Yourselves, KORAH and All Your Company, and Put FIRE in them, and Lay Incense upon them in the Presence of the LORD Tomorrow; and the Man whom the LORD Chooses, shall be the One Who is Holy. YOU HAVE GONE FAR ENOUGH, YOU SONS OF LEVI!"

Then MOSES Said to KORAH, "Hear Now, You Sons of Levi, Is it Not Enough for YOU, that the GOD of ISRAEL has Separated You from the Rest of the Congregation of ISRAEL, to bring you near to HIMSELF, to do the Service of the Tabernacle of the LORD, and to Stand before the Congregation, to Minister to Them; And that HE has brought you near, KORAH, and All Your Brothers, Sons of Levi, with You? AND ARE YOU SEEKING THE PRIESTHOOD ALSO?

Then MOSES sent a Summons to DATHAN and ABIRAM, the Sons of ELIAB; But they Said, "WE will not Come Up. Is it not ENOUGH that you have BROUGHT US UP, OUT OF A LAND FLOWING WITH MILK AND HONEY, to have Us DIE IN THE WILDERNESS, but YOU would ALSO LORD it OVER US? Indeed, YOU HAVE NOT BROUGHT US into a Land Flowing with MILK and HONEY, NOR have YOU GIVEN US AN INHERITANCE of FIELDS and VINEYARDS. WOULD YOU PUT OUT THE EYES OF THESE

MEN? We will not COME Up!"

Then MOSES Became Very ANGRY and Said to the LORD, "Do NOT Regard their Offering! I have not taken a Single Donkey from them, NOR HAVE I DONE ANY HARM TO ANY OF THEM."

And MOSES Said to KORAH, "You and All Your Company be Present before the LORD Tomorrow, Both YOU and THEY along with AARON. And Each of YOU take His FIRE Pan and Put Incense on it, and Each of YOU Bring His Censer before the LORD, Two Hundred and Fifty FIRE Pans; also YOU and AARON shall Each bring His Fire Pan."

So they each took His Own Censer and Put FIRE on it, and Laid Incense on it; and THEY stood at the Doorway of the TENT of MEETING, with MOSES and AARON. Thus KORAH Assembled All the Congregation AGAINST THEM at the Doorway of the Tent of Meeting. And the GLORY of LORD appeared to ALL THE CONGREGATION.

Then the LORD Spoke to MOSES and AARON, Saying, "'SEPARATE YOURSELVES FROM AMONG THIS CONGREGATION, THAT "I" MAY CONSUME THEM INSTANTLY.'" But They Fell on their Faces, and Said. "O GOD, THOU """GOD OF THE SPIRITS OF ALL FLESH"""', When One Man Sins, Wilt THOU be ANGRY with the Entire Congregation?"

Then the LORD Spoke to MOSES, Saying, 'Speak to the Congregation, Saying, "' GET BACK FROM AROUND THE DWELLINGS OF KORAH, DATHAN, AND ABIRAM." Then MOSES Arose, and went to DATHAN, and ABIRAM, with the ELDERS OF ISRAEL Following Him, and He Spoke to the Congregation, Saying, "Depart Now FROM THE TENTS Of These Wicked Men, And TOUCH NOTHING THAT BELONGS TO THEM. LEST YOU BE SWEPT AWAY IN ALL THEIR SIN."

So they got back from around the Dwellings of KORAH, DATHAN, and ABIRAM; and DATHAN and ABIRAM Came Out, and Stood at the Doorway of their Tents, along with Their Wives, and Their Sons, and Their Little Ones. And MOSES Said, "By this You Shall Know, that the LORD has Sent Me to Do All these Deeds; For This is Not My Doing. If these Men DIE, the Death of All Men, Or if they SUFFER the Fate of All Men, then the LORD has Not Sent Me. But if the LORD brings about An Entirely New Thing, and the Ground Opens its Mouth, and Swallows Them Up with ALL THAT IS THEIRS, and They Descend ALIVE into SHEOL,

Then You will Understand, that These Men have SPURNED THE LORD."

Then It Came About, as He Finished Speaking All these Words, that the Ground that was Under Them Split Open; and the EARTH Opened Up its MOUTH and SWALLOWED THEM UP, AND THEIR HOUSEHOLDS, AND ALL THE MEN WHO BELONGED TO KORAH, WITH THEIR POSSESSIONS. So THEY, and All that belonged to THEM, went alive to SHEOL; and the Earth Closed over Them, and They Perished from the Midst of the Assembly. And All Israel, Who were Around Them Fled at their OUTCRY, for they Said, "THE EARTH MAY SWALLOW US UP!"

FIRE also came forth from the LORD, and CONSUMED the Two Hundred and Fifty men, WHO were OFFERING the Incense. [Numbers 16. Verses 1 to 35.]

The EARTH Opened Up its MOUTH and SWALLOWED THEM UP, AND THEIR HOUSEHOLDS, AND ALL THE MEN WHO BELONGED TO KORAH, WITH THEIR POSSESSIONS. [Numbers 16. Verses32]

Then It Came About, as He Finished Speaking All these Words, that the Ground that was Under Them Split Open; and the EARTH Opened Up its MOUTH and SWALLOWED THEM UP, AND THEIR HOUSEHOLDS, AND ALL THE MEN WHO BELONGED TO KORAH, WITH THEIR POSSESSIONS. So THEY, and All that belonged to THEM, went alive to SHEOL; and the Earth Closed over Them, and They Perished from the Midst of the Assembly. And All Israel, Who were Around Them Fled at their OUTCRY, for they Said, "THE EARTH MAY SWALLOW US UP!" FIRE also came forth from the LORD, and CONSUMED the Two Hundred and Fifty men, WHO were OFFERING the Incense. [Numbers 16. Verses 31,32,33,34,35]

Ark of the Covenant

The Children of Israel being carried away in exile, out of their land to Assyria

Regarding the Children of Israel, since the ancient times of their Ancestor "NOAH", with Whom the Great LORD OF THE FLAMES, the Creator of the Universe, for the First Time made 'HIS COVENANT' along with His Children, and His Future Descendant Generations to Come, as recorded in the Very First Book "Genesis 9. 8, 9" of the Holy Bible, the Great LORD, also reverently known as the "MOST HIGH" has always been Most Loving, Most Benevolent, Most Patient, as HE Kept an Watchful Eye toward the Descendants of NOAH, but since NOAH'S Time, many of His Descendant Children. wrongfully went Astray by Willfully Breaking the "LORD'S COVENANT", as clearly stated by JOSHUA in "Joshua 24. 2" of the Holy Bible, and thus Started Worshiping HIS mere Creations, the so called other GODS.

So the Great LORD then again Chose from the Descendants of "NOAH", a Faithful Servant, named ABRAM, whom the LORD named ABRAHAM, a direct descendant of NOAH, and then renewed HIS HOLY COVENANT with Him, as mentioned in the Chapter "Genesis 17. 2, 4." of the Holy Bible, and then also Continued Renewing HIS COVENANT with His Descendants ISAAC, and JACOB as mentioned in "Genesis 26. 24", and in "Genesis 28. 13, 14, 15" of the Holy Bible, and JACOB, after LORD'S renewing of HIS HOLY COVENANT, changed the name of Place from "LUZ" to "BETHEL", meaning the "HOUSE OF 'EL'" or the House of the Almighty "LORD - GOD", where He Envisioned the Great LORD and HIS Evolutionary Plan and Purpose, shown to Him in the form of an 'Heavenly Ladder' passing through the various dimensional planes of this Planet Earth, stretching from the lowest Dense Physical plane, the plane of Incarnated Human Beings, known to the enlightened Seers and Sages as the Dimensional Plane of ASSIAH, reaching all the way to the Higher Heavenly Plane of "BRIAH", above which JACOB Saw the Domain of GOD'S Radiant Grace, existing in the Dimensional Plane of ATZILUTH.

But after JACOB'S Children, whom the Great LORD named as ISRAEL, under the influence of Material Mind Animal desires filled with Corrupt "Thought Forms" of Materialistic Jealousy and Hatred, did an AWFUL thing to their Own Younger Blood Brother, 'JOSEPH', by "WILLFULLY" Selling Him into Slavery, they after passing of Sometime, were then later on Forced to go to the Land of Egypt in search of Food, due to the onslaught of a Great Drought, where the LORD – GOD'S grace made their enslaved brother JOSEPH a "Mighty and High Positioned Trusted Officer" of the Ruling Pharaoh of Egypt, Who even in the "Time of his Great Afflictions" FAITHFULLY Served the LORD, in the Land of many So Called "'Gods and Goddesses'", Daily Worshiping HIM, and Thanking HIM from bottom of His Heart, for "HE" being His "ONE AND ONLY", the Great LORD – GOD, and this entire Episode is detail fully mentioned in "Genesis, Chapters 39 to 46" of the Holy Bible.

After Settling of JACOB and His Descendants in the Land of Egypt, over the Passing of 430 years as mentioned in "Exodus 12. 40, 41." of the Holy Bible, Many of the Descendant Children of Israel almost forgot their HOLY COVENANT, which was reverently made Earlier by their Ancestor's with the "MOST HIGH" and thus fell into great Despair and Afflictions of Oppression in the Land of Pharaohs. But the Great Lord never forgot HIS COVENANT made with their Patriarchs, and thus Chose MOSES to lead them out from their afflictions as clearly mentioned in "Exodus 3. 7, 8, 9.", but even after their deliverance with the Ineffable Grace of MOST HIGH, the Children of Israel having "Lower Material Mind or Animal Mind Desires", constantly grumbled for "Petty Things", and thus Rebelled "Time and Again" against the LORD and HIS Chosen Faithful Servant MOSES.

So at the Holy Mountain HOREB, whose Holy Peak is adjacent to the Flaming MOUNTAIN OF GOD, the Mount SINAI, situated in the Wilderness of "ARABAH", the Great LORD, looking at the FORGETFULNESS of the Children of Israel, then for the First time made """"A WRITTEN COVENANT"""""" with the Children of Israel having HIS IMPORTANT COMMANDMENTS Etched upon two tablets of Stone, which he Gave to MOSES for their Safekeeping, and which were then put as per HIS Instructions in an "'ARK OF THE COVENANT'".

His faithful Servant MOSES reminded ALL CHILDREN of ISRAEL About this "'WRITTEN COVENANT'" of the LORD, after they took possessions of various lands including all the ARABAH, which they acquired as per the Instructions of the LORD, regarding which the Holy Bible States:

'And they took Possession of His Land, and the Land of OG King of BASHAN, the Two Kings of Amorites, who were Across the JORDAN to the East, from AROER, which is on the Edge of the Valley of ARNON, even as far as MOUNT SION [that is MOUNT HERMON], with ALL THE

"ARABAH" ACROSS THE JORDAN TO THE EAST, EVEN AS FAR AS THE SEA OF "ARABAH", AT THE FOOT OF THE SLOPES OF PISGAH'. [Deuteronomy 4. 47, 48, 49.]

'Then MOSES Summoned All Israel, and Said to them, "Hear O Israel, the STATUTES and the ORDINANCES, Which I am Speaking Today in Your HEARING, that You may 'LEARN' them and 'OBSERVE' them Carefully.

"THE LORD OUR GOD MADE A 'COVENANT' WITH US AT HOREB. THE LORD "DID NOT" MAKE THIS COVENANT WITH OUR FATHERS, BUT WITH 'US', WITH ALL THOSE OF US, ALIVE HERE TODAY."

'The LORD Spoke to You 'FACE TO FACE' at the Mountain from the Midst of the "'FIRE'", while I was Standing between the LORD and YOU at that Time, to Declare to You, THE WORD OF THE LORD, for You were Afraid because of the "FIRE", and did not Go Up the Mountain.

He Said, "I AM THE LORD YOUR GOD, WHO BROUGHT YOU OUT OF THE LAND OF EGYPT, OUT OF THE HOUSE OF SLAVERY. YOU SHALL HAVE "NO OTHER GODS" BEFORE ME. YOU SHALL "NOT MAKE FOR YOURSELF 'AN IDOL', OR ANY LIKENESS OF 'WHAT IS IN "'HEAVEN'" ABOVE', OR 'ON THE EARTH' BENEATH, OR 'IN THE WATER' UNDER THE EARTH. YOU SHALL 'NOT WORSHIP THEM' OR SERVE THEM; FOR "'I'", THE LORD YOUR GOD, AM A JEALOUS GOD, VISITING THE 'INIQUITY OF THE FATHERS ON THE CHILDREN', AND ON THE 'THIRD AND THE FOURTH GENERATIONS' OF THOSE WHO 'HATE ME', BUT SHOWING LOVING - KINDNESS TO 'THOUSAND', TO THOSE WHO 'LOVE ME', AND KEEP MY COMMANDMENTS.

You Shall NOT take the NAME OF THE LORD YOUR GOD IN VAIN, For the LORD WILL NOT LEAVE HIM "'UNPUNISHED'", WHO TAKES HIS NAME IN VAIN". [Deuteronomy 5. Verses 1 to 11.]

'These WORDS of the LORD Spoke to All Your Assembly at the Mountain from the Midst of the 'FIRE', of the 'CLOUD' and of the 'Thick Gloom', with a 'Great Voice', and HE added 'NO MORE'. And HE wrote THEM on 'Two Tablets' of Stone, and Gave Them to ME. And it came about, when YOU Heard the VOICE from the Midst of the DARKNESS, while the Mountain was BURNING WITH FIRE that YOU came Near to Me, All the Heads of Your Tribes, and Your Elders. And You Said, Behold. THE LORD OUR GOD HAS SHOWN US HIS GLORY AND HIS GREATNESS, AND WE

HAVE HEARD HIS VOICE FROM THE MIDST OF THE 'FIRE'; WE HAVE SEEN TODAY, THAT THE '"GOD SPEAKS WITH MAN"', YET HE LIVES.

Now then Why Should We DIE? For this great 'FIRE' will Consume Us; if WE Hear the Voice of the LORD Our GOD Any Longer, Then We Shall DIE. For WHO is There of All Flesh, Who has HEARD the VOICE of the LIVING GOD, Speaking from the Midst of the FIRE, As WE Have, and LIVED? Go Near and Hear All that the LORD Our GOD Says; then Speak to US ALL, that the LORD will Speak to YOU, and We will Hear and Do it.

And the LORD Heard the Voice of Your Words, when You Spoke to Me, and the LORD Said to Me. '"I HAVE HEARD THE VOICE OF THE WORDS OF THIS PEOPLE, WHICH THEY HAVE SPOKEN TO YOU. THEY HAVE "DONE WELL", IN ALL THAT THEY HAVE SPOKEN. 'OH' THAT THEY HAD SUCH A HEART IN THEM, THAT THEY WOULD 'FEAR ME', AND KEEP "MY COMMANDMENTS ALWAYS", THAT IT MAY BE WELL WITH THEM, AND WITH THEIR SONS FOREVER! GO, SAY TO THEM, 'RETURN TO YOUR TENTS,'

BUT AS FOR YOU, STAND HERE BY ME, THAT "I" MAY SPEAK TO YOU, '"ALL THE COMMANDMENTS"', AND '"THE STATUTES"', AND '"THE JUDGMENTS"', WHICH YOU SHALL 'TEACH' THEM, THAT THEY MAY OBSERVE THEM IN THE LAND, WHICH "I" GIVE THEM TO POSSESS"'.

So You Shall OBSERVE to do Just as the LORD Your GOD has Commanded You; YOU shall NOT Turn ASIDE, to the RIGHT or the LEFT. You shall WALK in ALL THE WAY, which the LORD Your GOD has COMMANDED You, THAT YOU MAY LIVE, and that it may be 'WELL with YOU', and that YOU may PROLONG Your DAYS in the LAND, which YOU Shall Possess'. [Deuteronomy 5. Verses 22 to 33.]

But from the later Chapters of Holy Bible, We all Very Well Know that after the Passing Away of the "CHOSEN SON OF GOD", the GREAT KING SOLOMON, as clearly mentioned about Him in "1 Chronicles 17.13", who brought World Renowned Justice, Great Riches, Fame and Glory to the Promised Land, the Children of Israel Willfully Rebelled against the House of Judah, and instead installed JEROBOAM as their Chosen King, who Willfully Breaking the HOLY """'WRITTEN COVENANT"'"", WHICH WAS ESTABLISHED BY THE "LORD - GOD" WITH MOSES about 516 Years Earlier in the Wilderness, at the Holy Mount HOREB, then WRONGFULLY installed a GOLDEN CALF, by Deceitfully claiming it to be the "DELIVERER GOD OF ISRAEL", and then by illegally establishing it at the same very HOLY SPOT OF "BETHEL", which was established almost a MILLENNIAL earlier by JACOB in the ancient times, as the Venerated Holy Spot of the 'MOST HIGH', Who also named it as the "HOUSE OF EL" [430 years Passed since time of JACOB, when Exodus took Place, and King Solomon Started Building the Temple Building 480 years later in his fourth year of rule in Jerusalem, and ruled for another 36 years, as total years of his rule was of 40 years, and after his passing away Children of Israel Revolted, and instead of His Son REHOBOAM, they then Installed JEROBOAM as their New King to rule them. So Since the time of JACOB more than 946 years had passed, [430 + 480 + 36 = 946 Years], when JACOB passing through that Land of 'Luz', rested and Slept there having a 'Divine Vision', and then named this place of 'LUZ" with a New Holy Name, given to it as the holy "BETHEL", meaning the "House of El or the House of LORD - GOD".

And more or less Every King of Israel ruling in SAMARIA, who followed after the King JEROBOAM, till the time of King HOSHEA, willfully went on "DOING EVIL" IN THE SIGHT OF THE LORD, when through their Such Continuous Wrong doings, they then Finally LOST THE INVISIBLE PROTECTION, which the LORD – GOD Provided them 'ALL ALONG', because of the "Holy Covenant", which HE made earlier with their Faithful Ancestor's, and then All of them were Captured by the KING OF ASSYRIA, Who then Forcefully Carried them Away, these Rebel "CHILDREN OF ISRAEL", 'AS SLAVES' into EXILE, and settled them IN THE LANDS OF ASSYRIA, as mentioned in "2 Kings 17.6".

In the 12th year of Ahaz king of Judah, Hoshea the son of Eliah became king over Israel in Samaria, and reigned 9 years and he did evil inthe sight of the Lord. [2 Kings 17.1,2].

The Elohim group of Angels, which attend to the needs of the humans on the physical dense plane, known as the Nephilm appearing before a woman.

Part 45

Since the Very Ancient times of this Planet Earth, when the Creator LORD – GOD started the Grand Experiment of Consciousness Expansion upon this Planet Earth, which is supposed to take Place in its 4 Main Differentiated Frequency Levels of 'Vital Evolutionary Consciousness', known by the Seers and Sages in the Hebrew Language as the Dimensional Spheres of "ASSIAH, YETZIRAH, BRIAH, AND ATZILUTH", the Great LORD by using its aggregated dense materials, which were originally Objectively Formed due to the Coagulation of the Rarer Matter of SPIRIT, which thus are in FACT, a "PART AND PARCEL" of the VAST VITAL ETHEREAL SPACE, which is commonly termed by Human Beings as the CELESTIAL SPACE OF THE HEAVENLY SKIES, and this Grand Feat to start this Experiment of Consciousness Expansion upon this Planet earth, was achieved by the Desire Mind of the Unknowable LORD, through the Joint Action of the Spiral, Cyclic and Circular motions of the VITAL ETHEREAL MATTER, which is the BASIC COMPONENT of the VAST CELESTIAL SPACE itself.

But before the "LORD OF FLAMES" Created the Mankind in His Own Image, and other Visible Kingdoms of Nature to Coexist with the Human Beings, in its Differentiated Physical Plane Boundaries, known in Hebrew Language as the Densest Plane of ASSIAH, thus having the Most Coarse Parametric Space of the Objectively Manifested Planet Earth, this evolutionary Plan was put in place as per those requirements, which were Needed for their GRADUAL EVOLUTION, which has to be attained in certain CYCLIC PERIODS, known as the 'Wheels of Time".

These cyclic "Wheels of Time" Primarily corresponded to the everyday "FORWARD MOTION OF OBJECTIVELY VISIBLE CELESTIAL BODIES, PRIMARILY "THE SUN AND THE MOON", thus Continuously Moving Onward through a Gradual series of "SPIRAL MOTIONS", which are created due to the ANGULAR WOBBLING OF THE PLANET EARTH, as well as, the Similar Wobble Vibrations of SUN and the MOON, which geometrically synchronize with the Wobble Vibrations of this Planet Earth, and are thus being carried on in its Particular ELECTRO – MAGNETIC Radius of INFLUENCE, as these Electro-Magnetic frequency Vibrations are the Basis of ALL CONSCIOUSNESS EXPANSION, taking place in the Vast Ethereal Space, or in the Unfathomable Ethereal Space of the Celestial Skies commonly known as the 'COSMOS.'

The Created and thus Objectively Manifested Human Beings of this Planet Earth were then bestowed by the Great LORD OF FLAMES, with the Attribute of "Individualized Mind", as to Embody the five types of Electro – Magnetic Sensations, which are Primarily related to the INDIVIDUALIZED OBJECTIVE MATERIAL MIND known as the indwelling "PERSONALITY CONSCIOUSNESS", which Primarily works with the VITAL MAGNETIC IMPULSES of this Planet Earth, which are constantly emanating from its CENTER, and which also HELP All the Manifested Visible And Invisible Kingdoms to "Gradually Evolve" in its densest and Most Slower Vital Frequency Vibrations, which through their various interactions create the MATRIX of the Physical Plane.

The Great LORD OF FLAMES through the use of HIS Desire Minds Vital Energy, thus put in Motion the Vital Ethereal Matter of Space, which is Abundantly Available in the COSMOS, and forms it's so called UNIMAGINABLE VAST SPACE, and through such desired motions HE Achieved by the action of the "SPIRALING VIBRATIONS", known as the Process of "Thought Forming" or the "EVENTUATION PROCESS".

This EVENTUATION PROCESS during its "First Phase", MUCH EARLIER than the CREATION OF HUMAN BEINGS, Similarly Subjectively Manifested Various Other Types of Differentiated Consciousness level Entities and Beings, known to Hebrew Seers and Sages as the "ELOHIM", the Hebrew Word 'Elohim' meaning the "Children of "EL"', as the Title name "EL" denotes the "Greatness" of the Almighty "MOST HIGH".

The MOST HIGH thus Created these "ELOHIM'S" to assist HIM, to act as HIS Trusted Children, and to Faithfully carry on their Required Duties to fullness in All Related Aspects of the Various Evolutionary Cycles, which were to be gradually carried upon this Planet Earth, and which are as per HIS EVOLUTIONARY PLAN and PURPOSE, based upon the Universal Law of 'Will to do Good'. And thus each of their Hierarchical Groups were Given Certain Types of Powers, to Enable them to Preform "independently" their Required Duties, along with simultaneously upholding the Universal Law of 'will to do GOOD'.

These "ELOHIMS" existing as the Invisible 'Children of God" were thus given various duties to look after the Differentiated Evolving Kingdoms of this Planet, who during the course of their cyclic evolution are having their visible and invisible forms, in which the Densest Most Visible kingdom of this planet earth is the Mineral Kingdom, and the Evolving Crystals of this Kingdom possesses the Highest Conscious Vibrations, as they are not yet effected by the Vices which consist of the Animal Desires of the Polluted Mind, which is much more Prevalent in other Evolving Manifested Kingdoms of this planet Earth, which are represented by their attained "Color Frequencies", and the Crystals of the Mineral Kingdom also Grow just like any other animated form of differentiated kingdoms of nature upon this planet earth.

The 12 Crystals which were chosen by the LORD to be PUT in the BREAST PLATE of AARON, their Colors Primarily Resonated with the Cosmic Energies of the 12 Constellations, Which are Constantly Absorbed by the Sun and Moon, acting as the receptive Focal Points in our Solar Universe, before they Electro – Magnetically distribute them out throughout the Solar Universe acting as the "Energy Distribution Transformers".

A Particular Hierarchical Order of this Created Servant Group of the "Elohim", whom the Holy Bible denoted in Genesis as the "NEPHILIM", were given the Duties to act out as the "Care Takers" of the "Evolving Human Race" upon this Planet Earth, after the Creation started to further evolve upon this Planet Earth, and these "NEPHILIMS" to understand the intricate qualities of the "Individualized Human Mind", then as a part of their required duty, willfully started interacting with the objective "Human Forms", which were manifested and evolving, upon the dense plane of ASSIAH, of this Planet Earth.

But the evolving Human Beings, in their early stages of Evolution were then totally unable to understand the Plan and Purpose of the Unknowable LORD, and thus also started calling these Servant children of the MOST HIGH as their caretaker GODS and GODDESSES, and these Mighty and Powerful NEPHILIMS, who in reality are in fact HERMAPHRODITE BEINGS, thus Started to "Like" their Venerated status as the Gods and Goddesses of the evolving Human Being, which was ignorantly Given to them by their evolving Human Subjects of this Planet, and such undue glorification's then Corrupted the minds of these Elohim Servants of the LORD, who then slowly went astray from their required duties, as well as also made their Human Subjects to Stumble from their Evolutionary Paths, who became Wicked and Evil in their Thoughts, regarding which the Holy Bible States:

'Now it came about, when Man Began to Multiply on the Face of the Land, and Daughters were Born to them that the 'Sons of God' saw that the Daughters of Men were Beautiful; and they took Wives for themselves, whomever they chose. Then the LORD Said, "MY SPIRIT SHALL NOT STRIVE WITH MAN FOREVER, BECAUSE HE IS ALSO FLESH; NEVERTHELESS HIS DAYS SHALL BE ONE HUNDRED AND TWENTY YEARS.'

The NEPHILIM were on the EARTH in those days, and also afterward, when the Sons of GOD came into the Daughters of Men, and they Bore Children to them. Those were the Mighty Men, who were Old Men of Renown.

Then the LORD Saw that the Wickedness of Man was GREAT, and that Every Intent of the thoughts of His Heart was Only Evil Continually. And the LORD was SORRY, that He had made Man on Earth, and He was Grieved in HIS Heart. [Genesis 6. Verses 1 to 6.]

But many people may not know this Fact, that the major problem behind their such Wicked Behavior, was due to the illegal wrongdoings of the "Elohim" whom the LORD – GOD fully Trusted as His Trustworthy Helper Children, without checking their Illegal Behavior, who became the So Called Gods and Goddesses of this Physical World.

The presence of a light being known as Elohim or Angels, which attend to the needs of humans on the physical dense plane, known as the Nephilm.

Part 46

The Children of Israel, after the passing of 40 years in the Wilderness, which they spent during their time of Exodus, and then their subsequent establishment in the Promised Land, their Later Descendant Children and also Most of their Governing Kings did not honored their Holy Covenant with THE LORD, but instead went on following the Prescribed Rituals as per their own wishes and fancies, by not paying any heed to the required SPIRITUAL DEVOTION as Commanded by the LORD, as it was important for them to 'Spiritually and Not Religiously' Engage in the rules of Written Covenant, which was made Earlier at the Holy Mountain HOREB – SINAI, by the LORD HIMSELF with MOSES, which as per the Holy Bible clearly states:

'Then the LORD Spoke to MOSES, Saying, "Speak to ALL the Congregation of the Sons of Israel, and Say to Them, "'YOU SHALL BE HOLY, FOR ""I"" THE LORD YOUR GOD AM HOLY. EVERY ONE OF YOU SHALL REVERENCE HIS MOTHER AND HIS FATHER, AND YOU SHALL KEEP MY SABBATHS; I AM THE LORD YOUR GOD. DO NOT TURN TO IDOLS OR MAKE FOR YOURSELF MOLTEN GODS; I AM THE LORD YOUR GOD. NOW WHEN YOU OFFER A SACRIFICE OF PEACE OFFERINGS TO THE LORD, YOU SHALL OFFER IT SO THAT YOU MAY BE ACCEPTED.' [Leviticus 19. Verses 1 to 5.]

But among their ongoing Generations, there were still a "Chosen Few" who were fully devoted to the LORD their GOD, the "MOST HIGH", and thus were spiritually inclined to the Desire Mind Vibrations of the MOST HIGH, and were able to directly get HIS Divine Messages by talking to Him through Visions and Dreams, with the Holy Power of their Enlightened Minds, and then after receiving Such Messages they would spiritually Discern them, and then pass them on to the rest of the Children of Israel. These Chosen Ones were thus known to the Children of Israel, as the Holy Prophets of GOD.

These Chosen Prophets were thus Established as LORD'S Humble Servants upon this Planet Earth during their Incarnated Lives, by the Desired Will of the Almighty LORD - GOD, Who through their Continuous Efforts 'Time and Again' Warned the Children of Israel and their Evil Kings, for their Willful Wrongdoings against the Wrath of GOD, but they were mostly not listened to or paid attention to, by the so called Mighty Rulers of Israel, who got swayed by their Own Animal Mind Desires embodied as the Lower grade "PERSONALITIES" of wickedness and deceit in their Human Forms, which were totally drenched in the Worldly Desires of Illusory Material Glamour, and thus generally ignored their Prophesies, till the Death and Doom Occurred to them as well as their followers, just according to the warnings, which were rendered by these Holy Prophets. But even though Most of their Warnings and Divine Messages thus obtained from the LORD, were not properly followed or paid Timely attention, thus causing Doom and Destruction to the Children of Israel, the later Priestly Scribes noted and compiled them to become a Part and Parcel of the Holy Bible.

Most Human Beings of this Planet are still unaware of this underlying fact that after the Passing away of the Most Wise and Just King Solomon, the Demonic Invisible Entities and Beings, the so called Gods and Goddesses of Mighty and Powerful Egypt, who were looking for an ample opportunity to take their long due revenge upon the unwary Children of Israel, who got away with the intervention of their LORD from Serving Them during the Time of MOSES, then put their deceitful plans with full force in motion.

During the 40 years rule of His Rule, the Great King Solomon expanded the boundaries of His Kingdom and thus ruled over various New Kingdoms, which became part of His Vast Territory regarding which the Holy Bible states:

'Judah and Israel were as numerous as the Sand that is on the Seashore in Abundance; they were EATING, and DRINKING, and REJOICING. Now SOLOMON ruled over ALL THE KINGDOMS, from the River to the Land of the PHILISTINES, and to the Border of Egypt; they brought Tribute and Served Solomon All the Days of His Life.

For He had Dominion over Everything West of the River, from TIPHSAH even to GAZA, over All the KINGS WEST OF THE RIVER; and He had Peace on All Sides around about Him. So JUDAH and ISRAEL Lived in Safety, Every Man under His Vine, and His Fig Tree, from DAN even to BEERSHEBA, All the Days of Solomon. [1 Kings 4. 20, 21, 24, 25.]

And It was the Great King Solomon, who for the First Time Reverently Established the Grand House of the LORD in Jerusalem, and the Evil

Gods and Goddesses of this Earth, at the time of King Solomon, were already firmly rooted and established in all those Captured Lands, which were in the East and West of His Kingdom, and were thus falling now inside the Newly Enlarged boundaries of His Vast Domain, where these Gods and Goddess were highly revered and worshiped by their Materially Minded Followers, and their Just King Solomon being occupied with the governing of these Newly acquired Vast areas, thus became Lenient about their such practices, as it is hard for people to instantly leave their established faiths, even if they get occupied by the conquering forces, which aroused the Anger of his "Divine father", the MOST HIGH. But the same Kind of Situation was faced for 40 Years by MOSES in the Wilderness, about five centuries earlier, when the Children of Israel who were delivered from their Afflictions in Egypt by the "MOST HIGH", were Continuously Grumbling and Rebelling Against the Commands of their Unknowable LORD, His Chosen Leader MOSES as well as His Brother AARON, and Moreover they made a Molten GOD for themselves in the shape of a GOLDEN CALF, and similar situations were faced by King Solomon, in His Newly Occupied Territories, but the LORD was Unsatisfied, and regarding the Anger of the MOST HIGH, the Holy Bible States:

"Because they have Forsaken ME, And have Worshiped ASHTORETH, THE GODDESS of the SIDONIANS, CHEMOSH the GOD of MOAB, and MILCOM, the GOD of the Sons of AMMON; and they have Not Walked in MY Ways Doing 'WHAT IS RIGHT' in 'MY SIGHT' and OBSERVING MY STATUES, and MY ORDINANCES, as His Father David did. Nevertheless "'I'" will not take the whole Kingdom out of His hand, but "I" will make Him Ruler All the Days of His Life, for the Sake of MY Servant DAVID, Whom "'I'" Chose, Who Observed MY Commandments and MY Statutes." [1 Kings 11. 33, 34.]

And unknown to many Human Beings these so called Gods and Goddesses are nothing but Material Minded Invisible Conscious Existences, commonly referred in a Negative way as the "DEMONS", who having Deformed and Mutated Consciousness, due to the Misuse of their Vested Powers, which were originally trustfully given to them by their CREATOR LORD – GOD of the Universe, the MOST HIGH to look after evolving Human Race, then in their Wide Spread Heinous Conspiracy, by Willfully Back- Stabbing the LOVE and TRUST of their CREATOR LORD, thus ILLEGALLY Hijacked the Evolutionary Plan and Purpose of the MOST HIGH, but even through their All Evil Efforts, they could not Harm the "Chosen Son of God", the Great King SOLOMON, Who through His Divine Wisdom Easily Subdued them, and then kept them in Bondage's during the Entire Tenure of his Glorious Reign.

But after the passing away of the Great King SOLOMON, they found an Ample Opportunity to reestablish themselves as the GODS in the Promised Land for the Children of Israel, and thus devised a deceitful plan to support their Incarnated Stooge JEROBOAM, the Son of Nebat, who during the Time of Solomon under the Influence of their mind control "Thought Form" Frequency Vibrations, thus Foolishly Rebelled against the Great King Solomon and then took Refuge in the Land of Pharaoh's, which was under their Invisible Control for a Long Period of Time, as they Easily Controlled the Evolving Minds of their Subject Pharaohs without any Exceptions, but Only they could not control the Higher Conscious Mind of the Pharaoh Akhenaten, who being Spiritually Minded, believing in ONE LORD of this Solar Universe, then openly rebelled against their Wrongful Material Glamour Policies, deceitfully carried forward through their Well Established Corrupt Priesthood, which were harmful to the indwelling Evolutionary SOLAR Conscious of the evolving human beings of this Planet Earth.

And just like these So called Gods and Goddesses destroyed the Very Name and Fame of Pharaoh AKHENATEN from the Egyptian Records, and completely destroyed his Glorious City of AMARNA, after his passing away, through the Gruesome Actions of their Incarnated Henchmen Pharaoh Followers, who acted in conjunction with the supportive actions of their Corrupt Priesthood, they did the Same to the Glory of King Solomon after his Passing away from this world, by gradually destroying his famous cities, Particularly the cities of HAZOR, MEGIDDO, and GEZER, which He Built, regarding which the Holy Bible states:

'Now this is the account of forced labor, which King Solomon levied to build the House of the LORD, His own house, the MILLO, the Wall of JERUSALEM, HAZOR, MEGIDDO, and GEZER. For Pharaoh King of Egypt had Gone up and Captured GEZER, and burned it with FIRE, and killed the Canaanites who lived in the City, and had given it as a Dowry to His Daughter, Solomon's Wife. So Solomon rebuilt GEZER and the Lower BETH –HORON, and BAALATH and TAMAR in the Wilderness, in the Land of JUDAH, and All the Storage Cities which Solomon had, even the Cities for His Chariots, and the Cities for His Horsemen, and All that Pleased

Solomon to build in JERUSALEM, in LEBANON, and in All the Land under His Rule.' [1 Kings 9. Verses 15 to 19.].

But even after the Entire City of Amarna was Methodically razed to the Ground, by the Deceitful and Heinous actions of these Invisible Gods and Goddesses of this planet Earth, which were willfully Carried Out by their Corrupt Followers, most of the records about Pharaoh Akhenaten's Existence as well as His Family, were still later found in the last few Centuries, thus Firmly reestablishing his Existence in this World, but None of the Records related to the Glory of Solomon were ever found till to date, for the Very Basic FACT, that the Great King Solomon, Himself being a Humble Believer and Obedient Servant of the MOST HIGH never Glorified His OWN name, but Dedicated All His Actions to the Glory of the LORD, and in the Biblical Writings of Ecclesiastes claimed himself just as "A PREACHER" instead of His True Glorious Title of 'KING'. Also the Ancient Hebrews except glorifying the name of their LORD, did not etched their Personal Glories on Monument's, just like their Counterpart Egyptians did, through Elaborate Glories mentioned in their Hieroglyphic Language depictions, and thus etched on their Vast Monuments, and that is the very reason that even after the total destruction of Akhenaten Great Monuments and His Name's Permanent Elimination from the Egyptian History, the very pieces of his buildings, which were reused by their Ruthless and Greedy Destroyers, brought Him back to LIGHT, and for this very reason of Injustice done to Him, He is much more widely Known now in this World, than many of the Other Dynastic Pharaohs, whose Names and Glories were methodically recorded by the Ancient Scribes in the Egyptian Histories.

But as far as the Great King Solomon is Concerned, the Only Place One Can Find the Detailed Glories of King Solomon upon this physical world plane, Known to the HEBREW Seers as the Material Plane of ASSIAH, is the Holy Bible, which got Preserved even in the Times of Utmost Afflictions, which the Children of Israel faced due to the Wrongdoings of their Many Kings, the So called Political Leaders of their Times, who willfully worshiped the Molten Gods, against the Clear Mandates of their LORD- GOD, the MOST HIGH.

Regarding the rebellion of Jeroboam against the Great King Solomon, the Holy Bible states:

Then Jeroboam the Son of Nebat, an Ephraimite of Zeredah [Ephraimite means belonging to the Tribe of Ephraim], Solomon's Servant, whose mother's name was Zeruah, [Zeruah is an ancient Hebrew name for Venus], a widow, also Rebelled against the King. Now this was the reason, why He rebelled against the King; Solomon built the Milo, and closed up the Breach of the City of His Father David.

Solomon sought therefore to put Jeroboam to death; but Jeroboam arose and Fled to EGYPT to SHISHAK, KING OF EGYPT, and He was in Egypt until the death of SOLOMON. [1 Kings 11. 26, 27, 40.]

Since the Evil King Jeroboam started the Wrongful worship of Molten Gods in form of a Golden Calves among the Children of Israel, many of the Priestly Children of LEVI Clans, who on the Whole were a Group of RELIGIOUS People", but "NOT SPIRITUAL" as required by their LORD -GOD, were thus unable to figure out the Evil Workings of these Invisible Demonic Entities and Beings, as their Evolving Minds were Totally Set in the Religious Aspects of their Prescribed Rituals, and were thus not able to Comprehend the TRUE SPIRITUAL ASPECTS OF THEIR HOLY COVENANT.

In their later Histories, Only a handful of them, who through their SPIRITUAL EYES willfully looked beyond their Religious Mind, were thus able to understand the Desire Mind Vibrations of their MOST BELOVED LORD, and thus were consciously able to communicate with HIS Commandments, and were then known to all others in their own times as the Chosen Prophets of the LORD.

Even though the Great King Solomon, who established the Great and Glorious House of LORD in Jerusalem, and acted performing His Main Duties as the World famous King of the Israelite's during His Life, apart from being their Wisest King, He was also a Preacher for preaching the "Hidden Wisdom" of their LORD, a Title which was Claimed by him in the Book of Ecclesiastes of the Holy Bible. Regarding which it States:

'The Words of the Preacher, the Son of David, King in Jerusalem. "Vanity of Vanities", Says the Preacher, "Vanity of Vanities! All is Vanity." [Ecclesiastes 1. 1, 2.]

And the Great King Solomon apart from being the Chosen Son of the LORD as mentioned in "1 Chronicles 17.13", He was also a Prophet of the LORD, as He had Special Abilities provided to Him by the Lord to

Converse and understand the thoughts and feelings of both the Visible and Invisible Kingdoms of this Planet Earth, regarding which the Holy Bible States:

"Now GOD gave SOLOMON Wisdom, and Very Great Discernment and 'Breadth of Mind', like the Sand that is on the Seashore.

And He Spoke of Trees, From the Cedar that is in Lebanon, Even to the Hyssop that Grows on the Wall; He Spoke also of Animals and Birds, and Creeping Things and Fish. And Men came from All Peoples to hear the Wisdom of Solomon, From All the Kings of the Earth, Who had heard of His Wisdom." [1 Kings 4. 29, 33, 34.].

Even though the Great King Solomon, Himself Established Sacrifices to be performed on a Grand Scale in the Glorious House of the LORD, with Godly Wisdom, He Himself informed the Children of Israel, those Important Secrets, which were related to such Ritual Practices which involved "A Huge Slaughter of Innocent Animals", by revealing them in HIS Most Valuable Preaching's, which were later Compiled to be known as the Holy "Book of Ecclesiastes", regarding which the Holy Bible States:

"Guard Your Steps, as You Go to the HOUSE of GOD, and DRAW NEAR TO '"LISTEN"' rather than to OFFER THE '"SACRIFICE OF FOOLS"'; FOR THEY DO NOT KNOW, '"THEY ARE DOING EVIL"'. [Ecclesiastes 5. 1.]

A depiction of the King Solomon seated on the Left, the High Priest Zadok in the Center, and the Prophet Nathan seated on the Right.

233

The Great King Solomon, "Son of God" as mentioned in 1 Chronicles 17.13 and Preacher in the chapter of Ecclesiastes 1.1 of the Holy Bible, whose great monuents were Erased from the Material History of this world.

The Great King Akhenaten, High Priest Pharaoh of ancient Egypt, whose monuments were also Erased from the Material History of ths world.

The High Priest, [Kohen Gadula] of LORD being consulted by a
Temple Priest [Kohen]

Most Human Beings of this Planet Earth are unaware of this Hidden Fact, that by the Time of Exodus, Most of LORD'S Created Invisible Servant Helpers, 'The ELOHIM'S' went Astray from HIS Evolutionary Plan and Purpose, which HE established for this Planet Earth, and Willfully Misusing their Vested Powers in the name of their Assigned Duties, then in a Defiant Way, ILLEGALLY AND DECEITFULLY, themselves became the so called 'GODS and GODDESSES" of the evolving Human Races, and thus Wrongfully Established themselves with a title of a so called GOD, Parallel to their OWN CREATOR FATHER, who is the ONE AND ONLY, THE TRUE ALMIGHTY LORD – GOD OF THE UNIVERSE, WHO IS ALSO KNOWN AS "THE MOST HIGH".

The Creator Lord of the Universe, the MOST HIGH, at the Particular Time of EXODUS, Established Two Categories of Human Beings as HIS Chosen People, so as to Lead their Fellow Human Beings, upon the Established Evolutionary Path, for which HE first Chose MOSES and His Brother AARON, and Utilized their Humble Services to reestablish HIS Evolutionary Plan and Purpose upon this Planet Earth.

Thus during the time of Exodus, MOSES became the First "PROPHET" of the LORD thus Reestablishing the "HOLY ORDER of SPIRITUAL PROPHET'S" after the much earlier Times of their forefathers, NOAH, ABRAHAM, ISAAC and JACOB, with whom LORD could also Directly Communicate through Holy VISIONS, DREAMS as Well as DIRECT COMMUNICATION THROUGH A VARIETY OF "THOUGHT FORMS" having Vital Frequency Vibrations of HIS Desire Mind, during which they involved the Bluish Light in the Bottom Center of HIS FIERY Appearance, just like the Bluish Glow which exists in the bottom center of a Burning Candle Flame, which having blue frequencies represent the Ethereal Vitality permeated through its "Inherent Radiant Heat of Devotion", which thus expanded their Mind Consciousness , and the Fearful Sounds of the CLOUDS, which affected their Perception Senses thus making them Humble to the Presence of the MOST HIGH, and the Great LORD Vested in MOSES "HIS RADIANT FORCE", which was "'Equal and Above'" in Powers to these So Called Gods and Goddesses of the Ancient World. And also the Great LORD Chose AARON, to become the First "RELIGIOUS HEAD" of His Chosen Group as a Care taker of the Prescribed Rituals, with the TITLE OF "A HIGH PRIEST", the main difference between these two groups formed by the LORD being, that the Chosen PROPHETS only appeared out of ordinary Human Beings during those times, when Most of the Evolving Humanity of this Planet Willfully went Astray from their Established Evolutionary Path, which was clearly underlined in their Holy texts through His Earlier Chosen Prophets, and their Holy Messages were then Written down and thus Compiled in their HOLY BOOKS, even though the Lineages of the Second established Group having the HIGH PRIEST and His Helper Priesthood continued through their Birth Lineages, thus continuously performing their required duties, as being the Care Takers of the Prescribed Rituals as mentioned in their Holy Texts.

So to communicate with this Second Group, which was always headed by the HIGH PRIEST, the Great LORD established a way of DIVINATION which was totally different from the ways and means of Communication with his Chosen Prophets, and starting with AARON, the Great LORD provided His first HIGH PRIEST with "Two Holy Objects", which were known as the "'Holy Objects of Divination'", in which the First Holy Object known in Hebrew Language as 'THE URIM' provided the established HIGH PRIEST, the Spiritual Understanding of any Matter, through Visual Expansion of His Mind, which was related to the involved subject matter, and which is known since ancient times as the "LIGHT OF MIND, or the "ENLIGHTENMENT", thus providing the High Priest those 'Glimpses of Divination', which answered His questioning Mind about the Spiritual aspect of the Subject Matter, which was in Question, and mostly all such "Matters in Question" were related to the densely manifested Physical plane of ASSIAH, and the Second Holy Object known in Hebrew Language as 'THE THUMMIM' provided the HIGH PRIEST, the "'Perfect Material Understanding'" of any Subject Matter, which became totally Clear and thus Perfectly Visible in the Shining Spiritual Light, which was provided to Him by the first Holy Object "THE URIM" to His Expanded Mind, which thus gave Him the "'Proper and Perfect'" answers which were related to the involved subject matter of the material aspects, which was thus known as the "PERFECTIONS OF THE PERSONALITY MIND", or the "MATERIAL WORLD PERFECTIONS" which thus gave Him a "Total Understanding" through ENLIGHTENMENT thus provided by "THE URIM", and the PERFECT SOLUTION provided by "THE THUMMIM". Out of these Two Holy Objects, the "URIM" was of more importance, as it could work for all Spiritual Matters by itself, while THUMMIM denoting the Material World Perfections, depended entirely upon the Truthful 'SPIRITUAL' Light of the "URIM", and thus THUMMIM Could Only work in Conjunction with the URIM, but as far as the Children of Israel were concerned, both of these Holy Objects were of Divine Nature, as given by the LORD to HIS Chosen High Priest AARON.

By Providing these Two Holy Objects of Divination to His HIGH PRIEST AARON, which are Clearly mentioned in the Holy Bible as "THE URIM and THE THUMMIM", the Great LORD Commanded MOSES to tell the Children of Israel not to Indulge in Any Other Type of Divination Practices from that point onward, which were then illegally practiced in all other lands including Egypt where they were Most Popular among their People, where the Corrupt Gods and Goddesses invisibly dwelt expanding their Illegal and deceitful agendas, which were contrary to the SPIRITUAL EVOLUTION of SOUL CONSCIOUSNESS, Who with their Mutated Minds willfully betrayed HIS "Love and Trust", and thus Hijacked the Evolutionary Spiritual Path, by replacing it with Dense Material Path of "Illusory Glamour and Virtual Reality MATRIX", and regarding the LORD'S Command, which was Humbly Conveyed by MOSES to the Children of Israel, in this respect the Holy Bible states:

'If a Prophet or a Dreamer of dreams arises among you, and gives you a sign of wonder, and the Sign or the Wonder comes True, concerning which He Spoke to you, Saying, "Let us go after '"OTHER GODS"' [Whom you have Not Known] and Let Us Serve them". You shall not listen to the Words of that Prophet or that Dreamer of dreams; for the LORD your GOD is testing you to find out, IF YOU LOVE THE LORD YOUR GOD WITH ALL YOUR HEART AND WITH ALL YOUR SOUL. You shall follow the LORD your GOD and fear HIM; and you shall KEEP HIS Commandments, Listen to HIS Voice, Serve HIM, and cling to HIM. But that Prophet or that Dreamer of Dreams shall be put to Death, because He has Counseled Rebellion against the LORD your GOD, who brought you from the Land of Egypt, and redeemed you from the HOUSE of SLAVERY, to SEDUCE you from the way in which the LORD your GOD Commanded you to Walk. So you shall PURGE the EVIL from among you. [Deuteronomy 13. Verses 1 to 5.]

'When you enter the Land, which the Lord Your God gives you, you shall NOT Learn to IMITATE the Detestable things of those Nations. There shall NOT be Found Among you Anyone, who makes His Son or His Daughter pass through the FIRE, One who uses DIVINATION, One who

Practices WITCHCRAFT, or One who interprets OMENS, Or a SORCERER, or One who Casts SPELLS, or a MEDIUM, or a SPIRITIST, or One WHO CALLS UP THE DEAD.

For whoever does these Things is Detestable to the LORD; and because of these Detestable Things, THE LORD YOUR GOD WILL DRIVE THEM OUT BEFORE YOU. You shall be blameless before the LORD your GOD. For All the Nations, which you shall DISPOSSESS, Listen to those who practice WITCHCRAFT and to DIVINERS, but as for you, THE LORD YOUR GOD HAS NOT ALLOWED YOU TO DO SO. The LORD your GOD will raise up for you a PROPHET LIKE 'ME' from among you, from your Countrymen, YOU SHALL LISTEN TO HIM.

This is according to all, that you asked of the LORD your GOD in HOREB on the Day of the Assembly, Saying, "Let me Not Hear again the Voice of the LORD My GOD, Let Me NOT See this Great FIRE Anymore, LEST I DIE." And the LORD Said to Me, "THEY have Spoken Well. "'I'" will Raise UP a PROPHET from among their Countrymen like YOU, and "'I'" will PUT MY WORDS in His Mouth, and He shall speak to Them ALL THAT "'I'" COMMAND HIM. And it shall come about that WHOEVER will NOT LISTEN TO MY WORDS, Which He shall Speak in MY NAME, "'I'" MYSELF WILL REQUIRE IT OF HIM.

But the PROPHET, Who shall SPEAK a WORD 'PRESUMPTUOUSLY' in MY NAME, WHICH "'I'" HAVE NOT COMMANDED HIM TO SPEAK, OR WHICH HE SHALL SPEAK IN THE NAME OF "'OTHER GODS'", THAT PROPHET SHALL DIE. [Deuteronomy 18. Verses 9 to 20.]

These so called Gods and Goddesses. Who willfully defiled everything upon this Planet Earth, against the wishes of their Most Benevolent and Trusting Creator LORD – GOD, THE MOST HIGH in the Entire Universe, they did so for the very basic reason of their ILLEGAL CONTROLS, so that the Evolving Human Beings of this Planet, can be deceitfully controlled through the services of their Incarnated Henchmen, whom they illegally put as the heads of the evolving Human Societies in their controlled lands, who by their illegally enacted rules, put in place by the Cruel acts of force, and other Ruthless regulations, they could thus easily control their fellow Human subjects, as per the wishes of their deceitful Masters, just like any other Controlled Lower Species of the evolving Animal Kingdom, thus forcing them to spend their incarnated lives by living under their illegal controls in the territories of their Corrupted

World, and thus these controlled Human Beings then willingly or unwillingly, should perform those very acts, which are Contrary to their Prescribed Holy Texts.

These unfortunate Human Beings thus always stayed Constantly under their Demonic Control, even after the Physical Death of their Material Bodies, with "Absolutely No Chance" whatsoever to receive their SPIRITUAL ENLIGHTENMENT'S, which were clearly prescribed by the MOST HIGH in the Established Evolutionary Plans, which are meant for this Beautiful Planet Earth.

For these both Holy objects, "The URIM and the THUMMIM", the Great LORD instructed MOSES to put them inside the """BREAST PIECE OF JUDGMENT"""", in its Left Side Pocket's designated area, which is right over a Human Heart, so as to be Worn by AARON over His Heart for all Purposes of Divination, which Practically Gave Him LORD'S JUDGMENT regarding All the Important Matters, when He entered into HIS Holy Presence, which were then Clearly Visualized by Him through those Visions, Which Concerned the Sons of Israel, regarding which the Holy Bible States:

"'And YOU shall PUT in the Breast Piece of Judgment, the URIM and the THUMMIM, and they shall be over AARON'S Heart, when He goes in Before the LORD; and AARON shall Cary the Judgment of the Sons of Israel over His Heart, before the LORD Continually." [Exodus 28. 30.]

And both these URIM and THUMMIM along with the Breast Plate and other Priestly Garments were later transferred from AARON to His Son ELEAZAR, as per the Command of the LORD on MOUNT HOR, which was Situated by the Border of the Land of EDOM, regarding which the Holy Bible States:

'Then the LORD Spoke to MOSES and AARON at Mount HOR by the border of the Land of EDOM, Saying, "'AARON shall be Gathered to His People; for He shall not Enter the Land, which "I" have given to the Sons of Israel, because YOU Rebelled against MY Command at the Waters of MERIBAH.

Take AARON and His Son ELEAZAR, and bring them up to Mount HOR; and STRIP AARON OF HIS GARMENTS, and PUT them on His Son ELEAZAR. So AARON will be gathered to His People, and will DIE there."

So MOSES did as the LORD had commanded, and they went up to Mount HOR in the Sight of All the Congregation. And after MOSES had Stripped AARON of His Garments, and Put them on His Son ELEAZAR, AARON Died there ON THE MOUNTAIN TOP. Then MOSES and ELEAZAR Came down from the Mountain. And when all the Congregation saw that AARON had Died, all the House of Israel Wept for AARON Thirty Days. [Numbers 20. Verses 23 to 29.]

The LORD'S Prophet MOSES constantly reminded the Children of Israel, that they were just mere Slaves earlier in the Lands of Pharaoh, where their daily lives were mostly filled with Afflictions, from where their Great Merciful LORD with HIS Ineffable Grace, then delivered them, regarding which the Holy Bible states:

'And you shall Remember that YOU were a SLAVE in the Land of Egypt, and the LORD your GOD brought you OUT of There by a MIGHTY HAND, and by an Outstretched Arm; therefore the LORD your GOD Commanded you to observe the SABBATH Day.' [Deuteronomy 5. 15.]

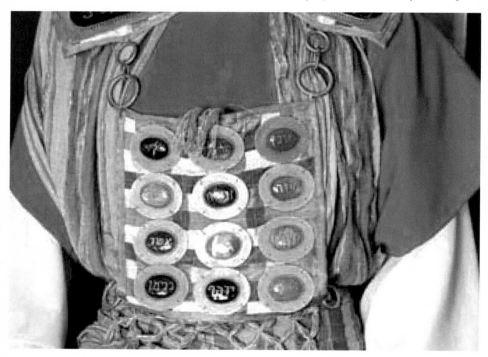

The Breast Plate of the High Priest [Kohen Gadula], showing 12 precious stones as commanded by LORD-GOD, representing the 12 Tribes of Israel, which also correspond to the 12 Cosmic Energies of the Zodiacal Constellations

During the time of Exodus, the So Called Divination through Wrong methods was carried out by Various Human societies, as clearly mentioned in "Deuteronomy 18. 9, 10, 11." of the Holy Bible, which primarily employed the services of Dead, Witchcraft, Mediums, Sorcery, Interpreting the Omens etc. and was thus in Full Swing at that time in many Places of this Planet Earth, Especially in those Lands where the Worship of So called Gods and Goddesses was Openly and Rigorously Practiced by Ignorant Human Beings, whose 'Personality Minds' although were Materially Smart and Advanced in all their outlooks in worldly matters, which were related to the affairs of this Dense Physical world, which objectively exists manifested in the dimensional plane of ASSIAH of this Planet Earth, but they were totally unaware and thus ignorant of the Various Spiritual Understandings, which pertained to their Own Higher Selves existence in the Invisible Higher Dimensional planes of this Planet, and also were Totally Unaware of their One and Only, True LORD - GOD Creator, who since ancient times is known as the MOST HIGH, and who to start with brought into manifestation, the various types of subjective and objective, conscious and unconscious Hierarchical Existences, to consciously evolve in their Cyclic Duration's, as per HIS Evolutionary Plan and Purpose.

These So Called Gods and Goddesses, many of whom were depicted by their devotees in Various Animal forms or having Animal faces and Human Bodies or Vice a Versa, or just Plainly in Elaborated Male or Female Human forms appearing like themselves, and who thus created by their Fellow Human Beings were then venerated by the great numbers of Human Masses, as their So Called GODS and GODDESSES, Depicted in their Various Shapes as the Decorated Carved statues or as Molten Figures of Precious Metals, and these ignorant people of this Earth thus failed to understand this secret fact, that these so called Gods and Goddesses, who were established by the Hands of their Fellow Human beings in their such various Elaborated form depictions, mostly made out of lifeless pieces of wood, metal or stones etc., got charged with their own Human thought form energies, which are composed of Magnetic Energy Vibrations, which they unknowingly created through Devotional Mental Sensation of "Feelings and Emotions", which were focused toward these Idol Statues with full venerated consciousness, which were related to their desires and wishes of their lower or material minds, and were thus formed with the onslaught of Venerated Prayers, Chanting's Dancing and Singing, and concentrated Veneration Mindful thoughts formed toward their so called Gods and Goddesses.

Through these powerful magnetic energy thought forms, which were thus created over many long periods due to such Human worship, the devoted Human Beings thus unknowingly made these So called Lifeless GODS and GODDESSES Statues, as the Storehouses of Powerful Vibrating Magnetic Energies, which are composed of Live Elemental essences of the 4 Invisible ethereal sub planes of ASSIAH, as well as the Conscious and Unconscious Elemental essences, and a variety of other Conscious and Unconscious Entities and Beings of the 7 sub planes, which exist in the Next Higher Dimensional Plane of YETZIRAH, whose dimensional boundaries interpenetrate our dense physical plane of ASSIAH upon this Planet Earth.

In the Very Early stages of Evolution upon this Planet Earth, The Creator LORD - GOD OF THE FLAMES, temporarily allowed these misguided practices upon the request of his Created Servants, who are commonly known as the "ELOHIMS", which were then carried out in many places by the ignorant evolving Humanity, as these Invisible Entitles and Beings known as the "ELOHIMS", easily managed their Human Subjects through these Human Desire Mind Energy Creations which now independently existed in the various 'Thought Forms' of Magnetic Energies created through Human Devotion and continuous Worship, and were then invisibly collected in these Statues, which thus became the Invisible "Energy Store Houses", and these 'Invisible Elohim's' then distributed these thus collected energies, in various quantities to their praying worshipers, as per their needs in the physical world, which solved their DENSE MATTER related Problems, including the curing of Physical Ailments etc., which thus appeared to the Ignorant Human Beings as if these GOD STATUES and MOLTEN IDOLS were Living, and thus Alive answering their Prayers, because praying to them, their desired wishes got fulfilled. This underlying Secret Fact is still unknown to many human beings, who still reverently Worship in this advanced 'Age of Science and Technology', the so called GODS and GODDESSES in many parts of the Physical World, instead of their ONE AND ONLY "True Creator" LORD – GOD, "THE MOST HIGH", the Unknowable Creator-Observer LORD of this Subjectively and Objectively Manifested Universe, whom the Ancient Vedic Hindu Scriptures could only define at their best as the "UNKNOWABLE TATTA", or the "GREAT LORD".

These Elohim's, who existing in their various Numerous Hierarchical Groups are themselves the '''DESIRE MIND CREATIONS''' of the Great LORD – GOD of the Universe, reverently known among HIS Followers as the '''MOST HIGH''', after passing of time, then became Totally Corrupt and Conceited after the widespread Misuse of their Vested Powers, and started enjoying their Glorious Status as the So called 'Gods and Goddesses' among Ignorant Human Beings, and thus became Openly Rebellious to their OWN CREATOR LORD, and have WILLFULLY IGNORED, since ancient times the 'Universal Demand' to stop their EVIL WAYS, and WRONGFUL PRACTICES upon this Planet Earth, as well as THE CELESTIAL COMMAND of "RETURN and SURRENDER".

The Most Benevolent LORD – GOD, "THE MOST HIGH", to protect His Chosen People, the Children of Israel, from such Demonic Divination Practice's, and to properly answer their Questions which were related to the ensuing "Spiritual" and "Worldly Matters", then gave the 2 Holy Objects known as "THE URIM and THE THUMMIM" to MOSES, so that He can Put them in the "BREAST PLATE OF JUDGEMENT" over the body area of AARON'S Heart, who was the First Chosen High Priest by the LORD and thus established for the Children of Israel, regarding which the Holy Bible States:

'MOSES said to the Congregation, "THIS is the Thing, which the LORD has Commanded to do." Then MOSES had AARON and His Sons come NEAR, and WASHED them with Water. And He Put the TUNIC on Him, and Girded Him with the Sash, and clothed Him with the Robe, and put EPHOD on Him; and He Girded Him with the Artistic Band of the EPHOD, with which He Tied it to Him.

He then Placed the BREASTPIECE on Him, and IN THE BREASTPIECE, HE PUT '''THE URIM AND THE THUMMIM.'''' [Leviticus 8. Verses 5 to 8.]

During those Times, when matters related to SPIRIT were Concerned by the Children of Israel, the SPIRITUAL LIGHT OF 'URIM'', then answered their such Questions, regarding which the Holy Bible states:

'Then MOSES Spoke to the LORD, Saying, "MAY the LORD, the GOD of the SPIRITS OF ALL FLESH, Appoint a Man over the Congregation, Who will go out and come before them, and Who will Lead them Out and

Bring them in, that the Congregation of the LORD may not be like the Sheep, which has No SHEPHERD."

So the LORD Said to MOSES, "Take JOSHUA, the Son of NUN, a Man in whom is the SPIRIT, and Lay your Hand on Him; and have Him stand before ELEAZAR the Priest, and before all the Congregation; and Commission Him in their Sight. And you shall Put Some of Your Authority on Him, in order that All the Congregation of the Sons of Israel may Obey Him.

Moreover, He shall stand before ELEAZAR the Priest, WHO SHALL INQUIRE FOR HIM, BY THE ""JUDGEMENT OF THE URIM"" BEFORE THE LORD. At His Command they shall Go Out, and at His Command they shall Come In, BOTH He and the Sons of Israel with Him, Even All the Congregation.

Then MOSES did just as the LORD Commanded Him; and He took JOSHUA and Set Him before ELEAZAR the Priest, and before All the Congregation.' [Numbers 27. Verses 15 to 22.]

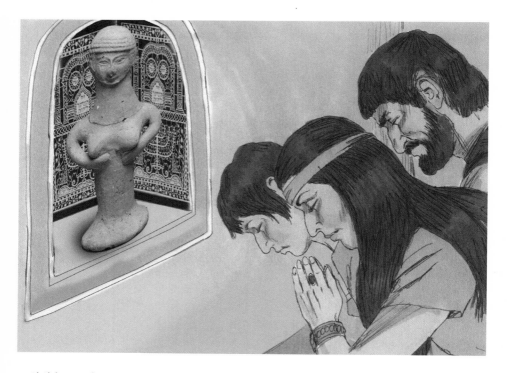

Children of Israel wrongfully worshiped the "Goddess Asherah - Ashtaroth".
"So they forsook the LORD and served Baal and the Ashtaroth" [Judges 2.13]

Moses showing the Ten Commandments of the LORD, etched on 2 stone
tablets, to the rebellious children of Israel in the wilderness of Sinai.

'FLAMING SWORDS"

Then the LORD Said to MOSES, "Make a FIERY SERPENT, and Set it on a Standard; and it shall come about, that everyone who is BITTEN, when He LOOKS at it, HE SHALL LIVE." And MOSES made a Bronze SERPENT, and Set it on the Standard; and it came about, that if a SERPENT Bit any Man, when He Looked to the Bronze SERPENT, He Lived.' [Numbers 21. Verses 8, 9.]

Part 49

All Human Beings, whom the LORD of FLAMES Created in HIS own Image upon this Planet Earth as mentioned in "Genesis 1. 27." of the Holy Bible, they were supposed to 'Gradually Evolve' enhancing their "SPIRIT CONSCIOUSNESS", as well as their "HIGHER MIND" commonly known as "THE SOUL", by gaining Spiritual Experiences in the 3 dimensional worlds of this Planet Earth, through the Cyclic Periods of Limited 'Time Duration's', which defined the so called 'Birth and Death" of their animated Incarnated Forms manifested upon the 3 Dense Dimensional Planes of this Planet Earth [ASSIAH, YETZIRAH, and BRIAH], which were composed of variegated subject matter made of unconscious elemental essences, which were related to these 3 Main Dimensional planes of Existence.

ALL Human Beings were thus supposed to evolve in various Human Races of Colors and Sizes, through the 'CONSCIOUS ATTRIBUTE OF WELL DEFINED "'INDIVIDUALIZED MIND'"', commonly known as the "FREE WILL", which Clearly Distinguished and thus Separate them from all other Species of Animal Kingdom, which were Introduced by the LORD of Flames as per HIS Evolutionary Plan and Purpose.

The LORD OF FLAMES Servant Helpers known as the 'ELOHIMS' meaning the Children of GOD, exist in their Two Major HERMAPHRODITE Varieties, which are Invisible to the Human Beings, and are known as the "SERAPHIM" meaning the "FIERY ONES OR THE BURNING ONES", who since ancient times have been Known to Advanced Seers as the "FIERY SERPENTS" or the "FLAMING SWORDS", and the "CHERUBIM'S" meaning the " WINGED CREATURES".

Both of these Main Angelic Varieties are supposed to Faithfully Serve their Creator LORD – GOD with FULL CONSCIOUSNESS OF THEIR "HEART AND MIND", especially through their Hierarchical Sub Group known as the 'NEPHILIM' who are mentioned in 'Genesis 6.4.' of the Holy Bible, as ALL OF THEM were Created by THE MOST HIGH, before the Creation of Human Beings took Place upon this Planet earth.

Both SERAPHIM and CHERUBIM are mentioned in the Holy Bible, for the First Time in its very first chapter called as "The Chapter of Creation", which is commonly known as the Chapter of "Genesis", although the SERAPHIM'S are ONLY mentioned by their 'Codified Quality Name' as the "FLAMING SWORD", regarding which the Holy Bible States:

"'Then the LORD GOD Said, "Behold, the Man has become Like One of US, knowing GOOD and EVIL; and now, Lest He Stretch out His Hand, and take also from the 'TREE OF LIFE', and Eat and Live Forever" – therefore the LORD GOD Sent Him out from the Garden of Eden, to cultivate the ground from which He was taken. So He drove the Man out; and at the East of the Garden of Eden HE STATIONED THE "CHERUBIM", AND THE "FLAMING SWORD" WHICH TURNED EVERY DIRECTION, TO GUARD THE WAY TO THE TREE OF LIFE.'" [Genesis 3. Verses 22 to 24.]

The Seraphim are mentioned again in the Holy Bible, at the time of MOSES in the Wilderness, by their 'Codified Quality Name' as the "FIERY SERPENTS", regarding which the Holy Bible states:

'And the LORD Sent FIERY SERPENTS among the People, and They BIT the People, so that Many People of Israel DIED. So the People came to Moses and Said, "WE have SINNED, because WE have Spoken against the LORD and YOU; Intercede with the LORD, that HE may Remove the SERPENTS from US." And MOSES interceded for the People. Then the LORD Said to MOSES, "Make a FIERY SERPENT, and Set it on a Standard; and it shall come about, that everyone who is BITTEN, when He LOOKS at it, HE SHALL LIVE." And MOSES made a Bronze SERPENT, and Set it on the Standard; and it came about, that if a SERPENT Bit any Man, when He Looked to the Bronze SERPENT, He Lived.' [Numbers 21. Verses 6 to 9.]

Since the ancient times of this Planet Earth, Various Evolving Human Races living upon its Huge Continents, which are Separated by the Huge Oceans, have Depicted these FIERY SERPENTS as the Holy Symbols of Protection in their Places of Worship, sometimes Etched as the "FIERY DRAGONS", and the Feminine Deities as the Symbols of Sleeping KUNDALINI FORCE, which are required for the PRESERVATION of their "VITAL ETHEREAL LIFE ESSENCE", and which thus provides them "FIERY HEAT OF MIND SENSES", which are essentially required for the ANIMATION ASPECT of their densely formed Material Bodies, which allows the Functioning of their Human Forms during their Incarnated Lives.

These SERAPHIM'S OR THE INVISIBLE FIERY SERPENTS are also known as " THE BURNING ONES of LOVE and PASSION", as their Consciousness is Primarily Composed of Magnetic Ethereal Energies, which emanate from the Central Core of this Planet Earth, and thus they are the Primary Care takers of the Astral Plane known in the Hebrew Language as the Dimensional Sphere of YETZIRAH, which is Primarily the Dimensional Plane of LOWER MIND DESIRES, known to Human Beings as the Liquid "Feelings and Emotions", Which get aroused pertaining to the "Dense Material World's Subjects and Objects". These "Feelings and Emotions" of Human Beings, which gets Created and Formulated as the "Live Thought Forms", being related to the Dense Material "Subjects and Objects", have their own independent "Life Periods" whose life time duration depends upon the Concentrated Efforts of the "Desire Mind" of the Involved Human Beings, which is generally termed as their "One Pointed WILL POWER", and usually stay as frequency vibrations in the ether's till their desired GOAL is Fulfilled.

Many of the Ill Minded Human Desires, which never got FULFILLED and thus their "THOUGHT FORMS" Never got DISSIPATED, then existing in their such 'Collective Group Formations', they became the PRIME SOURCE OF ALL CORRUPTION upon this Planet Earth, which through their HIGH CONCENTRATION LEVELS then permeated the Higher Dimensional Ethereal Matter thus existing as "'THE UNDESIRED COLLECTIVE CONSCIOUSNESS", which working its way out both Upward and Downward thus entered the "Interpenetrating Dimensional Zones" of this Planet Earth, which appear like the Shape of an EYE, and then also thus CORRUPTED the MIND CONSCIOUSNESS of these Various Hierarchical Groups of "ELOHIM", who are considered by the Evolving Human Beings of this Planet as their revered GODS and GODDESSES, because they being the 'CARETAKERS OF VITAL ENERGY RESERVOIRS" were Utilizing as well as Redistributing these "Magnetic Liquid Energies" for the benefit of evolving Human Beings, who thus fell from their GRACE, and since then are known in the Holy Texts as the "Fallen Angels".

These SERAPHIM'S as FIERY SERPENTS are again mentioned in the Chapter of Deuteronomy in the Holy Bible, in which MOSES is reminding the Children of Israel about the LORD'S Good DEEDS, which HE Earlier Performed for them, regarding which the Holy Bible States:

"He Led YOU through the Great and Terrible Wilderness, with its

'FIERY SERPENTS', and Scorpions, and Thirsty Ground, where there was No Water; He Brought Water for You out of the Rock of FLINT. " [Deuteronomy 8.15.]

The Great LORD Trustfully gave these "ELOHIM" independent POWERS to become the 'CARE TAKER GUIDES' of the evolving Human Races, and to look after their 'Gradual Conscious Expansion's', which were supposed to take place during their Cyclic Evolutionary Periods of Limited Time duration's upon this Planet Earth, in which the Human Races through their ENHANCED SPIRITUAL MINDS were Supposed to Gradually unravel the Hidden Mysteries of the Invisible Dimensions of this Planet Earth, but when their care takers the "Elohim" themselves stumbled from their required duties, then this Established Evolutionary Process got Totally Corrupted, and came in the hands of SO CALLED MASTERS, the INVISIBLE HEADS OF SECRET SOCIETIES, Who illegally wanted to RULE THIS PLANET for themselves, instead of their MOST BENEVOLENT CREATOR, "THE MOST HIGH".

After passing of many centuries the LORD himself gave a Vision to His Chosen Prophet ISAIAH about these SERAPHIM'S, regarding which the "Holy Bible" States:

'In the Year of King UZZIAH'S Death, I Saw the LORD Sitting on a Throne, Lofty and Exalted, with the Train of HIS Robe filling the Temple. SERAPHIM Stood above HIM, Each having Six Wings; with Two He Covered His Face, and with Two He Covered His Feet, and with Two He Flew. And One called out to ANOTHER and Said, "HOLY, HOLY, HOLY, IS THE LORD OF HOSTS, THE WHOLE EARTH IS FULL OF HIS GLORY." [Isaiah 6. 1, 2, 3.]

[Unknown to many Human Beings, Six is the Mathematical Number of Solar Consciousness]

The Holy Bible Further States about this episode:

"And the Foundations of the Thresholds Trembled at the Voice of Him who called out, while the Temple was filling with Smoke. Then I Said, "WOE to Me, for I am Ruined! Because I am a Man of Unclean Lips, and I Live among a People of Unclean Lips; For My Eyes have Seen the KING, the LORD of HOSTS." Then one of the SERAPHIM Flew to Me, with a Burning Coal in His Hand, which He had taken from the Altar with Tongs.

252

And He Touched My MOUTH with it and Said, "Behold this has Touched YOUR Lips; and you Iniquity is taken away, and your SIN is Forgiven." [Isaiah 6. 4, 5, 6, 7.]

King David also mentioned CHERUB in His Song which He sang for the Glory of the Almighty LORD, regarding which the Holy Bible States:

'And David SPOKE the words of this Song to the LORD in the Day that the LORD Delivered Him from the Hand of All his Enemies, and from the Hand of Saul. And He Said, "THE LORD is My ROCK, and My FORTRESS, and My DELIVERER. In My Distress, I called upon the LORD, YES I Cried to My GOD; And from HIS Temple HE Heard My Voice. And My Cry for HELP came into HIS Ears. Then the Earth Shook and Quaked. The Foundations of Heaven were Trembling, and were SHAKEN, because HE was Angry. Smoke went up out of HIS Nostrils, and FIRE from HIS Mouth Devoured' Coals were Kindled by it. He Bowed the Heavens also, and came down with Thick Darkness under His Feet. And HE rode on a '"CHERUB"' and Flew; and HE appeared on the Wings of the Wind.' [2 Samuel 22. 1, 2, 7, 8, 9, 10, 11.]

Psalm 18 in the Holy Bible repeat the same words, which state:

"And HE rode on a '"CHERUB"' and Flew; and HE appeared on the Wings of the Wind." [Psalm 18. 10.]

During the Time of Prophet ISAIAH, King HEZEKIAH also mentioned CHERUBIM, while praying to the LORD, regarding which the Holy Bible states:

And HEZEKIAH Prayed to the LORD Saying, "O LORD of HOSTS, the GOD of ISRAEL, Who art Enthroned above the CHERUBIM, Thou art the GOD, THOU ALONE, of All the Kingdoms of the Earth. THOU HAST MADE HEAVEN AND EARTH." [Isaiah 37. 15, 16.]

The Prophet EZEKIEL also mentioned CHERUBIM in His Vision, regarding which the Holy Bible States:

"These are the Living Beings, that I Saw beneath the GOD of Israel, by the River Chebar; So I Knew that they were CHERUBIM. Each one had Four Faces, and Each one Four Wings, and beneath their Wings was the Form of Human Hands. As for the Likeness of their Faces, they were the same faces, whose appearance I had seen by the River Chebar. Each one went Straight Ahead." [Ezekiel. 10, 20, 21, 22.]

In His letter to HEBREWS, the Great Apostle PAUL, a Servant of LORD JESUS CHRIST, originally a Pharisee Jew from Tarsus in Cilicia, whose earlier name was Saul, mentions CHERUBIM depictions being in the Holy of Holies, regarding which the Holy Bible States:

"And behind the Second Veil, there was a Tabernacle which is called the 'Holy of Holies', having a Golden Altar of Incense, and the 'Ark of the Covenant' covered on All Sides with GOLD, in which was a Golden Jar holding the MANNA, and AARON'S ROD which budded, and the Tables of the Covenant.

And above it were the CHERUBIM OF GLORY, overshadowing the Mercy Seat; but of these things we cannot speak in Detail". [Hebrews 9. 3, 4, 5.]

The Beloved Apostle JOHN also had a Vision of the LORD OF THE FLAMES, with flashes of Lightening and Sounds of Thunder, just as in the ancient times MOSES witnessed the Great LORD on MOUNT SINAI – HOREB, which got first Revealed to His Chosen Son JESUS CHRIST and then communicated to JOHN by an angel of the LORD, in which he similarly saw the CHERUBIM'S, as mentioned much earlier by Prophet EZEKIEL in His Visions of GOD, but in this Vision JOHN saw them having them Six Wings like that of SERAPHIM, which were envisioned by Prophet ISAIAH, instead of the Four Wings which were envisioned by Prophet EZEKIEL, but in his Vision Apostle JOHN instead of Seeing the Human Hands, like the Prophet EZEKIEL earlier saw in His Vision, instead Saw Two more Wings, regarding which the Holy Bible States:

"'The Revelation of JESUS CHRIST, which GOD gave HIM to Show to HIS Bond – Servants, the Things which must Shortly take Place; and HE Sent and Communicated it by HIS Angel to HIS Bond – Servant JOHN, Who bore Witness to the WORD OF GOD and to the Testimony of JESUS CHRIST , even to ALL that He Saw.'" [Revelation 1. 1, 2.]

"'And from the Throne Proceed Flashes of Lightning and Sounds, and Peals of Thunder. And there were Seven Lamps of FIRE burning before the Throne, which are the Seven SPIRITS of GOD; And before the Throne there was, as it were, a Sea of Glass Like Crystals; and in the Center and around the Throne, Four Living Creatures full of Eyes in Front and BEHIND. And the First Creature was Like a LION, and the Second Creature like a CALF, and the Third Creature had a Face Like that of a MAN, and the Fourth Creature was Like a Flying Eagle.

And the Four Living Creatures, Each One of Them having Six Wings, are Full of Eyes around and within; and Day and Night they do not Cease to Say , "HOLY, HOLY, HOLY, IS THE LORD GOD, THE ALMIGHTY, WHO WAS AND WHO IS, AND WHO IS TO 'TO COME."

And When the Living Creatures give GLORY, and HONOR, and THANKS, to HIM, Who SITS on the THRONE, to HIM, WHO LIVES FOREVER AND EVER.'" [Revelation 4. Verses 5 to 9.]

"And HE rode on the "'CHERUB'" and Flew; and HE appeared on the Wings of the Wind." [Psalm 18. 10.]

"These are the Living Beings, that I Saw beneath the GOD of Israel, by the River Chebar; So I Knew that they were CHERUBIM. Each one had Four Faces, and Each one Four Wings, and beneath their Wings was the Form of Human Hands. As for the Likeness of their Faces, they were the same faces, whose appearance I had seen by the River Chebar. Each one went Straight Ahead." [Ezekiel. 10, 20, 21, 22.]

Children of Israel wrongfully worshiped "Baal" instead of their LORD the MOST HIGH in the "Promised Land". "So they forsook the LORD and served Baal and the Ashtaroth" [Judges 2.13]

Even though the Great LORD – GOD of ABRAHAM, ISSAC and JACOB, through the Services of HIS Humble Servant MOSES and His brother AARON, freed the Physical Incarnated Bodies of the 'Children of Israel' from the Afflicting hands of the Mighty Pharaoh and His innumerable Deities, the so called GODS and GODDESSES of the Land of Egypt, their indwelling "Personality Minds" were still Craving the Lower Mind Desires, like any other members of the Animal Kingdom, and were still Polarized in the Next Invisible Higher plane, which is known to the Seers as the Dimensional world of YETZIRAH, which is composed of both Conscious and Unconscious Invisible Elemental Essences, which create its liquid magnetic frequency Vibrations Vital Material, and which since the 'Time of Creation" upon this Planet Earth, has been designated by "THE MOST HIGH" to be under the control of HIS Creator Servant Helpers, the so Called Gods and Goddesses, who are None other than the Hermaphrodite ELOHIM'S of Various Hierarchical Orders, commonly known to Humans as the "Angelic Beings, who invisibly exist in its 7 main Dimensional Sub Planes, to look after the Gradual Evolution of Conscious Expansion, which since the Time of Creation is taking place in the Various Visible and Invisible Differentiated Evolving Kingdoms of the Densest Dimensional Plane of this Planet Earth, known in Hebrew Language as the 'SEPHIROT of ASSIAH', of which the Normally Visible to the Human Eyes are 'THE MINERAL KINGDOM', 'THE VEGETABLE OR PLANT KINGDOM', 'THE ANIMAL KINGDOM', and 'THE HUMAN KINGDOM', but with the Aid of Science and Technology now the Humans can also See, the differentiated World of Tiny Microbial Species, as well as those Micro Elemental Lives, which form the Various 'Cells' and 'Tissues' of a Human Body itself.

The Cravings of the Lower Mind Desires, which Since ancient Times of this Planet Earth have been under the domain of these So called Invisible Gods and Goddesses, thus constantly made the Children of Israel Stumble from the Commands of the LORD, due to Which they again and again Grumbled under their MAGNETICALLY IMPULSED "'CORRUPT MIND CONTROL'", and thus Rebelled Against the Commands of their Most Benevolent LORD – GOD, and then faced the Dire Consequences.

The Great LORD – GOD, after delivering them from the 'Mental and Physical' Bondage's of the Pharaoh, and the so called 'Gods and Goddesses' of Egypt, Knowingly took the Children of Israel for 40 Years in the Wilderness, under the Leadership of HIS Humble Servant MOSES, so that they being the Members of HIS chosen Human Race, could thereby DEVELOP their Higher Mind Energies, which are Commonly Termed as the Human "WILL POWER", and which is the SECRET KEY to connect to their "SPIRITUAL MIND also known as their HIGHER SELVES, so they Would not Scum like all other Evolving Human Beings of this Planet, who Constantly Stumble during their Incarnated Lives from their 'WRITTEN DOWN HOLY TEXTS', due to the Same Reason of having their "Evolving Personality Minds Firmly Polarized in the Desires of the Lower Mind", and thus living, just like all other Evolving Animal Species, who are also Polarized during their incarnated lives in such Lower Mind Attractions, or in the Liquid Magnetic Desires, which are commonly Termed as the Sensations of "EMOTIONS and FEELINGS", which are related to the ILLUSORY GLAMOUR of the DENSE MATERIAL WORLD [ASSIAH] upon this Planet Earth.

After the passing away of JOSHUA, The Children of Israel again Went Astray, and Willfully Forsook their LORD, the "MOST HIGH", the LORD – GOD of their Forefathers, Who brought them out of the Land of Egypt, and they thus willfully Engaged themselves again in Doing Evil against their LORD, by serving So called Other GODS, Especially the "BAAL" and "ASHTAROTH", The Female Goddess, which aroused the Anger of LORD, and to teach them a Bitter Lesson, HE took away HIS Umbrella Protection from them, so that they could not stand anymore before their Enemies, which caused them Severe Distress, and also made them CRY to the LORD. Then the Great LORD MERCIFULLY took Pity on them, and for the first time HE raised up "JUDGES" among them, so as to deliver them out of the Hands of their Enemies, regarding which the Holy Bible States:

""""Then JOSHUA, the Son of NUN, the Servant of the LORD Died at the Age of One Hundred and Ten. And they buried Him in the Territory of His Inheritance in TIMNATH – HERES, in the Hill Country of Ephraim, North of Mount GAASH. And All That GENERATION also were Gathered to their Fathers; and there Arose ANOTHER GENERATION AFTER THEM, 'WHO DID NOT KNOW THE LORD', NOR YET THE WORK, WHICH HE HAD DONE FOR ISRAEL.

Then the Sons of Israel did EVIL in the SIGHT OF THE LORD, and Served "THE BAALS", and they Forsook the LORD, the GOD OF THEIR FATHERS, Who had Brought them Out of the Land Of Egypt, and Followed OTHER GODS from Among the GODS of Other Peoples Who were Around Them, and Bowed themselves Down to them; thus they Provoked the LORD to Anger.

So they Forsook the LORD and Served 'BAAL' and the 'ASHTAROTH', And the Anger of the LORD Burned Against Israel, and HE Gave them into the Hands of Plunderers, Who Plundered them; and HE Sold them into the Hands of their Enemies around them, so that they could No Longer Stand before their Enemies.

Wherever they went, the Hand of the LORD was AGAINST them for EVIL, as the LORD had SPOKEN and as the LORD had SWORN to them, SO they were SEVERELY DISTRESSED. Then the LORD Raised UP "'JUDGES'", WHO DELIVERED them from the Hands of those, who PLUNDERED them.

And YET they did Not Listen to their JUDGES, for they PLAYED the Harlot after OTHER GODS, and BOWED themselves DOWN to them. They Turned Aside QUICKLY from the Way, in which their FATHERS had WALKED in Obeying the Commandments of the LORD; THEY DID NOT DO AS THEIR FATHERS.

And When the LORD raised up JUDGES for them, the 'LORD WAS WITH THE JUDGE', and DELIVERED them from the Hand of their Enemies, All the DAYS of the JUDGE; For the LORD was Moved to Pity by their Groaning because of those, Who OPPRESSED and AFFLICTED them.

But it came about when the JUDGE Died, that they would TURN BACK AND "ACT MORE CORRUPTLY THAN THEIR FATHERS", IN FOLLOWING OTHER GODS TO SERVE THEM, AND BOW DOWN TO THEM; THEY DID NOT ABANDON THEIR PRACTICES OR THEIR STUBBORN WAYS.

So the Anger of the LORD Burned Against Israel, and HE Said, "'BECAUSE THIS NATION HAS TRANSGRESSED 'MY COVENANT', WHICH "I" COMMANDED THEIR FATHERS, AND HAS NOT LISTENED TO 'MY VOICE', "I" ALSO WILL "NO LONGER" DRIVE OUT BEFORE THEM, ANY OF THE NATIONS, WHICH 'JOSHUA' LEFT, WHEN HE DIED, IN ORDER TO TEST 'ISRAEL' BY THEM, WHETHER THEY WILL KEEP THE 'WAY OF THE LORD', TO WALK IN IT AS THEIR FATHERS DID, OR NOT.'"

So the LORD allowed those Nations to Remain, Not driving them out quickly; and HE did not give them into the Hand of JOSHUA.'''" [Judges 2. Verses 8 to 23.]

Clay statuette of Asherah

Part 51

Even When the LORD raised JUDGES among the Children of Israel from Time to Time, after Listening to their Wailing's and Crying's, who ALWAYS Mercifully delivered them from their Afflictions, just like during in earlier times the Humble Servant of the LORD, MOSES, also with LORD'S intervention delivered them again and again from their Afflictions, the Children of Israel for various reasons, forgetting their LORD - GOD, Still Willfully went on Doing Again and again 'EVIL' in the Sight of the LORD.

And the PRIME REASON for their Such EVIL Treachery against the LORD was, that they were following their "LOWER MIND DESIRE'S", when they wrongly 'INTERMARRIED' those in the Lands of their Occupation, who Worshiped Other GODS and GODDESSES, Especially the GODS known as the "BAALS" and the GODDESS "ASHEROTH" regarding which the Holy Bible States:

'"And the Sons of Israel Lived among the Canaanites, the Hittites, the Amorites, the Perizzites, the Hivites, and Jebusites; and they took their daughters for themselves as Wives, and gave their Own Daughters to their Sons, and Served their GOD'S.

And the Sons of Israel did, what was EVIL in the Sight of the LORD, and FORGOT the LORD their GOD, and SERVED the 'BAALS', and the 'ASHEROTH'. Then the Anger of the LORD was KINDLED Against Israel, So that HE sold them into the Hands of CUSHAN – RISHATHAIM King of MESOPOTAMIA; and the Sons of Israel Served CUSHAN – RISHATHAIM Eight Years.

And when the Sons of Israel Cried to the LORD, the LORD raised up a DELIVERER for the Sons of Israel to deliver them, 'OTHNIEL' the Son of KENAZ, CALEB'S Younger Brother. And the SPIRIT of the LORD Came upon Him, and He JUDGED Israel. When He went out to War, the LORD Gave CUSHAN – RISHATHAIM King of MESOPOTAMIA into His Hand, so that He Prevailed Over CUSHAN – RISHATHAIM. Then the Land had rest Forty Years. And 'OTHNIEL' the Son of KENAZ Died.

Now the Sons of Israel again did EVIL in the Sight of the LORD. So the

LORD Strengthened EGLON, the King of MOAB against Israel, BECAUSE they had done EVIL in the SIGHT OF THE LORD. And He Gathered to Himself, the Sons of AMMON and AMALEK; And He went and Defeated Israel, and they Possessed the City of the Palm Trees. And the Sons of Israel Served EGLON, the King of MOAB Eighteen Years.

But when the Sons of Israel CRIED to the LORD, the LORD Raised Up a Deliverer for them, EHUD the Son of GERA, the BENJAMITE, a Left Handed Man. And the Sons of Israel Sent Tribute by Him to EGLON, the King of Moab.'" [Judges 3 Verses 5 to 14.]

And Later On, even when EHUD Killed King EGLON, and the Sons of Israel under His Command, then Struck down about Ten Thousand Moabites, who were then followed also by SHAMGAR, the Son of ANATH, who Struck Down Six Hundred PHILISTINES with an 'OX – GOAD'; After Just Passing of Mere Only Eighty Year's, the Sons of Israel, then Again Went Astray, and did EVIL in the Sight of the LORD, regarding which the Holy Bible States:

"'Then the Sons of Israel again did EVIL in the SIGHT OF THE LORD, after EHUD Died. And the LORD sold them into the Hand of JABIN King of CANAAN, Who reigned in HAZOR; and the Commander of His Army was SISERA, Who lived in Harosheth – hagoyim. And the Sons of Israel CRIED to the LORD, for He had Nine Hundred Iron Chariots, and He OPPRESSED the Sons of Israel SEVERELY for Twenty Years.

Now DEBORAH, a PROPHETESS, the Wife of LAPPIDOTH, was JUDGING Israel at that time. And she used to SIT under the Palm Tree between RAMAH and BETHEL in the Hill Country of EPHRAIM; and the Sons OF Israel came up to Her for JUDGMENT.

Now She Sent and Summoned BARAK, the Son of ABINOAM from Kedesh- naphtali, and Said to Him, "BEHOLD, the LORD, the GOD OF ISRAEL has COMMANDED, "Go and March to Mount TABOR, and Take with YOU Ten Thousand Men from the Sons of NAPHTALI and from the Sons of JEBULUN. And "I" will Draw Out to You SISERA, the Commander of JABIN'S Army, with His Chariots, and His Many Troops to the River KISHON; and "I" will Give Him into Your Hand.'" [Judges 4. Verses 1 to 7.]

The Children of Israel with the INVISIBLE HELP, which was again

MERCIFULLY provided to them by their LORD, thus Prevailed in the Battle against the Armies of 'SISERA', and DESTROYED "JABIN", the King of CANAAN, and their Land remained Undisturbed for Forty Years. BUT the Children of Israel, Whose Evolving "PERSONALITY MIND" was Still Polarized in the "'LOWER MIND DESIRES'", which were related to the Worldly Glamour, then went on Repeating their Mistakes Again and Again, by Willfully Doing EVIL in the Sight of the LORD, regarding which the Holy Bible Further States:

"Then the Sons of Israel did what was EVIL in the SIGHT OF THE LORD; and the LORD gave them into the Hands of MIDIAN Seven Years. And the Power of MIDIAN Prevailed Against ISRAEL. Because of MIDIAN, the Sons of Israel MADE for themselves the DEN'S, which were in the MOUNTAIN'S, and the CAVE'S, and the STRONGHOLD. For it was when Israel had Sown, that the MIDIANITES would Come UP with the AMALEKITES, and the Sons of East, and Go against them. So they would Camp against them, and DESTROY the Produce of the Earth as far as GAZA, and leave No Sustenance in Israel, as well as NO Sheep, Ox, or Donkey. For they would Come Up with their LIVESTOCK and their TENTS, they would Come In Like LOCUSTS for Number, both They and Their CAMEL'S were INNUMERABLE, and they came into the Land to DEVASTATE it.

So ISRAEL was Brought Very Low, because of MIDIAN, and the Sons of Israel CRIED to the LORD. Now it came about, when the Sons of Israel Cried to the LORD on account of MIDIAN, that the LORD Sent a PROPHET to the Sons of Israel, and He Said to Them. "Thus Says the LORD, the GOD OF ISRAEL, "' IT WAS 'I' WHO BROUGHT YOU UP FROM EGYPT, AND BROUGHT YOU OUT FROM THE "HOUSE OF SLAVERY". AND 'I' DELIVERED YOU FROM THE HANDS OF EGYPTIANS, AND FROM THE HANDS OF ALL YOUR OPPRESSORS, AND DISPOSED THEM BEFORE YOU, AND GAVE YOU THEIR LAND, AND 'I' SAY TO YOU, """I AM THE LORD YOUR GOD; YOU SHALL NOT FEAR THE 'GODS OF THE AMORITES', IN WHOSE LAND YOU LIVE. BUT YOU HAVE NOT 'OBEYED ME'.'" [Judges 6. Verses 1 to 10.]

After the Passing away of MOSES and JOSHUA, although the Great LORD raised JUDGES among Children of Israel, to SPIRITUALLY Guide and also lead them out of their Daily Troubles; BUT in the Times of Great Afflictions, Which were Again Caused to them, when they WILLFULLY NOT PAYING MUCH ATTENTION TO THEIR JUDGES, DISOBEYED THEM, BY

AGAIN AND AGAIN DOING 'EVIL' IN THEIR LORD'S SIGHT; The Merciful LORD, then listening to their CRIES, still Sent them Many a Times His 'Chosen Prophets', to Wake them UP from their SPIRITUAL SLUMBER, of Whom Many a Times were OUTSIDERS rather than the PROPHETS, who were raised Among Themselves, the Prime Such Example being the Prophet 'ELIJAH', an Humble Servant of the LORD, who was a TISHBITE, as A NEW FACE thus used by the LORD was Much More Effective under such Conditions, to raise their Heavily Polarized MATERIAL MIND CONSCIOUSNESS, toward Heavenly Comforts of True 'SPIRITUAL GLORY'.

Judge 'OTHNIEL' the Son of KENAZ, CALEB'S Younger Brother

Deborah, a Prophetess, the Wife of Lappidoth, was JUDGING Israel, as she sat under the Palm Tree between RAMAH and BETHEL in the Hill Country of EPHRAIM; and the Sons OF Israel came up to Her for JUDGMENT.

Cave at Mount Tabor, Israel, now a church temple

Israel ancient Cave

Caves of the Medianites in Saudi Arabia at Mount Horheb

Israel ancient Cave

'So the King Consulted, and made Two Golden Calves, and He Said to them, "It is too much for you to go up to JERUSALEM; Behold YOUR GODS, O ISRAEL, THAT BROUGHT YOU UP FROM EGYPT." And He set one in 'BETHEL', and the other He put in 'DAN'. Now this Thing became a "'SIN'", for the People went to Worship before the ONE as far as 'DAN'. And He Made Houses on High Places, and made Priests from among all the People, who were NOT THE SONS OF LEVI. [1 Kings 12. Verses 28 to 31.]

The Secret of the Breast Plate
Part 52

During the Time, when the Great Lord Mercifully Raised JUDGES among the Sons of Israel, so as to deliver them from their Ensuing Afflictions, there were No Kings at that time in Israel, and Almost Every Man among the Children of Israel including Certain Members of the Priestly Levite Clan, willfully "'Forgetting their LORD'S Most Important Command'", Which Clearly Stated, "YOU SHALL HAVE 'NO OTHER GODS' BEFORE ME. YOU SHALL NOT MAKE FOR YOURSELF 'AN IDOL', OR ANY LIKENESS, OF WHAT IS IN HEAVEN ABOVE, OR ON THE EARTH BENEATH, OR IN THE WATER UNDER THE EARTH," [Deuteronomy 5. 7, 8.], then became CORRUPT in their MINDS due to their ensuing LOWER MIND DESIRES, and they thus became the Idol worshipers, just like all other People, who were already Dwelling in their Promised Land, as well as in the Eastern lands, which existed beyond the Euphrates and Tigris Rivers, all the way to Fertile Lands of INDIA.

These Dwellers of the Eastern Lands also became CORRUPTED much Earlier, Like their Counterpart Egyptians, Sumerians, and Chaldean's, over the Passing of Time, because being under the Corrupt Mind Control Vibration Impulses of the LORDS FIRST CREATED SERVANT HELPERS, The So Called Invisible "GODS and GODDESSES", Who willfully Back Stabbing HIS LOVE AND TRUST, through the MISUSE of their VESTED POWERS, thus HIJACKED HIS EVOLUTIONARY "SPIRITUAL PLAN AND PURPOSE" from this beautiful Planet Earth, and instead Illegally Introduced deceitful Practices through Magnetic Energy Impulses of 'Emotions and Feelings", which caused their Controlled Human Subjects to GO ASTRAY from their Evolutionary SPIRITUAL PATH, and thus instead of Showing their Humble Devotion to the Unknowable LORD OF THE FLAMES, Commonly Known as the "MOST HIGH", whom the Ancient Vedic Seers, of the Far Away Land of INDIA, Reverently Addressed as the "GREAT LORD- GOD", or the "MAHA - ISHVARA" in their Sanskrit Language, Who is always Present in SPIRIT Next to his Continuous Burning "SACRED GLOWING FIRE" known in Sanskrit as "DHUNI", then Violating their ANCIENT VEDIC RITUAL TEXTS, started the ILLEGAL Worship Practices of Serving their Man made Molten Idols, and Graven Images of the so called 'GODS and GODDESSES', and willfully stopped the Burnt offering Practices of their Ancestors in the Sacred FIRE, as Per their LORDS COMMAND, which were earlier offered by their Ancient Ancestor's through their DEVOTIONS of BURNT OFFERINGS in the Sacrificial FIRE, which were Ritually Prescribed and Practiced Wholeheartedly in the Ancient Times by their VEDIC ANCESTORS, known as the 'Aryan's' meaning the 'Children of the ARYA' or the 'Lion Race', as the Word 'Arya' in the Ancient Aramaic or Chaldean Language's means a "LION", and till to date NONE of their Incorruptible Children Followers, thus Worship Any Graven or Molten Image during their Vedic Ritual Practices, but MOST HINDUS Since Ancient times have "Ignorantly Gone Astray" from their Ancestral Vedic Path, and have thus Primarily Indulged in the Wrongful Worship of the 'Molten Idols and Graven Images', which keeping them mentally Polarized in the 'WORLDLY DESIRES' during their Entire Incarnated lives, thus makes their Evolving Desire Mind 'PERSONALITY' 'Totally Corrupt' and also BLIND toward their Evolutionary Goals, which is to Join with their Own 'SOLAR CONSCIOUS' Higher Selves, which is the Main Part of their SPIRITUAL EXISTENCE upon this Planet Earth.

During the Times of JUDGES, the Children of Israel were doing whatever was Right in their Own Eyes, especially Wrongfully Worshiping the 'Graven and Molten Images', which were Created by the Hands of Just Mere Mortal Human Beings Like Themselves, and thus forgetting their Holy Covenant, they willfully went against the Command of their LORD - GOD, regarding which the Holy Bible States:

"'Now there was a Man of the Hill Country of EPHRAIM, whose name was MICAH. And He Said to His Mother, "The Eleven Hundred Pieces of Silver, which were taken from you, about which you uttered a Curse in My Hearing, Behold, the Silver is with Me; I took it." And His Mother Said, "BLESSED be My Son by the LORD."

He then returned the Eleven Hundred Pieces of Silver to His Mother, and His Mother Said, "I Wholly Dedicate the Silver from My Hand to the LORD, for My Son to make a GRAVEN IMAGE, and a MOLTEN IMAGE; now therefore, I will return them to you."

So when He returned the Silver to His Mother, His Mother took Two Hundred Pieces of Silver and gave them to the SILVERSMITH, Who made them into a GRAVEN IMAGE, and a MOLTEN IMAGE, and they were in the House of MICAH.

And the Man MICAH had a Shrine, and He made an EPHOD, and

Household IDOLS, and consecrated one of His Sons, that He Might become His Priest.

In those Days there was No King in Israel; Every Man did what was RIGHT in His Own Eyes.

Now there was a Young Man from Bethlehem in JUDAH, who was a LEVITE; and He was staying there. Then the Man departed from the City, from Bethlehem in Judah, to stay wherever He might find a Place; and as He made His Journey, He came to the Hill Country of Ephraim, to the House of Micah. And Micah Said to Him, "Where do you come from?" And He Said to Him. "I am a LEVITE from Bethlehem in Judah, and I am going to STAY, wherever I may find a Place."

Micah then Said to Him, "Dwell with ME, and be a 'FATHER', and a 'PRIEST' to me, and I will Give you Ten Pieces of SILVER a YEAR, and a Suit of Clothes, and your MAINTENANCE." So the LEVITE went in. And the LEVITE agreed to live with the Man; and the Young Man became to Him like One of His Sons. Then the MICAH said, "NOW I know that the LORD will Prosper Me, Seeing I have a LEVITE as Priest.'" [Judges 17. Verses 1 to 13.]

[The Term "Father" is not Just a Christian term used for their 'Priesthood', as mentioned in this episode of the Holy Bible, it was already in use in the ancient times, as a term of Respect and Reverence for the members of the "Priesthood".]

According to the Holy Bible, later on the Members of the Israelite Tribe of DAN raided Micah's House and took away His Idols, for their "Own Worship" along with the Levite Priest, regarding which the Holy Bible States:

"And when these went into Micah's House, and took the Graven Image, the Ephod, and Household Idols, and the Molten Image, the Priest Said to them, "What are you Doing?" And they Said to Him, "Be Silent, Put Your Hand over Your Mouth, and Come with US, and be to us, 'A FATHER AND A PRIEST'. Is it better for you to be a PRIEST to the House of One Man, or to be PRIEST to A TRIBE, and Family in ISRAEL?"

And the Priest's heart was Glad, and He took the Ephod, and the Household Idols, and the Graven Image, and went among the People.

Then they turned and departed, and put the Little Ones and the Live Stock, and the Valuables in front of them.

When they had gone some distance from the House of Micah, the Men who were in the Houses near Micah's House, assembled, and Overtook the Sons of Dan. And they cried to the Sons of Dan, who turned around and Said to Micah, "WHAT is the Matter with you, that you have assembled together?" And He Said, "You have taken away 'My GODS', Which I Made, and the PRIEST, and have Gone Away, and WHAT do I have besides? So how can You Say to ME, "WHAT is the Matter with You?"

And the Sons of DAN Said to Him, "DO not let Your Voice be Heard among US, LEST Fierce Men Fall upon YOU, and You LOSE your LIFE, with the lives of YOUR HOUSEHOLD." So the Sons of DAN went on their Way; and when Micah saw that they were Too Strong for Him, He turned and went back to his house. Then they took what Micah had made, and the Priest who had belonged to him, and came to LAISH, to a People quiet and SECURE, and STRUCK them with the Edge of the SWORD; and they BURNED the CITY with FIRE. And there was No One to DELIVER them, because it was far from Sidon, and they had No dealings with ANYONE, and it was in the Valley, which is near Beth – rehob. And they rebuilt the City and lived in it.

And they called the name of the City 'DAN', after the Name of "DAN" their Father, who was Born in Israel; however, the name of the City formerly was LAISH. And the Sons of DAN, set up for themselves, THE GRAVEN IMAGE; and JONATHAN, the Son of GERSHOM, the Son of MANASSEH, He and His Sons were Priests to the Tribe of the DANITES, until the DAY of the CAPTIVITY OF THE LAND.

So they SET up for themselves, Micah's GRAVEN IMAGE, which He had made, All the Time that the HOUSE of GOD, was at SHILOH." [Judges Verses 18 to 31.]

And because the People of the City of DAN, which after being Burned Down, was reestablished by the members of the 'Israelite Tribe of DAN', who also changed its Earlier Name of 'LAISH' to their own Tribal name, thus renaming it as the City of 'DAN', were thus very much used to the worship of GRAVEN and MOLTEN IDOLS, in defiance to their LORD'S Commandment, and for this very reason, after the Passing away of the

Wisest and LORD'S 'Chosen Son', the King SOLOMON, it became much easier for the Sinner King JEROBOAM to Falsely Establish there a 'Golden Calf', as the 'Deliverer God of Israel', a Heinous feat which he easily realized by the Invisible Support, which was Provided Magnetically to Him, through the Corrupt Mind Control Impulses sent to overpower the Children of Israel, by the Demonic Egyptian Gods, as well as he was able to easily secure the required priesthood to Serve the Newly established GOLDEN CALF GOD, because they already existed in the City of Dan, Serving thereby the Molten Gods and Goddesses, as mentioned in the above Paragraph of the Holy bible which Clearly Stated, that JONATHAN, the Son of GERSHOM, the Son of MANASSEH, He and His Sons were 'Priests' to the Tribe of the DANITES, until the DAY of the CAPTIVITY OF THE LAND.

Regarding the Willful Treachery of King Jeroboam against the "True and Most High", the LORD – GOD of ISRAEL, the Holy Bible States:
'So the King Consulted, and made Two Golden Calves, and He Said to them, "It is too much for you to go up to JERUSALEM; Behold YOUR GODS, O ISRAEL, THAT BROUGHT YOU UP FROM EGYPT." And He set one in 'BETHEL', and the other He put in 'DAN'. Now this Thing became a "'SIN'", for the People went to Worship before the ONE as far as 'DAN'. And He Made Houses on High Places, and made Priests from among all the People, who were NOT THE SONS OF LEVI. [1 Kings 12. Verses 28 to 31.]

Members of the Israelite Tribe of DAN raided Micah's House and took away His Idols, for their "Own Worship" along with the Levite Priest.

Hannah, with her son Samuel and Priest Eli
"For this BOY I PRAYED, and the LORD has given me MY PETITION, which I asked of HIM. So I have DEDICATED Him to the LORD; AS LONG AS HE LIVES, HE IS DEDICATED TO THE LORD." And He Worshiped the LORD there.
[1 Samuel 1. 27, 28.]

Part 53

After the Great Lord – God raised His Judges among the Children of Israel, and they were still Rebellious against the "Commandments" of their LORD, So once again the Merciful LORD established His Humble Servants as PROPHETS among them, just like in the ancient times during the time of great Afflictions, HE established MOSES among them, and such was the Great Prophet SAMUEL, an EPHRAIMITE, with whom the LORD could easily Converse with HIS ineffable GRACE, by revealing and conveying to Him, the Evolutionary Plans and Purpose, which HE devised for the Children of Israel.

Prophet Samuel was born to a pious lady named HANNAH, who was married to ELKANAH from RAMATHAIM - ZOPHIM, the Hill Country of Ephraim, and she was CHILDLESS for a long time. But regarding her such condition she was bitterly provoked regularly by her rivals through their hurting taunts. So being greatly depressed and distressed, SHE went to the Temple of the LORD in SHILOH and PRAYED to the LORD by WEEPING bitterly about her such Condition, and the Priest ELI, who was then sitting by the Doorpost of the LORD'S Temple, saw her quietly seated just moving her lips with no voice, and after Inquiring from her, He blessed her, regarding which the Holy Bible States:

'Then ELI answered and said, "GO in Peace; and May the GOD OF ISRAEL Grant YOUR Petition, that you have asked of HIM."

And it came about in due Time, after HANNAH had Conceived, that She gave Birth to a Son; and she named Him "'SAMUEL'", Saying, "BECAUSE I HAVE ASKED HIM OF THE LORD".

Now when she had weaned Him, she took Him up with her, with a three year old bull, and One EPHAH of Flour, and a Jug of Wine, and brought Him to the HOUSE OF THE LORD in SHILOH, although the Child was Young. Then they slaughtered to bull, and brought the boy to ELI.

And she said, "OH My LORD! AS YOUR SOUL LIVES, MY LORD, I am the Women Who stood beside You, PRAYING TO THE LORD. For this BOY I PRAYED, and the LORD has given me MY PETITION, which I asked of HIM. So I have DEDICATED Him to the LORD; AS LONG AS HE LIVES, HE

IS DEDICATED TO THE LORD." And He Worshiped the LORD there. [1 Samuel 1. 17, 20, 24, 25, 26, 27, 28.]

And in due time, the Great LORD started conversing with his New Chosen Prophet, His Humble Servant SAMUEL, regarding which the Holy Bible further States:

'Now the boy SAMUEL was ministering to the LORD before ELI. And WORD FROM THE LORD WAS 'RARE' IN THOSE DAYS, VISIONS WERE INFREQUENT. And it happened at that time, as ELI was Lying down in His Place [Now his eyesight had begun to grow dim and he could not see well], and the Lamp of GOD had not Yet Gone Out, and SAMUEL was Lying down in the Temple of the LORD, where the ARK OF GOD was, that the LORD called SAMUEL; and He Said, "HERE I AM". Then He Ran to ELI and said, "Here I am, for you called Me." But He said, "I did not call, lie down again." So he went and lay down.

And the LORD Called Yet again, "SAMUEL!" So Samuel arose and went to Eli, and Said, "Here I Am, for You Called ME." But He answered, "I did not call you My Son, Lie down Again."

Now SAMUEL did not Yet Know the LORD, NOR had the WORD OF THE LORD yet been revealed to Him.

So the LORD called SAMUEL Again for the THIRD TIME. And He arose and went to ELI, and Said "Here I am, for YOU called ME". Then Eli DISCERNED, that the LORD was calling the Boy. [1 Samuel 3. Verses 1 to 8.]

Unknown to 'Most', which include the Invisible Entities and Human Beings of this Planet, the three times calling of the LORD in this above mentioned episode of the Holy Bible, till finally the Priest ELI discerned that it was the LORD'S Calling, also in a CODIFIED WAY, represents LORD'S three Main Energy Frequency Motions, Willfully Established at the VERY START, by HIS DESIRE MIND in the Entire Manifested Universe, which are Vibrations of the SPIRAL, CYCLIC and CIRCULAR Motions, perceived by Various Hierarchical Entitles and Beings as the "TONAL KEY NOTES" of Colors and Sounds", which are thus related to HIS 'Three Way Differentiated Consciousness', which is known to all in their Holy Scriptures, as the "HOLY TRINITY".

Regarding this Episode, The Holy Bible further States:

'And Eli Said to Samuel, "Go Lie Down, and It shall be if HE Calls YOU, that YOU shall Say, "SPEAK LORD, FOR THY 'SERVANT IS LISTENING'." So SAMUEL went and lay down in HIS Place. Then the LORD Came and Stood and called as at other Times, "SAMUEL! SAMUEL!" And Samuel Said, "SPEAK, FOR THY SERVANT IS LISTENING."

And the LORD Said to SAMUEL, "Behold, "I" AM ABOUT TO DO A THING IN ISRAEL, AT WHICH, BOTH EARS OF EVERYONE, WHO HEARS IT, WILL TINGLE. In that day "I" will Carry Out against ELI, all that "I" have Spoken Concerning His House, from Beginning to End. For "I" have told Him, that "I" am about to JUDGE His House forever, for the INIQUITY Which He Knew, because His Sons brought a CURSE Upon themselves, AND HE DID NOT 'REBUKE' THEM. And therefore "I" HAVE 'SWORN', to the House of ELI, that the INIQUITY of Eli's house, shall not be ATONED, for by SACRIFICE OR OFFERING FOREVER."

So SAMUEL lay down until Morning. Then He Opened the Doors of the House of the LORD. But SAMUEL was Afraid to Tell the VISION to Eli. Then Eli Called SAMUEL and Said, "SAMUEL MY SON." And He Said, HERE I AM." And He Said, "WHAT is the WORD, that HE Spoke to YOU? Please do not HIDE it from Me. May GOD do so to YOU, and More also, if you Hide anything from ME, all the WORDS that HE Spoke to YOU."

So Samuel told Him Everything, and Hid Nothing from Him. And He Said. "IT IS THE LORD; LET HIM DO, WHAT SEEMS GOOD TO HIM." Thus SAMUEL Grew, and the LORD WAS WITH HIM, and Let NONE OF HIS WORDS 'FAIL'.

And All ISRAEL, From DAN Even to Beersheba KNEW, that SAMUEL was CONFIRMED as a 'PROPHET OF THE LORD'. And the LORD Appeared again at SHILOH, because the LORD revealed HIMSELF to SAMUEL at SHILOH, by the WORD OF THE LORD.' [1 Samuel Verses 9 to 21.]

It is an UNDENIABLE FACT, that it was Always the PROPHETS of the LORD, Who being Simple Humble Servants of the LORD, Kept the LORD'S COMMANDS, and were thus the Chosen People of THE MOST HIGH', Who thus being IN-TUNED with the DESIRE MIND Vibration frequencies of the LORD, Clearly received HIS Messages through their INNER MIND HEARINGS and DIVINE VISIONS, also sometimes given to them by the

LORD in their DREAMS, based upon Which, as per HIS COMMAND, they PROPHESIED in their TIMES to "ALL THE RICH AND FAMOUS PEOPLE" in the Promised Land, just like the Well Established People of OUR OWN TIMES, Who willfully went Astray against the LORD'S WRITTEN COMMANDS, by becoming CORRUPT to acquire the Material Riches, and thus wasted their short lived times in mundane affairs of so called FAMILY and FRIENDS, which ALL HUMAN BEINGS INCLUDING THE WELL RESPECTED AND REVERED "PRIESTHOOD" of ALL FAITHS AND CREEDS, "Finally Leave Behind", including their BELOVED PHYSICAL BODIES, Which they Constantly NOURISH and CHERISH through ALL WAYS AND MEANS, during their Short Lived Incarnated LIVES, thus passing their Time in the Dense Physical Plane of ASSIAH, which after their PHYSICAL DEATH, then fall apart to become, 'DUST TO DUST and ASHES TO ASHES'.

And as SAMUEL Turned to go, SAUL Seized the Edge of His ROBE, and it TORE. So SAMUEL Said to Him, "The LORD has TORN the KINGDOM of ISRAEL from you today, and has GIVEN to your Neighbor, who is Better than YOU." [1 Samuel 15. Verses 10 to 28.]

Part 54

During the Time of Exodus, the Great LORD Commanded MOSES to Put TWO HOLY OBJECTS known in the Holy Bible as the "URIM and THUMMIM" in the BREAST PIECE OF JUDGEMENT, so that they should be worn by AARON, the Chosen High Priest, over the area of his HUMAN HEART, because the Objectively Manifested Heart Organ in the Human Form in reality corresponds to the particular area in the "Vital body" or the "Body Double", which is the Main Energy Distribution Center of the Vital Life Consciousness Force, and thus exists in the Human Body as the "Personality Conscious Center" or the Basic Architectural Spiritual Conscious Energy Reservoir, known as the Sacred Heart Center, which subjectively exists in the framework of the Objectively Manifested Dense Human Form, thus incarnated in the Dense Material Dimensional Plane of ASSIAH.

And for this very reason MOSES was COMMANDED by the LORD in the Wilderness, that the High Priest AARON, through these Two Holy Objects thus worn upon His Heart, should carry the JUDGMENT of the LORD toward the SONS of ISRAEL, which was then conveyed to them by the HIGH PRIEST, as the 'Divination Judgment' of the Great LORD to the Children of Israel.

All the Later High Priests of the Children of Israel also followed the 'Holy Divination Tradition', by always wearing in LORD'S presence, the required BREAST PLATE having the "URIM and THUMMIM", carried in the Pocket of their BREAST PIECE OF JUDGEMENT, and then following the Command of the LORD, they later Conveyed HIS Divine Judgments to the Children of Israel, especially to their Leaders, and Much later also to their Kings.

But whenever the LORD became UNHAPPY toward the Children of Israel, especially toward their Kings, Who WILLFULLY Broke the Rules and Regulations' of HIS 'HOLY COVENANT' which were Earlier Handed Down for the First Time in its "WRITTEN DOWN FORM" to the Children of ISRAEL, at the HOLY MOUNT SINAI, through HIS Humble Servant MOSES, then in those Later Troubled Times, when the Children of Israel willfully rebelled against the Great LORD, then as a Last Resort HE raised HIS Chosen PROPHETS to DIRECTLY WARN the Children of Israel of the 'Dire Consequences', who Being in Direct Communication with the 'Desire Mind Instructions' of the "MOST HIGH", then conveyed HIS 'Harsh Judgments' to the Children of Israel.

Thus the "WORDS" of All Chosen PROPHETS of the Great LORD – GOD, "THE MOST HIGH", were considered Superior to even the Divine Judgments of the "URIM and THUMMIM", by all the Children of Israel as well as their Ruling Kings, because these Powerful Leaders, who became the Kings of the Children of Israel, being 'Politically MINDED' were thus 'Very Forceful' in the Dense Material World, and they were able to easily Control and Manipulate the LORD'S "Priesthood" as clearly mentioned in the Various Episodes of Holy Bible. The Rebellion against the Great Lord commands was Openly Started right from the Time of Children of ISRAEL'S Very First King named SAUL, Whom LORD'S Humble Prophet SAMUEL Strongly Warned about 'LORD'S JUDGMENT', when Saul willfully did not carried out LORD'S Command, regarding which the Holy Bible States:

'Then the Word of the LORD came to SAMUEL, Saying, "I REGRET THAT I HAVE MADE SAUL KING, FOR HE HAS TURNED BACK FROM FOLLOWING ME, AND HAS NOT CARRIED OUT MY COMMANDS." And SAMUEL was DISTRESSED and CRIED Out to the LORD All Night.

And SAMUEL rose early in the morning to meet SAUL; and it was told SAMUEL, Saying, "SAUL came to Carmel, and behold, He set up a MONUMENT for Himself, then turned and proceeded on down to Gilgal."

And SAMUEL came to SAUL, and SAUL Said to Him, "BLESSED are you of the LORD! I have carried out the Command of the LORD." But SAMUEL Said, "WHAT then is this Bleating of the Sheep in My Ears, and the lowing of the Oxen which I HEAR?" And Saul Said, "THEY have brought them from AMALEKITES, for the People spared the best of the Sheep and Oxen, to Sacrifice to the LORD your GOD; but the rest we have utterly destroyed." Then SAMUEL Said to SAUL, "Wait, and let me tell you, What the LORD Said to me Last Night." And He Said to Him, "Speak!"

And SAMUEL Said, "IS it not True, though YOU were LITTLE in YOUR Own Eyes, you were MADE the Head of the Tribes of ISRAEL? And the LORD Anointed you KING over ISRAEL, and the LORD Sent you on a MISSION, and Said, "Go and Utterly DESTROY the 'SINNERS', the Amalekites, and Fight against them Until they are EXTERMINATED. Why then did YOU Not Obey the VOICE of the LORD, but Rushed upon the SPOIL, and did what was EVIL in the Sight of the LORD?"

Then Saul Said to SAMUEL, I did obey the Voice of the LORD, and went on the Mission, on which the LORD sent me, and have brought back AGAG, the King of AMALEK, and have utterly destroyed the AMALEKITES. But the People took some of the Spoil, Sheep and Oxen, the Choicest of the things devoted to Destruction, to Sacrifice to the LORD Your GOD at Gilgal."

And SAMUEL Said, "HAS THE 'LORD' AS MUCH 'DELIGHT' IN 'BURNT OFFERINGS AND SACRIFICES', AS 'OBEYING' THE 'VOICE OF THE LORD'? BEHOLD, TO 'OBEY' IS 'BETTER' THAN 'SACRIFICE', AND TO 'HEED' THAN THE 'FAT OF THE RAMS'. FOR 'REBELLION' IS AS THE "'SIN'" OF "'DIVINATION'", AND 'INSUBORDINATION' IS AS 'INIQUITY' AND 'IDOLATRY'.

Because YOU have REJECTED the WORD of the LORD, HE has also REJECTED YOU From Being KING."

Then SAUL Said to SAMUEL, "I have SINNED; I Have Indeed Transgressed the Command of the LORD, and your Words, BECAUSE I Feared the People, and LISTENED TO THEIR VOICE. Now therefore PLEASE Pardon My SIN, and Return with me, that I may Worship the LORD."

But SAMUEL Said to SAUL, "I Will Not Return with you; for you have REJECTED the 'WORD OF THE LORD', and the LORD has REJECTED YOU from being KING OVER ISRAEL."

And as SAMUEL Turned to go, SAUL Seized the Edge of His ROBE, and it TORE. So SAMUEL Said to Him, "The LORD has TORN the KINGDOM of ISRAEL from you today, and has GIVEN to your Neighbor, who is Better than YOU." [1 Samuel 15. Verses 10 to 28.]

These above Verses Clearly explain to Delusional Mankind, that the Great LORD of the Universe is not MUCH INTERESTED in their "OFFERINGS AND SACRIFICES", but wishes them to follow HIS VOICE, which for a long time has been Commanding them to 'Return from the Path of CORRUPTION' upon this Planet, and thus Totally Surrender themselves to their Creator LORD - GOD, and many of the WORLD LEADERS since ancient times, listening to their People have willfully forgotten the WRITTEN COMMANDS of the LORD , just like what King SAUL Said to SAMUEL, "BECAUSE I Feared the People, and LISTENED TO THEIR VOICE", to which Prophet SAMUEL Said, "Because YOU have REJECTED the WORD of the LORD, HE has also REJECTED YOU From Being KING."

So Samuel did what the LORD Said, and came to Bethlehem. And the Elders of the City came TREMBLING to meet Him and Said, "Do you come in Peace?" And He Said, "In Peace; I have come to Sacrifice to the LORD. Consecrate yourselves, and come with me to the Sacrifice." He also consecrated JESSE and His Sons, and invited them to Sacrifice.

Part 55

According to Holy Bible, during the Time of NOAH, a Great Deluge took Place upon the Physical Plane of Planet Earth, which is also recorded in various other Holy Texts of the Human Beings, and in this Great Deluge as per the Holy Bible, Most of the Human Beings and Animal Species were totally Wiped Out.

And according to Holy Bible, this Great Deluge took Place when the evolving Human Beings, who were CREATED by the GREAT LORD OF FLAMES in HIS Own Image, being Totally Polarized in their LOWER MIND Consciousness, created those Lower Mind thought Forms, which Erupted in its Collective State as the Undue 'Corruption' upon the Physical Plane of this Planet Earth, and then under the ILLUSORY MAGNETIC ENERGY MIND IMPULSES of their Care Takers "ELOHIM'S", the So Called GODS and GODDESSES, Who also Willfully misused their Individualized Vested Powers, thus openly rebelled against LORD'S SPIRITUAL PLAN and PURPOSE, which in the Very Beginning was Trustfully Established in their care for this Planet Earth.

After the Great Deluge the LORD OF FLAMES, then made a Covenant with NOAH and His Children, so that He and Descendants should Properly Follow the Established Evolutionary Spiritual Plan, but over passing of some generations, his descendants again started wrongfully worshiping the so called GODS and GODDESSES, when in fact these invisible entities and beings known as the "ELOHIM'S" were just mere HIS Created Servant Helpers, who themselves are having their Own Parallel Evolution along with their Visible Counterpart Human Beings, in the three Dimensional Spheres [ASSIAH, YETZIRAH, and BRIAH], of this Planet Earth.

So in the time of NOAH'S Descendant ABRAHAM, the "MOST HIGH" again made a Covenant with HIM, when the Evolving Human Beings of this Planet Earth existing on both the EAST and WEST Sides of Euphrates and Tigris Rivers, whose lands extended all the way to the Materially Prosper Countries of India and Egypt, heavily indulged again in the wrongful practices of worshiping these so called Man Made Gods and Goddesses, depicted under a variety of their Attributed Names, and thus this Holy Covenant made with the LORD by ABRAHAM was

The Great Deluge, which is also recorded in various other Holy Texts
and in this Great Deluge as depicted per the Holy Bible.

also revered by his descendants ISSAC and JACOB, who was named as 'ISRAEL' by the LORD. But after settling of JACOB in the Land of Egypt, a Materially Prosper Country, whose people since ancient times were heavily indulged in the worship of GODS and GODDESSES, in the following Period of 430 years, many of ISRAEL Descendant forgot about the Holy Covenant, which their ancestors reverently made with the "MOST HIGH".

Then in the Time of MOSES, for the first time, the Great LORD – GOD made a "Written Covenant" with the Children of Israel, which was Etched in the form of 'Ten Commandments' upon 'Two Stone Tablets', so that the Children of Israel and all their Future Descendants, being the Members of a Chosen race, thus evolving among rest of the Human Beings of this Planet, having a 'Written Covenant', should never again involve themselves in Material World Corruption, which Magnetically erupts due to Lower Mind Animal Instincts, and rather become the Leaders for Everyone's Spiritual Evolution upon this Planet Earth. Most People of this Planet Earth are Unaware of this Fact that the mathematical number '2' of the Stone Tablets, is the IMPORTANT number, Which represents the 'Solar Logos Consciousness' in our SUBJECTIVELY and OBJECTIVELY Manifested Current Solar Universe, thus Existing in the Vast Ethereal Space.

But just after passing of few Centuries, after the Children of Israel got established with LORD'S Help in the Promised Land, they started intermarrying those very people who being polarized in Animal Mind Instincts of the dense Material Plane, were wrongfully indulged in the worship of so called GODS and GODDESSES, and thus again went astray from their required 'Spiritual Goals'.

Starting from the first King SAUL, who as per "1 Samuel 15. 24" FEARED THE PEOPLE, AND LISTENED TO THEIR VOICE, rather than listening to the 'VOICE OF THE LORD', many later Kings of the Children of Israel did even worse than what King Saul did during His time, who openly established the Worship of Molten GODS and GODDESSES for the Children of Israel in their ruling Territory, thus willfully rejecting the Commands of their ALMIGHTY LORD – GOD and His Holy Covenant.

When King SAUL, willfully went against the VOICE OF THE LORD, then Prophet SAMUEL went and conveyed Him LORD'S Decision, to punish him for His such Treachery, and then He grieved over Saul's mistake, regarding which the Holy Bible states:

"Now the LORD Said to SAMUEL, "How long will you GRIEVE over SAUL, since I have rejected Him from being King over Israel? Fill your Horn with Oil, and Go; I will send you to JESSE the BETHLEHEMITE, for I have selected a King for MYSELF among His Sons."

So Samuel did what the LORD Said, and came to Bethlehem. And the Elders of the City came TREMBLING to meet Him and Said, "Do you come in Peace?" And He Said, "In Peace; I have come to Sacrifice to the LORD. Consecrate yourselves, and come with me to the Sacrifice." He also consecrated JESSE and His Sons, and invited them to Sacrifice.

Then it came about when they entered, that He Looked at ELIAB and thought, "Surely the LORD'S Anointed is before Him." But the LORD Said to SAMUEL, "DO NOT Look at His APPEARANCE or at the HEIGHT of His STATURE, because I have Rejected Him; FOR GOD SEES NOT AS MAN SEES, FOR MAN LOOKS AT THE OUTWARD APPEARANCE, BUT THE LORD LOOKS AT THE 'HEART'."

Thus Jesse made Seven of His Sons Pass before SAMUEL. But Samuel said to Jesse, "The LORD has not Chosen these." And Samuel Said to Jesse, "Are these All the Children?" And He Said, "There remains yet the YOUNGEST, and behold, He is tending the Sheep." Then Samuel Said to Jesse, "Send and bring Him; for WE will not Sit down until He Comes Here." So He Sent and brought Him in. Now He was ruddy, with Beautiful Eyes and a Handsome Appearance. And the LORD Said, "ARISE, ANOINT HIM; FOR THIS IS HE." Then Samuel took the Horn of Oil and anointed Him in the Midst of His Brothers; and the SPIRIT OF THE LORD came MIGHTILY upon "DAVID" from that Day Forward. And SAMUEL arose and went to Ramah. Now the SPIRIT OF THE LORD Departed from SAUL, and an EVIL SPIRIT FROM THE LORD Terrorized Him. [1 Samuel 16. 1, 4, 5, 6, 7, 10, 11, 12, 13, 14.]

The above verses of the Holy Bible clearly state, that the HEART ORGAN of the Human Form, in the EYES OF THE LORD, is the Venerated Seat of SPIRITUAL "SOLAR" CONSCIOUSNESS, and No Matter How Beautiful, Strong, Rich and Religiously or Politically Effective a Person Might Be in His Outer Appearance, if His Heart is Darkened and thus Maligned with 'Material Greed' and Filled with Lower Mind 'Animal Desire Ambitions' of the 3 Dense Material Plane Worlds, then That Person is Totally UNFIT to receive LORD'S Spiritual Grace, which is FREELY AVAILABLE to all Human Beings of this World, who instead of Worshiping the so called GODS and GODDESSES, thus Reverently keep HIS Evolutionary Spiritual COMMANDS.

A depiction of the "Sacred Heart Center" of Jesus Christ

Since the Very Beginning, When the Unknowable Creator of the UNIVERSE, Started His Grand Experiment of Consciousness Expansion, which is commonly Understood by Highly Evolved "Entities and Beings" as the "'Gradual Cyclic SPIRITUAL EVOLUTION", and who HIMSELF is commonly termed by All Hierarchies of Various 'Entities and Beings' as the Great LORD OF THE FLAMES, or the "MOST HIGH", then to start with, the GREAT LORD OF FLAMES, basically utilized two Main Attributes of HIS Unfathomably Huge Desire Mind, the first being the "LIGHT OF MIND" or the "Particular Segmentation of the Ethereal Frequency Vibrations", which could be "'Consciously, Unconsciously or Sub Consciously'" Perceived as the enlightening "LIGHT", by HIS Subjectively and Objectively Manifested Creations, who are evolving in their formulated existence, or as the energy frequency Vibrations of "TONAL KEY NOTES OF COLORS AND SOUNDS", and thus Provide the Necessary COMPREHENSION to all the Visible and Invisible Evolving Entities and Beings, which HE introduced in HIS Creations.

In the Creation Process, the 'Particular Segmentation' of the 'Ethereal Frequency Vibrations' was achieved by the GREAT LORD through the three Motions of Vital Energy, commonly known as the "Spiral", "Cyclic", and "Circular" Motions, which through their repeated Interactions Created the required "GEOMETRIES" known by the SEERS as the Angular "SCIENCE OF LIGHT", and "MATHEMATICS" which being the PERFECTIONS of the Various Manifestations, and represented by the Mathematical Numbers, then through their various Permutation and Combinations, thus provided the Required Perfections in HIS Creations, which are known as the Subjectively and Objectively manifested "Differentiated Conscious" Dimensional Spheres.

The gradual Comprehension of the "INDWELLING SPIRIT", which is an "INHERENT ASPECT" of the "ETHEREAL VITALITY", which is wrongly perceived by many of the evolving Entities and Beings as just being the GREAT VOID, and is commonly known to them as the CELESTIAL SPACE of the "ENTIRE UNIVERSE", can only be thus attained by the first aspect of "LIGHT OF MIND", and the Second being the "ACHIEVED PERFECTIONS", which manifests as the SUBJECTIVE and OBJECTIVE results of the "LIGHT OF MIND", in the Dense Frequency Vibrations of the "VITAL ETHER," which manifests due to the action of "LIGHT OF MIND" impulses, which form the Electric and Magnetic Conscious Actions and Reactions of HIS Manifested Creations, who are the Visible and Invisible Various Differentiated Conscious Entities and Beings, who upon their own Hierarchical levels according to their attained Evolutionary Conscious Capacities, during their Evolutionary Life Duration's, are supposed to act as the "Co – Creators" in HIS manifested domains according to HIS established Evolutionary Plans and Purpose.

During the Time of Exodus, the Two Holy Objects known as "THE URIM and THE THUMMIM" meaning the "LIGHT and PERFECTIONS", which the GREAT LORD instructed MOSES to Put in the "BREAST PLATE OF JUDGMENT", and were instructed to be Worn over the Area of the Physical Heart, by the High Priest of HIS Chosen Race, in a Way were those 'Special Objects', which existed as the Micro level representations of HIS MACRO Level Evolutionary Plan and Purpose, which was taking place in the Dense Physical Plane of ASSIAH upon this Planet Earth, and through which LORD'S Desire Mind impulses were conceived by the 'SPIRITUAL MIND' of the Inquiring HIGH PRIEST', as the JUDGMENTS of THE LORD – GOD, toward all the Actions, which were carried out by the Members of the Chosen Race of LORD in the Physical World, who were None other than the 'Children of Israel', whom HE Earlier Delivered out of their Slavery Bondage's.

The URIM, providing the 'LIGHT of MIND' acted as the Formulating devise for the Architectural Plans, which were to be followed by the 'Children of Israel', as the received JUDGMENTS OF THE LORD, and thus became the basis for the Children of Israel to Achieve the Perfections through the THUMMIM in the dense Physical Plane World. So Most of the Time just URIM was First Consulted, at the Start of, or at the Beginning of a New Undertaking, and THUMMIM was later on Consulted for the PERFECTIONS of their Such Undertakings, to ACHIEVE the PERFECT Desired Results.

The Consulting of 'URIM and THUMMIM' by the HIGH PRIEST was of Great Importance, especially during the Absence of Any LORD'S 'CHOSEN PROPHET', which was lacked among the Children of Israel. But when the Governing Ruler Kings of the Children of Israel, listening to the VOICE OF THE PEOPLE rather than their LORD - GOD, thus willfully rejected the VOICE OF THEIR MOST BENEVOLENT LORD – GOD, and then due to their such Corrupt Behavior, the Consulting of the URIM by them, did not anymore Provide them the Divine Judgment, as required answers from the LORD, regarding which the Holy Bible States:

'Now SAMUEL was DEAD, and all Israel had Lamented Him and Buried Him in RAMAH, His Own City. And SAUL had removed from the Land those, who were Mediums and Spiritists. So the PHILISTINES gathered together and came and camped in SHUNEM; and Saul gathered all Israel together, and they camped in GILBOA. When Saul Saw the Camp of the Philistines, He was Afraid, and His Heart Trembled Greatly.

When Saul inquired of the LORD, the LORD DID NOT ANSWER HIM, EITHER BY 'DREAMS' OR BY ""'URIM'"", OR BY PROPHETS.

Then Saul Said to His Servants, "Seek for a Woman, who is a Medium, that I may go to her and inquire of Her." And his Servants Said to Him, "Behold, there is a Woman, who is a Medium at En–dor." Then Saul disguised himself by putting on other clothes, and went, he and two other men with him, and they came to the woman by night, and He Said, "Conjure up for ME, please, and bring for me Whom I shall Name to you." But the woman said to him, "Behold, you know what Saul has done, how he has cut off those, who are Mediums and Spiritists from the Land. Why are you then laying a Snare for My Life, to bring about My Death?" And Saul Vowed to her BY THE LORD, Saying, "As the LORD Lives, there shall No Punishment come upon you for this thing."

Then the woman said, "WHOM shall I bring up for you?" And He Said, "Bring up SAMUEL for ME." When the woman Saw SAMUEL, She CRIED Out with a LOUD VOICE; and the woman spoke to SAUL. Saying, "Why have you Deceived me? For you are Saul." And the King said to her, "DO not be afraid; but what do you See?" And the woman said to SAUL, "I See a 'DIVINE BEING' Coming Up out of the Earth."

And He Said to her, "WHAT is His Form?" And She Said, "An Old Man is Coming Up, and He is Wrapped with a Robe." And Saul knew that it was SAMUEL, and He Bowed with His face to the Ground and did Homage. Then SAMUEL Said to SAUL, "Why have You DISTURBED me by bringing ME up?" And Saul answered, "I am Greatly DISTRESSED; for the Philistines are waging War Against me, and GOD HAS DEPARTED FROM ME, AND ANSWERS ME NO MORE, Either through Prophets, or by Dreams; therefore I have called you, that you may MAKE KNOWN to me, what should I DO."

And SAMUEL Said, " Why then do you ask me, SINCE THE LORD HAS DEPARTED FROM YOU, AND HAS BECOME YOUR ADVERSARY? And the LORD has done accordingly as HE Spoke through ME; for the LORD has TORN the KINGDOM Out of Your Hand, and GIVEN it to Your Neighbor, to DAVID. As you did not 'OBEY THE LORD', and did not EXECUTE HIS FIERCE WRATH on AMALEK, so the LORD has done this thing to YOU this day.

Moreover the LORD will also give over Israel along with you into the Hands of the Philistines, therefore TOMORROW YOU AND YOUR SONS WILL BE WITH ME. Indeed the LORD will give over the Army of Israel into the Hands of the Philistines!'' Then Saul immediately fell FULL LENGTH UPON THE GROUND, and was Afraid because of the WORDS OF SAMUEL, also there was no strength in him, for he had eaten no food all day and all night.' [1 Samuel 28. Verses 3 to 20.]

David, son of Jesse, being annointed by Prophet Samuel

292

Then the woman said, "WHOM shall I bring up for you?" And He Said, "Bring up SAMUEL for ME." When the woman Saw SAMUEL, She CRIED Out with a LOUD VOICE; and the woman spoke to SAUL. Saying, "Why have you Deceived me? For you are Saul." And the King said to her, "DO not be afraid; but what do you See?" And the woman said to SAUL, "I See a 'DIVINE BEING' Coming Up out of the Earth." [1 Samuel 28..11,12,13]

Seraphim

Part 57

The Unknowable LORD – GOD, the CREATOR – OBSERVER of the UNIVERSE, who is commonly referred to as "THE MOST HIGH" or the "ADONAI" in Aramaic and Hebrew Languages, remembering His Holy Covenant which HE ESTABLISHED with ABRAHAM, ISAAC, AND JACOB, during the time of Exodus, HE clearly explained their Descendant and HIS Chosen and Humble Servant MOSES, that even though HE appeared to them, HE NEVER LET THEM KNOW HIS NAME, regarding which the Holy Bible States:

'Then the LORD Said to MOSES, "Now YOU shall SEE, What "I" will do to Pharaoh; for under COMPULSION, He shall let them GO, and under COMPULSION He shall DRIVE them OUT of his LAND."

GOD Spoke further to MOSES, and Said to Him, " I AM THE LORD; AND I APPEARED TO ABRAHAM, ISAAC, AND JACOB, AS GOD ALMIGHTY, BUT MY NAME ""LORD"", I DID NOT MAKE MYSELF KNOWN TO THEM. AND I ALSO ESTABLISHED "'MY COVENANT"' WITH THEM, TO GIVE THEM THE "'LAND OF CANAAN"', THE LAND IN WHICH THEY SOJOURNED. AND FURTHERMORE, I HAVE HEARD, THE GROANING OF THE 'SONS OF ISRAEL', BECAUSE THE 'EGYPTIANS' ARE HOLDING THEM IN 'BONDAGE'. AND "'I"' HAVE "'REMEMBERED MY COVENANT"'.

SAY THEREFORE, TO THE 'SONS OF ISRAEL', "'I AM THE LORD, AND I WILL BRING YOU OUT FROM UNDER THE BURDENS OF THE EGYPTIANS, AND I WILL DELIVER YOU FROM THEIR BONDAGE. I WILL ALSO REDEEM YOU WITH AN 'OUTSTRETCHED ARM', AND WITH ""GREAT JUDGMENTS"".

THEN "I" WILL TAKE YOU FOR 'MY PEOPLE', AND "I" WILL BE YOUR GOD; AND YOU SHALL KNOW, THAT "I" AM THE 'LORD YOUR GOD', WHO BROUGHT YOU 'OUT' FROM UNDER THE 'BURDENS' OF THE EGYPTIANS. AND "I" WILL BRING YOU TO THE LAND, WHICH "I" SWORE TO GIVE TO GIVE TO 'ABRAHAM', 'ISAAC', AND 'JACOB', AND "I" WILL GIVE IT TO YOU FOR A "'POSSESSION"; "'I AM THE LORD.'" [Exodus 6. Verses 1 to 8.]

These Above Verses of the Holy Bible also Clearly State, that the Great Lord has been constantly observing the Descendants of NOAH, with

Whom in the Ancient times after the Great Deluge, HE made HIS Holy Covenant, and then again renewed HIS Covenant with Noah's Descendant. whom HE named from his given name ABRAM to ABRAHAM.

In this Modern world of Technological Advances, in which the Indwelling PERSONALITY SPIRIT embodied in the Human Form, which is Just a Very Tiny Insignificant Ethereal Conscious Energy Part of the "HIGHER SELF", which since very ancient times of this PLANET EARTH HISTORY has been termed by the 'SEERS AND SAGES' as the "SOUL" or the "SOLAR SPIRIT CONSCIOUSNESS", In reality is a Tiny Conscious Part of "Great Significance", which has been willfully sent by the "HIGHER SELF" on the SPIRALING EVOLUTIONARY ENERGY WAVES provided in this Universe by the "MOST HIGH", to Experience SPIRITUALITY IN THE 3 DENSE PLANE WORLD'S, which are known as the 3 Dimensional Worlds or the SEPHIROTS [LOKAS IN SANSKRIT] OF "ASSIAH, YETZIRAH, AND BRIAH", which has been willfully DERAILED with the WRONGFUL AND CORRUPT UNDERTAKINGS OF THESE "SO CALLED GODS AND GODDESSES", which are TOTALLY CONTRADICTORY TO ALL THE "SPIRITUAL" HOLY SCRIPTURES of the World, which in their Holy Texts PORTRAY THE DESIRE MIND THOUGHT FORMS OF THE CREATOR LORD GOD OF THIS UNIVERSE, DETAILING HIS EVOLUTIONARY PLAN AND PURPOSE, and thus over the passing of time, the Evolving Human Societies of Differentiated Human Race has Gradually fallen to New Lows of the dense Material Plane Mind Instincts, and even with Such Technological advances, they still exist "Materially Polarized" in their form bodies upon the Physical Plane [ASSIAH], just like any other Lower Mind Animal Species of this Planet.

But Most Incarnated Human Beings of this Planet, who usually being Religious and thus having Great Reverence for the Holy Bible, Clearly FAIL to 'Spiritually Examine' this Most Important Verse, which is written its Very First Chapter of its First Book named "Genesis" meaning "Creation" of the Holy Bible, which States:

"And GOD Created MAN in 'HIS OWN IMAGE', IN THE IMAGE OF GOD HE 'CREATED' HIM; MALE AND FEMALE "'HE'" CREATED THEM." [Genesis 1. 27.]

If the Incarnated Humans of this Planet earth should pay Little Close Attention, with their SPIRITUAL Mind fully OPEN, to receive this

Particular VERSE'S Codified Wisdom, who during their limited duration incarnated lives, mostly being mentally polarized in the Material World Glamour, thus fail to raise THIS IMPORTANT EVOLUTIONARY QUESTION in their evolving Minds, as to WHERE DO THEY COME FROM?, When they incarnate in their Human Forms, and WHERE DO THEY GO?, After their Conscious Connection with their Physical Bodies gets Finally SEVERED.

If with their "Inner Mind" Consciousness they may Question and thus pay their Undivided Clear Attention to this Important Subject, then through their 'SPIRITUAL EYES' they will FIND out its IMPORTANT MESSAGE, that the GREAT LORD - GOD Created the Human Beings in "HIS OWN IMAGE", to exist upon the Physical Plane of this Planet Earth as "HIS MOST IMPORTANT ANIMATED CREATION", and the 'MAIN HEAD' OF ALL THE FOUR MANIFESTED VISIBLE KINGDOMS OF THIS PLANET EARTH ['1' Mineral, '2' Plant and Vegetable, '3' Animal, and '4' The Poverty Stricken Evolving their Fellow Human Beings, whose Consciousness existing as the ' NEW SOULS', through the Evolutionary Process were thus granted the Consciousness Attribute of 'Individualized Mind", and then entered from the Various Species of Evolving Animal Kingdom into the Human Kingdom as New Students to learn Spirituality], and then Faithfully LOOK AFTER THEM with their "Attribute of Individualized Mind', Just like THE GREAT CREATOR – OBSERVER LORD GOD Himself Looks after all the Innumerable Visible and Invisible Hierarchical Existences, who exist in the Various Dimensional Planes as the Subjectively and Objectively Manifested "Entities and Beings".

But just Like the King SAUL of the Israelite's, as mentioned in the Holy Bible, Many of the World Leaders of the Materially advanced Modern world, listening to the Voices of their Masses, who although incarnated in an HUMAN FORM, are still having the Lower Type of ANIMAL MIND DESIRES, and then to please them, they by creating favorable Laws, Mandates, Rules and Regulations, have thus Gone ASTRAY from the 'HOLY TEXTS', which in a Codified Way define the EVOLUTIONARY PLAN and Purpose of the MOST HIGH, which is 'Much Needed' For their Spiritual Advancement, and which was recorded by the Holy Scribes, Seers and Sages, who Visualizing the "Thought Forms" provided to them by the Ineffable GRACE OF THE UNKNOWABLE 'MOST HIGH', and then understanding their TONAL KEY NOTES as Colors and Sounds, without the fear of their counterpart evolving human races and their LEADERS, who were totally immersed in Corrupt Desires of Animalistic

Instincts through polarization of their Desire Minds in the Magnetic World Glamour of the ASTRAL PLANE also known as the Dimensional Sphere of YETZIRAH, then by Humbly paying total obedience to their LORD- GOD Wrote Down HIS Wished Commands, which became the "Holy Texts", so that the Evolving Human Beings can "Spiritually" follow them during their Short Lived Incarnated lives upon the dense dimensional Physical world of ASSIAH.

Also many People of this Earth existing in their own dimensional levels, as well as their counterpart Invisible Angelic Beings, Overlook the Various Important Verses of the Holy Bible, that Clearly Inform them, that NOT ONLY THE 'GREAT LORD', also Known as the MOST HIGH, is the 'ONE AND ONLY' CREATOR LORD OF HIS UNIVERSE, BUT HE IS ALSO THE "CONSTANT OBSERVER" of HIS ENTIRE CREATION, and thus accordingly also constantly Pass HIS JUDGMENTS upon not only the HUMAN BEING, but also upon HIS INVISIBLE SERVANT HELPERS, THE SO CALLED "GODS AND GODDESSES" also known as "THE ELOHIMS", whenever they go ASTRAY from HIS Evolutionary Plan and Purpose.

Some of the Important Verses regarding HIS 'Constant Observation' upon this Planet Earth, also include this Verse, which State: " Then the LORD """SAW""" that the Wickedness of MAN was GREAT on the Earth, and that Every Intent of the THOUGHTS of HIS HEART was ONLY EVIL Continually." [Genesis 6. 5.]

And Regarding the So called GODS and GODDESSES, HIS 'JUDGMENTS' are Clearly Stated in this Verse of Holy Bible, which State: " For '''I''' will go through the 'Land of Egypt' on that Night, and will STRIKE DOWN all the First – Born in the Land of Egypt , both MAN and BEAST; and '''AGAINST ALL THE 'GODS' OF EGYPT, I WILL EXECUTE 'JUDGMENTS' – '''I AM THE LORD''' " [Exodus 12. 12.]

Prophet Samuel announcing to Children of Israel, about their King Saul

298

GOD Spoke further to MOSES, and Said to Him, " I AM THE LORD; AND I
APPEARED TO ABRAHAM, ISAAC, AND JACOB, AS GOD ALMIGHTY, BUT MY
NAME ""'LORD'"', I DID NOT MAKE MYSELF KNOWN TO THEM. AND I ALSO
ESTABLISHED "'MY COVENANT'" WITH THEM, TO GIVE THEM THE "'LAND
OF CANAAN'"', THE LAND IN WHICH THEY SOJOURNED. AND FURTHERMORE,
I HAVE HEARD, THE GROANING OF THE 'SONS OF ISRAEL', BECAUSE
THE 'EGYPTIANS' ARE HOLDING THEM IN 'BONDAGE'. AND "'I'" HAVE
"'REMEMBERED MY COVENANT'"'. '[Exodus 6.2,3,4,5.]

'And SAMUEL Said, "HAS THE 'LORD' AS MUCH 'DELIGHT' IN 'BURNT OFFERINGS AND SACRIFICES', AS 'OBEYING' THE 'VOICE OF THE LORD'? BEHOLD, TO 'OBEY' IS 'BETTER' THAN 'SACRIFICE', AND TO 'HEED' THAN THE 'FAT OF THE RAMS'. FOR 'REBELLION' IS AS THE "'SIN'" OF "'DIVINATION'", AND 'INSUBORDINATION' IS AS 'INIQUITY' AND 'IDOLATRY.'"
[1 Samuel 15. 22, 23.]

Part 58

The Holy Bible is a Great Book of compiled 'Spiritual Wisdom', which was Periodically received by the Chosen Prophets of the Great LORD - GOD, after they Faithfully Humbly received it Directly from their LORD – GOD, as well as sometimes by the intervention of His Faithful Servant Helpers, known as the Angelic Beings, who Performing their own prescribed duties as per the Commands of the MOST HIGH conveyed them HIS Prophetic Messages, and the Chosen Prophets always considered this Evolutionary Spiritual Wisdom as HIS direct Commands, which according to HIS Evolutionary Plan and Purpose are meant for the Benefit of HIS 'Subjective and Objective' Creations, which HE Willfully Manifested involving various differentiated invisible "Elemental Essences", who exist in the 3 main categories of their Hierarchical Existence, existing as the Conscious, Semi – Conscious and Unconscious "Elemental Lives", who following HIS Command Impulses, received and perceived by them as the Tonal Frequency Vibration of 'Colors and Sounds', then accordingly Perform their Required Duties in the three dense dimensional Plane Worlds of ASSIAH, YETZIRAH and BRIAH.

When looking at the Holy Bible Verses, One should examine them only with their 'SPIRITUAL EYES - FULLY OPEN', rather than visually looking at These Holy Texts just through our "Material or Religious Eyes", which are usually totally Blinded with the "Illusory Material World Glamour, or with our "Selfish Material World Needs"

Starting from MOSES, the Chosen Humble servant of the Great LORD, for the first time He narrated LORD'S Commandments to the 'Children of Israel', which He received in a 'Written Form' upon the TWO STONE TABLETS from the LORD, on HIS Flaming Mountain SINAI in the wilderness of ARABAH.

And even though MOSES Established the rules and regulations of 'BURNT OFFERINGS AND SACRIFICES', as per LORD'S Instructions, He Himself Saw that how the 'Children of Israel' got Wiped out with a Plague, when their Lower Desire Mind Craved for 'Meat', and Grumbled, even when their LORD - GOD was Constantly Providing them the Nutritious and Healthy food of "MANNA", during their entire 40 Year Stay in the Wilderness. This Entire Episode is well recorded in great details of the 11th Chapter of 'Numbers' in the Holy Bible.

Later on, when the Children of Israel got established in the Promised Land, then HIS Chosen Prophet SAMUEL also stressed upon this Important Point to the first King Saul, that the LORD Himself 'DO NOT CRAVE' for any such 'Meat Offerings', but Obeying HIS VOICE is of Primary Concern and of 'Most Importance' to HIM, as HE established such rules only to Satisfy the Lower Mind Cravings of HIS Chosen People, who Grumbled and Craved such foods during their wanderings in Wilderness, regarding which the Holy Bible States:

'And SAMUEL Said, "HAS THE 'LORD' AS MUCH 'DELIGHT' IN 'BURNT OFFERINGS AND SACRIFICES', AS 'OBEYING' THE 'VOICE OF THE LORD'? BEHOLD, TO 'OBEY' IS 'BETTER' THAN 'SACRIFICE', AND TO 'HEED' THAN THE 'FAT OF THE RAMS'. FOR 'REBELLION' IS AS THE '''SIN''' OF '''DIVINATION''', AND 'INSUBORDINATION' IS AS 'INIQUITY' AND 'IDOLATRY.'' [1 Samuel 15. 22, 23.]

The Great and Wisest King Solomon, the 'Chosen Son of GOD', as mentioned in the '1 Chronicles 17. 13' of the Holy Bible, in His Instructional Wisdom Writings to the 'Children of Israel' also raised the Sentiments of Prophet SAMUEL, by clearly explaining to 'Children of Israel', that when they GO to the House of GOD, they should LISTEN TO THE VOICE OF LORD, which are written as HIS Commands in their HOLY TEXTS, rather than to Offer Sacrifices, regarding which the Holy Bible States:

'Guard YOUR Steps, AS YOU GO TO THE HOUSE OF GOD, and DRAW near to LISTEN, rather than to OFFER the SACRIFICE of FOOLS; for THEY DO NOT KNOW, they are DOING EVIL.' [Ecclesiastes 5. 1.]

In this Regard Prophet ISAIAH also shared His Divine VISION, to the 'Children of Israel' concerning JUDAH and JERUSALEM, which He SAW, when it was provided to Him by the Grace of LORD – GOD, during the reigns of Uzziah, Jotham, Ahaz, and Hezekiah, Kings of JUDAH, regarding which the Holy Bible States:

'''What are your Multiplied Sacrifices to ME?'' Says the LORD. ''I'' have ''''''ENOUGH'''''' of Burnt Offerings of Rams, and the fat of Fed Cattle. And ''I'' take 'NO PLEASURE' in the Blood of Bulls, Lambs, or Goats.

When You Come to Appear before ME, WHO Requires of YOU this TRAMPLING of MY Courts? BRING YOUR 'WORTHLESS OFFERINGS' """"NO LONGER"""", THEIR INCENSE IS AN 'ABOMINATION' TO ME.

New MOON and SABBATH, the Calling of Assemblies – "I" Cannot Endure INIQUITY and the SOLEMN ASSEMBLY. "I" HATE your NEW MOON FESTIVALS, AND YOUR 'APPOINTED FEASTS', THEY have become a BURDEN to ME. I am WEARY OF BEARING THEM.

So when YOU spread out YOUR Hands in PRAYER, "I" will HIDE MY EYES from YOU, Yes, Even though YOU Multiply PRAYERS, "I" will NOT LISTEN. YOUR Hands are 'FULL OF BLOODSHED'. WASH YOURSELF, MAKE YOURSELVES 'CLEAN'; Remove the 'EVIL' of YOUR DEEDS from MY SIGHT. CEASE TO DO 'EVIL', LEARN TO DO GOOD; SEEK JUSTICE, REPROVE THE 'RUTHLESS'; DEFEND THE 'ORPHAN', PLEAD FOR THE 'WIDOW'. [Isaiah 1. Verses 11 to 17.]

Many Leaders of this Modern World, to save their so called 'Prestigious Positions' or 'Elected Seats' in the Evolving Human Societies, during their Limited Time Life Duration, using their 'VESTED POWERS' make so called Human Laws, defining the 'RULES and REGULATIONS' in the Name of 'CIVILIZATION' upon the Physical Plane of this Planet Earth, which are TOTALLY CONTRADICTORY to "The Commands" of their CREATOR LORD – GOD, which are based upon HIS Evolutionary Plan and Purpose for this Planet, Who thus foolishly 'FORGET', that their SHORT LIVED HUMAN LIVES are 'For Sure' ANSWERABLE TO THEIR 'CREATOR LORD', after they Depart 'ONE DAY' from this Physical Plane World, regarding which the 'Holy Bible' clearly States:

'The FOOL has Said in His HEART, "THERE IS NO GOD." They are "CORRUPT", they have Committed Abominable DEEDS; There is 'NO ONE' who does GOOD.

The LORD has LOOKED DOWN from HEAVEN upon the SONS OF MEN, To SEE if there are ANY WHO UNDERSTAND, WHO SEEK AFTER GOD.

They have ALL TURNED ASIDE; 'TOGETHER' THEY HAVE BECOME '''CORRUPT'''; THERE IS 'NO ONE' WHO DOES "GOOD", """"NOT EVEN ONE"""". [Psalm 14. 1, 2, 3.]

The Holy Bible also confirms that in its Codified Verses, the Holy Bible contains the 'Secret of the LORD', regarding which the Holy Bible States:

'The "SECRET" of the "LORD" is for THOSE, WHO FEAR "HIM". And 'HE' will Make Them Know "HIS COVENANT". [Psalm 25. 14.]

Since the time of Exodus, the Great LORD - GOD has been Fully Aware of this fact, that the 'Meat Cravings' of HIS Grumbling Chosen Race were very much there, and this Particular Problem could be taken Care of through their PEACE OFFERINGS, regarding which the Holy Bible States:

"'Now when YOU OFFER a SACRIFICE of 'PEACE OFFERINGS' to the LORD, you shall offer it so that YOU may be ACCEPTED. It shall be EATEN the "Same Day" YOU OFFER IT, and the 'Next Day'; BUT WHAT REMAINS UNTIL THE THIRD DAY SHALL BE BURNED WITH FIRE. So if it is EATEN at all on the Third Day, it is an 'OFFENSE'; IT will NOT BE ACCEPTED. And EVERYONE, who eats it will Bear His INIQUITY, for He has PROFANED THE HOLY THING OF THE LORD; and that PERSON shall be CUT OFF from His People.'" [Leviticus 19. 5, 6, 7, 8.]

But Later on, when the Great LORD became ANGRY, due to the Willful rejection of HIS Holy Commandments by the Evolving Descendants of 'ABRAHAM' upon this Planet Earth, then HIS Chosen Prophet 'JEREMIAH' Conveyed HIS 'Dire Warnings' to the 'Children of Israel', regarding which the Holy Bible States:

"AND "I" Shall make them 'EAT' the FLESH OF THEIR SONS, AND THE FLESH OF THEIR DAUGHTERS, AND THEY WILL EAT ONE ANOTHER'S 'FLESH' IN THE SIEGE, AND IN THE DISTRESS, with which their Enemies, and THOSE, Who Seek their LIFE will DISTRESS them." [Jeremiah 19. 9.]

And according to Holy Bible, this DIRE WARNING OF THE LORD did come TRUE and Such things did happened to the Children of Israel, because When through HIS Chosen Prophet the GREAT LORD Gave Ample warnings, and the "CORRUPT ONES" Still Did NOT HEED TO HIS WARNINGS, AND THUS CORRECTED THEMSELVES, by FULFILLING HIS DEMAND OF "RETURN and SURRENDER", then the PROPHECIES Conveyed to them became an UNDENIABLE FACT upon this Planet Earth, regarding which the Holy Bible States:

'Now it came about after this, that Ben – Hadad King of Syria, gathered all His Army and went up and besieged SAMARIA. And there was a Great Famine in Samaria; and behold, they Besieged it, until a Donkey's Head was SOLD for 'EIGHTY SHEKELS' of SILVER, and a Fourth of a Kab of 'DOVE'S DUNG' for 'FIVE SHEKELS' of Silver.

And the KING OF ISRAEL was passing by, on the Wall, a Woman Cried Out to Him, Saying, "Help, My Lord, O King!" And He Said, "IF the LORD does not HELP you, from where shall I Help You? From the Threshing Floor, or from the Wine Press?"

And the King Said to Her, "WHAT is the Matter with YOU?" And She Answered, "THIS WOMAN SAID TO ME, 'GIVE YOUR SON, THAT WE MAY """EAT""" HIM TODAY, AND WE WILL 'EAT MY SON' TOMORROW. 'SO WE """BOILED MY SON, AND ATE HIM"""'; AND I SAID TO HER ON THE NEXT DAY, 'GIVE YOUR SON, THAT WE MAY EAT HIM'; BUT SHE HAS 'HIDDEN HER SON''. [2 Kings. 6. Verses 24 to 29.]

'Now it came about after this, that Ben – Hadad King of Syria, gathered all His Army and went up and besieged SAMARIA. [2 Kings. 6.24]

'For What Great Nation is there, that has a GOD So Near to it, as is the LORD our GOD, Whenever we call on HIM? Or What Great Nation is there, that has Statutes and Judgments as RIGHTEOUS, as this 'WHOLE LAW', which I am setting before YOU today?

Only GIVE HEED TO YOURSELF and '''KEEP YOUR 'SOUL' DILIGENTLY''', lest YOU Forget the Things, which Your Eyes have SEEN, and lest they DEPART from your Heart, all the days of your LIFE; but make them KNOWN to your SONS and GRANDSONS.
[Deuteronomy 4. Verses 7,8,9]

The Secret of the Breast Plate
Part 59

According to the Holy Bible, during the time of Exodus, LORD'S Humble Servant MOSES clearly reminded the Children of Israel, their Important status as a Chosen Race, as the Great LORD made a Holy Covenant with their Ancestors and then again with them, and since they did not SEE any FORM of the LORD in the Midst of FIRE, when HE Spoke to them at Holy Mountain "HOREB -SINAI", they Should NEVER make a Graven Image, lest they act "CORRUPTLY", and thus willfully 'REBEL' against the Commands of their Compassionate GOD, and then for their such Heinous actions, FACE the Dire Consequences as a repercussion.

Also MOSES Stressed to them about an Important Point, which was for them to always keep 'DILIGENTLY' in touch with their Spiritual 'SOUL', known to the Seers and Sages as the "Solar Conscious', or the "Higher Self", which is a combination of "CHAYAH' meaning the 'Causal Body', which act as the Bridge to 'Transcendence', and the "YECHIDAH", meaning the Spiritual 'Oneness' with the Desire Mind of their CREATOR LORD-GOD, and both of these Higher or Spiritual Conscious bodies, which are composed of 'vital ethereal substance' or the 'Rare or Pure Consciousness Electric Ether' are supported in their 'SPIRITUAL CONSCIOUS STATE' by their "NESHAMAH" Body meaning the Mental Body, which reacting upon the conscious impulses of "CHAYAH, and YECHIDAH" then create the required 'Thought Forms', which get embodied in their body forms to exist as the 'RUACH' body, meaning the Emotional Body, or the Astral Body of Feelings and Emotions, which many people 'Consciously or Unconsciously' use as their Dream Body during their Physical Sleep, and the 'NEFESH' body, which is a 2 part 'Invisible and Visible' Physical body, existing in their Totality as an Incarnated Human Being upon the densest plane of this Planet Earth.

These 3 dense material plane bodies are controlled from an extremely tiny particular point, which is first established in the "CHAYAH", which being less than a 'Pin Point', then corresponding to the Five fold MATRIX of the Objective Universe, first differentiate itself in five ways, and then keeping 1/5th of its force in the firmly established point itself to gain 'material world experiences', and for this very reason thus established in "CHAYAH" [Causal Body], then with the second its 1/5th Vital force it creates an 'Extendable Vital Cord of Life Force Energy', known to the

Prophets and Seers as the "SILVER CORD", which is also mentioned by King Solomon in "Ecclesiastes 12. 6" of the Holy Bible, which stay connected to 3 dense plane bodies by helping them first to manifest, and then also provide them the Vital Force required for their animations during their Cyclic Life Duration's.

These 3 dense plane bodies which are known as the 'NESHAMAH' meaning the body of 'Spiritual Desire Mind' seeking Enlightenment, 'RUACH' meaning the body of 'Lower Desire Mind' analyzing through Liquid and Magnetic Sensations of the dense material world, commonly known as the "Feelings and Emotions", and 'NEFESH' which is the Incarnated Human Body living in the Dense Physical World, having its two parts, of which the first Part is known as the Invisible "Vital body" or the Body Double", which acts as an 'Architectural Framework' for the Dense Human Shell to incarnate, as well as helps to keep it in animation for the Cyclic Life Duration of the Visible Human body till the time of its Physical Death, during which the 'Silver Cord' gets Severed from it.

The 3 dense plane bodies of "NESHAMAH', 'RUACH', and 'NEFESH', of which 'each one' of them have 1/5th of the Differentiated Vital Force pouring out of the 'Pin Point' which is established in the Egg Shaped Sphere of fairly large body, known as the 'CHAYAH', which is thus Established in 'CHAYAH' [Causal Body], as per the 'evolutionary Plan and Purpose' of the LORD, for the 'Spiritual Consciousness Expansion' of the evolving "SOUL' to have its required Spiritual Experience in the 3 dense worlds of this Planet Earth, and all these bodies, which are connected with this 'Pin Point" through the vital energy "Silver Cord", are composed of the Differentiated Matter containing conscious, semi – conscious, and Unconscious elemental essences, of the corresponding 3 dense material planes of this Planet Earth, which are known as the Dimensional Sephirots of "BRIAH", YETZIRAH" and "ASSIAH".

And in the body of 'NEFESH' the 1/5th part of vital force coming down from "CHAYAH" through the "SILVER CORD" is equally shared by the Physical Body and its Body Double, which is also known to the SEERS as the 'Vital Body', as for the Dense Physical Body incarnated upon the densest physical plane, its source of animating force is the Vital body, which in its turn gets required vital impulses from the 'Pin Point' established in the "CHAYAH", and are received through the "Silver Cord".

So our "Personality consciousness" Embodied in our Dense Human

Form is a very tiny part of "A Spiritual investment", which is willfully invested by the "Soul Consciousness", who for its 'SPIRITUAL CONSCIOUS EXPANSION IN THE THREE DENSE WORLDS' willfully establishes this "Pin Point" in the "CHAYAH" Body, and then differentiates its tiny parted Spiritual energy, which to start with established itself, as an ethereal 'Pin Point" to further differentiate in a five fold manner as explained above, and when an Incarnated Human Being WILLFULLY WASTES its short lived life, consciously stuck in the "Material World Glamour", rather than attaining " the required Spiritual Experiences", for which PURPOSE, the evolving "Soul" sent it out to the densest Plane material world, then just like any other "Investment" it may not reap its rewards, and if the "Personality Consciousness" of a Human Being during its incarnated life, being polarized in 'Lower Mind Desire' gets 'carried away' by the Human Vices, then this Vital Investment" becomes an undesired "LOSS" for the Evolving SOUL", as in the End [Death] of every incarnated Human Life, the SOUL requires its 'Total Investment Back' filled with Gained 'SPIRITUAL EXPERIENCES'.

MOSES being the Humble Servant of the LORD, clearly informed the "Children of Israel" about the importance of "SOUL", in a Codified Way, as during those times, they were Continuously Grumbling and being Rebellious regarding Material aspects of Life, they were still not ready, and Mentally 'Matured and Developed', to receive its "Secret Wisdom", regarding which the Holy Bible States:

'For What Great Nation is there, that has a GOD So Near to it, as is the LORD our GOD, Whenever we call on HIM? Or What Great Nation is there, that has Statutes and Judgments as RIGHTEOUS, as this 'WHOLE LAW', which I am setting before YOU today?

Only GIVE HEED TO YOURSELF and '"KEEP YOUR 'SOUL' DILIGENTLY"', lest YOU Forget the Things, which Your Eyes have SEEN, and lest they DEPART from your Heart, all the days of your LIFE; but make them KNOWN to your SONS and GRANDSONS.

Remember the Day you Stood before the LORD your GOD at HOREB, when the LORD Said to Me, '"Assemble the People to ME, that "I" may let them Hear 'MY WORDS', SO they may 'LEARN TO FEAR ME', all the days they Live on the Earth, and that they may teach their CHILDREN."

And you came near and Stood at the Foot of the Mountain, and the

Mountain 'BURNED WITH FIRE' to the very heart of the Heavens; Darkness, Cloud, and Thick Gloom. Then the LORD Spoke to you from the Midst of the FIRE; you heard the 'SOUND OF WORDS', But You SAW NO FORM – ONLY A VOICE. So HE Declared to You HIS COVENANT, which HE Commanded you to PERFORM, that is, 'The Ten Commandments'; and HE Wrote them on Two Tablets of Stone. And the LORD Commanded Me at that Time to Teach You 'STATUTES and JUDGMENTS', that you might perform them in the LAND, where you are going over to POSSESS it.

So watch yourself carefully, since you Did Not 'SEE ANY FORM', on the Day the LORD Spoke to YOU at HOREB from the MIDST OF THE FIRE, lest you act 'CORRUPTLY' and make a Graven Image for YOURSELVES in the form of ANY FIGURE, the likeness of a MALE or FEMALE, the LIKENESS OF ANY ANIMAL that is on the Earth, the LIKENESS OF ANY WINGED BIRD that flies in the Sky, the LIKENESS OF ANYTHING THAT CREEPS on the Ground, the LIKENESS OF ANY FISH that is in the Water below the Earth.

And BEWARE, lest you Lift up YOUR EYES to Heaven, and SEE the SUN, and the MOON, and the STARS, ""''ALL THE HOST OF HEAVEN''"", and be 'DRAWN AWAY' AND 'WORSHIP THEM', and SERVE THEM, those which the 'LORD YOUR GOD' has Allotted to ALL THE PEOPLES UNDER THE WHOLE HEAVEN.

But the LORD has 'TAKEN YOU', and brought you out of the 'IRON FURNACE', from Egypt, to be a PEOPLE FOR HIS OWN POSSESSION, as today. [Deuteronomy 4. Verses 7 to 20.]

But as the later Chapters of the Holy Bible tells us, that even with the "GRAVE WARNINGS OF MOSES", the Children of Israel and their Descendant Generations fell from the GRACE, and willfully went ASTRAY, and thus being polarized in their 'Lower Mind Desires', they got 'carried away' by the Human Vices, which caused their 'Evolving SOULS" to lose their 'Vital Consciousness Investments", which became to them an undesired "LOSS" not able to get back even their 'Initial Investment', which being a chosen race of the LORD was supposed to be 'retrieved back', much more filled with Gained 'SPIRITUAL EXPERIENCES' than all other People.

All the Subjective and Objective manifestations of the Universe, which manifested according to LORD'S Desire Mind, were created by HIM through the Vibration Frequencies of Energy, which were started by HIM through the introduction of three important 'Energy Motions' [Spiral, Cyclic, and Circular], in the 'Vital Ethereal Essence', which compose the unimaginable Huge Cosmic "SPACE", and these Vibration Frequencies started by HIS Desire Mind, are known to the Seers since very ancient times as the Tonal Keynotes of "Colors and Sounds", regarding which the Holy Bible States:

"By the 'WORD OF THE LORD', the Heavens were Made, AND by the BREATH of HIS MOUTH, ALL THEIR 'HOST'." [Psalms 33. 6].

In this above Verse, the embedded Codified Wisdom, clearly Points Out to all, who examine this Important Verse through their "Spiritual Eyes", that the 'WORD OF THE LORD' represents the 'Tonal Sound Vibration Frequencies', which were started by LORD'S Desire Mind as the 'SPIRALING MOTION in the "VITAL COSMIC ETHEREAL SPACE', which then Manifested Various Star Solar Systems, which were later grouped together by the evolutionary Minds of "Entities and Beings", through their envisioned forms as the various 'Constellations', which thus exist manifested in the 'LIGHT SPIRALS', which extend outward from the Center of this 'MILKY WAY GALAXY'.

And the 'BREATH OF HIS MOUTH' represents the CYCLES of 'INTAKE and OUTTAKE' of the 'VITAL ETHER', which are known to the SEERS and Sages as the Cyclic "WHEELS OF TIME", which manifest the Various Hierarchical levels of Differentiated Consciousness, who have been commonly termed by the Seers and Sages as the "HOSTS", so they can experience during their Limited Life Cycle Duration's, their Subjective and Objective Worlds, which are meant for their Required Spiritual Conscious Expansion.

Much later Apostle JOHN, the Humble Disciple of LORD'S Chosen Son JESUS CHRIST, started His Gospel with this Same Important Information, in which He called the Vital Ethereal Space as the 'DARKNESS', and its Separated ETHEREAL Consciousness, which was Manifested by the DESIRE MIND of GOD, as the "LIGHT", which represents the 'ENLIGHTENED SPIRITUAL CONSCIOUSNESS', regarding which the Holy Bible States:

"In the Beginning was the WORD, and the WORD was with GOD, and the 'WORD WAS GOD'. HE was in the Beginning with GOD, ALL THINGS CAME INTO BEING BY HIM; AND APART FROM HIM, NOTHING CAME INTO BEING, THAT HAS COME INTO BEING.

IN HIM WAS LIFE; AND THE LIFE WAS THE "LIGHT" OF MEN. AND THE 'LIGHT' SHINES IN THE DARKNESS; and the DARKNESS did not COMPREHEND it. [John 1. Verses 1 to 5.]

LORD'S Humble Servant DAVID, the Son of JESSE whom LORD chose to be a KING over the Children of Israel, he with LORD'S grace also became aware of LORD'S True Desires, which are based upon the Universal Law of 'Will to do Good', regarding which the Holy Bible States:

"Sacrifice and Meal Offerings, THOU HAST NOT DESIRED; MY EARS THOU HAST OPENED; BURNT OFFERING AND SIN OFFERING YOU HAVE 'NOT REQUIRED'.

I have not Hidden Thy RIGHTEOUSNESS within My Heart; I Have Spoken of Thy Faithfulness, and Thy Salvation; I have not Concealed Thy Loving Kindness, and THY TRUTH from the Great Congregation." [Psalm 40. 6, 10.]

In the Psalm of ASAPH of the Holy Bible, the Same Message of the LORD is again delivered to the 'Children of Israel', which states:

"Hear, O MY PEOPLE, AND 'I' WILL SPEAK; O ISRAEL, 'I' WILL TESTIFY AGAINST you; 'I AM GOD, YOUR GOD'.

I 'DO NOT' REPROVE YOU FOR YOUR SACRIFICES, AND YOUR BURNT OFFERINGS ARE CONTINUALLY BEFORE ME. I SHALL TAKE 'NO YOUNG BULL' OUT OF YOUR HOUSE, 'NOR MALE GOATS' OUT OF YOUR FOLDS.

FOR EVERY BEAST OF THE FOREST IS '"MINE"', THE CATTLE ON A THOUSAND HILLS. I KNOW EVERY BIRD OF THE MOUNTAINS, AND EVERYTHING THAT MOVES IN THE FIELD IS '"MINE"'.

IF 'I' WERE HUNGRY, 'I' WOULD NOT TELL YOU; FOR 'THE WORLD IS MINE', AND 'ALL IT CONTAINS'.

Shall 'I' EAT THE FLESH OF BULLS, OR DRINK THE BLOOD OF MALE GOATS?

OFFER TO GOD, 'A SACRIFICE OF THANKSGIVING', AND PAY YOUR 'VOWS' TO THE 'MOST HIGH'; AND CALL UPON 'ME' IN THE 'DAY OF TROUBLE'; 'I' SHALL 'RESCUE' YOU, AND YOU WILL 'HONOR ME'." [Psalm 50. Verses 7 to 15.]

King DAVID also understood the Treachery of So Called "GODS and GODDESSES", who wrongly influence the Lower Desire Minds of evolving Human Beings, regarding which the Holy Bible States:

"Do You Indeed Speak Righteousness, O GODS? Do You Judge Uprightly, O SONS OF MEN?

NO, IN HEART YOU WORK 'UNRIGHTEOUSNESS'; ON EARTH YOU WEIGH OUT THE VIOLENCE OF YOUR HANDS." [Psalm 58. 1, 2.]

Although Psalm 2 of the Holy Bible does not talk about its authorship, the ACTS 4 Verses 25, 26 has clearly attributed them to King DAVID, which state:

'Who by the Holy Spirit, through the Mouth of our Father David Thy Servant, Didst Say, "Why did the Gentiles Rage, and the Peoples Devise FUTILE THINGS? The Kings of the Earth took their Stand, and the Rulers were Gathered Together against the LORD, and Against His CHRIST [Anointed].' [Acts 4. 25, 26.]

But the Psalm 2 of the 'Holy Bible' also Points out its authorship to the KING SOLOMON, as it corroborates with the information written in '1 Chronicles 17. 13', which clearly states SOLOMON being as the 'Chosen Son of God', regarding which the Holy Bible States:

" I Will SURELY tell of the Decree of the LORD; He Said to ME, ""'THOU ART MY SON', TODAY 'I' HAVE BEGOTTEN THEE"""".

ASK OF ME, AND 'I' WILL SURELY GIVE THE NATIONS AS THINE INHERITANCE, AND THE VERY ENDS OF THE EARTH AS THY

POSSESSIONS. THOU SHALT BREAK THEM WITH A 'ROD OF IRON', THOU SHALT SHATTER THEM LIKE EARTHENWARE." [Psalm 2. 7, 8, 9.]

"Sacrifice and Meal Offerings, THOU HAST NOT DESIRED; MY EARS THOU HAST OPENED; BURNT OFFERING AND SIN OFFERING YOU HAVE 'NOT REQUIRED'' [Psalm 40.6].

Part 61

The Great King DAVID, Son of Jesse, a Commoner, who as Per the Great LORD'S Instructions after being ANOINTED by Prophet SAMUEL, then reverently served the LORD according to HIS 'Desired Wishes', and Wisely Praised 'Glories' of the Creator LORD – GOD, who is Known to all as the Unknowable "MOST HIGH", and HIS Various 'Divine Attributes', he compiled as the 'Psalms' in Total Humility, regarding which the Holy Bible states:

'The Earth is the LORD'S, and ALL it Contains, THE World, and those who DWELL in it.' [Psalm 24. 1.]

'The SORROWS of Those, who have 'BARTERED' for 'ANOTHER GOD' will be MULTIPLIED; I shall Not Pour out their Libations of Blood, nor shall I take their Names upon My Lips.' [Psalm 16. 4.]

For who is GOD, But the LORD? And who is a Rock, except our GOD. [Psalm 18. 31.]

'Now I know, that the LORD Saves HIS Anointed; HE will answer HIM from HIS Holy Heaven, with the Saving Strength of HIS Right Hand. [Psalm 20. 6.]

'Your Hand will find out all your Enemies; Your Right Hand will find out THOSE, who HATE you. You will make them as a Fiery Oven in the time of your ANGER; The LORD will SWALLOW them up in HIS Wrath, and 'FIRE' will DEVOUR them.

Their OFFSPRING Thou Wilt DESTROY from the EARTH, and their DESCENDANTS from among the Sons of Men. Though they intended EVIL AGAINST Thee, and '''DEVISED A PLOT''', 'THEY WILL NOT SUCCEED.'' [Psalm 21. 8, 9, 10, 11.]

'The "SECRET OF THE LORD" is for THOSE, WHO FEAR HIM, AND HE WILL MAKE THEM KNOW "HIS COVENANT'''. [Psalm 25. 14.]

'One thing I have asked from the LORD, that I shall SEEK; that I may DWELL in the House of the LORD all the Days of My Life, to behold the

Beauty of the LORD, and to """"MEDITATE"""" in HIS Temple.' [Psalm 27. 4.]

'Do not Drag Me away with the WICKED, and with Those Who work INIQUITY; Who SPEAK Peace with their NEIGHBORS, While "EVIL IS IN THEIR HEARTS."' [Psalm 28. 3.]

'What Profit is there in My Blood, if I GO Down to the Pit? Will the DUST Praise Thee? Will it Declare Thy FAITHFULNESS?' [Psalm 30. 9.]

'I Hate those, who REGARD Vain "IDOLS"; But I TRUST in the LORD.

Let the Lying LIPS be DUMB, Which Speak ARROGANTLY against the RIGHTEOUS, with PRIDE and CONTEMPT.' [Psalm 31. 6, 16.]

'How Blessed is the MAN, to whom the LORD does not Impute INIQUITY, and in whose "SPIRIT", THERE IS NO DECEIT!'

Do not be as the 'HORSE', or as the 'MULE', WHICH HAS "NO UNDERSTANDING", Whose Trappings include 'BIT' and 'BRIDLE' to "HOLD" them in CHECK, otherwise they will not come near you. MANY are the SORROWS of the WICKED; But He Who TRUSTS in the LORD, Loving Kindness shall Surround Him.' [Psalm 32. 2, 9, 10.]

"For HE 'SPOKE', and it was 'DONE'; HE Commanded, and it STOOD Fast.

Blessed is the Nation, whose GOD is the LORD, the PEOPLE, Whom HE has Chosen for HIS Own Inheritance." [Psalm 33. 9, 12.]'

'O Fear the LORD, You HIS "'Saints'"; FOR THOSE who fear HIM, There is "NO WANT".

The young LIONS do LACK, and Suffer Hunger; BUT THEY WHO "SEEK THE LORD", SHALL "NOT BE IN WANT" OF ANY GOOD THING.'

Keep your Tongue from EVIL, and keep Lips from Speaking DECEIT. Depart from EVIL and """"DO GOOD""""; Seek PEACE and PURSUE IT.

The LORD redeems the 'SOUL' of HIS Servants; and NONE of THOSE Who Take REFUGE in HIM will be CONDEMNED.' [Psalm 34. 9, 10, 13, 14, 22.]

"And My 'SOUL' shall REJOICE in the LORD; IT shall EXULT in HIS Salvation. All My BONES will Say, "LORD, WHO IS LIKE THEE", WHO DELIVERS the AFFLICTED from Him, who is TOO STRONG for Him, and the Afflicted and the NEEDY from Him, who ROBS Him?" [Psalm 35. 9, 10.]

'Transgression Speaks to the "'UNGODLY'" within His HEART; THERE is No FEAR of GOD before HIS Eyes. For it Flatters Him in His own Eyes, Concerning the Discovery of His INIQUITY and the HATRED of it. The Words of His Mouth are WICKEDNESS and DECEIT; HE has CEASED to be WISE, and to DO GOOD. He Plans WICKEDNESS upon His Bed; HE Sets himself on a PATH that is NOT GOOD; HE does not Despise 'EVIL'. [Psalm 36. 1, 2, 3, 4.]

'Trust in the LORD, and 'DO GOOD'; Dwell in the Land, and Cultivate FAITHFULNESS.

Better is the LITTLE of the RIGHTEOUS, than the ABUNDANCE of Many WICKED. For the Arms of the Wicked will be Broken; But the LORD Sustains the RIGHTEOUS.

Depart from EVIL, and DO GOOD, SO you will abide FOREVER. For the LORD loves JUSTICE, and DOES NOT FORSAKE HIS GODLY ONES; THEY are PRESERVED Forever; BUT the Descendants of the WICKED will be CUT OFF.

The WICKED Spies upon the RIGHTEOUS, and He 'SEEKS TO KILL HIM'. The LORD will Not Leave HIM in His Hand, or Let Him be CONDEMNED, When He is JUDGED.

But TRANSGRESSORS will be ALTOGETHER DESTROYED; THE POSTERITY of the WICKED will be CUT OFF.' [[Psalm 37. 3, 16, 17, 27, 28, 32, 33, 38.]

'The "FOOL" has Said in His HEART,"THERE IS NO GOD". They are "CORRUPT", and have Committed "ABOMINABLE INJUSTICE"; THERE is NO ONE, Who does 'GOOD'. GOD has looked down from Heaven upon the 'SONS of MEN', to SEE if there is ANYONE who Understands, Who SEEKS after GOD. Every ONE of THEM has TURNED ASIDE; together they have become CORRUPT; THERE is NO ONE, who SEEKS GOOD, NOT EVEN ONE. [Psalm 53. 1, 2, 3.]

These Above Verses are of LORD'S Humble Servant King DAVID, in whose LINEAGE were born the Chosen Sons of GOD, the First being the Famous and Wisest King SOLOMON, and Much Later the Second Being JESUS CHRIST, the 'KING OF HEAVENS', which Clearly Point Out that King DAVID, through DEEP MEDITATION upon the grace of "LORD, the MOST HIGH", thus with HIS Grace, Understood many of the 'Secrets of Wisdom', which are Blissfully Governed by the Desire Mind of the LORD – GOD, and For the Benefit of Humanity King DAVID Compiled His 'Found Wisdom', which are known to all as His Psalms in the Holy Bible.

The Main SECRET about LORD'S Creation is, that All Manifestation came into EXISTENCE through "Eventuation Process", which reflects the DESIRE MIND ENERGY REFLECTIONS OF THE UNKNOWABLE 'GREAT LORD', REGARDING which KING DAVID WROTE: "'For HE ""SPOKE"'", and it was ""DONE""'; HE Commanded, and it STOOD fast.'" [Psalm 33. 9.]

'How Blessed is the MAN, to whom the LORD does not Impute INIQUITY, and in whose "SPIRIT", THERE IS NO DECEIT!' [Psalm 32. 2].

Most People of this dense Physical Plane World of ASSIAH, who during their 'Short Lived Incarnated Lives' are 'Very Religious', and thus 'Reverently and Faithfully' stick to their 'Personal Belief's', but do not clearly understand the Hidden "Spiritual Wisdom", which is Embedded in their 'Religious Texts', can thus Innocently Pass Away their Short Lived lives stuck in the Material World Glamour, which makes them 'SPIRITUALLY VERY POOR', as they, having 'No Concept' of the SPIRIT [Solar Consciousness], thus during their Incarnated Lives, do not consciously connect with their 'Higher Selves', which is commonly known as their 'SOULS', which exist in the Higher Dimensional world of 'BRIAH', commonly known as the "HEAVENLY WORLD", and in such cases during their 'Short Lived Incarnated Lives', their "Spiritual Consciousness' expansion does not take place, and their Incarnated Lives which they mostly spend in accumulating "Material World Objects', which are Desired by them due to their Lower Minds Polarized in "Feelings and Emotions', they at the Time of Passing Away from this Dense Dimensional World, then LEAVE ALL SUCH MATERIAL THINGS "BEHIND" Including their "MUCH CHERISHED PHYSICAL FORM", when their 'Silver Cord' of animating Vitality gets Broken.

The Holy Bible, which is a 'Store House" of Codified "Spiritual Wisdom" mentions that LORD'S Servant JOB, who was Righteous in HIS own EYES, was 'Rebuked and Reproved' by another servant of GOD named ELIHU, who was impulsed by the Desire Mind conscious reflections of the LORD —GOD, to Speak on HIS behalf to JOB, regarding which the Holy Bible States:

'Then these three men ceased answering JOB, because He was Righteous in His Own EYES. But the anger of ELIHU, the son of BARACHEL the BUZITE, of the Family of RAM burned, because He JUSTIFIED Himself before GOD. And His anger burned against His three friends, because they had found No Answer, and yet had Condemned JOB. Now ELIHU had waited to speak to JOB, because they were Years Older than He. And when ELIHU saw that there was NO ANSWER in the Mouth of the Three Men, His Anger Burned.

So ELIHU the Son of BARACHEL the BUZITE spoke out and Said, "I am Young in Years, and you are Old; THEREFORE I was Shy and Afraid to Tell you what I Think. I thought AGE Should SPEAK, and Increased Years should teach WISDOM. BUT IT IS ""'SPIRIT'"" IN MAN, AND THE "'BREATH OF THE ALMIGHTY'" GIVES THEM "'UNDERSTANDING'". The Abundant in Years may "'NOT BE WISE'", NOR MAY "ELDERS" UNDERSTAND "'JUSTICE'". So I Say, 'Listen to Me, I Too will TELL, what I Think.

For I am Full of WORDS; the "'SPIRIT'" within Me Constrains Me.

Let ME now be PARTIAL to no one; NOR Flatter any Man. For I do not know how to FLATTER, ELSE MY 'MAKER' would SOON Take Me Away.' [Job. 32, Verses 1 to 10, 18, 21, 22.]

ELIHU filled with SPIRIT of GOD, further informed JOB about GOD'S workings, regarding which the Holy Bible States:

However now JOB, Please HEAR My SPEECH, and LISTEN to My WORDS. Behold now, I Open My Mouth, my Tongue in my Mouth Speaks. My WORDS are from the Uprightness of My HEART; AND my Lips speak KNOWLEDGE Sincerely.

THE "'SPIRIT'" OF GOD HAS 'MADE' ME, AND THE BREATH OF THE 'ALMIGHTY' GIVES ME 'LIFE'. Refute me if YOU can: ARRAY YOURSELF before me, take Your Stand. Behold I BELONG TO GOD LIKE YOU; I TOO HAVE BEEN FORMED 'OUT OF THE CLAY'.

Behold, Let Me Tell You, YOU ARE NOT RIGHT IN THIS, FOR "GOD" IS GREATER THAN 'MAN'. Why do you COMPLAIN AGAINST HIM, THAT HE DOES NOT 'GIVE AN ACCOUNT OF HIS DOINGS?' INDEED GOD SPEAKS ONCE, OR TWICE, YET "'NO ONE NOTICES IT'". In a DREAM, A VISION OF THE NIGHT, when Sound Sleep falls on Men, while they SLUMBER in their BEDS, then HE Opens the Ears of Men, and SEALS THEIR INSTRUCTION, that HE May Turn MAN aside from His CONDUCT, and keep Man from PRIDE; HE keeps back His "'SOUL'" from the PIT, and His LIFE from Passing into SHEOL.

Man is also CHASTENED with Pain on his BED, and with Unceasing Complaint in his Bones; SO THAT HIS 'LIFE' LOATHES BREAD, AND HIS 'SOUL' FAVORITE FOOD. His Flesh WASTES Away from SIGHT, and His BONES, which were Not Seen, STICK OUT. Then His "'SOUL'" Draws near to the PIT, and His LIFE to those, WHO BRING DEATH.' [Job 33. Verses 1 to 6, and Verses 12 to 22.]

ELIHU Continued to explain JOB about the workings of LORD – GOD, regarding which the Holy Bible further states:

'Then ELIHU Continued and Said, "Hear my Words, you Wise men, and Listen to Me, YOU WHO 'KNOW'. For the EAR tests WORDS, as the PALATE tastes FOOD. Let US Choose for ourselves, WHAT IS RIGHT; Let us KNOW Among ourselves, WHAT IS GOOD.

SURELY GOD WILL NOT ACT WICKEDLY, AND THE ALMIGHTY WILL NOT PERVERT JUSTICE. Who gave HIM Authority over the EARTH? And who has laid on HIM the Whole WORLD?

IF HE SHOULD DETERMINE TO DO SO, IF HE SHOULD GATHER TO HIMSELF "'HIS SPIRIT AND HIS BREATH'", ALL FLESH WOULD PERISH TOGETHER, AND MAN WOULD RETURN TO DUST.' [Job 34. Verses 1, 2, 3, 4, 12, 13, 14, 15.]

ELIHU further explained JOB, that when a Man CONSCIOUSLY Stuck in the "Material World Glamour" does not Follow LORD'S Commands and thus willfully "SINS", it does not Affect the UNKNOWABLE ALMIGHTY CREATOR LORD, but HIS OWN "HIGHER CONSCIOUS SELF", commonly known to the Seers and Sages as the "'SPIRIT'", which has sent a Very Small or a Tiny Part of itself like the tiny 'Point of a Pin' or of a 'Needle' Size Ethereal Segment from the egg shaped expanding ethereal body of "CHAYAH" [Causal Body], to Experience "Spirituality " in the 3 dense Material Planes Worlds of this Planet Earth [BRIAH, YETZIRAH, and ASSIAH], through animated material forms, which are composed of related dimensional plane matters, and thus are supposed to attain Various Spiritual Experiences during their limited Life Span Duration's. And if YOU FOLLOW THE UNIVERSAL LAW OF "'WILL TO DO GOOD'", then YOU ALSO HELP YOUR "OWN SPIRIT", regarding which the Holy Bible States:

'Then ELIHU Continued and Said, "Do you think, this is according to JUSTICE? Do you Say, "My RIGHTEOUSNESS is MORE THAN GOD'S?"

IF YOU HAVE "'SINNED, WHAT DO YOU ACCOMPLISH AGAINST HIM? AND IF YOUR TRANSGRESSIONS ARE MANY, WHAT DO YOU DO TO HIM?

IF YOU ARE RIGHTEOUS, WHAT DO YOU GIVE TO HIM? OR WHAT DOES HE RECEIVE FROM YOUR HAND?

Because of the Multitude of OPPRESSION'S they CRY OUT; THEY CRY FOR HELP, because of the ARM OF THE MIGHTY. But "NO ONE" Says, "WHERE IS 'GOD MY MAKER'", Who gives SONGS IN THE NIGHT, WHO TEACHES US '"MORE THAN THE BEASTS'" OF THE EARTH, AND MAKES US '"WISER"' THAN THE 'BIRDS' OF THE HEAVENS?"

There they CRY OUT, but HE does not ANSWER, because of the PRIDE OF EVIL MEN. Surely GOD will NOT LISTEN to an EMPTY CRY, NOR will the ALMIGHTY REGARD IT.' [Job 35. 1, 2, 6, 7, and Verses 9 to 13.]

In this chapter of JOB like in any other Chapter of the Holy Bible, if any Longing Person, Who is just casually looking through it with only their Physical or Religious Eyes, INSTEAD should have His Spiritual Eyes FULLY Open, and if in such state of "Spiritual Mind", He is consciously looking for LORD'S Codified Wisdom, then He will surely find it, as all chapters of the Holy Bible, through various Narrations contain it, just like these next Following Verses of the Holy Bible also State:

'BEHOLD, GOD IS 'EXALTED' IN HIS POWER; WHO IS A '"TEACHER"' LIKE HIM?

BEHOLD, GOD IS EXALTED, AND WE DO NOT KNOW HIM; THE NUMBER OF HIS YEARS IS '"UNSEARCHABLE"'.' Job 36. 22, 26.]

'The ALMIGHTY – We cannot FIND HIM; HE is EXALTED in POWER; AND HE WILL 'NOT DO VIOLENCE' TO JUSTICE AND 'ABUNDANT RIGHTEOUSNESS'. Therefore Men 'FEAR HIM'; HE does not regard any, WHO ARE WISE OF HEART.' [Job 37. 23, 24.]

THE "'SPIRIT'" OF GOD HAS 'MADE' ME, AND THE BREATH OF THE 'ALMIGHTY' GIVES ME 'LIFE'. Refute me if YOU can: ARRAY YOURSELF before me, take Your Stand. Behold I BELONG TO GOD LIKE YOU; I TOO HAVE BEEN FORMED 'OUT OF THE CLAY'.

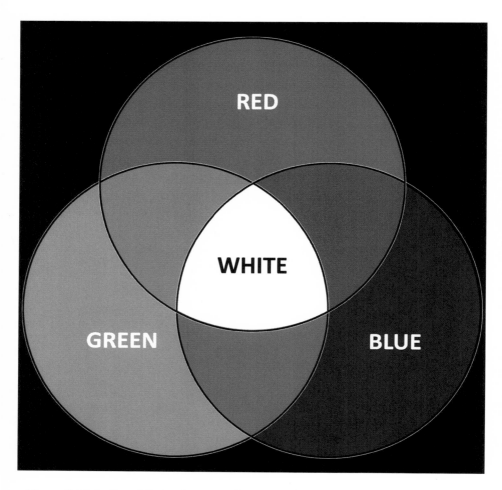

These 3 Main Tonal Color Frequencies upon this dense Physical Plane of this Planet Earth, which are perceived by Various Creatures and the Evolving Human Beings, as well as their Counterpart Invisible Entities and Beings are the Tonal Colors of [1] "RED", [2] "GREEN", and [3] "BLUE", which are in FACT the 3 basic Tonal Ingredients of "LIGHT".

The Secret of the Breast Plate

Part 63

In the Most Dense Plane, which is known as the Dimensional Sphere of ASSIAH of this Planet Earth, or for the evolving Human Beings as the Plane of their Short Lived "Incarnated Life Existence", the Great LORD-GOD through HIS Desire Mind Impulse Actions, Created the 3 Main Energy Motions known to the Enlightened "Seers and Sages" as the "Spiral, Cyclic and Spherical" Energy motions of the "Ethereal Vitality", which thus introduced in the "Cosmic Ethereal Space' 'created the 3 Main Tonal Color Vibration Frequencies, which through their Joint Interactions thus performed between themselves, Created the ""LIGHT""" to appear in HIS Subjective and Objective Manifestations, which since the Start of His Great Conscious Expansion Experiment in the Very Ancient Past, Provides the "Sense of Differentiation" to the Evolving Consciousness of all "Visible and Invisible" Dimensional Plane existences, which are commonly termed as the evolving "Entities and Beings" of the Universe.

These 3 Main Tonal Color Frequencies upon this dense Physical Plane of this Planet Earth, which are perceived by Various Creatures and the Evolving Human Beings, as well as their Counterpart Invisible Entities and Beings are the Tonal Colors of [1] "RED", [2] "GREEN", and [3] "Blue", which are in FACT the 3 basic Tonal Ingredients of "LIGHT".

The "RED" Color, which is the COLOR of "BLOOD", is related to the Metal "IRON", which the Wise King Solomon Associated with the "Planet MARS" in our Solar Universe [Iron + Oxygen creates the Red color], which provides the needed "VITALITY" to the Physical Bodies of Human Beings, as well as to the Bodies of Various Incarnated Members of the Most Species, who are evolving in the "Animal Kingdom". In the Red Blood, there is a Protein named HEMOGLOBIN Which carries OXYGEN to provide the Vital "'SPIRIT'" Force to the Incarnated Body, which is required for its Animation, and for this Codified Reason, the Great Lord Commanded MOSES, to Inform the 'Children of Israel' NEVER to EAT the "BLOOD" of Animals, regarding which the Holy Bible States:

"So when any Man, from the 'Sons of Israel', or from the Aliens, who Sojourn among them, in Hunting Catches a BEAST or a BIRD, which may be EATEN, He should POUR OUT its BLOOD, and cover it with Earth.

For as for the LIFE OF ALL FLESH, its BLOOD is IDENTIFIED with its LIFE. Therefore "'I'" Said to the 'Sons of Israel', "'YOU ARE NOT TO EAT THE BLOOD OF ANY FLESH'", FOR THE LIFE OF ALL FLESH IS ITS 'BLOOD'; WHOEVER EATS IT, SHALL BE CUT OFF.'" " [Leviticus 17. 13, 14.]

The Color "GREEN", is also the COLOR of "BLOOD", in Certain Species of the Animal Kingdom, which are Primarily known as the Insect Species of the Land, Air, and Water, upon this Dense Plane of Planet Earth, is related to the Metal "COPPER", which the Wise King Solomon Associated with the "Planet VENUS" in our Solar Universe [Copper + Oxygen Creates Green Color], and which provides "VITALITY" to the Physical Bodies of these ARTHROPODS and MOLLUSKS, who are also evolving in the "Animal Kingdom".

In the GREEN Blood, there is a Protein named 'HEMOCYANIN' which carries OXYGEN to provide the Vital 'BLUE' Force to the Incarnated Body required for its Animation. The Animal Kingdom Species which have 'Green' or 'Greenish – Blue' Blood are Horseshoe Crabs, Burgundy Snails, various Octopus and Squid Species, Crabs, Crayfish, Lobsters, Shrimps, Spiders, Scorpions, and various Flying Insects, whose bodies many a times leave their greenish blood residues on the Car's Windshield, when they get Hit by the windshield of a moving car.

The Joining of these 2 Vital Tonal Color Frequencies of "Red" and "Green" or the Vital Tinting Forces of MARS and VENUS, thus created the Tonal Color Frequencies of "YELLOW", which is the Color of Nobel Metal "GOLD", which also represents the Brightness of the Solar SUN in our Manifested Solar Universe.

The Codified Combination of these two Universal Tonal Color energy frequencies was mathematically known to the Wise King Solomon as '5.25', in which '5' represented the Planetary Consciousness of Mars and '.25' represented the Planetary Consciousness of Venus, whose Mathematical number is '7' [2+5= 7], and this 5.25 ratio is manifested in the animated animal species of this planet earth, in which Most Species incarnate with RED BLOOD, while compared to them only a Small Fraction of Species incarnate with the 'GREEN' OR 'GREENISH – BLUE' BLOOD upon this Physical Plane of ASSIAH.

To have this Mathematical Ratio objectively Manifest upon this Planet

Earth, to exist as the Various forms of Invisible and Visible Entities and Beings, the GREAT LORD OF FLAMES, created a "Wobbling Spiral Motion" in the 360 degree 'Circular Motion' of this Planet Earth, which through the Created Spiraling Wobble thus added 5.25 additional days in their Lunar Calendar Year of 360 days, and Since ancient times this Information was Codified in the Ancient Egyptian Ritual texts, which stated, that during these Extra Five days, at the End of their 360 day Lunar Calendar, the Great LORD of the Universe CREATED rest of all their GODS and GODDESSES, who have been referred to in the Holy Bible Simply as the 'GODS' or the 'ELOHIM'S', and thus these Five Days were Considered as the Holy Days in Ancient Egypt, and during these five days, which were added at the End of their Lunar Calendar Years, the Ancient Egyptians used to Celebrate their "Ritualistic Festivities" with great Pomp and Show, which were dedicated to the Birth of their GODS and GODDESSES.

The "BLUE" Color, which is also the COLOR of Copper based "BLOOD" in Certain Species of the Animal Kingdom, which are Primarily known as the Insect Species of the Land, Air, and Water, upon this Dense Plane of Planet Earth, is primarily related to the Metal "Tin", which the Wise King Solomon Associated with the "Planet JUPITER" in our Solar Universe, and Since ancient Times, the "BLUE" Color has been Considered by the SEERS and SAGES as the Basic Color of the 'FIERY SPIRIT', which provides "VITALITY" to the "Animated Forms" of all Hierarchical Entities and Beings. Our Planet Earth, when Observed from the Space appears as the "Blue Planet", which is the Color of it's "Collective Spiritual Consciousness".

The Combination of RED Color Frequencies of MARS and the BLUE Tonal Color Frequencies of JUPITER create the Color PURPLE, which is Mostly the Color of Manifested Invisible Entities and Beings, commonly known to Human Beings as the Hermaphrodite Angels, who existing as the Counterpart 'Beings' to the Visible Evolving Human Beings, are also evolving for their Own Consciousness Expansion upon this Planet Earth.

The Spiraling Motion, which the Great CREATOR LORD – GOD has created and used through HIS Desire Mind to subjectively and objectively manifest all Hierarchical Entities and Beings upon this Planet Earth has been codified in the Holy Bible as the "WHIRLWIND", through Which the Great LORD asked HIS Servant JOB an Important Question, which in fact is geared toward all invisible and Visible Hierarchical

Entities and Beings of various Dimensional Spheres of their Planet Earth, whether they KNOW of the True Expanse of its Invisible Dimensions, or Like HIM, Can Anyone Control the Emitted Cosmic Energies of Various CONSTELLATIONS, or the Vital Energy Forces of the Manifested COSMIC PLANES, Namely OF ORION, PLEIADES, URSA MINOR and URSA MAJOR [Bears], Which Cyclically Move in Set Mathematical and Geometrical Orders [Ordinances] in the Universe, and also Reach this Planet earth to effect it's Evolutionary Process, by ruling the Evolving Consciousness of differentiated Hierarchical Entities and Beings.

The Great LORD also Questioned all Humanity through JOB, whether they were Aware of their Own "HIGHER SELF", whom HE Addressed as the 'INNERMOST BEING', regarding which the Holy Bible States:

'Then the LORD answered JOB out of the 'WHIRLWIND', and said, "WHO is this, that Darkness Counsel, by WORDS without KNOWLEDGE?"

Where were YOU, when "I" Laid the FOUNDATION ON THE EARTH! Tell ME if YOU have UNDERSTANDING, WHO SET its Measurements, Since YOU Know? Or Who Stretched the Line on it? On WHAT were its BASES Sunk? Or Who Laid its Cornerstone.

Have the Gates of DEATH been REVEALED to You? Or have YOU Seen the Gates of Deep Darkness? Have you understand the Expanse of the EARTH? Tell ME, if YOU know all This.

Where is the Way to the Dwelling of Light? And Darkness, Where is its Place, that YOU may take it to its Territory, and YOU may Discern the Paths to its HOME?

Where is the Way, that the LIGHT is DIVIDED, OR the EAST Wind SCATTERED on the EARTH?

Can YOU Bind the Chains of the PLEIADES, Or Loose the Cords of ORION? Can YOU Lead forth a CONSTELLATION in its Season, and Guide the BEAR with Her SATELLITES?

Do YOU know the ORDINANCES of the HEAVENS, Or FIX their RULE over the EARTH?

Who has Put WISDOM in the "INNERMOST BEING", OR has Given

Understanding to the MIND?
[Job 38. 1, 2, 4, 5, 6, 17, 18, 19, 20, 24, 31, 32, 33, 36.]

'Then the LORD answered JOB out of the 'WHIRLWIND', and said, "WHO is this, that Darkness Counsel, by WORDS without KNOWLEDGE?"

Where were YOU, when "I" Laid the FOUNDATION ON THE EARTH! Tell ME if YOU have UNDERSTANDING, WHO SET its Measurements, Since YOU Know? Or Who Stretched the Line on it? On WHAT were its BASES Sunk? Or Who Laid its Cornerstone. [Job 38, 1, 2, 4, 5, 6]

So Give THY SERVANT an '''UNDERSTANDING HEART''' to JUDGE Thy People, to DISCERN between GOOD and EVIL. For WHO is Able to JUDGE this GREAT PEOPLE OF THINE?' [1 Kings 3.9]

Part 64

When any One Incarnates upon the Physical Plane [ASSIAH] of this Planet Earth, then according to the 'Evolutionary Plan and Purpose' of the Unknowable LORD – GOD, He / She incarnates with a 'SPECIFIC PURPOSE' of their "SOLAR CONSCIOUSNESS", which is Meant for the "ATTAINMENT OF 'MUCH NEEDED' SPIRITUAL EXPERIENCES" during His / Her Short Lived Human Life Duration, of which Most People are Totally UNAWARE, and then Going Astray from their Incarnated Lives "Spiritual Goal's" and 'Purposeful Spiritual Objectives', thus FOOLISHLY WASTE the Short Duration 'LIMITED TIME' of their "Most Valuable Human Life".

The Wise King SOLOMON, being the Chosen Son of LORD – GOD during His Time Upon this Planet Earth, when He became the King of Israel, as Per the Established Role of His Incarnated Life upon this Planet Earth, when the GREAT LORD appeared to Him in a Dream at GIBEON and asked Him of His Desired Wishes, then King SOLOMON Only Asked for a "'WISE AND DISCERNING HEART'", and 'NOTHING ELSE', regarding which the Holy Bible States:

'In Gibeon, the LORD Appeared to SOLOMON in a Dream at Night: and GOD Said, 'Ask What You WISH ME TO GIVE YOU.' Then SOLOMON Said, "Thou hast shown great Loving Kindness to THY SERVANT DAVID My Father, according as He Walked before Thee in TRUTH and RIGHTEOUSNESS, and UPRIGHTNESS of HEART toward THEE; and THOU hast GIVEN HIM a SON to Sit on His Throne, as it is this Day. And Now, O LORD MY GOD, Thou hast made THY SERVANT KING in place of My Father David, 'YET I AM BUT A LITTLE CHILD'; I do not know how to 'Go Out or Come In'. And Thy Servant is the Midst of THY PEOPLE WHICH THOU HAST CHOSEN, A GREAT PEOPLE WHO CANNOT BE 'NUMBERED OR COUNTED' FOR MULTITUDE.

So Give THY SERVANT an "'UNDERSTANDING HEART'" to JUDGE Thy People, to DISCERN between GOOD and EVIL. For WHO is Able to JUDGE this GREAT PEOPLE OF THINE?'

And it was Pleasing in the SIGHT OF THE LORD, that SOLOMON had asked this Thing. And GOD Said to Him, "BECAUSE YOU HAVE ASKED THIS THING, AND 'HAVE NOT' ASKED FOR YOURSELF 'LONG LIFE',

NOR HAVE ASKED 'RICHES' FOR YOURSELF, NOR HAVE YOU ASKED FOR THE 'LIFE' OF YOUR ENEMIES, BUT HAVE ASKED FOR YOURSELF '"DISCERNMENT TO UNDERSTAND JUSTICE"', BEHOLD. '"I"' HAVE DONE ACCORDING TO YOUR WORDS. BEHOLD, '"I"' HAVE GIVEN YOU A '"WISE AND DISCERNING HEART"', SO THAT THERE HAS BEEN '"NO ONE"' LIKE YOU, BEFORE YOU, NOR SHALL ONE LIKE YOU ARISE, AFTER YOU.

AND '"I"' HAVE ALSO GIVEN YOU WHAT YOU HAVE NOT ASKED, BOTH "RICHES AND HONOR", SO THAT THERE WILL NOT BE ANY, AMONG THE 'KINGS' LIKE YOU, ALL YOUR DAYS. AND IF YOU WALK IN MY WAYS, KEEPING MY 'STATUTES AND COMMANDMENTS', AS YOUR FATHER DAVID WALKED, THEN "I" WILL PROLONG YOUR DAYS.' [1 Kings 3. Verses 5 to 14.]

And because during King Solomon's Time, Apart from Him, Most of Evolving Humanity including the 'Priests and Prophets' of the Chosen Race, were not bestowed by the LORD, with the Divine Gift of "DISCERNMENT AND SPIRITUAL UNDERSTANDINGS", the Great King SOLOMON Himself Wrote Down for the Benefit of the 'Children of Israel', his 'Acquired Wisdom', which in the Holy Bible is known as the "Chapter of Ecclesiastes", which is 'TOTALLY FILLED WITH THE CODIFIED WISDOM OF THE UNIVERSE.'

For the Benefit of the "Children of Israel", and their 'Future Descendant Generations' to Come, The Chosen 'Son of GOD', known to the Whole World as the Wise King SOLOMON, being a Mighty and Famous King of His Times, Still Willfully undertook the Role of a Humble "Spiritual Preacher", regarding which the Holy Bible States:

'I the Preacher, have been King Over Israel in Jerusalem. And I set My Mind to "SEEK AND EXPLORE" by "WISDOM", Concerning ALL that has been DONE UNDER HEAVEN. It is a Grievous Task, which GOD has given to the 'SONS OF MEN' to be AFFLICTED with. I have SEEN all the WORKS, which have been done under the SUN, and behold, ALL is VANITY and STRIVING after WIND.

What is Crooked cannot be Straightened, and what is Lacking cannot be Counted. I Said to Myself, Behold, I have Magnified and Increased WISDOM More than ALL, who were over JERUSALEM before Me; AND MY MIND HAS 'OBSERVED' A WEALTH OF 'WISDOM AND KNOWLEDGE'. And I set My Mind to KNOW WISDOM, and to KNOW "MADNESS AND

FOLLY'; I realized that this also is STRIVING AFTER WIND. Because in 'Much Wisdom', there is 'Much Grief', and INCREASING KNOWLEDGE RESULTS IN INCREASING PAIN. [Ecclesiastes 1, Verses 12 to 18.]

In the above Verses King Solomon Clearly shared His Experiences which are related to the Discernment of "Knowledge and Wisdom", of all the Works, which had been done by the Various Visible and Invisible Hierarchical Entities and Beings, under the Plan and Purpose of the "Solar Logos", whose Objectively Manifested 'Heart and Mind' Organ Body in 'Our Solar Universe' is the Visible Solar SUN.

Also King SOLOMON clearly explained in these above Verses, that to properly understand and to FULLY KNOW the "MADNESS AND FOLLY" of Human Beings, he had to willfully Indulge in certain behavior aspects, which the Priesthood of His time may have considered as HIS WRONGDOINGS, because without Proper Experience, One Cannot become a Wise Person to deliver any Type of 'SPIRITUAL JUSTICE', as He further stated that after such Indulging experiments "He realized that it was also like STRIVING AFTER WIND. Because in 'Much Wisdom', there is 'Much Grief', and INCREASING KNOWLEDGE RESULTS IN INCREASING PAIN".

The Great King did not HIDE from the World about His Material World Indulges, to PROVE, that ONE is WRONGLY and FOOLISHLY Considered as GREAT in this Physical World, when He has Acquired Material World RICHES, and also Acquired a Great Number of Ways and Means for Various Pleasures, which in FACT "ALL ARE VANITY", as Only the 'TRUE RICHES' are those, which Enhance the SPIRITUAL ASPECT of the PERSON'S "Solar Consciousness", which is also Termed by the Sages as the "HIGHER SELF", which at the Start of any Human Incarnation sends a very tiny needle point portion of its Ethereal Consciousness from the Causal Body [CHAYAH] to Acquire Spiritual Experiences, by existing as the "Human Personality" in the 3 dense Dimensional Plane Worlds [BRIAH, YETZIRAH, and ASSIAH], and the "Higher Consciousness" HIMSELF resides in the Innermost Body of "YECHIDAH".

And The Great King Solomon, the Chosen SON of GOD, with the LORD'S GRACE, after Gaining both the Worldly and Spiritual Experiences, thus Wrote Down his 'GOD GIFTED WISDOM', known as "ECCLESIASTES", which is a Store House of "MOST VALUABLE and DEEP ROOTED KNOWLEDGE" of the 'Holy Bible', regarding which the Holy Bible States:

"All things are Wearisome; MAN is not able to tell it. THE EYE IS NOT SATISFIED WITH SEEING, NOR IS THE EAR FILLED WITH HEARING." [Ecclesiastes 1. 8.]

And Regarding His Material World Indulgences, the Great King Solomon Further States:

'I Said to MYSELF, "Come now, I will test you with PLEASURE. So ENJOY YOURSELF." And behold, it too was "'FUTILITY'". I Said of LAUGHTER, "It is MADNESS", and of 'PLEASURE', "WHAT does it ACCOMPLISH?"

I Explored with MY MIND, how to STIMULATE My Body with WINE, While My MIND was GUIDING ME WISELY, AND HOW TO 'TAKE HOLD OF FOLLY', UNTIL I COULD SEE, What GOOD there is, for the Sons of Men to Do Under HEAVEN, the Few Years of their LIVES.

I Enlarged My Works; I Built Houses for Myself, I Planted Vineyards for Myself; I made Gardens and Parks for Myself, and I Planted in them All Kinds of Fruit Trees; I made Ponds of Water for Myself from which to Irrigate a Forest of Growing Trees.

I Bought Male and Female Slaves, and I had Home born Slaves. Also I Possessed Flocks and Herds larger than ALL, who preceded ME in JERUSALEM. Also I Collected for Myself Silver and Gold, and the Treasure of Kings and Provinces. I Provided for Myself Male and Female Singers, and the Pleasures of MEN – Many Concubines.

Then 'I BECAME GREAT', and increased MORE than ALL, Who Preceded ME in JERUSALEM. My WISDOM also STOOD BY ME. And ALL that My Eyes DESIRED, I did NOT REFUSE Them. I did NOT WITHHOLD My HEART from ANY PLEASURE, for My Heart was PLEASED because of All My Labor, and this was My Reward for All My Labor.

Thus I Considered All My Activities, Which My Hands had DONE, and the LABOR which I had Exerted, AND BEHOLD, ALL WAS ""''VANITY''"" and "''STRIVING AFTER WIND'''", and there was "''NO PROFIT'''" Under the SUN. [Ecclesiastes 2. Verses 1 to 11.]

The Secret of the Breast Plate

Part 65

Most People of the World are Still Not Aware of this HIDDEN FACT that the Great King Solomon, Who asked the Great LORD for DISCERNMENT between GOOD and EVIL as His ONE AND ONLY DESIRED WISH, during His Incarnated Life upon this Planet Earth, was in fact "CHOSEN" by the UNKNOWABLE CREATOR GOD, also referred to by the Seers and Sages as the LORD OF THE FLAMES, to be "'HIS SON'" upon this Physical Plane [ASSIAH] of this Planet Earth, and the LORD – GOD, also known by All HIS Humble Servants as the "MOST HIGH" revealed this IMPORTANT SECRET to His Humble Servant PROPHET NATHAN during Night in a VISION, regarding which the Holy Bible States:

'And it came about, when DAVID dwelt in His House, that DAVID Said to 'NATHAN THE PROPHET', Behold, I am dwelling in a House of Cedar, but the ARK OF THE COVENANT of the LORD is Under Curtains." Then Nathan Said to DAVID, "Do All that is in Your HEART, for GOD is with YOU."

And it came about the same Night, that the WORD OF GOD came to NATHAN, Saying, "Go and Tell DAVID My Servant, 'Thus Says the LORD, "YOU shall Not Build a House for ME to DWELL IN; FOR I have Not Dwelt in a House, since the Day that I brought up Israel to this Day, but I have Gone from Tent to Tent, and from One Dwelling Place to Another.

And it shall come about, when Your Days are Fulfilled, that You must Go to be with Your Fathers, that I WILL SET UP ONE OF YOUR DESCENDANTS AFTER YOU, WHO SHALL BE OF YOUR SONS; AND I WILL ESTABLISH HIS KINGDOM.

HE SHALL BUILD FOR ME A 'HOUSE', AND 'I' WILL ESTABLISH HIS THRONE FOREVER. """'I WILL BE HIS FATHER, AND HE SHALL BE MY SON'"""; AND 'I' WILL NOT TAKE MY LOVING KINDNESS AWAY FROM HIM, AS 'I' TOOK IT FROM HIM, WHO WAS BEFORE YOU. BUT 'I' WILL SETTLE HIM IN MY HOUSE AND IN 'MY KINGDOM' "'FOREVER'", AND HIS 'THRONE' SHALL BE ESTABLISHED "FOREVER". [1 Chronicles 17. 1, 2, 3, 4, 5, 11, 12, 13, 13, 14.]

And the Great LORD thus PROVIDED HIS Chosen Son SOLOMON His

Desired Wish of DISCERNMENT between the GOOD and EVIL, and apart from this Great Boon, the Unknowable LORD – GOD also provided Him the Secret Understanding of the Solar Universe, in which the UNKNOWABLE LORD'S Desire Mind Consciousness acts as its Caretaker LORD, who is Commonly Known to the Seers and Sages as the "SOLAR LOGOS".

With the "MOST HIGH'S" Grace, which was AMPLY provided to SOLOMON by the LORD OF FLAMES through the Spiraling FLAMING SOLAR WINDS, which having the "Electric Mind Spiritual Consciousness" originated from the SUBJECTIVELY and OBJECTIVELY manifested SOLAR SUN, which is the 'HEART AND MIND' Organ of this Particular Solar Universe, in which our Planet Earth Exists, and from where the Conscious Electric Mind Waves thus Originate from its Magnetic Solar Spots to reach this Planet and thus Effect the evolutionary Minds of various evolving Entities and Beings of this Planet Earth, the Inquiring Mind of King Solomon then also Properly Understood about the 9 Main Huge Spherical Organs, which are Manifested in the Huge Subjective and Form which exists as the manifested body of Our 'Solar Logos' in the Celestial Space, and these 9 Main Huge Spherical Energy Distribution Organs, King Solomon Wisely Envisioned as the Huge Celestial "POMEGRANATES".

Due to the Double Role of Pomegranate shaped Huge Organ of SATURN, Whose Consciousness acts just like Him, existing as the "JUSTICE ORIENTED CHIEF SON" of the SOLAR LOGOS in this Solar Universe, the Wise Solomon thus clearly understood that the Total Number of Energy distribution Centers were not Just 9 but in a Practical manner were instead 10, due to the Governing Double Role of 'Saturn's Collective Consciousness' Energy. The Wise King Solomon also came to know the Physical Plane Name of Saturn's Collective Consciousness as the Mighty "EL", and His Mighty Servants as the "ELOHIM", who were supposed to be the Caretakers of JUSTICE upon this Planet Earth.

The reason for King SOLOMON'S understanding of these Huge Energy distribution Centers of our Solar Universe as the Celestial "Pomegranates" was due to this FACT, that just like a Physical Plane Pomegranate which has "Juicy Seeds of Vitality", these Celestial Pomegranates also Contained in them innumerable number of VITAL LIFE MONADIC ESSENCES, which based upon "Wheels of Time", Subjectively and Objectively, Cyclically Manifested in the various

Dimensional Planes [ATZILUTH, BRIAH, YETZIRAH, and ASSIAH] of the Solar Universe.

The Great King Solomon having this Divine Celestial Wisdom depicted in the Temple House of the LORD, 200 Pomegranates, in rows around the capitals of Two Pillars, the Right Pillar He named JACHIN, and the Left Pillar He named BOAZ, and the number 200 He devised by Multiplying the number 10 of Energy Distribution Organ Centers of our Solar Universe, by the Mathematical number '20' [10 x 20 = 200], as the Number 20 in a Codified way represented the Inherent Duality aspect of the 'Cosmic Energies', which Originate from the GEMINI CONSTELLATION of the Zodiac, which since ancient times on this Physical plane the 'Constellation of GEMINI'' has been represented by the Symbolic Sign of "TWO PILLARS", as well as the Mathematical Number of Our Current Solar Universe is also '2', and when this mathematical number '2' is multiplied with the number of its 10 conscious centers, one can obtain the Mathematical number 20, and this number when thus achieved, gets further multiplied to their 10 Conscious Differentiation's, which exist as the 10 Differentiated Planes of Existence, the Great King Solomon thus Obtained the Mathematical Number of 200 [2 x 10 x 10 = 200].

The Wise King Solomon also learned, that Out of these 10 Energy Distribution Organ Centers of Our Solar Universe, Only 7 Energy Distribution Centers Actively Participated in the Evolutionary Conscious Expansion Process while the other 3 Energy Distribution Organ Centers of Our Solar Universe which also included one of its center which is None other than the Duality Aspect of SATURN, these 3 Organ Centers worked in the End of Evolutionary Process as the Synthesizing Energy Centers. These 7 Energy Distribution Centers, which Actively Participated in the Evolutionary Conscious Expansion Process of this Solar Universe, as well as in the Evolutionary aspects of this Planet Earth, during their such Active Participation's, they acted in their both "Positive and Negative Aspects", and in a Codified way the Great King also Depicted them as the Nets of Network and Twisted Threads of Chain work for the Capitals, which were on the Top of the Pillars; SEVEN for the One Capital and SEVEN for the other Capital, regarding which the Holy Bible States:

'Now King SOLOMON sent and brought HIRAM from TYRE. He was a Widow's Son from the Tribe of NAPHTALI, and His father was a Man of TYRE, a Worker in Bronze; and He was filled with Wisdom and Understanding and Skill for doing any work in Bronze. So He came to King SOLOMON and Performed all His Work. And He fashioned the Two Pillars of Bronze, Eighteen Cubits was the Height of One Pillar, and a Line of Twelve Cubits measured the Circumference of both. He also made Two Capitals of molten bronze to set on Tops of the Pillars; the Height of the One Capital was Five Cubits, and the Height of the other Capital was Five Cubits. There were Nets of Network and Twisted Threads of Chain work for the Capitals, which were on the Top of the Pillars; SEVEN for the One Capital and SEVEN for the other Capital.

So He made the Pillars, and Two Rows Around on the One Network to cover the Capitals, which were on top of the POMEGRANATES; and so He did for the other Capital. And the Capitals which were on the Top of the Pillars in the Porch were of Lily Design, four Cubits.

And there were Capitals also on the Two Pillars, close to the rounded Projection, which was beside the Network; and the POMEGRANATES NUMBERED TWO HUNDRED in Rows around both Capitals. Thus He Set up the Pillars at the Porch of the Nave; and He Set Up the Right Pillar and named it JACHIN, and He Set up the Left Pillar and named it BOAZ.' [1 Kings 7. Verses 13 to 21.]

Majority of the flowers and POMEGRANATE fruits have a crown with 6 points.

BOAZ Left Pillar

TWO PILLARS OF JACHIN
Solomon's Temple Right Pillar

LILY WORK

NETS OF CHECKER WORK

WREATH OF CHAIN WORK

POMEGRANATES

BRONZE

"And there were Capitals also on the Two Pillars, close to the rounded Projection, which was beside the Network; and the POMEGRANATES NUMBERED TWO HUNDRED in Rows around both Capitals. Thus He Set up the Pillars at the Porch of the Nave; and He Set Up the Right Pillar and named it JACHIN, and He Set up the Left Pillar and named it BOAZ.'" [1 Kings 7. Verses 20,21.]

'A Generation Goes and a Generation Comes, BUT the EARTH remains FOREVER. Also, the SUN rises and the SUN Sets; and Hastening to its Place, it rises Again, Blowing toward the South, then turning toward the North, the Wind continues SWIRLING Along; and on its Circular Courses the Wind Returns.

All the Rivers Flow into the Sea, Yet the Sea is not FULL. To the Place where the Rivers flow, there they flow again.

That which has been is that which will be, and that which has been done is that which will be done. So there is Nothing New under the Sun.
[Ecclesiastes 1. 4, 5, 6, 7, 9.]

The Secret of the Breast Plate

Part 66

The Great King Solomon, through Divine Grace of the LORD Very Well Understood this Hidden Secret, that out of the Manifested Spherical Celestial Energy Distribution Centers in Our Solar Universe, the "Saturn Sphere" whose objectively manifested Visible body known to Human Beings as the 'Planet Saturn' Wore a Kingly Crown just like Him, also acted just like Him in a Double role to properly discern between GOOD and EVIL, so that its Collective Consciousness can be an EFFECTIVE CHIEF JUSTICE OF OUR ENTIRE SOLAR UNIVERSE.

The Objectively Manifested body of SATURN which is Visible to Human Beings in the Celestial Skies, while exerting its Invisible force upon the evolving beings and entities of this Planet Earth, takes 30 Years to orbit around the "Heart and Mind Center" of our Solar Universe, which happens to be our Solar SUN, whose Mathematical number is 6, a number which is symbolically represented by a spiraling limb extending out of a spherical point, and the King SOLOMON also understood that when the mathematical number 30 gets numerically reduced, it becomes the Basic Mathematical Number '3' [3 + 0 =3], which is the mathematical number of Saturn's Collective Consciousness.

The number '3', which Represents the "SATURN'S COLLECTIVE CONSCIOUSNESS", is also the Number of Holy Trinity, whose Vital Energies are represented by the three basic energy motions, which are known as the "Spiral, Cyclic, and Circular Motions", which govern the Totality of all the Evolutionary Processes, which take place in the Entire Universe, including the Formation and Manifestations of Differentiated Consciousness Planes and Sub Planes, and their Numerous Indwelling Hierarchical Entities and Beings.

The Great and Wise King also Understood that the 5.25 ratio which manifested various species of Animal Kingdom and their counterpart Angelic Beings upon this Planet Earth has in it the Mathematical number '5' which represents the consciousness of Mars, and '.25' in a Codified way represents the Consciousness of Venus, as 2 + 5 equals to 7, which represents the Number of 'Venus Collective Consciousness', but when 5.25 number is subtracted from the Solar Sun's Consciousness Number of '6', then a residue of .75 is left, which in a Codified Way represents

341

the Consciousness of Saturn, as 7 + 5 equals to 12, which when further reduced then becomes the mathematical number '3' [1 + 2 = 3], and thus the Great King Solomon clearly understood this Hidden Fact that Saturn's Vital Energies act out their Intended role in the Capacity of Solar Universe's Chief Justice, and thus exerts their Invisible Judiciary Influence upon both the Animal and Human Kingdoms, which are manifested in the 5.25 ratio, as well as their Counterpart Invisible Entities and Beings, Especially the 'Elohim's', who are also having their Own Evolutionary Process of Conscious expansion, which is parallel to the Evolving Human Beings upon this Planet Earth.

Thus during His Incarnated Life, the Great King Solomon with the Divine Grace of the "MOST HIGH", was Very Well able to 'COMPREHEND' LORD'S Desire Mind, and HIS Evolutionary Plan and Purpose, and also clearly UNDERSTOOD the Secret of the three Universal "Energy Motions", and out of these Three Motions, He Wisely DECIPHERED, that the CYCLIC MOTION of Vital Energy was the 'ONE', which kept all Manifestations in Proper 'BALANCE', through its Descending and Ascending Modes, which are also known as the Up and Down Energy Curves or the "Frequency Vibrations" of Ethereal Vitality. The Cyclic Motion thus created the Cyclic Time Periods, also known as the 'Wheels of Time', which were Clearly Visible to King Solomon in all aspects of Nature, and the Great King Solomon with the Grace of the LORD – GOD, after understanding all which took place since the evolution of Humanity began upon this Planet Earth, then Wisely Compiled, His all Such Observations, which pertained to the Cycles thus created by the Preserving Cyclic motion, regarding which the Holy Bible States:

'A Generation Goes and a Generation Comes, BUT the EARTH remains FOREVER. Also, the SUN rises and the SUN Sets; and Hastening to its Place, it rises Again, Blowing toward the South, then turning toward the North, the Wind continues SWIRLING Along; and on its Circular Courses the Wind Returns.

All the Rivers Flow into the Sea, Yet the Sea is not FULL. To the Place where the Rivers flow, there they flow again.

That which has been is that which will be, and that which has been done is that which will be done. So there is Nothing New under the Sun.

Is there ANYTHING of Which One might Say, "See this, it is NEW?"

Already it has EXISTED for AGES, which were before US. There is No Remembrance of Earlier Things; AND also of the Later Things which will Occur, There will be for them No Remembrance among those, WHO will Come Later Still. [Ecclesiastes 1. 4, 5, 6, 7, 9, 10, 11.]

In reference to the Cyclic Time, the Wise King Solomon further Explained about its Creation by the "MOST HIGH" through which HE Governs the Manifested UNIVERSE, regarding which the Holy Bible States:

'There is an Appointed Time for EVERYTHING. And there is a Time for every Event under Heaven – A Time to Give Birth, and a Time to DIE; A Time to Plant, and a Time to UPROOT what is PLANTED.
A Time to Tear APART, and a Time to SEW Together; A Time to be Silent, and a Time to Speak. A Time to LOVE and a Time to Hate; A Time for WAR, and a Time for Peace.

I have SEEN the TASK, which GOD has given the Sons of Men to Occupy Themselves. HE has made EVERYTHING Appropriate in its Time. HE has also Set Eternity in their HEARTS, yet so that MAN WILL NOT FIND OUT THE 'WORK' WHICH GOD HAS DONE FROM THE BEGINNING, EVEN TO THE END.

I know that there is NOTHING BETTER for Them to Rejoice 'AND TO DO GOOD' IN ONE'S LIFETIME'; MOREOVER, that Every Man who eats and drinks sees GOOD in All His LABOR – IT IS THE GIFT OF GOD.

I KNOW THAT '''EVERYTHING GOD DOES''' WILL REMAIN FOREVER; THERE IS NOTHING TO ADD TO IT, AND THERE IS NOTHING TO TAKE FROM IT, FOR GOD HAS SO WORKED, THAT MEN SHOULD 'FEAR HIM'. THAT WHICH IS, HAS BEEN ALREADY, AND THAT WHICH WILL BE, HAS ALREADY BEEN, FOR 'GOD SEEKS', WHAT HAS PASSED BY.' [Ecclesiastes 3. 1, 2, 7, 8, 10, 11, 12, 13, 14, 15.]

'I Said to myself, "GOD will JUDGE both the RIGHTEOUS MAN and the WICKED MAN", for a Time, for Every MATTER, and for Every DEED, is there. I Said to myself Concerning the Sons of Men, "GOD has SURELY TESTED them in Order for them to See that, THEY ARE BUT BEASTS." For the Fate of Sons of Men and the Fate of Beasts is the SAME. As One DIES, so DIES the OTHER; indeed, THEY ALL HAVE THE "'SAME BREATH'", and there is No Advantage for Man over Beast, for all is Vanity. ALL GO TO THE SAME PLACE. All came from the DUST, and all Return to the DUST.

WHO KNOWS, THAT THE "BREATH OF MAN" ASCENDS 'UPWARD', AND THE "BREATH OF THE BEAST" DESCENDS 'DOWNWARD' TO THE EARTH?'
[Ecclesiastes 3. Verses 17 to 21.]

The Great King Solomon, after Consciously Equipped with the Divine Grace of the LORD – GOD, and then looking through His Spiritual Eyes by Utilizing His "INNER MIND", while Discerning all Universal Affairs, also understood this Hidden fact of the Subjectively and Objectively Manifested Universe, that the Cyclic Motion was the "Basic Reason" for All 'Subjective and Objective' Reincarnations of "Entities and Beings", which continually took Place in the Micro to Macro Visible and Invisible Dimensional Levels of the Universe, as the Cyclic Motion Energy, which is Controlled by the Unknowable LORD – GOD'S Desire Mind Conscious Reflections, thus Governed all Actions and Reactions, which took place due to Intake of Vitality and then its Outward Dispersion in the Universe, and thus the 'Cyclic Vitality' is the True Basis for the Process of Evolving Consciousness, and its "CYCLIC WHEELS OF TIME" are commonly known as the Divine Mandates of 'Attraction and Repulsion', which are Primarily the Basis of all JUDGMENTS OF THE 'MOST HIGH', and regarding His Such Observations, the Holy Bible States:

'I Said to myself, "GOD will JUDGE both the RIGHTEOUS MAN and the WICKED MAN", for a Time, for Every MATTER, and for Every DEED, is there. I Said to myself Concerning the Sons of Men, "GOD has SURELY TESTED them in Order for them to See that, THEY ARE BUT BEASTS." For the Fate of Sons of Men and the Fate of Beasts is the SAME. As One DIES, so DIES the OTHER; indeed, THEY ALL HAVE THE "'SAME BREATH'", and there is No Advantage for Man over Beast, for all is Vanity. ALL GO TO THE SAME PLACE. All came from the DUST, and all Return to the DUST.

WHO KNOWS, THAT THE "BREATH OF MAN" ASCENDS 'UPWARD', AND THE "BREATH OF THE BEAST" DESCENDS 'DOWNWARD' TO THE EARTH?' [Ecclesiastes 3. Verses 17 to 21.]

Regarding the Actions and Reactions, which constantly take Place in the Dense Dimensional Planes of this Planet earth, especially in Physical Plane of ASSIAH, the Wise King Solomon made Great Observations, and found that Most People Stuck in the MATERIAL WORLD ILLUSORY GLAMOUR, thus during their Incarnated Lives, instead of Learning about the SPIRITUAL EXPERIENCES, were Foolishly Engaged in Rivalries, which

Created "'Unending Actions and Reactions'" between the Rivaling Factions. Which caused them to reincarnate Again and Again, to SETTLE their Folly's.

The Great King SOLOMON also found out the benefits of those 'Entities and Beings' who attained their SALVATION'S and thus FREED themselves from the Material World Bondage's. And attaining SUCH DIVINE FREEDOM, they thus did not EXISTED anymore, to NEED further Incarnations of Cyclic "Birth and Deaths" upon this Planet Earth, regarding which the Holy Bible States:

"Then I LOOKED again at all the ACTS of OPPRESSION, which were being DONE under the SUN. And behold, I SAW the TEARS of the OPPRESSED, and that they had no one to COMFORT THEM, and on the Side of their OPPRESSORS was "'POWER'", but they had NO ONE TO COMFORT THEM.

So I Congratulated the DEAD, who were Already Dead More than the LIVING, who are STILL LIVING. But ""'BETTER OFF THAN BOTH OF THEM'"" IS THE ONE, WHO HAS NEVER EXISTED, WHO HAS NEVER SEEN THE EVIL ACTIVITY THAT IS DONE UNDER THE SUN.

And I have SEEN that EVERY LABOR and EVERY SKILL, WHICH IS DONE, IS THE RESULT OF ""'RIVALRY'"" BETWEEN A MAN AND HIS NEIGHBOR. This too is VANITY and STRIVING after Wind.

One Hand FULL OF REST is BETTER than Two Fists Full of LABOR and STRIVING after WIND.

There was a Certain Man WITHOUT a DEPENDENT, having Neither a SON nor a BROTHER, YET there was "'NO END'" to His LABOR. Indeed, His 'EYES' WERE NOT SATISFIED WITH "'RICHES'", and He NEVER ASKED, "AND FOR 'WHOM' AM 'I' LABORING, and DEPRIVING Myself of Pleasure?" This too is Vanity, and it is a Grievous Task.

A POOR, YET WISE 'LAD' IS BETTER THAN AN OLD AND FOOLISH 'KING', WHO 'NO LONGER' KNOWS 'HOW TO RECEIVE INSTRUCTION' ". [Ecclesiastes 4. 1, 2, 3, 4, 6, 8, 13.]

The Great King Solomon also observed, that Most Human Beings, who are INCARNATED upon this Dense Physical Plane World of ASSIAH, because of their Unfamiliarity about their Own "SOLAR CONSCIOUS - HIGHER SELVES" were thus IGNORANTLY being POLARIZED in their Lower Desire Minds, and were thus More Interested in Performing Material Mind "'Religious Rituals'", rather than attaining the In-depth Spiritual Wisdom, which Abundantly Exists in their Holy Texts, regarding which the Holy Bible States:

'Guard Your STEPS, as you Go to the HOUSE OF GOD, and DRAW NEAR TO LISTEN, rather than to OFFER THE SACRIFICE of FOOLS; for they DO NOT KNOW, they are DOING EVIL. Do not be HASTY in 'WORDS' or IMPULSIVE in 'THOUGHT', to Bring up a MATTER in the 'PRESENCE OF GOD'. For GOD is in Heaven, and you are on the Earth; therefore LET YOUR WORDS 'BE FEW'. For the 'DREAM COMES THROUGH MUCH EFFORT', and the 'VOICE OF A FOOL' through 'MANY WORDS'.

When YOU make a 'VOW TO GOD', DO NOT BE "'LATE'" IN "PAYING IT'", FOR HE takes 'NO DELIGHT IN FOOLS'. PAY WHAT YOU "'VOW"'! It is BETTER that you should Not Vow than, THAT YOU SHOULD "'VOW"' and "'NOT PAY'".

If YOU See OPPRESSION of the POOR, and DENIAL of 'JUSTICE AND RIGHTEOUSNESS' in the Province, Do not be SHOCKED at the SIGHT, for 'ONE OFFICIAL WATCHES OVER ANOTHER OFFICIAL', AND THERE ARE "HIGHER OFFICIALS" OVER THEM.

He WHO Loves MONEY, will not be SATISFIED with MONEY, NOR HE, Who 'LOVES ABUNDANCE', with its INCOME. This too is VANITY.

When GOOD THINGS 'INCREASE', those WHO Consume Them 'INCREASE'. So what is the Advantage to their Owners, except to LOOK ON? The Sleep of a Working Man is Pleasant, whether He Eats LITTLE or MUCH. But the FULL STOMACH of the RICH MAN does not ALLOW HIM TO SLEEP.

There is a Grievous EVIL, Which I have SEEN under the SUN; Riches being 'HOARDED' by their OWNER to His HURT. When those RICHES were LOST through a BAD INVESTMENT, and He had fathered a SON, then there was NOTHING to SUPPORT Him. As He had Come Naked from His Mother's WOMB, so will He RETURN as He Came. He will TAKE 'NOTHING' from the FRUIT OF HIS LABOR that He can CARRY in His HAND. And this also is a Grievous EVIL – EXACTLY as a Man is BORN, thus will He DIE. So, WHAT is the ADVANTAGE TO HIM, Who Toils for the Wind?

Furthermore, as for Every Man, to WHOM GOD has given Riches and Wealth, HE has also Empowered Him to EAT from them, and to receive His reward and Rejoice in His Labor; this is the Gift of God. For HE WILL NOT 'CONSIDER' THE '''YEARS OF HIS LIFE''', BECAUSE GOD ''''''KEEPS HIM OCCUPIED'''''' WITH GLADNESS OF HIS 'HEART'.' [Ecclesiastes 5. 1, 2, 3, 4, 5, 8, 10, 11, 12, 13, 14, 15, 16. 19, 20.]

If a Man fathers a Hundred Children, and Lives Many Years, however MANY they be, but His SOUL is NOT SATISFIED with GOOD THINGS, and He does not even have a Proper Burial, then I Say. "BETTER the MISCARRIAGE than He, for it Comes in FUTILITY and Goes into Obscurity; and its name is Covered in Obscurity. It Never SEES the SUN and IT NEVER KNOWS ANYTHING; it is Better Off than He. Even if the other man Lives a Thousand Years Twice, and does not Enjoy GOOD THINGS – DO NOT ALL GO TO ONE PLACE? [Ecclesiastes 6.3,4,5,6.]

The Great and Wise King Solomon, through indulging in both Negative and Positive Experiments, which He Willfully carried Out throughout His Incarnated Life, in which the Negative Experiments were related to His Lower Desire Mind, and the Positive Experiments were related to His Higher Desire Mind, then by Thoughtfully DISCERNING His experiences of such Indulgences through "Intuitional Wisdom", which was Gracefully Provided to Him by the "MOST HIGH", thus Clearly UNDERSTOOD, that rather than Indulging in MATERIAL WORLD AFFAIRS of the Physical Plane [ASSIAH] of this Planet Earth, which is carried out by Most Humans following the PASSIONS of embodied "PERSONALITY", known as the "ANIMAL 'SOUL' MIND", in total Contrast to such Indulgences, the 'TRUE GOAL' of Incarnated Human Lives", was to willfully Connect with their "Higher Selves' having the "SPIRITUAL SOLAR CONSCIOUSNESS", which since ancient Times has been Termed by Seers and Sages, as to be known as the real "SOUL", and regarding this Hidden Fact He made Many Great Observations regarding which the Holy Bible States:

'A Man, to whom GOD has given RICHES, and WEALTH, and HONOR, so that His 'SOUL" lacks NOTHING of All that He Desires, but GOD has Not EMPOWERED Him to Eat from them, for a Foreigner ENJOYS them. This is Vanity and a SORE AFFLICTION.

If a Man fathers a Hundred Children, and Lives Many Years, however MANY they be, but His SOUL is NOT SATISFIED with GOOD THINGS, and He does not even have a Proper Burial, then I Say. "BETTER the MISCARRIAGE than He, for it Comes in FUTILITY and Goes into Obscurity; and its name is Covered in Obscurity. It Never SEES the SUN and IT NEVER KNOWS ANYTHING; it is Better Off than He. Even if the other man Lives a Thousand Years Twice, and does not Enjoy GOOD THINGS – DO NOT ALL GO TO ONE PLACE?

All the Man's Labor is for His 'Mouth', and yet the APPETITE is NOT SATISFIED, FOR what Advantage does the WISE Man have over the FOOL? What Advantage does the POOR Man have, knowing how to Walk before the LIVING?

What the Eyes See is BETTER than WHAT THE 'SOUL' DESIRES. This Too is "FUTILITY", and Striving after Wind. Whatever exists has already been NAMED, and it is known WHAT MAN IS; for He cannot DISPUTE with Him, WHO IS STRONGER THAN HE IS. For there are MANY WORDS, which INCREASE FUTILITY. What then is the Advantage to a Man?

For WHO KNOWS WHAT IS "'GOOD'" FOR A MAN DURING HIS 'LIFETIME', DURING THE 'FEW YEARS' OF HIS 'FUTILE LIFE'? He will SPEND them Like a SHADOW. For WHO can TELL a Man, what will be after Him under the SUN? [Ecclesiastes 6. Verses 2 to 12.]

The Wise King Solomon acting in the Role of the GOD'S Preacher, explained to the Evolving Human Beings of this World, the Basic Differences Between their "PERSONALITY CONSCIOUSNESS" embodied in a Human Form, which in Most Evolving Humans of the dense Physical Planes of this Planet Earth is CONSTANTLY ENTANGLED in the 'Magnetic Emotions and Feeling', which are the 'Desires of the Lower Mind', and their "SOUL CONSCIOUSNESS", also known as the 'Higher Self'. which Tries its Level Best to Fulfill the Role of a "SPIRITUAL MENTOR", by Vitally Sending its 'Higher Mind Desire Impulses' to the Embodied Evolving Human "Personality" Consciousness during its Incarnated Life Duration, through the means of the Vital Conscious 'Silver Cord' to influence the HEART, and thus Requires a Human Being to SPIRITUALLY GROW AND EVOLVE IN THE DENSE PLANES of this Planet Earth, during their Short Lived Incarnated Lives, so He can become Enlightened and Spiritually WISE, regarding which the Holy Bible States:

'Sorrow is Better than Laughter, for when a Face is SAD, A HEART MAY BE HAPPY. The Mind of the WISE is in the HOUSE OF MOURNING, WHILE the Mind of FOOLS is in the HOUSE OF PLEASURE. It is BETTER to LISTEN to the 'REBUKE' of a 'WISE MAN', than for One to LISTEN to the SONG OF FOOLS.

For OPPRESSION Makes a WISE Man MAD, and a BRIBE Corrupts the HEART. The End of MATTER is BETTER than its BEGINNING; 'PATIENCE' OF "'SPIRIT'" IS BETTER THAN 'HAUGHTINESS' OF "'SPIRIT'".

Wisdom along with an INHERITANCE is GOOD, and an Advantage to those, WHO SEE THE 'SUN'. For WISDOM is PROTECTION just as MONEY is PROTECTION. But the Advantage of "'KNOWLEDGE'" is that "'WISDOM'" PRESERVES the Lives of its POSSESSORS.

Wisdom Strengthens a WISE Man more than TEN RULERS, Who are in a CITY. Indeed, there is not a Righteous Man on Earth, who CONTINUALLY does GOOD and who Never SINS. Also, Do Not take SERIOUSLY all 'WORDS', which are SPOKEN, lest you HEAR Your Servant cursing you. For YOU also have 'REALIZED' that YOU likewise have MANY TIMES Cursed Others.

I TESTED ALL THIS WITH WISDOM, and I Said, "I will be WISE," But it was FAR FROM ME. What has been is REMOTE and EXCEEDINGLY MYSTERIOUS. Who can DISCOVER IT?

I Directed MY MIND to KNOW, to INVESTIGATE, and to SEEK WISDOM, and an EXPLANATION, and to Know the 'EVIL OF FOLLY', and the 'FOOLISHNESS of MADNESS'.

And I DISCOVERED MORE "BITTER" than "DEATH", the "'WOMAN'", whose HEART is SNARES and NETS, whose HANDS are CHAINS. One WHO IS PLEASING TO GOD, will 'ESCAPE FROM HER', but the SINNER will be 'CAPTURED by HER'.

'Behold, I have DISCOVERED THIS', Says the PREACHER, Adding one thing to ANOTHER, to find an EXPLANATION, which 'I' am still Seeking, but have NOT FOUND. I have Found ONE Man among a Thousand, BUT I HAVE "NOT FOUND" A 'WOMAN' AMONG ALL THESE. Behold, I have found ONLY this, that GOD made Men UPRIGHT, but THEY HAVE SOUGHT OUT MANY DEVICES.' [Ecclesiastes 7. 3, 4, 5, 7, 8, 11, 12, 19, 20, 21, 22, 23, 24, 25, 26, 27, 28, 29.]

The Wise Preacher King SOLOMON using His INNER MIND CONSCIOUSNESS, Clearly Stated in His Observations, that No Matter What the Human Beings May Try Employing their UTMOST Methods, to UNRAVEL and Discover the Workings of Unknowable CREATOR LORD- GOD of the Universe, they will NEVER SUCCEED in their Such Undertakings, regarding which the Holy Bible States:

'All this I have SEEN, and applied my MIND to Every Deed that has been DONE under the SUN, wherein a Man has Exercised AUTHORITY over ANOTHER Man to His HURT.

So then, I have seen the Wicked Buried, those WHO USED TO GO IN AND OUT FROM THE "'HOLY PLACE'", and THEY ARE SOON FORGOTTEN

351

IN THE CITY WHERE THEY DID THUS. This Too is Futility. Because the Sentence AGAINST an EVIL DEED is NOT EXECUTED QUICKLY, therefore the HEARTS of the Sons of Men among them are given FULLY TO DO EVIL. Although a SINNER does EVIL a HUNDRED TIMES, and may 'LENGTHEN his LIFE', still I KNOW that it will be WELL for those WHO FEAR GOD, who fear him 'OPENLY'.

When I gave My Heart to 'KNOW WISDOM', and to SEE THE TASK which has been DONE on the Earth [Even though One should Never Sleep Day or Night], and 'I SAW EVERY WORK OF GOD', I '''CONCLUDED''' that Man CANNOT DISCOVER THE WORK, which has been DONE under the SUN. Even though Man should SEEK LABORIOUSLY, HE WILL NOT 'DISCOVER'; AND THOUGH THE WISE MAN SHOULD SAY, '''I KNOW''', HE '''CANNOT DISCOVER'''.' [Ecclesiastes 8. 9, 10, 11, 12, 16, 17.]

The '''WORDS OF WISE''' are like '''GOADS''', and 'MASTERS OF THESE COLLECTIONS' are like 'WELL - DRIVEN NAILS'; they are Given by '''ONE SHEPHERD'''.

But beyond this My Son, Be WARNED; the WRITING OF 'MANY BOOKS' is 'ENDLESS', and EXCESSIVE DEVOTION to BOOKS is 'WEARING TO THE BODY'.

THE CONCLUSION, when all has been HEARD, is:

'''FEAR GOD, AND KEEP HIS COMMANDMENTS, BECAUSE THIS APPLIES TO EVERY PERSON.'' Because, GOD WILL BRING '''EVERY ACT''' TO JUDGMENT, EVERYTHING WHICH IS HIDDEN, WHETHER IT IS ''GOOD OR EVIL''.' [Ecclesiastes 12. Verses 11 to 14.]

The Wise King SOLOMON, after reaping the Benefits of His WISE AND DISCERNING HEART, which the "MOST HIGH" gracefully gave Him, then willfully took the 'ROLE OF A PREACHER' to preach about 'GODLY WISDOM' to the Children of Israel, and also to the Entire Humanity of this World, for the benefit of their SPIRITUAL ENHANCEMENT, Most of Whom are Still Ignorant of this UNDENIABLE FACT, that in their Short Life Duration's, they are Cyclically evolving for the Conscious expansion, which is their "SOUL'S Ultimate Goal, to attain 'SPIRITUAL WISDOM' upon this Planet Earth, regarding which the Holy Bible States:

'Whatever Your Hands find to do, VERILY, do it with all YOUR Might; FOR there is No Activity or Planning or Wisdom in SHEOL, where YOU are GOING. I again SAW under the SUN, that the Race is not with the SWIFT, and the BATTLE is Not to the Warriors, and Neither is BREAD to the WISE, Nor WEALTH to the DISCERNING, Nor FAVOR to Men of ABILITY; for "'TIME AND CHANCE'" OVERTAKE ALL.

Moreover, Man does not KNOW HIS TIME; Like Fish CAUGHT in a Treacherous Net, and Birds TRAPPED in a Snare, so the Sons of Men are ENSNARED at an 'EVIL TIME', when it SUDDENLY FALLS ON THEM.

So I Said, "WISDOM is BETTER than STRENGTH." But the WISDOM of the POOR MAN is DESPISED, and His WORDS are NOT HEEDED. The WORDS of the WISE Heard in Quietness are BETTER than the SHOUTING of a RULER among FOOLS.

WISDOM IS BETTER THAN 'WEAPONS OF WAR', BUT ONE 'SINNER' DESTROYS MUCH GOOD.' [Ecclesiastes 9. 10, 11, 12, 16, 17, 18.]

The Wise King Solomon was also very much aware of the Right hand Practices and the Left Hand Practices, which have been carried out Since Ancient Times, by Human Beings of Various Faiths in the Name of 'Religions and Spirituality' upon this Planet Earth, and He made His close Observations, regarding which the Holy Bible States:

'A WISE Man's HEART Directs Him to the RIGHT, but the FOOLISH Man's HEART Directs Him toward the LEFT. Even when the FOOL walks along the Road, His SENSE is LACKING, and He Demonstrates to everyone, that He is a FOOL.

Words from the Mouth of a WISE Man are GRACIOUS, while the LIPS of a FOOL Consume Him; the Beginning of His Talking is Folly, and the End of it is Wicked Madness. Yet the Fool Multiplies WORDS. No Man KNOWS what will HAPPEN, and WHO can Tell Him what will come after Him?

The Toil of a FOOL so WEARIES Him that He does not Know How to go to a City. [Ecclesiastes 10. 2, 3, 12, 13, 14, 15.]

The Great King Solomon also observed that since Ancient Times through various Faith related Practices, Many People by Willfully forgetting the JUDGMENTS of the LORD, have thus FOOLISHLY tried to Figure out the Desire Mind Activities of Unknowable 'MOST HIGH, LORD – GOD', regarding which the Holy Bible States:

'Just as YOU Do Not Know the Path of the Wind, and How BONES are Formed in the Womb of the Pregnant Woman, so you do not KNOW the '''ACTIVITY OF GOD''', WHO MAKES ALL THINGS.

The Light is Pleasant, and it is GOOD for the EYES to SEE the 'SUN'. Indeed, if a Man should Live Many Years, let him Rejoice in them all, and let Him 'REMEMBER THE DAYS OF DARKNESS', for they shall be MANY. Everything that is to come will be FUTILITY.

Rejoice, young man, during your Childhood, and let your Heart be Pleasant during the Days of Young Manhood. And Follow the Impulses of Your Heart and the Desires of Your Eyes. YET Know that '''GOD WILL BRING YOU TO JUDGMENT FOR ALL THESE THINGS'''.

So, remove Vexation from Your HEART, and Put away Pain from Your Body, because Childhood and the Prime of Life are "FLEETING".' [Ecclesiastes 11. 5, 7, 8, 9. 10.]

In the End the Wise King Solomon, acting as a Self-Established Preacher of GOD'S WISDOM to the Children of Israel, being the 'Chosen Son of GOD', also explained His Role as a SHEPHERD to His Human Flock, which as per the Evolutionary Plan and Purpose of the "MOST HIGH" is Evolving for their "SPIRITUAL CONSCIOUS EXPANSION" through "VITAL

354

ENERGY CYCLES" Upon this Planet Earth, regarding which the Holy Bible States:

'In Addition to being a WISE MAN, the PREACHER also taught the People KNOWLEDGE, and HE "'PONDERED'", SEARCHED OUT, and arranged MANY "'PROVERBS'".

The Preacher SOUGHT to FIND "DELIGHTFUL WORDS", AND TO WRITE "'WORDS OF TRUTH'" CORRECTLY. The "'WORDS OF WISE'" are like "'GOADS'", and 'MASTERS OF THESE COLLECTIONS' are like 'WELL - DRIVEN NAILS'; they are Given by "'ONE SHEPHERD'".

But beyond this My Son, Be WARNED; the WRITING OF 'MANY BOOKS' is 'ENDLESS', and EXCESSIVE DEVOTION to BOOKS is 'WEARING TO THE BODY'.

THE CONCLUSION, when all has been HEARD, is: "'FEAR GOD, AND KEEP HIS COMMANDMENTS, BECAUSE THIS APPLIES TO EVERY PERSON." Because, GOD WILL BRING "'EVERY ACT'" TO JUDGMENT, EVERYTHING WHICH IS HIDDEN, WHETHER IT IS "GOOD OR EVIL".' [Ecclesiastes 12. Verses 9 to 14.]

Rejoice, young man, during your Childhood, and let your Heart be Pleasant during the Days of Young Manhood. And Follow the Impulses of Your Heart and the Desires of Your Eyes. YET Know that "'GOD WILL BRING YOU TO JUDGMENT FOR ALL THESE THINGS'". [Ecclesiastes 11. 9.]

When the ASHDODITES arose Early the Next MORNING, behold, DAGON had fallen on His FACE to the Ground, before the 'ARK OF THE LORD'. So they took DAGON and Set him in His Place Again. But when they arose early the Next Morning, behold, DAGON had fallen on His FACE to the Ground, before the ARK OF THE LORD. And the HEAD of DAGON, and both the PALMS of His HANDS were CUT OFF on the Threshold; only the TRUNK of DAGON was left to Him. Therefore Neither the Priests of DAGON, Nor all who enter DAGON'S House, tread on the Threshold of DAGON in ASHDOD to this Day.

[1 Samuel 5. Verses 3, 4, 5.]

Part 70

Apart from what happened to the GODS and GODDESSES of EGYPT, and its ruling PHARAOH during the Time of EXODUS, against WHOM, the "MOST HIGH", the UNKNOWABLE LORD – GOD of the Universe, when PASSED HIS JUDGMENTS, it caused their Entire Religion to systematically and Totally Collapse over the Passing of TIME, which was Especially Geared toward their WORSHIP in Famous and Elaborated Temple Centers of EGYPT, and was in effect for such ritual practices during quite a Few Millenniums. And due to LORD – GOD'S Judgments in the end the Religion having Worship of Human Hand's made GODS – GODDESSES did not Survive in the Land of Egypt, and many other parts, like Mesopotamia and Babylon of this Planet earth.

During the time of Prophet SAMUEL, the Creator LORD, again PROVED HIS Superiority OVER All So Called GODS and GODDESSES of this WORLD, especially the Mighty God "DAGON" of the PHILISTINES, when the PHILISTINES took away the 'ARK OF THE COVENANT' from the Children of Israel, by defeating them during the Battle of EBENEZER, regarding which the Holy Bible States:

'Now the Philistines took the ARK OF GOD, and brought it from EBENEZER to ASHDOD. Then the Philistines took the ARK OF GOD, and brought it to the 'HOUSE OF DAGON', and set it by 'DAGON'.

When the ASHDODITES arose Early the Next MORNING, behold, DAGON had fallen on His FACE to the Ground, before the 'ARK OF THE LORD'. So they took DAGON and Set him in His Place Again. But when they arose early the Next Morning, behold, DAGON had fallen on His FACE to the Ground, before the ARK OF THE LORD. And the HEAD of DAGON, and both the PALMS of His HANDS were CUT OFF on the Threshold; only the TRUNK of DAGON was left to Him. Therefore Neither the Priests of DAGON, Nor all who enter DAGON'S House, tread on the Threshold of DAGON in ASHDOD to this Day.

Now the HAND of the LORD was heavy on ASHDODITES, and HE Ravaged them, and SMOTE them with TUMORS, both ASHDOD and its Territories. When the Men of ASHDOD SAW that it was so, they Said, "THE ARK OF THE GOD OF ISRAEL Must Not Remain with US, for 'HIS HAND is SEVERE' on us and DAGON OUR GOD". So they sent, and gathered all the Lords of the Philistines to them. And Said, "WHAT Shall WE Do with the ARK OF THE GOD OF ISRAEL?" And they Said, "Let the ARK OF THE GOD OF ISRAEL be brought around to GATH." And they brought the ARK OF THE GOD of Israel Around. And it came about, that after they had brought it around, the Hand of the LORD was 'AGAINST the CITY' with very great confusion; and HE SMOTE the Men of the City, BOTH Young and OLD, so that TUMORS broke on them.

So they Sent ARK OF GOD to EKRON. And it Happened as the ARK OF GOD came to EKRON, that the EKRONITES cried out, Saying, "THEY have brought the ARK OF GOD OF ISRAEL around us, to KILL US, and OUR PEOPLE." They Sent therefore and gathered all the Lords of Philistines and Said, "Send away the ARK OF GOD OF ISRAEL, and let it Return to its own Place." For there was a Deadly Confusion throughout the City; the HAND of the LORD was Very HEAVY there. And the Men, who did not DIE, were SMITTEN with TUMORS, and the Cry of the City went up to Heaven. [1 Samuel 5. Verses 1 to 12.]

Now the ARK OF THE LORD had been in the Country of the Philistines Seven Months. And the Philistines called for the Priests and the Diviners, Saying, "WHAT shall we do with the ARK OF THE LORD? Tell us HOW we shall send it to its Place." And they Said, "IF you Send away the ARK OF THE GOD OF ISRAEL, DO not SEND it 'EMPTY'; but you shall surely return to Him a 'GUILT OFFERING'. Then YOU shall be HEALED, and it shall be KNOWN to you WHY His HAND is not removed from you. Then they Said, "WHAT shall be the GUILT OFFERING which we shall return to Him?" And they Said, "FIVE GOLDEN TUMORS, and FIVE GOLDEN MICE according to the Number of the LORDS of the Philistines, for One PLAGUE was on all of you and on your LORD'S. So you shall make likeness of Your TUMORS, and likenesses of your MICE that ravage the Land, and you shall give GLORY to the GOD OF ISRAEL; perhaps "HE" will EASE HIS Hand from You, YOUR GODS, and your Land.

WHY THEN DO YOU HARDEN YOUR HEARTS, AS "EGYPTIANS AND PHARAOH" HARDENED THEIR HEARTS? WHEN "HE" HAD SEVERELY DEALT WITH THEM, DID THEY NOT ALLOW THE PEOPLE TO GO, AND THEY DEPARTED?

Now therefore take and Prepare a New Cart, and Two Milch Cows on which there has NEVER been a YOKE; and Hitch the Cows to the Cart and take their Calves Home away from them. And take the ARK OF THE LORD and Place it on the CART; and put the Articles of GOLD, which you return to HIM as a GUILT OFFERING in a BOX by its Side. Then Send it away that it may go. And watch, if it goes up by the way of its own territory to BETH-SHEMESH, then HE has done us this great EVIL. But if not, then we shall know that it was Not HIS HAND that STRUCK us; it HAPPENED to us by CHANCE."

Then the Men did so, and took two Milch Cows, and HITCHED them to the Cart, and Shut up their Calves at Home. And they put the ARK OF THE LORD on the Cart, and the BOX with the Golden Mice, and the Likeness of their Tumors. And the Cows took the Straight Way in the direction of BETH – SHEMESH; they went along the Highway, lowing as they went, and did not turn aside to the Right or to the Left. And the Lords of the Philistines followed them to the Border of BETH – SHEMESH.

Now the People of BETH – SHEMESH were reaping their Wheat Harvest in the Valley, and they raised their Eyes and SAW the ARK, and were Glad to SEE it. [1 Samuel 6. Verses 1 to 13.]

The above passages from Holy Bible Clearly defines the Supremacy of the CREATOR LORD – GOD over His Entire Creation, which includes the So Called GODS and GODDESSES of this Planet Earth.

Now the People of BETH – SHEMESH were reaping their Wheat Harvest in the Valley, and they raised their Eyes and SAW the ARK, and awere Glad to SEE it. [1 Samuel 6. 13.]

Aaron, the High Priest, wearing the Breast piece of Judgment offering
incense to the "MOST HIGH"

The Secret of the Breast Plate

Part 71

The Unknowable Creator GOD also known as the "MOST HIGH - LORD OF THE FLAMES", Who SUBJECTIVELY and OBJECTIVELY created the Invisible and Visible UNIVERSE, to MANIFEST through the formation of 'THOUGHT FORMS in HIS DESIRE MIND', which were EVENTUATED in HIS HUGE 'RADIUS OF INFLUENCE' through the Utilization of THREE ENERGY MOTIONS [Spiral, Cyclic, and Circular Motions] in the VITAL ETHEREAL MATTER, which Exists as the 'Unfathomable and Huge' SPACE and is thus composed of "'RARE VITAL ETHEREAL MATTER'", always have known since the Very Beginning, the 'PAST, PRESENT and FUTURE' Simultaneously, as HE Individually Controls and Operates the INNER MOST "STARTING POINT" of All Creations.

And thus the Great LORD Knowing Full Well, that the Descendant Members of His Evolving Chosen Race under the Negative Influence of CORRUPT Hermaphrodite Entities and Beings, who are commonly referred to as the so called GODS and GODDESSES, will STUMBLE from His Commandments in the Future, HE during the establishment of Covenant in the Wilderness, then willfully Provided them with the two Holy Object, which are known as the "URIM and THUMMIM", to be Worn inside the BREAST PLATE OF JUDGMENT by the HIGH PRIEST on top of His HEART area, and for the First Time for the Children of Israel, the Important role of a High Priest was Served by MOSES Brother AARON.

These Two Holy Objects, known as the "URIM and THUMMIM", provided the Needed Help to the Children of Israel, during the times of Absence from their Midst of a CHOSEN PROPHET, as these Two Holy Objects provided the Required Answers to the Children of Israel, in times of their Dire Needs, through the Spiritual LIGHT of 'URIM', which reflected the LORD'S DESIRE MIND through the 12 Important Stone Crystals, which were Skillfully Mounted in the four Rows upon the BREAST PLATE OF JUDGMENT, and was Perceived as CLAIRVOYANCE by the High Priest, and the second Holy Object known as the 'THUMMIM', provided LORD'S VERDICT to the inquiring mind of the High Priest through CLAIRAUDIENCE, which answered the Inquired Questions of the High Priest, so that He can get the Proper Understanding of the "Right Way" to Acquire Needed "PERFECTIONS" in their Intended Objective

Actions, or Reactions, which may be related to any Important Subject Matter. After the Passing away of the Great and Wise King SOLOMON from this World, When the Various Kings of Israel, who starting with King JEROBOAM inherited the Kingdom of Israel, they went on Willfully Defiling LORD'S COMMANDMENTS one after another, thus Unnecessarily Provoking the Most Merciful "MOST HIGH", and then in the End, LORD'S MIGHTY HAND Finally FELL upon them as a Dire Punishment, regarding which the Holy Bible States:

'In the Ninth Year of HOSHEA, the King of ASSYRIA Captured SAMARIA, and Carried ISRAEL Away into Exile to ASSYRIA, and SETTLED them in HALAH and HABOR, on the River of GOZAN, and in the Cities of the MEDES.

Now this came about, because the Sons of Israel had SINNED against the LORD their GOD, who had brought them up from the LAND OF EGYPT, from under the hand of PHARAOH, King of EGYPT, and they had 'FEARED OTHER GODS', and walked in the Customs of the Nations, whom the LORD had Driven Out before the Sons of Israel, and in the Customs of the Kings of Israel, which they had introduced.

And the Sons of Israel did things SECRETLY, WHICH WERE NOT RIGHT, AGAINST THE 'LORD THEIR GOD'. Moreover, they BUILT for themselves High Places in all their Towns, from Watchtower to Fortified City. And they SET for themselves 'Sacred Pillars', and "'ASHERIM'" on EVERY HIGH HILL, and UNDER EVERY GREEN TREE, and they BURNED INCENSE on all the HIGH PLACES as the Nations did, which the LORD had carried away to EXILE before them; and they did EVIL things PROVOKING the LORD.

And they Served IDOLS, concerning which the LORD had Said to them, "YOU SHALL NOT DO THIS THING". Yet the LORD Warned ISRAEL and JUDAH through ALL HIS "'PROPHETS'" and Every "'SEER'" Saying, "TURN FROM YOUR EVIL WAYS AND KEEP MY 'COMMANDMENTS', MY STATUES ACCORDING TO ALL THE "LAW" WHICH I COMMANDED 'YOUR FATHERS', AND WHICH I SENT TO YOU THROUGH 'MY SERVANTS', THE 'PROPHETS'."

However, they did NOT LISTEN, but STIFFENED their NECK like their Fathers, who did not believe in the LORD their GOD. And they rejected HIS 'Statutes', and HIS 'Covenant', which HE MADE with their Fathers, and HIS Warnings, with which HE Warned them. And they followed "'VANITY'', and became 'VAIN', and Went after the NATIONS which Surrounded them, concerning which the LORD had Commanded them Not to DO LIKE THEM.

And they FORSOOK all the COMMANDMENTS of the LORD their GOD, and MADE for themselves 'MOLTEN IMAGES', Even Two 'CALVES', and MADE an "'ASHERAH'", and WORSHIPED "'ALL THE HOST'" of HEAVEN, and SERVED 'BAAL'.

Then they MADE their Sons and their Daughters PASS through the FIRE, and Practiced DIVINATION and ENCHANTMENTS, and "'SOLD THEMSELVES'" TO DO 'EVIL' in the Sight of the LORD, PROVOKING HIM.

So the LORD was Very Angry with ISRAEL, and REMOVED THEM FROM HIS SIGHT; NONE was Left except the TRIBE OF JUDAH. Also JUDAH Did Not Keep the Commandments of the LORD their GOD, but WALKED IN THE CUSTOMS, which ISRAEL had INTRODUCED.

And the LORD Rejected ALL THE DESCENDANTS OF ISRAEL, and AFFLICTED them, and gave them into the Hand of PLUNDERERS, until HE had CAST them OUT OF HIS SIGHT.

When HE had TORN ISRAEL from the 'HOUSE OF DAVID', they made JEROBOAM, the Son of NEBAT King. Then JEROBOAM drove ISRAEL Away from Following the LORD, and made them COMMIT A GREAT SIN. And the Sons of Israel walked in all the SINS of JEROBOAM which HE DID, they did not DEPART from them, until the LORD removed ISRAEL from His Sight, as HE Spoke through all HIS Servants the PROPHETS. So ISRAEL was Carried Away into "'EXILE'" from their Own Land to ASSYRIA until this Day.

And the King of ASSYRIA brought Men from Babylon, and from Cuthah, and from Avva, and from Hamath, and Sephar- Vaim, and SETTLED them in the Cities of SAMARIA, in Place of the Sons of ISRAEL. So they POSSESSED SAMARIA, and Lived in its Cities. [2 Kings 17. Verses 6 to 24.]

The above Verse Clearly State, that Not Only the 'ISRAEL', but also the 'Tribe of JUDAH', DID NOT Keep the Commandments of the LORD their GOD, but WALKED IN THE CUSTOMS, which ISRAEL had 'WRONGFULLY INTRODUCED' against the Commands of the LORD their GOD. And they put Statues of the GODDESS "'ASHERIM'" on EVERY HIGH HILL, and UNDER EVERY GREEN TREE, and they BURNED INCENSE on all the HIGH PLACES as the Surrounding Nations did, which the LORD had carried away to EXILE before them; and they willfully did EVIL things, thus unnecessarily PROVOKING the LORD, and faced the Dire Consequences. And as a result the LORD Rejected ALL THE DESCENDANTS OF ISRAEL, and AFFLICTED them, and gave them into the Hand of PLUNDERERS.

'In the Ninth Year of HOSHEA, the King of ASSYRIA Captured SAMARIA, and Carried ISRAEL Away into Exile to ASSYRIA, and SETTLED them in HALAH and HABOR, on the River of GOZAN, and in the Cities of the MEDES.
[2 Kings 17. 6.]

And they SET for themselves 'Sacred Pillars', and '''ASHERIM''' on EVERY HIGH HILL, and UNDER EVERY GREEN TREE, and they BURNED INCENSE on all the HIGH PLACES as the Nations did, which the LORD had carried away to EXILE before them; and they did EVIL things PROVOKING the LORD.
[2 Kings 17. verses 10, 11.]

And the LORD Rejected ALL THE DESCENDANTS OF ISRAEL, and AFFLICTED them, and gave them into the Hand of PLUNDERERS, until HE had CAST them OUT OF HIS SIGHT. [2 Kings 17. 20]

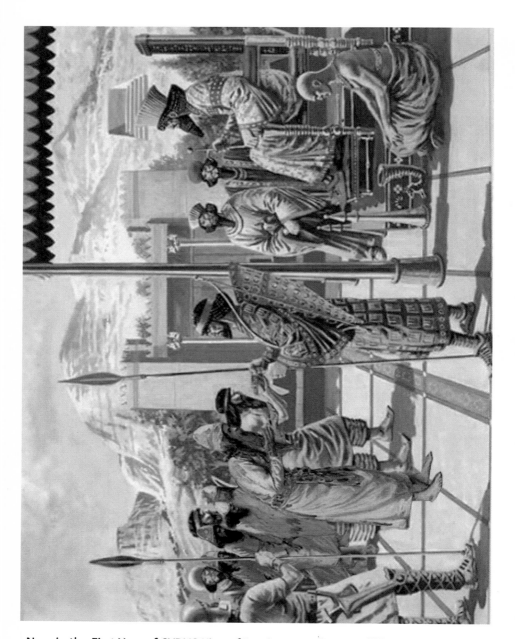

Now in the First Year of CYRUS King of Persia – In order to Fulfill the WORD of the LORD by the Mouth of JEREMIAH – the LORD Stirred up the SPIRIT of CYRUS King of Persia, so that He Sent a PROCLAMATION throughout His Kingdom, and also put in writing, Saying, "THUS Says CYRUS King of Persia, 'THE LORD, THE GOD OF HEAVEN, has given me all the Kingdoms of the Earth, and HE has Appointed Me to Build HIM a HOUSE in JERUSALEM, which is in JUDAH. Whoever there is Among You of all HIS People, May the LORD His GOD be with Him, and let Him Go Up!' "
[2 Chronicles 36. Verses 22.].

The Secret of the Breast Plate
Part 72

The Great LORD-GOD of the Universe, under whose Desire Mind Impulse Commands, the Various Visible and Invisible Kingdoms having their Innumerable Hierarchical Entities and Beings existing in their differentiated conscious roles, manifested in the Differentiated Dimension Levels of this Planet Earth, HE Patiently and Compassionately kept his PROMISE with His Chosen People, the Children of Israel, whom HE Chose to be Beacons of LIGHT for all other Evolving Human Races, who were Stuck in the Illusory Glamour of this Dense World due to Polarization of their "Evolving Personalities Desire Mind" in Lower Material Mind "Animal Passions", and Again and Again Sent Among them HIS Chosen PROPHETS, to Clearly Show their Deluded Mind's, the Proper Evolutionary Path, which they were supposed to 'Tread Upon' during their Short Lived Incarnated Human Lives, which could be beneficial to their evolving "Solar Conscious SPIRIT".

But over the Passing of Time, their descendant Generations became so CORRUPT, that all the people including the OFFICIALS of the PRIESTHOOD followed ABOMINATIONS of those NATIONS, whose Human Beings having Human Forms had more or less 'Animal Desire Minds', and thus acted with Strong 'Animal Passions' rather than utilizing their 'Higher Minds' in their daily lives.

The Children of Israel Unfortunately MOCKED their PROPHETS, and DESPISED their SPIRITUAL WORDS, thus making their Most Benevolent LORD – GOD Angry, regarding which the Holy Bible States:

'Furthermore, all the Officials of the Priests, and the People were Very Unfaithful following all the Abominations of the Nations; and they DEFILED the House of the LORD, which HE had SANCTIFIED in JERUSALEM. And the LORD, the GOD of their Fathers, Sent WORD to them Again and Again by HIS MESSENGERS, because HE had COMPASSION on HIS PEOPLE, and on HIS DWELLING PLACE; but they Continually MOCKED 'THE MESSENGERS OF GOD', DESPISED HIS WORDS, AND SCOFFED AT HIS 'PROPHETS', until the WRATH of the LORD AROSE against HIS People, until there was 'NO REMEDY'.

Therefore HE brought up against them the KING OF CHALDEAN'S, who SLEW their Young Men with the SWORD in the HOUSE OF THEIR

SANCTUARY, and had NO COMPASSION on Young Man or Virgin, Old Man or Infirm; HE Gave them ALL into His HAND. And all the Articles of the HOUSE of GOD, Great and Small, and the TREASURES of the King and of His Officers, He brought them ALL to BABYLON. Then they BURNED the House of GOD, and broke down the WALL OF JERUSALEM, and Burned all its Fortified Buildings with FIRE, and DESTROYED all its VALUABLE ARTICLES.

And those, who had escaped from the SWORD, He Carried Away to BABYLON; and they were SERVANTS to Him, and to His SONS, until the Rule of the Kingdom of Persia, to fulfill the WORD of the LORD by the Mouth of JEREMIAH, until the Land had Enjoyed its Sabbaths. All the Days of its Desolation it kept Sabbath until SEVENTY YEARS were Complete.

Now in the First Year of CYRUS King of Persia – In order to Fulfill the WORD of the LORD by the Mouth of JEREMIAH – the LORD Stirred up the SPIRIT of CYRUS King of Persia, so that He Sent a PROCLAMATION throughout His Kingdom, and also put in writing, Saying, "THUS Says CYRUS King of Persia, 'THE LORD, THE GOD OF HEAVEN, has given me all the Kingdoms of the Earth, and HE has Appointed Me to Build HIM a HOUSE in JERUSALEM, which is in JUDAH. Whoever there is Among You of all HIS People, May the LORD His GOD be with Him, and let Him Go Up!' " [2 Chronicles 36. Verses 14 to 23.].

The Holy Bible again Mentions the Two Holy Objects '"URIM and THUMMIM"' of the BREAST PLATE OF JUDGMENT, Whose Use was SUGGESTED by the SHESHBAZZAR, the PRINCE of JUDAH, who was Appointed GOVERNOR by the King CYRUS of BABYLON, Regarding which the Holy Bible States:

'However, in the First Year of CYRUS King of BABYLON, King CYRUS issued a DECREE to REBUILD this HOUSE of GOD. And also the Gold and Silver Utensils of the House of GOD, Which NEBUCHADNEZZAR had Taken from the Temple in JERUSALEM, and brought them to the Temple of BABYLON, these King CYRUS took from the Temple of BABYLON, and they were given to One, whose Name was SHESHBAZZAR, whom He Appointed GOVERNOR. And He Said to Him, "Take these Utensils, Go and Deposit them in the Temple in Jerusalem, and let the House of GOD be REBUILT in its PLACE." [Ezra 5. Verses 13 to 15.]

'Then the Heads of Father's Households of JUDAH and BENJAMIN and the PRIESTS, and the LEVITES Arose, even EVERYONE, Whose 'SPIRIT'

GOD had Stirred to Go Up and Rebuild the House of the LORD, which is in JERUSALEM.' [Ezra 1. 5.]

'Now these are the People of the Province, who came up out of the Captivity of the EXILES, whom NEBUCHADNEZZAR the King of Babylon had Carried Away to BABYLON, and Returned to JERUSALEM and JUDAH, each to His CITY. These came with ZERUBBABEL, JESHUA, NEHEMIAH, SERAIAH, REELAIAH, MORDECAI, BILSHAN, MISPAR, BIGYAI, REHUM, and BAANAH. The Number of the Men of the People of Israel: And of the Sons of the Priests: the Sons of HABAIAH, the Sons of HAKKOZ, the Sons of BARZILLAI, who took a WIFE from the Daughters of BARZILLAI the GILEADITE, and He was Called by their Name.

These Searched among their Ancestral Registration, but they could Not be Located; therefore they were Considered Unclean, and were EXCLUDED from the PRIESTHOOD. And the GOVERNOR Said to them, that they should NOT EAT from the MOST HOLY THINGS, until a PRIEST STOOD with 'URIM and THUMMIM'. [Ezra 2. 1, 2, 61, 62, 63.]

So the above Verses of the Holy Bible clearly 'POINT OUT', that the Two Holy Objects 'URIM and THUMMIM'', which belonged to the 'BREAST PIECE OF JUDGMENT', were still Available to the Returning Priesthood of the LORD, as they headed back to JERUSALEM from their EXILE in BABYLON, and their Newly Appointed Governor SHESHBAZZAR, the Prince of JUDAH, suggested their Use by a 'Standing Priest' wearing the BREAST PIECE OF JUDGMENT, to find out Someone's Ancestral Lineage, as to whether they Rightfully Belonged to the Priesthood Clan or Not, as they had Originally Claimed.

Newly Appointed Governor SHESHBAZZAR, the Prince of JUDAH, suggested using a 'Standing Priest' wearing the BREAST PIECE OF JUDGMENT, to find out Someone's Ancestral Lineage, as to whether they Rightfully Belonged to the Priesthood Clan or Not, as they had Originally Claimed.

And AARON shall CARRY the Names of the Sons of Israel in the Breast Piece of Judgment over His Heart, when He ENTERS the Holy Place, for a Memorial before the LORD Continually. And You Shall put in the Breast Piece of Judgment, the 'URIM', and the 'THUMMIM', and they shall be 'OVER AARON'S HEART', when He Goes in before the LORD; and AARON shall Carry the JUDGMENT of the Sons of Israel 'OVER HIS HEART', before the LORD Continually.' [Exodus 28. 29, 30.]

During the Time of Exodus, When the 'MOST HIGH' for the First Time made a WRITTEN 'Holy Covenant' with the Children of Israel, they were engraved Upon Two Stone Tablets which were composed of the material of His Holy Mountain, and received by His Humble Servant MOSES on Behalf of Children of Israel, which were then taken down by MOSES as the Written down Guiding Commands of the LORD, from His Holy Mountain "HOREB – SINAI" to Properly Guide the Children of Israel and their future descendants, as how to live the life of Chosen Human Beings, so they can become EXAMPLES for the rest of Evolving Humanity, whose evolving minds were being Wrongfully Polarized in the Illusory Glamour of the Dense Material Planes of this Plant Earth, which were illegally Controlled by the So called GODS and GODDESSES, who themselves became CORRUPT, and supported those Left Hand Practitioners, which are commonly known as the BLACK MAGICIANS, whose Selfish Mind Personalities embodied in their NEFESH [Dense Physical] Bodies through Various EVIL Practices, Overpowered their own RUACH [Astral] Bodies, and thus Forcefully cut themselves off from the Vital Conscious Connections of their Evolving "Higher Self's" Collective Conscious, the 'CHAYAH BODY' and the 'YECHIDAH BODY', which utilize the 'Electric Ethereal Matter' of the 1st and 2nd Higher Sub Planes of the Dimensional Sphere BRIAH [Mental Plane], and thus due to this very reason by becoming a 'LOST SOUL', and totally cut from the Evolutionary Vital Force Impulse of the "MOST HIGH", they Illegally and Deceitfully Propagated those 'ILLEGAL DIVINATION PRACTICES' in the evolving Human Races, which were Totally Contrary to the LORD'S Original Evolutionary Plan, and were thus Truly DEMONIC in Nature, which caused the DOOM and GLOOM of the "SPIRITUAL EVOLUTION" of the Evolving Humanity of this Planet Earth.

The Great LORD – GOD, for the Purpose of Conveying HIS Desire Mind JUDGMENTS toward all the 'Intended Actions' of the Descendant Children of the 12 Sons of ISRAEL [Jacob], then commanded MOSES to make a 'BREAST PLATE OF JUDGMENT' to be made by a skilled Goldsmith, upon which He should Mount 12 Stone Crystals, in Four Rows, of which each row having the 3 Precious Crystal Stones, should have upon them Engraved, the Corresponding Names of the 12 Sons of Israel upon them.

Each of these Stone Crystal were supposed to have ONE of the Sons of

Israel Name Engraved upon them, just like the Engravings which Normally Appeared on a Signatory SEAL, and these were the Given Names of the 12 Sons of JACOB [Israel], upon which the Original 12 TRIBES OF ISRAEL were BASED, regarding which the Holy Bible States:

'And YOU shall make a Breast Piece of Judgment, the Work of a Skillful Workman; like the work of the Ephod you shall make it; of Gold, of Blue, and Purple, and Scarlet Material, and Fine Twisted Linen you shall make it. It shall be Square and Folded Double, a Span in Length, and a Span in Width. And you shall Mount on it Four Rows of Stones; the First Row shall be a Row of 'Ruby', 'Topaz', and 'Emerald'; and the Second Row, a 'Turquoise', a 'Sapphire', and a 'Diamond'; and the Third Row, a 'Jacinth', an 'Agate', and an 'Amethyst'; and the Fourth Row, a 'Beryl' and an 'Onyx', and a 'Jasper'; they shall be set in Gold Filigree. And the Stones shall be according to the names of the Sons of Israel; Twelve, according to their Names; they shall be like the Engravings of a Seal, each according to His Name for the Twelve Tribes.

And AARON shall CARRY the Names of the Sons of Israel in the Breast Piece of Judgment over His Heart, when He ENTERS the Holy Place, for a Memorial before the LORD Continually. And You Shall put in the Breast Piece of Judgment, the 'URIM', and the 'THUMMIM', and they shall be 'OVER AARON'S HEART', when He Goes in before the LORD; and AARON shall Carry the JUDGMENT of the Sons of Israel 'OVER HIS HEART', before the LORD Continually.' [Exodus 28. 15, 16, 17, 18, 19, 20, 21, 29, 30.]

Basically the LORD – GOD suggested these 12 Stone Crystals to be used in the BREAST PIECE OF JUDGMENT, as the Evolution of Crystals is mainly of the Highest Consciousness levels in the First Evolutionary Visible Kingdom of this Planet Earth, which is termed as the "Densest Mineral Kingdom", and these 12 Stone Crystals Commanded by the LORD, sub consciously corresponded to the 'Emanated Vital Cosmic Frequency Vibrations' of the 12 Zodiacal Constellations of the Celestial Skies, which first being absorbed by the Subjectively and Objectively Manifested Various 'Planets' of our Solar UNIVERSE, who in this Solar Universe of LORD - GOD, played their Intended Roles as the "FOCAL POINTS OF ENERGY RECEPTION AND DISTRIBUTION" Primarily acted as the 'Energy Distribution Transformers', after being Stepped Down to be useful for Conscious Evolution, then finally reached our Planet Earth, thus affecting the "DESIRE MIND CONSCIOUSNESS" of Various Evolving Hierarchical 'Entities and Beings', and of these "Energy Distribution Centers, the "SUN and MOON" played their Important roles as the 'Main Energy Distribution Centers', which affected the daily lives of evolving Human Beings upon this Planet Earth.

Many People of this Illusory World, who Look at these Holy Verses with just their Physical Eyes or Religious Minds rather than looking at them with their 'Spiritual Eyes' or being consciously connected with their 'Higher Minds', usually Wonder, that HOW IT WAS POSSIBLE to Engrave a name upon hard Crystal like 'DIAMOND' in those times?, thus fail to understand this BASIC POINT, that Behind all these Instructions given to MOSES, was the Mighty Hand of the LORD – GOD Himself, who earlier Provided them WATER, just out of a ROCK in the Wilderness of HOREB, regarding which the Holy Bible States:

'Then all the Congregation of the Sons of Israel Journeyed by stages from the Wilderness of SIN, according to the Command of the LORD, and Camped at REPHIDIM, and there was No Water for the People to Drink. Therefore the People Quarreled with MOSES and Said, "Give US Water, that WE may DRINK". And MOSES Said to them, "WHY do you Quarrel with ME? Why do you TEST the LORD?" But the People Thirsted there for Water; and they GRUMBLED against MOSES and Said, "WHY, now, have YOU brought us up from EGYPT, to Kill US and Our Children, and Our Livestock with THIRST?"

So MOSES Cried out to the LORD, Saying, "What Shall I Do to this People? A LITTLE MORE, AND THEY WILL STONE ME." Then the LORD Said to MOSES, "PASS before the People, and take with you some of the Elders of Israel; and take in your HAND your STAFF, with which you STRUCK the Nile, and Go.

Behold, "I" will Stand before you on the ROCK at HOREB; and you shall STRIKE the ROCK, and WATER will come out of it, that the PEOPLE may DRINK." And MOSES did so in the Sight of the ELDERS of ISRAEL. And He Named the Place MASSAH and MERIBAH, because of the Quarrel of the Sons of Israel, and because they TESTED THE 'LORD', Saying, "IS THE LORD AMONG US, OR NOT?" [Exodus 17. Verses 1 to 7.]

So it is very important for the Evolving Humanity of this Planet Earth, to 'Spiritually Understand' before it is Too Late this FACT, that for the 'VITAL PRESERVATION OF THEIR EVOLVING PERSONALITY CONSCIOUSNESS' after their Physical Death, which is Embodied in their Incarnated Human Form during their Incarnated Lives, they should "Look and Listen very carefully", examining all Physical Plane "ILLUSORY PROPAGANDA'S' with their Spiritual Eyes fully OPEN, instead of willfully following the CORRUPT AGENDAS of their Visible Leaders, and their INVISIBLE 'BLACK – MAGIC' MASTERS of this Physical Plane World, who acting as the So called GODS and GODDESSES in Various Cultures are themselves DOOMED from any SPIRITUAL PROGRESS, and they are Illegally keeping the Innocent Evolving Humanity of this Planet, indulged in "MATERIAL WORLD GLAMOUR" during their short lived Incarnated Lives, and who in the name of Material Human Progress just since the Last few Centuries, have been illegally Promoting "MATERIALISM" with FULL SPEED, including the Popular "One Life Concept" of Evolving Consciousness in Human Beings, which is TOTALLY UNTRUE.

The Rock split by water on top of Mount Horeb / Sinai in the WILDERNESS of Saudi Arabia, [Modern day Mount Jebel el Lawz].

Behold, "I" will Stand before you on the ROCK at HOREB; and you shall STRIKE the ROCK, and WATER will come out of it, that the PEOPLE may DRINK." And MOSES did so in the Sight of the ELDERS of ISRAEL. And He Named the Place MASSAH and MERIBAH, because of the Quarrel of the Sons of Israel, and because they TESTED THE 'LORD', Saying, "IS THE LORD AMONG US, OR NOT?" [Exodus 17. Verses 6,7.]

And Solomon built a High Place for 'CHEMOSH', the Detestable IDOL of MOAB, on the MOUNTAIN which is EAST OF JERUSALEM, and for MOLECH, the Detestable IDOL of the Sons of AMMON. Thus also He Did for All His Foreign Wives, who BURNED INCENSE and SACRIFICED TO THEIR 'GODS'. [1 Kings 11.7,8.]

The Secret of the Breast Plate
Part 74

According to the Holy Bible, the Great LORD OF FLAMES, Clearly Instructed MOSES upon HIS Holy Mountain, regarding the Offerings, which were to be raised as CONTRIBUTIONS from the Children of Israel, which Included the 'ONYX Stones' for the 'EPHOD', as Well as the 12 'SETTING Stones', which were Supposed to be Set in the BREAST PIECE OF JUDGMENT, regarding which the Holy Bible States:

'Then the LORD Spoke to MOSES, Saying, "Tell the Sons of Israel, to RAISE a CONTRIBUTION for ME; from EVERY MAN, whose HEART moves Him, YOU shall Raise MY Contribution.

And this is the Contribution which YOU are to RAISE from them; Gold, Silver, and Bronze, Blue, Purple, and Scarlet Material, Fine Linen, Goat Hair, Ram's Skin Dyed Red, Porpoise Skins, Acacia Wood, Oil for Lighting, Spices for the Anointing Oil, and for Fragrant Incense.

ONYX STONES, AND SETTING STONES, FOR THE EPHOD, AND FOR THE BREAST PIECE.

And let them Construct a SANCTUARY for ME, that "I" May DWELL AMONG THEM.' [Exodus 25. Verses 1 to 8.]

Toward the Very End of Holy Bible, in the Revelation of JESUS CHRIST, which the LORD – GOD Gave Him, to Show to His Bond – Servants, the THINGS, Which MUST shortly take place, and these Divine Revelations JESUS Communicated to His Beloved Apostle JOHN through His Angel, which came to be known as the 'Chapter of Revelation' in the Holy Bible. In this Particular Chapter, Apostle John Similarly Mentioned the 12 Precious Stones, which corresponded to the 12 SETTING STONES of the BREAST PIECE OF JUDGMENT. Apostle JOHN called them the 12 FOUNDATION STONES of the CITY WALL of LORD'S JERUSALEM, regarding which the Holy Bible States:

'And He Carried Me Away in the "SPIRIT" to a Great and HOLY MOUNTAIN, and Showed Me the Holy City, 'JERUSALEM', Coming Down out of HEAVEN from GOD.

And the Walls of the City had Twelve Foundation Stones, and on them were the Twelve Names of the Twelve Apostles of the Lamb. The Foundation Stones of the City Wall were adorned with every kind of Precious Stone. The First Foundation Stone was JASPER; the Second, SAPPHIRE; the Third, CHALCEDONY; the Fourth, EMERALD; the Fifth, SARDONYX; the Sixth, SARDIUS; the Seventh, CHRYSOLITE; the Eighth, BERYL; the Ninth, TOPAZ; the Tenth, CHRYSOPRASE; the Eleventh, JACINTH; the Twelfth, AMETHYST.' [Revelation 21. 10, 14, 19, 20.]

The Great King Solomon who was gracefully given by the Most Benevolent LORD, a WISE AND UNDERSTANDING HEART, to DISCERN Between "'GOOD AND EVIL'", then Equipped with Extraordinary Divine Wisdom, wanted to LEARN more about the HIDDEN SECRETS of the BREAST PIECE, which gracefully PROVIDED the Inquiring High Priest, LORD'S JUDGMENTS toward the Children of Israel.

But Most People, who were living in His New Expanded Territories were Using EVIL METHODS for their Divination Purposes, which were part of their Various Ritual Practices, which were GEARED Toward their So Called GODS and GODDESSES.

So to Clearly Understand the DIFFERENCE between the GOOD Judgments of the LORD toward the Children of Israel, which were received by their High Priest wearing the BREAST PIECE OF JUDGMENT, through the use of Two Holy Objects, the 'URIM', and 'THUMMIM', and the EVIL Divination Practices of His Subjects, which invoked the Invisible Demonic SPIRITS, and the Spirits of DEAD, which worked through their venerated MOLTEN GODS and GODDESSES, as well as their Graven Images, the Great King Solomon being a Wise Judge, Just to Learn their Hidden SECRET of Evil Practices, HE acting as an "DISCERNING EXAMINER" willfully indulged in Marrying the Women, who came from those Lands where they reverently worshiped the IDOL'S of their So Called GODS and GODDESSES, and His Such ACTS, especially during his Old Age, were Not Spiritually UNDERSTOOD by the Priesthood or Comprehended by the People of His Times, Especially those, who were His Kingly Subjects.

Although even the Great LORD, fully knew the Underlying MOTIVES of His Chosen Son, the Wise King SOLOMON, which were behind His Such Wrong Acts, but these Very Acts made the LORD 'Very Unhappy', as His such acts added Unnecessary Confusion to the Evolving Minds of Children of Israel, who could not Figure out His TRUE DISCERNING MOTIVES, which were behind his such Strange Acts, and which were Totally Contradictory to LORD'S GIVEN COMMANDS, so the great Lord appeared to him, and told Him to refrain from such acts, but the King SOLOMON, to wisely differentiate between the GOOD and EVIL, having the 'DISCERNING MIND given to Him by the Great LORD Himself, wanted to go deep into Bottom of these So Called GODS and GODDESSES Mind Controlling "INFLUENCING SECRETS", and did not wanted to leave His Experiments "'Half Way Done'", regarding which the Holy Bible States:

'For it came about, when SOLOMON was OLD, His wives Turned His HEART away after OTHER GODS; and His HEART was not WHOLLY Devoted to the LORD his GOD, as the HEART of DAVID His Father had been.

For SOLOMON went after 'ASHTORETH', the 'GODDESS' of the SIDONIANS, and after 'MILCOM', the Detestable IDOL of the AMMONITES.

And Solomon built a High Place for 'CHEMOSH', the Detestable IDOL of MOAB, on the MOUNTAIN which is EAST OF JERUSALEM, and for MOLECH, the Detestable IDOL of the Sons of AMMON. Thus also He Did for All His Foreign Wives, who BURNED INCENSE and SACRIFICED TO THEIR 'GODS'.

Now the LORD was Angry with SOLOMON, because His Heart was Turned Away from the LORD, the GOD OF ISRAEL, who had APPEARED TO HIM 'TWICE', and had Commanded Him Concerning this thing, that He should not go after other 'GOD'S'; but He did not Observe, what the LORD had Commanded. So the LORD Said to Solomon, "BECAUSE you have DONE this, and you have not kept my Covenant, and My Statutes, which "I" have Commanded You. "I" will Surely TEAR the Kingdom from you, and will give it to your Servant. Nevertheless 'I WILL NOT DO IT IN YOUR DAYS', for the sake of your father DAVID, but I will tear it out of the Hand of your Son. However, "I" will Not Tear Away all the Kingdom, but I will Give One Tribe to Your Son, for the Sake of My Servant David, and for the Sake of 'JERUSALEM', WHICH I HAVE CHOSEN".' [1 Kings 11. Verses 4 to 13.]

Although in the End, the Great and Wise King SOLOMON, to clear all the Confusion from the Minds of His Subjects, Especially the Children of Israel, after Wisely Discerning between "GOOD and EVIL", now acting in the Role of a "PREACHER", the Old King Solomon then Openly Proclaimed about His Many Observations, which are His Valuable Writings to be known as the "ECCLESIASTES", and which are Part of the Holy Bible, in which He Stated, that all His Such WORLDLY ACTS were in fact FUTILE, which he carried on to become WISE.

The Great King Solomon also mentioned that he was able to TALK to the Dead, and thus CONGRATULATED them, as they were already dead to the Evils of OPPRESSION'S, which were willfully carried on by the LIVING of the Dense Material World, due to the Polarization of their Desire Minds in the MANY VICES, which are related to the ILLUSORY GLAMOUR of the Dense Material Plane World, regarding which the Holy Bible States:

'Then I LOOKED at all the ACTS of OPPRESSION, which were being done under the SUN. And behold, I SAW the Tears of the OPPRESSED, and that had 'NO ONE' to Comfort them; and on the Side of their OPPRESSORS was POWER, but THEY had NO ONE to COMFORT THEM.

So I Congratulated the DEAD, who are Already 'DEAD MORE THAN THE LIVING', who are Still Living. But BETTER Off than BOTH OF THEM, is the ONE, who has NEVER Seen the Evil Activity, that is DONE UNDER THE SUN. [Ecclesiastes 4. Verses 1 to 4.]

The Great King Solomon also Acknowledged that He had Many CONCUBINES, but in the Final Verdict He Clearly Explained Stating, that a Woman is MORE BITTER THAN DEATH, whose Heart is 'SNARES AND NETS', and whose Hands are like Chains, and ONLY that Person can Escape from HER BONDAGE'S, WHO IS "Pleasing to GOD', regarding which the Holy Bible States:

'Also I Collected for Myself, SILVER and GOLD, and the TREASURE of Kings and Provinces. I Provided for Myself Male and Female Singers, and the PLEASURES OF MEN – MANY CONCUBINES. Then I became GREAT, and increased more than all, who PRECEDED Me in JERUSALEM. My Wisdom also STOOD by ME.' [Ecclesiastes 2. 8, 9.]

'I Directed My Mind to KNOW, to INVESTIGATE, and to Seek WISDOM and an EXPLANATION, and to KNOW the EVIL of FOLLY, and the FOOLISHNESS of MADNESS. And I Discovered More Bitter than "DEATH" the Woman, Whose Heart is 'Snares and Nets', and whose Hands are Chains. One who is Pleasing to GOD will ESCAPE from HER, but the Sinner will be CAPTURED by Her.' [Ecclesiastes 7. 25, 26.]

And by Carefully Discerning between the 'GOOD and EVIL', and then Contemplating upon them during His Life, the Great King Solomon Wisely

Concluded, that all Material Plane World Activities, in which the Most of the Incarnated Human Beings of this Planet Earth Foolishly Indulged themselves, due to their LOWER MIND DESIRE'S, during their Short Lived Lives, and if these Activities were not Consciously Oriented toward their "SPIRITUAL PROGRESS", then they were thus 'TOTALLY IN-VAIN', and also like "Striving after Wind". And "Spiritual Progression" was Only Possible by 'FEARING GOD, AND KEEPING HIS HOLY COMMANDMENTS', because they Applied to Each and Every Person, who incarnated in the 3 Dense Material Plane Worlds of this Planet Earth, regarding which the Holy Bible States:

'I the Preacher, have been King over ISRAEL in JERUSALEM. And I Set My Mind to 'SEEK and EXPLORE' by WISDOM Concerning All that has been DONE UNDER HEAVEN. It is a GRIEVOUS TASK, which GOD has given to the Sons of Men, to be AFFLICTED with. I have SEEN, ALL THE WORKS, which have been DONE under the SUN, and Behold, "ALL IS VANITY AND STRIVING AFTER WIND".' [Ecclesiastes 1. 12, 13, 14.]

'The CONCLUSION, when ALL has been heard, is: 'FEAR GOD, AND KEEP HIS COMMANDMENTS', because this APPLIES TO EVERY PERSON. Because GOD will bring Every Act to JUDGMENT, EVERYTHING which is HIDDEN, whether it is "GOOD or EVIL".' [Ecclesiastes 12. 13, 14.]

The Holy Commandments

FIVE BODY'S OF A HUMAN BEING

[1] NEFESH / Physical body
[2] RUACH / Desire Mind Form
[3] NESHAMAH / Mental Body
[4] CHAYAH / Causal Body
[5] YECHIDAH / Body of
Collective Consciousness

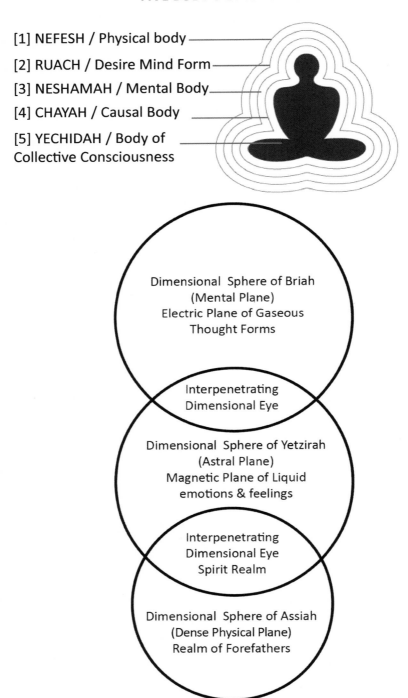

Dimensional Sphere of Briah
(Mental Plane)
Electric Plane of Gaseous
Thought Forms

Interpenetrating
Dimensional Eye

Dimensional Sphere of Yetzirah
(Astral Plane)
Magnetic Plane of Liquid
emotions & feelings

Interpenetrating
Dimensional Eye
Spirit Realm

Dimensional Sphere of Assiah
(Dense Physical Plane)
Realm of Forefathers

Three Dense Dimensional Spheres known as Planes

The Great King SOLOMON having a Wise Heart, which was fully EQUIPPED with LORD'S graceful Boon of DISCERNMENT between GOOD and EVIL, after Carefully Examining the EVIL PRACTICES of FOOLISH HUMAN BEINGS, who being Polarized in their Lower Minds "Material World Desires", and filled with 'Concentrated Animal Passions', were Faithfully Worshiping their so Called GODS and GODDESSES in the Form of MOLTEN IDOLS and GRAVEN IMAGES, which were created by just Mere HUMAN HANDS of the POOR WORKERS, to which Later On Many Well Established Noble and Rich People of their Human Societies BOWED DOWN in reverence and Awe, Solomon then with His Acquired Wisdom Found Out, that behind the Statues of these so called GODS and GODDESSES, were the Corrupt Consciousness of those Active Invisible 'Entities and Beings', who were commonly termed in the Human Societies as the "EVIL BLACK MAGICIANS", who Illegally Controlled those Innocent Human Societies, who during their Short Lived Incarnated Lives were Totally IGNORANT of these INVISIBLE DARK Entities and Beings, who being Extremely EVIL in their DECEITFUL AGENDAS, which were Against the Evolutionary Plan and Purpose of their "CREATOR LORD – THE 'MOST HIGH', were thus TOTALLY CUT OFF from their Own Higher Selves, and due to their such Deranged Material Minds, their Conscious Energies were Permanently Stuck in the Lower Dense Dimensional Levels of this Planet Earth, whose Dense MATTER vibrated at Much Slower Pace in Comparison to the Higher Dimensional Ethereal Planes of the Manifested Universe.

These CORRUPT Entities and Beings of this Planet Earth having totally DERANGED and MUTATED Consciousness were generally Invisible to the Evolving Human Beings of the dense Physical Plane, which Primarily and Solely being composed of their Lower Mind's Worldly Desires, which Polarized their evolving PERSONALITY Consciousness in the Wrong Vices, related to the Passions of the Lower Species of Animal Kingdom, were in fact a Part and Parcel of their "NEFESH and RUACH" Bodies Matter, which got TOTALLY CUT from the Radiant Consciousness of their HIGHER SELF, and were thus Permanently Stuck Mostly in the lower Sub Levels of the Dimensional Spheres of ASSIAH [Vital/Physical Plane], and YETZIRAH [Astral Plane] of this Planet Earth.

The Most Benevolent LORD – GOD of the Universe understating their 'Ensuing Dilemma', who is known to All 'Visible and Invisible' Entities and Beings as "THE MOST MERCIFUL" still did not wanted to "'DESTROY'" them yet, and Hoping that they like the 'FAILED STUDENTS IN AN EDUCATIONAL CLASS' Might REFRAIN from their EVIL WAYS Sometime in the DISTANT FUTURE, when a New Evolutionary Wave Impulse Emanating from HIS DESIRE MIND through SPIRALING - CYCLIC MOTION is Introduced upon this Plant Earth as a New "WHEEL OF TIME". The "MOST HIGH" in the Meanwhile to keep them busy in some Sort of Productive work, then Gave them Temporary Jobs of TESTING Incarnated Human Beings, especially those Evolving Human Beings, whose Desire Minds Polarized in ANIMAL PASSIONS wanted to do Wrong and EVIL things like them, during their Short Lived Incarnated Lives, and to refrain them from the EVIL WORKS due to their MATERIAL MIND NEEDS, the So called 'GODS and GODDESSES' Concept came in Existence Upon this Planet Earth.

But the PROPHETS, SEERS and SAGES, who being Humble Servants of the 'LORD OF THE FLAMES', thus having their 'Elevated Spiritual Consciousness', were always in close contact with their 'HIGHER SELVES', and were also Totally Aware, that these So called Invisible 'GODS and GODDESSES' were in fact the "Solar Conscious Fallen Angels", who due to their "NEGATIVE and EVIL WAYS of LEFT HAND PRACTICES", due to their Polarized Lower Desire Minds filled with Animal Passions, and Vices of Unquenchable ANGER, GREED and LUST, were Now Permanently Stuck during the current "CYCLIC EVOLUTIONARY WAVE", to exist as the 'GHOSTS and DEMONS' of Various Hierarchical Varieties in the Dense Dimensional Planes of this Planet Earth, whose Collective Consciousness Hierarchical In charge was termed to be known as the "SATAN and DEVIL".

The Holy Bible Clearly Mentions in many Places about their Such Roles of Testing, in which they EVEN Tested LORD'S Chosen Prophets, as well as HIS Chosen Son JESUS CHRIST, regarding which the Holy Bible States:

'Again there was a DAY, when the Sons of God came to PRESENT THEMSELVES BEFORE THE 'LORD', and 'SATAN' also came Among Them to PRESENT HIMSELF BEFORE THE LORD.

And the LORD Said to SATAN, "Where have YOU Come from?" Then 'SATAN' answered the LORD and Said, "From Roaming About on Earth, and Walking Around on it."

And the LORD Said to SATAN, "Have YOU Considered MY Servant JOB? For there is NO ONE LIKE HIM ON THE EARTH, a BLAMELESS and UPRIGHT MAN FEARING GOD, and Turning Away from EVIL. And He Still Holds FAST His INTEGRITY, although YOU INCITED ME AGAINST HIM, to RUIN Him Without CAUSE."

And SATAN Answered the LORD and Said, "SKIN FOR SKIN! Yes, All that a MAN has He will Give for His LIFE. However, Put forth THY Hand, Now, and Touch his Bone and His Flesh; He will CURSE THEE TO THY FACE." So the LORD Said to SATAN, "Behold, He is in your POWER, Only SPARE HIS LIFE."

Then SATAN went out from the Presence of the LORD, and SMOTE 'JOB' with 'Sore Boils' from the Sole of His FOOT to the CROWN of His HEAD. And He took a POTSHERD to Scrape Himself, while He was sitting among the ASHES.

Then His 'WIFE' Said to Him, 'DO YOU STILL HOLD FAST YOUR INTEGRITY? CURSE '''GOD''' AND "DIE"!' But He Said to Her. "YOU SPEAK AS '''ONE OF THE FOOLISH WOMEN SPEAKS. SHALL WE INDEED ACCEPT ''GOOD'' FROM '''GOD''', AND NOT ACCEPT '''ADVERSITY'''?' In ALL this 'JOB' did NOT 'SIN' with His LIPS.

Now when JOB'S Three Friends HEARD of all this Adversity that had come Upon Him, they came Each One from His Place, ELIPHAZ the TEMANITE, BILDAD the SHUHITE, and ZOPHAR the NAAMATHITE; and they made an Appointment together to come to SYMPATHIZE with Him, and Comfort Him. And when they Lifted up their Eyes at a Distance, and DID NOT RECOGNIZE HIM, they raised their Voices and Wept. And each of them TORE his Robe, and they threw DUST OVER THEIR HEADS, toward the Sky. Then they sat DOWN on the ground with Him for SEVEN Days and SEVEN Nights, with No One Speaking a WORD to Him, for they SAW that His PAIN was Very GREAT. [Job 2. Verses 1 to 13.]

And just Like King Solomon, who through the GIFT OF DISCERNMENT, found out the DARK SECRETS about the 'Hermaphrodite Angelic Beings' acting as the so called GODS AND GODDESSES upon this Planet Earth, who originally having the Radiant 'Solar Consciousness' later on became 'TOTALLY CORRUPT', and then Deceitfully Misusing their Vested Powers Illegally Rebelled Against the 'HOLY EVOLUTIONARY PLAN AND PURPOSE' of their CREATOR LORD-GOD, Similarly much Later LORD'S Humble Servant Prophet 'EZEKIEL', with LORDS Divine Clairaudience Words, also came to know about this 'HIDDEN FACT', regarding which the Holy Bible States:

'Again the WORD of the LORD came to Me Saying, "Son of Man, take up a LAMENTATION over the King of TYRE, and Say to Him, 'THUS Says the LORD GOD, "'YOU had the SEAL of PERFECTION, FULL of WISDOM and PERFECT in BEAUTY. You were in EDEN, the GARDEN of GOD; Every 'PRECIOUS STONE' was Your Covering: THE 'RUBY', the 'TOPAZ', and the 'DIAMOND'; THE 'BERYL', the 'ONYX', and the 'JASPER'; the 'LAPIS LAZULI', the 'TURQUOISE', and the 'EMERALD'; and the 'GOLD', the Workmanship of Your Settings and Sockets, was in YOU. On the Day that YOU were Created, THEY WERE PREPARED.

YOU were the Anointed CHERUB who COVERS, and 'I' Placed YOU there. You were on the Holy Mountain of GOD; YOU walked in the Midst of the STONES OF FIRE, You were BLAMELESS in your Ways from the Day YOU WERE CREATED, until 'UNRIGHTEOUSNESS' was FOUND IN YOU.

By the ABUNDANCE of your Trade, YOU WERE INTERNALLY FILLED WITH 'VIOLENCE', AND YOU 'SINNED'; THEREFORE "I" CAST YOU AS PROFANE, FROM THE 'MOUNTAIN OF GOD'. And "I" have DESTROYED you, O COVERING CHERUB, from the MIDST OF THE 'STONES OF FIRE'. Your HEART was lifted up because of Your Beauty; YOU CORRUPTED YOUR WISDOM BY REASON OF YOUR SPLENDOR. 'I' CAST you to the GROUND; 'I' put you before Kings, that they may SEE YOU.

By the Multitude of Your INIQUITIES, in the UNRIGHTEOUSNESS of your TRADE, YOU 'PROFANED' YOUR 'SANCTUARIES'. Therefore 'I' have brought 'FIRE' from the 'MIDST OF YOU'; IT has CONSUMED You, AND 'I' have TURNED you to ASHES on the EARTH, in the EYES of ALL Who SEE You.

All who KNOW you Among the PEOPLES are APPALLED at YOU; 'YOU HAVE BECOME TERRIFIED', And You will be 'NO MORE'.'" [Ezekiel 28. Verses 11 to 19.]

Also just like King Solomon, ISAIAH, the Chosen Prophet of LORD, with HIS Ineffable grace also came to know the Secrets Facts about ALL THOSE GODS AND GODDESSES including their Follower Human Beings, who with their Deranged Minds and Mutated Consciousness, Deceitfully Plotted against their "'ONE AND ONLY'" CREATOR LORD, by WILLFULLY BACKSTABBING HIS 'LOVE AND TRUST', having an ILLEGAL DESIRE to become just like the "MOST HIGH" HIMSELF, but instead were thrown DOWN TO THE RECESS OF THE "SHEOL'S PIT", to Permanently become the Undesirable 'GHOSTS and DEMONS' of Various Hierarchical Varieties in the Dense Dimensional Planes of this Planet Earth, regarding which the Holy Bible States:

'How YOU have FALLEN from Heaven, O Star of the MORNING, Son of the DAWN! You have been CUT DOWN to the Earth, YOU WHO has 'WEAKENED' the NATION'S! But YOU Said in Your Heart, "I WILL ASCEND TO HEAVEN; I WILL RAISE 'MY THRONE' ABOVE THE 'STARS OF GOD', AND I WILL SIT ON THE 'MOUNT OF ASSEMBLY', IN THE 'RECESSES OF THE NORTH'. I WILL ASCEND ABOVE THE 'HEIGHTS OF THE CLOUDS'; I WILL MAKE "MYSELF" LIKE THE """MOST HIGH""".

Nevertheless YOU will be 'THRUST' Down to SHEOL, to the RECESSES of the PIT. Those WHO SEE YOU will GAZE at YOU, They will PONDER over YOU, Saying, "IS this the MAN, who made the Earth TREMBLE, WHO Shook KINGDOMS, WHO made the WORLD like a WILDERNESS, and OVERTHREW its CITIES, WHO DID NOT ALLOW HIS PRISONERS TO ""GO HOME""?'. [Isaiah 14. Verses 12 to 17.]

Regarding the TESTING of LORD'S Chosen SON 'JESUS CHRIST', by the 'DEVIL', WHO being the Hierarchical Ring Leader of "Ghosts and Demons', who deceitfully act as the GODS AND GODDESSES for the Ignorant Human Races, who are Innocently Evolving upon the Dense Physical Plane World of this Planet Earth, and is also named to be known as the 'SATAN', the 'Holy Bible' states:

'Then JESUS was led up by the 'SPIRIT' into the WILDERNESS to be TEMPTED by the 'DEVIL'. And after He had Fasted FORTY DAYS and FORTY NIGHTS, HE then became HUNGRY. And the TEMPTER came and Said to Him, "IF YOU ARE THE 'SON OF GOD', Command that these STONES become BREAD." But He Answered and Said, "IT is WRITTEN, Man shall NOT LIVE ON BREAD ALONE, but on Every WORD THAT PROCEEDS OUT OF THE 'MOUTH OF GOD'."

Then the DEVIL took Him into the Holy City; and He Stood on the Pinnacle of the Temple, and Said to Him, "IF YOU ARE THE 'SON OF GOD', Throw YOURSELF Down; for it is WRITTEN, "He will give HIS ANGELS Charge Concerning YOU; AND on their HANDS they will Bear You Up, lest you Strike your Foot against a Stone." JESUS Said to Him, "On the Other Hand, it is WRITTEN, "YOU shall NOT 'TEMPT' THE LORD YOUR GOD".

Again, the DEVIL took Him to a Very High Mountain, and Showed Him all the Kingdoms of the WORLD, and their Glory; and He Said to Him, "ALL these things will I give YOU, IF YOU FALL DOWN AND 'WORSHIP ME'." Then JESUS Said to Him, "Behold, SATAN! FOR it is Written, "YOU shall Worship the LORD Your GOD, and 'SERVE HIM ONLY'."

Then the DEVIL left Him; and Behold, Angels came and began to Minister to Him. [Matthew 4. Verses 1 to 11.]

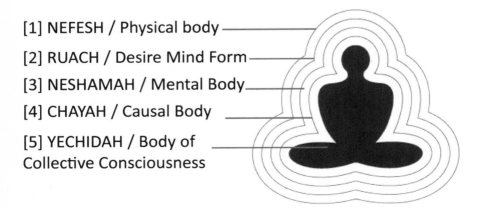

[1] NEFESH / Physical body

[2] RUACH / Desire Mind Form

[3] NESHAMAH / Mental Body

[4] CHAYAH / Causal Body

[5] YECHIDAH / Body of Collective Consciousness

FIVE BODY'S OF A HUMAN BEING

Again, the DEVIL took Him to a Very High Mountain, and Showed Him all the Kingdoms of the WORLD, and their Glory; and He Said to Him, "ALL these things will I give YOU, IF YOU FALL DOWN AND 'WORSHIP ME'." Then JESUS Said to Him, "Behold, SATAN! FOR it is Written, "YOU shall Worship the LORD Your GOD, and 'SERVE HIM ONLY'." [Matthew 4. Verses 8 to 10.]

These CORRUPT Demonic Beings and Soulless Entities acting as the so called GODS and GODDESSES, then using the Vital consciousness of the 'ANIMAL GROUP CONSCIOUS RESERVOIR' then illegally sent them in the Dense Physical Planes of the Planet Earth as the "TINY PARTS" of their Own Distorted and Mutated Consciousness, mirroring their Corrupt Agendas to Incarnate as those "Human Beings", who in the First Place were Totally Unqualified to Become any Type of LEADERS of the Evolving Human Societies, but they Still ILLEGALLY Placed them upon HIGH POSITIONS with RULING VESTED POWERS in the Evolving Human Societies.

Part 76

Although the "MOST HIGH" Showed HIS Graceful Lenience toward these CORRUPT FALLEN ANGELS, who Misusing their "VESTED POWERS" thus failed to Perform according to HIS Evolutionary Plan and Purpose upon this Planet Earth, and the Merciful LORD instead of Permanently DESTROYING their 'Evolved and Evolving' "'CONSCIOUS EXISTENCE'" through Universal Mandates, which are based upon the Universal Law of "WILL TO DO GOOD", and are Known to ALL Invisible Entities and Beings as the "NEUTRALIZATION PROCESSES', HE Still gave them a ONE MORE CHANCE to Permanently Refrain from such Illegal and Deceitful activities,after they Soulfully gave HIM their Such Promises and Assurances.

But as their Polarized Minds were Still Stuck in Worldly Desires of "DENSE MATTER,which moves at a very Slow Vibration Frequency Rate, they QUICKLY Forgot their Such Promises and Assurances, which they WILLFULLY MADE TO THE "MOST HIGH", and instead they willfully Backstabbing His "LOVE AND TRUST", through Illegal and Deceitful Means, then Conspired against HIM.

In this Widespread Conspiracy, they illegally used the "Group Conscious Reservoir"of the Lower Desires Mind "Animal Kingdom", who as per the 'Evolutionary Plan of the "MOST HIGH", through innumerable various incarnations, finally incarnated to Exist as the Evolving Domesticated and Pet Animals of the Evolving Human Races, and thus coming in "Close Contact" with the 'Individualized Mind Human Species', then Slowly Started to learn the Sign and Sound Language "Techniques of the Individualized Human Mind", and over such CLOSE CONTACTS, they themselves thus became Eligible to become Human Beings in the "NEXT ROUND" of"LORD'S DESIRE MIND VITAL EVOLUTIONARY WAVE".

These CORRUPT FALLEN ANGELS, then Misusing their 'VESTED POWERS' then Deceitfully Started using this Animal Group Conscious reservoir Vital Energies, which as Per the LORDS Evolutionary Plan and Purpose were not supposed to be released till the NEXT Evolutionary ROUND, as it will be like Putting a New Kid in An EDUCATIONAL CLASS, which has already Covered

Two third of a School Year Period, which will SURELY make that KID to FAIL in the Final Exams.

These CORRUPT Demonic Entities acting as the so called GODS and GODDESSES, then using the Vital consciousness of the 'ANIMAL GROUP CONSCIOUS RESERVOIR' then illegally sent them in the Dense Physical Planes of the Planet Earth as the "TINY PARTS" of their Own Distorted and Mutated Consciousness, mirroring their Corrupt Agendas to Incarnate as those "Human Beings", who in the First Place were Totally Unqualified to Become any Type of LEADERS of the Evolving Human Societies, but they Still ILLEGALLY Placed them upon HIGH POSITIONS with RULING VESTED POWERS in the Evolving Human Societies.

These 'DEFORMED MIND'S' Leaders full of "ANIMAL PASSIONS", who were the PUPPET STOOGES of their INVISIBLE MASTERS, were thus fully Supported by their"Invisible Henchmen Controllers" in their "MIGHT IS RIGHT" Policies, to achieve the "MATERIAL WORLD RICHES", who then Utilized them Mostly for their Own "Animal Passions and Related Pleasures", as well as to Openly Propagate the DECEITFUL AGENDAS of their "INVISIBLE MASTERS", the so called "GODS and GODDESSES", for which they Dedicated "Elaborate and Huge Temples of Worship",where they Installed their GRAND STATUES created and fabricated by Mere Mortal Human Hands, having ANIMALS SHAPES, AND ANIMAL FACED HUMAN SHAPE BODIES, ALONG WITH JUST HUMAN SHAPED DEPICTIONS HAVING MULTIPLE HANDS, WINGS, OR BOTH", which were Elaborately Covered with Expensive Regalia's, and Precious and Semi-Precious Jewels, along with Classy Ornaments of Gold and Silver.

When the Most Benevolent LORD JUDGED THEM for their Such Ruthless BEHAVIOR in the Dense Material Plane World, they all "TREMBLED" at their FATE with Great Fear,and then FACING A "PERMANENT DEATH AND COMPLETE EXTINCTION FROM THE UNIVERSE" as per the "UNIVERSAL LAW", they Cried and asked for HIS MERCIFUL FORGIVENESS", in Lieu of which the Great LORD again Temporarily FORGAVE them, but through His Limited Actions instead of Destroying them, HE Instead Systematically over the Passing of Time, then Totally ERADICATED THEIR 'DECEITFUL AGENDAS' which included the "GODS AND GODDESSES CONCEPT" from the Ancient Lands of EGYPT,MESOPOTAMIA, BABYLON, GREECE, ROME, ANATOLIA, and

Other Related Areas, which were Under their Corrupt Domains.

But some of HIS Ancient Servants, who were MOST CUNNING, then taking FULL ADVANTAGE OF HIS INEFFABLE "LOVE AND TRUST", then Quietly Started Conspiring Behind his Back to become like the "MOST HIGH" themselves, and then MISUSING THEIR"VESTED POWERS" and "UNIVERSAL ENERGIES", also Quietly Experimented ILLEGALLY with the "Animal Conscious Human Species", to whom they Provided with Ample Material Riches, and High Positions of 'NOBILITY' and "CELEBRITY STATUS" in their Evolving Human Societies, so they can Easily Propagate their Deceitful Agendas of "NO GOD EXISTENCE CONCEPT" by openly becoming "AGNOSTICS and ATHEISTS" in their Elite Society Circles.

But these STUPID Servants of the "MOST HIGH", WHO were "ILLEGALLY AND DECEITFULLY" Engaged in Such Heinous Activities of BETRAYAL against the "LOVE AND TRUST" of the "MOST HIGH" Completely Failed to understand and Comprehend the "GRAVE RESULTS OF THEIR SUCH ACTIONS", and MISCALCULATED that the Great """UNKNOWABLE CREATOR LORD""", who CREATED THEM BY BRINGING THEM INTO"SUBJECTIVE AND OBJECTIVE" MANIFESTATION'S, has Constantly Given them SO MANY CHANCES, AGAIN and AGAIN, for a VERY LONG TIME, in fact was Really HOPING that they Sooner or Later will MEND THEIR EVIL WAYS, and ALSO CONTRARY TO THEIR "'FALSE BELIEF", was in fact "FULLY AWARE OF THEIR SUCH DECEITFUL AGENDAS", and thus to UPHOLD THE UNIVERSAL LAW OF "WILL TO DO GOOD" was ready to Permanently ERADICATE THEM without ANY FURTHER NOTICE, along with their Complete Elimination, and Extinction, which involved the TOTAL DESTRUCTION of their 'ARCHETYPE CONSCIOUS PATTERNS', which is now taking place in the Manifested Universe in Full Swing.

Regarding the Deceitful Agendas of "NO GOD EXISTENCE CONCEPT" propagated by the Foolish "AGNOSTICS and ATHEISTS" Human Agents of the INVISIBLE CORRUPT MASTERS, upon this Glamour filled Material Plane World, who knowingly or unknowingly acted as the Front Men and Stooges of these Invisible FALLEN ANGELS, during their Short Lived incarnated Lives upon the dense Material Plane of this Planet Earth, the 'MOST MERCIFUL LORD OF FLAMES' Filled with Divine "LOVE FOR ALL ENTITIES AND BEINGS" who are His Experimental Creations, since Ancient Past has Faithfully

WARNED them MANY a TIMES through His Chosen Prophets, Seers, and Sages, regarding which the Holy Bible States:

"The FOOL has Said in His Heart, "THERE IS NO GOD", THEY are 'CORRUPT', and have'COMMITTED ABOMINABLE INJUSTICE'; There is 'NO ONE', who does GOOD.

GOD has LOOKED DOWN FROM HEAVEN upon the Sons of Men, to SEE if there is Anyone WHO UNDERSTANDS, who SEEKS AFTER GOD. Every ONE of them has Turned Aside; together they have become CORRUPT; THERE is 'NO ONE' who does GOOD, not even 'ONE'."[Psalm 53. Verses 1 to 3.]

'Now Consider this, 'YOU WHO FORGET "GOD", LEST "I" TEAR YOU IN PIECES, AND THERE BE NONE TO DELIVER'. He who offers a Sacrifice of 'THANKSGIVING' Honors Me; AND to Him, Who Orders His Way Aright, 'I' shall show the Salvation of GOD.' [Psalm 50. 22, 23.]

'Be Careful, "DO NOT TURN TO EVIL'; FOR you have Preferred this to Affliction. Behold, GOD is EXALTED in HIS POWER; WHO IS A "TEACHER" like HIM? Behold, GOD is Exalted, and WE do not Know HIM; THE NUMBER of "HIS YEARS" is"UNSEARCHABLE".' [Job 36. 21, 22, 26.]

'The ALMIGHTY — We Cannot Find HIM; HE is EXALTED IN POWER; AND HE will Not Do VIOLENCE to "JUSTICE" and "ABUNDANT RIGHTEOUSNESS". Therefore MEN Fear HIM; HE does not regard any WHO are WISE OF HEART.' [Job 37. 23, 24.]

'TREMBLE, and do not "SIN"; MEDITATE in Your HEART upon your BED, and be STILL. Offer the Sacrifices of "RIGHTEOUSNESS", and TRUST IN THE LORD.' [Psalm 4. 4, 5.]

'The Nations have SUNK Down in the PIT, which THEY have MADE; In the Net which they HID, their Own Foot has been CAUGHT. The LORD has MADE HIMSELF KNOWN; HE has Executed JUDGMENT. In the Works of HIS

Own Hands, the WICKED is SNARED.' [Psalm 9. 15, 16.]

'For the Wicked BOASTS of His Heart's Desire, AND the GREEDY Man CURSES and SPURNS THE LORD. The Wicked, in the "HAUGHTINESS OF HIS COUNTENANCE", DOES NOT"SEEK HIM". All His Thoughts are, "THERE IS NO GOD".' [Psalm 10. 3, 4.]

'The HEAVENS are telling of the GLORY of GOD; and their EXPANSE is DECLARING the WORK OF 'HIS HANDS'. The Law of the LORD is PERFECT, restoring the "'SOUL'";THE Testimony of the LORD is SURE, making Wise the " SIMPLE".' [Psalm 19. 1, 7.]

'The EARTH is LORD'S, and ALL it CONTAINS, the WORLD, and THOSE who DWELL in it.'[Psalm 24. 1.]

'Transgression speaks to the UNGODLY within His Heart; THERE is 'NO FEAR' of GOD before His EYES.' [Psalm 36. 1.]

'If we had FORGOTTEN the NAME of Our GOD, or EXTENDED our Hands to a Strange God; WOULD not GOD find this OUT? For HE Knows the 'SECRETS OF THE HEART'.' [Psalm 44. 20, 21.]

'Their Inner Thought is, that their HOUSES are FOREVER, and their Dwelling Places to ALL GENERATIONS; THEY have called their LANDS after their NAMES. But Man in His POMP will not ENDURE; HE is like the Beast that PERISH.

Do not be Afraid, when a Man becomes RICH, when the Glory of His House is INCREASED; FOR when He 'DIES', he will CARRY NOTHING AWAY; HIS Glory will Not Descend After HIM.' [Psalm 49. 11, 12, 16, 17.]

'And they Say, "How Does GOD Know? And is there KNOWLEDGE with the 'MOST HIGH'? "Behold, these are the WICKED; AND always at EASE, they have INCREASED in WEALTH.' [Psalm 73. 11, 12.]

'Yet they Still Continued to 'SIN AGAINST HIM', to Rebel Against the "MOST HIGH' in the Desert. And in their Heart they PUT GOD to TEST, by Asking FOOD according to their DESIRE.

How often they REBELLED Against HIM in the WILDERNESS, and GRIEVED HIM in the DESERT! And Again and Again they Tempted GOD, and PAINED the Holy One of ISRAEL.

Yet they TEMPTED and REBELLED Against the "MOST HIGH GOD", and Did Not KEEP HIS TESTIMONIES, but Turned Back and Acted TREACHEROUSLY like their "FATHERS"; THEY turned aside like a Treacherous BOW. For they PROVOKED HIM with their High Places, and Aroused HIS JEALOUSY with their GRAVEN IMAGES.' [Psalm 78. 17, 18,40, 41, 56, 57, 58.]

'But they Mingled with the NATIONS, and LEARNED their Practices. And SERVED their 'IDOLS',which became a SNARE to them. They Even SACRIFICED their "'SONS and DAUGHTERS'" to the ""''DEMONS"''', and SHED Innocent BLOOD, the BLOOD of their "SONS and DAUGHTERS", whom they "SACRIFICED" to the "IDOLS OF CANAAN"; AND the LAND was POLLUTED with the BLOOD. Thus they became UNCLEAN in their Practices, and Played the Harlot in their DEEDS. Therefore the Anger of the LORD was KINDLED against His People, and HE ABHORRED HIS INHERITANCE.' [Psalm 106. Verses 35 to 40.]

'Hear,O MY People, and I will ADMONISH YOU; O Israel, if YOU would LISTEN to ME! LET there be "NO STRANGE GOD" AMONG YOU; NOR shall YOU Worship ANY "FOREIGN GOD".'[Psalm 81. 8, 9.]

'I Said, YOU are God's, and All of YOU are Sons of the "MOST HIGH". NEVERTHELESS YOU WILL "'DIE" LIKE MEN, and 'FALL' Like Any One of the PRINCES".' [Psalm 82. 6, 7.]

'That they may KNOW, that """"THOU ALONE"""", whose Name is the "LORD", ART the """""MOST HIGH""""" OVER ALL THE EARTH.' [Psalm 83. 18.]

'Let All those be ASHAMED, who Serve 'GRAVEN IMAGES', WHO BOAST THEMSELVES OF 'IDOLS'; WORSHIP '"HIM"' ALL YOU "GODS".' [Psalm 97. 7.]

'Do not TOUCH MY Anointed Ones, and Do MY PROPHETS NO HARM.' [Psalm 105. 15.]

'The FEAR OF THE LORD is the Beginning of KNOWLEDGE; FOOLS Despise WISDOM and INSTRUCTION.' [Proverbs 1. 7.]

'The SACRIFICE of the WICKED is an ABOMINATION to the LORD, but the PRAYER of the UPRIGHT is HIS DELIGHT.' [Proverbs 15. 8.].

'TREMBLE, and do not "SIN"; MEDITATE in Your HEART upon your BED, and be STILL. Offer the Sacrifices of "RIGHTEOUSNESS", and TRUST IN THE LORD.' [Psalm 4. 4, 5.]

'Now the SERPENT was more Crafty than Any Beast of the Field, which the LORD GOD had made. And He said to the Woman, "Indeed has GOD Said, "'You shall not EAT from Any TREE of the GARDEN"'? And the Woman said to the SERPENT, "From the Fruit of the Trees of the Garden we may Eat; but from the Fruit of the Tree,which is in the Middle of the Garden, GOD has Said, "YOU shall not EAT from it or Touch it, LEST YOU DIE". [Genesis 3 verses 1,2,3.]

Part 77

The Creator LORD OF FLAMES, who upon HIS 'Holy Mountain' Commanded MOSES to make a BREAST PIECE OF JUDGEMENT for His Chosen High Priest AARON, has been known to all HIS Visible and Invisible Creations since the Very Ancient Times, as the 'ONE AND ONLY 'LORD OF JUDGMENT', who as per the "EVOLUTIONARY PLAN AND PURPOSE', based upon the Universal Law of "Will to do Good", Periodically makes HIS 'JUDGMENTS'for the Entire 'Subjectively and Objectively Manifested "SOLAR UNIVERSE", and thus has at HIS Disposal, THOSE UNKNOWABLE EXTRAORDINARY "Energies, Forces,and Powers" about which HIS Created Servants, the so called "ELOHIM'S" have Absolutely "NO IDEA".

And even when they collectively CONSPIRED against their 'GREAT LORD's' LOVE and TRUST, and thus by willfully Betraying HIM they HIJACKED the Proper Evolution,which was supposed to take Place upon this Planet Earth, they being DECEITFUL THIEVES,were still TOTALLY UNABLE to Find Out or Comprehend all the Details of those UNKNOWABLE EXTRAORDINARY "Energies, Forces, and Powers" of the Great LORD, and their Discrete OPERATIONS, which can ONLY BE USED by the GREAT LORD Himself and 'NO ONE ELSE'.

With the Deceitful and Illegal Introduction of Animal Consciousness by these UNFAITHFUL SERVANTS OF THE 'LORD', who are commonly termed as the so called GODS and GODDESSES upon this Planet Earth, they by illegally taking out certain parts from the "Collective Animal Group Consciousness" which exist as their "Huge Reservoir of ETHEREAL VITALITY" upon this Planet Earth, thus FORCED them to Incarnate in Human Forms upon this Planet Earth, who were Not Supposed to be introduced as the Human Beings till the NEXT 'EVOLUTIONARY CYCLIC VITAL WAVE' emanated as per the DESIRE MIND OF THE LORD, and is very much required for attaining their 'Conscious Expansion' as per HIS Evolutionary Plan and Purpose.

The'HUMAN FORM' out of All Animal Species is only considered as "HOLY" as it was created by LORD Himself in "HIS OWN IMAGE" as thus considered as "A TEMPLE OF GOD", regarding which the Holy Bible States:

'And GOD Created Man in HIS OWN IMAGE, in the Image of GOD HE created Him; MALE and FEMALE HE CREATED them.' [Genesis 1. 27.]

'Or Do You Not Know that Your body is a Temple of the Holy Spirit who is in You,whom you have from GOD, and that you are NOT YOUR OWN?' [1 Corinthians 6. 19.]

'Or what Agreement has the "Temple of GOD" with IDOLS? FOR we are the TEMPLE OF THE LIVING GOD; just as GOD Said, "I Will DWELL in them and WALK Among them;AND I will be their GOD, and they shall be MY PEOPLE".' [2 Corinthians 6. 16.]

These Evolving 'Infant Personalities' who by the WRONGFUL ACTIONS OF CORRUPT ANGELIC BEINGS were thus Illegally forced before their TIME to Incarnate as Human Being's in the Dense Physical Plane of Planet Earth were PRIMARILY composed of Animal Consciousness, who now being Incarnated as the Evolving Humans were also provided with Conscious Attribute of 'Individualized Mind', and thus have been commonly termed since then as the NEW SOULS', were still DRENCHED in their "ANIMAL PASSIONS", and for that Very Reason according to LORD'S Evolutionary Plan and Purpose, they had to WAIT till the NEXT 'EVOLUTIONARY CYCLIC VITAL WAVE' of 'Conscious Expansion' occurs.

These Low Level Desire Mind Human Beings still Polarized in their Animal Passions, with the given attribute of Co – Creatorship, then Created those Wrong Desire "THOUGHT FORMS" related to their Animalistic Minds, which became the LIVE ELEMENTAL ENTITIES in the Vital ethereal Matter of Dimensional Planes of YETZIRAH [Astral Plane],and ASSIAH [Vital/Physical Plane], which were in TOTAL CONTRADICTION to the Evolutionary Plan and Purpose of their CREATOR LORD – GOD, and many of these WRONGFUL DESIRE 'THOUGHT FORMS' composed of Elemental Lives, thus STAYED "UNFULFILLED",and over the Passing of Time Aggregated themselves as 'UNDESIRABLE VICES' to become a "Collective Consciousness of "MURKY ETHEREAL VITAL MATTER" and thus started Circulating in Spiraling Cyclic Circular motion around this Planet Earth, which became "A VITAL SOURCE OF ALL CORRUPT IDEAS", Which Caused the Dense Physical Planes of this Planet Earth to become an Undue Place of "Pain and Sufferings".

This Detestable Circulating Matter appearing like a "Huge Ethereal SERPENT" moving around the EARTH, was then wrongfully used for their "ILLEGAL AGENDAS" by those Deceitful ELOHIM'S, who Misusing their Vested Powers Willfully Betrayed the"LOVE AND TRUST" of their Creator "LORD – GOD", which were in total Contrast to HIS Beautiful Evolutionary Plan and Purpose.

The SERPENT mentioned in Genesis was not a regular Serpent but was made of this Detestable Circulating Matter of Live Elemental "Thought Forms", appearing like a "Huge Ethereal SERPENT", Who being composed of Deranged Mental "Thought Forms"through "Clairaudience" then Deceitfully talked to the Woman, who was fashioned by the LORD - GOD, as we all know this fact that no Regular Serpent of LORD'S Creation can Converse in Human Tongue, regarding which the Holy Bible States:

'Now the SERPENT was more Crafty than Any Beast of the Field, which the LORD GOD had made. And He said to the Woman, "Indeed has GOD Said, "'You shall not EAT from Any TREE of the GARDEN"'? And the Woman said to the SERPENT, "From the Fruit of the Trees of the Garden we may Eat; but from the Fruit of the Tree,which is in the Middle of the Garden, GOD has Said, "YOU shall not EAT from it or Touch it, LEST YOU DIE".

And the SERPENT Said to the Woman, "YOU surely shall Not DIE! FOR GOD Knows that in the Day you EAT from it, YOUR Eyes will be Opened, and you will be LIKE 'GOD',knowing "GOOD AND EVIL".

When the Woman Saw that the TREE was Good for Food, and that it was a Delight to the Eyes, and that the TREE was Desirable to make one WISE, she took from its Fruit and Ate; and she Gave also to her Husband with her, and He ATE.' [Genesis 3.Verses 1 to 6.]

In these above verses, is Embedded the Codified Information about the "Tree of Life", which also explains the Central Point 'EIN SOPH' of Vital Ethereal Energy , which in a codified way is mentioned as the Central "TREE, which is in the Middle of the Manifested Universal "Garden", and whose Fruits are the Vital frequency Evolutionary waves, which cyclically provide

403

the Necessary 'Spiritual Wisdom' to all Evolving Entities and Beings of our Solar Universe, especially the Mentally Evolved Human Beings of the 3 Dense Planes, who being freed from the Illusory Glamour are thus 'Willing and Ready' to receive it.

These Deranged Mind Entities and Beings referred to as the "FALLEN ANGELS" in the Holy Book, acting as the so called Gods and Goddesses on this Planet Earth Overlooked this FACT, that for their Such Heinous ACTION'S and Misuse of their Vested Powers, they according to their Own Evolutionary Cycle will also be Ultimately JUDGED by their 'CREATOR LORD', Whose Conscious Attributes are "ALWAYS UNKNOWABLE" to all of HIS CREATION'S.

In the Past History of this Planet Earth, the Great LORD as per HIS Promise to MOSES has surely JUDGED all the so called GODS and GODDESSES of Ancient Egypt as well as Else ware in the Middle East and Neighboring Lands, making their Centuries Old Religion to Totally Collapse and Disappear from this Planet Earth, causing their Huge Elaborate Temples to become Just Historical Ruins and Sites, regarding which the Holy Bible States:

'AGAINST'"ALL THE GODS OF EGYPT"' I WILL EXECUTE ""'JUDGMENTS"""' – 'I AM THE LORD'.[Exodus 12. 12.]

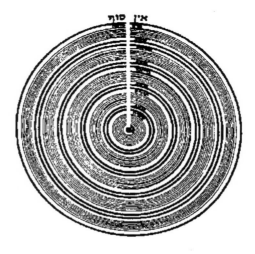

Ein Sof

404

In the Past History of this Planet Earth, the Great LORD as per HIS Promise to MOSES has surely JUDGED all the so called GODS and GODDESSES of Ancient Egypt as well as Else ware in the Middle East and Neighboring Lands, making their Centuries Old Religion to Totally Collapse and Disappear from this Planet Earth, causing their Huge Elaborate Temples to become Just Historical Ruins and Sites, regarding which the Holy Bible States:

'AGAINST'''ALL THE GODS OF EGYPT''' I WILL EXECUTE '''''JUDGMENTS'''''
– 'I AM THE LORD'.[Exodus 12. 12.]

Then it came about as He Finished Speaking all these WORDS, that the Ground that was under them SPLIT OPEN; and the EARTH OPENED ITS MOUTH and SWALLOWED THEM UP, and their Households, and all the Men who belonged to KORAH, with their Possessions. [Numbers 16. 31,32.]

Isis and Osiris – Gods of Egypt

The Unknowable 'CREATOR – OBSERVER' LORD of the Universe, also being the Merciful PRESERVER of HIS 'CREATION' is the Only SUPREME JUDGMENT Authority in the Subjectively and Objectively Manifested UNIVERSE, who Clearly Understands that any Manifested "Entity or Being" existing with or without a dense FORM in HIS Creation, according to HIS Evolutionary Plan and Purpose acting in their OWN CAPACITY as a "CO – CREATOR" having an "Unconscious, Sub Conscious, Semi - Conscious, Conscious, Elevated Conscious, Super Conscious, or Ultra Conscious"level of Mind, utilizing the HIGHER MIND, knowingly or unknowingly "'Support or Create'" those "THOUGHT FORMS" in the Vital Ethereal Matter of Infinite Space, which are BENEFICIAL for ALL MANIFESTATIONS, who are existing in their COLLECTIVE CONSCIOUS ENERGY GROUP RESERVOIRS, and thus they being Beneficial for their CONSCIOUS EXPANSION are considered "GOOD".

And utilizing the LOWER MIND knowingly or unknowingly they "'Support or Create'"those Particular "THOUGHT FORMS" in the Vital Ethereal Matter of Infinite Space, which being of LOWER MIND PASSIONS are basically SELFISH in Nature, and thus may be HARMFUL for the Evolving MASSES belonging to Collective Consciousness,and thus they are considered "EVIL". So the "MOST HIGH", the LORD – GOD of the Universe Periodically Judge all Creations, WHO SUBJECTIVELY and OBJECTIVELY Existing in their Own Levels thus pass through their RESPECTIVE EVOLUTIONARY CYCLES OF CONSCIOUS EXPANSION, which Continue in the Infinite Universe, regarding which the Holy Bible States:

'But the LORD abides FOREVER; HE has ESTABLISHED HIS Throne for JUDGMENT, and HE will 'JUDGE THE WORLD' in Righteousness; He will Execute JUDGMENT for the PEOPLES with EQUITY.' [Psalm 9. 7, 8.]

For the Preservation Purpose of the Evolutionary MASSES, the Creator LORD Periodically Passes HIS Beneficial JUDGMENTS toward HIS Manifested Creations,who are existing in the Visible or Invisible frequency Dimensions of the Differentiated Planes and their Sub Planes, which act out as HIS "'Balancing Decisions'", and May be HARMFUL to those Very FEW, who Misusing their VESTED POWERS may Foolishly Engage themselves in ILLEGAL and DECEITFUL "EVIL" ACTS,which may be CONTRADICTORY to the UNIVERSAL MANDATES of the Evolutionary Plan and Purpose of the LORD - GOD, which Clearly Requires the Gradual "'SPIRITUAL CONSCIOUS ENERGY EXPANSION'" of all Evolving Entities and Beings, which exist in the Manifested Universe.

Just like in the Dense Physical Plane, where the Judgments are usually Passed based upon Various Actions of the Incarnated People, as to if they were GOOD or EVIL, similarly the Judgments based upon the "Life Actions" thus await the "Personality Conscious" of Incarnated Human Beings of this Planet Earth,after their Life Duration Tenure in the Dense Physical Plane Finally Ends. And that is why the Great LORD is also known as the JUDGMENT LORD OF THE "SHEOL",which is the abode of those Dead Conscious Beings, who do not possess a Dense Body any more in the Physical Plane of ASSIAH, but now exist in the Various Lower Sub Planes of YETZIRAH which are known as the Domains of the NETHERWORLD, and in them the Judging LORD Redeems the Righteous, regarding which the Holy Bible States:

'This is the way of those who are FOOLISH, and of THOSE after them, WHO APPROVE THEIR WORDS. As Sheep they are APPOINTED for SHEOL; Death shall be their SHEPHERD;and the UPRIGHT shall rule over them in the MORNING; and their FORM shall be for SHEOL to Consume, so that they have No Habitation. But GOD will REDEEM My SOUL from the POWER of SHEOL; FOR HE WILL RECEIVE ME.' [Psalms 49. 13, 14, 15.]

The Prophet ISAIAH also clearly warned all those OPPRESSING LEADERS of the HUMAN RACES about the JUDGMENT'S of the LORD, Who like the Great King of BABYLON'S Desire Mind Passions, were Foolishly Polarized in POMP and SHOW of the Illusory World Glamour of this Planet Earth, thus Oppressing the Downtrodden POOR and NEEDY,regarding which the Holy Bible States:

'That YOU will take up this TAUNT against the King of BABYLON and

Say, "How the OPPRESSOR has Ceased, and how FURY has Ceased! THE LORD Has '"BROKEN THE STAFF"' of the WICKED, the SCEPTER of RULERS.

SHEOL from Beneath is Excited over YOU to Meet You, when YOU Come; IT Arouses for you the 'SPIRITS OF THE DEAD', all the 'LEADERS' of the EARTH; IT Raises all the Kings of the Nations from their Thrones.

They will all Respond and Say to You, Even YOU have been MADE WEAK as WE, YOU have become like US Your POMP and the Music of your HARPS have been brought down to SHEOL; MAGGOTS are SPREAD out as YOUR BED beneath YOU, and WORMS are YOUR COVERINGS.' [Isaiah 14. 4, 5, 9, 10, 11.]

The Great Creator LORD has reserved His SEVERE JUDGMENTS for all those, who having Animal Mind DESIRES thus FOOLISHLY worship the IDOLS of those Invisible"Entities and Beings" who are HIS MERE CREATIONS, and thus Not 'GOD',regarding which the Holy Bible States:

'They have made ME Jealous with what is "NOT GOD"; THEY have Provoked ME to Anger with their IDOLS. So "I" will make them Jealous with those, who are Not a PEOPLE; "I" will Provoke them to Anger with a Foolish Nation, FOR a FIRE is Kindled in MY Anger, and Burns to the Lowest Part of SHEOL, and Consumes the Earth with its Yield, and Sets on FIRE the Foundations of the MOUNTAINS.[Deuteronomy 32. 21, 22.]

'The WICKED will Return to SHEOL, EVEN all the NATIONS, who Forget GOD.' [Psalm 9.17.]

'Though they DIG into SHEOL, from there shall MY Hand take them; AND though they Ascend to HEAVEN, from there will 'I" Bring them DOWN.' [Amos 9. 2.]

During the Times of MOSES, the CHILDREN of ISRAEL witnessed with their Own Eyes the Harsh JUDGMENTS of their LORD – GOD, when some of their Members Foolishly Rose Up AGAINST LORD'S Humble Servant MOSES, and for their Such unworthy Behavior, LORD'S Anger Kindled against them, and as HIS Harsh Judgment Against them, the Earth Opened up and they Went Down ALIVE to the SHEOL, regarding which the Holy Bible States:

'And MOSES Said, "By this you shall KNOW, that the LORD has Sent Me to do ALL HIS DEEDS; for this is Not My DOING. If these Men DIE the Death of All Men, or if they SUFFER the FATE of All Men, then the LORD has not Sent Me. But if the LORD brings about an Entirely NEW THING, and the GROUND OPENS ITS MOUTH and SWALLOWS THEM UP with all that is theirs, and they 'DESCEND ALIVE INTO SHEOL', then You will UNDERSTAND that these Men have SPURNED THE 'LORD'.

Then it came about as He Finished Speaking all these WORDS, that the Ground that was under them SPLIT OPEN; and the EARTH OPENED ITS MOUTH and SWALLOWED THEM UP,and their Households, and all the Men who belonged to KORAH, with their Possessions.

So they and all that belonged to them Went DOWN ALIVE TO SHEOL; and the EARTH CLOSED OVER THEM, and they PERISHED from the MIDST OF THE ASSEMBLY.' [Numbers 16 Verses 28 to 33.]

During the Glorious times of Ancient Egypt, in their Wide Pantheon of so called GOD'S and GODDESSES, their Important GOD OSIRIS was considered as the MAIN JUDGING GOD of the NETHERWORLD [SHEOL], and He was Also their ONLY GOD, against whom the Jealous God SETH and His Evil Group Conspired, and Unjust fully Murdered HIM and then cut his Body of Consciousness into many pieces, after which His Wife ISIS located HIS Body Parts, and restored Her Husband's Body.

In the Land of Ancient Egypt, GOD OSIRIS'S MAIN TEMPLE was in ABYDOS, and as He was considered as the LORD of the NETHERWORLD, which was entered by the Departed Peoples "Personality Conscious" through the Portals of SHEOL, for this very reason, Many People in the

Old Kingdom of Ancient Egypt thus preferred to get their Dead Bodies buried in the Vicinity of Abydos.

But because the Judging GOD OSIRIS of the Netherworld had a wife named ISIS, for this reason many Children of Israel over the Passing of Time, then wrongfully got Carried Away with this False Notion, that their LORD GOD of JUDGMENT, who upon HIS Holy Mountain commanded HIS Servant MOSES to make 'A BREAST PIECE OF JUDGMENT' similarly also had a WIFE.

And as the Goddess ISIS was the wife of Egyptian God OSIRIS, the Children of Israel under the Negative Mind Control Impulses of the Invisible Corrupt Hermaphrodite Angelic Beings, then Wrongfully and Foolishly Associated Goddess ASHERIM with their "MOST HIGH" considering her to be HIS Consort, but they Quickly forgot this undeniable FACT that upon His Flaming Mountain, the Great LORD – GOD, clearly Commanded MOSES to Totally DESTROY all the Sacred Pillars and Altars of the 'GODDESS ASHERIM', regarding which the Holy Bible States:

'Watch YOURSELF that YOU make NO COVENANT with the Inhabitants of the Land into which you are going, lest it become a 'SNARE' in your MIDST. BUT RATHER, YOU ARE TO'TEAR DOWN THEIR ALTARS, AND SMASH THEIR SACRED PILLARS, AND CUT DOWN THEIR""'ASHERIM'''' – For You shall not WORSHIP Any Other GOD, for the LORD,whose name is JEALOUS, is a Jealous GOD.' [Exodus 12, 13, 14.]

But the Children of Israel, even before the Establishment of Any Kings among them, due to their Polarization in the LOWER DESIRE MIND PASSIONS after settling in the Promised Land, Soon Forgot LORD'S Holy Command, and then Wrongfully Started worshiping Goddess ASHEROTH, which was against the Commands of their MOST BENEVOLENT LORD. Regarding which the Holy Bible States:

'And the Sons of Israel Lived among the Canaanites, the Hittites, the Amorites, the Perizzites, the Hivites, and the Jebusites: and they took their Daughters for themselves as Wives, and gave their Own Daughters to their Sons, and Served their God's.

And the Sons of Israel did what was EVIL in the Sight of the LORD, and FORGOT the LORD their GOD, and SERVED the BAALS and the "ASHEROTH".' [Judges 3. 5, 6,7.]

But the Most Merciful LORD - GOD, understanding the wrong behavior of the Children of Israel, which was due to their LOWER MIND DESIRE PASSIONS, then raised among them a JUDGE named GIDEON, the Son of JOASH the ABIEZRITE, and instructed Him in the Night to DESTROY the Altar of BAAL and to CUT Down the Wooden Statue of ASHERAH that was Beside it, regarding which the Holy Bible States:

'Then the Angel of the LORD came and Sat under the OAK that was in OPHRAH, which belonged to JOSH the ABIEZRITE as His Son GIDEON was beating out Wheat in the Wine Press in order to Save it from the Midianites. And the Angel of the LORD Appeared to Him and Said to Him, "THE LORD is with YOU, O Valiant Warrior". Then GIDEON Said to Him, "Oh My Lord, if the LORD is with US, WHY then has all THIS HAPPENED to US? And WHERE are All HIS Miracles which Our Fathers Told US About, Saying, "'Did Not the LORD bring us up from EGYPT?'" But now the LORD has ABANDONED us and GIVEN us into the Hand of Midian."

Now the Same Night it came about, that the LORD Said to Him, "Take your Father's Bull and a Second Bull SEVEN Years Old, and PULL DOWN THE "'ALTAR OF BAAL'" which Belongs to Your FATHER, and CUT DOWN THE "'ASHERAH'" that is Beside it; and Build an Altar to the "'LORD Your GOD'" on Top of this Stronghold in an Orderly Manner, and take a Second Bull and Offer a Burnt Offering with the "'WOOD OF THE ASHERAH'" which You shall CUT DOWN."

Then GIDEON took Ten Men of His Servants and DID as the LORD had SPOKEN TO HIM; and it came about, because He was Too Afraid of His Father's Household and the Men of the City to Do it by DAY, that He did it by NIGHT. When the Men of the City Arose Early in the Morning, behold, the Altar of BAAL was TORN DOWN, and the ASHERAH which was beside it, was CUT DOWN,and the Second Bull was offered on the Altar which had been BUILT.

And they SAID to One Another, 'Who did this Thing?' And when they SEARCHED About and INQUIRED, they Said, "GIDEON the Son of JOASH Did This Thing." Then the Men of the City said to JOASH, "BRING Out Your Son, that He may DIE, for He has TORN DOWN the Altar of BAAL, and INDEED, He has CUT DOWN THE 'ASHERAH' which was beside it."

But JOASH Said to ALL who Stood Against Him, "WILL You CONTEND for BAAL, or will you Deliver Him? WHOEVER will PLEAD for Him shall be PUT to DEATH by Morning. IF He is a "'GOD'", let Him Contend for Himself, because SOMEONE has TORN DOWN His Altar." Therefore on that DAY He Named Him 'JERUBBAAL, that is to Say, "Let BAAL Contend Against Him," because He had TORN DOWN His Altar.' [Judges 6. 11, 12, 13, 25, 26, 27, 28, 29, 30, 31, 32.]

Then GIDEON took Ten Men of His Servants and DID as the LORD had SPOKEN TO HIM; and it came about, because He was Too Afraid of His Father's Household and the Men of the City to Do it by DAY, that He did it by NIGHT. When the Men of the City Arose Early in the Morning, behold, the Altar of BAAL was TORN DOWN, and the ASHERAH which was beside it, was CUT DOWN,and the Second Bull was offered on the Altar which had been BUILT. [Judges 6. 27.]

413

'MANASSEH was Twelve Years Old when He became King, and He Reigned Fifty – Five Years in Jerusalem. And He did EVIL in the Sight of the LORD according to the Abominations of the Nations, whom the LORD Dispossessed before the Sons of Israel. For he Rebuilt the High Places which HEZEKIAH His Father had BROKEN DOWN; HE also Erected Altars for the BAALS and made ASHERIM, and Worshiped all the HOST OF HEAVEN and Served them. And He built altars in the House of the LORD, of which the LORD had Said, "My Name shall be in JERUSALEM FOREVER". For He Built Altars for All the HOST OF THE HEAVEN in the Two 'COURTS OF THE HOUSE OF THE LORD.' [2 Chronicles 33 Verses 1 to 5.]

When the Children of Israel entered the Promised Land, which as per the HOLY COVENANT was Faithfully Provided to them by their Most Merciful LORD- GOD, then even with HIS Repeated warnings Conveyed through His Prophets and JUDGES, they still fell from their Evolutionary Path of becoming a 'CHOSEN RACE', and Miserably Failed to exist as a 'Beacon of Light' for rest of Evolving Humanity of this Planet Earth, as they instead Willfully adopted those Wrong Customs of the Lands, against which the GREAT LORD – GOD Specifically Commanded them Not to Indulge in. And afterward they also asked LORD'S Humble Servant, their Prophet- Judge SAMUEL, to install a Human King to Rule over them, instead of the INVISIBLE LORD Himself, who since the times of their Forefathers NOAH, ABRAHAM, ISAAC, and JACOB, without their Knowledge, through His Extended Hand of Mercy, was constantly ruling and watching over them, and also Judging them as their MOST BENEVOLENT KING, regarding which the Holy Bible States:

'But the Thing was DISPLEASING in the Sight of SAMUEL, when they Said, "Give US a King to JUDGE US." And Samuel Prayed to the LORD.

And the LORD Said to SAMUEL, "Listen to the Voice of the People in regard to ALL that they Say to YOU, for they have Not Rejected You, but '"THEY HAVE REJECTED ME FROM BEING KING OVER THEM"'. Like All the DEEDS which they have DONE, since the Day that "I" BROUGHT THEM UP FROM EGYPT EVEN TO THIS DAY – in that 'THEY HAVE FORSAKEN ME', and 'SERVED OTHER GODS' – So they are DOING to YOU Also. Now then LISTEN to their Voice; HOWEVER, You shall SOLEMNLY WARN them and tell them of the Procedure of the King, who will Reign over them."

So SAMUEL SPOKE all the WORDS of the LORD to the People who had asked of Him a King. And He Said, "THIS will be the Procedure of the King who will Reign over YOU; He will take YOUR Sons and Place them for Himself in His Chariots and among His Horsemen, and they will run before His Chariots. And He will APPOINT for Himself Commanders of Thousands and of Fifties, and some to do His Plowing and to REAP his Harvest, and to make His Weapons of War, and Equipment for His Chariots. He will also take YOUR Daughters for Perfumers, and Cooks, and Bakers. And He will take the Best of Your Fields, and Your Vineyards, and Your Olive Groves, and give them to His Servants. And He will take a Tenth of Your SEED, and of Your Vineyard, and give to His Officers, and to His Servants. He will also take Your Male Servants, and Your Female Servants, and Your Best Young Men, and Your Donkeys, and use them for His Work. He will take a TENTH of YOUR Flocks, and YOU YOURSELVES will Become His SERVANTS.

Then YOU will CRY OUT in THAT DAY, because of YOUR KING, whom YOU have CHOSEN for YOURSELVES, BUT THE 'LORD' WILL NOT ANSWER 'YOU' IN THAT DAY."

Nevertheless, the People REFUSED to LISTEN to the Voice of SAMUEL, and they Said, "NO, But there shall be a King over US, that We also may be like All the NATIONS, that our King may JUDGE US, and GO Before US, and Fight Our Battles".' [1 Samuel 8.Verses 6 to 20.]

But after LORD installed Kings among the Children of Israel, Hoping that they will mend their EVIL Ways, the Later KINGS did even more Abominations against Him, regarding which the Holy Bible States:

'MANASSEH was Twelve Years Old when He became King, and He Reigned Fifty – Five Years in Jerusalem. And He did EVIL in the Sight of the LORD according to the Abominations of the Nations, whom the LORD Dispossessed before the Sons of Israel. For he Rebuilt the High Places which HEZEKIAH His Father had BROKEN DOWN; HE also Erected Altars for the BAALS and made ASHERIM, and Worshiped all the HOST OF HEAVEN and Served them. And He built altars in the House of the LORD, of which the LORD had Said, "My Name shall be in JERUSALEM FOREVER". For He Built Altars for All the HOST OF THE HEAVEN in the Two 'COURTS OF THE HOUSE OF THE LORD.'

And He made His Sons Pass through the FIRE in the Valley of

BENHINNOM; and He Practiced WITCHCRAFT, Used DIVINATION, Practiced SORCERY, and Dealt with MEDIUMS and SPIRITISTS. He Did Much EVIL in the Sight of the LORD, Provoking Him to Anger.

Then He PUT THE CARVED IMAGE OF THE 'IDOL' which He had Made in the HOUSE of GOD, of which the GOD had Said to 'DAVID', and to SOLOMON His Son, "IN THIS HOUSE AND IN JERUSALEM, WHICH "I" HAVE CHOSEN FROM "ALL" THE TRIBES OF ISRAEL, "I"WILL PUT MY NAME FOREVER; and "I" will Not again Remove the Foot of ISRAEL from the Land, which "I" Appointed for Your Fathers, if Only they will Observe to do All that "I" have Commanded them according to all the LAW, the STATUTES, and the ORDINANCES given through MOSES. Thus MANASSEH Mislead JUDAH, and the Inhabitants of JERUSALEM to DO MORE 'EVIL' than the Nations whom the LORD DESTROYED before the Sons of ISRAEL. [2 Chronicles 33 Verses 1 to 9.]

But when King JOSIAH, who keeping the LORD'S Commandments Destroyed the IDOLS of Various GODS including GODDESS ASHERAH, and Stopped the worship being performed by the IDOLATROUS PRIESTS to the SUN, and to the MOON, and to the CONSTELLATIONS, and to ALL THE HOST OF HEAVEN, which were ILLEGALLY and WRONGFULLY Established in the HOUSE OF LORD in Jerusalem by the Earlier EVIL Kings, at that time, the Temple of "MOST HIGH", due to these IDOLATROUS Activities was in a Very SAD Condition, regarding which the Holy Bible States:

'Then the King Commanded HILKIAH the High Priest, and the Priests of the Second Order and the Door – Keepers, to Bring Out of the Temple of the LORD, all the Vessels that were made for BAAL, for ASHERAH, and for all the HOST OF HEAVEN; and He burned them outside Jerusalem in the Fields of the KIDRON, and carried their Ashes to BETHEL. And He did away with the IDOLATROUS PRIESTS, whom the Kings of Judah had appointed to Burn Incense in the HIGH PLACES in the Cities of JUDAH and in the Surrounding Area of Jerusalem, also those who Burned Incense to BAAL, to the SUN, and to the MOON, and to the CONSTELLATIONS, and to ALL THE HOST OF HEAVEN.

And He Brought out the "'ASHERAH'" from the "HOUSE OF THE LORD" outside JERUSALEM to the Brook KIDRON, and BURNED it at Brook KIDRON, and Ground it to DUST, and Threw its DUST on the GRAVES of the Common People. He also BROKE DOWN the HOUSES OF THE MALE CULT PROSTITUTES, which were in the 'HOUSE OF THE LORD', Where the WOMEN were Weaving HANGINGS for the "ASHERAH".'

He also defiled TOPHETH, which is in the Valley of the Son of HINNOM that No Man might make His Son or His Daughter PASS through the FIRE for MOLECH. And He did away with the Horses which the Kings of JUDAH had GIVEN to the SUN, at the Entrance of the HOUSE OF THE LORD, by the Chamber of Nathan – Melech the Official, which was in the Precincts; and He burned the CHARIOTS OF THE SUN with FIRE. And the Altars which were on the Roof, the Upper Chamber of AHAZ, which the Kings of JUDAH had made, and the Altars which MANASSEH had made in the TWO COURTS of the HOUSE OF THE LORD, the King Broke Down; and He ran from there, and threw their DUST into the Brook KIDRON.

And the High Places which were before JERUSALEM, which were on the Right of the Mount of Destruction, which Solomon the King of Israel had built for ASHTORETH the Abomination of the SIDONIANS, and for CHEMOSH the Abomination of MOAB, and for MILCOM the Abomination of the Sons of AMMON, the King Defiled. And He Broke in Pieces the Sacred Pillars, and CUT DOWN THE ASHERIM, and filled their places with Human Bones.

Furthermore,the Altar that was at BETHEL and the HIGH PLACE which JEROBOAM the Son of NEBAT, who made ISRAEL 'SIN', had made, even that Altar and the High Place He Broke Down. Then He Demolished its Stones, Ground them to DUST, and BURNED THE 'ASHERAH'. [2 Kings 23. Verses 4 to 7, and Verses 10 to 15.]

'Then the King Commanded HILKIAH the High Priest, and the Priests of the Second Order and the Door – Keepers, to Bring Out of the Temple of the LORD, all the Vessels that were made for BAAL, for ASHERAH, and for all the HOST OF HEAVEN; and He burned them outside Jerusalem in the Fields of the KIDRON, and carried their Ashes to BETHEL. [2 Kings 23. 4]

'Then JACOB Summoned His Sons and Said, "Assemble YOURSELVES that I may TELL YOU, what shall BEFALL YOU in the Days to COME. Gather Together and HEAR, O SONS OF JACOB; AND LISTEN TO ISRAEL YOUR FATHER. [Genesis 49. 1.]

Part 80

The Wise King Solomon, the Chosen Son of GOD, after He was made the KING to Rule over ISRAEL, Only asked the Great LORD – GOD, the "SUPREME JUDGE" OF THE UNIVERSE, for an "Understanding Heart" to DISCERN BETWEEN GOOD AND EVIL, when the "MOST HIGH" Appeared to Him in a Dream at Night in GIBEON, so that He can Wisely JUDGE HIS Chosen People on HIS BEHALF in this Physical World, Whom NO ONE ELSE, BUT THE GREAT LORD HIMSELF was ONLY able to JUDGE, regarding which the Holy Bible States:

'And THY Servant is in the Midst of THY PEOPLE, which THOU hast CHOSEN, a Great People WHO cannot be Numbered or Counted for MULTITUDE.

So GIVE THY SERVANT an UNDERSTANDING HEART to '"JUDGE"' THY PEOPLE to Discern between GOOD and EVIL. For WHO IS ABLE TO "JUDGE", THIS GREAT PEOPLE OF'"THINE"'.' [1 Kings 3. 8, 9.]

Thus Being a Judge Himself for the 'Children of Israel', the Wise King who with Discerning and Understanding Heart Deciphered some of the Secrets of the Manifested Universe, then shared with all Humanity HIS GODLY WISDOM, and Some of His Great Works are now Part of the Holy Bible, which are Known as the"Ecclesiastes", Psalms, Proverbs, and "Song of Solomon", regarding which the Holy Bible States:

'Now GOD gave Solomon WISDOM, and Very Great Discernment and BREADTH OF MIND, like the SAND that is on the SEASHORE. And Solomon's Wisdom SURPASSED the Wisdom of All the Sons of the EAST, and All the WISDOM OF EGYPT. For He was Wiser than ALL MEN, than ETHAN the EZRAHITE, HEMAN, CALCOL, and DARDA, the Sons of MAHOL; and His FAME was KNOWN in ALL THE SURROUNDING NATIONS.

He also SPOKE 3000 PROVERBS, and His SONGS were 1005.

And He Spoke of Trees, from the Cedar that is in LEBANON, Even to the HYSSOP that Grows on the Wall; HE Spoke also of ANIMALS and BIRDS, and CREEPING THINGS, and FISH.And Men came from All Peoples to HEAR the 'WISDOM of SOLOMON', from All the KINGS of the EARTH, WHO had HEARD of His WISDOM.' [1 Kings 4. Verses 29 to 34.]

The Great King Solomon being a Wise Judge installed by the LORD for the 'Children of Israel, thus with His Discerning Mind became very much Interested to Learn the SECRET OF THE BREAST PIECE OF JUDGMENT, which having the 12 Stones was Set in a GOLD Filigree, upon which were engraved the names of the 12 Tribes of ISRAEL, each Precious Stone looking like an Engraved Seal, along with having the 2 Holy Objects "URIM and THUMMIM" tucked inside the Breast Piece, which was Continually worn by the HIGH PRIEST of LORD'S Holy Temple over His Heart,when He Entered the Holy Place of the LORD, and through which the High Priest of the GREAT LORD Received and Carried Out the Judgments of the LORD, which were meant for the Sons of Israel.

The Wise King Solomon was Well Aware of this fact that His Great Ancestor Patriarch JACOB, who was named by the "MOST HIGH" as "ISRAEL", was the First Person of the LORD'S CHOSEN RACE, Whom the Great and UNKNOWABLE LORD – GOD through a Divine Vision showed HIS Manifested Differentiated Dimensions, which were Interpenetrating and thus Connected through Energy Linkages, which appeared to the Discerning Mind of JACOB as the Celestial Ladder, or the HEAVENLY LADDER, upon which the Angelic Personalities Embodying SOLAR CONSCIOUS were Cyclically Descending in the Dense Dimensional Planes of this Planet Earth, and then after Acquiring the Necessary Spiritual Experiences, which are needed for their Conscious Expansion, they were Ascending Back again upon this Vital Energy Ladder toward the Higher Ethereal Dimensional Plane, which is the DOMAIN of their Spiritual 'COLLECTIVE CONSCIOUSNESS" ruled by the UNKNOWABLE "MOST HIGH".

The Evolution taking Place in these Differentiated Dimensional Planes, which in Hebrew Language are known as the "SEFIRAH or SEPHIROT", is Constantly Affected by the Invisible Cosmic Radiations of the 12 Zodiacal Constellations which reach our SOLAR UNIVERSE, and then also Come to OUR PLANET EARTH, and the Great LORD – GOD Blessed JACOB [ISRAEL] with 12 Sons, so that they being Unique in their Evolutionary Capacities could Consciously Correspond to the 12 MAIN COSMIC ENERGY RADIATIONS, which constantly effect the Evolution of this Planet Earth, and can thus be the Starting Heads of the 12 Tribes of HIS Chosen Race upon the Physical Plane of this Planet Earth, regarding which the Holy Bible States:

'Then JACOB was left Alone, and a Man Wrestled with Him until Day Break. And when He Saw that HE had Not Prevailed AGAINST Him, He touched the Socket of His Thigh; so the Socket of JACOB'S THIGH was DISLOCATED while He Wrestled with HIM.

Then HE Said, "LET Me Go, for the DAWN is Breaking". But He Said, "I will Not let YOU Go unless YOU BLESS ME." So HE Said to Him, "WHAT is Your Name?" And He Said, "JACOB". And He Said, "YOUR Name shall NO LONGER be JACOB, but ISRAEL; for YOU have 'STRIVEN WITH GOD', and with 'MEN' and have 'PREVAILED'.

Then JACOB asked Him and Said, "Please Tell Me Your NAME". But HE Said, "WHY is IT, that YOU ASK MY NAME?" And He Blessed Him there.' [Genesis 32. Verses 24 to 29.]

'Then JACOB Departed from BEERSHEBA and went toward HARAN. And He came to a Certain Place and Spent the Night there, because the SUN had SET; and He took one of the Stones of the Place, and Put it under His HEAD, and lay down in that Place.

And He had a DREAM, and behold, a LADDER WAS SET ON THE EARTH WITH ITS TOP REACHING TO HEAVEN; AND BEHOLD, THE ANGELS OF GOD WERE ASCENDING AND DESCENDING ON IT. And behold, the LORD Stood Above it and Said, "I AM THE LORD, THE GOD OF YOUR FATHER ABRAHAM, AND THE GOD OF ISAAC; the LAND on which You LIE, I will

Give it to You and to Your DESCENDANTS.' [Genesis 28. Verses 10 to 13.]

Upon waking up, JACOB remembered His DREAM, and named that Place as 'BETHEL' meaning the "HOUSE OF 'EL'", the name "EL" of the LORD meaning the "GREAT AND MIGHTY ONE", regarding which the Holy Bible States:

'So JACOB Rose Early in the Morning, and took the Stone that He had PUT UNDER HIS HEAD, and SET it up as a PILLAR, and POURED OIL ON ITS TOP. And He called the Name of that place "BETHEL"; HOWEVER, Previously the Name of the City had been 'LUZ'.' [Genesis 28. 18, 19.]

Regarding His 12 Sons, JACOB was Very well Aware with LORD'S GRACE about them, that they being Unique in their Evolutionary Capacities, had thus Different Types of Qualities, which were according to the Evolutionary PLAN AND PURPOSE of the GREAT LORD –GOD, which was to be carried out through them upon the Physical Plane of this Planet Earth, and in a CODIFIED WAY Jacob EXPLAINED their Qualities having HIDDEN MEANINGS in Form of His BLESSINGS, which corresponded to the 12 Cosmic Energies, regarding which the Holy Bible States:

'Then JACOB Summoned His Sons and Said, "Assemble YOURSELVES that I may TELL YOU, what shall BEFALL YOU in the Days to COME. Gather Together and HEAR, O SONS OF JACOB; AND LISTEN TO ISRAEL YOUR FATHER.

"REUBEN", you are My First – Born; My Might and the Beginning of My Strength, PREEMINENT in DIGNITY and PREEMINENT in POWER. Uncontrolled as WATER, YOU shall NOT have PREEMINENCE, because YOU went up to Your Father's Bed; THEN You DEFILED IT – He went up to My Couch.

"SIMEON" and "LEVI" are Brothers; THEIR SWORDS are IMPLEMENTS of VIOLENCE. Let MY"SOUL" NOT Enter into their COUNCIL; LET not My GLORY be UNITED with their Assembly; because in their ANGER they

Slew Men, and in their Self – Will they Lamed Oxen. Cursed be their Anger, for it is FIERCE; AND their WRATH, for it is CRUEL. I will DISPERSE them in JACOB, and SCATTER them in ISRAEL.

'JUDAH'', Your Brothers shall Praise You; YOUR Hand shall be on the Neck of YOUR ENEMIES; YOUR Father's Sons shall BOW DOWN to You. JUDAH is a Lion's Whelp; FROM the PREY, MY Son, YOU have Gone Up. He Couches, He Lies Down as a LION, and as a LION, who DARES ROUSE Him UP? The SCEPTER shall Not Depart from JUDAH, Nor the Ruler's Staff from between His Feet, until SHILOH Comes, and to Him shall be the Obedience of the Peoples. He ties his Foal to the Vine, and His Donkey's Colt to the Choice Vine; HE Washes His Garments in Wine, and His Robes in the Blood of Grapes. His Eyes are Dull from Wine, and His Teeth White from Milk.

''ZEBULUN'' shall Dwell at the Seashore; AND He shall be a Heaven foe Ships, and His Flank shall be Toward SIDON.

''ISSACHAR'' is a Strong Donkey, lying Down between the Sheepfolds. When He Saw that a Resting Place was GOOD, and that Land was Pleasant. He bowed His Shoulder to Bear Burdens, and became a SLAVE at Forced LABOR.

''DAN'' shall JUDGE His People, as One of the Tribes of ISRAEL. 'DAN' shall be a SERPENT in the WAY, a HORNED SNAKE in the Path that BITES the HORSE'S HEELS, so that His Rider Falls Backward. For THY SALVATION I WAIT, O LORD.

As for ''GAD'', Raiders shall Raid Him, but He shall Raid at their Heels.

As for ''ASHER'', His Food shall be RICH, and He shall Yield ROYAL DAINTIES.

''NAPHTALI'' is a DOE let LOOSE, HE GIVES BEAUTIFUL 'WORDS'.

"JOSEPH" is a Fruitful Bough, a Fruitful Bough by a SPRING; Its Branches Run OVER a Wall. The Archers Bitterly Attacked Him, and SHOT at Him and HARASSED Him; but His BOW remained FIRM, and His Arms were AGILE, from the Hands of the MIGHTY ONE OF JACOB [From there is the Shepherd, the Stone of Israel], from the GOD OF YOUR FATHER, WHO HELPS YOU, and by the ALMIGHTY WHO BLESSES YOU WITH BLESSINGS OF HEAVEN ABOVE, Blessings of the DEEP that LIES BENEATH, Blessings of the BREASTS, and of the WOMB. The BLESSINGS of YOUR FATHER have SURPASSED the BLESSINGS of MY ANCESTORS, up to the UTMOST BOUND of the EVERLASTING HILLS; MAY they be on the HEAD of JOSEPH, and on the CROWN of the HEAD of the ONE DISTINGUISHED Among His Brothers.

"BENJAMIN" is a Ravenous WOLF; In the Morning He DEVOURS the PREY, and in the Evening He DIVIDES the SPOIL.

All these are the Twelve Tribes of Israel, and this is what their FATHER Said to THEM, when He BLESSED them. He BLESSED them, EVERY ONE WITH THE BLESSING "'APPROPRIATE TO HIM'".' [Genesis 49 Verses 1 to 28.]

The Great King Solomon through His Intellectual Observations, made a Note of these Sacred Wordings of His Ancestor JACOB, and with His Discerning Mind then Figured OUT the Secret of the 12 Cosmic Energies, which Corresponded to the Specific Blessings of JACOB [ISRAEL], and thus for Him were a Valuable Key to the Secret of the Breast Piece of Judgment, which Held the 12 Precious Stones, with the Engraved Names of the 12 Sons of ISRAEL [JACOB].

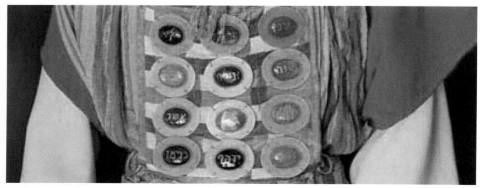

The wise King Solomon having a Discerning Heart and Inquiring Mind, which was gracefully gifted to Him by the MOST HIGH, wanted to Understand the Secrets of so called GODS and GODDESSES, whom so many people of the Neighboring Lands IGNORANTLY Worshiped, and thus their Man Made IDOLS and GRAVEN IMAGES were Faithfully Served, and Reverently Bowed Down to, by vast amounts of Evolving Humanity, as well as their Ruler Kings and Nobles and Installed Priests, who were living in those Lands.

The Wise King SOLOMON being a Faithful Humble Servant of the MOST HIGH, the CREATOR – OBSERVER LORD – GOD of the UNIVERSE, fully UNDERSTOOD this Important FACT, which was Deep Rooted in His Heart Consciousness right from His Early Childhood, after he was Chosen by the Great LORD Himself as His Own SON, as Clearly mentioned in "1 Chronicles 17. 13." of the Holy Bible, that HIS LORD - GOD, for WHOM He Constructed the Most Elegant TEMPLE HOUSE in JERUSALEM, was the "ONLY TRUE LORD - GOD" of the Universe, who HIMSELF Created it with HIS DESIRE MIND, and thus is also its SOLE PRESERVER and the SUPREME JUDGE, as King Solomon Very Well Knew the Sayings of the LORD, which the Great LORD Himself told to his Ancestor MOSES, that "HE WILL JUDGE ALL THE MIGHTY AND POWERFUL GODS OF EGYPT", which is recorded and written Down in the Holy TORAH as LORD'S Statement to MOSES, regarding which the Holy Bible States, " AGAINST ALL THE GODS of EGYPT, I WILL EXECUTE JUDGMENTS – I AM THE LORD". [Exodus 12. 12]

But for His Learning Purposes of the Secrets, of these So Called GODS and GODDESSES and their Corrupt 'MODUS OPERANDI', the Great King SOLOMON willfully Indulged in their Ritual Practices, because to CATCH a "GROUP OF THIEVES", the Wise POLICE as Under Cover becomes a Part of them, and Join them to become One of their Members, and Willfully Indulge and Engage themselves in their Wrong Operations to LEARN THE SECRETS OF THEIR OPERATIONAL MODES, and their HIDDEN WAYS and MEANS.

This wise King SOLOMON with His Discerning Mind knew this fact that No Human in their Proper Mind Follows any kind of 'Faith or

Religion', till they get their DESIRED WISHES FULFILLED, and thus for the MOST DIFFICULT TASK of UNCOVERING their SECRETS the great King SOLOMON Wisely Figured Out, that Only He having LORD'S GRACE could Fulfill this Most Difficult Task, as otherwise Being just a Normal Human Being, it was IMPOSSIBLE for Anyone Else to Learn the SECRETS of these INVISIBLE ENTITIES, who Deceitfully Operated in their Followers Mind Consciousness, through their ESTABLISHED IDOLS and GRAVEN IMAGES, and Illegally Controlled the Desire Minds of Evolving Human Beings in their LAND'S, just Like the Human Beings Control the Unwary Animals of the Animal Kingdom upon this Planet Earth.

The Great King Solomon, having LORD'S Intuitional Wisdom, by Willfully Indulging in Such Wrong Practices, which were against the Commandments of the LORD - GOD, thus Raised Various DOUBTS in the Evolving Minds of PRIESTHOOD and His Contemporary Prophets of the LORD, who FAILED to NOTICE with their "Inner Spiritual Mind Consciousness", this DEEP and IMPORTANT FACT that, NO MATTER WHAT Solomon Experimented with, for His Underlying Quest for Attaining the "Knowledge and Wisdom" pertaining to the SECRETS of these So Called GODS and GODDESSES, HE Still Preached to all the "Children of Israel" to remember the "FEAR OF THE LORD", as everything Else in every Type of Sense was Nothing but Just "VANITY", regarding which the Holy Bible States:

'The WORDS of the PREACHER, the Son of DAVID, King in JERUSALEM, "Vanity of Vanities", Says the PREACHER, "Vanity of Vanities! ALL is Vanity.' [Ecclesiastes 1. 1.]

And the ABOVE VERSE from the Chapter of Ecclesiastes is its Very First Verse, and the Very Last Verse of this Chapter SUMS UP King SOLOMON'S CONCLUSION, regarding which the Holy Bible States:

'The CONCLUSION, when all has been HEARD, is: FEAR GOD and KEEP HIS COMMANDMENTS, because this APPLIES to EVERY PERSON. Because GOD will BRING every ACT TO JUDGMENT, Everything which is HIDDEN, whether it is GOOD or EVIL.' [Ecclesiastes 12. 13, 14.]

The Great King Solomon Very Carefully OBSERVING all these illegal Rituals of GOD'S and GODDESSES Worship, which was taking place in the Territories of His DOMAIN as well as in the Neighboring Lands like that of EGYPT, then with DISCERNING MIND He finally UNRAVELED their

SECRETS, by finding out that these So Called GODS and GODDESSES were Absolutely NOT the DESIRED MIND CREATIONS of the "MOST HIGH", which Manifested as Per HIS Evolutionary Plan and Purpose upon the 3 Dense Dimensional Planes of this Planet Earth, as the "UNKNOWABLE CREATOR LORD – GOD" through HIS DESIRE MIND VITAL REFLECTIONS, Only Created in the Ethereal Matter, the Differentiated Conscious Hierarchical "BEINGS", which belong to the Various Evolving Kingdoms upon this Planet Earth.

But Many of these so Called GODS and GODDESSES, which Prevailed upon this Planet Earth since a LONG TIME, were Just Mere Formed "ENTITIES", Without having any "SOUL CONSCIOUSNESS", which came in Existences, due to the Collection of the VITAL THOUGHT FORMS, composed of unconscious live Elemental's of Ethereal Matter, which were in fact created by the DESIRE MIND MAGNETIC ENERGIES of the Ignorant Human Beings, who being Deeply Polarized in the Lower Mind Desires related to their ANIMAL PASSIONS, thus acting as the CO – CREATORS with Limited Abilities in the Evolutionary Process of the Great LORD, then Unknowingly CREATED THEM through their 'Wished Desire Energies' which caused the corresponding MAGNETIC VIBRATIONS in the Differentiated Ethereal Matter of the 2 Dense Planes of the Planet Earth manifesting the related "Thought Forms" in their ETHEREAL MATTER, which are known as the Dimensional Spheres of YETZIRAH and ASSIAH, of which the Plane of YETZIRAH is Primarily the Magnetic Plane of 'EMOTIONS and FEELINGS".

And they unknowingly created these Vibrations related to their Desired Wishes in the Ethereal Matter, by MENTALLY Concentrating upon these Man Made IDOLS and GRAVEN IMAGES of so called GODS and GODDESSES, thus Unknowingly Charging them with their Vital Emotional Energies of EXPECTATIONS. And over the Time with Singing, Dancing, and Chanting Rituals dedicated to these Molten and Graven GODS and GODDESSES thus passed on their Mind's Vital Magnetic Energies, in which many Ignorant Human Beings having Reverence for these Statues, thus Willfully took part along with the Ambiance of Pleasant Smells which were due to the Floral Offerings, the Perfumes and the Incense, and in this way they Unknowingly Created Powerful ENERGY THOUGHT FORMS, which over the Passing of Time made these MAN MADE IDOLS, to Exist as Huge Store Houses of Live Elemental Ethereal Energy Reservoirs, and thus these Invisible Live Energies collected in these IDOL's Energy reservoirs then started affecting the

Desired Wishes of their Human Subjects which were 'NOT AT ALL SPIRITUALLY ORIENTED', but were Only related to the 'Dense Physical Material World Need's', thus creating More and More Firm Belief for the Material Minded Human Beings in these so called GODS and GODDESSES, whose Material Desire wishes thus got Fulfilled.

Many Human Beings of this Planet Earth are STILL UNAWARE of their CONSCIOUS MIND'S Capacities, as the "Evolving Mind" known as the Human "PERSONALITY" being an "'Individualized or Segmented part of their SOUL Conscious Energy'" which being "'ETHEREAL'" in Nature is NOT a Part of the 'HUMAN BRAIN ORGAN', although it Fully Utilizes it during an INCARNATED HUMAN LIFE as its MAIN ORGAN of PERCEPTION and CREATION ACTIONS, and for its various other Functions in the Dense Physical Plane.

The GOOD FEELINGS and EMOTIONS of a Prayer which create "BENEFICIAL LIVE THOUGHT FORMS" meant for the Well Being of Someone, and the BAD FEELINGS and EMOTIONS commonly known as the "EVIL EYE", which can Negatively Affect or HURT Someone, are also based upon this Principle of "Invisible Live Thought Formations", which being COMPOSED OF ELEMENTAL LIVES can travel through the Interpenetrating dimensional Zones of ASSIAH and YETZIRAH, and thus according to the 'Desired Wishes' then manifest the DESIRED RESULTS wherever they DIRECTED and thus Sent with a STRONG WILL FORCE. And those 'Thought Forms' which are Created by the "Collective Consciousness Desire Minds of MASSES" are More Powerful than those which are Created by just an INDIVIDUAL or a SMALL NUMBER OF PEOPLE.

These "Soulless" ENTITIES known as the GODS AND GODDESSES, whose Established IDOLS are Still Prevalent in many Zones of the Dense Physical Plane of this Plant Earth are Similar to the Formed "ENTITIES" in the Business World, willfully formulated by the Evolving Human Beings, which are known as the "MULTINATIONAL CORPORATIONS", which in Reality are NOT HUMAN BEINGS THEMSELVES, but the Mere Mind Creations of the HUMAN BEINGS and thus in their own Might become "POWERFUL ENTITIES, but have Many Human Beings Running them, and can still Continue to Exist due to the Constant Investing of the material energies of Human Beings known as the "SHARES", even when their "ORIGINAL CREATORS and FORMULATORS" since long have PASSED AWAY from this Physical Plane World of Planet Earth, and thus can Continue to Act Like a HUGE Group of the Collective Consciousness, Embodying the Hearts, Minds and Bodies of their Incarnated Human Being Worker's. Thus these CORPORATE ENTITIES being Constantly Supported and Fed by the Material Energies of New Human Generations over the PASSING OF TIME become MORE AND MORE POWERFUL, and can Continue to Exist as Such for Very LONG PERIODS, till the Evolving Human Society themselves for any Particular Reason May STOP to Invest their MATERIAL ENERGIES [MONEY] in them.

The Ancient Egyptian Religion as well as many other World Religions of GODS and GODDESSES, having their Priesthood as their Employees, which Prospered upon this Planet Earth by acting out their Roles as the SOULLESS POWERFUL ENTITIES, similar to these Modern Day Multinational Corporations, were being thus constantly FED by the VITAL ENERGIES OF THE DESIRE MIND THOUGHT FORMS of their Respective Human Races, and Finally Ended to EXIST, when the REAL CREATOR, THE UNKNOWABLE LORD – GOD OF THE UNIVERSE, THE "MOST HIGH" THEN APPROPRIATELY "JUDGED THEM', and regarding the Great King Solomon's Various Observations, which are known as the PROVERBS, the Holy Bible States:

'The Proverbs of SOLOMON, the Son of DAVID, King of ISRAEL:
To Know WISDOM and INSTRUCTION, TO Discern the SAYINGS
OF UNDERSTANDING, TO Receive Instruction in WISE BEHAVIOR,
RIGHTEOUSNESS, JUSTICE, and EQUITY; TO Give PRUDENCE to the
NAIVE, TO the YOUTH KNOWLEDGE and DISCRETION, A Wise Man will
HEAR and INCREASE in LEARNING, AND a Man of UNDERSTANDING will
ACQUIRE Wise COUNSEL, TO Understand a PROVERB and a Figure, THE
WORDS of the Wise and their RIDDLES.

The FEAR of the LORD is the BEGINNING of KNOWLEDGE; FOOLS
Despise WISDOM and INSTRUCTION.

Wisdom SHOUTS in the Street, SHE Lifts her Voice in the Square; AT the
Head of the Noisy Streets, she Cries Out; AT the Entrance of the Gates
in the City, SHE Utters Her Sayings; "HOW long, O Naive Ones, will You
Love SIMPLICITY? And Scoffers DELIGHT themselves in Scoffing, AND
FOOLS HATE KNOWLEDGE?

Turn to My Reproof, Behold, I will Pour OUT My SPIRIT on YOU; I will
Make My WORDS Known to You. Because I called, and you REFUSED;

I Stretched Out My Hand, and NO ONE Paid Attention; AND You NEGLECTED All My COUNSEL, and DID NOT Want My REPROOF; I will Even LAUGH at your CALAMITY; I will MOCK when Your DREAD Comes like a STORM, AND Your CALAMITY Comes On like a WHIRLWIND, when DISTRESS and ANGUISH come on YOU.

Then they will CALL on ME, but I will NOT ANSWER; THEY will Seek Me DILIGENTLY, but they shall NOT FIND ME, BECAUSE they hated KNOWLEDGE, AND they DID NOT CHOOSE '''THE FEAR OF THE LORD'''. [Proverbs 1. Verses 1 to 7, and Verses 20 to 29.]

The Secret of the Breast Plate

Part 82

The Great King Solomon after His Discerning Explorations pertaining to the SECRETS of these So Called GODS and GODDESSES, through His Close Observations also found out, that MANY of their Incarnated Human FRONTS, who were NONE OTHER than their Faithful Worshipers, knowingly or unknowingly were also Involved in the DARK ARTS, which were carried on through the LEFT HAND RITUAL PRACTICES, commonly known as the BLACK MAGIC, especially by the SERVING PRIESTHOOD of these GODS and GODDESSES, who were the willful Practitioners of these Wrongful and Illegal Dark MAGICAL Arts, against which the GREAT BENEVOLENT and MERCIFUL LORD GOD Overwhelmingly Commanded MOSES for the 'Children of Israel' NEVER TO INDULGE in such EVIL PRACTICES, Because of Such EVIL Practices willfully Carried Out in the TEMPLES OF WORSHIP, in the Lands of so called GODS and GODDESSES thus became the Places of "DARK DOMAINS", frequented by the Invisible "DISEMBODIED SOUL PERSONALITIES", who were ILLEGALLY TRAPPED AND CONTROLLED after their Physical Deaths in the Dense Physical Plane, by the Roving BLACK MAGICIANS, who Deceitfully Utilizing the Astral Plane Ethereal Matter took the Preferred Animated Shapes of their Worshiped IDOLS, deceitfully appearing to them their Venerated GODS and GODDESSES and thus Deceitfully through these Illusory Forms appearing and acting for them like their Venerated So called GODS and GODDESSES whom they remembered during their Incarnated Lives from their IDOL SHAPES, then Illegally Trapped them to make them as their PERMANENT SLAVE Followers, and these 'DISEMBODIED SOUL PERSONALITIES" Existing in their AFTER LIFE CONSCIOUSNESS BODIES, then believing them as their Living GODS and GODDESSES Innocently got Stuck in their DECEITFUL TRAPS, and thus getting CUT OFF from their "RADIANT SOUL CONSCIOUS HIGHER SELVES", then themselves also became the 'DOOMED CONSCIOUS EXISTENCES FOREVER' which various Scriptures since Ancient Times have termed as the 'NIGHT GHOSTS OR THE SHADY CREATURES' or the 'SPIRITS OF THE DEAD'. And in such DREADFUL STATES OF CONSCIOUS EXISTENCE, they PERMANENTLY Got Stuck in the Dense Ethereal Sub Plane Dimensions of the "ASSIAH and YETZIRAH" SPHERES, NEVER TO ASCEND BACK AGAIN UPON THE EVOLUTIONARY LADDER TOWARD THE "HIGHER DIMENSIONAL PLANES", which are THE SPIRITUAL DOMAINS OF THEIR "TRUE SOLAR CONSCIOUSNESS EXISTENCE", which the

""""TRUE LORD GOD OF THE UNIVERSE"""" AS PER HIS EVOLUTIONARY PLAN AND PURPOSE, IN THE "VERY BEGINNING" JOYFULLY ESTABLISHED FOR THEM.

And THIS was the MAIN REASON for the MOST MERCIFUL LORD GOD to WARN HIS CHOSEN RACE, the Children of Israel and their Future Descendant Generations, through the Services of His Humble Servant MOSES, by STRESSING AGAIN AND AGAIN and REMINDING THEM to Always KEEP HIS COMMANDMENTS, and "NOT TO MAKE OR WORSHIP 'GODS AND GODDESSES IDOLS", so that they DO NOT Ignorantly become an Innocent Victim and FALL PREY to these DERANGED MIND BLACK MAGICIANS, who were Truly Active behind the CONSPIRACY of these so called GODS and GODDESSES, deceitfully carried out by them against the MOST HIGH upon the Dense Physical Plane of this Planet Earth.

And all those who by FOOLISHLY worshiping these MAN MADE GODS and GODDESSES IDOLS become the 'NIGHT OR THE SHADY CREATURES' or the 'SPIRITS OF THE DEAD' after their Passing away from the Dense Physical Plane, never Got LIBERATED AGAIN, regarding which the Holy Bible States:

'Then GOD Spoke all these WORDS, Saying, "I AM THE LORD YOUR GOD, Who brought YOU Out of the Land of Egypt, out of the House of Slavery. YOU SHALL HAVE NO OTHER GODS BEFORE ME. You shall NOT MAKE for YOURSELF AN IDOL, or Any LIKENESS of what is in HEAVEN Above or on the EARTH BENEATH or in the WATER UNDER THE EARTH.

You shall NOT WORSHIP THEM or SERVE THEM; for "I", the LORD YOUR GOD, am a Jealous GOD, Visiting the INIQUITY of the FATHERS on the CHILDREN, on the THIRD and the FOURTH GENERATIONS of those who HATE ME, but Showing LOVING KINDNESS to THOUSANDS who LOVE ME, and KEEP MY COMMANDMENTS.' [Exodus 20. Verses 1 to 6.]

'For MY Angel will GO Before YOU and Bring You in to the Land of the AMORITES, the HITTITES, the PERIZZITES, the CANAANITES, the HIVITES, and the JEBUSITES; AND "I" WILL COMPLETELY DESTROY THEM.

You shall NOT WORSHIP their GODS, NOR SERVE THEM, NOR DO ACCORDING TO THEIR DEEDS; BUT YOU SHALL UTTERLY OVERTHROW THEM, AND BREAK THEIR 'SACRED PILLARS' IN PIECES. But YOU shall

'''SERVE the LORD YOUR GOD''', and HE will BLESS YOUR BREAD, AND YOUR WATER; and "I" will REMOVE SICKNESS from YOUR MIDST.' [Exodus 23. Verses 23, 24, 25.]

'Watch YOURSELF that You MAKE NO COVENANT with the INHABITANTS OF THE LAND, into which YOU are GOING, lest it become a SNARE in Your Midst. But Rather, You are to TEAR DOWN THEIR ALTARS and SMASH their SACRED PILLARS, and CUT DOWN their '''ASHERIM'''.

You shall MAKE for YOURSELF 'NO MOLTEN GODS'.' [Exodus 34. 12, 13, 17.]

'Do not TURN to IDOLS or Make for Yourselves MOLTEN GODS; I AM THE 'LORD YOUR GOD'. [Leviticus 19. 4.]

'You shall NOT MAKE for YOURSELVES 'IDOLS', Nor shall YOU Set Up for YOURSELVES An IMAGE or a SACRED PILLAR, Nor shall YOU PLACE a FIGURED STONE in Your Land to BOW DOWN to it; for I AM THE 'LORD YOUR GOD'.' [Leviticus 26. 1.]

'So WATCH Yourself CAREFULLY, Since You Did NOT SEE 'ANY FORM' on the DAY the LORD SPOKE to YOU at HOREB from the Midst of the FIRE, lest YOU ACT CORRUPTLY, and MAKE A 'GRAVEN IMAGE' for YOURSELVES in the FORM of Any FIGURE, the Likeness of MALE or FEMALE, the LIKENESS of Any ANIMAL that is on Earth, the LIKENESS of Any WINGED BIRD that Flies in the Sky, the LIKENESS of ANYTHING that Creeps on the Ground, the LIKENESS of Any FISH that is in the WATER Below the Earth.

And Beware, lest YOU Lift up YOUR EYES to HEAVEN and SEE the SUN and the MOON and the STARS, all the HOST of HEAVEN, and be Drawn Away and WORSHIP THEM and SERVE Them, those which the LORD your GOD has Allotted to all the PEOPLES under the Whole Heaven.' [Deuteronomy 4. Verses 15 to 19.]

'I am the LORD Your GOD, who brought You Out of the Land of EGYPT, Out of the House of Slavery. You shall have NO OTHER GODS before ME.

You shall NOT make for YOURSELF Any IDOL, or any Likeness of what is in HEAVEN Above, or on the EARTH Beneath or in the WATER under the EARTH.' [Deuteronomy 5. 6, 7, 8.]

'But thus YOU shall do to them; YOU shall TEAR Down their Altars, and SMASH their SACRED PILLARS, and HEW Down their "ASHERIM", and BURN their GRAVEN IMAGES with FIRE.

For YOU are a HOLY PEOPLE to the LORD Your GOD; the LORD Your GOD has "CHOSEN YOU" to be a PEOPLE for HIS Own POSSESSION out of ALL THE PEOPLES, who are on the FACE OF THE EARTH.' [Deuteronomy 7. 5, 6.]

The LORD - GOD in a Codified Way Again and Again Stressed, and thus Clearly Emphasized upon this Most Important Point to MOSES, that these MOLTEN IDOLS and GRAVEN IMAGES, Elaborately Decorated with Precious Gold and Silver, by just being Store Houses of "INVISIBLE" NEGATIVE ENERGY "THOUGHT FORMS", were thus Completely Filled and Fully Saturated with the "ANIMAL MIND PASSIONS" of the 'LOST SOULS', and they thus being HEINOUS WORKS OF "ABOMINATIONS", they should NEVER be Brought into their HOUSES, by the Evolving Children of Israel, as they can NEGATIVELY AFFECT THEIR MINDS and thus their INNER or HIGHER MIND SPIRITUAL CONSCIOUSNESS EVOLUTION, and then Abruptly Stop their "SPIRITUAL GROWTH" as well as their OVERALL "WELL – BEING", but instead they should be TOTALLY DESTROYED and BURNT WITH "FIRE", regarding which the Holy Bible States:

'The GRAVEN IMAGES OF THEIR GODS, YOU ARE TO BURN WITH 'FIRE"; YOU shall NOT COVET the "SILVER" or the "GOLD" that is on THEM, NOR take it for YOURSELVES, lest YOU be "SNARED" by it, for it is an ABOMINATION to the LORD Your GOD.

And YOU shall NOT Bring an ABOMINATION into YOUR HOUSE, and become a DEVOTED THING LIKE IT; YOU shall UTTERLY DETEST it, and YOU shall UTTERLY ABHOR IT, for it is a DEVOTED THING.' [Deuteronomy 7. 5, 6, 25, 26.]

'BEWARE lest YOU Forget the LORD Your GOD by NOT KEEPING HIS COMMANDMENTS, and HIS ORDINANCES, and HIS STATUTES, which I am Commanding YOU Today; lest when YOU have EATEN and are SATISFIED, and have Built GOOD HOUSES and Lived in THEM, and when YOUR HERDS and YOUR FLOCKS Multiply, and YOUR SILVER and GOLD Multiply, and All that YOU have MULTIPLIES, then YOUR HEART becomes PROUD, and YOU FORGET THE LORD YOUR GOD, Who brought YOU Out from the Land of EGYPT, Out of the HOUSE OF SLAVERY.

And it shall COME About if "YOU EVER FORGET" THE LORD YOUR GOD, and "GO AFTER OTHER GODS AND SERVE THEM, AND WORSHIP THEM", I TESTIFY AGAINST YOU TODAY THAT YOU SHALL """"SURELY PERISH"""". [Deuteronomy 8. 11, 12, 13, 14, 19.]

'Circumcise then YOUR "HEART", and STIFFEN Your NECK NO MORE. For the LORD Your GOD is the """"GOD OF GODS"""", and the """"LORD OF LORDS"""", the GREAT, the MIGHTY, and the AWESOME GOD, Who does not Show "PARTIALITY, NOR TAKE A BRIBE".' [Deuteronomy 10. 16, 17.]

'These are the STATUTES and the JUDGMENTS which YOU shall CAREFULLY Observe in the Land, which the LORD, the GOD of YOUR FATHERS, has Given YOU to POSSESS as Long as YOU Live on the EARTH.

YOU shall UTTERLY DESTROY all the PLACES, where the NATIONS whom YOU shall DISPOSSESS SERVE their GODS, On the HIGH MOUNTAINS, and On the Hills, and Under Every Green Tree. And YOU shall TEAR DOWN their Altars and SMASH their SACRED PILLARS and BURN their "'ASHERIM'" with "'FIRE'", and YOU shall CUT DOWN the ENGRAVED IMAGES of their GODS, and YOU shall "OBLITERATE" THEIR NAME from that PLACE.

YOU shall NOT ACT Like this toward the LORD Your GOD. But YOU shall SEEK the LORD at the Place, which the LORD Your GOD shall "CHOOSE" from ALL Your TRIBES, to ESTABLISH HIS Name there for HIS Dwelling, and there YOU shall COME.' [Deuteronomy 12. Verses 1 to 5.]

The Great LORD OF FLAMES in a Codified Way also gave them a 'GRAVE WARNING', about the "'LOSS OF THEIR PERSONALITY SOULS" whose Conscious Energies could be "EATEN UP" after their Physical Death by the Corrupt Invisible Dark Entities and Beings, whose Deranged Consciousness composed of THE LIVE MURKY THOUGHT FORMS Is always lurking for their INNOCENT VICTIMS, if the 'Children of Israel" acting Just Like the Rest of Evolving Humanity, Willfully Disobeyed HIM, and DID NOT Carried Out HIS COMMANDMENTS, regarding which the Holy Bible States:

'But if YOU Do Not OBEY ME and Do Not CARRY OUT all these COMMANDMENTS, If, Instead, YOU REJECT MY STATUTES, and if Your

"'SOUL'" Abhors MY ORDINANCES So as Not to Carry Out ALL MY COMMANDMENTS, and So Break "'MY COVENANT'", "I", in Turn will do this to YOU; I will Appoint Over YOU a SUDDEN TERROR, CONSUMPTION and FEVER, that shall WASTE Away the EYES, and Cause the """"SOUL TO PINE AWAY""""; Also, YOU shall SOW Your SEED Uselessly, for YOUR ENEMIES shall "'EAT IT UP'". [Leviticus 26. 14, 15, 16.]

And it shall COME About if "YOU EVER FORGET" THE LORD YOUR GOD, and "GO AFTER OTHER GODS AND SERVE THEM, AND WORSHIP THEM", I TESTIFY AGAINST YOU TODAY THAT YOU SHALL """""SURELY PERISH""""." [Deuteronomy 8. 11, 12, 13, 14, 19.]

The Secret of the Breast Plate
Part 83

When the Children of Israel, under the Ill Governance of their Successive CORRUPT KINGS, by Willfully worshiping the so called GODS and GODDESSES Went Astray from the LORDS Intended Evolutionary Path for their SPIRITUAL Conscious Expansion, which the MOST BENEVOLENT AND MERCIFUL CREATOR LORD GOD OF THE UNIVERSE Set for HIS CHOSEN RACE during their Deliverance from the "Slavery Bondage's in Egypt", and went on doing REPEATED ABOMINATIONS against their LORD – GOD, then the MERCIFUL LORD – GOD Time and Again SENT Among them HIS CHOSEN PROPHETS, SEERS AND SAGES, to "STRONGLY WARN" them, about the DIRE CONSEQUENCES as Reactions for their such DETESTABLE BEHAVIOR, of which the Wise King Solomon after His Wrong and Right Experiments to Discern the Underlying Truth about such DETESTABLE BEHAVIOR of the Human Beings with His Understanding HEART, then during His Own Times also played His Role as a "Prophet Preacher" for the 'Children of Israel' Conveyed the Same Message, but His Deep Rooted Wisdom SAYING'S were OVERLOOKED by Many Narrow Minded People, who were Incapable to SEE THROUGH His Valuable Preaching's.

During their 40 Years' Time Period in the WILDERNESS, in which the 'Children of Israel' Regularly STUMBLED Many a Times, the Most MERCIFUL LORD – GOD, through the WRITTEN Commandments, which were Given to HIS Humble Servant MOSES upon the Holy Mountain 'HOREB – SINAI", thus went Continually Forgiving them and reestablishing them, to Exist as the Members of HIS CHOSEN RACE, to live their Evolutionary LIVES in a Proper Manner as per HIS EVOLUTIONARY PLAN AND PURPOSE, as they were meant to SERVE AS the "Beacons of Light" in the Promised Land to the rest of FAILING HUMANITY of this World, who IGNORANTLY got Totally DECEIVED by the Invisible "FALLEN ANGELS" and their DARKENED HEARTS "MAGICIANS", ACTING IN THE ROLES OF THE 'VENERATED PRIESTHOOD' for these so called MAN MADE "'GOD AND GODDESSES'" IDOLS. Which were carefully installed in their STRUCTURED TEMPLE ESTABLISHMENTS, which were the ELABORATE POWER HOUSES OF THEIR ' "ORGANIZED RELIGIONS'".

And these CORRUPT ENTITIES were the STUMBLING BLOCKS for the SPIRITUAL GROWTH and CONSCIOUS EXPANSION of the Evolving Human Races, who through their DECEITFUL CORRUPT BEHAVIOR, thus brought Down upon the Physical Plane of this Planet Earth, in its Ignorant EVOLVING HUMANITY, those Wrong and Forbidden Practices and Rituals, which involved first creating the Molten Idols, and Graven Images, and Various Other TYPES OF "' ICONS'" and "SYMBOLIC DEPICTIONS", and then Established those ILLEGAL RITUALS related to the ANIMAL MIND PASSIONS, which involved SEX AND PROSTITUTION as their SACRED RITUALS, as well as the Heinous Acts of CHILDREN AND HUMAN SACRIFICES, which were GRAVE ABOMINATIONS to the MOST BENEVOLENT CREATOR LORD GOD OF THE UNIVERSE, and thus Caused them to Overwhelmingly SIN against the ONE AND ONLY, THE ALMIGHTY "UNKNOWABLE CREATOR - OBSERVER LORD – GOD" OF THE UNIVERSE, who Since Ancient Times has been known to All HIS VISIBLE AND INVISIBLE CREATIONS as the "MOST HIGH".

The Chosen PROPHETS of the LORD, Time and Again tried to Convey LORD'S MESSAGE to the FAILING CHILDREN OF ISRAEL, which were always made FUN OFF, and thus LORD'S MESSAGE was Willfully REJECTED by all those, WHOSE DESIRE MINDS gave away to their 'EMBODIED PERSONALITY CONSCIOUSNESS, LOWER MIND ANIMAL - PASSIONS', and regarding LORD'S POWERFUL MESSAGE, which was passed on to them through His Humble Servants, the Holy Bible Clearly States:

'Sacrifice and Meal Offerings THOU hast NOT DESIRED; MY Ears THOU hast OPENED; BURNT OFFERING and SIN OFFERING THOU HAST NOT REQUIRED' [Psalm 40. 6.]

When the Great LORD'S Dire Warnings were Continuously being willfully REJECTED by the CHILDREN OF ISRAEL, who under the MIND CONTROL SPELLS of these INVISIBLE DARK "ENTITIES" who were behind the so called GODS and GODDESSES IDOLS, GRAVEN IMAGES, IDOLS, STATUES, and Various Other Types of ICONIC and SYMBOLIC DEPICTIONS, which were also ILLEGALLY Established inside the 'HOUSE OF THE LORD' in JERUSALEM, and were VITALLY POWERED by the Wrongful Invisible Lower Mind THOUGHT FORMS of the Children of Israel by their

UNQUENCHABLE GREED, LUST, and ILLEGAL DESIRE TO CONTROL ALL OTHERS for the Sake of their ILLUSORY NAME AND FAME, then the Great LORD who is the MOST MERCIFUL in the ENTIRE UNIVERSE, who even then under such Detestable Conditions was Staying in the Midst of HIS Chosen Race, with HIS Holy Presence Embodied through the "ARK OF COVENANT", then Sent Among Them His Humble Servant and CHOSEN PROPHET JEREMIAH to Give them a """"DIRE AND FINAL WARNING"""", that if they DO NOT Change their EVIL WAYS, then they were GOING TO LOOSE their MOST HOLY OBJECT, THE "ARK OF COVENANT", which was a Symbol of HIS Presence Among them, and after its Such GREAT LOSS was not GOING TO BE MADE AGAIN, regarding which the Holy Bible States:

'As a THIEF is SHAMED When He is Discovered, SO the House of ISRAEL is SHAMED; THEY, their KINGS, their PRINCES, and their PRIESTS, and their PROPHETS, WHO Say to a TREE, "YOU ARE MY FATHER", and to a STONE, "YOU GAVE ME BIRTH".

For they have TURNED their BACK to ME, and NOT their FACE; BUT in the Time of their TROUBLE they will Say, "ARISE AND SAVE US". But WHERE are YOUR GODS, which YOU made for YOURSELF? Let them ARISE, if they can SAVE YOU in the TIME of YOUR TROUBLE; FOR according to the NUMBER of YOUR CITIES are YOUR GODS, 'O JUDAH'.

Why do YOU Contend with ME? You have ALL TRANSGRESSED AGAINST ME, Declares the LORD. In Vain "I" have STRUCK Your Sons; THEY Accepted No CHASTENING. Your SWORD has DEVOURED Your PROPHETS like a Destroying Lion. O Generation, Heed the WORD of the LORD. Have "I" been a WILDERNESS TO ISRAEL, Or a LAND OF THICK 'DARKNESS'? Why do MY PEOPLE Say, WE are FREE TO ROAM; WE will COME NO MORE TO THEE?

"Why do YOU go AROUND so MUCH Changing YOUR Way? Also, YOU shall be put to SHAME by EGYPT as YOU were put to SHAME by ASSYRIA. From this PLACE also YOU shall GO OUT with YOUR HANDS ON YOUR HEAD; FOR the LORD has REJECTED THOSE in WHOM YOU 'TRUST', and YOU shall Not Prosper with them"'.' [Jeremiah 2. Verses 26 to 31, and 36, 37.]

And in the End Prophet JEREMIAH Conveyed LORDS FINAL WARNING to the Children of Israel, which CLEARLY Warned them about LOOSING their ARK OF COVENANT through which they always Felt LORD'S HOLY PRESENCE AMONG THEM, and After Not Paying Any HEED by the 'Children of Israel to the LORD'S GRAVE WARNING, it Ultimately DID HAPPENED, when they Finally LOST LORD'S HOLY ARK OF COVENANT, and regarding LORD'S GRAVE AND DIRE WARNING which was Conveyed by Prophet JEREMIAH to the Children of Israel, the Holy Bible States:

"And it shall be in THOSE DAYS, when YOU are MULTIPLIED and INCREASED in the LAND", Declares the LORD, "THEY shall Say No MORE, 'THE Ark of the Covenant of the LORD'. And it shall NOT COME TO MIND, NOR shall THEY REMEMBER IT, NOR shall THEY MISS IT, NOR SHALL IT BE MADE AGAIN.' [Jeremiah 3. 16.]

And as per LORD'S WARNING King NEBUCHADNEZZAR, the KING OF CHALDEAN'S, Attacked JERUSALEM, and DESTROYED the CITY and its INHABITANTS, regarding which the Holy Bible States:

'Therefore HE Brought up against them, the KING of the CHALDEAN'S, who Slew their Young Men with the SWORD in the "HOUSE OF THEIR SANCTUARY", and had NO COMPASSION on Young Man or Virgin, Old Man or Infirm; HE Gave them All into His HAND.

Then they BURNED the "HOUSE OF GOD", and BROKE DOWN the Wall of Jerusalem and Burned All its Fortified Buildings with FIRE, and DESTROYED ALL ITS """"VALUABLE ARTICLES"""".' [2 Chronicles 36. 17, 19.]

Later on, when the Children of Israel Overwhelmingly CRIED to the Unknowable LORD - GOD in CAPTIVITY for 70 Years, then to FULFILL JEREMIAH'S PROPHECY, the Great LORD Stirred up the SPIRIT OF CYRUS King of Persia, during the First Year of His Reign, who like the Great King SOLOMON was thus moved by the LORD – GOD, and with returning all the Articles of the House of the LORD, Which King NEBUCHADNEZZAR had earlier carried away from JERUSALEM to be Put in the House of His GODS, CYRUS King of Persia, then issued a DECREE to Build the 'HOUSE

OF THE LORD' in JERUSALEM regarding which the Holy Bible States:

'To Fulfill the WORD of the LORD by the Mouth of JEREMIAH, until the Land had enjoyed its Sabbaths. All the Days of its DESOLATION it Kept Sabbath, until SEVENTY Years were Complete. Now in the First Year of Cyrus King of Persia – In Order to Fulfill the WORD of the LORD by the Mouth of JEREMIAH – The LORD Stirred up the Spirit of CYRUS King of PERSIA, so that He Sent a PROCLAMATION throughout His Kingdom, and also PUT IT IN WRITING, Saying, " THUS Says CYRUS King of PERSIA, 'THE LORD, THE GOD OF HEAVEN, has GIVEN Me All the Kingdoms of the Earth, and He has Appointed Me to BUILD HIM A '''HOUSE IN JERUSALEM''', which is in JUDAH. Whoever there is Among You of ALL HIS PEOPLE, May the LORD HIS GOD be with Him, and let Him Go Up!'.' [2 Chronicles 36. 21, 22, 23.]

The Most Corrupt Dark Entities of the Dense Plane Worlds [ASSIAH and YETZIRAH] of this Planet Earth, who are NONE other than the Deranged Mind Existences, Invisibly Circulating around this Planet in Ethereal Frequencies with their Mutated Consciousness, Deceitfully operating as the PART and Parcel of the Collective Consciousness Dark Forces of the Material Minded Animalistic Passions, which were created as the Magnetic "THOUGHT FORMS" of Unfulfilled Desires of Human LUST, GREED and FALSE PRIDE over Long Periods of Evolutionary Time upon this Planet Earth, and have been thus Invisibly Operating since Ancient Times till Now, through the "GRAVEN IMAGES and ICONIC SYMBOLS" of the so called Man Made Venerated GODS and GODDESSES of the "ORGANIZED RELIGIONS" in the Evolving Human Races, in fact Did not wanted the LORD – GOD'S House to be REBUILT in JERUSALEM, which they had DECEITFULLY Taken Over Earlier, by Overpowering the Material Minds of the Evil Kings of His Chosen Race, so with their Deceitful Intention's, they also Overpowered the Enemies of LORD'S Chosen People as well as the Mind of King ARTAXERXES of PERSIA, and made Him Issue a Decree to Stop Rebuilding the House of GOD in JERUSALEM, regarding which the Holy Bible States:

'REHUM the Commander and SHIMSHAI the Scribe Wrote a Letter against JERUSALEM to King ARTAXERXES as Follows –

443

Let it be KNOWN to the King, that the JEWS who came Up from YOU have COME to US at JERUSALEM; THEY are REBUILDING the REBELLIOUS and EVIL CITY, and are FINISHING the WALLS and REPAIRING the FOUNDATIONS. Now let it be KNOWN to the KING, that if that CITY is REBUILT and the WALLS are FINISHED, they will NOT PAY TRIBUTE, CUSTOM or TOLL, and it will DAMAGE the REVENUE of the KINGS.

We inform the KING that if that City is REBUILT and the WALLS Finished, as a Result YOU will have NO POSSESSION in the Province beyond the RIVER.

Then the King Sent an ANSWER to REHUM the Commander, to SHIMSHAI the Scribe, and to the Rest of their Colleagues who Live in SAMARIA and in the Rest of the PROVINCES Beyond the RIVER: "Peace. And now the Document which YOU Sent to US has been Translated and Read before Me. And a DECREE has been ISSUED by ME, and a SEARCH has been Made and it has been DISCOVERED that, THAT CITY has RISEN Up against the KINGS in the PAST Days, that REBELLION and REVOLT have been PERPETRATED in it, that Mighty Kings have Ruled Over JERUSALEM, Governing all the PROVINCES beyond the RIVER, and that TRIBUTE, CUSTOM, and TOLL were PAID to THEM. So now ISSUE a DECREE to Make these Men 'STOP WORK', that the CITY may NOT BE REBUILT Until a Decree is ISSUED by Me. And BEWARE of Being NEGLIGENT in Carrying Out this Matter; WHY SHOULD DAMAGE INCREASE TO THE DETRIMENT OF THE KINGS?"

Then as soon as the COPY of King ARTAXERXES Document was read before REHUM and SHIMSHAI the Scribe and their Colleagues, they went in HASTE to JERUSALEM to the JEWS, and STOPPED them by FORCE OF ARMS. Then WORK on the HOUSE OF GOD in JERUSALEM Ceased, and it was STOPPED until the Second Year of the Reign of DARIUS King of PERSIA. [Ezra 4. 8, 12, 13, and Verses 16 to 24.]

Then they BURNED the "HOUSE OF GOD", and BROKE DOWN the Wall of
Jerusalem and Burned All its Fortified Buildings with FIRE, and DESTROYED
ALL ITS """"VALUABLE ARTICLES""""." [2 Chronicles 36. 19.]

The Great King Solomon also came to know about this Hidden Universal Fact, that the UNKNOWABLE LORD'S DESIRE MIND was DIFFERENTIATED in its 10 Major Aspects, which created the Universal TREE OF LIFE having 10 Major COSMIC DIMENSIONS, which were Known as the 10 HUGE UNFATHOMABLE COSMIC SPHERES of DIFFERENTIATED ETHEREAL VITALITY commonly referred to as the 10 WAY DIFFERENTIATED MIND CONSCIOUSNESS, which are known in the Hebrew Language as the "SEFIRAHS OR SEPHIROTS" of the UNIVERSAL TREE OF LIFE.

The Holy Bible, unknown to many Human Beings is a Collection of CODIFIED SPIRITUAL WISDOM having the Embedded Secrets of the UNIVERSAL MATRIX, which Contains in it the Wisdom of Dimensional Matrix Boundaries, a Number of Invisible HOSTS, and Various Other Evolving Visible and Invisible Kingdoms, Composed of Individualized BEINGS, and the Corporate Conscious "Soulless Existences" known as the "ENTITIES", the Information about which the Unknowable Creator LORD – GOD through HIS Humble PROPHETS, SEERS, and SAGES, Periodically Conveyed to HIS Chosen Race, which became their Grouped Compilations to exist as the Holy Texts, to be Known among the Incarnated Human Beings and their Corresponding Invisible Entities and Beings as the HOLY BOOK or the HOLY BIBLE.

These Holy Texts having Codified Wisdom of the Unknowable LORD – GOD, were meant for all the LORD'S Worshipers to Gradually DISCERN them with an UNDERSTANDING HEART in conjunction with their Evolving PERSONALITY CONSCIOUSNESS, which has been freed from the Material World Illusory Glamour in relationship with their Higher Conscious "SOUL" Mind, and which is also Part and Parcel of their ' Solar Consciousness'.

Thus looking at them through their SPIRITUAL EYES by Utilizing the Conscious Attributes of their INNER MINDS, and not just Looking at it with their Mere Physical Eyes, which are just a part and Parcel of their Lower Material Conscious "PERSONALITY MINDS", which Most Humans Constantly utilize during their Short Lived Incarnated Human Form Lives as their "Lower Mind Senses" Consciously Stuck in its ILLUSORY GLAMOUR, which affect them MOST in the Dense Physical Plane World, and they thus FOOLISHLY ACT just like All other Evolving Animal Species due to their Unquenchable ANIMAL PASSIONS, in which they stay Mentally Polarized during their Incarnated Form Lives upon this Planet Earth.

The Great King Solomon, Who Humbly Asked the Great LORD

GOD during His Incarnated life, for ONLY ONE DESIRED WISH of DISCERNMENT to UNDERSTAND "UNIVERSAL JUSTICE", which as per LORD'S Evolutionary Plan and Purpose is the True Basis of Spiritual Conscious Expansion, to be carried FORWARD CYCLICALLY upon this Planet Earth through Spiraling Motions of ACTIONS and REACTIONS, thus with LORD'S GRACE the Wise King Solomon Paid Close ATTENTION to the "MATHEMATICAL NUMBERS" which are the Basis of All GEOMETRIES, which SUBJECTIVELY and OBJECTIVELY Manifested LORD'S All DESIRE MIND CREATIONS in the VITAL ETHEREAL SPACE to be Known as the INFINITE UNIVERSE.

King Solomon then Further Found out, that the Mathematical Number "5" was of Utmost Importance as it was the Basis of the FIVE-FOLD UNIVERSAL MATRIX, which was Consciously Experienced by the Evolving Human Beings through their FIVE EMBODIED SENSES OF MIND, as well as this MATRIX was Similarly Experienced by their Counterpart Invisible Beings and Entities, who were Commonly Referred to as the LORD'S HOSTS, and are in fact a Countless Varieties of Hierarchical Servants of the "MOST HIGH" LORD – GOD, and they all were thus related to the BASIC UNIVERSAL NUMBER "5", which also Corresponded to the FIVE HOLY BOOKS OF MOSES, which are known to the Children of Israel as the 'HOLY TORAH', and are filed with LORD'S CODIFIED WISDOM, which apart from the Codified FACTS of the CREATION HISTORY, they repeatedly Stressed upon the KEEPING of LORD'S COMMANDMENTS, which HE Especially FORMULATED for the Children of Israel, the Evolving MEMBERS of HIS CHOSEN RACE.

Through Close Observations the Great King Solomon also found out that the Mathematical Number "5" Provided a FIVE POINTED Geometrical shape known as a "PENTACLE or a PENTAGON", with which the Ancient Egyptians, in their Numerous Symbolic Depictions represented the INNUMERABLE "STARS" OF THE CELESTIAL SKIES, and to soak their Beneficial Cosmic Energies they created their "Pentacle Shaped Amulets".

The Great King Solomon also UNDERSTOOD that all incarnated Human Beings of this Planet Earth also Possessed Not Just One, but FIVE BODIES, composed of their Related Dimensional ETHEREAL

MATTERS containing LIVE ELEMENTAL ESSENCES, all of which were of DIFFERENTIATED DENSITIES. And apart from the Dense Physical Body of a Human Being, which is composed of LIVE ELEMENTAL ESSENCES each having its own level of CONSCIOUS EXISTENCE, which form its DNA, CELLS, TISSUES, and VARIOUS BODY ORGANS, to EXIST in its Entirety as the Complete HUMAN FORM, which stay ANIMATED during its INCARNATED LIFE due to the VITAL CURRENTS which are constantly Provided to it through the Invisibly Connected VITAL SILVER CORD, the rest of other 4 Bodies are Generally INVISIBLE to the Human Eye, and Since Ancient Times these FIVE BODIES are known to SEERS and SAGES in HEBREW language as the Human Bodies of [1] NEFESH, [2] RUACH, [3] NESHAMAH, [4] CHAYAH, [5] YECHIDAH.

The Great King Solomon also came to know about this Hidden Universal Fact, that the UNKNOWABLE LORD'S DESIRE MIND was DIFFERENTIATED in its 10 Major Aspects, which created the Universal TREE OF LIFE having 10 Major COSMIC DIMENSIONS, which were Known as the 10 HUGE UNFATHOMABLE COSMIC SPHERES of DIFFERENTIATED ETHEREAL VITALITY commonly referred to as the 10 WAY DIFFERENTIATED MIND CONSCIOUSNESS, which are known in the Hebrew Language as the "SEFIRAHS OR SEPHIROTS" of the UNIVERSAL TREE OF LIFE.

Then King Solomon also Paying Close Attention to LORD'S HOLY WORDS as Instructed to His Great Ancestor MOSES, and written Down in the Chapter of LEVITICUS then found out, that when the 10 Major Aspects of LORD'S DESIRE MIND were Multiplied with this Universal Number of 5, which Originally Created the Five-fold Universal MATRIX required for the LORD'S Evolutionary Purposes of 'Conscious Expansion', it resulted to give the Mathematical Holy Number of 'FIFTY' [10 x 5 = 50], which through SPIRAL, CYCLIC, CIRCULAR Motions thus Completed the UNIVERSAL EVOLUTIONARY PROCESS, and the Great LORD knowing the Importance of this Resulted Mathematical Number '50', which Defined the Universal Evolutionary Completion in its Entirety, then through HIS Humble Servant MOSES Commanded the Children of Israel to Celebrate the 50th Year as a Year of Release from BONDAGE'S of the Dense Material World, and the 50th Year should be thus Considered as the "'HOLY YEAR OF JUBILEE'", regarding which the Holy Bible States:

'You are also to Count off SEVEN SABBATHS of YEARS for YOURSELF, SEVEN TIMES SEVEN YEARS, so that YOU have the TIME of SEVEN SABBATHS of YEARS, Namely Forty – Nine Years. You shall then Sound a Ram's Horn ABROAD on the Tenth Day of the SEVENTH MONTH; on the 'DAY OF ATONEMENT' YOU shall SOUND A HORN ALL THROUGH YOUR LAND.

You shall thus "CONSECRATE THE FIFTIETH YEAR" and "'PROCLAIM A RELEASE'" through the Land to 'ALL ITS INHABITANTS'. It shall be a ""'JUBILEE'"" FOR YOU, and EACH OF YOU shall RETURN TO 'HIS OWN PROPERTY', and EACH OF YOU shall RETURN TO 'HIS FAMILY'.

You shall have the 'FIFTIETH YEAR' as a "'JUBILEE'"; YOU shall NOT SOW, NOR REAP its After Growth, NOR Gather in from its UNTRIMMED VINES. For it is a "'JUBILEE'"; IT SHALL BE "'HOLY TO YOU'". You shall EAT its CROPS Out of the FIELD. On this Year of "JUBILEE" Each of YOU shall return to HIS Own Property.

If YOU make a Sale, Moreover, to Your Friend, or Buy from Your Friend's Hand, YOU SHALL "'NOT WRONG ONE ANOTHER'", CORRESPONDING to the Number of Years after the 'JUBILEE', you shall BUY from Your Friend; HE is to SELL to YOU according to the Number of Years of CROPS. In PROPORTION to the EXTENT of the YEARS YOU shall Increase its PRICE, and in PROPORTION to the FEWNESS of the YEARS, YOU shall DIMINISH its PRICE; FOR IT IS A "NUMBER OF CROPS" HE IS SELLING TO YOU.

So YOU shall "NOT WRONG ONE ANOTHER", but YOU shall "FEAR YOUR GOD"; FOR "'I'"AM THE "'LORD YOUR GOD'". You shall thus Observe 'MY STATUTES', and KEEP MY ""'JUDGMENTS'"", so as to Carry Them Out, that YOU may Live "'SECURELY'" on the Land.' [Leviticus 25. Verses 8 to 18.]

But Unfortunately in the Name of so called MODERN CIVILIZATION, which has been introduced upon this Planet Earth by the Visible and Invisible MOST CORRUPT, NOW RICHLY ORGANIZED AND POWERFUL ""'SOULLESS'" CORPORATE "'ENTITIES'", who in Fact are Powered by the

Unquenchable MATERIAL MINDED "GREED" of the Incarnated BEINGS, Many of the LORD'S IMPORTANT COMMANDMENTS are now Willfully Ignored By Most Human Beings during their Short Lived Incarnated Lives.

Because these CORRUPT "SOULLESS" ENTITIES Very Well know this UNDENIABLE FACT that the Evolving Human Beings Live their Incarnated DAILY LIVES in Various Lands based upon the "IMPORTANT FACTOR OF TIME", and these Corrupt ENTITIES existing as POWERFUL ORGANIZATIONS, who Willfully Back-Stabbed the LOVE and TRUST of their CREATOR LORD – GOD, then according to their DECEITFUL and ILLEGAL RUTHLESS AGENDAS, which are Totally Against the SPIRITUAL EVOLUTIONARY PLAN AND PURPOSE of the "MOST HIGH", in their First "EFFECTIVE ACTION" they first made 2000 years ago PLANETS EARTH TIME as "ZERO" AD, even when there were Many Time Calendars with Rich Heritage Already in Effect, so that their Evolving Evolutionary Consciousness over the Passing of Cyclic Time should For Sure Become the "LOST SOULS", and Unknowingly their Evolving Consciousness thus become PERMANENTLY Captives in the Illusory Glamour GRIP of these "Soulless Entities", and thus FORCED to become an INTEGRAL Part and Parcel of the Extended Arms of their CORRUPT EXISTENCES upon this Planet Earth.

Then King Solomon also Paying Close Attention to LORD'S HOLY WORDS as Instructed to His Great Ancestor MOSES, and written Down in the Chapter of LEVITICUS then found out, that when the 10 Major Aspects of LORD'S DESIRE MIND were Multiplied with this Universal Number of 5, which Originally Created the Five-fold Universal MATRIX required for the LORD'S Evolutionary Purposes of 'Conscious Expansion', it resulted to give the Mathematical Holy Number of 'FIFTY' [10 x 5 = 50].

And they Made a Proclamation throughout JUDAH and JERUSALEM to all the EXILES, that they should Assemble at JERUSALEM, and that whoever would not Come within Three Days, according to the COUNSEL of the LEADERS and the ELDERS, all His POSSESSIONS should be FORFEITED and He Himself EXCLUDED from the Assembly of the EXILES. [Ezra 10. 7, 8.]

The Secret of the Breast Plate
Part 85

When the Children of Israel, due to their Willful ABOMINATIONS against the MOST HIGH were taken in Captivity by the Chaldean King NEBUCHADNEZZAR, after He Destroyed the Walled City of JERUSALEM, the Chaldean King took them as the SLAVE - SERVANTS to BABYLON, and during those Difficult Times they finally Came Back to their Senses, and UTTERLY WEPT and CRIED to their Merciful LORD GOD for His KIND HELP, and HIS Graceful Intervention to FREE them Again, but this time from the Slavery Bondage's of BABYLON, like He Earlier FREED THEIR ANCESTORS from Egypt's Slavery during the Times of His Humble Servant MOSES.

The Great LORD Knowing full well, that just as the BEASTS of HIS Manifested WORLD having ANIMAL PASSIONS were HARD TO CONTROL due to their LOW LEVEL DESIRE MINDS polarized in MATERIAL WORLD DESIRES, similarly it was TRUE for His Created Human Beings, who during their Short Lived Incarnated Lives were Primarily having ANIMAL MIND PASSIONS, and thus for them, this Wise Statement was Absolutely True that the "OLD NATURE DIES HARD', Especially among all those Children of Israel, who by Continuously listening to their FALSE PROPHETS'S DREAM DIVINATION'S, then willfully Indulged in Abomination Rituals against Him, even when they were Time and Again WARNED by his CHOSEN Messengers and Prophets, and for this Very Reason they ALL thus Needed a Minimum time period of 70 Years for a New Generation of Children of Israel to COME UP, who may NOT thus INDULGE in those Abomination Rituals, which their FATHER'S before their CAPTIVITY were Foolishly Practicing along with their CORRUPT KINGS and their "GONE ASTRAY PRIESTHOOD" in HIS Sanctified Chosen Holy Place of JERUSALEM, as during those Difficult Times, a 70 Years Period was Normally Considered a TOTAL TIME PERIOD OF AN INCARNATED HUMAN LIFE upon this Physical Plane of Planet Earth, regarding which the Holy Bible states:

'As for DAYS OF OUR LIFE, they contain """"SEVENTY YEARS"""', or if due to Strength Eighty Years, YET their "PRIDE" is but LABOR and SORROW; FOR Soon it is GONE, and WE Fly AWAY.' [Psalms 90. 10.]

Thus Listening to the CRIES of the EXILES, the WORDS of LORD came to LORD'S CHOSEN PROPHET "JEREMIAH", who as per LORD'S COMMAND then sent a "LETTER OF HOPE" to all the EXILES in BABYLON, regarding which the Holy Bible States:

'Now these are the WORDS of the LETTER which JEREMIAH THE PROPHET Sent from JERUSALEM to the rest of the ELDERS of the EXILE, the PRIESTS, the PROPHETS, and all the PEOPLE whom NEBUCHADNEZZAR had taken into EXILE from JERUSALEM to BABYLON.'

'Thus Says the LORD of HOSTS, the GOD of ISRAEL, to all the EXILES whom "I" have Sent into EXILE from JERUSALEM to BABYLON, "Build Houses and Live in them; and Plant Gardens, and Eat their Produce. TAKE WIVES AND BECOME THE FATHERS OF "SONS AND DAUGHTERS", AND TAKE WIVES FOR YOUR SONS AND GIVE YOUR DAUGHTERS TO HUSBANDS, THAT THEY MAY BEAR "'SONS AND DAUGHTERS'"; AND MULTIPLY THERE AND DO NOT "'DECREASE'". And Seek the Welfare of the CITY WHERE "I" HAVE SENT YOU IN EXILE, and PRAY TO "LORD" on its BEHALF; FOR IN ITS "WELFARE YOU WILL HAVE WELFARE".

For thus Says the LORD OF HOSTS, the GOD OF ISRAEL, "DO NOT let YOUR PROPHETS who are in Your MIDST and YOUR DIVINERS DECEIVE YOU, and DO NOT LISTEN TO THE "DREAMS", which they DREAM. For they 'PROPHESY FALSELY' to "YOU IN MY NAME"; "I HAVE NOT SENT THEM", Declares the LORD.

For thus Says the LORD, "WHEN """SEVENTY YEARS"""" HAVE BEEN COMPLETED FOR BABYLON. "I" WILL VISIT YOU AND 'FULFILL MY GOOD WORD' TO YOU, TO BRING YOU BACK TO THIS PLACE. FOR "I" KNOW THE PLANS THAT "I" HAVE FOR YOU", Declares the LORD. "PLANS FOR WELFARE" AND NOT FOR CALAMITY TO "GIVE YOU A FUTURE AND A HOPE".

'Then YOU will CALL UPON ME and COME and PRAY TO ME, and "I" will LISTEN TO YOU. And YOU will SEEK ME and FIND ME, when 'YOU SEARCH FOR ME WITH ALL YOUR HEART. AND "I" WILL BE FOUND BY YOU', Declares the LORD, 'AND "I" WILL RESTORE YOUR FORTUNES, AND

WILL GATHER YOU FROM ALL NATIONS, AND FROM ALL THE PLACES, WHERE "I" HAVE DRIVEN YOU', Declares the LORD, 'AND "I" WILL BRING YOU BACK TO THE PLACE FROM WHERE "I" SENT YOU IN EXILE'.' [Jeremiah 29. 1, and Verses 4 to 14.]

Then Later On, after the passing over of ''''70 YEAR'S PERIOD''''' during the Reign of King ARTAXERXES of PERSIA, the Great LORD - GOD CHOSE a Humble Servant named "EZRA" son of SERAIAH, who was SCRIBE Skilled in the Commandments of the LORD, which were known in His Times as the "LAW OF MOSES", so that He Could again STIR UP the SLEEPING SPIRITS of the Children of Israel and their DESCENDANT CHILDREN, who over the Passing of Time got Carried Away in the DELUSIONS of this "ILLUSORY WORLD MATRIX" of the Dense Physical Plane, and willfully Rejected their "MOST HIGH" by Foolishly Indulging in those ABOMINATION RITUALS, about which their LORD – GOD through His Chosen PROPHETS, Time and Again Warned them.

With LORD'S Grace, the HOLY SPIRIT OF EZRA Made the Children of Israel feel REMORSE and thus CRY ALOUD About their WRONG DOINGS, which they had Foolishly Done Against their LORD'S COMMANDS, when they all with their Full Attention EMOTIONALLY Listened to Him with their Heavy Hearts Contemplating on His WORDS, which were related to LORD'S COMMANDS, which Temporarily Opened their Spiritual Eyes, regarding which the Holy Bible States:

'Now after these things, in the Reign of ARTAXERXES King of PERSIA, there went up "EZRA" Son of SERAIAH, Son of AZARIAH Son of HILKIAH.

This EZRA went up from Babylon, and He was a SCRIBE Skilled in the Law of MOSES, which the LORD GOD of Israel had Given; and the King Granted Him all He Requested because the 'HAND OF THE LORD HIS GOD' was Upon Him. And some of the Sons of Israel and Some of the Priests, the Levites, the Singers, the Gatekeepers, and the Temple Servants went up to Jerusalem in the Seventh Year of King ARTAXERXES. And He came to JERUSALEM in the Fifth Month, which was in the Seventh Year of the King.

For on the First of the First Month He began to go up from Babylon; and on the First of the Fifth Month He came to JERUSALEM, because the Good hand of His GOD was upon Him. For EZRA had Set His Heart to Study the Law, and to Practice it, and to TEACH His STATUTES and ORDINANCES in ISRAEL. [Ezra 7. 1, and Verses 6 to 10.]

'Now while EZRA was Praying and Making Confession, WEEPING and PROSTRATING Himself before the HOUSE of GOD, a Very Large Assembly, Men, Women, and Children, gathered to Him from Israel, for the "PEOPLE WEPT BITTERLY".

And SHECANIAH the Son of JEHIEL, one of the Sons of ELAM, answered and Said to EZRA, "WE have been "UNFAITHFUL TO OUR GOD", and have married Foreign Women from the Peoples of the Land; YET Now there is """HOPE"""" for Israel in SPITE of this. So now let us MAKE A COVENANT with our GOD to Put Away all the Wives and their Children, according to the Counsel of MY LORD and of those who TREMBLE at the COMMANDMENT of Our GOD; and let it be DONE According to the Law. ARISE! For this Matter is YOUR Responsibility, but WE will be with YOU; BE Courageous and Act."

Then EZRA Rose and Made the Leading PRIESTS, the LEVITES, and ALL ISRAEL, TAKE OATH that they would DO According to this Proposal; SO they TOOK THE OATH. Then EZRA Rose from Before the House of GOD and went into the Chamber of JEHOHANAN the Son of ELIASHIB. Although He went there, HE did Not EAT BREAD, Nor Drink WATER, for HE was MOURNING Over the "UNFAITHFULNESS OF THE EXILES".

And they Made a Proclamation throughout JUDAH and JERUSALEM to all the EXILES, that they should Assemble at JERUSALEM, and that whoever would not Come within Three Days, according to the COUNSEL of the LEADERS and the ELDERS, all His POSSESSIONS should be FORFEITED and He Himself EXCLUDED from the Assembly of the EXILES.

So all the Men of JUDAH and BENJAMIN assembled at JERUSALEM with in the THREE DAYS. It was the Ninth Month on the Twentieth of the Month, and all the People SAT in the OPEN SQUARE before the HOUSE of GOD, TREMBLING because of this Matter and the Heavy Rain. Then EZRA the Priest Stood Up and Said to them, "YOU have been UNFAITHFUL and have Married Foreign Wives ADDING TO THE GUILT OF ISRAEL. Now therefore Make CONFESSION to the LORD GOD OF YOUR FATHERS, and DO HIS WILL; and Separate YOURSELVES from the PEOPLES OF THE LAND and from the FOREIGN WIVES."

Then all the Assembly Answered and Said with a LOUD VOICE. "THAT'S RIGHT! AS YOU HAVE SAID, 'SO IT IS OUR DUTY TO DO.' But there are Many People, it is the RAINY SEASON, and we are not able to STAND in the OPEN. Nor can the TASK be DONE in One or Two Days. For WE HAVE "'TRANSGRESSED'' GREATLY IN THIS MATTER. Let Our LEADERS Represent the Whole Assembly and LET all those in OUR CITIES who have Married Foreign Wives Come at Appointed Times, together with the ELDERS and JUDGES of Each City, until the "FIERCE ANGER OF GOD" on Account of this Matter is TURNED AWAY from US. [Ezra 10. Verses 1 to 14.]

Chaldean King NEBUCHADNEZZAR, who took the Children of Israel as the SLAVE - SERVANTS to BABYLON.

Then NEHEMIAH, who was the GOVERNOR, and EZRA THE PRIEST AND
SCRIBE, and the LEVITES WHO TAUGHT THE PEOPLE, Said to ALL THE PEOPLE,
"This DAY is HOLY TO THE LORD YOUR GOD; Do Not MOURN or WEEP." For
All the PEOPLE were WEEPING when they HEARD the WORDS OF THE LAW.
[Nehemiah 8. 9.]

The Secret of the Breast Plate

Part 86

When the Chaldean King NEBUCHADNEZZAR Destroyed Jerusalem and took Most of the Children of Israel into Captivity, then there were a few JEWS Still left, who escaped and Survived their CAPTIVITY, but lived in Depleted State of GREAT FEAR AND DISTRESS, about which the GOOD KEEPERS of the LORDS COMMANDMENTS Bitterly WEPT and MOURNED, and such was a HUMBLE MAN Named NEHEMIAH, regarding whom the Holy Bible States:

'The Words of NEHEMIAH the Son of HACALIAH. Now it HAPPENED in the Month CHISLEY, in the Twentieth Year, while I was in "SUSA" the CAPITOL, that HANANI, one of My Brothers, and Some Men from JUDAH Came; and I asked them Concerning the JEWS who had ESCAPED and had SURVIVED the CAPTIVITY, and about JERUSALEM.

And they Said to ME, "THE REMNANT there in the PROVINCE who SURVIVED the CAPTIVITY are in GREAT DISTRESS and REPROACH, and the Wall of Jerusalem is BROKEN Down and its Gates are BURNED with FIRE". Now it came about when I heard these Words, I Sat Down and WEPT and MOURNED for Days; and I was FASTING and PRAYING before the GOD OF THE HEAVEN.

And I Said, "I Beseech THEE, O LORD GOD OF HEAVEN, THE GREAT AND AWESOME GOD, WHO PRESERVES THE COVENANT AND LOVING KINDNESS FOR THOSE 'WHO LOVE HIM' AND KEEP 'HIS COMMANDMENTS', Let THINE EAR Now be ATTENTIVE and THINE EYES OPEN to HEAR the PRAYER of THY SERVANT which I am Praying before THEE Now, Day and Night, on Behalf of the 'SONS OF ISRAEL' THY SERVANTS, Confessing the SINS of the Sons of Israel which WE have SINNED Against THEE; I and My Father's House have SINNED.'

We have ACTED Very CORRUPTLY Against THEE and have NOT KEPT THE COMMANDMENTS, NOR THE STATUTES NOR THE ORDINANCES WHICH THOU DIDST COMMAND THY SERVANT MOSES.

Remember the WORD which THOU Didst COMMAND THY Servant MOSES, Saying, "IF YOU ARE UNFAITHFUL "'I'" WILL SCATTER YOU AMONG THE PEOPLES' BUT IF YOU RETURN TO ME AND KEEP MY COMMANDMENTS AND DO THEM, THOUGH THOSE OF YOU WHO HAVE BEEN SCATTERED WERE IN THE "'MOST REMOTE PART OF THE HEAVENS", I WILL GATHER THEM FROM THERE AND WILL BRING THEM TO THE PLACE WHERE "I" HAVE CHOSEN TO CAUSE MY NAME TO DWELL".

And they are THY Servants and THY People WHOM THOU Didst Redeem by THY GREAT POWER and by THY STRONG HAND. O LORD I Beseech THEE, May THINE EAR be ATTENTIVE and THINE EYES OPEN to HEAR the PRAYER of THY SERVANT, and the Prayer of THY SERVANT'S Who DELIGHT to REVERE THY NAME, and Make THY Servant SUCCESSFUL Today, and GRANT Him COMPASSION before this Man." Now I was the Cup Bearer to the King. [Nehemiah 1.Verses 1 to 11.]

These Above Important Verses of the Holy Bible contain the CODIFIED UNIVERSAL WISDOM about the CREATOR 'LORD – GOD', and about ALL HIS CREATIONS, which Manifested to Exist as THE HIERARCHICAL ORDERS OF THE "ANGELIC HOSTS", about which obviously LORD'S Worshiper NEHEMIAH was Fully Aware of, as HE openly stated them Reverently Mainly in Two places of these Above Verses, the first being this Statement, which States, "Let THINE "'EAR Now be ATTENTIVE'" and THINE "'EYES OPEN to HEAR'" the PRAYER of THY SERVANT", which Clearly Explains this "HIDDEN FACT" that Contrary to the Human Beings, the Invisible Angelic Beings who are also having their "CONSCIOUS EXPANSION EVOLUTION" Parallel to the Human Beings upon this Planet Earth, they in an Opposite Way to the Evolving Human Beings INSTEAD Utilize their SENSORY PERCEPTIONS in Such a Way, with which they "SEE THE SPOKEN WORDS", and HEAR THE TONAL FREQUENCIES OF "WRITTEN WORDS" as well as Various OTHER TYPES OF "SYMBOLIC DEPICTIONS", so they can "'VISUALLY SEE'" THE SPOKEN PRAYERS AND CHANTING'S, and HEAR THE "FORMULATED OBJECTS".

And the Second being this Important Statement, which States, " THOUGH THOSE OF YOU WHO HAVE BEEN SCATTERED WERE IN THE "'MOST REMOTE PART OF THE HEAVENS", I WILL GATHER THEM FROM

THERE AND WILL BRING THEM TO THE PLACE WHERE "I" HAVE CHOSEN TO CAUSE MY NAME TO DWELL". This Particular Statement talks about the Lower Dimensional Sub Planes of ASSIAH and YETZIRAH, which Composed of Unlikable, Detestable, ROUGH and COARSER MATTER have been named in a Codified way by NEHEMIAH as the "'MOST REMOTE PART OF THE HEAVENS'".

During the Times of Nehemiah, the Scribe Priest EZRA with LORD'S Help, also fulfilled His role as a Humble Servant of the "MOST HIGH", to Wake Up the Descendant Children of Israel from their SPIRITUAL SLUMBER, Most of whom Returned to the PROMISED LAND From their 70 Year Exile in Babylon, and made them Willfully Comprehend and Fully Understand LORD'S COMMANDS, which were the HOLY WORDS OF THE LAW, just like about 800 Years before Him, His Great Ancestor MOSES with LORD'S Grace also Similarly Fulfilled His Role in the Wilderness to explain the WORDS of the LAW to the Children of Israel as per the LORD'S COMMAND.

When the People Gathered in the Square and ATTENTIVELY and Reverently Listened to the WORDS OF THE LAW, they Started WEEPING and CRYING, regarding which the Holy Bible States:

'And all the People gathered as ONE MAN at the SQUARE which was in front of the WATER GATE, and they Asked EZRA the SCRIBE to bring the "BOOK OF THE LAW OF MOSES", which the LORD had GIVEN to ISRAEL.

Then EZRA the Priest brought the LAW before the ASSEMBLY of MEN, WOMEN, and All Who Could LISTEN with UNDERSTANDING, on the First Day of the Seventh Month.

And He read from it before the SQUARE which was in Front of the Water Gate from Early MORNING UNTIL MIDDAY, in the Presence of Men and Women, those who could UNDERSTAND; and all the PEOPLE were Attentive to the "BOOK OF LAW". And EZRA the Scribe STOOD at a Wooden Podium which they had made for the PURPOSE. And beside Him stood MATTITHIAH, SHEMA, ANAIAH, URIAH, HILKIAH, and

MAASEIAH, on His Right Hand; and PEDAIAH, MISHAEL, MALCHIJAH, HASHUM, HASHBADDANAH, ZECHARIAH and MESHULLAM on His Left HAND.

And EZRA Opened the BOOK in the 'SIGHT OF ALL THE PEOPLE' for He was STANDING Above All the People; and when He OPENED it, ALL THE PEOPLE STOOD UP. Then EZRA Blessed the 'LORD THE GREAT GOD'. And All the People Answered "AMEN, AMEN!" while Lifting their Hands; THEN they BOWED LOW and WORSHIPED THE LORD with their FACES TO THE GROUND.

Also JESHUA, BANI, SHEREBIAH, JAMIN, AKKUB, SHABBETHAI, HODIAH, MAASEIAH, KELITA, AZARIAH, JOZABAD, HANAN, PELAIAH, and the LEVITES, Explained the LAW to the PEOPLE, while the PEOPLE Remained in their PLACE. And they Read from the Book, from the LAW OF GOD, TRANSLATING TO GIVE THE SENSE, SO THAT THEY UNDERSTOOD THE READING.

Then NEHEMIAH, who was the GOVERNOR, and EZRA THE PRIEST AND SCRIBE, and the LEVITES WHO TAUGHT THE PEOPLE, Said to ALL THE PEOPLE, "This DAY is HOLY TO THE LORD YOUR GOD; Do Not MOURN or WEEP." For All the PEOPLE were WEEPING when they HEARD the WORDS OF THE LAW.

Then He Said to them, "GO, Eat of the Fat, Drink of the Sweet, and Send PORTIONS to HIM WHO has NOTHING PREPARED; FOR this DAY IS HOLY TO OUR LORD. Do NOT be GRIEVED, for the JOY OF THE LORD IS YOUR STRENGTH".

So the LEVITES CALMED ALL THE PEOPLE, Saying, "BE Still, for the DAY IS HOLY, Do NOT BE GRIEVED". And All the PEOPLE Went Away to EAT, to Drink, to Send PORTIONS, and to CELEBRATE a GREAT FESTIVAL, because "'THEY UNDERSTOOD THE WORDS, WHICH HAD BEEN MADE KNOWN TO THEM"''. [Nehemiah 8. Verses 1 to 12.]

The Above Verses Clearly State that Most Children of Israel were unaware of the IN DEPTH Details of the "LAW OF GOD", and became Very Happy and Joyful when '"THEY UNDERSTOOD THE WORDS, WHICH HAD BEEN MADE KNOWN TO THEM'".

But it is NOT SO NOW in our Own Modern Times, in which Most of the Evolving Human Beings of this Planet are Now Able to READ and WRITE, and thus Can Easily READ their Holy Scriptures, but in the NAME OF SO CALLED "CIVILIZATION" which is now Primarily Composed of Various "SOULLESS EXISTENCES" KNOWN AS the Man Made Group FORMATIONS of Various Existence's, which exist in their formulated structures with "IMMENSE POWERS" given to them by the Evolving HUMAN BEINGS THEMSELVES, which are the Famous "CORPORATIONS, GOVERNMENTS, AND ORGANIZATIONS OF ALL TYPES", who now Directly or Indirectly Totally Control the Evolving Human Beings in their Evolutionary Daily Lives, who have thus NO TIME to READ IN DEPTH THEIR LORD'S GIVEN "CODIFIED WISDOM" and thus Properly Understand their Hidden Secrets.

We have ACTED Very CORRUPTLY Against THEE and have NOT KEPT THE COMMANDMENTS, NOR THE STATUTES NOR THE ORDINANCES WHICH THOU DIDST COMMAND THY SERVANT MOSES. [Nehemiah 1. 7.]

And an ANGEL OF THE LORD Appeared to Him, Standing to the Right of the
ALTAR OF INCENSE. And ZACHARIAS was TROUBLED when He Saw Him,
and FEAR GRIPPED Him. But the ANGEL Said to Him, "Do NOT be AFRAID,
ZACHARIAS, for YOUR Petition has been HEARD, and Your Wife ELIZABETH will
Bear YOU a SON, and YOU will Give Him the Name "'JOHN'". And YOU will have
JOY and GLADNESS, and MANY will REJOICE at His Birth. [Luke 1. 11 to 14.]

The Secret of the Breast Plate

Part 87

Most People of this Planet Earth, during their Short Lived Human Lives have ABSOLUTELY "No IDEA" as to WHAT IS THE MAIN DIFFERENCE BETWEEN A "LIVING BEING AND A LIVING ENTITY"?

And the Proper Answer to this Very Important Question is that ALL the Incarnated "BEINGS" having Personality and SOUL Consciousness, and thus Existing With or Without a "DENSE FORM BODY" are Just a TINY EXTENDED PART OF THEIR "SPIRITUAL MIND ETHEREAL VITALITY" having "SOUL CONSCIOUS VITAL ENERGIES", while ALL So Called "ENTITIES" are JUST "SOULLESS EXISTENCES", formulated by the Evolving Consciousness of "BEINGS" themselves, who acting in their Limited Capacity Roles as the CO – CREATORS within Certain Limitations and Boundaries, brought them into Existence by Utilizing their Vested Powers of Evolutionary MIND Consciousness.

And these Manifested 'ENTITIES' thus Formulated by the Desire Minds of Co – Creator BEINGS are then Constantly EMPOWERED by them to Consciously Exist as "SOULLESS CREATIONS" through the SUPPORT of the Vital Energy "THOUGHT FORMS" of these Manifested "BEINGS", who themselves are Created in the First Place by the DESIRE MIND Vital Energies of the UNKNOWABLE LORD – GOD.

The COMPUTERS and ALL Other Types of "ARTIFICIAL INTELLIGENCE'S" Similarly brought into Existence throughout the UNIVERSE are thus the Living Heartless ENTITIES, which can Interact in their LIMITED CAPACITIES with the Evolving CONSCIOUSNESS of LORD'S CREATION, which Consist of Only the "SOUL" BEINGS.

And ALL BEINGS are thus Subjectively and Objectively Manifested due to the DESIRE MIND VITAL FORCE ACTION of the UNKNOWABLE 'CREATOR – OBSERVER', the ONE AND ONLY MOST HIGH – THE LORD GOD OF THE INFINITE UNIVERSE, and HIS "GOVERNING ORDER OF DIVINITY" is Commonly Referred to be known in Spiritual Terms as the "GOD" by all the "Beings and Entities" of the Universe, who are Hierarchically placed in Differentiated Dimensional Spherical Levels Composed of Conscious and Unconscious Vital ELEMENTAL ESSENCES, who ACT according to their DIFFERENTIATED LEVELS OF ATTAINED "CONSCIOUSNESS EXPANSION", which Provide them Various Types of CONSCIOUS ATTRIBUTES to PERFORM their REQUIRED DUTIES acting as CO – CREATORS with VESTED POWERS, and according to HIS "MATHEMATICALLY and GEOMETRICALLY" induced EVOLUTIONARY PLAN AND PURPOSE, which is carried FORWARD in the VITAL ETHEREAL SPACE through the three Basic Universal Motions which are Understood as the SPIRAL, CYCLIC and CIRCULAR MOTIONS of VITAL ENERGY, which then through their interactions known as the ANGULAR MOVEMENTS thus created the GEOMETRIC FORMATIONS to Subjectively and Objectively MANIFEST as the GRAND ILLUSORY MATRIX, which Consciously keeps all Types of BEINGS Occupied during their Short Lived Cyclical Duration's, which are Commonly Known as the "LIFE PERIODS" of "PERSONALITY CONSCIOUS EXPANSION".

The Cyclic appearance of a Particular SOUL CONSCIOUSNESS to RE-MANIFEST itself again in the Dense Physical Plane, but with a Different PERSONALITY CONSCIOUSNESS embodied in a New Incarnated Dense Form Body, so as to Consciously Exist in the Differentiated Dimensional Planes of the SOLAR UNIVERSE as per the Evolutionary Plan and Purpose of Conscious Expansion, which in the Very Beginning was Put in Place by the Creator – Observer "MOST HIGH", is generally known as the "Reincarnation Process", as at the End of a "Cyclic Life Duration", the Evolving "PERSONALITY CONSCIOUSNESS" after its attained SPIRITUAL EXPERIENCES in the 3 Dense Plane Worlds of this Planet Earth, is then Supposed to Merge Back into its own "SOUL CONSCIOUS VITAL ENERGY SPHERICAL RESERVOIR, which since Ancient Times is known by the SEERS and SAGES in Hebrew Language as the "CHAYAH", and through this Consciousness MERGING then get DISSOLVED in it by Properly and thoroughly TINTING its Vital Ethereal Matter with its accumulated Spiritual Experience Homogeneously Diffused throughout it, which through the addition of Many Such Cyclic Experiences is known as the Gradual Conscious Expansion of the Evolutionary "SOUL MIND".

For the Attainment of Spiritual Experiences, the UNKNOWABLE LORD GOD thus WILLFULLY brought into MOTION the VITAL ETHEREAL

MATTER, which in its Entirety Composes the 'VITAL ETHEREAL SPACE', and thus HIS DESIRE MIND CONSCIOUS REFLECTIONS Formulated those Manifestations in it to Exist as the LIGHT and DARK Spirals to be known as a "GALAXY OF STAR SOLAR SYSTEMS", which are commonly termed as the MANIFESTATIONS of the "COSMOS" to Subjectively and Objectively Exist by the DESIRE MIND VITAL ENERGIES OF THE UNKNOWABLE "MOST HIGH".

The Cyclic appearance of a Particular SOUL CONSCIOUSNESS, which has been Considered as an ENLIGHTENED PROPHET of the "MOST HIGH" by the Evolving Human Races, thus to RE-MANIFEST itself in the Dense Physical Plane as per the Plan and Purpose of the LORD- GOD, but with a Different PERSONALITY CONSCIOUSNESS than His Earlier Birth, as His Earlier Manifested Personality Consciousness has been already Totally Dissolved in "CHAYAH BODY", and then again Reincarnated by being embodied in a New Incarnated Dense Form Body to Consciously Exist in the Differentiated Dense Dimensional Planes of this Planet EARTH, so that like His Earlier Efforts He can again SUPPORT the Conscious Expansion of LORD'S Chosen Race has been Clearly Mentioned in the HOLY BIBLE which is referred to as "THE ORACLE OF THE WORD OF THE LORD TO ISRAEL THROUGH "MALACHI", In which toward its End the LORD - GOD through MALACHI tells the Children of Israel about sending back ELIJAH'S Consciousness Among them, regarding which the Holy Bible States:

'Remember the LAW OF MOSES MY SERVANT, even the STATUTES and ORDINANCES which "I" Commanded Him in HOREB for all ISRAEL.

Behold "I" am Going to Send you 'ELIJAH the PROPHET' before the Coming of the Great and Terrible Day of the LORD.

And He will restore the Hearts of the Fathers to their Children, and the Hearts of the Children to their Fathers, LEST "I" COME and SMITE THE LAND with a CURSE.' [Malachi 4. Verses 4 to 6.]

And the Holy Bible Clearly Mentions that as per the GREAT LORD'S

HOLY WORDS Conveyed through MALACHI to the Children of Israel, the SPIRIT CONSCIOUSNESS OF 'ELIJAH' was REINCARNATED back upon this Physical Plane of Planet Earth as the "'PERSONALITY CONSCIOUSNESS OF JOHN THE BAPTIST'", regarding which it States:

'In the Days of HEROD, King of JUDEA, there was a Certain PRIEST Named ZACHARIAS, of the Division of ABIJAH; and He had a Wife from the Daughters of AARON, and Her Name was ELIZABETH. And they were both RIGHTEOUS in the Sight of GOD, Walking BLAMELESSLY in All the COMMANDMENTS and REQUIREMENTS of the LORD. And they had NO CHILD, because ELIZABETH was BARREN, and they were BOTH Advanced in YEARS.

Now it came about, while He was Performing His Priestly Service before GOD in the Appointed Order of His Division, according to the Custom of the PRIESTLY OFFICE, He was 'CHOSEN BY LOT' to Enter the TEMPLE OF THE LORD and BURN INCENSE. And the Whole Multitude of the PEOPLE were in PRAYER OUTSIDE at the HOUR OF INCENSE OFFERING.

And an ANGEL OF THE LORD Appeared to Him, Standing to the Right of the ALTAR OF INCENSE. And ZACHARIAS was TROUBLED when He Saw Him, and FEAR GRIPPED Him. But the ANGEL Said to Him, "Do NOT be AFRAID, ZACHARIAS, for YOUR Petition has been HEARD, and Your Wife ELIZABETH will Bear YOU a SON, and YOU will Give Him the Name "'JOHN'". And YOU will have JOY and GLADNESS, and MANY will REJOICE at His Birth.

For He will be GREAT in the SIGHT OF THE LORD, and He will Drink No Wine or Liquor; and He will be Filled with the HOLY SPIRIT, while YET IN HIS MOTHER'S WOMB. And He will Turn Back Many of the 'SONS of ISRAEL' to the "'LORD THEIR GOD'".

And it is HE Who will GO as a FORERUNNER before HIM in the "'SPIRIT and POWER'" of ""'ELIJAH'"", to TURN the HEARTS of the FATHERS back to the CHILDREN, and the DISOBEDIENT to the ATTITUDE of the RIGHTEOUS; SO as to MAKE READY a PEOPLE Prepared for the LORD".' [Luke 1. Verses 5 to 17.]

And it is HE Who will GO as a FORERUNNER before HIM in the "'SPIRIT and POWER'" of """'ELIJAH""", to TURN the HEARTS of the FATHERS back to the CHILDREN, and the DISOBEDIENT to the ATTITUDE of the RIGHTEOUS; SO as to MAKE READY a PEOPLE Prepared for the LORD".' [Luke 1.17.]

'For "I", THE LORD, Do Not CHANGE; therefore YOU, O Sons of JACOB, are "NOT CONSUMED". From the Days of YOUR FATHERS YOU HAVE TURNED ASIDE FROM "'MY STATUTES'", and HAVE NOT KEPT THEM. """RETURN to ME""", AND "'I'" WILL"'RETURN TO YOU'", Says the 'LORD OF HOSTS'. BUT YOU SAY, "'HOW SHALL WE RETURN?'"

"WILL A 'MAN' ROB "'GOD'"? YET YOU ARE ROBBING ME! BUT YOU SAY, "HOW HAVE WE ROBBED THEE?' IN "TITHES" AND "CONTRIBUTIONS".

YOU ARE CURSED WITH A """""CURSE""""", FOR YOU ARE ROBBING ME, THE WHOLE NATION OF YOU!!! [Malachi 3. Verses 6 to 9.]

The Secret of the Breast Plate

Part 88

Even when the Great LORD Reestablished Children of Israel back in the Promised Land after their 70 Years of Slavery in BABYLON, and with HIS Grace a Second Temple HOUSE OF LORD was Rebuilt in JERUSALEM, still the Undue CORRUPTION from the HEARTS of Many Thankless Members of HIS Chosen Race was Still NOT Totally REMOVED, Especially those who belonged to the PRIESTHOOD, about which the Great LORD - GOD Conveyed HIS Unhappiness to the Unworthy Children of Israel through MALACHI, known as the "'ORACLE OF WORD'", regarding which the Holy Bible States:

'The Oracle of the WORD of the LORD to ISRAEL through MALACHI. "I HAVE LOVED YOU", Says the LORD. But YOU Say, "HOW hast THOU LOVED US?" "WAS NOT ESAU JACOB'S BROTHER?" Declares the LORD. "YET I HAVE LOVED JACOB".'

"A Son HONORS His FATHER, and a SERVANT His MASTER. Then if "I" Am a FATHER, where is MY HONOR? And if "I" Am a MASTER, where is MY RESPECT? Says the LORD OF HOSTS to YOU, O Priests who DESPISE MY NAME. But YOU Say, "HOW have WE Despised THY NAME?" [Malachi 1, 2, 6.]

The Great LORD - GOD also Clearly CONVEYED to the Children of Israel through His Humble Servant PROPHET "ZECHARIAH" that HE wanted JERUSALEM to be "'THE CITY OF TRUTH'" upon this Planet Earth, where Everyone Living in HIS HOLY CITY was to be TRUTHFUL and HONEST to Each Other, as it was HIS Chosen Place to DWELL thus Manifested upon the Dense Physical Plane "ASSIAH" of this Planet EARTH, regarding which the Holy Bible States:

Then the WORD of the LORD of HOSTS came Saying, 'THUS Says the LORD OF HOSTS, "I AM EXCEEDINGLY JEALOUS FOR ZION, YES, WITH GREAT WRATH I AM JEALOUS FOR HER". Thus Says the LORD, "I WILL RETURN TO ZION AND WILL DWELL IN THE 'MIDST OF JERUSALEM'.

THEN JERUSALEM WILL BE CALLED THE 'CITY OF TRUTH', AND THE 'MOUNTAIN OF THE LORD OF HOSTS' WILL BE CALLED 'THE HOLY MOUNTAIN'.' [Zechariah 8. Verses 1 to 3.]

During the Time of the Second Temple, the CONDUCT of the PRIESTS, the Children of LEVI, toward their "MOST HIGH" became SO BAD, that the GREAT LORD was Left with Absolutely NO OTHER CHOICE but to CURSE them, which was an IRREMOVABLE CURSE which FINALLY Took its TOLL, when the LORD'S SECOND TEMPLE WAS ALSO DESTROYED, and has NOT BEEN REBUILT EVER SINCE THEN, EVEN UNTIL "NOW" in HIS Holy City of JERUSALEM, which HE Willfully Chose as a PLACE for HIS DWELLINGS, to be known upon this Planet Earth as a 'CITY OF TRUTH', regarding which the Holy Bible States:

'And NOW, this Commandment is for YOU, O PRIESTS. "IF YOU DO NOT TAKE IT TO "'HEART'" TO GIVE HONOR TO MY NAME", Says the LORD OF HOSTS, 'THEN "I" WILL SEND THE "CURSE UPON YOU", AND "I" WILL CURSE YOUR BLESSINGS; AND INDEED, "I" HAVE CURSED THEM """"ALREADY"""", BECAUSE YOU ARE NOT TAKING IT TO HEART.

BEHOLD,"I" AM GOING TO REBUKE YOUR "OFFSPRING", AND "I" WILL SPREAD REFUSE ON YOUR FACES, THE REFUSE OF YOUR FEASTS; AND YOU WILL BE TAKEN AWAY WITH IT.

THEN YOU WILL KNOW THAT "I" HAVE SENT THIS COMMANDMENT TO YOU, THAT MY COVENANT MAY CONTINUE WITH LEVI", Says the LORD OF HOSTS.

"MY COVENANT WITH HIM WAS ONE OF "'LIFE'" AND "'PEACE'", AND "I" GAVE "'THEM'" TO HIM AS AN """"OBJECT OF REVERENCE""""; SO HE REVERED ME, AND STOOD IN AWE OF MY NAME.' [Malachi 2. Verses 1 to 5.]

In these Most Important Verses of the Holy Bible, the Great LORD for the First Time HIMSELF, through MALACHI in a "'CODIFIED WAY'"

Mentioned Again the Importance of Both the Holy Objects of the "URIM" and the "THUMMIM", as being the "OBJECTS OF REVERENCE", as the GREAT LORD Clearly Stated to MALACHI by using the Plural WORDS "THEM", thus Saying 'AND "I" GAVE "'THEM'" TO HIM AS AN ""'OBJECT OF REVERENCE"'"'.

These Holy ""'OBJECTS OF REVERENCE"'"', which through HIS GRACE Provided HIS JUDGMENTS to the High Priest from the Tribe of "LEVI", so as to Continue "LIFE" and "PEACE" among the Incarnated Children of Israel, as the Word "URIM" meaning the "'LIGHT'" Provides "'LIFE'" to the Various Evolving Kingdoms Including the HUMAN BEINGS Incarnated upon this Planet EARTH, and the Word "'THUMMIM'" meaning "'PERFECTIONS'" Provides the True Harmony of "'PEACE'" among them.

And these above Verses in a Codified Way also Mention the Holy "ARK OF COVENANT", which was also the HOLY OBJECT OF REVERENCE for all the CHILDREN OF ISRAEL, whose PRESENCE Among them caused them to HUMBLY REVERE their LORD GOD, when their High Priest from the TRIBE of LEVI Reverently STOOD in its Presence, IN AWE OF HIS NAME in the HOLY OF HOLLIES.

The Great LORD further CONVEYED HIS Important Message to the PRIESTHOOD through His Humble Servant MALACHI, regarding which the Holy Bible States:

'TRUE Instruction was in His MOUTH, and UNRIGHTEOUSNESS was NOT FOUND on His LIPS; HE Walked with ME in PEACE and UPRIGHTNESS, and He TURNED Many BACK from INIQUITY.

For the LIPS OF A PRIEST should PRESERVE "'KNOWLEDGE'", and MEN should SEEK Instruction from His MOUTH; FOR HE IS THE "'MESSENGER'" OF THE 'LORD OF THE HOSTS'.

But as for YOU, You have TURNED ASIDE from the WAY; YOU HAVE CAUSED MANY TO STUMBLE BY THE INSTRUCTION; YOU HAVE

""""CORRUPTED""""" THE "COVENANT OF LEVI", SAYS THE 'LORD OF HOSTS'.

"So "'I'" also have MADE YOU 'DESPISED and ABASED' before ALL THE PEOPLE, JUST AS YOU ARE NOT KEEPING "'MY WAYS'", BUT ARE SHOWING "'PARTIALITY'" IN THE 'INSTRUCTION'."

DO WE NOT ALL HAVE ONE FATHER? HAS NOT """"ONE GOD""""" CREATED US? WHY DO WE DEAL TREACHEROUSLY EACH AGAINST HIS BROTHER SO AS TO "'PROFANE'" THE COVENANT OF 'OUR FATHERS'?' [Malachi Verses 6 to 10.]

The Great LORD by Utilizing the Services of HIS Humble Servant MALACHI through HIS ORACLE also ADMONISHED the CHILDREN OF HIS CHOSEN RACE, Commanding them to "'RETURN AND SURRENDER'", who having their Evolving PERSONALITY MINDS Polarized in the MATRIX OF ILLUSORY MATERIAL GLAMOUR of the DENSE PHYSICAL PLANE WORLDS, Especially of Both the "ASSIAH and YETZIRAH", thus became OVERWHELMINGLY GREEDY and Willfully Rejected the Commandments of their MOST BENEVOLENT LORD - GOD.

And Due to their Such Deranged Minds, they were willfully ROBBING THEIR LORD – GOD, the "MOST HIGH" of the UNIVERSE, regarding which the Holy Bible States:

'For "I", THE LORD, Do Not CHANGE; therefore YOU, O Sons of JACOB, are "NOT CONSUMED". From the Days of YOUR FATHERS YOU HAVE TURNED ASIDE FROM "'MY STATUTES'", and HAVE NOT KEPT THEM. """"RETURN to ME""""", AND "'I'" WILL"'RETURN TO YOU'", Says the 'LORD OF HOSTS'. BUT YOU SAY, "'HOW SHALL WE RETURN?'"

"WILL A 'MAN' ROB "'GOD'"? YET YOU ARE ROBBING ME! BUT YOU SAY, "HOW HAVE WE ROBBED THEE?' IN "TITHES" AND "CONTRIBUTIONS".

YOU ARE CURSED WITH A """"CURSE"""", FOR YOU ARE ROBBING ME, THE WHOLE NATION OF YOU!!!

Bring the "'WHOLE TITHE'" into the "'STOREHOUSE'", SO that there May be FOOD IN MY HOUSE, and "TEST ME NOW IN THIS",' Says the LORD OF HOSTS, "IF "'I'" WILL NOT OPEN FOR YOU THE WINDOWS OF 'HEAVEN', and "POUR OUT FOR YOU A BLESSING", UNTIL there is NO MORE NEED. Then "I" will REBUKE the "'DEVOURER'" for YOU, so that it may not DESTROY the FRUITS of the GROUND, NOR will YOUR VINE in the Field Cast its GRAPES", Says the LORD OF HOSTS. And all the NATIONS Will Call YOU 'BLESSED', for YOU SHALL be a "'DELIGHTFUL LAND'", Says the LORD OF HOSTS.

YOUR WORDS have been ARROGANT Against "ME", Says the LORD. 'YET YOU SAY, "WHAT HAVE WE SPOKEN AGAINST THEE?" You have Said, "IT IS VAIN TO SERVE "'GOD'"; AND WHAT PROFIT IS IT THAT 'WE' HAVE KEPT HIS CHARGE, AND THAT WE HAVE WALKED IN MOURNING BEFORE THE LORD OF HOSTS? So Now We Call the ARROGANT BLESSED; NOT ONLY are the DOERS of WICKEDNESS Built Up, but THEY also "'TEST'" GOD and ESCAPE."

Then THOSE WHO FEARED THE LORD SPOKE TO ONE ANOTHER, AND THE "'LORD'" GAVE 'ATTENTION' AND "'HEARD IT'", and a """"BOOK OF REMEMBRANCE"""" was "WRITTEN BEFORE HIM" for "'THOSE'" Who 'FEAR THE LORD', and Who 'ESTEEM HIS NAME'.

"'And THEY will be MINE'", Says the LORD OF HOSTS, "ON THE DAY THAT "'I'" PREPARE "MY OWN POSSESSION", AND "'I'" will "'SPARE THEM'", as a MAN SPARES HIS "OWN SON", WHO SERVES HIM. So YOU will Again DISTINGUISH between the RIGHTEOUS and the WICKED, between ONE who SERVES GOD, and ONE who DOES NOT SERVE HIM.' [Malachi 3. Verses 6 to 18.]

So the above Verses of the Holy Book Clearly COMMAND ALL HUMAN BEINGS, WHO Now being a Part and Parcel of Various Organized "SOULLESS STRUCTURES", known as the Living "ENTITIES" of the "'NEW

WORLD ORDER''', thus INNOCENTLY AND FOOLISHLY "CLAIM" TO FEAR THE LORD, as these Above Verses Command them to WILLFULLY '''RETURN AND SURRENDER''', All the Material World STOLEN MONIES WITH FULL RESPECT, which they being FILLED WITH ANIMAL MIND PASSIONS have ILLEGALLY AND DECEITFULLY Taken Away from HIM FOR THEIR OWN MATERIAL USE, AND THUS HAVE WILLFULLY ROBBED THEIR LORD – GOD, the "MOST HIGH" CREATOR – OBSERVER of the UNIVERSE.

The Performance of this '''RETURN AND SURRENDER''' Action by ALL as per the Above Verses of the Holy Bible is of UTMOST IMPORTANCE, If they also WANT to be Included in the MOST HOLY """"BOOK OF REMEMBRANCE""""", and thus ESCAPE the LOOMING PUNISHMENT, Which Awaits THEM after their PHYSICAL DEATHS.

'TRUE Instruction was in His MOUTH, and UNRIGHTEOUSNESS was NOT FOUND on His LIPS; HE Walked with ME in PEACE and UPRIGHTNESS, and He TURNED Many BACK from INIQUITY. For the LIPS OF A PRIEST should PRESERVE '''KNOWLEDGE''', and MEN should SEEK Instruction from His MOUTH; FOR HE IS THE '''MESSENGER''' OF THE 'LORD OF THE HOSTS'. But as for YOU, You have TURNED ASIDE from the WAY; YOU HAVE CAUSED MANY TO STUMBLE BY THE INSTRUCTION; YOU HAVE """""CORRUPTED""""" THE "COVENANT OF LEVI", SAYS THE 'LORD OF HOSTS'. [Malachi 2 Verses 6, 7, 8.]

[Depiction of the Destruction of the Second Temple of 70 AD]

"BEHOLD,"I" AM GOING TO REBUKE YOUR "OFFSPRING", AND "I" WILL SPREAD REFUSE ON YOUR FACES, THE REFUSE OF YOUR FEASTS; AND YOU WILL BE TAKEN AWAY WITH IT. THEN YOU WILL KNOW THAT "I" HAVE SENT THIS COMMANDMENT TO YOU, THAT MY COVENANT MAY CONTINUE WITH LEVI", Says the LORD OF HOSTS."

"MY COVENANT WITH HIM WAS ONE OF "'LIFE'" AND "'PEACE'", AND "I" GAVE "'THEM'" TO HIM AS AN """"OBJECT OF REVERENCE""""; SO HE REVERED ME, AND STOOD IN AWE OF MY NAME.' [Malachi 2. Verses 1 to 5.]

477

"But as for ME, this MYSTERY has NOT Been REVEALED to Me for Any WISDOM Residing in ME More than in Any Other Living Man, but for the Purpose of Making the Interpretation Known to the King, and that YOU MAY UNDERSTAND THE THOUGHTS OF YOUR MIND." [Daniel 2.30.]

The Secret of the Breast Plate

Part 89

Most People, WHO during their Short Lived Incarnated Lives, under the Tight Grip of Illusory Material World Glamour, thus Foolishly WASTE their Entire Life Time Period Totally ENTANGLED in Physical World Aspects, which are related to its Mundane Worldly affairs, rather than their EVOLUTIONARY GOAL of SPIRITUAL Consciousness expansion of their "ETHEREAL CHAYAH BODY" [CAUSAL BODY], and they Innocently do such Grave MISTAKE, because they are TOTALLY UNAWARE OF THIS "UNIVERSAL FACT" that their "Physical Body Form Existence" in the Dense Dimensional Plane World of ASSIAH is Incarnated Only for the Main Purpose of their 'CHAYAH BODIES "ETHEREAL MATTER" CONSCIOUS EXPANSION', Which as per the Evolutionary Plan and Purpose is related to the DESIRE MIND REFLECTIONS OF THE "UNKNOWABLE MOST HIGH", WHO IS THE LORD GOD OF THE ENTIRE UNIVERSE, and for this Very Reason, as per the Evolutionary Plan and Purpose of the MOST HIGH, their Evolving "SOUL MIND" has sent a Very Tiny Portion of its Own Vital Ethereal Matter as its "CONSCIOUS EXPANSION INVESTMENT" in the Dense Physical Plane World of this Planet Earth, to Temporarily exist as the "PERSONALITY MIND CONSCIOUSNESS" Embodied in an Incarnated Human Form for a SHORT and Limited DURATION, so that through its SPIRITUAL ACTIONS and REACTIONS in Physical World, it can achieve its SPIRITUAL GOALS by attaining the REQUIRED SPIRITUAL EXPERIENCES in the Dense Dimensional worlds of this Planet Earth.

But if the Incarnated Human Being after being Born with an INDIVIDUALIZED PERSONALITY MIND in the Dense Physical Plane Forgets His SPIRITUAL GOAL, and gets His Desire MIND Entangled in the Illusions and Delusions of the Material World Glamour, which are Related to His Lower or the ANIMAL MIND PASSIONS, then it can Negatively Affect His RUACH Body [Astral Body], which Exists in the Magnetic or the IONIZED Dimensional Plane of YETZIRAH, and if He continues to Stay PERSISTENTLY POLARIZED in these UNQUENCHABLE DESIRES of the LOWER MIND then He unknowingly can Permanently MALIGN His RUACH BODY [Astral Body also known as Dream Zone Body], and Eventually Cause the "Evolving SOUL" to Permanently LOOSE its Segmented INVESTMENT, and then gets SEVERED as "POLARIZED

PERSONALITY" to Slowly Degenerate by becoming a GHOST or an UNDEAD BEING, and then for its Unquenchable "WANTS and NEEDS" to be Illegally Captured by Ruthless and Deceitful BLACK MAGICIANS, who through LEFT HAND PRACTICES are SIMILARLY STUCK THEMSELVES FOREVER in the Dense Dimensional Plane Worlds, and in Many Rare Cases if the "PERSONALITY MIND CONSCIOUSNESS" Embodied in an Incarnated Human Form Becomes Totally "EVIL" in the Physical Plane World, Creating those Actions and Reactions which are Totally Contrary to the Spiritual Agendas of ITS HIGHER SELF, known to all as the "SOUL", then it may also Negatively affect the VITAL AREA OF THE "CHAYAH BODY", where it is connected at the STARTING POINT in the Higher Dimensional Plane of BRIAH with the Extending SILVER CORD of Vitality, which Connects all the Manifested Bodies of a Human Being with it, which Exist Manifested in the 3 Dense Dimensional Plane Worlds of this Planet Earth.

The Densifying of this CHAYAH MATTER is known as the "HARDENING OF THE SACRED HEART", and due to the HARDENING of the "VITAL AND CONSCIOUS" ETHEREAL MATTER which in fact Belongs to the YECHIDAH Body, Which is the "HIGHEST BODY CONTAINER OF THE PURE SOLAR CONSCIOUSNESS", then that Particular PORTION OF ETHEREAL MATTER in the CHAYAH BODY will also Get Permanently DETACHED from the CHAYAH BODY, Causing AN IRREPARABLE DAMAGE TO THE EVOLVING "SOUL" and thus Suffer the Dreadful CONSEQUENCES for a Very LONG PERIOD OF TIME, which for the "REMAINING DAMAGED SOUL" also Seems Like a PUNISHMENT PERIOD OF "ETERNITY".

The UNKNOWABLE and GREAT LORD – GOD being the CREATOR – OBSERVER of this GRAND EXPERIMENT thus KNOWING ALL THESE IMPORTANT FACTS PERTAINING TO THE REOCCURRING "STUMBLING OF THE EVOLVING HUMAN BEINGS" has thus the "MOST PATIENCE", which is Commonly termed as HIS "MERCY" toward HIS Manifested Creations, so that HIS Created BEINGS having "SOUL CONSCIOUSNESS" according to the EVOLUTIONARY PURPOSES of their CREATOR LORD, thus going through the CYCLIC INCARNATIONS in the DENSE DIMENSIONAL PLANES of this Planet Earth, can Properly Achieve their DESIRED SPIRITUAL GOALS, and to the LORD'S HUMBLE SERVANT, HIS CHOSEN PROPHET DANIEL many Such Mysteries were Revealed by LORD'S GRACE, so that DANIEL and His Friends can Save themselves from Such Destruction, when they were in the Service of Chaldean King NEBUCHADNEZZAR in the Land of SHINAR, [The Word "CHALDEAN" Denoted those People of BABYLON who were Willfully involved in the LEFT HAND Ritual Practices glorifying the INVISIBLE SOULLESS ENTITIES, AND THEIR INVISIBLE FOLLOWERS; THE BLACK MAGICIANS AND INNUMERABLE HOST'S OF "UNDEAD BEINGS"], regarding which the Holy Bible States:

'Now in the Second Year of the Reign of NEBUCHADNEZZAR, NEBUCHADNEZZAR had "DREAMS"; AND His "'SPIRIT'" was TROUBLED, and His SLEEP Left Him. Then the King Gave Orders to call in the MAGICIANS, the CONJURERS, the SORCERERS, and the CHALDEAN'S, to tell the King His Dreams. So they Came in and Stood before the King. And the King Said to them, " I HAD A DREAM, and My SPIRIT is ANXIOUS to Understand the DREAM".

The Chaldean's Answered the King and Said, "There is NOT A MAN ON EARTH Who could Declare the Matter for the King in as much as No Great King or Ruler has Asked anything like this of any MAGICIAN, CONJURER, OR CHALDEAN. Moreover, the thing which the King Demands is Difficult, and there is NO ONE ELSE who could Declare it to the King Except "GODS", Whose Dwelling Place is NOT with "MORTAL FLESH"."

Because of this the King became INDIGNANT and Very FURIOUS, and Gave Orders to DESTROY All the WISE MEN OF BABYLON.

Then DANIEL went to His House and informed His Friends HANANIAH, MISHAEL, and AZARIAH about the Matter, in order that they might Request "COMPASSION" from the GOD OF HEAVEN Concerning this MYSTERY, so that DANIEL and His Friends might NOT be DESTROYED with the Rest of the Wise Men of BABYLON. Then the MYSTERY was REVEALED to DANIEL in a NIGHT VISION.

Then DANIEL Blessed the GOD OF HEAVEN; DANIEL Answered and Said, "LET the Name of GOD be BLESSED FOREVER and EVER, for WISDOM and POWER Belong to HIM. And it is HE WHO Changes the "TIMES and the EPOCHS"; HE REMOVES KINGS AND ESTABLISHES KINGS; HE Gives WISDOM to WISE MEN, and KNOWLEDGE to MEN of UNDERSTANDING. It is HE WHO "REVEALS the PROFOUND and HIDDEN THINGS"; HE KNOWS WHAT IS IN THE "DARKNESS", and the LIGHT DWELLS WITH HIM.

To THEE, O GOD of MY FATHERS, I Give THANKS and PRAISE, For THOU hast Given Me 'WISDOM and POWER'; EVEN Now THOU hast Made KNOWN TO ME What We Requested of THEE, FOR THOU hast Made Known to US the King's MATTER."

DANIEL Answered before the King and Said, "AS for the MYSTERY about which the King has Inquired, Neither WISE Men, CONJURERS, MAGICIANS, Nor DIVINERS are Able to Declare it to the KING. However, there is a 'GOD in HEAVEN' Who Reveals MYSTERIES, and HE Has made Known to King NEBUCHADNEZZAR what will take Place in the LATTER DAYS. This was YOUR DREAM and the VISIONS in YOUR MIND while on Your BED. As for You, O King, While on Your BED Your THOUGHTS Turned to what would Take Place in the FUTURE; and HE Who Reveals MYSTERIES has made Known to YOU what will Take Place.

But as for ME, this MYSTERY has NOT Been REVEALED to Me for Any WISDOM Residing in ME More than in Any Other Living Man, but for the Purpose of Making the Interpretation Known to the King, and that YOU MAY UNDERSTAND THE THOUGHTS OF YOUR MIND. [Daniel 2. 1, 2, 3, 10, 11, 12, 17, 18, 19, 20, 21, 22, 23, 27, 28, 29, 30.]

The Great LORD also INSPIRED HIS Chosen PROPHET EZEKIEL, in a Codified Way about HIS WISDOM OF "MERCY", regarding which the Holy Bible States:

'Therefore thus SAYS the LORD GOD, "NOW "I" Shall RESTORE the FORTUNES of JACOB, and have MERCY on the 'WHOLE HOUSE OF ISRAEL'; and "I" shall be Jealous for MY HOLY NAME.

And they shall FORGET their DISGRACE and their TREACHERY which THEY "PERPETRATED"AGAINST "'ME'", when they LIVE SECURELY on their OWN LAND with NO ONE to Make them AFRAID.

When "I" Bring them BACK from the PEOPLES and GATHER them from the LANDS of their ENEMIES, then "I" shall be Sanctified through them in the SIGHT OF MANY NATIONS. Then they will know that "I AM THE LORD THEIR GOD, BECAUSE I MADE THEM GO INTO EXILE AMONG THE NATIONS, AND THEN GATHERED THEM AGAIN TO THEIR OWN LAND; AND 'I' WILL LEAVE 'NONE OF THEM' ANY LONGER. AND 'I' WILL NOT HIDE 'MY FACE' FROM THEM 'ANY LONGER', FOR 'I' SHALL HAVE "'POURED OUT MY SPIRIT'" ON THE "'HOUSE OF ISRAEL'", Declares the LORD GOD.' [Ezekiel 39. Verses 25 to 29.]

'Therefore thus SAYS the LORD GOD, "NOW "I" Shall RESTORE the FORTUNES of JACOB, and have MERCY on the 'WHOLE HOUSE OF ISRAEL'; and "I" shall be Jealous for MY HOLY NAME. And they shall FORGET their DISGRACE and their TREACHERY which THEY "PERPETRATED"AGAINST "'ME'", when they LIVE SECURELY on their OWN LAND with NO ONE to Make them AFRAID. [Ezekiel 39. Verses 25, 26.]

Many People are Still UNAWARE of this BIBLICAL FACT, that when MOSES was on the Holy Mountain of GOD, there with LORD'S GRACE He witnessed the "SEVEN HOLY FLAMES" of the "LORD GOD" as the BLAZING FIRE Appearing as the FLAMES from the MIDST OF A BUSH, of which ONE FLAME was in the Center and THREE FLAMES were on its One Side and the OTHER THREE FLAMES were on its OTHER SIDE, which even Burning did not Consume the BUSH.

The Secret of the Breast Plate

Part 90

The "MOST HIGH" LORD GOD of the CHILDREN of ISRAEL, being the One and ONLY CREATOR – OBSERVER LORD OF THE ENTIRE UNIVERSE is also known to HIS Chosen Humble Servants and all HIS HOSTS Including the PROPHETS, MESSENGERS, SEERS, and SAGES as the "GREAT LORD OF FLAMES".

The MOST HIGH is known as the GREAT LORD OF FLAMES for this PRIMARY REASON, that All Types of Manifested Visible and Invisible "SOUL BEINGS" existing With or Without Dense Forms in the Differentiated Dimensional Spheres of the Subjectively and Objectively Manifested UNIVERSE, having their Various Attained levels of EVOLUTIONARY VITAL CONSCIOUSNESS, are just the TINY SPARKS of HIS 'FLAMING' DESIRE MIND'S "INNUMERABLE CONSCIOUS REFLECTIONS", which are Part and Parcel of the 7 MAIN FLAMES of HIS ETHEREAL VITALITY, Which so appear in their SEVEN MAIN DIFFERENTIATION'S due to the 7 way Mathematically Differentiated Permutations and Combinations of HIS DESIRE MIND, which gets Differentiated in such a Way due to the 'Constant Mathematical Interactions' of the three Universal Energy Motions [Spiral, Cyclic, and Circular], which Create the so called "CONCEPT OF TIME" in the Vital Ethereal Unfathomable Space of the COSMOS, which is Commonly termed since Very Ancient Times by the Seers as the Huge Infinite Universe.

To Spiritually Understand the MOST DEEP AND IMPORTANT SECRET OF THE UNIVERSE, by Utilizing the HIGHEST Faculty of Our Inner Mind, If We Just Give Mathematical Numbers to the Three Basic Universal Motions, Starting with the Spiral Motion as "1", Circular Motion as "2", and Cyclic Motion as "3", in their Proper Mathematical and Geometrical Order which Exist in the VITAL ETHEREAL MATTER as the Universal MOTION FORCES started as "FREQUENCY VIBRATIONS" to be Conducted in the Ethereal Space by the Desire Mind Actions of the GREAT LORD - GOD, because after the Completion of A GREAT CYCLE represented by Mathematical number '3', then Only a New SPIRAL with Mathematical Number '1' Can Start Again, for the Purpose of New Subjective and Objective Manifestations in the Vital Ethereal Space of COSMOS, and then through their Mathematical and Geometrical Interaction Combinations known as the "PERMUTATIONS AND COMBINATIONS in the Vital Ethereal Space, they create 4 More FLAMING OUTBURSTS, thus to form a New Set of Total 7 ETHEREAL FLAMES OF VITALITY, which can be Spiritually Observed as the 7 Mathematical Combinations of the 3 Intersecting Basic Motions to Mathematically exist as the Blazing Flame Frequencies of "1","2","3", "1+2", "1+3", "2+3", and "!+2+3" only and No More.

If we Consider these to be a Pattern of their CLOCK WISE MOTIONS, then in an ANTI CLOCK WISE MOTION Concept their Permutation Combination results will still be the same as the "SEVEN" Flaming Combinations, and thus No Different than the Original Number "7", which Pertains to the 7 way Differentiated DESIRE MIND VITAL CONSCIOUS REFLECTIONS OF THE CREATOR – OBSERVER LORD GOD OF THE UNIVERSE thus Appearing like the 7 Holy Flames of BLAZING FIRE.

The Holy Bible in the Very Start of its Very First Chapter, known as the "CHAPTER OF GENESIS" [CREATION] in a Codified way explains the DESIRE MIND WORKINGS OF THE "MOST HIGH" as HIS 7 WAY DIFFERENTIATED DESIRE MIND ACTIONS to start the Grand Experiment of CONSCIOUS EXPANSION UPON THIS PLANET EARTH, regarding which the Holy Bible States:

'Thus the HEAVENS and the EARTH were Completed, and ALL THEIR "HOSTS". And by the SEVENTH DAY GOD COMPLETED HIS WORK which HE had DONE; and HE RESTED on the SEVENTH DAY from HIS work which HE had DONE. Then GOD Blessed the SEVENTH Day and SANCTIFIED it, BECAUSE in it HE Rested from All HIS Work which GOD had CREATED and MADE.' [Genesis 2. Verses 1 to 3.]

For this Very reason the GREAT LORD OF FLAMES is also known to the PROPHETS, MESSENGERS, SEERS, and SAGES as the "GREAT LORD OF SABBATH", and that is why the "MOST HIGH" also Commanded the Children of Israel, to Observe the SABBATH by following HIM in HIS FOOTSTEPS, because they being the Members of HIS Chosen Race and vested with Limited Powers of "INDIVIDUALIZED PERSONALITY MINDS" should wisely act as the CO – CREATORS in their Human Forms during their Incarnated Life Duration's in the Dense Physical Plane World of ASSIAH, which has been Manifested by LORD'S DESIRE MIND for them upon this Planet Earth, regarding which the Holy Bible States:

'And YOU shall SOW Your Land for SIX Years and GATHER in its YIELD, but on the SEVENTH Year YOU shall let it REST and LIE FALLOW, so that the NEEDY OF YOUR PEOPLE MAY EAT; and whatever they LEAVE, the BEAST of the FIELD MAY EAT. You are to do the SAME with YOUR VINEYARD and YOUR OLIVE GROVE.

SIX Days YOU are to DO YOUR WORK, But on the SEVENTH Day YOU shall CEASE from LABOR in Order that YOUR OX and YOUR DONKEY may REST, and the Son of YOUR Female SLAVE, as well as YOUR STRANGER, may REFRESH THEMSELVES.

Now Concerning EVERYTHING Which "I" have Said to YOU, BE ON YOUR GUARD; and DO NOT MENTION THE NAME OF OTHER "GODS", "NOR LET BE HEARD FROM YOUR MOUTH". [Exodus 23. Verses 10 to 13.]

The Above Verses also Clearly Explains that by the Time of EXODUS of Children of Israel Freed from their Slavery Bondage's of EGYPT upon this Planet Earth, Many of the "INVISIBLE HOSTS" who were Part of the LORD'S Creations which also included the HEAVENS and the EARTH, by Willfully MISUSING THEIR VESTED POWERS BECAME "TOTALLY CORRUPT", and thus for the Advancement of their DARK AGENDAS Started Illegally Maneuvering in a DECEITFUL WAY the COLLECTED THOUGHT FORM Energies of the Human Beings, which came in manifestation due to their Emotional Sentiments and Desired Feelings toward their so called MAN MADE GODS AND GODS IDOLS AND GRAVEN IMAGES Elaborately Installed in their Temples of Worship, and thus Utilizing these INVISIBLE ENERGIES illegally controlled the evolving Minds of Innocent Human Beings, to Propagate their OWN DECEITFUL AGENDAS Upon this PLANET EARTH against the Established Plan and Purpose of the "MOST HIGH", which Culminated to Manifest as the WRONGFUL "LEFT HAND PRACTICES" which were ILLEGALLY Carried Out in those Lands where the MAN MADE IDOLS of "GODS AND

GODDESSES" were Installed to be Worshiped, and then in those Lands, the Resident People including the Children of Israel during their Slavery Period in EGYPT laboriously worked all the 7 Days a Week.

The Great LORD in a Codified Way shared the Hidden Universal Wisdom with the Children of Israel as HIS COMMANDMENTS through HIS Humble Servant MOSES, in which the Seven Differentiated Vital Energies of HIS DESIRE MIND having the Attributes of Differentiated Consciousness, HE Equated them to the SEVEN Days of the Physical Plane World of this Planet Earth to be Celebrated among HIS CHOSEN PEOPLE AT HIS CHOSEN PLACE, which came to be known as the FAMOUS CITY OF JERUSALEM, and the Three Universal Motions, HE Equated with the Three Main Seasonal Movements, which Periodically took Place during THREE TIMES in a YEAR, regarding which the Holy Bible States:

'SEVEN DAYS YOU SHALL CELEBRATE a FEAST TO THE LORD YOUR GOD in the PLACE which the LORD CHOOSES, because the LORD YOUR GOD will BLESS YOU in ALL YOUR PRODUCE and in ALL THE WORK OF YOUR HANDS, so that YOU SHALL BE ALTOGETHER JOYFUL.

THREE TIMES IN A YEAR ALL YOUR MALES SHALL APPEAR BEFORE THE LORD YOUR GOD in the PLACE which HE CHOOSES, at the FEAST OF UNLEAVENED BREAD, and at the FEAST OF WEEKS and at the FEAST OF BOOTHS, and THEY shall NOT APPEAR Before the LORD EMPTY – HANDED.' [Deuteronomy 16. 15, 16.]

Many People are Still UNAWARE of this BIBLICAL FACT, that when MOSES was on the Holy Mountain of GOD, there with LORD'S GRACE He witnessed the "SEVEN HOLY FLAMES" of the "LORD GOD" as the BLAZING FIRE Appearing as the FLAMES from the MIDST OF A BUSH, of which ONE FLAME was in the Center and THREE FLAMES were on its One Side and the OTHER THREE FLAMES were on its OTHER SIDE, which even Burning did not Consumed the BUSH, regarding which the Holy Bible States:

'Now MOSES was Pasturing the Flock of JETHRO His Father – in – Law, the Priest of MIDIAN: and He Led the Flock to the West Side of the Wilderness, and Came to HOREB, the MOUNTAIN OF GOD. And the Angel of the LORD appeared to Him in a BLAZING FIRE from the MIDST of the BUSH; and He Looked, and Behold, the BUSH was BURNING with FIRE, yet the BUSH was NOT CONSUMED. So MOSES Said, "I Must Turn aside Now, and SEE this MARVELOUS SIGHT, why the BUSH is NOT BURNED UP." When the LORD Saw that He Turned Aside to LOOK , GOD Called to Him from the MIDST of the BUSH, and Said, "MOSES, MOSES!" And He Said, "HERE I AM"." [Exodus 3. Verses 1 to 4.]

And regarding MOSES witnessing the "SEVEN HOLY FLAMES" of the "LORD GOD" appearing as the FLAMES of the BLAZING FIRE in the MIDST OF the Burning BUSH upon the Mountain, the Great LORD Clearly REMINDED Him about it during HIS Command of Making the GOLDEN LAMP-STAND with the Seven Flames, regarding which the Holy Bible States:

'AND SEE THAT YOU MAKE THEM AFTER THE '''PATTERN''' FOR THEM, '''''WHICH WAS SHOWN TO YOU ON THE MOUNTAIN'''''." [Exodus 25. 40.]

Thus When Later on the "MOST HIGH", who is the Great "LORD OF FLAMES" Commanded MOSES to Make the GOLDEN LAMP STAND to have SEVEN LAMPS representing HIS SEVEN WAY DIFFERENTIATED "DESIRE MIND" VITAL ENERGY CONSCIOUS REFLECTIONS appearing like the 7 LIMB FLAMES of the BLAZING FIRE, which in a Codified Way also Represent the 7 Active Branches of the TREE OF LIFE IN OUR SOLAR UNIVERSE acting as the 7 Main Vital Energy Distribution Systems, and thus affect the Conscious Evolution of Spiritual Mind upon this Planet Earth, which the Great King Solomon Wisely Understood as the VITAL ENERGIES OF THE SEVEN PLANETARY SCHEMES, with the Solar SUN having its GOLDEN ENERGIES being in its Middle Center, and the Saturn, Jupiter and Mars as part of its 3 Branches on its one side and Venus, Mercury and Moon existing as its 3 Branches on the Other side, and their Synthesizing energy interactions and Reactions depicted in a Codified way as its Cups, its Bulbs and its Flowers, while the 7 Flames of the Lamp-stand themselves represented the 7 WAY SPLIT LORDS

DESIRE MIND VITAL CONSCIOUSNESS, representing their Differentiated Tinting Vital Energies manifested through their Subjective and Objective Celestial Bodies.

Thus the Golden Lamp-stand was to have the Six Branches Going Out from its Sides, of which Three Branches of the Lamp-stand were to GO OUT from its ONE SIDE and Three Branches of the Lamp-stand were to GO OUT from its OTHER SIDE, and at that Point of Commandment, the GREAT LORD – GOD also '"REMINDED MOSES"' that these SEVEN FLAMING LAMPS were to be MADE ACCORDING TO THE HOLY PATTERN, WHICH WAS SHOWN TO HIM IN THE BLAZING FIRE ON HIS HOLY MOUNTAIN, regarding which the Holy Bible States:

'Then YOU shall make a Lamp-stand of PURE GOLD. The Lamp-stand and its Base and its Shaft are to be Made of Hammered Work; its Cups, its Bulbs and its Flowers shall be of One Piece with it.

And Six Branches shall GO Out from its Sides; THREE Branches of the Lamp-stand from its One Side, and Three Branches of the Lamp-stand from its Other Side. Three Cups shall be SHAPED like Almond Blossoms in the One Branch, a Bulb and a Flower, and Three Cups Shaped Like Almond Blossoms in the Other Branch, a Bulb and a Flower – So for Six Branches Going out from the Lamp-stand; and in the Lamp-stand four Cups shaped like Almond Blossoms, its Bulbs and its Flowers.

And a Bulb Shall be under the First Pair of Branches Coming Out of it, and a Bulb under the Second Pair of Branches Coming Out of it, and a Bulb under the Third Pair of Branches Coming Out of it, for the Six Branches Coming Out of the Lamp-stand. Their Bulbs and their Branches shall be of One Piece with it; all of it shall be One Piece of Hammered Work of Pure Gold.

Then YOU shall MAKE its Lamps SEVEN IN NUMBER; and they shall MOUNT its Lamps so as to Shed LIGHT on the SPACE in front of it. And Its SNUFFERS and their TRAYS shall be of Pure GOLD. It shall be MADE from a TALENT of Pure GOLD, with ALL these UTENSILS.

AND SEE THAT YOU MAKE THEM AFTER THE "'PATTERN'" FOR THEM, """WHICH WAS SHOWN TO YOU ON THE MOUNTAIN""".' [Exodus 25. Verses 31 to 40.]

Then YOU shall MAKE its Lamps SEVEN IN NUMBER; and they shall MOUNT its Lamps so as to Shed LIGHT on the SPACE in front of it. And Its SNUFFERS and their TRAYS shall be of Pure GOLD. It shall be MADE from a TALENT of Pure GOLD, with ALL these UTENSILS. AND SEE THAT YOU MAKE THEM AFTER THE "'PATTERN'" FOR THEM, """WHICH WAS SHOWN TO YOU ON THE MOUNTAIN""".' [Exodus 25. Verses 37 to 40.]

Violet   Red   Orange   Yellow   Green   Blue   Indigo   Violet

The 7 Colors in the Visual Light Spectrum [VLS] and the 7 Sound Solfèges

'LISTEN to the WORD of the LORD, O SONS OF ISRAEL, for the LORD has a CASE AGAINST THE INHABITANTS OF THE LAND, because there is NO FAITHFULNESS or KINDNESS Or KNOWLEDGE of GOD in the LAND. There is SWEARING, DECEPTION, MURDER, STEALING, and ADULTERY. They Employ VIOLENCE, so that BLOODSHED FOLLOWS BLOODSHED. Therefore the LAND MOURNS, and Everyone WHO Lives in it LANGUISHES along with the BEASTS of the FIELD, and the BIRDS of the SKY; and also the FISH of the SEA DISAPPEAR.

Yet let No One Find FAULT, and let NONE Offer REPROOF; FOR Your PEOPLE are like those WHO CONTEND WITH THE PRIEST. So YOU will STUMBLE by DAY, and the PROPHET also will STUMBLE with YOU by NIGHT; and "I" will DESTROY your MOTHER. My PEOPLE are DESTROYED for Lack of KNOWLEDGE. Because YOU have REJECTED KNOWLEDGE, "I" Also will REJECT YOU from being MY PRIEST. Since YOU have FORGOTTEN the LAW of YOUR GOD, "I" will Also FORGET YOUR CHILDREN. [Hosea 4. Verses 1 to 6.]

The Great UNKNOWABLE LORD GOD of the Universe, whose DESIRE MIND VITAL CONSCIOUS REFLECTIONS are DIFFERENTIATED into SEVEN MAIN ACTIVE PARTS, and in our Solar Universe HIS VITAL ENERGIES thus affect the 7 Energy Distribution Centers of an Incarnated Human Vital Body, who during His Animated Life Duration is Evolving for the Spiritual Conscious Expansion upon this Planet Earth, and for this Very Reason HE then Strongly Emphasized through MOSES to the Members of His Chosen Race to MAKE SEVEN DAYS OF ATONEMENT, regarding which the Holy Bible States:

'For SEVEN Days YOU shall Make ATONEMENT for the ALTAR and CONSECRATE it; then the ALTAR shall be MOST HOLY, and Whatever TOUCHES the ALTAR shall be Holy.' [Exodus 29. 37.]

The Great LORD also Commanded Children of Israel through HIS Humble Servant MOSES that at the End of Every SEVEN Years CYCLIC Period, they have to be REMINDED Again about HIS LAWFUL COMMANDS, which are Based Upon the Universal LAW of "WILL TO DO GOOD", so they DO NOT GO ASTRAY from their CHOSEN Evolutionary Path, which HE Particularly Devised For them to Exist as the Members of HIS CHOSEN RACE upon this Planet Earth, regarding which the Holy Bible States:

'Then MOSES Commanded them Saying, "AT the End of Every SEVEN Years, at the Time of the YEAR OF REMISSION OF DEBTS, at the Feast of BOOTHS, When ALL ISRAEL Comes to APPEAR Before the LORD YOUR GOD at the PLACE which HE Choose, YOU shall read this LAW in Front of All Israel in their Hearing.

Assemble the PEOPLE, the Men, and the Women, and Children, and the Alien who is in your Town, in Order that they may HEAR and LEARN, and FEAR the LORD YOUR GOD, and be CAREFUL to OBSERVE all the WORDS of this LAW.

And their CHILDREN, who have NOT KNOWN, will HEAR and LEARN to FEAR the LORD YOUR GOD, as LONG as YOU Live on the LAND, which YOU are about to Cross the JORDAN to POSSESS.' [Deuteronomy 31. Verses 10 to 13.]

The LORD GOD keeping in mind the Importance of the Number SEVEN and the Number TEN which is an Important Mathematical Number depicting the 10 MANIFESTED SEPHIROTS of the TREE OF LIFE, also COMMANDED MOSES, for the Children of Israel to make a Permanent Statute to make ATONEMENT in the SEVENTH MONTH on its 10th Day Every Year, so they can Rejuvenate themselves by HUMBLING their SOULS, regarding which the Holy Bible States:

"'And this shall be a Permanent Statute for YOU; in the SEVENTH Month, on the Tenth Day of the Month, You shall Humble YOUR SOULS, and Not Do Any WORK, whether the Native or the Alien who Sojourns Among YOU; for it is on this Day that Atonement shall be Made for YOU to CLEANSE YOU; YOU Shall be Clean from ALL YOUR SINS BEFORE THE LORD.

It is to be a SABBATH of Solemn Rest for YOU, that YOU May Humble YOUR SOULS; IT IS A PERMANENT STATUTE. So the PRIEST who is ANOINTED and ORDAINED to Serve as Priest in His FATHER'S Place shall Make Atonement; HE shall thus put on the Linen Garments, the Holy Garments, and Make ATONEMENT for the HOLY SANCTUARY; and He shall Make Atonement for the TENT OF MEETING and for the ALTAR. He shall also make Atonement for the PRIESTS and for ALL THE PEOPLE OF THE ASSEMBLY.

Now YOU shall have this as a PERMANENT STATUTE, to Make Atonement for the Sons of Israel for ALL THEIR SINS ONCE EVERY YEAR.'' And JUST as the LORD had Commanded MOSES, So He DID.' [Leviticus 16. Verses 29 to 34.]

And regarding the Importance of the CYCLIC SEVENTH YEAR, being a YEAR OF 'SABBATH REST'', the Great LORD Gave HIS ASSURANCE to

MOSES for the Children of Israel, that on the SIXTH YEAR HE will Bless them with a Huge CROP, which will Last them for the Duration of ENTIRE THREE YEARS, regarding which the Holy Bible States:

'The LORD then SPOKE to MOSES at MOUNT SINAI, Saying, "SPEAK to the Sons of Israel, and Say to THEM, 'WHEN You COME into the LAND which I shall GIVE YOU, then the LAND shall have SABBATH to the LORD.

Six Years YOU shall SOW Your Field, and Six Years YOU shall PRUNE Your VINEYARD and Gather in its CROP, but during the SEVENTH Year the LAND shall have a SABBATH REST, a SABBATH to the LORD; YOU shall Not SOW YOUR FIELD NOR PRUNE YOUR VINEYARD.

YOU shall thus OBSERVE MY STATUTES, and KEEP MY JUDGMENTS, so as to CARRY THEM OUT, that YOU may LIVE SECURELY on the LAND. Then the Land will YIELD its PRODUCE, so that YOU can EAT YOUR Fill and LIVE SECURELY on it.

But if YOU SAY, "WHAT are we Going to EAT on the SEVENTH YEAR if WE DO NOT SOW or GATHER IN OUR CROPS?" THEN "I" will So ORDER MY BLESSING for YOU in the SIXTH YEAR that it will Bring Forth the CROP FOR THREE YEARS. When YOU are SOWING the EIGHTH YEAR, YOU can Still EAT Old Things from the CROP, Eating the OLD Until the NINTH YEAR when its CROP Comes in.' [Leviticus 25. 1, 2, 3, 4, 18, 19, 20, 21, 22.]

The Great Lord also COMMANDED MOSES about the Importance of the First Day of the SEVENTH Month, thus making it a Day of Holy Convocation, regarding which the Holy Bible States:

'Now in the SEVENTH Month, on the First Day of the Month, YOU shall also have a HOLY CONVOCATION; YOU shall DO NO LABORIOUS WORK. It will be to YOU a DAY for BLOWING TRUMPETS.' [Numbers 29. 1.]

But Even after Clearly Giving the COMMANDS and INSTRUCTIONS

to the Children of Israel through His Humble Servant MOSES, their Descendants born in the Promised Land Willfully did ABOMINATIONS against their "MOST HIGH", and their Women engaged themselves in Adultery giving Birth to Children of Harlotry, then the Great LORD Again Admonished them with Dire WARNINGS through HIS Chosen PROPHET HOSEA, regarding which the Holy Bible States:

'Also,"I" will have NO COMPASSION on Her CHILDREN, because they are CHILDREN OF HARLOTRY. For their MOTHER has PLAYED the HARLOT; SHE Who CONCEIVED THEM has Acted Shamefully. For She Said, I will GO after My LOVERS, WHO Give Me My Bread and My Water, MY Wool and My FLAX, MY Oil and My DRINK.' [Hosea 2. 4, 5.]

'LISTEN to the WORD of the LORD, O SONS OF ISRAEL, for the LORD has a CASE AGAINST THE INHABITANTS OF THE LAND, because there is NO FAITHFULNESS or KINDNESS Or KNOWLEDGE of GOD in the LAND. There is SWEARING, DECEPTION, MURDER, STEALING, and ADULTERY. They Employ VIOLENCE, so that BLOODSHED FOLLOWS BLOODSHED.

Therefore the LAND MOURNS, and Everyone WHO Lives in it LANGUISHES along with the BEASTS of the FIELD, and the BIRDS of the SKY; and also the FISH of the SEA DISAPPEAR.

Yet let No One Find FAULT, and let NONE Offer REPROOF; FOR Your PEOPLE are like those WHO CONTEND WITH THE PRIEST. So YOU will STUMBLE by DAY, and the PROPHET also will STUMBLE with YOU by NIGHT; and "I" will DESTROY your MOTHER.

My PEOPLE are DESTROYED for Lack of KNOWLEDGE. Because YOU have REJECTED KNOWLEDGE, "I" Also will REJECT YOU from being MY PRIEST. Since YOU have FORGOTTEN the LAW of YOUR GOD, "I" will Also FORGET YOUR CHILDREN. [Hosea 4. Verses 1 to 6.]

With these Dire Warnings, the MOST MERCIFUL LORD GOD OF ISRAEL STILL HOPING FOR THE MEMBERS OF HIS "CHOSEN RACE" TO CHANGE

FROM THEIR WRONG AND DECEPTIVE WAYS, AGAIN ADMONISHED the Children of Israel through HIS PROPHET JOEL to "RETURN AND SURRENDER", regarding which the Holy Bible States:

"'YET Even Now," declares the LORD, "RETURN TO ME WITH ALL YOUR HEART, and with FASTING, WEEPING, and MOURNING; and REND YOUR HEART AND NOT YOUR GARMENTS."

Now RETURN TO THE LORD YOUR GOD, For HE is GRACIOUS and COMPASSIONATE, SLOW TO ANGER, ABOUNDING IN LOVING KINDNESS, and RELENTING OF EVIL.' [Joel 2. 12, 13.]

Prophet Joel

497

'For "I" DELIGHT IN "'LOYALTY'" rather than 'SACRIFICE', and in the "'KNOWLEDGE OF GOD'" rather than 'BURNT OFFERINGS'. But Like ADAM they have TRANSGRESSED the COVENANT; there THEY HAVE DEALT TREACHEROUSLY AGAINST ME.' [Hosea 6. 6, 7.]

Many Incarnated Human Beings of this Planet Earth belonging to various Races, Casts and Creeds, who are Proud of their Material World Achievement's, which are related to their Physical World Educational Knowledge and Wisdom based upon the Science and Technology, which is Prevalent during their Incarnated Life TIME Duration in the Dense Dimensional Plane of ASSIAH, and the so called Glory of their Incarnated Bodies Name and Fame among other Human Beings, thus Innocently get their Evolving PERSONALITY MIND CONSCIOUSNESS, Entangled and Polarized in the Illusory Material World aspects of both the Dense Dimensional Planes of ASSIAH and the Liquid Magnetic Plane of YETZIRAH, and thus Totally Go ASTRAY from the Main Goal of Achieving the SPIRITUAL EXPERIENCES related to their SACRED HEART, during their Short Lived LIVES, for which they Basically Incarnated upon the Dense Planes of Planet Earth as per the Evolutionary Plan and Purpose of their SOUL CONSCIOUSNESS SPIRITUAL EXPANSION, which Existing in the Higher Sub Planes of the Dimensional Sphere of BRIAH belongs to one of the SEVEN WAY DIFFERENTIATED DESIRE MIND CONSCIOUS REFLECTIONS of the UNKNOWABLE CREATOR – OBSERVER of the UNIVERSE, who is Reverently known by HIS Visible and Invisible Creations as the "MOST HIGH".

And because the LORD – GOD, the MOST HIGH Chose the Children of Israel to be the Members of HIS Chosen Race to LEAD other Evolving Human Beings of this Planet Earth toward their SOUL'S SPIRITUAL EVOLUTION, whose PERSONALITY MINDS got Polarized for the Attainment of Material World Riches due to UNQUENCHABLE GREED, and were thus Foolishly Stuck in the Worship of Man Made IDOLS and GRAVEN IMAGES, and for this Very Reason the "MOST HIGH" dealt with the Children of Israel Since the Times of MOSES Very PATIENTLY by Constantly Warning them through His Chosen Judges, Prophets, Messengers and EVEN HIS BELOVED SON'S, Not to GO ASTRAY from HIS COMMANDMENTS, which He Gave them in Great Details through HIS Humble Servant MOSES, because if their SACRED HEARTS GOT HARDENED, they like All Other Evolving Human Beings of this Planet Earth Face the DIRE CONSEQUENCES of PERMANENTLY LOSING IMPORTANT ETHEREAL MATTER OF THEIR "CHAYAH BODIES", which to a Great Degree already Evolved during the Period of Many Thousands of Earth Years over Many Incarnations of Cyclic Lives, and thus had Gradually Evolved by Attaining VARIOUS SPIRITUAL EXPERIENCES in the Dense Planes of this Planet Earth to make the CHAYAH BODY ETHEREAL MATTER SPIRITUALLY RICH having Numerous Blazing TONAL COLOR VIBRATIONS, and Such a Great LOSS could Permanently Hamper the SPIRITUAL EVOLUTION OF their "SOLAR CONSCIOUSNESS" SOUL EXISTENCE for a VERY LONG TIME, which is termed by the SEERS AND SAGES as the "CYCLE OF ETERNITY".

The Sheepherder AMOS from TEKOA, who was CHOSEN by the Great LORD GOD as HIS PROPHET, had a Spiritual Vision Concerning the Children of Israel, and thus Clearly Understood the Extreme PATIENCE and MERCY of the Great LORD – GOD Toward them, even when they Willfully Committed those ABOMINABLE ACTS against HIM, by NOT KEEPING HIS Commandments, which Weighted the LORD DOWN Very HEAVILY due to their Such Evil Actions, as HE did not wanted them to Face the DIRE CONSEQUENCES of PERMANENTLY LOSING IMPORTANT ETHEREAL MATTER OF THEIR "CHAYAH BODIES", regarding which the Holy Bible States:

'Thus Says the LORD, "FOR Three TRANSGRESSIONS of ISRAEL and for FOUR, "I" will NOT REVOKE its PUNISHMENT, because THEY SELL RIGHTEOUS for "'MONEY'", and the NEEDY for A PAIR OF SANDALS.

These who PANT after the Very DUST OF THE EARTH on the HEAD OF "'HELPLESS'" also Turn ASIDE the Way of the HUMBLE; And a Man and His FATHER, RESORT to the SAME GIRL, in ORDER TO PROFANE "'MY HOLY NAME'".

And on GARMENTS taken as PLEDGES they STRETCH OUT beside EVERY ALTAR, and in the HOUSE OF THEIR GOD they DRINK THE WINE OF THOSE, Who have been FINED.

YET it was "I" Who DESTROYED THE AMORITE before them, though His Height was Like the Height of Cedars and He was STRONG as the OAKS;

"I" Even Destroyed His FRUIT ABOVE and His ROOT BELOW. And it was "I" who Brought YOU UP from the LAND OF EGYPT, and "I" Led YOU in the WILDERNESS FORTY YEARS that YOU MIGHT take POSSESSIONS of the Land of the AMORITE.

Then "I" Raised UP Some of YOUR Sons to be PROPHETS and Some of YOUR Young Men to be NAZIRITES, IS it NOT SO, O SONS OF ISRAEL?" Declares the LORD. But YOU Made the NAZIRITES Drink WINE, and YOU COMMANDED the PROPHETS Saying, 'YOU SHALL NOT PROPHESY!' BEHOLD, "I" AM WEIGHTED DOWN BENEATH YOU as a WAGON is WEIGHTED DOWN when FILLED WITH 'SHEAVES'." [Amos 2. Verses 6 to 13.]

The Humble Servant of LORD Prophet HOSEA also REMINDED CHILDREN OF ISRAEL as to what TRULY Makes their LORD GOD Joyful and Happy, which in Fact is Acquiring of the "'SPIRITUAL KNOWLEDGE", regarding which the Holy Bible States:

'For "I" DELIGHT IN "'LOYALTY"' rather than 'SACRIFICE', and in the "'KNOWLEDGE OF GOD"' rather than 'BURNT OFFERINGS'. But Like ADAM they have TRANSGRESSED the COVENANT; there THEY HAVE DEALT TREACHEROUSLY AGAINST ME.' [Hosea 6. 6, 7.]

But When the Children of Israel Willfully Committed Abomination's against their LORD GOD, many of their So Called Prophets WHO WERE NOT CHOSEN AT ALL BY THE "MOST HIGH", but Instead were Supported by those Invisible Existences which were the Hierarchical Groups of the Most CORRUPT SOULLESS ENTITIES, and also those DECEITFUL Maneuvering BEINGS, who were deceitfully working behind the MOLTEN IDOLS and GRAVEN IMAGES acting out as the so called GODS AND GODDESSES, Who also Played a Major Role to LEAD the Children of Israel Go ASTRAY, from the HOLY COMMANDMENTS of their LORD GOD.

These Hierarchical Groups of the Most CORRUPT SOULLESS ENTITIES, as well as those DECEITFUL Maneuvering BEINGS, who acting as the CO – CREATORS Created them with the MISUSE OF their Forceful Powers, which were Vested in them by the LORD GOD for Evolutionary Purposes, and thus WRONGFULLY MADE THE DENSE PHYSICAL PLANE OF THIS PLANET EARTH AS AN UNDUE PLACE OF "PAIN AND SUFFERINGS" in the Entire Creation, are also known in the Holy Texts as the "FALLEN ANGELS" who embodying the SOLAR CONSCIOUSNESS, which in the Very Beginning was Joyfully Given to them by the "MOST HIGH", so that they can serve HIM in their allotted Capacities as caretakers of HIS Evolutionary Plan and Purpose.

These Solar Conscious Angels, after their OWN FAILINGS to PROPERLY FOLLOW THE EVOLUTIONARY PLAN AND PURPOSE OF THE "MOST HIGH" due to the HARDENING OF THEIR SACRED HEARTS were already Facing the DIRE CONSEQUENCES, When during their Own Evolution they PERMANENTLY LOST the IMPORTANT ETHEREAL MATTER CONNECTION OF THEIR "CHAYAH BODIES", which DUE TO THEIR SUCH HARDENING OF HEART got SEVERED thus making them RUTHLESS "'INVISIBLE'" BLACK MAGICIANS, SORCERERS, DIVINERS and WITCH CRAFT PRACTITIONERS OF THE LEFT HAND PRACTICES, to Mainly Exist in the Lower Sub Plane Dimensions of ASSIAH and YETZIRAH Upon this Planet Earth specializing in ANIMAL MIND PASSIONS Especially of UNQUENCHABLE LUST and GREED till they According to the "UNIVERSAL LAW" FINALLY GET DESTROYED AND SENT TO TORTURE CHAMBERS for Purification Purposes, which takes place during the Very Long 'CYCLE OF ETERNITY'.

These INVISIBLE ONES, who are working for their Invisible DARK MASTERS are the Main Culprits, who made the Children of Israel GO ASTRAY FROM LORD'S COMMANDMENTS, whose Evolving PERSONALITY MINDS under their Invisible Influence of their CONSTANT FREQUENCY VIBRATIONS thus got Swayed by the UNQUENCHABLE GREED OF MATERIAL WORLD GLAMOUR AND RICHES, and these "Invisible Ones" by Misusing their Vested Powers and acting as the Co – Creator's in the Dense Planes of ASSIAH and YETZIRAH thus Deceitfully Back – Stabbed the LOVE AND TRUST OF THE "MOST HIGH", and WILLFULLY HIJACKED THE "SPIRITUAL EVOLUTIONARY PLAN", and Instead ILLEGALLY Installed a "MATERIAL MIND" EVOLUTIONARY PLAN for the 'ENTRAPMENT' of their 'PERSONALITY CONSCIOUSNESS", SO THAT THE UNAWARE EVOLVING HUMAN BEINGS AFTER THEIR PHYSICAL DEATH INSTEAD OF GOING TO THE HIGHER DIMENSIONAL 'HEAVEN WORLD'S of BRIAH and ATZILUTH, INSTEAD BECOME "DEMONS" LIKE THEM and stay STUCK in the Lower DIMENSIONAL WORLDS OF PAIN AND SUFFERINGS only to SERVE THEM in the Advancement of their ILLEGAL and DECEITFUL AGENDAS, which are Pertaining to the MATRIX of Illusory World Affairs, and the GREAT LORD GOD revealed this Hidden Secret to the Children of Israel by Conveying it through His Chosen Prophet MICAH of MORESHETH, so they do not FOOLISHLY FALL in the Deceitful TRAP of these so called Prophets and Diviners, regarding which the Holy Bible States:

'Thus Says the LORD Concerning the Prophets, WHO LED MY PEOPLE ASTRAY; WHEN they have SOMETHING to Bite with their Teeth, they Cry, "PEACE", BUT Against Him who PUTS NOTHING in their MOUTHS, they Declare HOLY WAR.

Therefore it will be NIGHT FOR YOU – WITHOUT VISION, and DARKNESS FOR YOU – WITHOUT DIVINATION. The SUN will GO DOWN ON THE PROPHETS, and the DAY WILL BECOME DARK OVER THEM.

The SEERS will be ASHAMED, and the DIVINERS will be EMBARRASSED. INDEED, they will COVER THEIR MOUTHS, because there is NO ANSWER FROM 'GOD'.' [Micah 3. Verses 5 to 7.]

503

'AND DO NOT FEAR THOSE WHO KILL THE BODY, BUT ARE "UNABLE TO KILL THE SOUL"; BUT RATHER FEAR 'HIM', WHO IS "ABLE TO DESTROY" BOTH "SOUL AND BODY" IN HELL.' [Matthew 10. 28.]

All Incarnated Human Beings of this Planet Earth during their Animated Life Duration's, Possess a Two Fold NEFESH BODY, of which One Part being Visible to the Human Eyes, is made up of Dense Plane's "Solid Matter", and thus have Innumerable Tiny Elemental Lives which compose the Physical Body's DNA, Cells and Tissues etc., and being Dense Solid is thus VISIBLE to their Eyes, while the other Part being Composed of Dense "'Ethereal Matter'" Contain Vital Elemental Lives, and thus is INVISIBLE to their Eyes, and Cannot be Noticed by them Until and Unless they Gradually Develop their SPIRITUAL EYESIGHT with the Grace of the "MOST HIGH".

The Ethereal Vital Part of the NEFESH BODY being intermingled with the Dense Human Form invisibly extends out Normally about a Quarter Inch from the Surface of the Physical body, and during Animated Life Duration of the Incarnated Human Form thus act as the Vital Energy Framework needed for the Live Animation of the Dense Incarnated Human Form, and this Invisible Part of NEFESH also known as the "BODY DOUBLE" apart from having many Small Energy Distribution Centers, which appear like Vortexes of Rotating energies, it has 7 Main Energy Centers, which act as the Main receivers of the 7 way differentiated VITALITY CONSCIOUSNESS Energies Circulating in our SOLAR UNIVERSE, which in reality are the 7 Way Differentiated Desire Mind Cosmic Energy Reflections of the "MOST HIGH", and thus Receive them at 90 Degree Right Angles, which are Focused through the existing SOUL MIND known as the "'YECHIDAH BODY ETHEREAL CONSCIOUSNESS'", which is established during the Entire Consciousness Expansion Time Period upon the Dimensional Sphere of BRIAH, and then acting out as the FOCAL POINT RECEIVER it then passes these ENERGIES Further on to the Manifested body of CHAYAH, from which they Vitally Animate the NESHAMAH, RUACH, and the NEFESH Bodies existing in the Dense Dimensional Level worlds of this Planet Earth, joined through the Extending CORD OF VITALITY, which the Great KING SOLOMON Termed as the "SILVER CORD", and the CHAYAH BODY He Termed as the GOLDEN BOWL which in the Very End gets Finally Crushed to release the Embodied 'SOLAR CONSCIOUS' to Finally Exist as an "Light Being" having Radiant Bluish – White Glowing SOUL,

Totally Filled and Absorbed with Spiritual Experiences thus gained through Cyclic Incarnations in the Dense Dimensional Spheres of BRIAH, YETZIRAH and ASSIAH, regarding which the Holy Bible States:

"THOU dost HIDE THY FACE, they are DISMAYED; THOU dost Take Away their "'SPIRIT'", they EXPIRE, and Return to their DUST. THOU dost Send Forth THY SPIRIT, they are CREATED; AND THOU dost RENEW the FACE OF THE GROUND." [Psalm 104. 29, 30.]

'Remember HIM before the SILVER CORD is BROKEN, and the GOLDEN BOWL is CRUSHED' [Ecclesiastes 12. 6.]

The Great LORD'S Humble Servants, which INCLUDED many of HIS Chosen Priests, Judges, Prophets, Messengers, Seers, and Sages, were Well Aware of their Evolving SOULS, which Being a Very Tiny Part of LORD'S UNFATHOMABLE SOLAR MIND DESIRE CONSCIOUSNESS was thus HIS Creation, which if NEEDED HE Could also DESTROY, if for any reason HIS Grand Experiment of Conscious Expansion upon this Planet Earth Gets Irrevocably CORRUPTED, with ABSOLUTELY NO FUTURE then to follow the Universal Law of "WILL TO DO GOOD", regarding which the Holy Bible States:

"Surely My SOUL Remembers and is Bowed Down within ME."

"The LORD is My PORTION", Says MY SOUL. "Therefore I have HOPE IN HIM"." [Lamentations 3. 20, 24.]

These Humble Servants of the LORD GOD were also aware of the LIQUID Magnetic Energy Waves of the Dimensional Plane of YETZIRAH, which is the IONIZED Dimensional Sphere of Live SENTIMENTS, EMOTIONS and FEELINGS composed of related Live Elemental Essences upon this Planet Earth, whose Dimensional Boundaries Invisibly Extend all the Way to the Dense Body of Our MOON, which being Composed of Sentimental Magnetic Liquid 'Thought Forms' thus Act Out as the Falling Waterfalls, and the Thundering Rolling Waves, which create Various Disturbances in the RUACH BODY and thus affect its Silver Cord Connection with the SOUL MIND, also termed as the Inner or the Higher Mind, which then as its Ongoing Reaction also effect the Embodied PERSONALITY MIND in the Dense Physical Form, which Vitally Exists as the Evolving Electromagnetic "SENSORY CONSCIOUSNESS" in the Animated Dense Human Form, regarding which the Holy Bible States:

'Why are YOU in DESPAIR, O MY SOUL? And WHY have Become DISTURBED within ME?

Deep Calls to DEEP at the Sound of THY WATERFALLS; ALL THY BREAKERS, and THY WAVES have ROLLED OVER ME.' [Psalm 42. 5, 7.]

"And Now My SOUL is POURED OUT WITHIN ME; Days of AFFLICTION have SEIZED ME. At NIGHT it PIERCES My Bones within ME, and MY GNAWING PAINS take NO REST." [Job 30. 16, 17.]

'Surely I have COMPOSED and QUIETED MY SOUL; Like a WEANED Child RESTS Against His Mother, MY SOUL is Like a WEANED Child WITHIN ME.' [Psalm 131. 2.]

'O LORD, THOU hast Brought UP My SOUL from SHEOL; THOU hast KEPT ME ALIVE, that I should NOT GO DOWN TO "PIT".' [Psalm 30. 3.]

'For THY Loving Kindness toward ME is GREAT, and THOU hast DELIVERED My SOUL from the DEPTHS OF SHEOL.' [Psalm 86. 13.]

'He KEEPS back His SOUL from the 'PIT', and His LIFE from PASSING OVER INTO SHEOL.' [Job 33. 18.]

'For THOU Wilt not ABANDON My SOUL TO SHEOL; NEITHER Wilt THOU ALLOW THY HOLY ONE TO UNDERGO "DECAY". [Psalm 16. 10.]

'DO NOT HOLD BACK DISCIPLINE FROM THE CHILD, ALTHOUGH YOU BEAT HIM WITH THE ROD, HE WILL NOT DIE. YOU SHOULD BEAT HIM WITH THE ROD, AND DELIVER HIS ""SOUL"" FROM SHEOL.' [Proverbs 23. 13, 14.]

In the Above Verses of the Holy Bible, the Humble Servants of LORD are Reverently Talking of their LORD'S Grace provided for their SOUL'S Protection, which through Timely Reprimands STOP the Hardening of their CHAYAH BODY'S ETHEREAL MATTER, which can Happen due to the Extreme Polarization of PERSONALITY MIND into Animal Passions of the MATERIAL WORLD'S ILLUSORY GLAMOUR, which as the LORD'S PROTECTION will thus Prevent the DECAY OF THEIR "SOULS", which the Great LORD provided them as a PRICELESS TREASURE with the Conscious Attributes of an "INDIVIDUALIZED MIND", to act out their Incarnated Life Roles as Co -Creator's with Limited Powers to Attain SPIRITUAL EXPERIENCES in the 3 Dense Dimensional Spheres [ASSIAH, YETZIRAH, and BRIAH] of this Planet Earth.

The Great LORD'S Humble Servants Time and Again Warned the Children of Israel about LORD'S Ability to DESTROY their SOULS, if through their Persistent WRONGDOINGS and due to the HARDENING OF THEIR SACRED HEARTS, they PERMANENTLY Lose their Connections with their SOULS, and become the Pawns of "SOULLESS ENTITIES" Controlled by the Dark Masters, regarding which the Holy Bible States:

'Then the LORD Said to Me, "EVEN though MOSES and SAMUEL were to Stand before ME, MY HEART would NOT be with this PEOPLE; Send them Away from MY PRESENCE, and LET THEM GO!

And it shall be that when they Say to YOU, 'WHERE should We GO?' Then YOU are to Tell THEM, "THUS Says the LORD; "THOSE DESTINED FOR DEATH, TO DEATH; AND THOSE DESTINED FOR THE SWORD, TO THE SWORD; AND THOSE DESTINED FOR FAMINE, TO FAMINE; AND THOSE DESTINED FOR CAPTIVITY, TO CAPTIVITY"'.' [Jeremiah 15. 1, 2.]

'Then the WORD of the LORD came to ZECHARIAH Saying, "THUS

has the LORD OF HOSTS Said, 'DISPENSE TRUE JUSTICE, and Practice KINDNESS and COMPASSION each to His Brother; and Do NOT Oppress the Widow or the Orphan, the Stranger or the Poor; and Do NOT Devise EVIL in Your HEARTS Against One Another'. But they Refused to Pay Attention, and Turned a STUBBORN Shoulder and STOPPED their EARS from HEARING.

And they MADE THEIR HEARTS LIKE '''FLINT''', SO they COULD NOT HEAR THE '''LAW''' and the WORDS which the LORD OF HOSTS had SENT by ''''HIS SPIRIT'''' through the Former PROPHETS; therefore GREAT WRATH came from the LORD OF HOSTS. And it Came ABOUT that Just as HE Called and they would NOT LISTEN, SO They Called and "I" would NOT LISTEN", Says the LORD of HOSTS; BUT "I" Scattered them with a STORM WIND AMONG ALL THE NATIONS Whom they have NOT KNOWN. Thus the Land is DESOLATED Behind them, so that NO ONE went BACK and FORTH, for They Made the PLEASANT LAND DESOLATE.' [Zechariah 7. Verses 8 to 14.]

Much LATER, when the LORD GOD after Sending back ELIJAH, who was sent to Incarnate as 'JOHN THE BAPTIST' among the Children of Israel, also along with Him Sent His Begotten Son JESUS CHRIST upon this Physical Plane of Planet Earth to Admonish the Children of Israel, so Listening to Him they may SAVE THEIR SOULS from the LOOMING EXTINCTION, and then JESUS CHRIST repeated the WORDS OF PROPHET ISAIAH for them to FEAR THEIR LORD – GOD, who is FULLY CAPABLE OF DESTROYING THEIR "SOUL CONSCIOUSNESS", IF IT BECOMES DAMAGED DUE TO LOSS OF ETHEREAL MATTER FROM THEIR Evolving "CHAYAH BODIES" DUE TO THE HARDENING OF THE SACRED HEART regarding which the Holy Bible states:

'And HE Will DESTROY the GLORY of His FOREST and of His Fruitful Garden, BOTH '''SOUL''' and "BODY".' [Isaiah 10. 18.]

'AND DO NOT FEAR THOSE WHO KILL THE BODY, BUT ARE "UNABLE TO KILL THE SOUL"; BUT RATHER FEAR 'HIM', WHO IS "ABLE TO DESTROY" BOTH "SOUL AND BODY" IN HELL.' [Matthew 10. 28.]

"For the Fate of the Sons of Men and the Fate of Beasts is the SAME. As One Dies so Dies the Other; INDEED, 'THEY ALL HAVE THE SAME BREATH', and there is No Advantage for Man over Beast, for All is Vanity." [Ecclesiastes 3. 19.]

The Secret of the Breast Plate

Part 94

Since the time of LORD'S Creation, all HIS Conscious Creations which include Innumerable Varieties of Hierarchical HOSTS and HIS Faithful Humble Servants, have very well KNOWN this UNDENIABLE FACT, that it is the VITAL SPIRIT ENERGY of the UNKNOWABLE LORD'S DESIRE MIND which Provide for all HIS Manifested Creations the "VITAL SOLAR CONSCIOUSNESS" to be EMBODIED into Various Animated Form Bodies for their Existence in the 3 Dense Dimensional Planes of this Planet Earth [ASSIAH, YETZIRAH and BRIAH], in which during their "Limited Time" Incarnated Lives they Exhibit Differentiated Levels of Evolving and Expanded Consciousness, who in fact are an Extended Part of their Group Conscious Reservoirs, to which they CONTINUE TO BELONG till they as per the Evolutionary Plan and Purpose of the LORD GOD after acquiring the REQUIRED Spiritual Experiences in HIS DENSE WORLDS then get Qualified to Join the Next Higher Level of LORD'S VITAL SPIRIT'S ETHEREAL VIBRATIONS, through the Conscious Energy Attributes of HIS NEXT EVOLUTIONARY "DESIRE MIND" VITAL WAVE, put in SPACE through the "SPIRAL MOTION" to Further their Conscious Evolution.

The Great LORD'S Humble Servants including Prophets, Seers and Sages who since Very Ancient Times have reverently known HIM as the UNKNOWABLE "MOST HIGH", have termed "HIS VITAL SPIRIT ENERGY" as the "LIFE FORCE" OR "THE BREATH OF LIFE IN ALL FLESH", which Provide the SOLAR CONSCIOUSNESS to be EMBODIED in Various Animated Form Bodies of the 3 Dense Dimensional Planes of this Planet Earth [ASSIAH, YETZIRAH and BRIAH], regarding which the Holy Bible States:

'Then the LORD Said, "MY SPIRIT shall NOT STRIVE WITH MAN FOREVER, BECAUSE HE IS ALSO "'FLESH'"; Nevertheless His Days shall be One Hundred and Twenty Years".' [Genesis 6. 3.]

"AND behold, "I", Even "I" am Bringing the Flood of Water upon the Earth, to 'DESTROY ALL FLESH' in which is the 'BREATH OF LIFE', from 'UNDER HEAVEN'; Everything that is on the Earth shall PERISH".' [Genesis 6. 17.]

The VITAL SPIRIT of the UNKNOWABLE "MOST HIGH" being "ETHEREAL" in Nature,which Compose the ENTIRE SPACE of the INFINITE UNIVERSE, can be Only brought in ANIMATION due to the 3 ACTIONS of HIS DESIRE MIND, which Produce the 3 UNIVERSAL MOTIONS in the COSMIC SPACE, and are known as [1] The Spiral Motion, [2] The Circular Motion, and [3] The Cyclic Motion.

The VITAL SPIRIT of the LORD GOD, PROVIDES the Sensory Consciousness Attributes to all VISIBLE and INVISIBLE Kingdoms of this Planet Earth, which are Governed by their GROUP SOUL MIND, which for their SPIRITUAL CONSCIOUSNESS EXPANSION as per LORD'S EVOLUTIONARY PLAN are thus SUBJECTIVELY and OBJECTIVELY Manifested in its 3 Dense Dimensional Planes [ASSIAH, YETZIRAH, and BRIAH], to Vitally Exist according to their Level of Attained Conscious Expansion WITH or WITHOUT their FORM BODIES, and in the Human Beings of this Planet Earth this Cosmic Vital Force of LORD'S DESIRE MIND First Provides Consciousness and then PRESERVES them but can also REMOVE LIFE according to the LORD'S DESIRED "WILL".

Prophet ISAIAH Clearly WARNED the Children of Israel, about the LORD'S BREATH OF VITALITY, as when they become WRONG and EVIL in their Ways, HE BLOWS it to REMOVE LIFE, regarding which the Holy Bible States:

'The Grass WITHERS, the Flower FADES, When the BREATH OF THE LORD BLOWS Upon it; SURELY the PEOPLE ARE GRASS. The Grass WITHERS, the Flower FADES, But the WORD OF OUR GOD STANDS FOREVER' [Isaiah 40. 7, 8.]

Since the Very Ancient Times, the SPIRIT ATTRIBUTES OF THE LORD GOD being ETHEREAL in Nature were EQUATED by the Seers and Sages of the Dense Physical World [ASSIAH] thus Incarnated upon this Planet Earth with the "'WIND'", which carries it to the Various Evolving Kingdoms of this Planet Earth as the INVISIBLE "BREATH OF LIFE", and After the GREAT FLOOD during NOAH'S TIME, to Reestablish Him, the Great LORD sent Forth a VITAL WIND to Pass Over the Earth having ETHEREAL VITALITY, regarding which the Holy Bible States:

'But GOD Remembered NOAH and All the Beasts and All the Cattle that were with Him in the ARK; and GOD CAUSED A "WIND" TO PASS OVER THE EARTH, and the Water Subsided.' [Genesis 8. 1]

In the Densest Dimensional Plane of this Planet Earth, which is KNOWN to the PROPHETS, MESSENGERS, SAGES and SEERS as the Physical Spherical Plane of ASSIAH, it has a total of 7 Main Sub Planes, of which the first 4 are ETHEREAL in Nature, and thus are Composed of 4 Types of Differentiated Ethereal Matter Invisible to Human Eyes in which various types of Conscious and Unconscious Elemental Lives always Exist, whose Main Role is to act out their Required Duties for the Formation of the INCARNATED FORMS to be Born in the Physical Plane World of this Planet Earth, as well as to Provide the 4 Types of Vital Ethereal Force, commonly termed as the "'FOUR WINDS'", which are Required for its ANIMATION and for the WORKING OF THE SENSORY ACTIVITIES of PERSONALITY MIND CONSCIOUS to keep the Incarnated "FORM PRESERVED" during its Incarnated LIFE DURATION PERIOD upon the Dense Physical Plane of this Planet Earth. The Great LORD gave HIS Chosen Prophet EZEKIEL an Important Vision about it regarding which the Holy Bible States:

"Thus Says the LORD GOD to these Bones, Behold, "I" will CAUSE BREATH TO ENTER YOU, THAT YOU MAY COME TO LIFE. And "I" will put SINEWS on YOU, Cover YOU with SKIN, and ""PUT BREATH IN YOU"" that YOU may Come ALIVE; and YOU will KNOW "I" AM THE LORD."

So I PROPHESIED as I was COMMANDED; and as I PROPHESIED, there was a Noise, and behold, a Rattling; and the Bones came Together, BONE to its BONE. And I Looked, and behold, SINEWS were on them, and Fresh Grew, and SKIN Covered Them; BUT THERE WAS "NO BREATH" IN THEM.

Then HE Said to Me, "PROPHESY TO THE 'BREATH', PROPHESY, SON OF MAN, AND SAY TO THE BREATH, """THUS SAYS THE LORD GOD, "'COME FROM THE FOUR WINDS'", O BREATH, AND BREATHE ON THESE SLAIN, THAT THEY COME TO LIFE"""'."

So I Prophesied as HE COMMANDED ME, and the "'BREATH CAME INTO THEM, AND THEY CAME TO LIFE'", and they STOOD on their Feet, an Exceedingly Great Army. [Ezekiel 37. Verses 5 to 10.]

The Prophets, Messengers, Seers and Sages of the Great LORD have Named the four Vital Ether's as the "FOUR WINDS OF THE HEAVEN", having 'LORD'S ETHEREAL VITALITY', Which First Creates, then Preserves, as Well as in the Very End Destroys the "INCARNATED FORM" Causing it's so called "PHYSICAL DEATH" and then SCATTER Back the COMPOSING ELEMENTAL LIVES to their "OWN GROUP RESERVOIRS of CONSCIOUSNESS VITALITY", regarding which the Holy Bible in a Codified Way States:

'And "I" shall BRING Upon ELAM the "'FOUR WINDS'" from the "FOUR ENDS OF HEAVEN", and shall "SCATTER THEM TO ALL THESE WINDS"; AND there will be 'NO NATION' to which the OUTCASTS of ELAM will NOT GO.' [Jeremiah 49. 36.]

"AND "'I'" WILL PUT 'MY SPIRIT WITHIN YOU', AND YOU WILL COME TO 'LIFE', AND "I" WILL PLACE YOU ON YOUR OWN LAND, THEN YOU WILL KNOW THAT "'I'", THE LORD,HAVE SPOKEN AND DONE IT," DECLARES THE LORD." [Ezekiel 37. 14.]

During the Time of EXODUS, both His Humble Servants MOSES and AARON were FULLY AWARE of this UNDENIABLE FACT that their LORD – GOD was the "SOLE PROVIDER" of "THE SPIRITS OF ALL FLESH", regarding which the Holy Bible States:

'Then the LORD Spoke to MOSES and AARON, Saying, "SEPARATE Yourselves from Among this CONGREGATION, that "I" may CONSUME them INSTANTLY."

But they FELL ON THEIR FACES, and Said, "O GOD, THOU ""GOD OF THE SPIRITS"" OF ALL FLESH, when One Man Sins, Wilt THOU be Angry with the Entire Congregation?"' [Numbers 16. Verses 20 to 22.]

All Created Beings of the Universe who by having the SPIRIT VITALITY are

Manifested upon this Planet Earth by the Desire Mind Vital Frequencies of the Unknowable "MOST HIGH", have the Same Vital Breath of the "SOLAR CONSCIOUSNESS", about which the Great Wise King Solomon Properly Understood, regarding which the Holy Bible States:

"For the Fate of the Sons of Men and the Fate of Beasts is the SAME. As One Dies so Dies the Other; INDEED, 'THEY ALL HAVE THE SAME BREATH', and there is No Advantage for Man over Beast, for All is Vanity." [Ecclesiastes 3. 19.]

All the SOULLESS CREATIONS of the MANKIND upon the Physical Plane of this Planet Earth, which Now Exists as POWERFUL ENTITIES IN THE FORM OF "MULTINATIONAL or GLOBAL CORPORATIONS", which Now Even Control the Leaders of the VARIOUS GOVERNING AGENCIES of ALL NATIONS, and THE OTHER SOULLESS GROUP CONSIST OF '''BREATHLESS''' MOLTEN AND GRAVEN IMAGES OF GODS AND GODDESSES and their Iconic Symbols, existing as Huge RELIGIOUS ORGANIZATIONS with a GREAT NUMBER OF FOLLOWERS, whose so called Fronts exist as the Incarnated Priesthood, then Control the Innocent Evolving Human Race in the Name of "SECTARIAN RELIGIONS", as MOST HUMANS are thus TOTALLY UNAWARE OF THE EVOLUTIONARY FACTS, as they Like in the Ancient Days of this Planet Earth, are NOT TAUGHT ANYMORE those IMPORTANT UNIVERSAL FACTS IN ANY OF THE MODERN DAY EDUCATIONAL UNIVERSITIES, which are RELATED TO THEIR INDWELLING "SOLAR CONSCIOUSNESS" which Embodied as the 'PERSONALITY MIND CONSCIOUSNESS' in their Physical Forms is ELECTROMAGNETIC in nature, and thus being Unaware of these SPIRITUAL FACTS, they are Illegally Maneuvered by the Invisible DARK BEINGS Who are Permanently Doomed to Exist in the Lower Worlds of ASSIAH and YETZIRAH, as they themselves became Permanently DISCONNECTED FROM THEIR 'SOUL CONSCIOUSNESS' which Exist in the COSMIC ELECTRICAL ETHER'S upon the Higher Dimensional Sphere of BRIAH, due to the HARDENING OF THEIR HEARTS, and their Incarnated Henchmen Now Sitting on TOP POSITIONS of the Human Societies, who through their Vested Powers DECEITFULLY Control the Human MASSES though the Artificial Flow of Money, and through the SOULLESS BANKING SYSTEM supported by the SOULLESS STOCK MARKETS which Globally Trade Daily their SOULLESS SHARES, and thus make them WORK DAY AND NIGHT, thus working under the ILLUSORY GLAMOUR, and without their Knowledge to Just Exist as Modern World "HUMAN SLAVES", and in the Name of "CIVILIZATION" keep them Mentally Polarized in Material World's Illusory Matters, so they can just Barely Survive in the Physical Plane World, or in an Opposite Situation get Drenched in Unquenchable GREED with Absolutely NO TIME or a Right Mental Framework to DEEPLY CONTEMPLATE upon the IMPORTANT SPIRITUAL MATTERS, as Now a Days in the Physical Plane World, the TIME IS EQUATED WITH MONEY with the Most Prevalent Saying, that the "TIME IS MONEY".

And thus the Incarnated Human Beings after coming to the Physical Plane have Totally Forgotten that in the Very First Place, as per the Evolutionary Plan of the "MOST HIGH" they were Sent to Incarnate upon the Dense Physical Plane by their "YECHIDAH SPIRIT CONSCIOUSNESS", and thus were Supposed to Acquire the NEEDED Spiritual Experiences for their SPIRIT'S CONSCIOUSNESS EVOLUTIONARY EXPANSION during their Short Lived Incarnated Lives in the Physical Plane World "ASSIAH" of this Planet Earth.

Prophet JEREMIAH, the Humble Servant of the LORD – GOD informed the Children of Israel with a GRAVE WARNING about these "BREATHLESS EXISTENCES", which were even Prevalent in Great Numbers during His Own Times, who were "TOTALLY DEVOID OF LORD'S SPIRIT", regarding which the Holy Bible States:

'All MANKIND IS "'STUPID'", DEVOID OF KNOWLEDGE; EVERY GOLDSMITH IS PUT TO SHAME BY HIS "'IDOLS'", FOR HIS MOLTEN IMAGES ARE "'DECEITFUL'", AND THERE IS "'NO BREATH'" IN THEM.' [Jeremiah 51. 17.]

LORD'S Humble Servant ELIPHAZ also told JOB about the DARKNESS caused by the DARK BEINGS, and the 'BREATH OF LIFE' which as a Result of their Deceitfulness, will then GO Away, regarding which the Holy Bible States:

"HE will NOT ESCAPE from DARKNESS; THE FLAME will WITHER His SHOOTS, and by the 'BREATH OF HIS MOUTH', HE will GO AWAY." [Job 15. 30.]

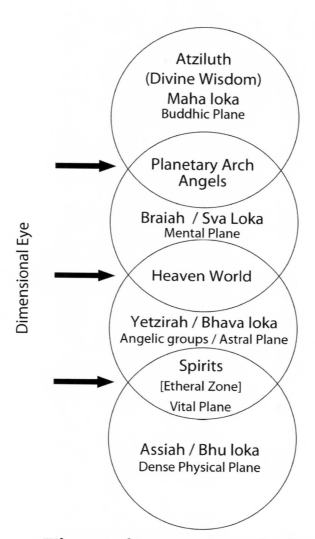

Dimensional Eye

Atziluth
(Divine Wisdom)
Maha loka
Buddhic Plane

Planetary Arch
Angels

Braiah / Sva Loka
Mental Plane

Heaven World

Yetzirah / Bhava loka
Angelic groups / Astral Plane

Spirits
[Etheral Zone]
Vital Plane

Assiah / Bhu loka
Dense Physical Plane

The 4 dimensional planes
of creation, related to evolution of planet Earth.

The VITAL SPIRIT of the LORD GOD, PROVIDES the Sensory Consciousness
Attributes to all VISIBLE and INVISIBLE Kingdoms of this Planet Earth, which
are Governed by their GROUP SOUL MIND, which for their SPIRITUAL
CONSCIOUSNESS EXPANSION as per LORD'S EVOLUTIONARY PLAN are thus
SUBJECTIVELY and OBJECTIVELY Manifested in its 3 Dense Dimensional Planes
[ASSIAH, YETZIRAH, and BRIAH], to Vitally Exist according to their Level of
Attained Conscious Expansion WITH or WITHOUT their FORM BODIES, and
in the Human Beings of this Planet Earth this Cosmic Vital Force of LORD'S
DESIRE MIND First Provides Consciousness and then PRESERVES them but can
also REMOVE LIFE according to the LORD'S DESIRED "WILL".

And GOD Made the EXPANSE, and SEPARATED THE WATERS, which were BELOW the EXPANSE from the WATERS which were ABOVE the EXPANSE; and IT WAS SO.' And GOD called the EXPANSE 'HEAVEN'. And there was Evening and there was Morning. [Genesis 1. 7, 8.]

Part 95

The Grand Experiment of SPIRITUAL CONSCIOUSNESS EXPANSION, which as Per the EVOLUTIONARY PLANS, the GREAT LORD Established upon this Planet Earth, for the Spiritual Advancement of ALL THE VISIBLE AND INVISIBLE KINGDOMS of its DIFFERENTIATED DIMENSIONS, which are having the 7 WAY DIFFERENTIATED SOLAR VITAL CONSCIOUSNESS, which also include HIS Created Hierarchy of Innumerable HOSTS as well as the Incarnated Human Beings created by HIM in HIS Own Image, as well Innumerable Species of Animal and Plant Kingdoms, and also the Extremely Slow Growth Evolution of the CRYSTALS belonging to the Mineral Kingdom, which also Grow like all other SPECIES, and they all are Evolving According to their Own Levels of Inherent SOLAR CONSCIOUSNESS, which range from PURE OR THE UNTAINTED CONSCIOUSNESS without any Dense Material World Experiences to the SUPER or ULTRA CONSCIOUS level Existences, which are Totally Drenched with Attained Spiritual Experiences in the Dense Material Worlds, so that the GREAT LORD can then Advance them on HIGHER SPIRALS to the RARE ETHEREAL and HIGHEST LEVELS OF COSMOS for the Further Advancement of their Conscious Attributes, so that in the Very END, they can FINALLY Attain their ULTIMATE FREEDOM from the DIMENSIONAL BOUNDARIES OF THE INFINITE UNIVERSE.

Regarding the Creation of the Various Dimension Levels and their Differentiated Conscious Inhabitants which Consciously or Unconsciously Exist IN THEM, for their Evolutionary Conscious Gradual Expansion in the Subjectively and Objectively Manifested Infinite Universe, the Holy Bible in a Codified Way States:

'Thus the HEAVENS and the EARTH were COMPLETED, AND ALL THEIR "'HOSTS"'.' [Genesis 2. 1.]

Also as per LORD'S EVOLUTIONARY PLAN AND PURPOSE, ALL MANIFESTATIONS CAME IN EXISTENCE First to Appear as the "THOUGHT FORMS", which were Created by the DESIRE MIND CONSCIOUS ENERGIES of the UNKNOWABLE LORD GOD in the VITAL ETHEREAL

MATTER through the Workings and the Utilization of the three Universal Motions [Spiral, Circular and Cyclic] in the UNFATHOMABLY HUGE SPHERICAL PARAMETERS, which Since Ancient Times has been Termed by LORD'S Humble Servants as the SPACE or the ETHEREAL COSMOS.

This Process of Creation by the DESIRE MIND OF THE "MOST HIGH" to Manifest HIS DESIRED WISHES AS THE "THOUGHT FORMS" having "LIGHT OF MIND CONSCIOUSNESS" in the VITAL ETHEREAL SPACE is known as the "EVENTUATION PROCESS", which created the LIGHTENED ARMS OF THE SPIRALING GALAXIES having INNUMERABLE NUMBER OF STAR SOLAR SYSTEMS, regarding which the Holy Bible States:

'Then GOD Said, "LET there be LIGHT"; and there was LIGHT.

And GOD Saw that LIGHT WAS GOOD; and GOD Separated the LIGHT from the DARKNESS.[Genesis 1. 3, 4.]

The EVENTUATION PROCESS, which involves the DESIRE MIND'S "STRONG WISHING POWER" ALSO KNOWN AS THE "WILL POWER" or THE "SOLAR CONSCIOUS SOUL'S THOUGHT FORMING FORCE" which according to the Desired Will Force related to any Subject or any Object then CREATES FREQUENCY VIBRATIONS in the Invisible VITAL ETHEREAL MATTER OF THE ETHEREAL SPACE, which Since Very Ancient Times have been DENOTED BY THE ONE POINTED 'HOLY WORDS' WHICH REPRESENT THE DESIRE MIND'S FOCUSED AND CONCENTRATED ENERGIES PERTAINING TO WISHFUL THINKING, which are ""LET IT BE"", and ""SO BE IT"".

As far as the CREATION upon this Planet Earth is Concerned, Most People are Unaware of this Supreme Fact, that when the Densest Part of Earth First Appeared Separated from its Liquid Waters, due to Forceful Action of the DESIRE MIND frequency Vibrations of the LORD – GOD "MOST HIGH", it First Appeared as a One Large Expanse of Dense Earth, or a SINGLE HUGE CONTINENT, which was Surrounded on its all Sides by the Huge Expanse of Liquid Water composed of Hydrogen and Oxygen Gases, a Supreme Fact about which the Ancient Vedic Seers and

Sages also knew, and called this LAND OF PLANET EARTH in the Sanskrit Language as the "JUMBUDVIPA" meaning "THE GREAT CONTINENT", which was Surrounded on its All Sides by the Huge Expanse of DEEP WATERS, whom they Called as the "ADI MAHA SAGARA".

The Holy Bible, which is A HUGE STORE HOUSE OF CODIFIED WISDOM, in its Very First Chapter of GENESIS [Creation] Clearly EXPLAINED the Creation of Great Expanse in the Midst of Waters, which also then SEPARATED the DRINKING WATERS from the OCEANIC WATERS as Part of the LORD'S EVENTUATION PROCESS, brought in Action by the DESIRE MIND OF THE GREAT LORD. And this Land Mass, which thus Appeared in the MIDST OF WATERS upon this Planet Earth, then became a Heaven Place World on the Physical Earth to be used for the Preservation and Continuation of all the 4 Evolving Visible Kingdoms of this Planet Earth, who were Manifested by the DESIRE MIND ACTION OF THE LORD GOD, having Embodied Vital Consciousness in their Incarnated Forms, which are known as the [1] Mineral Kingdom, [2] Plant Kingdom, [3] Animal Kingdom, and the [4] Human Kingdom.

The Great Ancient Expanse of this Planet Earth, which was brought into Manifestation by the GREAT LORD through HIS DESIRE MIND ACTIONS as ONE HUGE LAND MASS, is Now Currently DIVIDED into Great Continents, due to the Constant Movement of Tectonic Plates caused by the Planet Earth's 3 Energy Motions, but the OCEANIC WATERS Surrounding them are Still CONNECTED although their areas covering these Separated Continents have Now Different Names, which have been given by the Human Beings, regarding which the Holy Bible States:

'Then GOD Said, "LET THERE BE AN "EXPANSE" in the "MIDST OF THE WATERS", and Let it SEPARATE THE "WATERS FROM THE WATER".

And GOD Made the EXPANSE, and SEPARATED THE WATERS, which were BELOW the EXPANSE from the WATERS which were ABOVE the EXPANSE; and IT WAS SO.'

And GOD called the EXPANSE 'HEAVEN'. And there was Evening and there was Morning.

Then GOD Said, "Let THE WATERS BELOW THE HEAVENS BE GATHERED INTO ONE PLACE, AND LET THE DRY LAND APPEAR"; and IT WAS SO. And GOD called the DRY LAND EARTH, and the GATHERING OF THE WATERS HE CALLED SEAS; and GOD Saw it was GOOD.

Then GOD Said. "LET THE EARTH SPROUT VEGETATION, PLANTS YIELDING SEED, and FRUIT TREES BEARING FRUIT AFTER THEIR KIND, WITH SEED IN THEM, ON THE EARTH"; and IT WAS SO.

And the Earth Brought Forth VEGETATION, PLANTS YIELDING SEEDS AFTER THEIR KIND, and TREES BEARING FRUIT, with SEEDS IN THEM, after their KIND; and GOD Saw it was GOOD.' [Genesis 1. Verses 6 to 12.]

The Above Verses also Contain the Important Codified Information about the Creation of DIFFERENTIATED DIMENSIONS OF THE PLANET EARTH BY THE DESIRE MIND OF THE "MOST HIGH", as the Spherical Expanse in the Cosmic Ethereal Waters mentioned in the Above Verses of the Holy Bible also denotes the Manifestation of the Heaven World of BRIAH, and the Separation of Ethereal Waters denote the Separation of Liquid Magnetic waters of the Dimensional Sphere of YETZIRAH from the Electric Water Currents of the Heaven world of BRIAH. Similarly the Liquid waters of the Densest Dimensional World of ASSIAH, which Happens to be the Physical Plane World of All Incarnated Human Beings, also got Separated from the Sentimental Liquid Watery World of the Emotions and Feelings, which exists upon this Planet Earth as the Dimensional world of YETZIRAH, also commonly known as the "ASTRAL PLANE".

The Great LORD also ESTABLISHED the "'CONCEPT OF TIME'" for All Evolving Creatures of this Planet Earth existing in their Differentiated Conscious Hierarchical Groups, which is based on the Cyclic Movements of Various Visible Planets, the Solar Stars Like Our Own Sun, and Various Combined Star Groups of the Celestial Heavens known as the Zodiacal Constellations, which are Depicted as the Zodiacal SIGNS in the Celestial Skies having Various Shapes and Symbols, also existing as the HUGE ENERGY RESERVOIRS which represent the Negative and Positive Tinting Qualities of their Cosmic Energy Radiations, regarding which the Holy Bible States:

Then GOD Said, "LET there be "'LIGHTS'" in the EXPANSE OF THE HEAVENS to SEPARATE THE DAY FROM THE NIGHT, AND LET THEM BE FOR "'SIGNS'", AND FOR "'SEASONS'", AND FOR "'DAYS AND YEARS'"; AND LET THEM BE FOR "'LIGHTS IN THE EXPANSE OF THE HEAVENS TO GIVE "LIGHT ON EARTH"; and IT WAS SO. [Genesis 1. 14, 15.]

These Time Cycles are Practically Followed by all the Visible and Invisible Kingdoms of this Planet Earth, during which they PERFORM their DAILY DUTIES acting as the Co – Creators in their Limited Capacities as per the LORD'S EVOLUTIONARY PLAN AND PURPOSE, and thus LIVE OUT their Incarnated Lives upon this Planet Earth, their Main Goal of Incarnated Life being to Consciously ATTAIN and ACHIEVE the Required "'SPIRITUAL EXPERIENCES'".

In Our SOLAR UNIVERSE, the Two Main ENERGY LIGHTS brought into Manifestation by the DESIRE MIND OF THE "MOST HIGH", which Constantly affect the Evolutionary Conscious Expansion, as well as the Daily Lives of all Evolving Kingdoms of this Planet Earth, are Conveyed to this Planet Earth by their SUBJECTIVELY and OBJECTIVELY manifested Bodies in the Celestial Skies known as the SUN and MOON, which act as the FOCAL POINT RECEIVERS for ALL INCOMING COSMIC ENERGY RADIATIONS and then Act Out their Roles as HUGE ENERGY TRANSFORMERS to Convert them into those Useful Frequency Vibrations, which can be Consciously or Unconsciously Utilized for the Evolutionary Purposes by all Visible and Invisible Evolving Kingdoms of this Planet Earth, regarding which the Holy Bible States:

'And GOD Made the TWO GREAT LIGHTS, the GREATER LIGHT to GOVERN THE DAY, and the LESSER LIGHT to GOVERN THE NIGHT; HE Made the STARS Also. And GOD PLACED them in the EXPANSE of the HEAVENS to Give LIGHT ON EARTH, and to GOVERN the DAY and the NIGHT, and to SEPARATE the LIGHT from the DARKNESS; and GOD SAW that it was GOOD. [Genesis 16, 17, 18.]

The LORD is GOOD, a STRONGHOLD in the "'DAY OF TROUBLE'", and HE KNOWS THOSE WHO TAKE "'REFUGE IN HIM'". But with an OVERFLOWING FLOOD HE will Make a "'COMPLETE END'" of its SITE, and will "'PURSUE HIS ENEMIES'" into "DARKNESS"'.' [Nahum 1. Verses 7, 8.]

The Great LORD GOD of the UNIVERSE, being its SOLE CREATOR – OBSERVER with a Prestigious Title of "THE MOST HIGH", through HIS Humble PROPHETS Time and Again Patiently Warned All HIS Visible and Invisible Creations, Who by having the Conscious Attributes of INDIVIDUALIZED MINDS, are Evolving WITH or WITHOUT their Dense Form Bodies in Ethereally Differentiated Dimensions of this Planet Earth, which include ALL HIS CREATED HOSTS also Termed as the ANGELIC BEINGS of Various HIERARCHICAL ORDERS, who in their Limited Co – Creator Role Capacities as Per HIS Evolutionary PLANS were Maneuvering the Collections of the LIVE Vital Thought Form Energies, known as "THE ANIMAL MIND MAGNETIC FORCE", existing in their Categorized GROUP RESERVOIR FORMATIONS which have been Created by the INDIVIDUALIZED DESIRE MINDS OF THE EVOLVING HUMAN BEINGS, to Exist as the POLARIZED BUNDLES OF SENTIMENTS, EMOTIONS and FEELINGS Energies which are related to the Manifold DESIRES and WISHES of their "PERSONALITY MIND PASSIONS".

When SOME of the Angelic Beings WILLFULLY Betrayed their Creator LORD'S Trust, who themselves are Just Mere LORD'S Creations, and under their Illegal Mind Control Impulses the Children of Israel, the Members of HIS Chosen Race Willfully went ASTRAY from LORD'S Evolutionary Plans in BABYLON, then the Great LORD Conveyed His Warnings through Prophet NAHUM the ELKOSHITE in a Vision Provided to Him, which is known as the 'ORACLE OF NINEVEH", regarding which the Holy Bible States:

'The Oracle of NINEVEH. The Book of the Vision of NAHUM the ELKOSHITE.

A JEALOUS and AVENGING GOD is the LORD; THE LORD is '"AVENGING and WRATHFUL"'. THE LORD TAKES '"'VENGEANCE"'" ON HIS '"ADVERSARIES"'", AND HE "RESERVES WRATH" FOR "HIS ENEMIES".

THE LORD IS '''SLOW TO ANGER''' AND IS '''GREAT IN POWER''', AND THE LORD WILL '''BY NO MEANS LEAVE THE GUILTY UNPUNISHED'''. In "WHIRLWIND and STORM" is HIS WAY, and the "CLOUDS" are the DUST BENEATH HIS FEET.

HE REBUKES THE SEA and Makes it DRY; "HE DRIES UP ALL THE RIVERS". BASHAN and CARMEL "WITHER"; THE BLOSSOMS OF LEBANON WITHER.

MOUNTAINS QUAKE because of HIM, and the "HILLS DISSOLVE"; INDEED the EARTH is UP HEAVED by HIS PRESENCE, the WORLD and ALL THE INHABITANTS IN IT.

WHO CAN STAND BEFORE HIS INDIGNATION? WHO CAN ENDURE THE '''BURNING OF HIS ANGER'''? HIS WRATH IS POURED OUT LIKE '''FIRE''', AND THE ROCKS ARE '''BROKEN UP''' BY HIM.

The LORD is GOOD, a STRONGHOLD in the '''DAY OF TROUBLE''', and HE KNOWS THOSE WHO TAKE '''REFUGE IN HIM'''. But with an OVERFLOWING FLOOD HE will Make a '''COMPLETE END''' of its SITE, and will '''PURSUE HIS ENEMIES''' into "DARKNESS".' [Nahum 1. Verses 1 to 8.]

And Most of these Categorized GROUP RESERVOIRS of DESIRE MIND PASSIONS GOT FORMED around THE MAN MADE OBJECTS OF VENERATION'S, Which Mostly Consisted of BREATHLESS MOLTEN IDOLS AND GRAVEN IMAGES, which During the Earlier Stages of Human Evolution upon this Planet Earth, became the So Called PERSONALIZED GODS AND GODDESSES of Various Evolving Human Societies of this Planet Earth, to Exist as the STORE HOUSES OF INVISIBLE MAGNETIC FORCE which in the First Place was Created by the HUMAN BEINGS THEMSELVES, to be HOUSED in Elaborate and Grand Temples of Worship.

Many of the LORD'S CREATIONS, the INVISIBLE HIERARCHICAL ORDERS

OF '"HOSTS"' Commonly Known as THE ANGELIC BEINGS of VARIOUS TYPES who were GIVEN THE DUTIES to Act as the OVERSEERS and UNDERTAKERS of these GROUP RESERVOIR ENERGIES in FACT have Themselves """NEVER SEEN THE UNKNOWABLE LORD GOD""", as they also are JUST HIS MERE CREATIONS, and therefore it is TOTALLY IMPOSSIBLE FOR ALL OF THEM TO '"EVER KNOW HIM"', and Since the GRAND EXPERIMENT OF CONSCIOUS EVOLUTION BEGAN, they have ONLY UNDERSTOOD HIS "HOLY PRESENCE" AMONG THEM through HIS DESIRE MIND "THOUGHT FORMS", which Appear to THEM as THE "TONAL VIBRATIONS" OF DIFFERENTIATED '"COLORS AND SOUNDS"', and THESE TONAL FREQUENCY VIBRATIONS THUS APPROPRIATELY GUIDE THEM TO PERFORM THEIR RESPECTIVE DUTIES.

Even when the Great LORD appeared Many times in Front of MOSES and all the Children of Israel in the Wilderness, "NO ONE EVER SAW HIM", as they Only HEARD HIS VOICE and Understood HIS PRESENCE AMONG THEM through the CLOUD of SMOKE and FIRE, regarding which the Holy Bible States:

'Now MOSES used to take the Tent and Pitch it Outside the CAMP, A GOOD DISTANCE FROM THE CAMP, and He CALLED it the "TENT OF MEETING". And it CAME ABOUT, Whenever MOSES Went Out to the TENT, that ALL THE PEOPLE WOULD ARISE AND STAND, Each at the Entrance of His Tent, and "GAZE AFTER MOSES" until He ENTERED THE TENT. And it came about, Whenever MOSES Entered the TENT, the "PILLAR OF CLOUD" would DESCEND and "STAND AT THE ENTRANCE OF THE TENT "; and the "LORD WOULD SPEAK WITH MOSES".

When All the People SAW THE PILLAR OF CLOUD STANDING AT THE ENTRANCE OF THE TENT, ALL THE PEOPLE WOULD "ARISE AND WORSHIP", EACH AT THE ENTRANCE OF HIS TENT. Thus the LORD used to SPEAK TO MOSES '"FACE TO FACE"', JUST AS A MAN SPEAKS TO '"HIS FRIEND"'. When MOSES Returned to the Camp, His Servant JOSHUA, the Son of NUN, a Young Man, would not Depart from the Tent. [Exodus 33 Verses 7 to 11.]

When MOSES Reverently asked LORD GOD to Show HIS GLORY, then the

Great LORD Graciously Answered that "NO MAN COULD SEE HIM", and "'LIVE'", regarding which the Holy Bible States:

'Then MOSES Said, "I PRAY THEE, SHOW ME THY GLORY!" And HE Said, "I MYSELF WILL MAKE ALL "'MY GOODNESS'" PASS BEFORE YOU, AND WILL PROCLAIM THE NAME OF THE LORD BEFORE YOU; AND "I" WILL BE GRACIOUS TO WHOM "I" WILL BE GRACIOUS, AND WILL SHOW COMPASSION ON WHOM "I" WILL SHOW COMPASSION".

BUT HE SAID, "YOU CANNOT SEE MY FACE, FOR "'NO MAN'" CAN SEE ME AND "'LIVE'"!"

Then the LORD Said, "BEHOLD, there is a Place by ME, and YOU shall Stand there on the ROCK; and it will Come About, while MY GLORY IS PASSING BY, that "I" will PUT YOU IN THE CLEFT OF THE ROCK AND COVER YOU WITH MY HAND UNTIL "I" HAVE PASSED BY, THEN "I" WILL TAKE MY HAND AWAY AND YOU SHALL SEE "'MY BACK'", BUT "'MY FACE'" SHALL NOT BE "'SEEN'". [Exodus 33 Verses 18 to 23.]

BECAUSE ALMOST ALL THESE ANGELIC BEINGS, who as per their Assigned Duties were Managing the Energy Reservoirs of these So called MAN MADE MOLTEN GODS AND GODDESSES HAD ACTUALLY NEVER SEEN THEIR "'CREATOR LORD - GOD'" except HIS DESIRE MIND'S TONAL FREQUENCY VIBRATIONS APPEARING IN VARIOUS SHADES OF COLORS AND SOUNDS, A GROUP OF THEIR "'DERANGED MIND'" TOP LEADERS, WHO WERE ORIGINALLY TRUSTED BY THE LORD AND WERE THUS KEPT IN HIS HIGHEST SERVICE AS HIS "COUNSELORS", THEY ALL DUE TO THEIR "FALSE PRIDE" AFTER HAVING MUTATIONS IN THEIR EVOLVING CONSCIOUSNESS, WHICH WAS CAUSED DUE TO THE DEPLETION OF THE CONSCIOUS ENERGIES OF THEIR OWN "SACRED HEART'S LOVE FREQUENCIES" THEN BY WILLFULLY MISUSING THEIR ALLOTTED VESTED POWERS THUS BACK - STABBED HIS "'LOVE AND TRUST'", AND THEN STARTED a MOST HEINOUS CONSPIRACY AGAINST THE "'UNKNOWABLE MOST HIGH'", and Started this FOOLISH RUMOR Among them, that there was ABSOLUTELY "'NO SUCH THING'" AS THE "MOST HIGH", and thus "'THEY THEMSELVES'" were the HIGHEST AUTHORITY in ALL THE DIMENSIONAL PLANE WORLDS OF THIS PLANET EARTH, which thus STARTED THE ONSLAUGHT OF THEIR DECEITFUL AGENDAS to be ROOTED among the Various Hierarchical Levels of INVISIBLE BEINGS, which Culminated in UTMOST CORRUPTION, thus Making All Dimension Levels Under their ILLEGAL CONTROL as the Places of "PAINS AND SUFFERINGS", which is Now Prevalent in a VERY BIG WAY in All THE DIMENSIONAL CORNERS of this Planet Earth. The Great LORD again DIRELY WARNED ALL THESE INVISIBLE CONSPIRATORS and their INCARNATED HUMAN HENCHMEN WHO were ILLEGALLY SEATED AND POSITIONED by them on the TOP LEVELS OF THE EVOLVING HUMAN SOCIETIES including Various RELIGIOUS ORGANIZATIONS through His Chosen Prophet NAHUM, regarding which the Holy Bible States:

'WHATEVER YOU DEVISE "'AGAINST THE LORD'", HE WILL MAKE "'A COMPLETE END'" OF IT. DISTRESS WILL NOT RISE UP "'TWICE'".

FROM YOU HAVE GONE FORTH ONE WHO "'PLOTTED EVIL AGAINST THE LORD'", A WICKED "'COUNSELOR'".

'Now MOSES used to take the Tent and Pitch it Outside the CAMP, A GOOD DISTANCE FROM THE CAMP, and He CALLED it the "TENT OF MEETING".
[Exodus 33 Verses 7]

Then the LORD answered Me and Said, "RECORD THE VISION, AND INSCRIBE IT ON '''TABLETS''', THAT THE ONE WHO READS IT MAY RUN. For the VISION is YET FOR THE APPOINTED TIME; IT HASTENS TOWARD THE GOAL, AND '''IT WILL NOT FAIL'''. Though it TARRIES, Wait for IT; FOR IT WILL '''CERTAINLY COME''', IT WILL NOT '''DELAY'''." [Habakkuk 2. 2, 3,]

During those Dark Times, when the Children of Israel under the Mind Control Influence of the Corrupt HOSTS being Totally Unaware of the HIGHER DIMENSIONAL REALMS, which Exist upon THIS PLANET EARTH, thus Went ASTRAY from the LORD'S COMMANDMENTS, then these DARK MASTERS of so called BROTHERHOOD'S and belonging to Various Hierarchical Orders of Invisible Beings, who acted as the So Called GODS and GODDESSES upon this Planet EARTH, and Willfully Conspired Against the Evolutionary Plan and Purpose of the "MOST HIGH", by STRATEGICALLY PLACING WICKED PEOPLE as RELATIVES, FRIENDS, ACQUAINTANCES, AND A WHOLE MYRIAD OF OTHER INFLUENTIAL PEOPLE AROUND THE "'RIGHTEOUS PEOPLE'" upon the Physical Plane of this Planet Earth, thus Deceitfully Surrounding them in their Daily Lives, So as to also PULL them Down Like themselves into ANIMAL MIND ACTIVITIES OF LOW GRADE PASSIONS, regarding which the Holy Bible States:

'Therefore the LAW is IGNORED, and JUSTICE is NEVER UPHELD, FOR THE "'WICKED'" SURROUND THE "'RIGHTEOUS'"; THEREFORE, JUSTICE COMES OUT "'PERVERTED'".' [Habakkuk 1. 4.]

The Great LORD of UNIVERSE having UTMOST PATIENCE for HIS Chosen Race, then to Properly Guide the Children of Israel thus raised HIS Chosen Prophets Among them, and Such was a PROPHET named HABAKKUK, who was the FIRST PROPHET SINCE MOSES TIME, WHOM THE LORD while giving Him a VISION OF ORACLE, also COMMANDED HIM TO "RECORD" THE VISION BY "'INSCRIBING IT ON THE TABLETS'", just like MOSES in Earlier Times Wrote Down the "LORD'S COMMANDS" upon TWO TABLETS upon HIS Holy Mountain, regarding which the Holy Bible States:

"The Oracle which HABAKKUK THE PROPHET SAW. [Habakkuk 1. 1.]

Then the LORD answered Me and Said, "RECORD THE VISION, AND

INSCRIBE IT ON "'TABLETS'", THAT THE ONE WHO READS IT MAY RUN."

"For the VISION is YET FOR THE APPOINTED TIME; IT HASTENS TOWARD THE GOAL, AND "'IT WILL NOT FAIL'". Though it TARRIES, Wait for IT; FOR IT WILL "'CERTAINLY COME'", IT WILL NOT "'DELAY'"'." [Habakkuk 2. 2, 3,]

In this MOST IMPORTANT ORACLE, which the GREAT LORD COMMANDED HABAKKUK to INSCRIBE ON THE TABLETS, the Great LORD also Clearly Explained to HIS Chosen Prophet HABAKKUK, that the "FALSE PRIDE" is the "MAIN REASON" for the "'DOWNFALL OF BOTH THE VISIBLE AND INVISIBLE BEINGS'" of Various DIMENSIONAL LEVELS, Who Subjectively and Objectively Exists Manifested in HIS ALL CREATIONS, as it HARDENS THE ETHEREAL MATTER OF THEIR "'SOUL'" CONSCIOUSNESS, WHICH THUS BECOMES "TOTALLY MALIGNED" and FINALLY GETS CUT OFF FROM THE "SOUL'S ETHEREAL MATTER", and then the Manifested SOUL Could be "LOST FOR AN ETERNAL CYCLE", regarding which the Holy Bible States:

"BEHOLD, as for the 'PROUD ONE', HIS "'SOUL'" IS "NOT RIGHT" WITHIN HIM; but the "RIGHTEOUS" will "LIVE BY HIS FAITH" [Habakkuk 2. 4.]

The HARDENING OF THE "ETHEREAL HEART CENTER", which is the "SACRED CENTER" EXISTING AS THE INDWELLING PLACE OF THE SOLAR CONSCIOUS ENERGY, known as THE "'SOUL MIND'" OR THE "'CONTEMPLATING CONSCIOUSNESS'" then CAUSES the ONSLAUGHT OF "'UNQUENCHABLE GREED in the Evolving "PERSONALITY MIND" of an Incarnated Human Being, and the Great LORD GOD Commanded Prophet HABAKKUK to make a PERMANENT RECORD of it by INSCRIBING ON THE TABLETS, regarding which the Holy Bible States:

'Because YOU have LOOTED MANY NATIONS, ALL THE REMAINDER OF THE PEOPLES WILL "LOOT YOU"– BECAUSE OF HUMAN BLOODSHED AND VIOLENCE DONE TO THE LAND, TO THE TOWN AND ALL ITS INHABITANTS.

Woe to Him who GETS "'EVIL GAIN'" for His House to PUT NEST ON HIGH to be delivered from the Hand of CALAMITY! YOU have DEVISED a SHAMEFUL THING FOR YOUR HOUSE BY "'CUTTING OFF MANY PEOPLES"; SO YOU ARE "'SINNING'" AGAINST "YOURSELF". Surely the STONE will CRY OUT from the WALL, and the RAFTER will ANSWER IT FROM THE FRAMEWORK.

Woe to Him who Builds a City with BLOODSHED and FOUNDS a TOWN with VIOLENCE! IS IT NOT INTENDED FROM THE "LORD OF HOSTS" THAT PEOPLE TOIL FOR "FIRE", and NATIONS GROW WEARY FOR 'NOTHING'?

For the EARTH will be FILLED with the "'KNOWLEDGE OF THE GLORY OF THE LORD'", as "WATERS COVER THE SEA".' [Habakkuk 2. Verses 8 to 14.]

AND as far as the BREATHLESS MOLTEN IDOLS and GRAVEN IMAGES of so called GODS and GODDESSES are CONCERNED, which are created Just by Mere Human Hands, the GREAT LORD GOD COMMANDED His Chosen Prophet HABAKKUK to "INSCRIBE HIS COMMANDS ON THE TABLETS", regarding which the Holy Bible States:

'What PROFIT is the "IDOL" when its MAKER has CARVED it, OR an "IMAGE", a "'TEACHER OF FALSEHOOD'"? For its Maker Trusts in His "OWN HANDIWORK" when He FASHIONS "'SPEECHLESS IDOLS'".

Woe to Him WHO SAYS TO A 'PIECE OF WOOD', "AWAKE"! TO A 'DUMB STONE', "ARISE"! And that is "YOUR TEACHER"? Behold, it is OVERLAID with GOLD and SILVER, and there is "'NO BREATH AT ALL INSIDE IT'".

But the LORD is in HIS HOLY TEMPLE. LET all the EARTH be "SILENT BEFORE HIM".' [Habakkuk 2. Verses 18 to 20.]

The Great LORD also gave a VISION to Holy Servant Prophet OBADIAH, so that through Him the Children of Israel should KNOW that all the Other Human Beings who being ALLIED WITH THEM are being ILLEGALLY

CONTROLLED by these MOST CORRUPT INVISIBLE BEINGS and thus they have NO TRUE UNDERSTANDINGS, as these are the Same CORRUPT BEINGS Who established for them the "BREATHLESS AND SOULLESS ENTITIES" to EXIST as their Revered MOLTEN AND GRAVEN IMAGES OF "'GODS AND GODDESSES '", So that they under their Negative Influence can also BACK – STAB them and thus Hurt them, and all their Negative Actions will BRING BACK NEGATIVE REACTIONS, regarding which the Holy Bible States:

'All the Men ALLIED WITH YOU will Send YOU Forth to the BORDER, and the Men at PEACE with YOU will DECEIVE YOU AND OVERPOWER YOU. They WHO EAT YOUR BREAD will SET AN AMBUSH FOR YOU. [There is NO UNDERSTANDING IN HIM.]

For the DAY OF LORD DRAWS NEAR ON "'ALL THE NATIONS'". AS YOU HAVE "'DONE'", IT WILL BE DONE TO YOU. YOUR DEALINGS WILL RETURN ON YOUR OWN HEAD. [Obadiah 1. 7,15.]

Although the Incarnated Human Beings of this Planet Earth belonging to Various Races, Casts and Creeds, whom the LORD GOD in the Very Beginning Created in HIS OWN IMAGE, are the MOST INTELLIGENT SPECIES AMONG ALL OTHER SPECIES OF THE '"ANIMAL KINGDOM"' having the Conscious Attribute of "INDIVIDUALIZED MIND", but they are "STILL UNAWARE" OF THIS "SUPREME FACT", that their Embodied "PERSONALITY CONSCIOUSNESS" evolving in their Animated Forms has been Incarnated for the Main Purpose of Attaining SPIRITUAL EXPERIENCES in the Dense Plane Worlds, and their Indwelling PERSONALITY is Just a Very Tiny and Just a Minute Part of their "SOLAR ETHEREAL CONSCIOUSNESS", which is also a PART AND PARCEL OF THE SEVEN WAY DIFFERENTIATED DESIRE MIND CONSCIOUS REFLECTIONS OF THE UNKNOWABLE '"MOST HIGH"', and BECAUSE the "MOST HIGH", who is THE SOLE CREATOR – OBSERVER, PRESERVER AND DESTROYER OF THIS UNIVERSE IS UNKNOWABLE TO '"ALL HIS CREATIONS"' INCLUDING ALL THE MEMBERS OF THE "VISIBLE KINGDOMS" AND THE "INVISIBLE HIERARCHICAL ANGELIC BEINGS", for this being the MAIN REASON, since Very Ancient Times of this Planet Earth EVEN TILL NOW, the Incarnated Human Beings Have Been '"WRONGFULLY AND IGNORANTLY WORSHIPING"' the MAN MADE OBJECTS, SYMBOLS, AND VARIOUS GRAVEN IMAGES, as well as the "NATURAL FORMATIONS OF STONES, HILLS AND TREES", as "HIS TRUE FORM REPRESENTATIONS", which are Total ABOMINATIONS TO THE "MOST HIGH", because they are JUST HIS MERE CREATIONS, and thus Just a MINUTE MANIFESTED PART DUE TO THE "DESIRE MIND" OF THE UNKNOWABLE "WHOLE". The Humble Servant of the LORD Prophet ISAIAH Clearly Understood these Undeniable FACTS that the People's Personality Mind's Being Captive in their IGNORANCE, were thus FOOLISHLY WORSHIPING THE GRAVEN IMAGES OF SO CALLED GODS AND GODDESSES, WHO WERE 'CONSIGNED TO THE BEASTS AND THE CATTLE" to be carried on to Different Places, and were thus THEMSELVES CAPTIVES as the "BURDENSOME LOADS" FOR THE WEARY BEASTS, and Prophet Isaiah thus Conveyed LORD'S MESSAGE to the Children of Israel, regarding which the Holy Bible States:

'BEL has BOWED DOWN, NEBO STOOPS OVER; THEIR IMAGES ARE

"CONSIGNED TO THE BEASTS AND THE CATTLE". The THINGS You CARRY are "'BURDENSOME'", A LOAD FOR THE WEARY BEAST. They STOOPED OVER, they have BOWED DOWN TOGETHER; THEY COULD NOT RESCUE THE BURDEN, BUT HAVE "'THEMSELVES'" GONE INTO CAPTIVITY. [Isaiah 46. 1, 2.]

The GREAT AND UNKNOWABLE LORD – GOD, after HE Established HIS Chosen Race Upon the Physical Plane [ASSIAH] of this Planet Earth, Hoping for them to Exist as the "SHINING BEACONS OF LIGHT" as well as the Guiding Symbols for All other EVOLVING HUMAN RACES of this Planet Earth, then through His Various Humble Prophets Time and Again "'DID HIS UTMOST EFFORTS'" to Convey HIS SPIRITUAL MESSAGES to them, who Under the CORRUPT MIND CONTROL TECHNIQUES OF THE "'INVISIBLE FALLEN ANGELS'", EASILY GOT SWAYED TO THEIR DECEITFUL TECHNIQUES, WHICH WERE RELATED TO THE "'ANIMAL MIND PLEASURES AND PASSIONS", and For this Very Reason these Invisible Existences Deceitfully Incited them to Create their so called MAN MADE "'GODS AND GODDESSES'" IN FORMS OF ANIMALS LIKE A BULL WHO "'LUSTS AND FIGHTS'", as well various other Type of ANIMAL HEADS having HUMAN FORMS and BODIES, thus Showing and Reminding them of their Lower Mind Animal Passions, which "FEEL EXCITING AND PLEASURABLE" to their Evolving "PERSONALITY MINDS", so as to Keep them LOST in the Material World Illusory Glamour during their Short Lived Human Lives Upon this Planet Earth, about which LORD'S Chosen Prophet ISAIAH as Per LORD'S Command Humbly Conveyed HIS MESSAGE to the Children of Israel, regarding which the Holy Bible States:

'I AM THE LORD, AND THERE IS "'NO OTHER'"; BESIDES ME THERE IS "'NO GOD'".

"I" WILL GIRD YOU, THOUGH YOU HAVE "'NOT KNOWN ME'"; THAT MEN MAY KNOW FROM THE RISING TO THE SETTING OF THE SUN, THAT THERE IS "'NO ONE BESIDES ME'". I AM THE LORD, AND THERE IS "'NO OTHER'", THE ONE "'FORMING LIGHT AND CREATING DARKNESS", "CAUSING WELL – BEING" AND "CREATING CALAMITY"; I AM THE LORD WHO DOES "'ALL THESE'". [Isaiah 45. Verses 5 to 7.]

These ABOVE MOST IMPORTANT VERSES OF THE HOLY BIBLE Clearly

State that the GREAT AND UNKNOWABLE LORD "'FIRST'" CREATED THE "'DARK ETHEREAL SPACE OF THE INFINITE UNIVERSE'", IN WHICH "'HE FORMED THE LIGHT'", because after the CREATION OF THE "DARK ETHEREAL SPACE HAVING VITAL CONSCIOUSNESS" then Manifested the GREAT "CHAOS" appearing as the "CALAMITY", Without having Any "'MATHEMATICAL and GEOMETRICAL ORDER in the DARKNESS'", which was Removed after the "FORMATION OF LIGHT", WHICH THROUGH ITS CYCLIC "'FREQUENCY VIBRATIONS'" BROUGHT A PROPER "'MATHEMATICAL AND GEOMETRICAL ORDER IN THE DARKNESS OF ETHEREAL VITALITY'", thus MANIFESTING the DIFFERENTIATED "VISIBLE AND INVISIBLE" DIMENSIONAL LEVELS and thus CAUSING the "WELL BEING" OF ALL CONSCIOUS AND UNCONSCIOUS MANIFESTED EXISTENCES TO HARMONIOUSLY "CO - EXIST" IN THEM.

Regarding the HAUGHTINESS of the "'REBELLIOUS HOSTS'" and the FOOLISHNESS OF THEIR CONTROLLED HUMAN BEINGS Incarnated Upon this Planet Earth, the GREAT LORD further CONVEYED to the Children of Israel as well as THE ENTIRE MAN KIND through HIS Prophet ISAIAH, regarding which the Holy Bible States:

'WOE to the "ONE" Who "'QUARRELS WITH HIS MAKER'" – AN EARTHENWARE VESSEL AMONG THE VESSELS OF EARTH!

WILL THE "CLAY" SAY TO THE "POTTER", "WHAT ARE YOU DOING?" OR THE "THING" YOU ARE MAKING SAY, "HE HAS NO HANDS"?' [Isaiah 45. 9.]

For the FOOLISH HUMANS OF THIS PLANET EARTH, who Instead of REVERENTLY WORSHIPING their 'ONE AND ONLY' THE "MOST HIGH'", the CREATOR LORD GOD of the UNIVERSE, Ignorantly started Worshiping HIS Mere Servants, the Invisible Groups of Hierarchical "HOSTS", who were Behaving as the So called GODS AND GODDESSES, the GREAT LORD then Conveyed to them the required "KNOWLEDGE AND WISDOM" ABOUT HIS EVOLUTIONARY "PLAN AND PURPOSE" ESTABLISHED BY HIS "DESIRE MIND", through HIS Chosen Prophet ISAIAH, regarding which the Holy Bible States:

'TO WHOM WOULD YOU "LIKEN ME", AND MAKE ME "EQUAL" AND COMPARE ME, THAT WE SHOULD BE ALIKE?

Those who Lavish GOLD from the PURSE and WEIGH SILVER ON THE SCALE HIRE A "'GOLDSMITH'", AND HE MAKES "IT INTO A GOD"; THEY BOW DOWN, INDEED THEY WORSHIP IT.

THEY LIFT IT UPON THEIR SHOULDER AND CARRY IT; THEY SET IT IN ITS PLACE AND IT "STANDS THERE". IT DOES NOT MOVE FROM ITS PLACE. THOUGH ONE MAY "CRY TO IT", IT CANNOT ANSWER; IT CANNOT DELIVER HIM FROM HIS DISTRESS.

REMEMBER this, and be ASSURED; RECALL IT TO MIND, YOU "TRANSGRESSORS". Remember the FORMER THINGS LONG PAST, FOR "I" AM "GOD", AND THERE IS "'NO OTHER'"; 'I" AM "GOD", AND THERE IS "'NO ONE LIKE ME'", DECLARING "THE END" FROM THE "BEGINNING", AND FROM "ANCIENT TIMES" THINGS WHICH HAVE "NOT BEEN DONE", SAYING "'''MY PURPOSE WILL BE ESTABLISHED'''", AND "I" WILL ACCOMPLISH "'ALL MY GOOD PLEASURE'"; Calling a Bird of Prey from the EAST, THE MAN OF "'MY PURPOSE'" FROM A "FAR COUNTRY".

TRULY "I" HAVE SPOKEN; TRULY "I" WILL BRING IT TO PASS. "I" HAVE PLANNED IT, "'SURELY'" 'I' WILL DO IT. [Isaiah 46. Verses 5 to 11.]

LORD'S Chosen Prophet JEREMIAH also Boldly Declared LORD'S WARNINGS to the Children of Israel and their IDOL WORSHIPING PROPHET'S and PRIEST'S whose "PERSONALITY MINDS" UNDER THE GRIP OF MOST CORRUPT "INVISIBLE BEINGS" GOT TOTALLY POLLUTED, regarding which the Holy Bible States:

"For Both PROPHET and PRIEST are POLLUTED; EVEN in MY HOUSE "I" have found their WICKEDNESS", Declares the LORD.

'Moreover, Among the PROPHETS OF SAMARIA "I" SAW AN OFFENSIVE THING; They "'PROPHESIED BY BAAL'" and LED MY PEOPLE "'ISRAEL'"

ASTRAY. Also among the PROPHETS OF JERUSALEM "I" have SEEN A "HORRIBLE THING"; THE COMMITTING OF "'ADULTERY'" and "'WALKING IN FALSEHOOD'"; AND They Strengthen the "'HANDS OF EVILDOERS'", So that "'NO ONE HAS TURNED BACK FROM HIS WICKEDNESS". All of them have Become to ME LIKE SODOM, and Her Inhabitants LIKE GOMORRAH.

Thus Says the LORD OF HOSTS, "DO NOT LISTEN TO THE WORDS OF THE PROPHETS WHO ARE PROPHESYING TO YOU. THEY ARE LEADING YOU INTO "'FUTILITY'"; THEY SPEAK A VISION OF THEIR OWN "'IMAGINATION'", NOT FROM THE "'MOUTH OF THE LORD'".

"I" DID NOT SEND THESE PROPHETS, BUT THEY RAN. "I" DID NOT "SPEAK TO THEM", BUT THEY PROPHESIED.

Can a Man HIDE HIMSELF IN HIDING PLACES, SO "I" DO NOT SEE HIM?" Declares the LORD. "DO "I" NOT FILL THE HEAVENS AND THE EARTH?" Declares the LORD.

"I HAVE HEARD WHAT THE PROPHETS HAVE SAID WHO PROPHESY "'FALSELY IN MY NAME'", Saying, 'I HAD A DREAM, I HAD A DREAM!' How Long? Is there ANYTHING in the "HEARTS OF THE PROPHETS" Who PROPHESY FALSEHOOD, Even these PROPHETS of the "DECEPTION OF THEIR OWN HEART", WHO INTEND to Make "MY PEOPLE FORGET MY NAME" by their DREAMS which they RELATE TO ONE ANOTHER, JUST AS THEIR "'FATHERS FORGOT MY NAME BECAUSE OF BAAL'"?"

"Therefore behold, "I" AM AGAINST THE PROPHETS," Declares the LORD, "WHO STEAL MY WORDS FROM EACH OTHER". "Behold "I" AM AGAINST THE PROPHETS." Declares the LORD "WHO USE THEIR TONGUES AND DECLARE, "THE LORD DECLARES." "Behold, "'I' AM AGAINST THOSE WHO HAVE PROPHESIED FALSE DREAMS", Declares the LORD, "And RELATED THEM, AND LED MY PEOPLE ASTRAY BY THEIR FALSEHOODS AND RECKLESS BOASTING; YET "I" DID NOT SEND THEM OR 'COMMAND THEM', NOR DO THEY FURNISH THIS PEOPLE "'THE SLIGHTEST BENEFIT'", " DECLARES THE LORD." [Jeremiah 23. 11, 13, 14, 16, 21, 24, 25, 26, 27, 30, 31, 32.]

'Then JESUS Spoke to the MULTITUDES and to His DISCIPLES, Saying, "THE SCRIBES AND THE PHARISEES have SEATED THEMSELVES in the """CHAIR OF MOSES""""; THEREFORE All that they TELL YOU, "DO AND OBSERVE", but "DO NOT DO" ACCORDING TO THEIR DEEDS; FOR THEY "'SAY THINGS"', AND DO NOT DO THEM. [Matthew 23. Verses 1 to 3]

Although the Chosen Prophets of LORD GOD Time and Again Went on Conveying LORD'S Commands and Instructions to the Children of Israel, there was NOT MUCH Change to OCCUR in their Behavior Patterns, by the Time HIS SON JESUS CHRIST Incarnated Upon the Physical Plane of this Planet Earth.

When JESUS was Born, His Divine Birth apart from being Known to the Caretaker INVISIBLE BEINGS of this Planet Earth, was also NOTICED by Many Magicians and Wise Men of the East, who SAW A BRIGHT STAR IN THE EAST and being well TRAINED as the STARGAZER ASTROLOGERS, they were able to Interpret this HOLY CELESTIAL OMEN, and then Clearly Understanding Its IMPORTANCE, they Firmly Concluded that "A GODLY KING OF THE JEWS" was BORN AMONG THEM, regarding which the Holy Bible States:

'Now after JESUS was born in BETHLEHEM of JUDEA in the Days of HEROD THE KING, Behold, MAGI FROM THE EAST arrived in JERUSALEM, Saying. "WHERE is HE who has been BORN KING of the JEWS? For WE SAW HIS STAR IN THE EAST, and have COME to WORSHIP HIM".

And when HEROD THE KING HEARD it, He was TROUBLED, AND ALL JERUSALEM WITH HIM. And Gathering Together ALL THE '''PRIESTS AND SCRIBES''' OF THE PEOPLE, HE BEGAN TO '''INQUIRE OF THEM''', Where the CHRIST WAS TO BE BORN. And they SAID to Him, "IN BETHLEHEM OF JUDEA, FOR SO IT HAS BEEN WRITTEN BY THE PROPHET, 'And YOU, BETHLEHEM, LAND OF JUDAH, are by NO MEANS LEAST AMONG THE LEADERS OF JUDAH; FOR OUT OF YOU SHALL COME FORTH A '''RULER''', WHO WILL SHEPHERD MY PEOPLE ISRAEL''.' [Matthew 2. Verses 1 to 6.]

Many People are Not Aware of this Important Biblical Fact that "KING DAVID", Son of JESSE, and the Father of Wise KING SOLOMON, in Whose Lineage later on JESUS CHRIST was also BORN, was HIMSELF FROM THIS HOLY TOWN OF BETHLEHEM, AND THUS A '''BETHLEHEMITE''', where

He as per the LORD'S Command was ANOINTED by the Prophet SAMUEL to be the "KING OF ISRAEL", regarding which the Holy Bible States:

'Now the LORD Said to SAMUEL, "How Long will You GRIEVE over SAUL, SINCE "I" have Rejected Him from being KING OVER ISRAEL? Fill YOUR HORN WITH OIL, and GO; "I" will Send YOU to "JESSE THE BETHLEHEMITE", for "I" have SELECTED A KING FOR MYSELF AMONG HIS SONS".' [1 Samuel. 16. 1]

The Above Verses regarding JESUS'S Birth, which the Priests and Scribes Quoted to HEROD THE KING, were Uttered Much Earlier by the Prophet MICAH of MORESHETH, who Gracefully received LORD'S WORD during the Times of Kings JOTHAM, AHAZ, and HEZEKIAH, the Kings of JUDAH, regarding which the Holy Bible States:

'But as for YOU, "BETHLEHEM" EPHRATHAH, TOO LITTLE to be AMONG THE CLANS OF JUDAH, FROM YOU '"ONE'" WILL GO FORTH FOR ME TO BE RULER IN ISRAEL.

HIS GOINGS FORTH ARE FROM '"'"'LONG AGO'"'"', FROM THE '"DAYS OF ETERNITY'". Therefore, HE will GIVE them Up until the TIME, WHEN SHE '"WHO IS IN LABOR'" HAS BORN A CHILD. Then the Remainder of HIS Brethren will RETURN to the Sons of Israel.

And HE will Arise and '"SHEPHERD'" HIS "FLOCK" IN THE '"STRENGTH OF THE LORD'", IN THE MAJESTY OF THE '"NAME OF THE LORD HIS GOD'". And they will REMAIN, BECAUSE at that TIME '"HE WILL BE GREAT'" TO THE ENDS OF THE EARTH.' [Micah 5. Verses 2 to 4.]

Also the Great LORD himself TOLD King AHAZ Son of JOTHAM, the King of JUDAH about the Birth of JESUS CHRIST to Occur in the Distant Future, regarding which the Holy Bible States:

'Then the LORD Spoke Again to AHAZ, Saying, "ASK a SIGN for YOURSELF from the LORD YOUR GOD, MAKE it DEEP as SHEOL or HIGH as

HEAVEN''. But Ahaz Said, ''I will NOT ASK, NOR will I TEST THE LORD!''

THEN HE SAID, ''LISTEN NOW, O HOUSE OF DAVID! IS IT TOO SLIGHT A THING FOR YOU TO TRY THE '''PATIENCE OF MEN''', THAT YOU WILL TRY THE '''PATIENCE OF MY GOD AS WELL?

Therefore the LORD HIMSELF will GIVE You a SIGN; Behold, A ''VIRGIN WILL BE WITH CHILD'' AND BEAR A '''SON''', AND SHE WILL CALL HIS NAME '''EMMANUEL'''. He will EAT ''''''CURDS AND HONEY'''''' at the TIME HE KNOWS ENOUGH TO REFUSE '''EVIL AND CHOOSE GOOD'''. For before the BOY will KNOW ENOUGH TO ''REFUSE EVIL AND CHOOSE GOOD'', the LAND Whose TWO KINGS You DREAD WILL BE '''FORSAKEN'''.' [Isaiah 7. Verses 10 to 16.]

During the TIMES of JESUS CHRIST, a Tiny Part of the SOUL CONSCIOUSNESS of ''PROPHET ELIJAH'' also Reincarnated upon the Physical Plane as the Embodied ''PERSONALITY MIND'' of ''JOHN THE BAPTIST'', Who was Quoting the Words of Prophet ISAIAH asking the People of JUDEA to make a WAY FOR THE LORD IN THE WILDERNESS, regarding which the Holy Bible States:

'A Voice is Calling, CLEAR THE WAY FOR THE LORD IN THE WILDERNESS; Make SMOOTH in the DESERT A HIGHWAY FOR OUR GOD.' [Isaiah 40. 3.]

'Now in those Days JOHN THE BAPTIST Came PREACHING in the Wilderness of JUDEA, Saying, ''REPENT, for the Kingdom of Heaven is at Hand''. For ''THIS IS THE ONE'' Referred to by ISAIAH the PROPHET, Saying, ''THE Voice of ONE CRYING in the WILDERNESS, MAKE Ready the WAY OF THE LORD, MAKE HIS PATHS STRAIGHT!''

Now JOHN Himself had a Garment of Camel's Hair, and a Leather Belt about His Waist; and His Food was LOCUSTS and WILD HONEY. Then JERUSALEM was Going Out to Him, and All JUDEA, and all the District around the JORDAN; and they were being BAPTIZED by Him in the Jordan River, as they CONFESSED THEIR SINS. But When He Saw Many of the "PHARISEES and SADDUCEES" coming for BAPTISM, He Said to them, "YOU BROOD OF VIPERS, who Warned YOU to FLEE from the WRATH TO COME? Therefore bring Forth Fruit in KEEPING WITH YOUR REPENTANCE. [Matthew 3. Verses 1 to 8.]

JESUS CHRIST also exposed many of the SO called LEADERS of the "ORGANIZED RELIGION", which was Prevalent in the Hay DAY of His TIMES, Controlled by the Hierarchical SCRIBES and PHARISEES, Who during HIS Time Period were taking Full Advantage of the INNOCENT Children of Israel, as Most of The Children of Israel by being Themselves Remorseful in those TRYING TIMES under the Roman Rule, who themselves Worshiped the Images of so Called GODS AND GODDESSES, were thus Paying a Blind Eye to the Important Spiritual Matters which were Related to LORD'S COMMANDS, and for this Very Reason they Never Questioned the DEEDS OF THEIR RELIGIOUS LEADERS, who Like "MOSES" Said THINGS for Them to "DO", but they THEMSELVES NEVER DID THEM, and JESUS OPENLY CALLED THESE LEADERS OF THE "'ORGANIZED RELIGION'" as "'THE SONS OF HELL'", regarding which the Holy Bible States:

'Then JESUS Spoke to the MULTITUDES and to His DISCIPLES, Saying, "THE SCRIBES AND THE PHARISEES have SEATED THEMSELVES in the ""CHAIR OF MOSES""'; THEREFORE All that they TELL YOU, "DO AND OBSERVE", but "DO NOT DO" ACCORDING TO THEIR DEEDS; FOR THEY "'SAY THINGS'", AND DO NOT DO THEM.

And they TIE UP HEAVY LOADS, and "LAY THEM ON MEN'S SHOULDERS"; But they THEMSELVES are UNWILLING to MOVE THEM WITH SO MUCH AS A "'FINGER'". But they DO ALL THEIR DEEDS TO BE NOTICED BY MEN; FOR They BROADEN Their PHYLACTERIES, and LENGTHEN the TASSELS of their GARMENTS.

And they LOVE THE PLACE OF HONOR AT "'BANQUETS'", and the "'CHIEF SEATS'" IN THE 'SYNAGOGUES', and 'RESPECTFUL GREETINGS' in the MARKET PLACES, and being CALLED by Men, "'RABBI'".

But "WOE TO YOU", SCRIBES and PHARISEES, HYPOCRITES, because

"'YOU SHUT OFF THE KINGDOM OF HEAVEN FROM MEN'"; for YOU DO NOT ENTER IN YOURSELVES, NOR DO YOU ALLOW "'THOSE'" WHO ARE ENTERING TO GO IN.

[WOE TO YOU, "SCRIBES" AND "PHARISEES", HYPOCRITES, because YOU DEVOUR WIDOWS' HOUSES, Even While for a PRETENSE You MAKE LONG PRAYERS; therefore YOU shall Receive Greater CONDEMNATION.]

WOE to YOU, SCRIBES and PHARISEES, HYPOCRITES, because YOU Travel About on SEA and LAND to Make ONE "PROSELYTE"; and when He becomes ONE, YOU MAKE HIM "'TWICE AS MUCH'" a "'''SON OF HELL''''" as YOURSELVES.

Woe to YOU, "'BLIND GUIDES'", Who Say, "WHOEVER SWEARS BY THE "'TEMPLE'", THAT IS "'NOTHING'"; BUT Whoever Swears by the GOLD OF THE TEMPLE, HE is OBLIGATED". YOU "'FOOLS'" and "'BLIND MEN'"; WHICH IS MORE "IMPORTANT", the GOLD, or the TEMPLE that SANCTIFIED THE GOLD? [Matthew 23. Verses 1 to 7, and Verses 13 to 17.]

John the Baptist

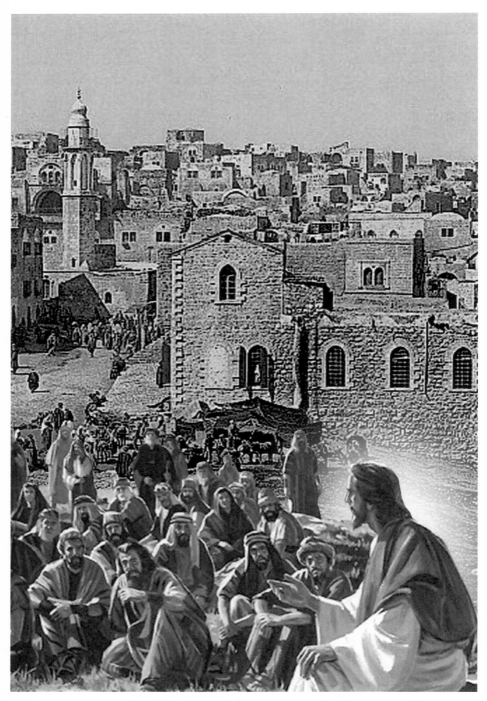

"And having Summoned HIS Twelve Disciples, HE Gave them AUTHORITY over UNCLEAN SPIRITS, TO CAST THEM OUT, AND TO HEAL "EVERY KIND OF DISEASE AND EVERY KIND OF SICKNESS"." [Matthew 10. 1]

The Wise King SOLOMON, who also PREACHED to the Children of Israel during His Life Time about his Acquired Knowledge and Wisdom, was Chosen by LORD GOD to be His SON upon this Planet Earth, which was Narrated to Prophet NATHAN by the LORD Himself and thus Recorded in '1 Chronicles 17. 13.' of the Holy Bible, the Great King with the LORD'S GRACE Clearly Understood, that to FIND "KNOWLEDGE" ABOUT ANYTHING, AND THUS TO ACQUIRE THE RELATED "WISDOM" HE HAD TO SET HIS MIND TO "SEEK IT", regarding which the Holy Bible States:

'I, the Preacher, have been King Over Israel in JERUSALEM. And I SET MY MIND TO "'SEEK"' and EXPLORE by WISDOM Concerning ALL that has been DONE under HEAVEN. It is a GRIEVOUS TASK Which GOD has GIVEN to the SONS of MEN to be AFFLICTED WITH.' [Ecclesiastes 1. 12, 13.]

Similarly Much Later LORD'S Son JESUS CHRIST Stressed Upon the Most Important Point, for Humans to Achieve their DESIRED WISHES by "'ASKING and SEEKING"', so they can "RECEIVE and FIND THEM" by the Grace of the GREAT LORD, Who is the FATHER IN HEAVEN, known to ALL as THE "MOST HIGH", Who Gracefully Provides according to the UNIVERSAL LAW OF "WILL TO DO GOOD", regarding which the Holy Bible States:

'ASK, and it shall be GIVEN TO YOU; SEEK, and YOU shall FIND; KNOCK, and it shall be OPENED to YOU. For Every One who Asks RECEIVES, and He Who SEEKS FINDS, and to Him Who KNOCKS it shall be OPENED.

Or What Man is there Among You, when His Son shall ASK Him for a LOAF, will GIVE HIM A STONE? Or if He shall ASK for a FISH, He will NOT GIVE HIM A SNAKE, Will He?

If YOU then "BEING EVIL", Know How to GIVE "GOOD GIFTS" TO YOUR

CHILDREN, HOW MUCH MORE SHALL """"YOUR FATHER WHO IS IN HEAVEN"""" GIVE WHAT is "GOOD TO THOSE" Who ASK HIM! Therefore Whatever You WANT Others to DO FOR YOU, DO SO FOR THEM, FOR THIS IS """"THE LAW"""" AND THE PROPHETS.' [Matthews 7. Verses 7 to 12.]

During the Times of JESUS CHRIST, when the FOOLISH HUMANITY of this Planet Earth, and their GLORIOUS KINGS SEATED ON THEIR PRESTIGIOUS THRONES with the Help of INVISIBLE CORRUPT ENTITIES AND BEINGS, who were Worshiped as the so called BREATHLESS GODS AND GODDESSES along with the MYRIAD of "SPIRITS OF THE DEAD", who were Reverently Worshiped through the Oracles of their "Skulls and Bones", and who were Constantly Glorified and Acclaimed by their BOUGHT OUT HISTORIANS for their "INHUMANE VIOLENT DEEDS" and RUTHLESS WARS FOUGHT FOR THE ACHIEVEMENTS OF THE "MATERIAL GAINS" AND TO CONTROL ACQUIRED LANDS, IN THE FALSE NAME OF "PATRIOTISM", and their Subservient so called POLITICAL AND RELIGIOUS WORLD LEADERS, being Consciously Stuck in the MATRIX OF ILLUSORY GLAMOUR of this DENSE PLANE WORLD OF "ASSIAH", were "'NOT READY'" AT "ANY COST TO ACCEPT'" JESUS'S AUTHORITY AS THE "CHIEF JUDGE OF THE UNIVERSE", But on the Other Hand the INVISIBLE DEMONS of this PLANET EARTH were FULLY AWARE OF HIS SUCH "HIGHLY EXALTED STATUS", and were thus CONSTANTLY "'AFRAID'" OF HIS PRESENCE UPON THE PHYSICAL PLANE [ASSIAH] OF THIS PLANET EARTH, Regarding which the Holy Bible States:

"And when HE had come to the Other Side into the Country of the GADARENES, Two Men Who were DEMON – POSSESSED met HIM as they were Coming Out of the Tombs; THEY were So Exceedingly VIOLENT that NO ONE could PASS by that Road.

And behold, they "'CRIED OUT'", Saying, "WHAT DO WE HAVE TO DO WITH YOU, SON OF GOD? HAVE YOU COME HERE TO TORMENT US """"BEFORE THE TIME""""?" [Matthew 8. 28, 29.]

During the Time of MOSES, the GREAT LORD HIMSELF TOLD MOSES about the IDOLS OF THE "ANIMAL FACED GODS AND GODDESSES", who were NOTHING BUT the FRONTS FOR THE INVISIBLE """"DEMONS"""", to whom the Foolish Humanity of this Planet Earth Ignorantly offered their Sacrifices, regarding which the Holy Bible States:

"And THEY shall No Longer Sacrifice their Sacrifices to the "'GOAT DEMONS'" with which they Play HARLOT. This shall be a "'PERMANENT STATUTE'" to them THROUGHOUT THEIR GENERATIONS." [Leviticus 17. 7.]

About 15 Centuries Later from the Ancient Times of MOSES, Apostle PAUL, by being a PHARISEE BY BIRTH Very well Remembered LORD'S WORD about the "DEMONS", who Invisibly act from behind the IDOLS AND GRAVEN IMAGES of the So Called GODS AND GODDESSES, and shared His Spiritual Wisdom with the People of CORINTH, regarding which the Holy Bible States:

'Look at the Nation ISRAEL; are Not Those WHO EAT THE SACRIFICES SHARERS IN THE ALTAR? What do I Mean then? That a Thing Sacrificed to IDOLS is ANYTHING, or that an IDOL is ANYTHING? No but I Say that the THINGS which the GENTILES SACRIFICE, they SACRIFICE to """"DEMONS"""", and NOT TO """"GOD""""; and I Do Not Want YOU to Become Sharers in DEMONS.' [1 Corinthians 10. Verses 18 to 20.]

JESUS CHRIST was well Aware of HIS Position as the "'CHIEF JUSTICE OF THE UNIVERSE'", and also about all the Illegal acts which have been Carried Out upon this Planet Earth by these DEMONIC BEINGS and their Corporate Soulless Group Configurations known as the "'INVISIBLE ENTITIES'" keeping the Evolving Humanity Illegally Bound in the ILLUSORY WORLD GLAMOUR through the Excessive Magnetic Energies, which are given to them IGNORANTLY by the Human Beings THEMSELVES, Created by them as the Magnetic Energies of their DESIRED THOUGHT FORMS, which are COMPOSED OF "SENTIMENTS AND FEELINGS" formulated by the Invisible Very Tiny Elemental Lives, so JESUS Gave HIS Twelve Disciples Authority over these DEMONS AND UNCLEAN SPIRITS, regarding which the Holy Bible States:

"And having Summoned HIS Twelve Disciples, HE Gave them AUTHORITY over UNCLEAN SPIRITS, TO CAST THEM OUT, AND TO HEAL "EVERY KIND OF DISEASE AND EVERY KIND OF SICKNESS"." [Matthew 10. 1]

Most People of this Modern World, even though they have Made Great Technical Advances, are Still Unaware of this SPIRITUAL FACT, that ALL KIND OF PHYSICAL AND MENTAL DISEASES AND THEIR RELATED SICKNESSES are in fact caused by a variety of these Invisible Hierarchical DEMONS who are differentiated in their Own Conscious Levels, Who first effect the INVISIBLE VITAL BODY OF THE HUMAN BEINGS, which then causes Sickness and Disease in the NEFESH BODY also known as the Physical Body, and also create a Hurdle in its Vital Connection with the RUACH BODY also known as the ASTRAL BODY, thus causing problems in the Proper Reception of Desire Mind Frequencies related to the "Common Sense" by the physical Human Brain, which is termed as the MENTAL SICKNESS.

And these Demonic Beings are in fact the "Partial Ethereal Consciousness" of the TRAPPED DEAD HUMAN BEINGS who after their Physical Death GOT STUCK IN THEIR UNFULFILLED DESIRES of this ILLUSORY DENSE PLANE WORLD due to their "STRONG WORLDLY DESIRES", thus Forcing them TO ABANDON THEIR "'EVOLUTIONARY PATH OF SPIRITUAL EVOLUTION", AND ALSO CAUSING A "GREAT LOSS" TO THEIR EVOLVING "SOUL MINDS"', WHO LOST their "'INITIAL ETHEREAL CONSCIOUSNESS ENERGY INVESTMENT PORTION"' WHICH IN THE FIRST PLACE WAS SENT TO INCARNATE AS A "HUMAN BEING" IN THE DENSE PHYSICAL PLANES FOR THE VERY PURPOSE OF ATTAINING "SPIRITUAL EXPERIENCES" IN THE DENSE MATERIAL PLANE WORLD'S [ASSIAH, YETZIRAH, AND BRIAH], DUE TO THE "RIGIDNESS OF THE EVOLVING PERSONALITY MIND'S"', Which Since Ancient Times, has been Written Down by the Prophets, Seers and Sages in the Holy Texts, who have Termed it as the "HARDENING OF THE HEART".

And after becoming the DEMONS having DEFORMED and Mutated Consciousness, they willfully go against the Spiritual Evolution of Human Consciousness, and CREATE Physical Health Related Hurdles in the Incarnated Human Beings through their Governing control of Tiny Elemental Lives, which form the Human Cells, as well as Myriad Varieties of Mutating VIRUSES, BACTERIA, FUNGUS AND YEASTS ETC. And these Demonic Beings and their Group Formations existing as the Corporate Soulless Entities Illegally Established as GODS AND GODDESSES in the Evolving Human Societies, and Reverently Worshiped by their FOLLOWER HUMAN BEINGS, WHO ARE STUCK IN UNQUENCHABLE LUST, GREED, AND FALSE PRIDE OF the So Called "'NAME AND FAME" are Very Well Aware of the UNIVERSAL LAW, which Clearly States that they will be "'JUDGED'" for their Heinous Crimes and will be SENT TO THE "TORTURE PITS" AND THE "PURIFICATION CHAMBERS" FOR THE UNFATHOMABLE "CYCLE OF ETERNITY", regarding which the Holy Bible States:

'FOR IF """'GOD"'"" DID NOT SPARE "'ANGELS'" WHEN THEY SINNED, BUT CAST THEM INTO "'HELL'" AND COMMITTED THEM TO "'PITS OF DARKNESS'", RESERVED FOR "'JUDGMENT'"; AND DID NOT SPARE THE ANCIENT WORLD, BUT PRESERVED "'NOAH'", A PREACHER OF RIGHTEOUSNESS, WITH SEVEN OTHERS, WHEN HE BROUGHT A FLOOD UPON THE WORLD OF THE UNGODLY; AND IF HE CONDEMNED THE CITIES OF "SODOM AND GOMORRAH" TO "'DESTRUCTION'" BY REDUCING THEM TO "ASHES", HAVING MADE THE MAN "EXAMPLE" TO THOSE WHO WOULD LIVE "'UNGODLY THEREAFTER'"; AND IF HE RESCUED "'RIGHTEOUS'" LOT, OPPRESSED BY THE ""SENSUAL CONDUCT OF UNPRINCIPLED MEN"" [FOR BY WHAT HE SAW AND HEARD THAT RIGHTEOUS MAN, WHILE LIVING AMONG THEM, FELT HIS "RIGHTEOUS SOUL" TORMENTED DAY AFTER DAY WITH THEIR "LAWLESS DEEDS"], THEN THE LORD KNOWS "'HOW TO RESCUE THE GODLY FROM TEMPTATION'", AND TO "'KEEP THE UNRIGHTEOUS UNDER PUNISHMENT FOR THE DAY OF JUDGMENT'", AND ESPECIALLY THOSE WHO INDULGE THE FLESH IN ITS "'CORRUPT DESIRES'" AND "'DESPISE AUTHORITY'". DARING, SELF – WILLED, THEY "'DO NOT TREMBLE'" WHEN THEY REVILE ANGELIC MAJESTIES, WHEREAS ANGELS WHO ARE "GREATER IN MIGHT AND POWER" DO NOT BRING A REVILING JUDGEMENT "AGAINST THEM BEFORE THE LORD".

But these, LIKE "UNREASONING ANIMALS", Born as "'CREATURES OF INSTINCT'" to be CAPTURED AND KILLED, REVILING where they have "NO KNOWLEDGE", will in the DESTRUCTION OF THOSE CREATURES "ALSO BE DESTROYED"." [2 Peter 2. Verses 4 to 12.]

'And HE Entered the Temple and began to Cast Out those who were Selling,
Saying to them, "IT is Written, 'AND MY HOUSE SHALL BE A HOUSE OF
PRAYER', but YOU have Made it a ROBBERS' DEN". And HE was Teaching Daily
in the Temple; but the CHIEF PRIESTS, and the SCRIBES, and the LEADING MEN
Among the People were Trying to "'DESTROY HIM'", and they Could Not Find
Anything that they Might Do, For ALL THE PEOPLE WERE HANGING UPON HIS
WORDS.' [Luke 19. Verses 45 to 48.]

The Problem of the "HARDENING OF THE HEART" occurring in Many of the Incarnated Human Beings of this Planet Earth, which Brought "'UNDUE CORRUPTION'" upon this Planet is "VERY OLD", as it came into Existence Due to the CORRUPT BEHAVIOR of the Certain Group of "FALLEN ANGELS" Who are "KNOWN AS "THE NEPHILIMS", their Very Name Meaning the "FIERY ONES", who having the Inherent Quality Attributes of both Visibility and Invisibility to Manifest upon the Dense Physical Plane, then "'ILLEGALLY INTERACTED'" WITH THE "DESIRE MINDS" OF THE EVOLVING HUMAN BEINGS, which Took Place AFTER THE CREATION OF HUMAN BEINGS, which was ACCOMPLISHED ACCORDING TO THE EVOLUTIONARY PLAN AND PURPOSE OF THE "UNKNOWABLE MOST HIGH" UPON THIS PLANET EARTH.

These Such Illegal Interactions of NEPHILIMS, who JUST BELIEVED IN THE "MIGHT AND POWER" OF "'THE INCARNATED PHYSICAL FORM'", thus Enhanced both the "'CORRUPTION and VIOLENCE'" upon this Planet Earth, which then CAUSED the Outburst of "'ANIMAL MIND PASSIONS'" RELATED TO THE LOWER MIND DESIRES, which GOT AROUSED in the Embodied PERSONALITY MINDS of the Incarnated Human Beings, Who thus started seeking for themselves Ways and Means to "ACQUIRE MIGHT AND POWER" upon the Dense Plane [ASSIAH], instead of the Needed "SPIRITUAL DESIRES", which were Absolutely Necessary for the "EVOLUTIONARY DIVINE PURPOSE" Requiring Evolutionary Growth of their "CHAYAH AND YECHIDAH BODIES", for which they in the Very First Place were CREATED BY THE GREAT LORD to Incarnate in the "FORM OF HUMAN BEINGS" upon this Planet Earth, which were Unique to the Entire Animal Kingdom with the INDIVIDUALIZED ATTRIBUTES OF "EVOLUTIONARY MINDS" and thus Differentiated From the All other ANIMAL SPECIES incarnated upon the Dense Physical Plane [ASSIAH] of this Planet Earth. And thus their INTENDED THOUGHT FORMS, which were based upon their Lower Mind Desires were FILLED Just ONLY with ANIMAL PASSIONS which were "NOT AT ALL SPIRITUAL" as REQUIRED by their "SOUL MINDS", BUT INSTEAD "ONLY EVIL AND WICKED", regarding which the Holy Bible States:

"The NEPHILIM were on the EARTH in those Days, '"AND ALSO AFTERWARD"', when the SONS OF GOD CAME INTO THE DAUGHTERS OF MEN, and they Bore Children to them.Those were the Mighty Men who were of Old, Men of Renown. Then the LORD SAW that the "WICKEDNESS OF MAN" was GREAT on the EARTH, and Every INTENT of the '"THOUGHTS OF HIS HEART" was ONLY EVIL "CONTINUALLY".

Now the Earth was CORRUPT in the SIGHT OF GOD, and the EARTH was "FILLED WITH VIOLENCE". And GOD Looked on the Earth, and behold, IT WAS CORRUPT; for ALL FLESH HAD CORRUPTED their Way UPON the Earth." [Genesis 6. 4, 5, 11, 12.]

After the Destruction of Humanity by the GREAT FLOOD, which took Place during the time of NOAH upon this Planet Earth, the Problem of CORRUPTION Even Got Worse and became More FIRM ROOTED and GREATLY ENHANCED in the Evolving Human Societies, when the Human Beings Started Worshiping BREATHLESS and SOULLESS Objects as the so called GODS and GODDESSES.

To Clean the Problem of CORRUPTION from this Planet Earth, the GREAT LORD chose a Descendant of NOAH whom he RENAMED from ABRAM to ABRAHAM to become a Pioneer for ""HIS CHOSEN RACE""', and thus told Him to LEAVE His FATHER'S HOUSE, HIS RELATIVES, and HIS COUNTRY. Because they ALL WORSHIPED these SO CALLED "OTHER GODS", regarding which the Holy Bible States:

'Now the LORD Said to ABRAM, "GO forth from '"YOUR COUNTRY", AND FROM '"YOUR RELATIVES"', AND FROM YOUR '"FATHER'S HOUSE"', to the "LAND" which "I" WILL SHOW YOU; AND "I" WILL MAKE YOU A GREAT NATION, AND "I" WILL BLESS YOU, AND MAKE YOUR NAME "GREAT"; AND SO YOU SHALL BE '"A BLESSING;"'.' [Genesis. 12, 1, 2.]

Much Later LORD'S Humble Servant JOSHUA Clarified LORD'S Intentions behind HIS Such Command which HE gave in the Much Earlier Times to their Patriarch ABRAHAM, through His Notable Address, which He Gave to the Children of Israel Gathered at SHECHEM, regarding which the

Holy Bible States:

'Then JOSHUA GATHERED all the Tribes of Israel to SHECHEM, and Called for the ELDERS OF ISRAEL, and for THEIR HEADS, and THEIR JUDGES, and THEIR OFFICERS; AND they PRESENTED "THEMSELVES BEFORE GOD".

And JOSHUA Said to All the People. "THUS Says the LORD, THE GOD OF ISRAEL, 'FROM ANCIENT TIMES "'YOUR FATHERS'" LIVED BEYOND THE RIVER, Namely "TERAH", the "FATHER OF ABRAHAM" and the "FATHER OF NAHOR", and they "'''SERVED OTHER GODS''''".

Then "I" Took "YOUR FATHER ABRAHAM" from Beyond the River, and Led Him through "ALL THE LAND OF CANAAN", and "MULTIPLIED HIS DESCENDANTS" and Gave Him "ISAAC". And to ISSAC "I" Gave "JACOB and ESAU", and to ESAU "I" Gave "MOUNT SEIR", to Possess it; but "JACOB AND HIS SONS" went Down to 'EGYPT'. Then "I" Sent "MOSES and AARON", and "I" Plagued EGYPT by 'WHAT "I" DID' in ITS MIDST; and Afterwards "I" BROUGHT YOU OUT".' [Joshua 24. Verses 1 to 5.]

As Mentioned in "1 Kings 4. 32" of the Holy Bible, "3000 PROVERBS" were Spoken by the GREAT KING SOLOMON and regarding the "HARDENING OF THE HEART", the Holy Bible States:

'How BLESSED is the Man WHO FEARS ALWAYS, BUT He Who "HARDENS HIS HEART" Will "'FALL INTO CALAMITY"'.' [Proverbs 28. 14.]

Apostle PAUL being a Humble Servant of JESUS CHRIST also CLEARLY EXPLAINED to the 'EPHESIANS' that the "HARDENING OF HEART" Produces the "FUTILITY OF MIND", which happened to all the GENTILES, who Worshiped the SOULLESS and BREATHLESS "'IDOLS and GRAVEN IMAGES'" of So Called "GODS AND GODDESSES", regarding which the Holy Bible States:

'This I Say therefore, and AFFIRM TOGETHER WITH THE "LORD", that

555

YOU WALK No Longer Just as the GENTILES also WALK, in the "'FUTILITY OF THEIR MIND'", being "DARKENED IN THEIR UNDERSTANDING", Excluded from the "'LIFE OF GOD'", because of the IGNORANCE that is in Them, BECAUSE OF THE "'"HARDNESS OF THEIR HEART'"'"; And they, having BECOME "'CALLOUS'", have Given themselves over to SENSUALITY, FOR THE PRACTICE OF EVERY KIND OF "'IMPURITY WITH GREEDINESS'"'.' [Ephesians 4. Verses 17 to 19.]

When JESUS CHRIST Incarnated upon this Physical Plane of this Planet Earth, the PROBLEM OF "'CORRUPTION" AMONG LORD'S CHOSEN RACE, BEING THE "CHILDREN OF ISRAEL", WAS AGAIN IN "FULL SWING", as Even in "THEIR GREAT LORD'S HOUSE" they were Making FOOLS OF INNOCENT PEOPLE THROUGH DECEITFUL MONEY CHANGING OPERATIONS AS WELL AS OVERCHARGING THEM FOR RELIGIOUS GOODS, WHO REVERENTLY CAME TO WORSHIP THE "MOST HIGH" IN JERUSALEM, regarding which the Holy Bible States:

"And JESUS Entered the Temple and Cast Out All THOSE, who were Buying and Selling in the Temple, and OVERTURNED THE TABLES OF THE MONEY CHANGERS, AND THE SEATS OF THOSE "WHO WERE SELLING DOVES". And HE Said to Them, "IT IS WRITTEN, 'MY HOUSE SHALL BE CALLED A HOUSE OF PRAYER' [Isaiah 56. 7]; BUT YOU ARE MAKING IT A "ROBBERS' DEN"'." [Matthew 21. 12, 13.]

'And they CAME to JERUSALEM. And HE Entered the TEMPLE and began to Cast Out those WHO were Buying and Selling in the Temple, and Overturned the Tables of the MONEY CHANGERS and the Seats of Those who were Selling DOVES; and HE would NOT Permit Any One to Carry Goods through the Temple.

And HE Began to TEACH and Say to THEM, "IS IT NOT WRITTEN, 'MY HOUSE SHALL BE CALLED A HOUSE OF PRAYER FOR "'ALL NATIONS'"'? But YOU have Made it a "'ROBBERS' DEN'"'." And the CHIEF PRIESTS and the SCRIBES HEARD THIS, and began SEEKING HOW TO "'DESTROY HIM'", for ALL MULTITUDE WAS "ASTONISHED AT HIS TEACHING"'.' [Mark 11. Verses 15 to 18.]

'And HE Entered the Temple and began to Cast Out those who were Selling, Saying to them, "IT is Written, 'AND MY HOUSE SHALL BE A HOUSE OF PRAYER', but YOU have Made it a ROBBERS' DEN". And HE was Teaching Daily in the Temple; but the CHIEF PRIESTS, and the SCRIBES, and the LEADING MEN Among the People were Trying to "'DESTROY HIM'", and they Could Not Find Anything that they Might Do, For ALL THE PEOPLE WERE HANGING UPON HIS WORDS.' [Luke 19. Verses 45 to 48.]

Apostle JOHN gave a More Detailed Version of what took place in the Temple, when JESUS Saw Abominations being done to the Holy House of the LORD, regarding which the Holy Bible States:

'And the PASSOVER of the JEWS was At Hand, and JESUS went up to Jerusalem. And He Found in the Temple those who were Selling Oxen and Sheep and Doves, and the MONEY CHANGERS Seated. And He made a Scourge of Cords, and DROVE THEM ALL OUT OF THE TEMPLE, with the Sheep and the Oxen; and HE POURED Out the COINS of the MONEY CHANGERS, and OVERTURNED THEIR TABLES; and to those who were Selling the DOVES HE Said, "TAKE these Things Away; Stop Making My Father's House a "'HOUSE OF MERCHANDISE'"." His Disciples REMEMBERED that it was Written, "ZEAL FOR THY HOUSE WILL CONSUME ME [Psalm 69.9]". The Jews therefore Answered and Said to Him, "WHAT Sign do YOU show to US, SEEING that YOU Do these Things?" JESUS Answered and Said to Them, "DESTROY this Temple, and in THREE DAYS "'I'" WILL RAISE IT UP". The Jews therefore SAID, "IT Took FORTY – SIX Years to Build this Temple, and YOU will Raise it Up in THREE DAYS?"

But HE was SPEAKING of the TEMPLE OF HIS BODY. When therefore HE was RAISED FROM THE DEAD. His Disciples remembered that "'HE SAID THIS'"; and they BELIEVED THE SCRIPTURE, AND THE WORD WHICH JESUS HAD SPOKEN.' [John 2. Verses 13 to 22.]

'In GIBEON the LORD Appeared to SOLOMON in DREAM at NIGHT; and GOD
Said, "ASK WHAT YOU WISH ME TO GIVE YOU". So Give THY Servant an
UNDERSTANDING HEART to JUDGE THY PEOPLE to DISCERN BETWEEN GOOD
AND EVIL, for WHO is ABLE to JUDGE this GREAT PEOPLE OF THINE?' [1 Kings 3.
5, 9.]

When the GREAT LORD appeared to SOLOMON in a Dream at Night in GIBEON, then LORD'S Chosen Son SOLOMON had Just Only "ONE DESIRE", about which He Humbly Asked of the MOST HIGH to Grant Him, which was AN UNDERSTANDING HEART to be the "WISE JUDGE" Upon this Planet Earth, So that He Could "'DISCERN BETWEEN GOOD AND EVIL'", regarding which the Holy Bible States:

'In GIBEON the LORD Appeared to SOLOMON in DREAM at NIGHT; and GOD Said, "ASK WHAT YOU WISH ME TO GIVE YOU".

So Give THY Servant an UNDERSTANDING HEART to JUDGE THY PEOPLE to DISCERN BETWEEN GOOD AND EVIL, for WHO is ABLE to JUDGE this GREAT PEOPLE OF THINE?' [1 Kings 3. 5, 9.]

But When LORD'S Chosen Son JESUS CHRIST Incarnated upon this Planet Earth, HE already had the FULL AUTHORITY TO ACT AS THE "CHIEF JUSTICE" UPON THIS PLANET EARTH, ESPECIALLY CONFINED WITH THE "IMPORTANT DUTY" TO CLEAN UP ALL "CORRUPTION", WHICH WAS CAUSED BY "INVISIBLE FIERY BEINGS", WHO DECEITFULLY ACTED AS THE SO CALLED DEMONIC "GODS AND GODDESSES", who had "'WILLFULLY HIJACKED'" the Evolutionary Plan and Purpose of the "MOST HIGH" through the DECEITFUL MISUSE OF THEIR "VESTED POWERS".

The "CHIEF JUSTICE OF THE UNIVERSE" DESIGNATION OF THE "JESUS CHRIST", WAS GIVEN TO HIM BY THE UNKNOWABLE LORD – GOD "MOST HIGH", LONG BEFORE HIS INCARNATION TOOK PLACE UPON THE DENSE PHYSICAL PLANE OF THIS PLANET EARTH IN AN HUMAN FORM, SO AS TO JUDGE "LORD'S ALL CREATIONS", which Included BOTH THE VISIBLE AND INVISIBLE "BEINGS AND SOULLESS ENTITIES", and JESUS CHRIST Openly Declared His Such Status to ALL HUMAN BEINGS being the "GOD'S JUDGE" to FULFILL THE LAW during this ESTABLISHED EVOLUTIONARY CYCLE WHICH LAWFULLY STAYS "'ENFORCED'" TILL THE "PASSING OF HEAVEN AND EARTH". JESUS CHRIST was Not Afraid of these DEMONS, even when the CORRUPT INVISIBLE DEMONIC HIERARCHIES had been Illegally Controlling Human Beings Just Like ANY OTHER ANIMAL SPECIES through their Deceitful Mind Control Techniques known as "TEMPTATIONS", WHO ALSO MADE SURE NOT TO MAKE HIM A '"KING AMONG HIS PEOPLE"' and Instead INCITED THEIR CORRUPT FOLLOWERS PLACED UPON THE "HIGH POSITIONS" OF HUMAN SOCIETY TO GO '"AGAINST HIM"', regarding which the Holy Bible States:

"Do Not Think that 'I' CAME TO ABOLISH THE LAW OR THE PROPHETS; 'I' DID NOT CAME TO "ABOLISH", BUT TO '"FULFILL". For Truly 'I' Say to You, UNTIL "HEAVEN AND EARTH PASS AWAY", NOT THE SMALLEST LETTER OR STROKE SHALL PASS AWAY FROM 'THE LAW', "UNTIL ALL IS ACCOMPLISHED"." [Matthew 5. 17, 18.]

JESUS CHRIST IN THE FIRST PLACE WAS '"SUPPOSED TO BE"' THE "KING" UPON THE "PHYSICAL PLANE OF THIS PLANET EARTH", JUST AS THE CELESTIAL STAR DECLARED THIS "UNDENIABLE FACT" TO THE "MAGI'S" FROM THE EAST, and the Main Reason For HIM Not becoming a KING upon this Physical Plane was that the INVISIBLE "CONTROLLING DEMONS" OF THIS PLANET EARTH HAVE BEEN CONTINUOUSLY "MAKING ONLY" THOSE AS THE "KINGS" OR ESTABLISHING TILL NOW MOSTLY THOSE ON THE "HIGH PLACES" OF THE HUMAN SOCIETIES, WHO CAN WILLFULLY "ADVANCE THEIR "ILLEGAL AND DECEITFUL AGENDAS" WHICH INVOLVE "CORRUPTION AND VIOLENCE" AT ALL LEVELS OF THE HUMAN SOCIETIES, IN THE NAME OF SO CALLED ADVANCEMENT OF HUMAN "CIVILIZATION", SO these DEMON MASTERS Instead of Making HIM a KING Willfully MOCKED HIM as "THE KING OF JEWS" through their Human Followers, who Foolishly acted under their INVISIBLE THOUGHT FORMS ENERGY INFLUENCE, when they Illegally Crucified Him Just like any "Death Penalty Criminal" of HIGH OFFENCE, regarding which the Holy Bible States:

'"And WHEN they had CRUCIFIED Him, they Divided up HIS Garments AMONG Themselves, Casting LOTS; and Sitting Down, they began to Keep Watch Over HIM there. AND they Put Up ABOVE HIS HEAD the Charge AGAINST HIM which Read, "THIS IS JESUS THE KING OF THE JEWS". At that Time Two Robbers were CRUCIFIED with HIM, ONE on the RIGHT and ONE on the LEFT.

And THOSE who were Passing By were HURLING ABUSE AT HIM, Wagging their HEADS, and Saying, "YOU WHO DESTROY THE TEMPLE AND REBUILD IT IN THREE DAYS, SAVE YOURSELF! IF YOU ARE THE SON OF GOD, COME DOWN FROM THE CROSS".

In the Same Way the "CHIEF PRIESTS", ALONG WITH THE "SCRIBES AND ELDERS", WERE MOCKING HIM, AND SAYING, "HE SAVED OTHERS; HE CANNOT SAVE HIMSELF. '"HE IS THE KING OF ISRAEL'"; LET HIM NOW COME DOWN FROM THE CROSS, AND WE SHALL BELIEVE IN HIM. HE TRUSTS IN GOD; LET HIM DELIVER HIM NOW, IF HE TAKES PLEASURE IN HIM; FOR HE SAID, 'I AM THE SON OF GOD'."

And the Robbers also, who had been CRUCIFIED with HIM were CASTING THE SAME 'INSULT' AT 'HIM'.'" [Matthew 27. Verses 35 to 44.]

The "DEMONIC BEINGS AND SOULLESS ENTITIES" COLLECTIVELY TERMED AS "THE DEVIL" wanted to THOROUGHLY CHECK "JESUS CHRIST" through Illegal Methodical Testing Procedures Known as the "TEMPTATIONS", whether He was "READY TO ADVANCE" their OWN "DECEITFUL AGENDAS" just like their Other Followers, which Including the "KING HEROD" and "THE CAESARS OF ROME" were Already Doing for them, but JESUS CHRIST PLAINLY REFUSED THEIR ALL SUCH TEMPTATIONS, regarding which the Holy Bible States:

'And the TEMPTER Came and Said to HIM, "IF YOU ARE THE SON OF GOD, COMMAND THAT THESE STONES BECOME BREAD". But HE Answered and Said, "IT IS WRITTEN, 'MAN SHALL NOT LIVE ON BREAD ALONE, BUT ON EVERY WORD THAT PROCEEDS OUT OF THE MOUTH OF GOD [Deuteronomy 8. 3.]'." Then the DEVIL took Him into the Holy City; and He Stood HIM on the Pinnacle of the Temple, and Said to HIM, "IF You are the Son of GOD Throw Yourself Down; FOR IT IS WRITTEN, 'HE WILL GIVE HIS ANGELS CHARGE CONCERNING YOU; AND ON THEIR HANDS THEY WILL BEAR YOU UP, LEST YOU STRIKE YOUR FOOT AGAINST A STONE [Psalm 91. 11, 12] '." JESUS Said to Him, "ON the Other

HAND, it is WRITTEN, 'YOU SHALL NOT TEMPT THE LORD YOUR GOD [Deuteronomy 6. 16]'." [Matthew 4. Verses 3 to 7.]

The Fallen Angels also COLLECTIVELY known as the "TEMPTER" OR THE "DEVIL", WHO IN THE VERY FIRST PLACE WERE MANIFESTED BY THE "MOST HIGH" THROUGH THE ACTIONS OF HIS "DESIRE MIND", then WILLFULLY Betraying the """LOVE AND TRUST""" OF THEIR "'CREATOR LORD GOD'" through the "MISUSE OF THEIR VESTED POWERS" THUS "BACK STABBED HIM" and ILLEGALLY TOOK OVER THE "CONTROL OF ALL THE KINGDOMS OF THIS WORLD" TO ILLEGALLY AND DECEITFULLY PUSH "ALL EVOLUTION" UPON A "DOWN HILL PATH" OF "MATERIAL PLANE BONDAGE'S" INSTEAD OF THEIR REQUIRED "SPIRITUAL ASCENSION'", SO THAT EVOLVING CONSCIOUSNESS OF "EVERYONE" GETS "DOOMED AND TRAPPED FOREVER" JUST LIKE THEY ARE DOOMED "'THEMSELVES'" IN THIS EVOLUTIONARY CYCLE UPON THIS PLANET EARTH. And because ALL THE "KINGDOMS" AND THEIR SO CALLED "GLORY" of This PHYSICAL PLANE WORLD is Still Under their ILLEGAL CONTROLS, thus the "'DEVIL'" FREELY "'OFFERED THEM" TO "JESUS CHRIST", IF HE WOULD "FOLLOW HIM" ON THE WRONG PATH AGAINST LORD'S ESTABLISHED EVOLUTIONARY PLAN, WHICH WAS ESTABLISHED FOR THE BENEFIT OF ALL EVOLVING BEINGS who are having Differentiated Levels of "'SOLAR CONSCIOUSNESS'", regarding which the Holy Bible States:

'Again the DEVIL Took HIM to a Very High Mountain, and Showed HIM "'ALL THE KINGDOMS OF THE WORLD, AND THEIR GLORY; and He Said to HIM, "ALL THESE THINGS WILL I GIVE YOU, IF YOU FALL DOWN AND WORSHIP ME". Then JESUS Said to HIM, "BEGONE SATAN! For it is WRITTEN, 'YOU SHALL WORSHIP THE LORD YOUR GOD, AND SERVE HIM ONLY [Deuteronomy 6. 13, and Deuteronomy 10. 20.]'."

Then the DEVIL Left HIM; and behold, ANGELS came and BEGAN TO MINISTER HIM.' [Matthew 4. Verses 8 to 11.]

These DEMONIC BEINGS Who Willfully Hijacked Planetary EARTH'S EVOLUTION, and Since Long are Collectively Known as the "DEVIL", thus knowing FULL WELL THAT "JESUS" WAS ORDAINED TO BE THE

"KING OF JEWS", thus "TESTED HIM" THROUGH THEIR "THOUGHT FORMS" METHODS which are also Known as the "MIND CONTROL TECHNIQUES" Commonly Known as the "'TEMPTATIONS'", in which they DECEITFULLY INDUCE "A LIVE THOUGHT FORM" IN THE INVISIBLE "HUMAN AURA", TO BE INSTANTLY FILTERED INTO THE "PHYSICAL HUMAN BRAIN", AND THEN "ANY IGNORANT HUMAN BEING" to whom they Might INTRODUCE SUCH TEMPTATIONS being UNAWARE OF THESE "'DEMONIC PROCEDURES'", WITHOUT EVER QUESTIONING AS TO "WHO GAVE HIM "ALL OF A SUDDEN" THIS INTENDING "THOUGHT" WHICH INSTANTLY AFFECTS AND GRIPS HIS HUMAN BRAIN, OR HOW ALL OF A SUDDEN "SUCH A THOUGHT" CAME TO HIS MIND", THEN IN MOST CASES "'FOOLISHLY ACCEPTS" IT AS "HIS OWN THINKING", AND THEN UNDER ITS "'NEGATIVE INFLUENCE'" WITHOUT ANY CONTEMPLATION TAKE SUCH "DRASTIC ACTIONS" WHICH ARE TOTALLY CONTRARY TO HIS NECESSARY AND REQUIRED "SPIRITUAL EVOLUTION". And after Completion of Such Drastic Action Which is TOTALLY Contrary to the Spiritual Values then Unknowingly Make Him a "'DISCIPLE MEMBER'" of the Invisible DEMONIC TEAM.

And also the Main Reason for Not Making JESUS A KING Upon the Physical Plane of this Planet Earth was that these "'CORRUPT ANGELIC BEINGS", Commonly Termed as the Hierarchical "DEMONS", who are Collectively Termed also as the "DEVIL'", have been Illegally Acting Since for a LONG TIME as the So Called GODS and GODDESSES of Many Faiths and Beliefs upon this Planet EARTH, which have been existing in their FOUR MAIN HIERARCHICAL DIVISIONS, known from Bottom to Top as the [1] Disciples, [2] Initiates, [3] Adepts, and the [4] Masters, of which Each group have Myriad of Members with further Hierarchical Sub Divisions, of which the Highest Level has Always been the So Called "'MASTERS LEVEL'", who Deceitfully Propagated the "'LEFT HAND PRACTICES" and Instituted the "DARK ARTS OF SOULLESS BEHAVIOR" in the Name of an "'DARK MIND MATERIAL ENERGY RESERVOIR'" Established "AT AN REMOTE PLACE" known as the "THE HEADQUARTERS OF THE GREAT BROTHERHOOD" in the INVISIBLE ETHEREAL DIMENSIONS OF THIS PLANET EARTH to Exist as a "GREAT SOULLESS ENTITY" LIKE A HUGE "SUPER ENERGY MIND COMPUTER", to which they all ADDED THEIR ATTAINED NEGATIVE EXPERIENCES, and also upon which was Based the Ancient Cult of "GODDESS ASHERAH" and Many Other Similar Established BLOOD THIRSTY GODDESSES CULTS upon the Physical Plane [ASSIAH] having their

Different Names to "'FOOL THE INNOCENT AND IGNORANT HUMANITY OF THIS WORLD'", and these FOUR MAIN HIERARCHICAL DIVISIONS of DEMONIC BEINGS Working as the Employees of AN CORPORATE GROUP UNDER THE PATRONAGE OF THIS "ESTABLISHED SOULLESS ENTITY" IN THE "HEADQUARTERS OF THE GREAT BROTHERHOOD" whom they Named as the "DARK MOTHER", then Propagated their DECEITFUL AGENDAS TO ENHANCE "'FULL SCALE CORRUPTION IN THE ESTABLISHED GROUPS OF THE "'SO CALLED ELITES'" to Carry Forward their DECEITFUL AGENDAS Operating from Behind their BREATHLESS IDOLS AND IMAGES, who Promoted the LUSTFUL BEHAVIOR Filled with the ANIMAL PASSION LIVE THOUGHT FORMS Induced in the Minds of Evolving Human Beings, which is Termed as the Various Grade Levels of the Demonic Possessions, which on the low levels exist as the ADDICTIONS OF VARIOUS HABITS, for which the Modern Physical Plane Doctors Well Versed in the PHYSICAL BODY ANATOMY, but Devoid of "SPIRITUAL WISDOM" Still have NO CLUE in these Ethereal Matters and thus call them as the "Psychological Problems", and on the Higher Level POSSESSIONS they create a LUNATIC STATE of Mind in the Human Beings regarded as the 'Personality Disorder' by the Physical World Doctors, regarding which the Holy Bible States:

'And when they came to the Multitude, a Man Came up to HIM, Falling on His Knees before HIM, and Saying, "LORD, have Mercy on My Son, for He is LUNATIC, and is Very ILL; for He Often Falls into the FIRE, and Often into the WATER. And JESUS REBUKED Him, and the DEMON Came OUT of Him, and the Boy was CURED AT ONCE. [Matthew 17. 14, 15, 18.]

When More than One DEMON Invisibly Influences the Human Mind to exist in their Group Formation, then to the Physical Plane World Doctors, it may APPEAR as a Case of "MULTIPLE PERSONALITY", but JESUS CHRIST was Fully Aware of these Invisible Matters which AFFECTED the "PERSONALITY MINDS" of Incarnated Human Beings, and removed 7 DEMONS Out of MARY MAGDALENE, regarding which the Holy Bible States:

"And it Came About Soon Afterwards, that HE began Going About from One City and Village to Another, Proclaiming and Preaching the Kingdom of GOD; and the TWELVE were with HIM, and also Some Women who had been HEALED OF '''EVIL SPIRITS AND SICKNESS'''; MARY who was called MAGDALENE, from whom SEVEN DEMONS had GONE OUT." [Luke 8. 1, 2.]

JESUS casting out SEVEN DEMONS from MARY MAGDALENE

He who is NOT WITH ME IS AGAINST ME; AND He who does NOT
GATHER with ME "SCATTERS". Therefore "I" Say to YOU, ANY "SIN"
AND "BLASPHEMY" shall be "FORGIVEN" Men, But BLASPHEMY Against
the """"SPIRIT"""" shall "'NOT BE FORGIVEN'". And WHOEVER shall Speak
a WORD AGAINST THE 'SON OF MAN', it shall be "FORGIVEN HIM"; BUT
WHOEVER SHALL SPEAK AGAINST THE "'HOLY SPIRIT'", IT SHALL """"NOT
BE FORGIVEN"""" HIM, EITHER IN """"THIS AGE"""", OR IN THE """"AGE TO
COME"""". [Matthew 12. Verses 30 to 32.]

JESUS CHRIST, the Son of GOD, who incarnated as the CHIEF JUDGE of All the Visible and Invisible Dimensional Worlds of this Planet Earth was SUPPOSED to be the King of JEWS upon the Physical Plane World Just like His Great Ancestors, the Great King DAVID and His Son Solomon, just as the Celestial Star Predicted to the MAGI from the EAST, and HE was Sent by the "FATHER IN HEAVEN" with JUST ONE GREAT MISSION to Liberate The "PERSONALITY MINDS" of the Ignorant Evolving Human Beings from the BONDAGE'S of these MOST CORRUPT 'INVISIBLE DEMONIC BEINGS', so as to Consciously Become One with their "SOLAR CONSCIOUSNESS" or the Radiant Ethereal "SPIRIT", also known as the "'SPIRIT OF THEIR FATHER GOD'", as these DEMONS by JESUS Time were Very Successful to Establish their Deceitful Agendas Especially of Firmly Setting a "'HUGE MATRIX OF SOULLESS ENTITIES'" toward their "'INTENDED GOAL'", which was to FINALLY SET DECEITFULLY "ONE WORLD ORDER" upon this Planet Earth, and Taking "TOTALLY OUT" the Required SPIRIT'S EVOLUTIONARY GOAL, for which REASON the Evolving Human Beings in the First Place Incarnated upon this Physical Plane World. They wanted to Achieve their NONSPIRITUAL GOALS, through the Establishment of GLOBALLY TRADED SOULLESS ENTITIES LATER TO BE KNOWN AS THE "'MULTIPLE CORPORATIONS'", Formulated through an Easy Duplication Process, Controlled by Just a "'POWERFUL INVISIBLE HANDFUL 'FEW' CORRUPT HEARTLESS CONTROLLERS'" AND THEIR FEW CHOSEN VISIBLE HUMAN STOOGES, VERY SMALL IN NUMBER COMPARED TO EVOLVING "'MASSES'" Some Time in the Distant Future, to First Exist as the Powerful Kingdoms Ruled by RUTHLESS and VIOLENT Greedy Kings in the Name of So Called GLORY, and Religious Organization of Mostly IDOLS and GRAVEN IMAGES Ruled by their CORRUPT PRIESTHOOD, who Especially Indulged in Those Magic Rituals of Tonal COLORS and SOUNDS, which brought them in CLOSE Contact with the Invisible DEMONIC BEINGS AND THEIR CREATED "SOULLESS ENTITIES" EXISTING AS THE "SO CALLED GODS AND GODDESSES", and thus made their ILLEGAL AND DECEITFUL STRONGHOLD More FIRM upon the INCARNATED HUMAN'S "PERSONALITY MINDS", who were Living Upon the Physical Plane [ASSIAH] of this Planet Earth.

JESUS CHRIST after His First Meeting with the "TEMPTER DEVIL" in the

Wilderness, was thus fully aware of HIS DECEITFUL CONTROL Upon the "ENTIRE EVOLVING HUMANITY", when SATAN OFFERED HIM "ALL THE KINGDOMS OF THE WORLD AND THEIR GLORY", and so JESUS CHRIST Strongly Warned His DISCIPLES about the DEVIL'S ILLEGAL CONTROL which even Infiltrated LORD'S CHOSEN RACE, regarding which the Holy Bible States:

'Behold, "I" Send YOU Out as SHEEP in the Midst of WOLVES; therefore be SHREWD as SERPENTS, and INNOCENT as DOVES. But Beware of MEN; for they will Deliver YOU up to the COURTS, and SCOURGE YOU in the SYNAGOGUES; and YOU shall EVEN be BROUGHT before "GOVERNORS and KINGS" for "MY SAKE", as a Testimony to Them and to the "GENTILES". But when They Deliver YOU UP, DO NOT Become ANXIOUS about HOW or WHAT YOU WILL SPEAK; FOR IT SHALL BE "'GIVEN TO YOU IN THAT HOUR WHAT YOU ARE TO SPEAK'''.

FOR IT IS NOT "'YOU WHO SPEAK'", BUT IT IS THE "'SPIRIT OF YOUR FATHER'", WHO "SPEAKS" IN YOU.

And Brother Will DELIVER UP Brother to DEATH, and a FATHER His Child; and Children will RISE UP AGAINST PARENTS, and Cause them to be Put to DEATH. And YOU will be HATED by ""ALL"" on Account of MY NAME, but it is the "'ONE'" WHO has ENDURED to the END, Who will be """SAVED"". [Matthew 10. Verses 16 to 22.]

JESUS CHRIST FULLY WELL Knew about the ILLEGAL CONTROL of Invisible DEMON'S upon the Evolutionary Lives of Human Beings, who Since Ancient Times are Collectively Termed as the "DEVIL", Because this UNDENIABLE FACT was FIRMLY ESTABLISHED IN FRONT OF "JESUS" BY THE "DEVIL HIMSELF", When HE "OPENLY OFFERED" JESUS CHRIST "ALL THE KINGDOMS OF THE WORLD, AND THEIR GLORY" as Clearly Mentioned in "Matthew 4. Verses 8, 9." of the Holy Bible, so HE Very Well Knew that It was NOT AN EASY TASK to MAKE HUMAN BEINGS Publicly Aware of this SECRET FACT, as DEMONIC INFLUENCE had Fully Infiltrated the FAMILY STRUCTURE of the Human Beings upon this Physical Plane World, and Many Members in the Human Families, Whose Personality Minds due to being Polarized in the ILLUSORY GLAMOUR COMMONLY KNOWN AS "'THE GLORY'" of Material World "'MATRIX'" were Fully Under Demonic Control, who Willfully made them FALL AWAY from their Established Evolutionary Path of "SPIRITUALITY", and thus Clearly Told HIS DISCIPLES that in HIS MISSION OF "SPIRITUAL AWARENESS", there was going to be SURELY CONFRONTATION between those Family Members who were Mostly Stuck in the So called NAME AND FAME "GLORY" of ILLUSORY MATERIAL WORLD GLAMOUR which was Totally Controlled by the DEVIL'S BRIGADE OF DEMONS, and THOSE Other Members Who as Per LORD'S Evolutionary Plan wanted to Carry Onward their "SPIRITUAL EVOLUTION" as they are Just a TINY PART OF THEIR "SOUL ENERGY" also known as "THE HOLY SPIRIT", which is EXISTING Due TO the Desire Mind of the UNKNOWABLE "MOST HIGH" who is Commonly known to All as the "HEAVENLY FATHER", and thus JESUS Repeated Prophet MICAH'S Words which Stated, "For SON Treats FATHER Contemptuously, DAUGHTER Rises Up Against Her MOTHER, DAUGHTER – IN – LAW Against Her MOTHER – IN – LAW; A MAN'S ENEMIES ARE THE "'MEN OF HIS OWN HOUSEHOLD [Micah 7. 6.]", regarding which the Holy Bible States:

"But WHOEVER shall Deny ME before MEN, I will also DENY Him before MY FATHER who is in HEAVEN. Do Not Think that "I" Came to Bring Peace, but a Sword. For I Came to Set a MAN AGAINST His FATHER, and a DAUGHTER AGAINST Her MOTHER, and a DAUGHTER – IN – LAW AGAINST HER MOTHER – IN – LAW; AND a MAN'S Enemies will be the "'MEMBERS OF HIS HOUSEHOLD'". He Who LOVES Father or Mother "MORE THAN ME" is "NOT WORTHY OF ME"; and He Who Loves SON or DAUGHTER "MORE THAN ME" is NOT WORTHY OF "'ME'".

He Who Receives a PROPHET in the Name of a PROPHET shall RECEIVE a PROPHET'S REWARD; AND He Who Receives a RIGHTEOUS MAN shall RECEIVE a RIGHTEOUS MAN'S REWARD. [Matthew 10. 33, 34, 35, 36, 37, 41.]

JESUS also Understood, that these Fallen Angels also Termed as the Hierarchical DEMONS ran their DECEITFUL OPERATIONS upon the Physical Plane by ILLEGALLY CONTROLLING the Solar Conscious Spirit's "SOUL ENERGY VITAL CONNECTION" which is Invisibly Connected to the Incarnated Human Body, and Many a Times the "'Blindness and Dumbness'" is Caused by these Invisible "Demonic Beings and Entities", who Illegally POSSESS the "Personality Minds" of the Evolving Human Beings, by Illegally Riding their Incarnated form body AURAS, just like All Human Beings Ride a "Vehicle", and thus JESUS Warned All the Human Beings that if they GO AGAINST their "'OWN HOLY SPIRIT'", which sent them from the DIMENSIONAL SPHERE OF BRIAH to Incarnate as a PERSONALITY MIND to be Embodied in an Incarnated Human Form upon the DENSE DIMENSIONAL SPHERE OF ASSIAH commonly known as the PHYSICAL PLANE, for the Main Purpose of Attaining "'SPIRITUAL EXPERIENCES'", which is the Only Plane which is Visible to the Physical EYES of Incarnated Human Beings, and if SOME ONE WILLFULLY GOES AGAINST THEIR "HOLY SPIRIT", THEN HE AS PER "'LORD'S EVOLUTIONARY PLAN'" SHALL NOT BE "'FORGIVEN IN THIS CYCLIC AGE" OR IN THE "NEXT AGE TO COME", regarding which the Holy Bible States:

'Then there was BROUGHT to HIM a "'Demon – Possessed Man'" WHO was a BLIND and DUMB, and HE Healed Him, so that the DUMB Man "SPOKE and SAW". And all the Multitudes were Amazed, and Began to Say, "THIS Man Cannot be the Son of David, Can He?" But when the Pharisees heard it, they Said, "THIS Man Casts OUT Demons Only by BEELZEBUL, the Ruler of DEMONS". And Knowing their Thoughts HE Said to them, "ANY KINGDOM DIVIDED AGAINST ITSELF IS LAID WASTE AND ANY CITY OR HOUSE DIVIDED AGAINST ITSELF SHALL NOT STAND. And if SATAN Casts Out SATAN, HE is DIVIDED Against Himself; HOW then shall His Kingdom Stand? And if "I" by BEELZEBUL Casts Out Demons, "'BY WHOM DO YOUR SONS CAST THEM OUT?'" Consequently they shall be "'YOUR JUDGES'".

But if "I" Cast OUT DEMONS by the "SPIRIT OF GOD", then the KINGDOM OF GOD has Come UPON YOU. Or how can Anyone Enter the Strong Man's House and CARRY OFF HIS PROPERTY, UNLESS HE FIRST "BINDS" THE STRONG MAN? And then He will PLUNDER HIS HOUSE.

He who is NOT WITH ME IS AGAINST ME; AND He who does NOT GATHER with ME "SCATTERS". Therefore "I" Say to YOU, ANY "SIN" AND "BLASPHEMY" shall be "FORGIVEN" Men, But BLASPHEMY Against the """SPIRIT"""" shall "'NOT BE FORGIVEN'". And WHOEVER shall Speak a WORD AGAINST THE 'SON OF MAN', it shall be "FORGIVEN HIM"; BUT WHOEVER SHALL SPEAK AGAINST THE "'HOLY SPIRIT'", IT SHALL """NOT BE FORGIVEN"""" HIM, EITHER IN """"THIS AGE"""", OR IN THE """"AGE TO COME"""". [Matthew 12. Verses 22 to 32.]

'Then there was BROUGHT to HIM a "'Demon – Possessed Man'" WHO was a BLIND and DUMB, and HE Healed Him, so that the DUMB Man "SPOKE and SAW". [Matthew 12. 22.]

"Then ONE of the TWELVE, Named JUDAS ISCARIOT, went to the Chief Priests, and Said, "WHAT are YOU Willing to Give Me to DELIVER HIM UP TO YOU?" And They Weighed Out to Him THIRTY PIECES OF SILVER. And from THEN ON He Began Looking for a Good Opportunity to "'BETRAY HIM'"." [Matthew 26. Verses 14 to 16.]

JESUS CHRIST Being the "CHIEF JUSTICE OF ALL VISIBLE AND INVISIBLE DIMENSIONS OF THIS PLANET EARTH" FULL WELL KNEW, that the Main Problem upon the PHYSICAL PLANE of this Planet Earth was NOT the MASSES of Incarnated HUMAN BEINGS, but their MIND CONTROLLERS, who were NONE OTHER than the CORRUPT AND EVIL INVISIBLE BEINGS Termed by HUMAN'S as the "DEMONS, SATAN, and DEVIL", and their "'SOULLESS'" GROUPED ENERGY FORMATIONS EXISTING AS THE VARIOUS BREATHLESS IDOLS AND GRAVEN IMAGES OF "GODS AND GODDESSES" upon the Physical Plane [ASSIAH], who taking Advantage of the "HUMAN IGNORANCE" ABOUT THEIR KNOWLEDGE OF THE EXISTENCE OF HIGHER DIMENSIONAL PLANES, Especially the 4 Ethereal Sub Planes of this Physical Plane World, which are INVISIBLE TO PHYSICAL HUMAN EYES, thus used them as their "'CONTROLLED PUPPETS'" through the IMPULSED THOUGHT FREQUENCIES, which were Illegally Bombarded to their Human Minds, as through these IMPULSED THOUGHTS Apart from Controlling the "PERSONALITY MINDS" of ELDERS, CHIEF PRIESTS and the SCRIBES, they were also Constantly Influencing the Minds of HIS DISCIPLES and their Family Relatives, and when these Illegal Thought Forms Invisibly IMPULSED by the "SATAN" griped the PERSONALITY MIND of His "DISCIPLE PETER", then JESUS REBUKED HIM in Front of His All Disciples as the PERSONIFICATION OF "SATAN", whose Personality Mind at that Particular Point was under the Influence of "SATAN'S MIND CONTROL THOUGHT FORMS", regarding which the Holy Bible States:

'From that Time JESUS CHRIST began to Show HIS Disciples that HE Must GO to JERUSALEM, and SUFFER Many Things from the ELDERS, and CHIEF PRIESTS, and SCRIBES, and be KILLED, and be RAISED UP on the THIRD DAY. And PETER took HIM aside and began to Rebuke HIM, Saying, "GOD Forbid it, LORD! This shall Never Happen to YOU".

But HE Turned and Said to PETER, "GET Behind ME, SATAN! You are a STUMBLING BLOCK to ME; for YOU are NOT Setting Your MIND on GOD'S INTERESTS, but MAN'S. [Matthew 16. Verses 21 to 23.]

This Same Incidence has been also Narrated in MARK'S GOSPEL, regarding which the Holy Bible States:

'And HE Continued by Questioning them, "BUT Who Do You Say that I AM?" Peter Answered and Said to HIM, "THOU ART THE CHRIST". And HE Warned Them to TELL "NO ONE" ABOUT HIM.

And HE began to TEACH them that the Son of Man Must Suffer Many Things, and be Rejected by the ELDERS, and the CHIEF PRIESTS, and the SCRIBES, and be KILLED, and after THREE DAYS RISE AGAIN. And HE was STATING the Matter Plainly. And PETER Took HIM aside and began to Rebuke HIM.

But Turning Around and Seeing HIS Disciples, HE Rebuked PETER, and Said, "GET Behind ME, SATAN; FOR YOU ARE NOT SETTING YOUR MIND ON GOD'S INTERESTS, BUT MAN'S".' [Mark 8. Verses 29 to 33.]

Similarly the MOTHER of the Sons of ZEBEDEE Came to JESUS and asked under the CORRUPT INFLUENCE of these Invisible Demonic Beings and their SOULLESS Corporate ENTITIES, for PREFERENTIAL TREATMENT for Her Sons, Who were HIS TWO DISCIPLES OUT OF THE TWELVE, regarding which the Holy Bible States:

'Then the Mother of the Sons of ZEBEDEE came to HIM with Her Sons, Bowing Down, and Making a Request of HIM. And HE Said to Her, "WHAT Do YOU Wish?" She Said to HIM, "COMMAND that in YOUR KINGDOM these TWO SONS of MINE may SIT, ONE on YOUR RIGHT and ONE on YOUR LEFT."

But JESUS Answered and Said, "YOU Do Not KNOW what YOU ARE ASKING FOR. Are YOU Able to DRINK the CUP that I AM ABOUT TO DRINK?" They Said to HIM, "WE ARE ABLE".

He Said to them, "MY CUP YOU SHALL DRINK; BUT TO SIT ON MY RIGHT AND ON MY LEFT, THIS IS NOT MINE TO GIVE, BUT IT IS FOR THOSE FOR WHOM IT HAS BEEN PREPARED BY MY FATHER".

And Hearing this, the TEN became INDIGNANT at the TWO BROTHERS. [Matthew 20. Verses 20 to 24.]

Peter also Under the MIND CONTROL Influence of these Corrupt INVISIBLE BEINGS on Behalf of All Disciples, also Inquired of JESUS as to WHAT WAS THEIR BENEFIT to be with HIM, because they Left EVERYTHING and FOLLOWED HIM, regarding which the Holy Bible States:

"Then PETER Answered and Said to HIM, "BEHOLD, We have Left Everything and Followed You; WHAT then will there be FOR US?" And JESUS Said to them, "Truly I Say to YOU, that YOU who have Followed ME, in REGENERATION when the Son of Man will Sit on HIS Glorious Throne, You also Sit upon Twelve Thrones, Judging the Twelve Tribes of Israel. [Matthew 19. 27, 28.]

The Invisible Demons through their MIND CONTROL TECHNIQUES were always Creating WRONG Questions of Undue Rivalry between the Twelve Disciples of JESUS CHRIST, regarding which the Holy Bible States:

'And they Came to CAPERNAUM; and When HE was in the HOUSE, HE Began to Question them, "WHAT were YOU Discussing on the WAY?" But they Kept SILENT, for On the Way THEY HAD DISCUSSED WITH "ONE ANOTHER" WHICH OF THEM WAS THE "'GREATEST'". And Sitting Down, HE Called the TWELVE and Said to them, "IF ANYONE WANTS TO BE FIRST, HE SHALL BE "LAST OF ALL", and "SERVANT OF ALL".' [Mark 9. Verses 34 to 35.]

JESUS CHRIST Very well knew that due to the Onslaught of Mind Control Frequencies of the Invisible DEMON MASTERS, the UNDERLYING FAITH of His Disciples was Still NOT STRONG ENOUGH to CAST OUT DEMONS, which JESUS termed as "A STRONG WILLFUL 'PRAYER' FROM THE SACRED HEART", regarding which the Holy Bible States:

'And JESUS Said to Him, "IF YOU CAN! All Things are Possible to Him WHO BELIEVES". Immediately the Boy's Father Cried Out and began Saying, "I DO BELIEVE; HELP MY UNBELIEF".

And When JESUS Saw that a Crowd was Rapidly Gathering, HE REBUKED the UNCLEAN SPIRIT, Saying to it, "YOU DEAF AND DUMB SPIRIT, I COMMAND YOU, COME OUT OF HIM AND DO NOT ENTER HIM AGAIN". And after Crying Out and Throwing Him into Terrible Convulsions, it CAME OUT; and the BOY became so Much Like a CORPSE that Most of Them Said, "HE IS DEAD!" But JESUS Took Him by the Hand; and He Got Up.

And when HE had Come into the House, HIS Disciples began Questioning HIM PRIVATELY, "WHY IS IT THAT WE COULD NOT CAST IT OUT?" And He Said to them, "THIS KIND CANNOT COME OUT BY ANYTHING, BUT 'PRAYER'".' [Mark 9. Verses 23 to 29.]

And in the Very End, the MIND CONTROL Influence of SATAN was so POWERFUL Upon JESUS'S Disciple JUDAS ISCARIOT, that HE was Greedily Led by the INVISIBLE DEMONS to their Religious Fronts, the CHIEF PRIESTS, who Offered Him Just Only "30 PIECES of SILVER", so that HE Could Willfully BETRAY HIS DIVINE MASTER, that Holy "SON OF GOD" known to ALL HIS Disciples as the "LORD CHRIST" Incarnated in an Ordinary HUMAN FORM, whom Even the SATAN Himself COULD NOT BUY with the "FULL OFFERING OF ENTIRE WORLD KINGDOMS, and their RICHES AND GLORY", regarding which the Holy Bible States:

"Then ONE of the TWELVE, Named JUDAS ISCARIOT, went to the Chief Priests, and Said, "WHAT are YOU Willing to Give Me to DELIVER HIM UP TO YOU?" And They Weighed Out to Him THIRTY PIECES OF SILVER. And from THEN ON He Began Looking for a Good Opportunity to "'BETRAY HIM'"'." [Matthew 26. Verses 14 to 16.]

JESUS CHRIST Being the "CHIEF JUSTICE" OF ALL THE "VISIBLE AND INVISIBLE BEINGS AND ENTITIES" OF THE UNIVERSE, Told His Disciples that when HE Sits on HIS GLORIOUS THRONE AS THE "SUPREME JUDGE KING", he will Separate THOSE on the RIGHT EVOLUTIONARY PATH OF "SPIRIT", to be Put on HIS Right Side, from the ONES Upon the Demonic Path of LEFT HAND PRACTICES, to be Put on HIS Left Side to be Sent into the "TORTURE CHAMBER OF ETERNAL FIRE", regarding which the Holy Bible States:

'But When the Son of Man Comes in HIS GLORY, and All the Angels with HIM, then HE will Sit on His Glorious Throne. And All the NATIONS will be GATHERED Before HIM; AND HE will Separate Them FROM One Another, as the SHEPHERD Separates the Sheep from the Goats; AND HE will Put the Sheep on HIS Right, and the Goats on the Left.

Then the KING will Say to those on HIS RIGHT, "COME, YOU WHO ARE BLESSED OF MY FATHER, INHERIT THE KINGDOM PREPARED FOR YOU FROM THE "FOUNDATION OF WORLD".

Then HE will also Say to those on HIS LEFT, "DEPART FROM ME, ACCURSED ONES, INTO THE "ETERNAL FIRE", WHICH HAS BEEN PREPARED FOR THE "'DEVIL AND HIS ANGELS"'.' [Matthew 25. 31, 32, 33, 34, 41.]

Jesus rebuking Peter

'Then the CHIEF PRIESTS and the ELDERS of the PEOPLE were Gathered Together in the Court of the HIGH PRIEST Named "CAIAPHAS"; AND they PLOTTED Together to SEIZE JESUS by STEALTH, and KILL HIM.' [Matthew 26. 3, 4.]

JESUS CHRIST also Being the GOD'S APPOINTED CHIEF JUDGE for all the Incarnated Human Beings of this Planet as well as for the INVISIBLE CORRUPT DEMONIC BEINGS, Collectively Known as the "DEVIL or the SATAN", who have been Invisibly Acting as the "ILLEGAL CONTROLLER AND PUPPET MASTERS" for all the Ignorant and Innocent EVOLVING HUMAN BEINGS, of the Physical Plane [ASSIAH] of the Planet Earth, by ILLEGALLY CONTROLLING THEIR "PERSONALITY MINDS" through the DECEITFUL Introduction of FORMULATED "EVIL DESIRE" THOUGHT FORMS in their INVISIBLE AURA BODIES which ILLEGALLY INCREASED AND ACTIVATED their INACTIVE AND RESIDUAL "ANIMAL PASSIONS", which All Human Beings Existing as the Highest Members of Animal Kingdom, thus Contain them as the "INACTIVE SPORES OF ANIMAL PASSIONS" in their "PERSONALITY MIND CONSCIOUSNESS", as the GREAT LORD GOD after creation of the ANIMAL KINGDOM Created Human Beings in HIS OWN IMAGE and Gave them THE HIGHEST CONSCIOUS ATTRIBUTE OF "'AN INDIVIDUALIZED PERSONALITY MIND'" to Rule over them.

After the "TEMPTER SATAN" Miserably Failed to INFLUENCE the PERSONALITY MIND of JESUS CHRIST as Mentioned in the Chapter of "Matthew 4. 8, 9." of the Holy Bible, when HE OFFERED JESUS All the WORLD'S KINGDOM'S AND THEIR SO CALLED "'ILLUSORY GLORY'", which ALL were WILLFULLY REJECTED by JESUS AS THE "MUNDANE ILLUSORY GLAMOUR" Compared to the GREAT LORD'S WORSHIP THROUGH "SPIRITS EVOLUTION" KNOWN AS the Path of "SPIRITUALITY", Since then HIS ADVERSARY SATAN was Continuously Looking for An Opportunity for an Appropriate REVENGE Against "'HIS TRUE SPIRITUAL MINISTRY'", and thus Deceitfully INCITING THE VARIOUS "NON SPIRITUAL FRONTS" who Existed as the INCARNATED PRESTIGIOUS LEADERS OF THE ORGANIZED RELIGION OF HIS TIMES, who being TOTALLY UNAWARE of these ILLEGAL MIND CONTROL OPERATIONS carried on by the CORRUPT INVISIBLE BEINGS, thus Under their Illegal Influence, then Plotted to SEIZE AND KILL THE "INCARNATED HUMAN FORM OF JESUS", regarding which the Holy Bible States:

'Then the CHIEF PRIESTS and the ELDERS of the PEOPLE were Gathered Together in the Court of the HIGH PRIEST Named "CAIAPHAS"; AND they PLOTTED Together to SEIZE JESUS by STEALTH, and KILL HIM.' [Matthew 26. 3, 4.]

But JESUS was Fully Aware of the OPERATIONAL MODE of these Invisible DEMONS and their ILLEGAL Mind Control, which WRONGFULLY has been in Existence For A VERY LONGTIME upon this Planet Earth and WRONGFULLY STILL CONTINUES, Especially through their Hold Upon the SOULLESS GOVERNING ORGANIZATIONS Formulated by the Human Beings Themselves to Exist as HUGE SOULLESS STRUCTURAL ESTABLISHMENTS, through which in the Name of So Called "FAME and GLORY", they Deceitfully Incited Hateful and Fighting ANIMAL PASSIONS of the LOWER MINDS, by Illegally Flaming them in the Personality Minds of Innocent and Ignorant Incarnated Human Beings, to GO Against ALL OTHER HUMAN BEINGS, who Did Not BELONGED to their Particular SOCIAL STRUCTURES OR BELIEF SYSTEM, and that is Why JESUS Propagated the DIVINE MESSAGE OF "TRUE SPIRITUAL LOVE" Among ALL HUMAN BEINGS, without Any Differentiation between RICH and POOR or a "JEW or a GENTILE", and Explained them through Parables that All Such Classifications of the DENSE PLANE WORLD were Only Related to the Incarnated Form Body and Its EMBODIED PERSONALITY MIND, and NOT TO THEIR TRUE "CONSCIOUS EXISTENCE", which is the SOLAR CONSCIOUS "ETHEREAL SPIRIT", a Divine Gift Bestowed Upon ALL VISIBLE AND INVISIBLE EVOLVING BEINGS OF THIS PLANET EARTH, Given to them FREELY by the UNKNOWABLE "MOST HIGH" as Per HIS EVOLUTIONARY PLAN AND PURPOSE.

So when People during JESUS Crucifixion under the ILLEGAL MIND CONTROL of these So Called "GODS and GODDESSES" WHO ARE NONE OTHER THAN INVISIBLE DEMONIC ANGELS, AND THEIR ASSOCIATED "DARK MASTERS" OF THE LEFT HAND PRACTICES, "SPAT ON HIM" and "BEAT HIM UP" and then divided HIS Garments Among themselves by Casting LOTS just as HIS Famous Ancestor KING DAVID Much Earlier Said in "Psalm 22. 18." of the Holy Bible which States: "THEY DIVIDE MY GARMENTS AMONG THEM, AND FOR MY CLOTHING THEY CAST LOTS".

JESUS KNOWING FULL WELL their IGNORANCE and UNAWARENESS

about these INVISIBLE DEMONS, AND THEIR DECEITFUL MIND CONTROL PRACTICES, Still Asked the CREATOR FATHER, the "MOST HIGH LORD GOD" to FORGIVE THEM, regarding which the Holy Bible States:

'Then the Soldiers of the GOVERNOR Took JESUS into the PRAETORIUM and Gathered the Whole ROMAN COHORT AROUND HIM. And They Stripped HIM, and Put a Scarlet Robe on HIM.

And after Weaving a CROWN OF THORNS, they Put it on HIS HEAD, and a REED in HIS RIGHT HAND; and they KNEELED Before HIM and MOCKED HIM, Saying, "HAIL, KING OF THE JEWS!" And they "'SPAT ON HIM'", AND TOOK THE REED AND BEGAN TO "BEAT HIM ON THE HEAD". And AFTER they had MOCKED HIM, they TOOK HIS Robe Off and Put HIS Garments on HIM, and Led HIM to CRUCIFY HIM.' [Matthew 27. Verses 27 to 31.]

'And when They Came to the Place Called "THE SKULL", there they CRUCIFIED HIM" and the Criminals, ONE on the Right and the OTHER on the Left. But JESUS was SAYING, 'FATHER FORGIVE THEM; FOR THEY """"DO NOT KNOW"""" WHAT THEY ARE DOING." And they CAST LOTS, Dividing Up HIS Garments AMONG Themselves.' [Luke 23. 33, 34.]

JESUS CHRIST was Fully Aware of His Healing Powers, and His Total Authority, bestowed upon Him by the "MOST HIGH", as to Be the "SUPREME JUDGE" Over All the VISIBLE AND INVISIBLE DOMAINS of This Planet Earth, but During His Incarnated Life He Never Misused HIS VESTED POWER, as HIS MAIN MISSION WAS TO PROPAGATE THE "SPIRITUAL LOVE", so that the PROBLEM OF THE "HARDENING OF HEART" IN EVOLVING HUMAN BEINGS Can be Totally Removed From this Planet Earth, to SAVE THEIR "ETHEREAL SOUL CONSCIOUSNESS" FROM ITS UNDUE TOTAL "ANNIHILATION AND EXTINCTION"' in this AGE AND AGES TO COME, which the DOOMED FALLEN ANGELS were NOT READY to AGREE Upon, as THEY BEING DOOMED THEMSELVES, AND NOT ABEL TO "SPIRITUALLY EVOLVE ANY FURTHER", THUS SINCE ANCIENT TIMES HAVE BEEN ILLEGALLY CONTROLLING THE "'PERSONALITY MINDS'" OF "IGNORANT HUMAN BEINGS" IN THE NAME OF "ORGANIZED RELIGIONS" Especially Those which PERTAINED

TO THE SO CALLED "GODS AND GODDESSES" represented through Breathless IDOLS AND GRAVEN IMAGES, Especially the Various Goddesses LIKE THE MOTHER "GODDESS ASHERAH", who even the Children of Israel also Started Foolishly Worshiping in their Temples of the Promised Land, knowing Full Well that "'NO SUCH GODDESS'" has been Ever Been Mentioned in their First BOOK OF TORAH [Genesis], as it was ONLY THEIR FATHER LORD GOD, who through the ACT OF HIS DESIRE MIND CREATED THEM WITH WHAT IS COMMONLY KNOWN AS "'THE EVENTUATION PROCESS'", FOR THEM TO THUS EXIST IN MALE AND FEMALE DENSE HUMAN FORMS UPON THIS PLANET EARTH, regarding which the Holy Bible States:

'In the Beginning GOD Created the Heavens and the Earth.

Then God "SAID", "LET the EARTH Bring Forth LIVING CREATURES after their KIND; Cattle and Creeping Things and Beasts of the Earth after their Kind", and IT WAS SO. And GOD Made the Beasts of the Earth after their KIND, and the Cattle after their KIND, and everything that CREEPS on the Ground after its KIND; and GOD SAW that it was GOOD.

Then GOD Said, "LET us Make MAN in Our Image, According to Our Likeness; and LET THEM Rule over the FISH of the SEA, and over the BIRDS of the SKY, and over the CATTLE and over ALL THE EARTH, and over Every CREEPING THING that CREEPS on the Earth". And GOD Created MAN IN HIS OWN IMAGE, in the IMAGE of GOD HE CREATED Him; MALE and FEMALE HE Created Them. [Genesis. 1. 1, 24, 25, 26, 27.]

The Crucifixion

'Then the Soldiers of the GOVERNOR Took JESUS into the PRAETORIUM and Gathered the Whole ROMAN COHORT AROUND HIM. And They Stripped HIM, and Put a Scarlet Robe on HIM.

And after Weaving a CROWN OF THORNS, they Put it on HIS HEAD, and a REED in HIS RIGHT HAND; and they KNEELED Before HIM and MOCKED HIM, Saying, "HAIL, KING OF THE JEWS!" And they "'SPAT ON HIM'", AND TOOK THE REED AND BEGAN TO "BEAT HIM ON THE HEAD". And AFTER they had MOCKED HIM, they TOOK HIS Robe Off and Put HIS Garments on HIM, and Led HIM to CRUCIFY HIM.' [Matthew 27. Verses 27 to 31.]

Now there was a HERD of Many "SWINE" Feeding there on the Mountain; And the DEMONS Entreated Him to PERMIT them to ENTER the SWINE. And HE GAVE them PERMISSION. And the DEMONS Came Out from the MAN and Entered the SWINE; AND the HERD Rushed Down the Steep Bank into the Lake, and were DROWNED. And when those who Tended THEM Saw what had Happened, they Ran Away and Reported it in the CITY and Out in the Country. And the People went out to See what had Happened; and they Came to JESUS, and Found the Man from Whom the DEMONS had Gone Out, "SITTING DOWN AT THE FEET OF JESUS", Clothed and in "HIS RIGHT MIND"; and they became Frightened. And those who had SEEN it REPORTED to Them HOW THE MAN WHO WAS "'DEMON – POSSESSED" had been MADE WELL.' [Luke 8. Verses 26 to 36.]

Part 106

JESUS CHRIST knowing Full Well about the Ignorance of Common People about the Invisible Frequency Dimensions of this Planet Earth, and the Illegal Operations of the "UNCLEAN SPIRITS" who Mostly Dwell Invisibly in the Lower Dense Ether's of this Physical World [ASSIAH], and being Themselves DOOMED from Any Further 'SPIRITUAL EVOLUTION' thus Illegally Overpower their Innocent Victims to Prolong their Own DOOMED Existence, then JESUS tried HIS Best to Explain their Wrong Operational Modes to the People, so that they can be CAREFUL from their Illegal and Deceitful Attacks, regarding which the Holy Bible States:

'ALL Things have Been Handed Over to ME by My Father; AND No One Knows the Son, Except the Father; NOR does ANYONE Know the Father, Except the Son, and ANYONE to Whom the Son Wills to Reveal HIM.' [Matthew 11. 27.]

"Now When the UNCLEAN SPIRIT Goes Out of a MAN, it PASSES through WATERLESS Places, Seeking REST, and DOES NOT Find it. Then It Says, "I will Return to My House FROM Which I Came"; AND when it COMES, it FINDS it UNOCCUPIED, SWEPT and Put in Order. Then it Goes, and Takes ALONG with it SEVEN OTHER SPIRITS, MORE WICKED THAN ITSELF, and They GO IN and LIVE THERE; and the LAST STATE of that MAN Becomes WORSE than the FIRST. That is the WAY it will ALSO be with this EVIL GENERATION". [Matthew 12. Verses 43 to 45.]

The Same Information, which was TOLD by JESUS about the Unclean Spirits is also recorded in the Gospel of Luke of the Holy Bible, which State:

"When the UNCLEAN SPIRIT Goes Out of a MAN, it PASSES through WATERLESS Places SEEKING REST, and Not Finding Any, It SAYS, "I will Return to My House From Which I Came'.

And when it COMES, it FINDS it SWEPT and Put in Order. Then it Goes and Takes ALONG SEVEN OTHER SPIRITS, MORE EVIL THAN ITSELF, and They GO IN and LIVE THERE; and the LAST STATE of that MAN Becomes WORSE than the FIRST."

And it came about while HE Said these Things, One of the Women in the Crowd raised Her Voice, and Said to Him, "BLESSED IS THE WOMB THAT BORE YOU, AND THE BREASTS AT WHICH YOU NURSED". But HE Said, "ON THE CONTRARY, BLESSED ARE THOSE WHO HEAR THE "'WORD OF GOD'", AND OBSERVE IT"." [Luke 11 Verses 24 to 28.]

JESUS Cured EVEN those Human Beings, who were POSSESSED by a Very Large Number of Demons, Many Fold MULTIPLES OF SEVEN OR EIGHT, like a Full LEGION of DEMONS, regarding which the Holy Bible States:

'And they SAILED to the Country of the GERASENES, which is Opposite GALILEE. And when HE had Come Out onto the Land, HE was MET by a CERTAIN MAN FROM THE CITY who was "POSSESSED with DEMONS"; and who had Not Put on Any Clothing for a Long Time, and was Not Living in a HOUSE, but in the "TOMBS".

And Seeing JESUS, He Cried Out and Fell before HIM, and Said in a LOUD VOICE, "WHAT Do I have to DO with YOU, JESUS, Son of the "'MOST HIGH GOD'"? I Beg You, Do Not TORMENT Me". For HE had been COMMANDING the "UNCLEAN SPIRIT" to COME OUT of the MAN. For it had SEIZED Him Many Times; AND He was Bound with CHAINS and SHACKLES and Kept UNDER GUARD; and Yet He would BURST His FETTERS and be DRIVEN by the DEMON into the DESERT.

And JESUS asked Him, "WHAT is Your Name?" And He Said, "LEGION"; FOR MANY DEMONS ENTERED HIM. And they were Entreating HIM Not to COMMAND Them to Depart into the ABYSS.

Now there was a HERD of Many "SWINE" Feeding there on the Mountain; And the DEMONS Entreated Him to PERMIT them to ENTER the SWINE. And HE GAVE them PERMISSION. And the DEMONS Came Out from the MAN and Entered the SWINE; AND the HERD Rushed Down the Steep Bank into the Lake, and were DROWNED.

And when those who Tended THEM Saw what had Happened, they Ran Away and Reported it in the CITY and Out in the Country. And the People went out to See what had Happened; and they Came to JESUS, and Found the Man from Whom the DEMONS had Gone Out, "SITTING DOWN AT THE FEET OF JESUS", Clothed and in "HIS RIGHT MIND"; and they became Frightened. And those who had SEEN it REPORTED to Them HOW THE MAN WHO WAS "'DEMON – POSSESSED" had been MADE WELL.' [Luke 8. Verses 26 to 36.]

All the Physical and Mental HEALING of the Human Beings is Related to "STRONG WILLED FAITH and BELIEF" in the "MOST HIGH", the "UNKNOWABLE CREATOR – OBSERVER, PRESERVER and DESTROYER OF THE MANIFESTED UNIVERSE", and Also in "HIS CHOSEN FRONTS", Who are HIS Humble Servants, who Incarnate as HIS Prophets and Messengers, Especially HIS SON'S WITH SPECIAL MISSIONS RELATED TO "'HIS JUDGMENTS'", WHO INCARNATE IN ORDINARY "HUMAN FORM" UPON THE PHYSICAL PLANE [ASSIAH] OF THIS PLANET EARTH, as Such "STRONG BELIEF" then CONNECTS THE "PERSONALITY MIND" EMBODIED IN AN INCARNATED HUMAN FORM, WITH HIS "HIGHER SELF OR THE YECHIDAH BODY" WHICH IS COMPOSED OF "PURE SOLAR ENERGY CONSCIOUSNESS", AND THUS ALSO TO THE DESIRE MIND CONSCIOUS REFLECTIONS OF THE UNKNOWABLE "MOST HIGH", Which Then CREATES the "'VIBRATING POSITIVE ENERGY THOUGHT FORMS IN THE VITAL ETHER'", WHICH THUS "TOTALLY NEUTRALIZES" THE NEGATIVE ENERGY THOUGHT FORMS, WHICH EXIST AS THE "'SOULLESS DEMONIC ENTITIES" HAVING CORPORATE STRUCTURES, having an ILLEGAL HOLD upon the "Personality Mind" of Incarnated Human Beings, regarding which the Holy Bible States:

'And JESUS Said to Him, "IF YOU CAN! ALL THINGS ARE POSSIBLE TO HIM, WHO BELIEVES".' [Mark 9. 23.]

All TYPES OF ILLNESSES and DISEASES are Related to NEGATIVE

THOUGHT FORM ENERGIES, which FIRST AFFECT THE INVISIBLE VITAL BODY, also known as the "BODY DOUBLE", which is Composed of Invisible DENSE ETHER'S [2nd, 3rd, and 4th Types of ETHER'S] OF THE PHYSICAL PLANE, Which the FALLEN ANGELS AND THEIR HIERARCHICAL DEMONIC GROUPS have been Illegally MISUSING for a Very Long Time Upon this Planet Earth.

The SENTIMENTAL DEPRESSIONS of ALL KINDS in the Personality Minds of Evolving Human Beings Create Such POWERFUL "'LIVE NEGATIVE THOUGHT FORMS", Which Cause ILL Effects in the Vital Energy Circulation of the Energy Distribution Centers, which are Situated at the Surface of the Manifested VITAL BODY, which is also known as the "ETHEREAL NEFESH", in which these MINOR and MAJOR ENERGY CENTER'S Appear like "Slow or Fast Rotating Vortex Depressions" or the Sephira's of the Circulating ELECTRIC and MAGNETIC Ethereal Currents, thus Causing HARMFUL UNDUE RESTRICTIONS in the VITAL ENERGY FLOW Circulation, which Gradually Cause Various Types of DISEASES and ILLNESSES to Slowly Manifest in the DENSE PHYSICAL FORM OF A HUMAN BEING, and if These Demonic Beings and their SOULLESS CREATIONS known as the DEMONIC ENTITIES, which get Empowered by the Live Energies of the "NEGATIVE THOUGHT FORMS" Somehow Get Illegally Attached to the INVISIBLE HUMAN AURA, they being Invisible to the Human Eye then Deceitfully Ride His Human Form by feeding upon his Vital Currents, and thus Negatively Affect His Brain Functions as well as His "PERSONALITY CONSCIOUSNESS", and in that Case the PERSONALITY OF THE HUMAN BEING is known as being "POSSESSED". But in the so called Modern World of Technology, the Physical Plane Doctors have Now Named them as Various Types of Mental Illnesses, which they Cure with Several Types of "NARCOTIC DRUGS" to Keep them Calm, which in FACT are THE REQUIRED "'NEGATIVE ENERGY FOOD'" FOR THESE "INVISIBLE DEMONIC BEINGS and ENTITIES", which keep them "SATISFIED" till their "NEXT DOSE", but the Proper Way of HEALING is to Permanently DESTROY their Illegal Hold, which is Wrongly Carried On and Affixed to the Human AURA through the Negative Thought Form live Energies of the Lower Desire Mind, Pinned upon the RUACH BODY and NEFESH BODY of the Incarnated Human Beings, and their Such Removal is Only Possible through the INTERVENTION OF THE UNIVERSAL VITAL ENERGIES OF THE "MOST HIGH", Which JESUS also Used to HEAL the Sick and also CURE the Possessed, as LORD'S VITAL ENERGIES Invisibly Circulated through HIS Incarnated Human Form, regarding which the Holy Bible States:

'And I Say to YOU, MY FRIENDS, DO not be Afraid of Those WHO KILL THE BODY, AND AFTER THAT HAVE "'NO MORE'" THAT THEY CAN DO. BUT "I" WILL WARN YOU WHOM TO FEAR; FEAR THE "'ONE'" WHO AFTER HE HAS KILLED HAS "'AUTHORITY TO CAST INTO HELL"'; YES, "I TELL YOU, FEAR HIM!"' [Luke 12. 4, 5.]

And Regarding JESUS even Bringing BACK THE DEPARTED "SPIRIT" in Incarnated Human Form, by Rejoining the Invisible SEVERED SILVER CORD, the Holy Bible States:

'And as JESUS Returned, the Multitude Welcomed Him, for they had ALL Been Waiting for HIM. And behold, there CAME a Man Named JAIRUS, and He was an "'OFFICIAL OF THE SYNAGOGUE'"; AND HE "FELL AT JESUS' FEET", and began to Entreat HIM to Come to His HOUSE; FOR He had an Only Daughter, about 12 Years Old, and She was DYING. But as He Went, the Multitudes were "PRESSING AGAINST HIM".

And a Woman who had A HEMORRHAGE for TWELVE YEARS, and Could Not be "HEALED BY ANYONE", Came up behind HIM, and TOUCHED THE FRINGE OF HIS CLOAK; and Immediately Her HEMORRHAGE STOPPED.

And JESUS Said, "WHO is the ONE who TOUCHED ME?" And while They All were DENYING IT, PETER Said, "MASTER, The Multitudes are Crowding and PRESSING Upon You". But JESUS Said, "SOMEONE Did Touch ME, FOR "I" was AWARE that POWER HAD GONE OUT OF "ME"."

And when the Woman Saw that She had Not ESCAPED NOTICE, SHE Came TREMBLING and FELL DOWN Before HIM, and DECLARED in the Presence of all the PEOPLE the "REASON WHY SHE HAD TOUCHED HIM", and How She had been IMMEDIATELY HEALED.

And HE Said to Her, "Daughter, YOUR FAITH HAS MADE YOU WELL; GO

IN PEACE". While HE was Still Speaking, Someone Came from the House of the SYNAGOGUE OFFICIAL, Saying, "YOUR Daughter has DIED; Do Not Trouble the TEACHER Any More". But when JESUS HEARD this, HE Answered Him, "DO NOT be AFRAID Any Longer; "'ONLY BELIEVE'", and SHE shall be Made WELL".

And when HE had COME to the House, HE Did Not Allow Anyone to Enter with HIM, Except PETER, JOHN, and JAMES, and the GIRL'S FATHER and MOTHER. Now they were ALL WEEPING and LAMENTING for Her; but HE Said, "STOP Weeping, for She has NOT DIED, but is ASLEEP". And they BEGAN LAUGHING at HIM, KNOWING THAT SHE HAD DIED.

HE, However, took her by the Hand and Called, Saying, "CHILD, ARISE!" And Her "'"'SPIRIT RETURNED"'"', and She Rose UP Immediately; and HE Gave Orders for Something to be GIVEN Her to EAT. And Her Parents were AMAZED; but HE INSTRUCTED them to "'TELL NO ONE WHAT HAD HAPPENED"''.' [Luke 8. Verses 40 to 56.]

JESUS, PETER, JOHN, and JAMES, and the GIRL & her FATHER and MOTHER

The Secret of the Breast Plate
Part 107

By the Time PROPHET ELIJAH'S SOUL CONSCIOUSNESS Incarnated again as an Enlightened "PERSONALITY MIND" Upon the Physical Plane [ASSIAH] to be Embodied in the Human Form of "JOHN THE BAPTIST", along with LORD'S Son to also Incarnate as the JESUS CHRIST, and Established their SPIRITUAL MINISTRIES to Enhance the "SOLAR SPIRIT CONSCIOUSNESS" of the Evolving Human Beings as per the LORD'S EVOLUTIONARY PLAN through the Proper Guiding of their PERSONALITY MINDS embodied in the Human Forms, whom The GREAT LORD CREATED IN HIS OWN IMAGE to Exist Upon this Planet Earth, because by then the CORRUPT CONTROL of the so Called BROTHERHOOD was Firmly Established as an HUGE SOULLESS CORPORATE ENTITY in the Invisible ETHEREAL FREQUENCIES of this Planet Earth, whose Corrupt MEMBERS, the So Called MASTERS, after Learning the SECRETS OF DIFFUSING THE "SOLAR LIGHT ENERGY" through LORD'S GIVEN "'VESTED POWERS AND DIVINE CONSCIOUS ATTRIBUTES'", whom they WILLFULLY MISUSED AND THUS BACK-STABBED HIS KINDNESS AND BENEFICIAL "LOVE AND TRUST", and Further More Apart from it They Also Illegally Termed THEMSELVES as the so called "LIGHT BEINGS", and were DECEITFULLY SUCCESSFUL to ESTABLISH """A NEW WORLD ORDER"'" in the Formulated Shape of a "HUGE SOULLESS ENTITY" to be Known as the "ROMAN EMPIRE", which by that time had a "FIRM GRIP" upon the PERSONALITY MINDS of the Evolving Human Beings, who during Those Times lived under Its CAPTURED DOMAINS upon the Physical Plane of this Planet Earth, and Their RULING LEADERS Seated by these INVISIBLE CORRUPT BEINGS Upon KINGLY THRONES AND ELEVATED POSITIONS to Act as their CORRUPT FRONTS, thus Wrongfully Promoted "BLOOD AND VIOLENCE" in the Name of So Called "FAME AND GLORY", and JESUS Himself Informed HIS Disciples about this Hidden Fact that the KINGDOM OF HEAVEN was SUFFERING "VIOLENCE", and about JOHN THE BAPTIST BEING PROPHET ELIJAH, regarding which the Holy Bible States:

'And from the Days of JOHN THE BAPTIST UNTIL NOW, the Kingdom of HEAVEN SUFFERS "VIOLENCE", AND VIOLENT MEN TAKE IT BY FORCE".

'For ALL PROPHETS and the LAW PROPHESIED Until JOHN. And if YOU CARE TO ACCEPT IT, HE HIMSELF IS """"ELIJAH"""", WHO was to COME. He WHO has "EARS to HEAR", Let Him HEAR.' [Matthew 11. Verses 12 to 15.]

JESUS being the LORD' CHOSEN CHIEF JUDGE OF THE UNIVERSE, was also DESTINED to be KNOWN as the CHRIST Among the Human Beings as well as the INVISIBLE ANGELS of this Planet Earth, also Clearly Explained About "HIMSELF" From the "Psalm 110.1" of DAVID as being "'THE ETERNAL LORD", which States: "The LORD Says to "'MY LORD'"; SIT at MY RIGHT HAND, UNTIL "I" MAKE "'THINE ENEMIES'" A "FOOTSTOOL FOR THY FEET".", and it is also A HIDDEN FACT that it was the "'SOUL CONSCIOUSNESS OF JESUS'" through Whom this "WORLD" was Made by the DESIRE MIND OF THE UNKNOWABLE "MOST HIGH", regarding which the Holy Bible States:

'And JESUS Answering began to Say, as HE Taught in the Temple, "HOW IS IT THAT THE SCRIBES SAY THAT THE CHRIST IS THE "SON OF DAVID"? David HIMSELF Said in the Holy Spirit. 'The LORD Said to "'MY LORD'"; "SIT at MY RIGHT HAND, UNTIL "I" Put "'THINE ENEMIES'" Beneath THY FEET". David Himself Calls HIM "LORD"; AND so in WHAT SENSE IS HE 'HIS SON'?" And the Great Crowd Enjoyed Listening to Him.

And in HIS Teaching HE was Saying; "BEWARE of the SCRIBES Who Like to Walk in "'LONG ROBES'", and LIKE RESPECTFUL GREETINGS in the Market Places, and CHIEF SEATS in the SYNAGOGUES, and PLACES OF HONOR at BANQUETS.' [Mark 12. Verses 35 to 39.]

'GOD After HE SPOKE Long Ago to the FATHERS, IN THE PROPHETS, IN MANY PORTIONS, AND IN MANY WAYS, in these LAST DAYS has SPOKEN TO US IN HIS SON, Whom HE Appointed "HEIR OF ALL THINGS", Through WHOM also "HE MADE THE WORLD".' [Hebrews 1. 1, 2.]

JESUS is the GOD'S CHOSEN HIGH PRIEST, and for the "12 JEWELS" OF HIS SACRED "BREAST PLATE" HE Consciously Used HIS Twelve Disciples as the 12 LIVING PIECES OF JUDGEMENT, as He Gave Them Judging

AUTHORITY Over All the "'UNCLEAN SPIRITS'", and thus to HEAL Every Kind of DISEASE and SICKNESS, which is Prevalent Upon this World, regarding which the Holy Bible States:

'And Having Summoned HIS Twelve Disciples, HE Gave Them Authority over "Unclean Spirits", to Cast them Out, and to HEAL Every Kind of DISEASE and Every Kind of SICKNESS.

Now the Names of the Twelve Apostles are these; THE First, SIMON, Who is called "PETER", and "ANDREW" His Brother; and "JAMES" the Son of Zebedee, and "JOHN" His Brother; "PHILIP" and "BARTHOLOMEW"; "THOMAS" and "MATTHEW" the Tax Gatherer; "JAMES" the Son of Alphaeus, and "THADDAEUS"; "SIMON" the Cananaean, and "JUDAS ISCARIOT", the One Who Betrayed HIM.

These Twelve JESUS Sent Out after Instructing Them, Saying, "DO NOT GO in the Way of the GENTILES, and DO NOT Enter Any City of the SAMARITANS; BUT Rather Go to the LOST SHEEP of the HOUSE of ISRAEL".' [Matthew 10. Verses 1 to 6.]

JESUS CHRIST after HIS Ascension from the Physical Plane World, also CHOSE a Zealot Pharisee Named "SAUL" later to be Renamed as the Apostle "PAUL", Who under the Invisible Mind Control of Hierarchical Demons, right from the Death of Jesus's Humble Follower STEPHEN, which Took Place in His Presence, then STARTED to ACT Even More CRUELLY TOWARD ALL JESUS FOLLOWERS by Persecuting them, regarding which the Holy Bible States:

'And SAUL was in Hearty Agreement with Putting HIM to Death. And on that Day a Great PERSECUTION AROSE against the CHURCH in JERUSALEM; and they were SCATTERED throughout the Regions of JUDEA and SAMARIA, Except the APOSTLES. And Some Devout Men BURIED STEPHEN, and Made Loud LAMENTATION over Him. But SAUL Began RAVAGING THE CHURCH, Entering House after House; and DRAGGING OFF Men and Women, He would PUT THEM IN PRISON.' [Acts 8. Verses 1 to 3.]

But JESUS being LORD'S SON, AS WELL AS HIS CHOSEN HIGH PRIEST Divinely Placed to Act Upon this Planet Earth, Gracefully Wanted the Zealot SAUL to Be Freed from the Invisible Mind Control of the DEMONIC HIERARCHY, and then Wanted Him to Become His Chosen Instrument as THE LIVING "LIGHT OF MIND", so that He could Properly ACT His NEW ROLE just Like the Holy Object "URIM" of the BREAST PLATE, existing for HUMANITY as a Beacon of "LIGHT" in the Form of a "LIVING URIM", for the Deliverance of both the JEWS AND GENTILES ALIKE by the SPIRITUAL ENERGIES OF THE "SACRED HEART", and for this reason JESUS Appeared to "SAUL" for the First Time as the "FLASHING LIGHT", So that He Himself Could "SHINE" Just Like the LIGHT of """"URIM"""", Fully Equipped with the "SPIRITUAL WISDOM OF THE LORD", and thus Act as a Spiritual Guide for All Those HUMAN'S, whose PERSONALITY MINDS were Stuck in the "DARKNESS OF DEMONIC INFLUENCE" and thus LOST in the "SPIRITUAL IGNORANCE", regarding which the Holy Bible States:

'Now SAUL, Still Breathing Threats and Murder AGAINST the Disciples of the LORD, went to the High Priest, and Asked for Letters from Him to the Synagogues at DAMASCUS , so that if He Found Any Belonging to the Way, BOTH Men and Women, He Might Bring them BOUND to JERUSALEM.

And it Came About that as He Journeyed, He was Approaching DAMASCUS, and Suddenly a LIGHT FROM HEAVEN FLASHED AROUND HIM; AND HE FELL TO THE GROUND, AND HEARD A VOICE SAYING TO HIM, "SAUL, SAUL, WHY ARE YOU PERSECUTING ME?" And He Said, "WHO ART THOU, LORD?" And He Said, "I AM JESUS WHOM YOU ARE PERSECUTING, BUT RISE, AND ENTER THE CITY, AND IT SHALL BE TOLD YOU WHAT YOU MUST DO". And the Men Who Traveled with Him STOOD SPEECHLESS, Hearing the Voice, but "SEEING NO ONE". And SAUL GOT UP from the Ground, and though His Eyes were OPEN, He could SEE NOTHING; and Leading Him by the Hand, they BROUGHT Him into DAMASCUS. And He was "'THREE DAYS" Without Sight, and Neither ATE NOR DRANK. [Acts 9 Verses 1 to 9.]

Regarding JESUS being the HIGH PRIEST OF GOD, His Humble Servant PAUL, who before His "Divine Choosing" was Earlier Known as the

Zealot Pharisee "SAUL from TARSUS", Humbly Informed all the HEBREW Brethren in Writing about JESUS'S Such Exalted Status, Clearly Stating that HE is the LORD'S MOST SACRED "HIGH PRIEST", regarding which the Holy Bible States:

'For Assuredly HE Does Not Give Help to Angels, but HE Gives Help to the "DESCENDANT OF ABRAHAM". Therefore, HE had to be Made LIKE His Brethren in ALL THINGS, that HE Might Become a MERCIFUL AND FAITHFUL "'HIGH PRIEST'" IN THINGS PERTAINING TO GOD, to Make PROPITIATION for the SINS OF THE PEOPLE.' [Hebrews 2. 16, 17.]

'Since then WE have a GREAT HIGH PRIEST who has PASSED through the HEAVENS, JESUS THE SON OF GOD, let US Hold Fast Our CONFESSION. For WE Do Not have a "HIGH PRIEST" Who Cannot SYMPATHIZE with Our Weakness, but One WHO has been TEMPTED in All Things as We Are, Yet WITHOUT SIN.' [Hebrews 4. 14, 15.]

JESUS'S Humble Servant PAUL, to Properly Explain the Role of JESUS CHRIST to His Hebrew Brethren, as being the Chosen HIGH PRIEST of the "MOST HIGH", thus Quoted "Psalm 2. 7.", which States: "I will Surely Tell of the Decree of the LORD; HE Said to ME, "THOU Art MY SON, TODAY I have Begotten THEE". And also Quoted "Psalm 110. 4" of King David, which States: "THE LORD has SWORN and WILL NOT CHANGE HIS MIND, THOU art a PRIEST FOREVER According to the ORDER of MELCHIZEDEK.", regarding which the Holy Bible States:

'So also CHRIST Did Not Glorify Himself so as to BECOME a HIGH PRIEST, but HE Who Said to HIM, "THOU ART MY SON, TODAY I HAVE BEGOTTEN THEE"; just as HE Says also in Another Passage, "THOU ART A PRIEST FOREVER ACCORDING TO THE ORDER OF MELCHIZEDEK".' [Hebrews 5. 5, 6.]

'Where JESUS has ENTERED as a FORERUNNER for US, having become a "HIGH PRIEST FOREVER" According to the ORDER OF MELCHIZEDEK.' [Hebrews 6. 20]

'For it was FITTING that WE should have Such a "HIGH PRIEST", Holy, Innocent, Undefiled, Separated from SINNERS and EXALTED ABOVE THE HEAVENS; WHO does Not Need DAILY, like Those High Priests, to OFFER UP SACRIFICES, First for His OWN SINS, and then for the SINS OF THE PEOPLE, BECAUSE This HE Did "'ONCE FOR ALL, WHEN HE OFFERED HIMSELF'".' [Hebrews 7. 26, 27.]

'But when CHRIST Appeared as a "HIGH PRIEST" of the GOOD THINGS to Come, HE Entered through the GREATER and More PERFECT Tabernacle, "NOT MADE WITH HANDS", that is to Say, NOT of this CREATION; and NOT THROUGH THE BLOOD OF GOATS AND CALVES, But Through "HIS OWN BLOOD", HE ENTERED THE HOLY PLACE "ONCE FOR ALL", HAVING OBTAINED "'"'ETERNAL REDEMPTION"'"'. [Hebrews 9. 11, 12.]

'And Since WE HAVE A "'GREAT PRIEST'" OVER THE "'HOUSE OF GOD'", let us Draw Near with a Sincere Heart in Full Assurance of FAITH, HAVING OUR HEARTS SPRINKLED CLEAN FROM AN "'EVIL CONSCIENCE'" and Our Bodies WASHED WITH "PURE WATER".' [Hebrews 10. 21, 22.]

Now the Names of the Twelve Apostles are these; THE First, SIMON, Who is called "PETER", and "ANDREW" His Brother; and "JAMES" the Son of Zebedee, and "JOHN" His Brother; "PHILIP" and "BARTHOLOMEW"; "THOMAS" and "MATTHEW" the Tax Gatherer; "JAMES" the Son of Alphaeus, and "THADDAEUS"; "SIMON" the Cananaean, and "JUDAS ISCARIOT", the One Who Betrayed HIM. [Matthew 10. Verses 2, 3, 4.]

And it Came About that as He Journeyed, He was Approaching DAMASCUS, and Suddenly a LIGHT FROM HEAVEN FLASHED AROUND HIM; AND HE FELL TO THE GROUND, AND HEARD A VOICE SAYING TO HIM, "SAUL, SAUL, WHY ARE YOU PERSECUTING ME?" And He Said, "WHO ART THOU, LORD?" And He Said, "I AM JESUS WHOM YOU ARE PERSECUTING, BUT RISE, AND ENTER THE CITY, AND IT SHALL BE TOLD YOU WHAT YOU MUST DO". And the Men Who Traveled with Him STOOD SPEECHLESS, Hearing the Voice, but "SEEING NO ONE". And SAUL GOT UP from the Ground, and though His Eyes were OPEN, He could SEE NOTHING; and Leading Him by the Hand, they BROUGHT Him into DAMASCUS. And He was "'THREE DAYS" Without Sight, and Neither ATE NOR DRANK. [Acts 9 Verses 3 to 9.]

"In the BEGINNING was the WORD, and the WORD was With GOD, and the WORD was GOD. HE was in the Beginning WITH GOD. All Things Came into Being by HIM; and APART from HIM '''NOTHING CAME INTO BEING''' THAT HAS '''COME INTO BEING'''. IN HIM WAS '''''LIFE'''''; AND the "LIFE" was the '''''LIGHT''''' of Men. And the "LIGHT" SHINES IN THE '''DARKNESS'''; and the DARKNESS Did Not COMPREHEND IT. [John 1. Verses 1 to 5.]

The Secret of the Breast Plate

Part 108

When the Great King SOLOMON'S Consciousness Incarnated in a Human Form, as the Son of King DAVID, then the UNKNOWABLE "MOST HIGH" Chose Him to be His Own SON as Clearly Mentioned in "1 Chronicles 17. 13." of the Holy Bible, as the GREAT LORD used His Son SOLOMON Later to be HIS "PREACHER" for the MANKIND, after He Acquired the 'Secrets of Wisdom' by LORD' GRACE, regarding which the Holy Bible States:

"The Words of the PREACHER, the Son of David, KING in JERUSALEM.' [Ecclesiastes 1. 1.]

"WISDOM" which is Based Upon "KNOWLEDGE" and "UNDERSTANDING", is the MAIN Conscious Attribute of LORD'S Begotten SON in the UNIVERSE, which Manifested IT From "HIS DESIRE MIND" to Exist as the Frequency Vibrations of "THE TREE OF LIFE", and with LORD'S GRACE, the Great King SOLOMON Very Well Came to Realize this "SUPREME and SECRET FACT" of the Universe, and then by Performing His DUTY as the Chosen Son of the "MOST HIGH", HE PREACHED this Hidden Knowledge to ALL the "MANKIND" in the Form of PROVERBS, regarding which the Holy Bible States:

'How BLESSED is the Man Who Finds WISDOM, and the Man Who "GAINS UNDERSTANDING".

She is the ""TREE OF LIFE"" to THOSE, who Take a HOLD of Her. And HAPPY are "ALL" who HOLD HER "FAST".

The LORD by "WISDOM" FOUNDED the EARTH; BY "UNDERSTANDING" HE ESTABLISHED THE HEAVENS. By HIS "KNOWLEDGE" THE DEEPS WERE BROKEN UP, AND THE SKIES DRIP WITH DEW.' [Proverb 3. 13, 18, 19, 20.]

Much Later when JESUS Incarnated also in the Lineage of King DAVID as

THE CHOSEN SON OF THE "MOST HIGH", to EXIST AS THE LORD'S "HIGH PRIEST" to the MANKIND, then the Living JEWEL of His "SACRED BREAST PLATE", HIS Humble Servant JOHN and the Living "URIM" OF THE "SACRED BREAST PLATE" HIS Humble Servant PAUL earlier known as "SAUL", Who Required "'3 DAYS'" for His TRANSFORMATION to Become LORD'S Chosen VEHICLE after He was BLINDED by Flashing LIGHT during which He Did Not Eat or Drink and thus His PERSONALITY MIND became Clean of ALL IMPURE THOUGHTS OF VIOLENCE, which were Related to His PERSECUTIONS of LORD'S Humble Followers, as "'EYES are the DOORWAY to the Solar Conscious Inner Mind SPIRIT'", and the Great LORD Chose this 3 Day Period for Him, just Like HIS MASTER JESUS rose from the DEAD After the Period of 3 DAYS.

Both JOHN and PAUL were Very Well Aware of 'JESUS "SOLAR SPIRIT" CONSCIOUSNESS' PRESENCE IN THE VERY "BEGINNING" AT THE TIME OF "CREATION OF THE WORLD", AS WELL AS HE WAS ALSO PRESENT WHEN THE MANKIND WAS CREATED UPON THIS PLANET EARTH as "'EVERYTHING WAS CREATED THROUGH HIM'", and Because of this FACT, the Verses in GENESIS Explaining "MAN'S CREATION BY THE LORD" are WRITTEN AS "US" Denoting the PLURALITY, as ALL MANIFESTATIONS APPEARED DUE TO THE ACTIVE PARTICIPATION OF HIS SON'S DESIRE MIND "TONAL FREQUENCY VIBRATIONS OF ETHEREAL VITALITY ", to Provide the REQUIRED "ANIMATING LIFE" to ALL CREATIONS, and Both of HIS HUMBLE SERVANTS "JOHN AND PAUL" Tried their UTMOST to Explain this HIDDEN SECRET to the MANKIND, regarding which the Holy Bible States:

"Then GOD Said, "LET ""'US'"" Make Man in """OUR""" IMAGE, According to """OUR""" LIKENESS." [Genesis 1. 26.]

"In the BEGINNING was the WORD, and the WORD was With GOD, and the WORD was GOD. HE was in the Beginning WITH GOD.

All Things Came into Being by HIM; and APART from HIM "'NOTHING CAME INTO BEING'" THAT HAS "'COME INTO BEING'".

IN HIM WAS """"LIFE""""; AND the "LIFE" was the """"LIGHT"""" of Men. And the "LIGHT" SHINES IN THE "'DARKNESS'"; and the DARKNESS Did Not COMPREHEND IT. [John 1. Verses 1 to 5.]

'In these LAST DAYS has Spoken to US in HIS Son, WHOM HE Appointed "HEIR OF ALL THINGS", Through WHOM Also "'HE MADE THE WORLD'".' [Hebrews 1, 2.]

King DAVID was also Aware of "MOST HIGH LORD'S" SON'S Ethereal Presence, which Guided Him During His Life as "HIS LORD", and He Clearly Wrote About it in His Psalm, regarding which the Holy Bible States:

'The LORD Says to "'MY LORD'"; SIT at MY RIGHT HAND.' [Psalm 110. 1.]

JESUS CHRIST was Well Aware of King SOLOMON being LORD'S Earlier Chosen Son and HIS Valuable Contributions as LORD'S "PREACHER to the MANKIND", but HIMSELF Apart from Being the LORD'S Begotten SON, His Role was also to be THE SACRED "'MOST HIGH PRIEST'" OF THE UNKNOWABLE "MOST HIGH" By Wearing a "SACRED BREAST PLATE" COMPOSED OF THE CONSCIOUSNESS OF "LIVE HUMAN BEINGS" in this WORLD, and thus Having "'A MUCH GREATER ROLE'" THAN THAT OF "'KING SOLOMON'" upon this Planet Earth, and JESUS HIMSELF INFORMED TO THE "ENTIRE MANKIND" about this Hidden Fact, regarding which the Holy Bible States:

'The Queen of the South shall Rise Up with this Generation at the JUDGMENT and shall CONDEMN it, because SHE Came from the ENDS OF THE EARTH to Hear "'WISDOM OF SOLOMON'"; and Behold, """"SOMETHING GREATER THAN SOLOMON IS HERE"""". [Matthew 12. 42.]

And this Above "'STATEMENT OF JESUS CHRIST'" IS ABSOLUTELY TRUE for ALL GENERATIONS TO COME.

But During the Earlier Times, the Great King Solomon also wanted to LEARN about the Hidden Wisdom, which was related to the "Secrets of the Breast Plate" worn by the HIGH PRIEST upon His Chest, and He Started Examining it "Mathematically and Geometrically", as It being An IMPORTANT SACRED OBJECT Existing Since the Times of HIS Ancestor's MOSES AND AARON as the 'LORD'S KEY OF JUDGEMENT" for the Children of Israel, and as this Breast Plate was Composed of 4 ROWS and 3 COLUMNS having "12 HOUSES OF VITAL ENERGY" [4 x 3 = 12.] represented by the 12 Precious Stones, the Great King Looked at it As a COMBINATION OF THE "SATURN AND JUPITER'S" KEYS OF CELESTIAL ENERGIES, which Circulated through our Solar Universe, as they also Heavily Influenced the "Conscious Evolution", which is still taking Place upon the Physical Plane of this Planet Earth. King SOLOMON with the Grace of the Most High Very Well knew that "SATURN" KNOWN IN HEBREW AS THE "SHABBATHAI" and also referred to as "EL" or "AL" Provides LAW AND ORDER of Governance, and All Kings of the Physical Plane World Wore a Circular Crown Upon their Heads Imitating SATURN'S KINGLY "'RING'", and JUPITER IN HEBREW IS KNOWN AS THE "TZEDEK" meaning the "RIGHTEOUS ONE". And the Circulating JUPITER Energies Provided "PEACE and HARMONY", through their Cyclic Checks and Balances in the Solar Universe, as well as in the Evolving Kingdoms, which are ANIMATED Upon this Planet EARTH.

The SATURN Consciousness has a Mathematical Number 3, and thus a SATURN KEY has 3 Rows and 3 Columns, and the JUPITER Consciousness has a Mathematical Number 4, and thus a JUPITER KEY has 4 Rows and 4 Columns. The Mathematical Number 4 also represents the Geometrical Shape of a SQUARE, which is also a Two Dimensional Depiction of a CUBE, which HAPPENS to be SIX SIDED, and thus Corresponds to Mathematical Number 6 of the SOLAR SUN. The Mathematical Number 4 of JUPITER also represented the Four Cardinal Directions as well as the 3 Celestial Crosses of Heavens, the MUTABLE CROSS, the RIGHTEOUS OR FIXED CROSS Required for SPIRITUAL SOUL ENHANCEMENT, which in a Codified Way is represented by MAN – Aquarius, LION – Leo, EAGLE – Scorpio, BULL – Taurus, and the CARDINAL CROSS.

SATURN Energies represented by the Mathematical Number 3, which is also the Number of Holy TRINITY, Corresponded to the THREE UNIVERSAL MOTIONS [Spiral, Cyclic, and Circular] through Which the

Balancing "'JUSTICE'" Prevailed in the 3 DENSE DIMENSIONAL SPHERES [ASSIAH, YETZIRAH and BRIAH] of this Planet Earth. The Wise King Solomon also Knew that the Sound Vibrations of 3 Important Hebrew Letters ALEPH [Aliph], LAMED [Lam], and MEM [Mem] Corresponded to the Frequency Vibrations of these 3 Celestial Motions, as the TONAL SOUNDS of "'ALEPH'" Corresponded to the LORD'S DESIRE MIND Spiral Motion, which Started all the SUBJECTIVE and OBJECTIVE Manifestations in the UNIVERSE. The Tonal Sounds of "'LAMED'" Corresponds to the LORD'S DESIRE MIND Cyclic Motion, which PRESERVES and ENDS all the SUBJECTIVE and OBJECTIVE Manifestations, which are thus MANIFESTED in the UNIVERSE through the Governance of Various SMALL and LARGE Cycles of "CONSCIOUS EVOLUTION'S", commonly referred to as the "WHEELS OF TIME". The OUROBOROS symbol Depicted by a Snake Eating its Tail is a Representation of CYCLIC LIFE DURATION'S, in which the HEAD represents the Starting "ALEPH" Point and the TAIL represents the Ending "TAV" Point.

The Tonal Sounds of "MEM" Corresponds to the LORD'S DESIRE MIND Circular Motion, which SEPARATES all the SUBJECTIVE and OBJECTIVE Manifestations from ONE ANOTHER through its Differentiation Process, which are thus MANIFESTED in the UNIVERSE, and through the Circular Motion controlled by the DESIRE MIND, the GREAT LORD Separated the LIGHT from DARKNESS, WATERS from the WATERS, and an EXPANSE in the Midst of the WATERS thus Creating the DENSE MATTER as mentioned in "Genesis 1. 3, 6, 7." of the Holy Bible.

The Great King Solomon being MARRIED to an Egyptian Princess thus also knew through the Acquired Wisdom of their Priesthood, that in Every 72 Years the SOLAR SUN Appeared to Move ONE DEGREE from ONE CONSTELLATION TO ANOTHER, which are 12 in Number. Similarly there were 12 Tribes of LORD'S Chosen Race, which were Under HIS Command to RULE them as their KING, and as the Mathematical Number of Solar Sun was 6, which being the "SACRED HEART AND MIND" CENTER OF THE SOLAR UNIVERSE Acted as the RECEIVING and TRANSFORMING ENERGY DISTRIBUTION FOCAL POINT CENTER, for the "CELESTIAL ENERGY EMANATIONS OF THE 12 ZODIACAL CONSTELLATIONS", and thus Multiplying the Mathematical Number 6 of the Solar Sun by the Total Number 12 of the Zodiacal Constellation's which EFFECT THE EVOLUTIONARY PROCESS OF ALL VISIBLE AND

INVISIBLE BEINGS also resulted in Mathematical Number 72 [6 x 12 = 72], and thus the Great King Solomon Dedicated each year of the 72 Years of the "ONE DEGREE CELESTIAL CYCLE" to One of the CONSCIOUS ATTRIBUTES OF THE "MOST HIGH", which became to be known as the "'72 NAMES OF GOD'", which represented the Holy Vibrations of HIS Conscious Attribute Frequencies.

The 12 STONES of Breast Plate, each representing the Differentiated Consciousness of One of the 12 Sons of ISRAEL [Jacob] which JACOB Himself Clearly Defined in "Genesis 49. Verses 1 to 28" of the Holy Bible, thus PRIMARILY Corresponded to the Celestial Energies of the 12 Constellations, which affected their "Personality Minds".

The Hebrew Gematria of LORD'S MOST HOLY NAME "YHVH" being "26" [Y = 10, H = 5,V = 6, H = 5, thus Totaling to 10+5+6+5 = 26], and King Solomon knowing this Mathematical FACT thus with LORD'S Grace then Figured out that the 3 Columns of the Sacred Breast Plate, each having 4 Precious Stones corresponding to the 4 HOUSES OF CELESTIAL ENERGIES, for this Very Reason, Each of these Vertical Column in their Mathematical Totality represented a Mathematical Number, which was Less than LORD'S Name NUMBER of "26". And the three Rows when Closely Observed by the King Solomon thus calculating from RIGHT to LEFT Came out to be 23, 25, and 24 thus providing a GRAND TOTAL of 23 + 25 + 24 = 72, which Equaled to the "72 NAMES OF MOST HIGH GOD".

Thus the Wise King SOLOMON was Able to CALCULATE and also Figure out the Mathematical Correspondence to the 4 Rows of the BREAST PLATE in which the Precious Stones were MOUNTED starting from Right to Left. In this LORD'S KEY OF JUDGEMENT, the First Row starting from Right to Left had thus these Mathematical Numbers: 6, 1, 8, which Corresponded to the Gematria of HEBREW LETTERS "VAV", "ALEPH", and "CHET". The Second Row starting from Right to Left had these Mathematical Numbers: 7, 5, and 3, which Corresponded to the Gematria of HEBREW LETTERS "ZAYIN", "HEH", and "GIMEL". The Third Row starting from Right to Left had these Mathematical Numbers: 2, 9, and 4, which Corresponded to the Gematria of HEBREW LETTERS "BET", "TET", and "DALET". The Last Fourth Row starting from Right to Left had these Mathematical Numbers: 8, 10, and 9, which Corresponded to the

Gematria of HEBREW LETTERS "CHET", "YOD", and "TET".

The Demonic Hierarchies of FALLEN ANGELS who WILLFULLY REBELLED AGAINST the EVOLUTIONARY PLAN AND PURPOSE of the MOST HIGH tried their LEVEL BEST to Figure OUT the "'SECRETS OF KING SOLOMON'S WISDOM'", but Failed Miserably in ALL THEIR EFFORTS. So unable to do Any Harm to the 72 Names of the "MOST HIGH", they created their Own 72 Demonic Hierarchies Against the "MOST HIGH", which were Easily Subdued by King Solomon, who Being the LORD'S APPOINTED JUDGE then APPROPRIATELY "PUNISHED THEM".

But after SOLOMON'S Passing Away from this Material Plane World, they TOOK THEIR REVENGE upon the Ignorant Children of Israel, who under their "Negative Mind Control" of Material Greed and Lust Willfully Involved themselves in the Abomination Practices Against the Commandments of their LORD - GOD, and thus Carried them on for Many Centuries, and Did Not LISTENED to the LAMENTATIONS of their HOLY PROPHETS by paying a DEAF EAR, which Ultimately Ended with the LOSS of BOTH THEIR HOLY OBJECTS, THE "URIM and THUMMIM" of the BREAST PLATE, as well as the LOSS of THE REVERED and the MOST SACRED OBJECT, which was the "LORD'S ARK OF COVENANT".

The End.

SOLOMON'S KEY OF LORDS BREASTPLATE COMMANDED BY THE LORD FOR THE HIGH PRIEST

8	1	6
3	5	7
4	9	2
9	10	8

[24] + [25] + [23]
=72

72 Holy names of "Most High"

Each of these Vertical Column in their Mathematical Totality represented a Mathematical Number, which was Less than LORD'S Name NUMBER of "26". And the three Rows when Closely Observed by the King Solomon thus calculating from RIGHT to LEFT Came out to be 23, 25, and 24 thus providing a GRAND TOTAL of 23 + 25 + 24 = 72, which Equaled to the "72 NAMES OF MOST HIGH GOD".

SOLOMON'S KEY OF LORDS BREASTPLATE COMMANDED BY THE LORD FOR THE HIGH PRIEST

CHET	ALEPH	VAV
GIMAL	HEH	ZAYIN
DALET	TET	BET
TET	YOD	CHET

$$[24] + [25] + [23]$$
$$=72$$

72 Holy names of "Most High"

Each of these Vertical Column in their Mathematical Totality represented a Mathematical Number, which was Less than LORD'S Name NUMBER of "26". And the three Rows when Closely Observed by the King Solomon thus calculating from RIGHT to LEFT Came out to be 23, 25, and 24 thus providing a GRAND TOTAL of 23 + 25 + 24 = 72, which Equaled to the "72 NAMES OF MOST HIGH GOD".

"Now BEZALEL, the Son of URI the Son of HUR, of the Tribe of JUDAH, Made ALL that the LORD had Commanded MOSES. And with Him was OHOLIAB, the Son of AHISAMACH, of the Tribe of DAN, an Engraver and a Skillful Workman and a Weaver in BLUE and in PURPLE and in SCARLET Material, and Fine Linen." [Exodus 38. 22, 23.]

EPILOGUE

The Holy Bible Contains All the Secrets of Universe, but can be only REVEALED to Those with SPIRITUAL EYES, Who are Humbly Examining it through the Contemplation's of their Inner Mind.

Apart from Doing the Physical Plane Duties, Most Humans Never Question about their Short Lived Incarnated Life Existence, as to Why In the First Place they Embodied a Human Form upon this Planet Earth?, or from where they Came to Incarnate in a Human form or Where they will Go when their ""Personality Mind's Evolving Consciousness" Leave their Physical Form, which takes place upon the Severance of their Invisible Silver Cord?, which during their Incarnated Human LIFE, Go on Providing the Vital Consciousness Energies for the Required Animation Purposes to their Dense Physical Form, although they See People being Born and also Dying EVERYDAY in their Relative Human Societies.

And if by Chance Some One Pays Any Attention to these Above Mentioned Questions, they Hardly Get Any PROPER ANSWERS to their Inquiring Mind's SATISFACTION, as Not Too Many People Can Answers

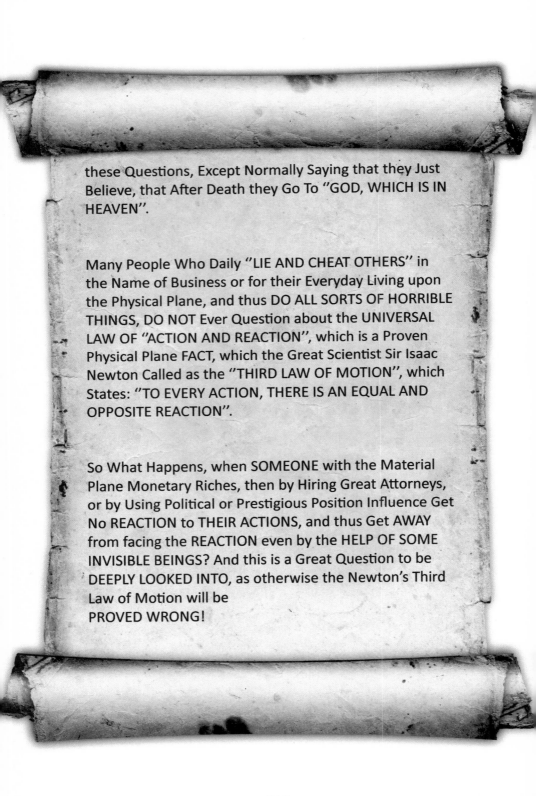

these Questions, Except Normally Saying that they Just
Believe, that After Death they Go To "GOD, WHICH IS IN
HEAVEN".

Many People Who Daily "LIE AND CHEAT OTHERS" in
the Name of Business or for their Everyday Living upon
the Physical Plane, and thus DO ALL SORTS OF HORRIBLE
THINGS, DO NOT Ever Question about the UNIVERSAL
LAW OF "ACTION AND REACTION", which is a Proven
Physical Plane FACT, which the Great Scientist Sir Isaac
Newton Called as the "THIRD LAW OF MOTION", which
States: "TO EVERY ACTION, THERE IS AN EQUAL AND
OPPOSITE REACTION".

So What Happens, when SOMEONE with the Material
Plane Monetary Riches, then by Hiring Great Attorneys,
or by Using Political or Prestigious Position Influence Get
No REACTION to THEIR ACTIONS, and thus Get AWAY
from facing the REACTION even by the HELP OF SOME
INVISIBLE BEINGS? And this is a Great Question to be
DEEPLY LOOKED INTO, as otherwise the Newton's Third
Law of Motion will be
PROVED WRONG!

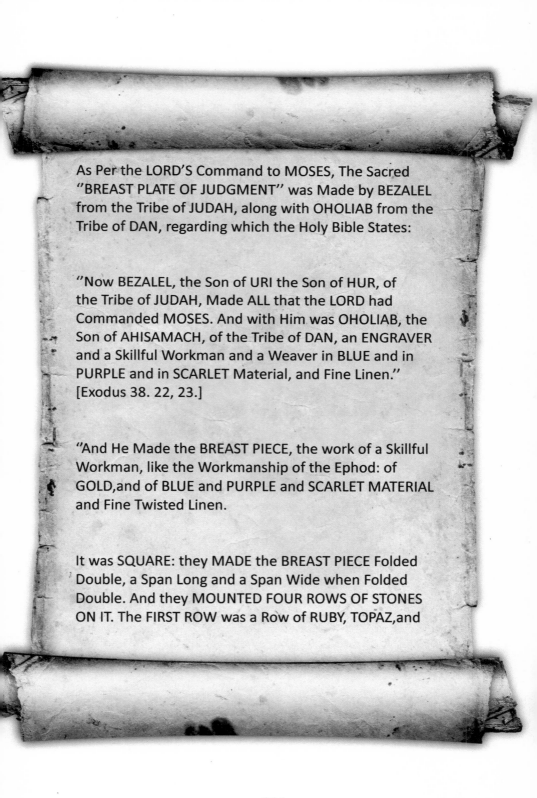

As Per the LORD'S Command to MOSES, The Sacred "BREAST PLATE OF JUDGMENT" was Made by BEZALEL from the Tribe of JUDAH, along with OHOLIAB from the Tribe of DAN, regarding which the Holy Bible States:

"Now BEZALEL, the Son of URI the Son of HUR, of the Tribe of JUDAH, Made ALL that the LORD had Commanded MOSES. And with Him was OHOLIAB, the Son of AHISAMACH, of the Tribe of DAN, an ENGRAVER and a Skillful Workman and a Weaver in BLUE and in PURPLE and in SCARLET Material, and Fine Linen." [Exodus 38. 22, 23.]

"And He Made the BREAST PIECE, the work of a Skillful Workman, like the Workmanship of the Ephod: of GOLD,and of BLUE and PURPLE and SCARLET MATERIAL and Fine Twisted Linen.

It was SQUARE: they MADE the BREAST PIECE Folded Double, a Span Long and a Span Wide when Folded Double. And they MOUNTED FOUR ROWS OF STONES ON IT. The FIRST ROW was a Row of RUBY, TOPAZ,and

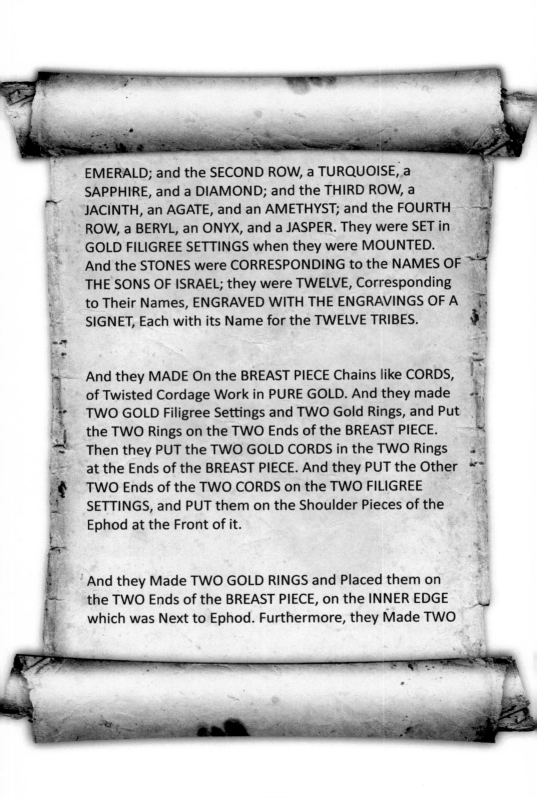

EMERALD; and the SECOND ROW, a TURQUOISE, a SAPPHIRE, and a DIAMOND; and the THIRD ROW, a JACINTH, an AGATE, and an AMETHYST; and the FOURTH ROW, a BERYL, an ONYX, and a JASPER. They were SET in GOLD FILIGREE SETTINGS when they were MOUNTED. And the STONES were CORRESPONDING to the NAMES OF THE SONS OF ISRAEL; they were TWELVE, Corresponding to Their Names, ENGRAVED WITH THE ENGRAVINGS OF A SIGNET, Each with its Name for the TWELVE TRIBES.

And they MADE On the BREAST PIECE Chains like CORDS, of Twisted Cordage Work in PURE GOLD. And they made TWO GOLD Filigree Settings and TWO Gold Rings, and Put the TWO Rings on the TWO Ends of the BREAST PIECE. Then they PUT the TWO GOLD CORDS in the TWO Rings at the Ends of the BREAST PIECE. And they PUT the Other TWO Ends of the TWO CORDS on the TWO FILIGREE SETTINGS, and PUT them on the Shoulder Pieces of the Ephod at the Front of it.

And they Made TWO GOLD RINGS and Placed them on the TWO Ends of the BREAST PIECE, on the INNER EDGE which was Next to Ephod. Furthermore, they Made TWO

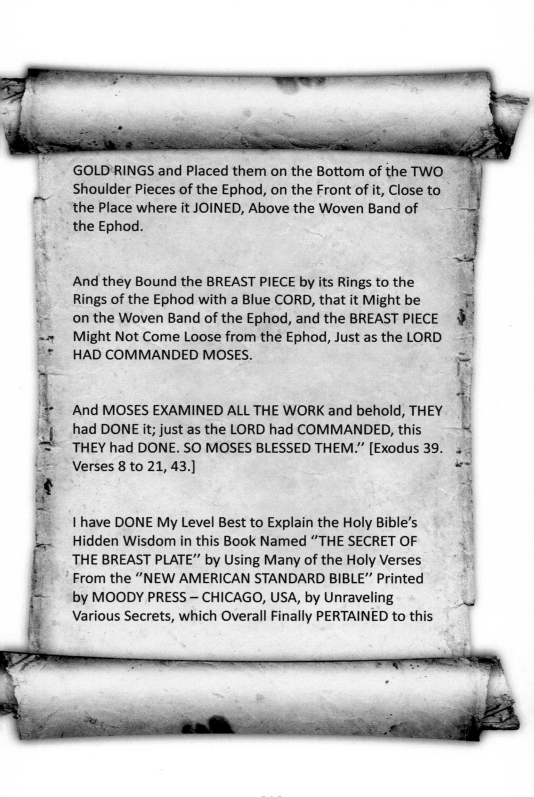

GOLD RINGS and Placed them on the Bottom of the TWO Shoulder Pieces of the Ephod, on the Front of it, Close to the Place where it JOINED, Above the Woven Band of the Ephod.

And they Bound the BREAST PIECE by its Rings to the Rings of the Ephod with a Blue CORD, that it Might be on the Woven Band of the Ephod, and the BREAST PIECE Might Not Come Loose from the Ephod, Just as the LORD HAD COMMANDED MOSES.

And MOSES EXAMINED ALL THE WORK and behold, THEY had DONE it; just as the LORD had COMMANDED, this THEY had DONE. SO MOSES BLESSED THEM." [Exodus 39. Verses 8 to 21, 43.]

I have DONE My Level Best to Explain the Holy Bible's Hidden Wisdom in this Book Named "THE SECRET OF THE BREAST PLATE" by Using Many of the Holy Verses From the "NEW AMERICAN STANDARD BIBLE" Printed by MOODY PRESS – CHICAGO, USA, by Unraveling Various Secrets, which Overall Finally PERTAINED to this

Important Subject Matter of Breast Plate, which was WORN by LORD'S HIGH PRIEST.

This is MY 20th and Last Book in the Spiritual Series, which May Bring the "'Needed Spiritual Awareness'" to the Embodied Personality Mind of Human Beings, which is having its "CONSCIOUS EXPANSION EVOLUTION" through the Incarnated Human Form thus Manifested upon the Dense Physical Plane of this Planet Earth.

The End.

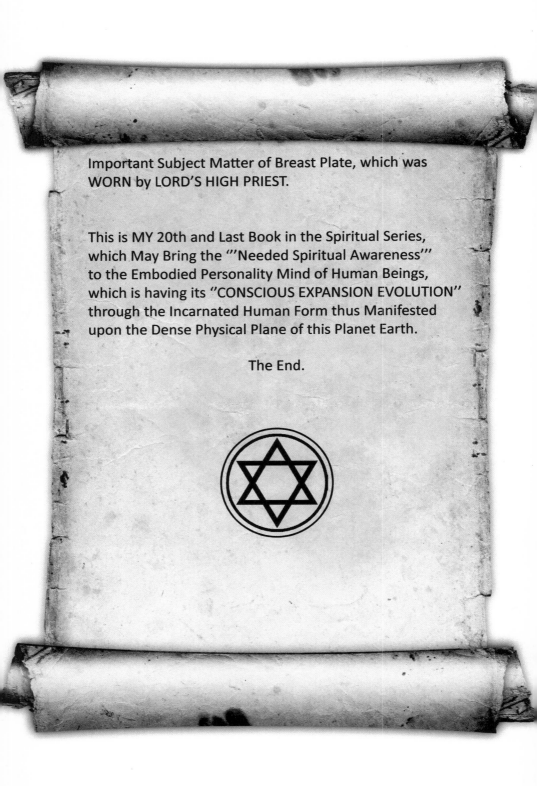

Sidon

PHOENICIA

SIDON

MANSUATE

Damascus

DAMASCUS

Litani River

Ijon

Abel-beth-maacah

Tyre

TYRE

ARAM

Kedesh

Lake Huleh

Hazor

Acco

Janoah   Merom

MEGIDDO

Chinnereth

KARNAIM

Kishon River

Sea of Galilee

Karnaim

Ashtaroth

Mt. Carmel

Hannathon

Jokneam

Mt. Tabor

Dor

Megiddo

Yarmuk River

HA

DOR

Beth-shan

Ramoth-gilead

GILEAD

Jordan River

Jabesh-gilead

Samaria

Mt. Ebal

Mahanaim

Mt. Gerizim

Jabbok River

Joppa

Aphek

ISRAEL

AMMON

A vassal of Assyria

Ahaz builds a pagan altar

Rabbah (Amman)

Gezer

Ekron

Aijalon

Ashdod

Jerusalem

hkelon

Gath

Lachish

Hebron

Aroer

ta

PHILISTIA

JUDAH   En-gedi

DEAD SEA

Arnon River

A vassal of Assyria

Arad

MOAB

N. Besor

Beersheba

Kir-haresEth

MEDITERRANEAN

SEA

35 E

36 E

35 E

36 E

615

FRIENDS OF
ISRAEL
SCOUTS, INC.
TZOFIM

June 30, 2015

Outfinite Visions
PO Box 07081-0416
Springfield, NJ 07081

To whom this may concern,

This letter is to inform you that we received a signed copy of "The Secret of the Breast Plate".

Thank you

Elad Sanderovich
Executive Director
Friends of Israel Scouts

www.israelscouts.org

Acknowledgment by Executive Director 2015
Elad Sanderovich from Friends of Israel Scouts, Inc.

UNITED NATIONS

Dag Hammarskjöld
L I B R A R Y

July 29, 2015

Greetings from the Dag Hammarskjöld Library,

This is to confirm our receipt of the book you generously donated to our library, The Secret of the Breast Plate. We thank you for your consideration.

Best Regards,

Ashley Rode
United Nations
Dag Hammarskjöld Library
Tel: +1 212 963-3290
Email : rode@un.org

email acknowledgment by Ashley Rode 2015
Dag Hammarskjöld Library | United Nations

August 3, 2015

Mr. Kevin Vancio
Outfinite Visions
P.O. Box 0416
Springfield, NJ 07081

Dear Mr. Vancio,

Thank you for sending a copy of the book *The Secret of the Breast Plate*. I appreciate that you thought of sending it to me.

Kind regards,

Kim S. Phipps
President

SHARPENING INTELLECT   DEEPENING CHRISTIAN FAITH   INSPIRING ACTION   SINCE 1909

One College Avenue Suite 3000 • Mechanicsburg Pennsylvania 17055 • 717.796.5085 Phone
717.691.6059 Fax • www.messiah.edu

Acknowledgment by President 2015
Kim Phipps of Messiah College

Baha'l Office of Education & Schools

Thank you for the
copy of "The Secret of the
Breast Plate" We will
include it in our library
selections.

Sincerely,

May Mais

BAHÁ'Í FAITH

Baha'i National Center
1233 Central Street
Evanston, IL 60201

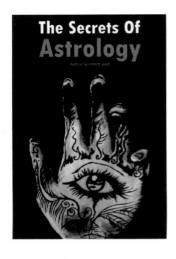

The Secrets of
Astrology
ISBN: 978-1-105-64530-3

$21.95

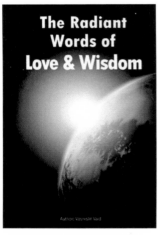

The Radiant Words of
Love & Wisdom
ISBN: 978-1-105-81701-4

$21.95

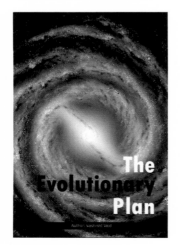

The Evolutionary
Plan
ISBN: 978-1-105-81713-7

$21.95

Who are Devas [Angels]
and what Happens
after Physical Death?
Vol I
ISBN: 978-1-105-81720-5
$21.95

Who are Devas [Angels]
and what Happens
after Physical Death?
Vol II
978-1-105-81726-7
$21.95

Who are Devas [Angels]
and what Happens
after Physical Death?
Vol III
ISBN: 978-1-105-81730-4
$21.95

Other Publications by the same author which are available:
www.OutfiniteVision.com

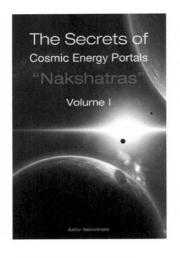

The Secrets of
Cosmic Energy Portals
"Nakshatras" book I

ISBN: 978-1-105-87471-0

$21.95

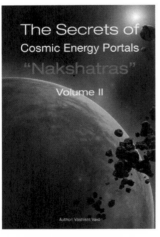

The Secrets of
Cosmic Energy Portals
"Nakshatras" book II

ISBN: 978-1-105-81701-4

$21.95

The Codified Mysteries

ISBN: 978-1-300-09987-1

$21.95

The Universal Knowledge

978-1-300-34605-0

$21.95

The Esoteric Collections book I

ISBN: 978-1-300-90734-3

$21.95

The Esoteric Collections book II

ISBN: 978-1-304-54952-5

$21.95

Other Publications by the same author which are available:
www.OutfiniteVision.com

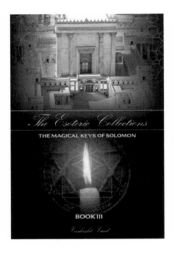

The Esoteric Collections book III
ISBN: 978-1-304-54953-2

$21.95

The Esoteric Collections book IV
ISBN: 978-1-304-54956-3

$21.95

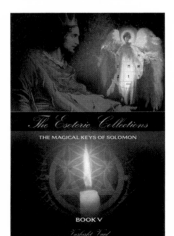

The Esoteric Collections book V
ISBN: 978-1-304-54958-7

$21.95

The Esoteric Collections book VI
ISBN: 978-1-312-68380-8

$21.95

The Esoteric Collections book VII
ISBN: 978-1-312-52625-9

$21.95

The Higher Self & Lower Self
ISBN: 978-1-312-57237-9

$21.95

The Esoteric Tidbits
$21.95

The Secret of the Breast Plate

ISBN: 978-1-329-04623-8
$21.95